Contemporary Living

Verdene Ryder, CFCS
Family Life Education Consultant
Houston, Texas

Marjorie B. Harter, Ph.D.
Family Life Education Consultant
Washington, D.C.

Publisher
The Goodheart-Willcox Company, Inc.
Tinley Park, Illinois

Cover: Robin Smith/Tony Stone Images
Part I:
    Miracles Studio, Cedar Rapids, IA
Part II:
    ©The Stock Market/William Roy, 1989
Part III:
    ©The Stock Market/Tom Steward, 1994
Part IV:
    ©The Stock Market/Chuck Savage, 1994
Part V:
    ©The Stock Market/George Disario, 1993
Part VI:
    ©The Stock Market/Ariel Skelley, 1994
Part VII:
    Tony Freeman/PhotoEdit

Library of Congress Catalog Card Number 94-30248
International Standard Book Number 1-56637-099-X

3 4 5 6 7 8 9 0 - 95 - 99 98 97

Library of Congress Cataloging-in-Publication Data

Ryder, Verdene.
Contemporary living / Verdene Ryder, [Marjorie B. Harter]. —
[New rev. ed.]
p.   cm.
Includes index.
1. Family life education—United States.   I. Harter, Marjorie B.
II. Title. ISBN 1-56637-099-X
HQ10.5.U6R93 1995
646.7—dc20

94-30248
CIP

Introduction

Contemporary Living is written for you. It presents a fresh look at life in today's world. It helps you understand your development as an individual, as a family member, and as part of society.

Life today offers more alternatives than ever before. This book helps you evaluate the alternatives you face. It does not tell you what to do or how to live. Rather, it gives you the information you need to make your own decisions.

Contemporary Living explores all aspects of life: personality development, health, communication, relationships with family and friends, mate selection, marriage, parenting,

handling crises, aging, death, and managing family living. Practical information is given to help you deal with real-life situations.

This new edition has been completely revised. Several new topics have been added, including deciding on a career, getting and keeping a job, lifestyle options and consequences, group behaviors involving violence, and characteristics of strong families. A new chapter on balancing family and work has been added.

This revised text is even more readable, and all photos are in full color. Each chapter begins with learning objectives and terms to know. Chapters end with review materials to make your task of learning more efficient and meaningful—and therefore, more enjoyable.

Verdene Ryder
Marjorie B. Harter

3

About the Authors ▪ ▪ ▪ ▪ ▪ ▪ ▪ ▪ ▪ ▪ ▪ ▪ ▪ ▪ ▪ ▪ ▪ ▪

Verdene Ryder, C.F.C.S., is a nationally recognized author and family life specialist. In addition to being an author of *Contemporary Living,* she is also the author of the popular parenting text, *Parents and Their Children,* and several booklets. She also writes a newspaper column for young teens and is often consulted in interviews on radio and TV relating to family life issues. Verdene Ryder has extensive teaching experience at both the high school and university levels. She is a member of several professional organizations and has received numerous academic and leadership awards. A scholarship has been named in her honor to enable low-income women to attend college.

Marjorie B. Harter, Ph.D., is a family life education and publications consultant who has written extensively and conducted numerous teacher education workshops on family life topics. A former family and consumer sciences teacher, she has developed classroom curricula for nonprofit organizations in the areas of teenage pregnancy prevention and population education as well as general family life education. Dr. Harter has also served as editor of several family and consumer sciences periodicals, including the former *Journal of Home Economics.*

Table of Contents

Part IV:
The Marriage Relationship

Part VI: Families Face Change

Personal Development

You: Growing and Changing

After studying this chapter, you will be able to

- identify the three forces that shape personality.

- describe six patterns of growth.

- define self-concept, self-esteem, and self-worth.

- explain how a person's character is revealed by his or her behavior.

- describe what it means to be a responsible adult.

- identify possible roadblocks to responsible adulthood.

The future holds many opportunities for you. It also may hold some roadblocks. The goal for you as you enter adulthood will be to overcome the roadblocks and seize the opportunities.

This can be a challenge. How you meet this challenge depends, in part, on how you feel about yourself.

You have been expressing yourself through your actions since you were born. You influence others you meet, and they, in turn, influence you. This "connectedness" with others is one of the basic fundamentals of life.

You are a unique individual, but you function within a family, a community, and a society. There are boundaries within which you must function, but you have freedom within these boundaries. As you grow and mature, you will learn to recognize the balance between rights and responsibilities that this freedom requires.

Terms to Know

personality	emotional growth
heredity	self-concept
environment	self-esteem
growth pattern	self-worth
puberty	character
pituitary gland	goal

Your Personality

In order to understand yourself and those around you, you need to understand the forces that help shape your personality.

Personality is defined as the group of behavioral and emotional traits that distinguishes an individual. It is all that a person has been, is now, and hopes to be. It can also be defined as the sum of all inherited and acquired characteristics.

This book will help you explore the many forces that shape your personality. Once you are familiar with the many aspects of your personality, you will be able to answer the important questions, "Who am I?" and "How do I deal with who I am?" You will learn to recognize the many possibilities that can be a part of your life.

Forces that Shape Personality

Heredity, the sum of the traits that are passed from your ancestors to you, has a great effect on your personality, 1-1. Because you are a human being, you have many traits in common with other human beings. You have two eyes, two ears, a nose, a mouth, two arms, and two legs. These are human traits determined by heredity.

Heredity also causes differences among humans. The color of eyes, the shape of ears, and the length of arms vary from person to person. How many of your classmates have black hair? How many have blue eyes?

Heredity influences more than your appearance. It also affects such traits as your attitude, intelligence, and behavior. Thus, heredity is one force in shaping your total personality.

Your environment also plays a major role in your personality development, 1-2. *Environment* is all of the conditions, objects, and circumstances that surround an individual. You and your classmates share parts of your environment. You attend the same school and have the same teachers. You participate in the same activities. Other parts of your environment are different from those of your

David Hopper

1-1
Family members tend to look alike because of their inherited characteristics.

classmates. Factors such as your family situation, neighborhood, religion, and friends make your environment unique to you. Your environment affects your thoughts, feelings, and actions. It helps shape your personality.

A third force that helps shape your personality is your response to your environment. In some situations, your responses may be like those of your peers. In other cases, your responses may be different. For instance, suppose you went with a group of your friends to a movie. You were all in the same theater, saw the same scenes, and heard the same words, but you may have had different responses. Some of your friends may have thought it was funny or boring or confusing. Some may have thought it was well written,

1-2

Cholla Runnels

Your peers, or persons in your age group, are part of your environment. They influence your personality development.

but poorly acted. Some may have paid special attention to the scenery, costumes, special effects, or music. Each person might have responded to the movie in a different way.

Both environmental and hereditary forces affect your personality development, but authorities disagree about how these forces affect personality development, 1-3. Some authorities think that environmental forces are more important. They say that people inherit only the potential for various personality traits. They think that a certain social environment is needed to develop these traits. Other authorities think that hereditary forces are more important.

You, as an individual, have inborn qualities determined by heredity. You are in a particular environment, and you respond uniquely to that environment. Together, these three forces shape your personality. They determine how you deal with the challenges, successes, and frustrations you meet

in your daily life. Much of your future will be determined by the decisions you make as you balance these three forces. Because of their importance, these forces will be discussed in more depth in the subsequent chapters.

Your Growth

Adolescence is a time of growth and change. It is a time for leaving childhood behind and becoming an adult. Although

1-3

Both heredity and environment play a role in personality development.

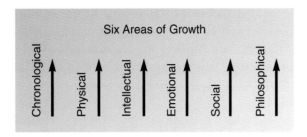

1-4
People grow in six different areas. The rate of growth varies from area to area as well as from person to person.

growth is usually measured in terms of age, height, and weight, people really grow in six different areas. They grow chronologically, physically, intellectually, emotionally, socially, and philosophically.

Each person grows at a unique pace, 1-4. For instance, one person's physical growth may be slow while intellectual growth is rapid.

Another person's physical growth may be rapid while intellectual growth is slow. The possible variations in growth rates are endless. The term *growth pattern* is used to describe the unique way a person grows. People's growth patterns and their responses to their growth patterns affect their personality development.

Chronological Growth

Everyone ages at the same chronological rate, 1-5. You grow older every minute and every day. Chronological age is determined at birth and cannot be altered. You add another year to your age with each calendar year.

Our culture has done much to form our attitudes toward age. The advertising industry and mass media make youth look appealing. Young people are pictured as having fun and being successful. The image of aging people in today's world has taken on a more

Evin Thayer

1-5
Each birthday adds another year to a person's chronological growth.

positive picture than that of previous generations. Today this age group is often portrayed as enjoying an active and abundant life. How you feel about your aging will affect your personality throughout your life.

Physical Growth

The physical growth of humans follows the same general pattern from childhood through puberty and adulthood. Changes in physical growth may happen at different times for different people, but the sequence of the basic changes will be the same.

Physical growth is the easiest to observe. For instance, by age three, children are twice as tall and four times as heavy as they were at birth. This rate of growth slows down and then remains steady until about the age of ten.

At puberty, the growth rates of boys and girls begin to differ. *Puberty* is the time when the body changes from that of a boy or girl to that of a man or woman. This sudden growth and change is triggered by the *pituitary gland* at the base of the brain. This gland secretes hormones that affect other parts of the body. At puberty, hormones from the pituitary gland stimulate the sex glands. The sex glands then produce other hormones that cause changes in bodies of boys and girls.

The age at which puberty begins varies. Most girls reach puberty at about age 12. Most boys reach puberty two years later, at about age 14. At puberty a girl grows rapidly in height and weight. Her hip cage widens, her breasts enlarge, and she begins her menstrual cycle. Hair appears in the pubic region, under the armpits, and on her legs.

A boy also undergoes many physical changes during puberty. He grows rapidly in height, his neck thickens and broadens, his shoulders widen, and his waist narrows. His muscles develop rapidly, and his strength virtually doubles between the ages of 12 and 16. See 1-6. His vocal cords lengthen, causing

Cholla Runnels

1-6
Muscle development allows strength in boys to double between the ages of 12 and 16.

squeaks as his voice deepens. Hair appears on his body, especially on his face and in the pubic region.

Physical growth is hardly noticeable in adulthood. Adults rarely grow in height, although they often gain weight. The body of an adult works to maintain itself rather than to grow in size.

Your response to your physical growth affects your personality development. You may be taller, shorter, heavier, or thinner than the average person. You may have reached physical maturity earlier or later than others. If you can accept your physical traits and growth pattern, this will have a positive effect on your personality.

Intellectual Growth

We inherit our potential for intelligence. However, we all grow differently in this area based on our environment and our response to that environment.

A person born with a high potential for intelligence can fail to be motivated and thus never develop a sharper mind. A person who has an average potential for intelligence can study hard and work hard to become successful—even in a career that requires a great deal of intelligence.

Environment can influence intelligence in other ways, too. Nutritious food and adequate rest and exercise make you feel better and allow you to learn more. Your family, friends, and school provide many opportunities for new learning experiences. Such experiences include everything from family talks, to a day out with friends, to a part in a school play. Every time you see something, read something, or talk with someone, you have the chance to expand your intellectual growth.

If you respond positively to your inherited potential and to the opportunities your environment offers you, you can increase your intellectual growth. This is probably the greatest step toward personal independence you can take. Intelligence gives you the capability to function well in the world around you.

Emotional Growth

Your emotions are your feelings. These feelings are often revealed to those around you through different behaviors. Many emotions are expressed outwardly for all to see.

Babies who are unhappy may cry uncontrollably. Happy children may laugh excitedly. Teens may be sullen and retiring when they feel sad. Other emotions are kept inside or suppressed, invisible to family and friends.

Emotional growth refers to the continuing refinement of emotions or mental states that causes an individual to act in a certain way. Each person has a unique timetable for learning to control and express emotions. Some people are emotionally mature at a fairly young age. On the other hand, some people act like children in the way they handle their emotions even after they become adults.

How you handle your emotions will be an indication of your emotional maturity. During your teen years you will experience many emotions, 1-7. You may also notice that your emotions change rapidly. You may be happy and excited one minute and sad and depressed the next. This is normal. The important thing is that you recognize these emotional shifts and learn to manage them to help you live an effective life. You also need to learn to express your emotions and to not

1-7   Cholla Runnels

Many new and different emotions may be felt during a dating relationship.

1-8
Dating gives you the chance to meet new people and to grow socially.

keep them bottled up inside. This, too, is a part of growing emotionally.

Another part of emotional growth is learning the best way to respond to emotional situations. For instance, if you feel anger toward someone, you will find a way to resolve this anger without using hurtful words or violent behavior. You may try mentally counting to ten rather than yelling out words you might regret later. You may even suggest that you both calm down and talk about the problem again when you aren't so upset. Learning to handle your feelings and actions in ways that are acceptable to others will help you grow emotionally.

Social Growth

You also grow socially as you learn to relate to others around you. This growth begins at an early age. Babies smile when parents or caregivers "talk" to them. Children first play alone, and then they learn the fun of playing with others. As a teen you are opening up new avenues for social growth, 1-8. This will continue throughout your life.

In your family you learn to grow in your roles as a child, son or daughter, and brother or sister as you pass through different stages of social growth. You grow from self-centeredness to being considerate of others. You learn to share and to take turns. You learn to listen to the views of others.

In your community you learn what is acceptable as a pattern for social behavior. These experiences in a social setting help you meet new people and learn behaviors that are acceptable and unacceptable. You mature socially as you adopt standards of responsibility for living in an organized society. You learn to adopt as your own the rules and guidelines that allow a society to function for the benefit of all.

Philosophical Growth

As you grow philosophically, you may search for deeper meaning and purpose in your life. You are learning to study truth and knowledge using reflective thinking and reasoned inquiry. As a child you related to specific objects. As a teen you are thinking more abstractly of things you cannot see or feel.

Questions such as "Who are you?" "Where are you from?" and "Where are you going?" were easy to answer when you were young. You simply stated your name, the city in which you lived, and the place you were going—to school, home, or to the store. As you grow philosophically, you sense there are other ways to answer these questions. You begin to think more deeply about who you are, why you are here, and your goals for life, 1-9.

Young people are looking for a sense of direction. They are also trying to gain deeper insight into other people and the world around them.

Your Self-Concept ■ ■ ■

Your *self-concept* is the way you see yourself. There is no one else in the world exactly like you. Look around and you will never find anyone quite like you. You may have your hair cut as your friends do, and you may wear the same styles of clothes. However, even if you try to look like others, you will never be like others. You are unique and this makes you special.

Cholla Runnels

1-9

As you mature, you begin to think more deeply about yourself and the world around you.

What is included in your self-concept— this picture you have of yourself? Several factors are a part of this image, such as your appearance, your personality traits, and your abilities.

Your appearance forms a part of your self-concept. Everyone has different physical characteristics. Some characteristics you may like about yourself and others you may not like. Maybe you think you're too tall or too short. Maybe you think your nose is too big. If you feel good about your appearance, you feel good about yourself. This leads to a positive self-concept. If you don't feel good about the way you look, you have a negative self-concept. If you don't care how you look, this too can be a part of your self-concept. Many things about your appearance you cannot change, but you can make the most of your good qualities. If you do this, you can still have a positive self-concept.

Another part of your self-concept is your personality. You have certain personality traits that are different from your friends. You may enjoy being with a lot of people and you may like to be involved with what is going on. On the other hand, maybe you feel more comfortable staying in the background, reading a book, or listening to music. These individual personality traits are a part of your self-concept. If you feel comfortable with your personality, you have a positive self-con-

cept, 1-10. If you wish you could change your personality, you may have a negative self-concept.

Each of you has certain skills that are different from those of your peers. You may already realize you cannot do a few things as well as some of your friends. Perhaps your ability to excel in a sport is not your main strength, but you may be at ease with the computer. You may be able to feed figures into a computer to show your sports friends the calculated speed of a slider or a fast-pitched softball. Each of you has different talents and skills, and these also form a part of your self-concept.

David Hopper

1-10
With a positive self-concept, a person has the confidence to accept challenges and try new things.

How Is Your Self-Concept Formed?

It is natural to compare yourself with others. This is one way your self-concept is formed. If you think you are as good as the next person, this shapes your self-concept. Even if you think you're not as good as others, this still influences the concept you have of your self. Knowing what you can and cannot do shapes your self-concept.

From the time you were very young, your parents, other family members, your teachers, and friends all have played a part in shaping your self-concept. They did this by reacting to your behavior. Sometimes they told you how well you were doing. You felt proud of yourself. You told yourself, "Hey, I can do this!" Sometimes they may have told you the opposite, and another image formed. That image was of someone who wasn't as good as others, and again, your self-concept was influenced.

You may be able to help shape another person's self-concept by giving compliments.

You may feel good about yourself when others recognize your abilities. You have your own strengths and weaknesses. Everyone does. If, however, you dwell on your weaknesses you will tend to feel overwhelmed. Others, as well, may not realize the strengths you do have. You will feel more worthwhile when you focus on your strengths.

What Is Self-Esteem?

Self-esteem is how you feel about your self-concept. If you have self-esteem, you feel that you are a good and worthwhile person. You believe in yourself. When you have self-esteem, you are able to accept your weaknesses but you do not dwell on them. You make the most of your strengths, and this is reflected in your attitudes.

Your self-esteem even influences your behavior. If you have self-esteem, you have confidence in yourself and believe in your ability to relate to others and to accomplish tasks. With self-esteem, you can learn new

---

How Self-Esteem Influences Behavior

With Self-Esteem	Without Self-Esteem
Can express strong opinions	Uncertain of own opinions
Trusts own judgment	Afraid to trust own judgment
Is not afraid of criticism	Overly sensitive to criticism
Accepts consequences of own behavior	May blame others or oneself too much
Enjoys being with others	May be shy and withdrawn
Self-confident	Reluctant to try new things
Independent	More dependent on others
Creative in problem solving	Lacks creativity in problem solving
Participates in a variety of activities	Participates in few activities
Shows initiative	Lacks initiative
May devote more time to others	Is preoccupied with self
Assertive	Unassertive
Can take leadership roles	More of a follower

1-11
Self-esteem, as well as a lack of self-esteem, influences a person's behavior.

1-12
People can like themselves even when something goes wrong.

skills and take reasonable risks as you seek new experiences. See 1-11.

Thousands of everyday occurrences influence how you feel about yourself. Your self-esteem may go up and down. One moment you may be upset by a negative remark someone made and judge yourself in the same way. The next hour someone may compliment you, and you feel fine again. This is normal. With time, however, you will be able to pay less attention to those events that lower your self-esteem. You will be able to focus more on your positive qualities and get on with your life. See 1-12.

What Is Self-Worth?

Self-worth is a feeling of worthwhileness, adequacy, and belonging. This feeling is influenced by a person's self-esteem. With self-worth, a teen can say "I count," "I have something to offer," "I am somebody." Without a feeling of self-worth, the words might be "I'll always be second rate" or "I don't deserve to be loved."

Many teens today do not seem to think their life has any value. Your feeling of self-worth holds a promise of what you can become. You are a worthwhile person. A feeling of self-worth empowers you to look ahead with promise. It expands your horizons and helps you focus on what you want to become. Self-worth can give you the feeling, "I am everything because of what I can become." You may not like everything about your life today, but your tomorrow will be what you want to make it. Your feeling of self-worth will help you look ahead and see the positive possibilities. It is up to you.

What are the steps to this feeling of empowerment? How can you catch hold of the feeling of self-worth? Begin with the following:

- Measure yourself honestly. Jot down your strengths and your weaknesses. You may ask a parent or a friend to help you. List your good qualities. Think about how these qualities can help you reach your goals. Be aware of your weaknesses, but do not dwell on them.

- Practice positive self-talk. Tell yourself there is promise in what you are doing. If you have a job, tell yourself, "I'm doing this job better everyday and I'm going to learn how to move ahead." This belief in your future will give you strength. Avoid negative self-talk. If you say to yourself, "I'm a loser," you give yourself an excuse for not trying.

- Accept the things about yourself you cannot change. Tell yourself, "This is the way it is for me now." Your success in the future will depend on what you can do. Part of this is learning to accept what you cannot do.

- Focus on the present, but keep an eye on the future. Dwelling on the past may increase feelings of helplessness. Do the best you can today, and keep your eye on the promise of the future.

- Take one step at a time. Many tasks may seem overwhelming during the teen years. Try taking small steps, but make each one count. Look ahead realistically to where you are headed.

- Be a friend to yourself. You have to like yourself before you can like others. If you feel inadequate or hopeless, pause and focus on something that you feel good about. Remember, a feeling of positive self-worth is within everyone's reach.

Your Character

Another important part of you is your character. *Character* can be defined as a sense of right and wrong that guides your behavior. It is the part of your personality that helps you make choices that are in line with your personal values.

Character development begins in childhood. As children interact with parents and other adults, they begin to learn which behaviors are acceptable and which are not. Children begin to accept these standards as their own. These acquired standards guide their behavior, and thus their character develops.

In the early years, children's behavior is often guided by forces outside their control. They try to conform to the behavior guidelines set by their parents in order to receive their praise. Children like to avoid punishment and to gain rewards. As they grow older, children's behavior is shaped by the approval or disapproval by others outside the family. Social pressures come into play. Behavior is influenced by what is socially acceptable or unacceptable.

Your behavior may often be guided by rules that have been established by authorities. Self-discipline in following these rules protects you in many ways. It also helps maintain order in our society. Obeying these rules will help you build character. When the controls become a part of you, character is developing. You will act in accordance with your own conscience. You will be able to control your own behavior as you meet new situations throughout your life.

As a human being, you have the freedom to decide your own fate. Your life will include many new and exciting experiences. You will meet new friends who will influence you. You will find yourself in many new environments. Your character will be revealed as you respond to all the new situations in your life.

Virtues are traits that indicate character. In 1-13, eight virtues and their definitions are listed. Read the definition of each virtue. Then review the descriptive phrases in the two columns. You will be able to evaluate whether or not your behavior enhances or impedes your character development.

Becoming a Responsible Adult ■ ■ ■ ■ ■ ■ ■

One of the tasks of adolescence is to become a responsible adult. Teens are capable of handling many new responsibilities. Fulfilling these responsibilities is the way you become more independent, 1-14.

Independence is something you earn by proving you can handle responsibility. Many teens wish they could press a button and be awarded instant independence, but it doesn't work that way. For instance, Jodi lamented that his parents never allowed him to take the family car anywhere without them. He was 16 and had his driver's license. Jodi couldn't understand why, so he asked his dad. His dad explained, "Jodi, we asked you to mow the yard every week and many weeks I had to do the job myself. We asked you to let us see your

homework. You always said you had done it. Then we were called by your teacher who said you might fail because you didn't turn in your homework. You have not followed through on these responsibilities. We can't give you any more freedom because you have not yet learned to act responsibly."

Greater rewards have to be earned by fulfilling responsibilities—big and small. Mowing the lawn may not seem important, but someone has to do it. You can't always pick and choose responsibilities. You accept what needs to be done to help your family. Then you fulfill the job to the best of your ability.

Becoming responsible is not simply a matter of performing tasks assigned to you. Responsible people also take charge of their conduct. They own up to their actions and answer for them. If your actions are questioned, or if your behavior is not acceptable, you may try to blame someone or something else. "He made me do it," you may say. If you fail a test, you may say your friend borrowed your book, or you had to work late. The truth is you did not find time to study.

Many people are ready to claim credit for successes, but if mistakes are made they try to disclaim any responsibility. Making mistakes is normal. By denying your mistakes, you give the impression that you believe you are above making mistakes. This is acting irresponsibly.

One of the most unkind things anyone can do is to take away your opportunity to be responsible. Some people trade responsibility for the crippling attitude, "I want someone to take care of me." They lose their desire to succeed on their own. They become content with letting others run their lives.

As a teen today, you have many opportunities to become a responsible adult. Take the opportunity to increase your freedom by becoming a responsible adult. Accept responsi-

Virtues that Help Build Character

Tends to Impede Character Development	Definition	Tends to Enhance Character Development
Finds difficulty in disciplining self to achieve goals. Unable to control behavior when pressured. Finds difficulty in setting goals and waivers in achieving them.	**Self-discipline** To be able to direct self and control behavior in achieving goals.	Believes self-discipline is the means for achieving goals. Able to discipline self in setting goals. Able to control behavior.
Shuns taking responsibility for any action. Finds excuses for not completing tasks. Blames others for own inadequacy.	**Responsibility** To be accountable for your actions.	Accountable for all tasks assigned. Completes tasks without being reminded. Thinks before acting and then accepts responsibility for own actions.
Thinks the end justifies the means if lying will help. Thinks lying is O.K. if no one is hurt. Thinks stretching the truth is justified.	**Honesty and Integrity** To be real, genuine, truthful. To respect self and others.	Word can be counted on. Fulfills promises. Knows the right thing to do and has the will to pursue it. Exhibits integrity in all relationships.
Places well-being of self above the well-being of others. Code of ethical conduct changes depending on situation. Cannot be counted on to react in an honorable way.	**Loyalty** To care sincerely about the well-being of family, friends, and country.	Exhibits steadfastness in attachments to others. Uses intellect in evaluating issue of loyalty. Can be counted on to act in an honorable way.
Self-centered; self-preservation is main objective. Unable to sense needs of others. Indifferent to needs of other human beings.	**Compassion and Mercy** To take seriously the realities of other persons, their lives, and their emotions, as well as their external circumstances.	Feels moral awareness of those around. Natural inclination to help those in distress. Supportive of others in distress.
Needs someone or something to cause person to start and to continue. Willing to settle for job half-done.	**Motivation and Hard Work** Inner urge that prompts individual into positive action.	Self starter. Wants to accomplish goals. Able to continue hard work even if no rewards given.
Tires of task or goal before finishing. No feeling of accomplishment. Unwilling to sacrifice own desires or comforts in order to finish tasks.	**Perseverance** Sets realistic goals and works hard to achieve them.	Sets realistic goals and works to finish. Persists in action to improve self and others. Willing to sacrifice own desires or comforts in order to finish tasks.

Adapted from *The Book of Virtues* by Wm. J. Bennett.

1-13

By reading the descriptive phrases, you can evaluate whether or not your behavior enhances or impedes character development.

1-14 David Hopper
Your responsibilities as a teenager include doing your best in school.

state, and national. Listen to the news, read newspapers, and become active in citizens' groups, 1-15. It is important that you maintain an ongoing interest in what is happening in your local community and in your country. Critical thinking about the issues will give you the background you will need to meet your citizenship responsibilities. You are only one person, but your vote can make a difference.

A Citizen of Your Local Community

Your local community is where you live and go to school or work. Every member of the community plays a part in keeping it a good place to live. In some communities, many people do not seem to care. In others, citizens have a real sense of community pride.

bility when you do make a mistake. Fulfill your responsibilities in your family, in your school, and in your community. You will be learning to fulfill your broader role as a responsible citizen.

What Does It Mean to Be a Good Citizen?

An important part of being a responsible adult is being a good citizen. Citizenship in our country gives you both rights and responsibilities. The rights of citizens are protected by the laws of our government. As a citizen, you are required to obey these laws. You also have the responsibility to pay taxes. These taxes are used to support government services from the local level to the federal level.

You will be reaching 18 in a short time. At that time you will gain the right to vote on government matters. You should be learning all you can about your government—local,

1-15
Reading newspapers will keep you informed of what is happening in your local community and in the world.

Contemporary Topics *of interest to teens*
Volunteering Benefits Everyone

You can return something to your community, your country, and your world by volunteering. Volunteering is choosing freely to provide a service for others without pay. Many community successes are the result of volunteers who decided to do something to make life better for the citizens of their community. Such projects range from beautification plans to recycling programs to garden plots for people to grow their own produce.

Globally, volunteerism is a growing movement. Across the world, people are in need. Governments are not able to help all who suffer. Volunteer organizations step in when needed to ease suffering wherever possible. All of these organizations rely on volunteer help, either to provide the aid directly or to raise funds to support the work of the organization.

Teens have youth and energy, and many young people want to help others. Volunteering is the answer for many. Once you start volunteering, you will discover that giving to others brings much personal satisfaction. Even though your time may be limited, every minute can count. With volunteer work, you can decide how much time you have to give.

By volunteering, you not only help others, but you also help yourself. You can develop a wide range of skills as you work to benefit others. You may ask, "What is in it for me?" There are several good reasons for young people to volunteer. Volunteering gives you the opportunity to

- learn to be responsible.

- put your special talents to use.

- test your skills and learn new ones.

- make new friends.

- explore a related career or field of work.

As you enter adulthood, you can begin to make a difference in your community. You can become more involved. You can play a role in keeping it, or making it, a good place to live.

You can begin now to make a difference in your community by showing that you care. Is an elderly person living alone in your neighborhood? Just picking up a carelessly delivered newspaper and placing it by the door is a simple, caring gesture. Perhaps you could offer to mow the lawn or shovel the snow. Just watching for the elderly person to see if he or she is up and about each day shows you care.

In one neighborhood, a young man was upset because of the accumulation of trash on the streets. He started picking up the trash on Saturday mornings. Children came out and helped him. Other teens and adults started picking up the trash in their yards. Within two months, the street was clean and orderly. A young teen showed he cared about his neighborhood, and he made a difference.

- work with people in different age groups.

- make important contacts in your community.

- be recognized for a job well done.

There are various ways you can volunteer. You can work through an already established organization that uses volunteer help. Such organizations include the American Red Cross, the Salvation Army, Habitat for Humanity, and Big Brothers/Big Sisters. Every community has programs already in place that always need volunteers. These include museums, zoos, animal shelters, libraries, park districts, and nursing homes. Some communities have Voluntary Action Committees to coordinate volunteer work in their area.

Another way to get involved as a volunteer is to work through organizations to which you already belong. Your group may wish to launch its own volunteer program to fill a need they see in your community.

The following are some ways teenagers have volunteered:

- Acting as counselors in camps for children with special needs.

- Planting trees in areas damaged by fire.

- Reading to elderly people in nursing homes.

- Cleaning beaches and roadsides.

- Helping with home construction as a part of community projects to build housing for low-income people.

- Tutoring elementary school children.

- Participating in clothing and food drives for the needy.

- Collecting materials for recycling.

Can you think of other ways you can volunteer to help make your community, country, and world a better place to live?

Your local community has many organizations that can use your help. They are always looking for volunteers. Show you care and take an active role in making your community better by volunteering your time and talents.

A Citizen of the Larger Community

The world is at your doorstep. What you do in your local community and what our society does as a nation impacts the world. Likewise, what happens in local communities around the world can impact you.

Many of the products you buy are imported from other countries. Likewise, many of the products made in this country are exported worldwide. You have only to look in your home to see the many items that are imported from other countries. Your television may have components that came from other countries. Fabrics may have come from mills in one country, but may be sent to other nations to be sewn into clothing. We live in a global economy that combines the raw materials from one country and the technology available in another country to produce a final product.

How we care for our environment today can affect the future quality of life on this planet. For example, both the production and use of fuel can damage the environment. Oil spills in the oceans can foul the waters. Fumes from burning fuels can pollute the air. Nuclear waste, if improperly handled, can have long-lasting environmental effects. These are concerns that can affect the entire world community. As a citizen of the world, you need to be informed of the environmental benefits and risks of energy production as well as other trends (such as population growth) that affect global well-being. You can then make your concerns known. Responsible adults need to be informed about what is happening in the world and how it impacts lives.

Taking a Leadership Role

Assuming responsibility sometimes means taking a leadership role. Leaders are needed within the local community, as well as in state and national forums. The role of a leader is one of the responsibilities you may assume as an adult.

You have many opportunities to develop leadership skills now as a teenager. You can exercise these skills in school, religious, and community groups to which you may belong. The experience you gain will be very useful in helping you reach later goals in life. As you continue your education or work after high school, your ability to lead will help you move ahead, 1-16.

What does it take to become a leader? You may become a leader if you are able to communicate your thoughts and those of others effectively. You are able to direct discussions. You are able to get people involved because you can motivate others. You have

Cholla Runnels

1-16
Leadership skills developed in school can help you in the working world.

the ability to look at the whole of a problem and break it down into parts that are solvable. You can work with group members to identify problems, find ways to solve them, and lead the group in carrying out solutions. You will learn more about developing leadership skills later in this book.

Meeting Personal Expectations

Each of you has expectations for your personal life. Some of your expectations are for what you hope to accomplish. For instance, today you may hope to pass your chemistry exam. If you don't pass this one, and you continue to have trouble, your future expectations may not be met. Your future expectations may include education, a career, marriage, and becoming a parent.

Some of your personal expectations may not be measurable. They may involve more abstract feelings that bring you contentment and satisfaction with your life. Your hopes for finding happiness, love, affection, and fulfillment are equally important expectations.

Goal-Setting in Your Teen Years

Expectations become your goals. A *goal* is something you want to achieve or to have. Maybe as a teenager you haven't spent much time thinking about goals, but you have probably thought about your future. If so, then some goals may have entered your mind. For instance, your parents have probably asked you what you plan to do when you get out of school. From an early age, others too may have asked, "What do you want to be when you grow up?" You probably have answered that question many times through the years, but now is the time to commit to an answer. If you do know what career field interests you, then you are ready to start setting some goals for yourself.

It is important to begin to focus on goals during your teen years. Goals help you steer toward a satisfying future. They can give you a purpose for making the most of every day. Goals help you think more critically when faced with decisions. Even if circumstances cause you to detour slightly, you know you can still reach your goals using other plans. With goals in mind, you can sense promise as you look toward your future.

Roadblocks to Responsible Adulthood ■ ■ ■ ■ ■

Every path to adulthood will have obstacles to overcome. These obstacles will require extra effort to find a way over them. Major roadblocks may cause some people to give up altogether. Other young people will be challenged all the more to do their best and try their hardest.

What Are the Roadblocks?

Every generation has roadblocks. Some roadblocks have been around for hundreds of years. Your parents faced them, and you may face them also. These are the roadblocks of poverty and unemployment, crime and violence in the home and on the streets, abuse of alcohol and other drugs, and sexual abuse. Sexually transmitted diseases have also been around for hundreds of years, but AIDS is the most recent killer. An unplanned pregnancy too early in life can also be a roadblock. More than one million of the U.S.'s nine million girls between the ages of 15 and 19 get pregnant every year. About half give birth. Nearly one-third of all babies are born out of wedlock.

Many young people today are overwhelmed by these roadblocks. Out of frustration, some drop out of school, run away, or join a gang where they hope to survive. Some become early victims. They may become victims of the gang violence that has been escalating in recent years. The abuse of drugs, including alcohol, claims some young lives.

Sexually transmitted diseases, especially HIV, may ultimately cause the death of other young people. Tragically, some take their own lives. For the survivors, the biggest roadblock may be the loss of faith in any promise of a better future.

1-17
Most young people find ways to overcome the roadblocks they encounter.

Somehow, though, these survivors have to find a way to move past these roadblocks. Many teens have found a formula that works for them, 1-17. Even with devastating problems, they recognize that their future depends on their ability to take responsibility for their own lives.

Concerns of Young Adults

Fortunately, not all young people are faced with these major roadblocks. All teens, however, have many of the same concerns. In a number of surveys, teenagers have consistently listed the following as their most important concerns:

Having enough money.
Staying healthy (and avoiding AIDS).
Avoiding wrong decisions.
The future of the country.
Choosing the right career.
Getting a good job.
Finding the right person to marry.
Dealing with family problems.

Finding Your Way

You can find a way around the roadblocks and there are ways of dealing with your concerns. Reading this book is a start. In the chapters to follow, you will learn more about yourself and your relationships with others. You will learn about the decisions facing you. You will find help in making these decisions. You will be learning about families—how they are changing and the responsibilities family members must share.

Your future depends on your ability to take responsibility for your life. You may think that life has not given you what others have. You may not have had a choice in some of the circumstances in your life, but you do have a choice about what you are going to do with your future.

There are many people who can help you sort out your options. Though many young people turn to their friends for advice, they also look to their parents. If you have a good relationship with your parents, you are more likely to turn to them for guidance. Other family members, too, can help you find answers. Don't be afraid to ask for help.

As you prepare for responsible adulthood, keep the following in mind:

- Seek reliable information resources and ask questions.

- Identify your options and think through possible consequences.

- If you make judgments, be responsible for the results.

- Have opinions, but listen to the opinions of others as well.

- Understand your values—that which is important to you.

- Respect your heritage.

- Be able to communicate, negotiate, and compromise.

- Learn how to create your future.

Your life is a continuum—a long, straight line. What happens to you today will always be a part of you. What you do today is a part of your future. Keep a vision for your entire life before you—not just today. You have positive possibilities!

Summary ■ ■ ■ ■ ■ ■ ■ ■ ■ ■ ■ ■ ■ ■

- Your personality development is dependent on three factors: your heredity, your environment, and your response to your environment.

- Growth may be measured in six ways: chronologically, physically, intellectually, emotionally, socially, and philosophically.

- The image that is your self-concept begins to form at an early age. Your parents, other family members, your teachers, and friends all play a part in shaping your self-concept.

- A positive self-concept leads to self-esteem. Your feeling of self-esteem influences your behavior.

- With a sense of self-worth, you feel confident in your ability to reach the goals you have set for your life.

- Character is the part of your personality that helps you make choices that are in line with your personal values.

- One of the tasks of adolescence is to become a responsible adult. As you take on more responsibilities, you will be given more independence.

- As a citizen, you have both rights and responsibilities. You can begin fulfilling your rights and responsibilities as a teenager.

- Your personal expectations are what you hope to accomplish. Some expectations are measurable and some are not. These expectations become your goals.

- It is not always easy to become a responsible adult. There are road-blocks, such as poverty, drug abuse, and violence, that can make the road difficult to travel.

- Your future will depend on your ability to take responsibility for your life.

To Review

1. Match the following terms and identifying phrases.
   _____ Heredity
   _____ Personality
   _____ Environment
   _____ Growth pattern
   _____ Self-concept
   _____ Self-esteem
   _____ Self-worth
   a. How you feel about yourself.
   b. The unique way a person grows.
   c. All of the conditions, objects, and circumstances that surround an individual.
   d. A sense of right and wrong.
   e. Feeling of adequacy.
   f. Group of behavioral and emotional traits that distinguish an individual.
   g. The way you see yourself.
   h. The sum of traits that are passed from your ancestors to you.

2. Name two similarities heredity causes in humans.

3. Name two differences heredity causes in humans.

4. List two parts of your environment that you share with your peers and two parts of your environment that are unique.

5. Match the following areas of growth with their definitions.
   _____ Chronological
   _____ Physical
   _____ Social
   _____ Emotional
   _____ Intellectual
   _____ Philosophical
   a. Development of a deeper feeling of meaning and purpose in life.
   b. Growth in months and years.
   c. Growth in height and weight.

    d. Development of ability to get along with other people.

    e. Growth in knowledge and mental abilities.

    f. Development of ability to control and express feelings.

6. When do the physical growth patterns of boys and girls begin to differ?

7. What is character?

8. Explain the relationship between responsibility and independence.

9. List two rights and two responsibilities of citizenship.

To Do

1. Discuss how your response to your environment can change some hereditary characteristics. Can these changes be beneficial or detrimental to your well-being?

2. Design a bulletin board titled "Six Ways We Grow." Find pictures to illustrate each type of growth.

3. Discuss how a feeling of self-worth can help you believe in your future. Cite examples of people who have had difficult childhoods, but have become successful.

4. Discuss how responsibility can be reflected in work habits, personal relationships, dating, family relationships, sports activities, and school government.

5. In small groups, develop lists of ways teens can volunteer in your local community.

6. Research one of the organizations listed in this chapter that use volunteer help. Prepare a report for the class on the organization's history, goals, and activities.

7. Make a list of roadblocks teens face in your community. Then make a list of suggestions for overcoming each of these roadblocks.

8. Conduct a survey of the students in your school on the concerns of teens. Use the list of concerns of teens given in this chapter, or make a list of your own. Have students rank the concerns in order of importance. After tabulating the results of the survey, write an article for the school paper.

Your Heredity

David Hopper

After studying this chapter, you will be able to

- explain the process of heredity.

- describe how twins and multiple births occur.

- identify the characteristics that a person inherits.

- explain the role of heredity as only one of many factors influencing life success.

Terms to Know

chromosomes

gene

dominant gene

recessive gene

mutations

fraternal twins

identical twins

mirror imaging

Siamese twins

autosomes

blood type

Rh factor

You have a heritage that has been given to you by your ancestors. Because of your family heritage, you have unique characteristics. Some of these characteristics are visible, 2-1, and some are invisible, but they all influence development. For instance, bone structure, musical ability, and certain diseases can be traced through generations of families.

As you study about heredity, you should consider your responsibilities to any future children you may have. Heredity is a repeti-

Cholla Runnels

2-1
Heredity has caused this mother, daughter, and granddaughter to have similar facial characteristics.

·tive cycle. Your hereditary potentials were determined by your parents, and through you, these potentials will be passed on to future generations.

The Process of Heredity

Hereditary information is contained in *chromosomes.* Humans have 23 pairs of chromosomes (46 total) in every cell of their bodies.

When a man and woman mate, both pass on half of their chromosomes to the offspring. The sperm from the father contains 23 chromosomes. The egg from the mother contains 23 chromosomes. Thus, when the sperm and egg unite, the new offspring receives 23 chromosomes from each parent, or 46 chromosomes in all. See 2-2. The chromosomes reproduce themselves, so each cell of the body contains 46 chromosomes that are identical to the original 46.

Chromosomes and Genes

A human chromosome is composed of a chemical called deoxyribonucleic acid (DNA). Each chromosome can be viewed as a strand of thousands of genes. The *gene* is the basic unit of heredity. Genes carry all the characteristics that will be transferred. Genes

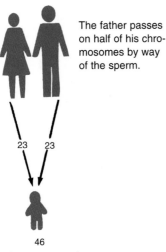

The mother passes on half of her chromosomes by way of the egg.

The father passes on half of his chromosomes by way of the sperm.

23   23

46

These 46 chromosomes determine the total heredity of the child.

2-2
As the chromosomes from the sperm and egg unite, they determine the total heredity of the offspring.

occur in pairs. In each pair of genes, one gene is from the mother, and one gene is from the father. Many pairs of genes work together to form each trait.

Dominant and Recessive Genes

The traits of each person are determined by the way genes from the two parents combine. Gregor Mendel, an Austrian monk, founded the laws of dominant and recessive genes in the 1800s. Mendel's laws are illustrated in 2-3. They can be summarized as follows:

1. Inherited traits are determined by genes. These genes are passed unchanged from generation to generation.

First generation
One parent has a pair of dominant genes (●●). The other parent has a pair of recessive genes(●●).

Second generation
Each offspring receives one dominant gene and one recessive gene. All offspring exhibit the dominant trait and are carriers of the recessive trait.

Third generation
If two people having genes like those of the second generation would mate, their offspring would have varying gene combinations. Statistically, one out of four would have a pair of dominant genes. Two out of four would have one dominant gene and one recessive gene. One out of four would have a pair of recessive genes and would exhibit the recessive trait.

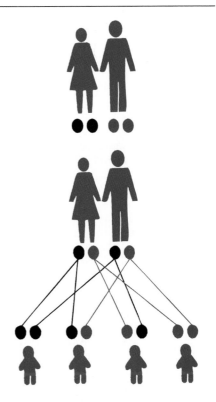

2-3
This is a representative view of how dominant and recessive genes work in the process of heredity.

2.   Genes occur in pairs. A parent gives one of each pair of genes to an offspring.

3.   Where the two genes in a pair act differently, one gene often dominates the other. Thus, one gene is *dominant* (more influential or prevalent) and the other is *recessive* (less influential or prevalent).

4.   The effect of a recessive gene may be masked by that of a dominant gene. However, if two recessive genes are paired, the effect will be noticed.

5.   When traits are governed by different genes, the genes for each trait are transmitted independently. Thus, the genes for one trait have no effect on the genes for other traits.

Mutations

The sperm and egg contain genes exactly like the genes that the man and woman received from their parents. The rare excep-

2-5
Fraternal twins may be of the same sex or of opposite sexes.

Fraternal twins are products of two different eggs fertilized by two different sperm.

The two fertilized eggs develop into two different persons. They carry different combinations of chromosomes and genes.

Thus, apart from having been born together, fraternal twins are no more alike than any two siblings. They may be two boys; two girls; or a boy and a girl.

2-4
The development of fraternal twins.

tions to this rule occur when genes have mutations. *Mutations* are chemical changes in genes. They are caused by either spontaneous error in genetic mechanisms or through some outside influence such as radiation. The atom bomb dropped in Japan during World War II caused severe radiation damage. As a result, many defective offspring were born.

Identical twins are products of a single egg fertilized by a single sperm.

 At an early stage, the developing embryo divides.

  The halves develop into two separate persons. The two twins carry the same genes and chromosomes.

  Thus, identical twins are always of the same sex. They are either two identical boys or two identical girls.

2-6
The development of identical twins.

Twins and Multiple Births

The role of heredity in twins remains uncertain. Medical scientists do know that once a mother has had twins, her chances of having twins again are three to ten times greater. The sister of a twin-bearing mother also has an above-average chance of having twins. Twinning (having twins) often "skips" generations. In other words, a woman who is a twin may not have twins, but may be the grandmother of twins.

Fraternal Twins

Fraternal twins are the products of two eggs fertilized by two sperm. They are no more alike than brother and sister except that they are born at the same time. They may be of the same sex or of opposite sexes. See 2-4 for an explanation of how fraternal twins develop. A set of fraternal twins is pictured in 2-5.

Identical Twins

Identical twins are products of a single fertilized egg that divides as shown in 2-6. They have the same hereditary factors, so they are always of the same sex. They also have identical physical traits. See 2-7. The only exception is that the fingerprints of identical twins are never the same.

Mirror imaging, or reverse patterning, sometimes occurs in identical twins. In mirror imaging, some body details that appear on the right side of one twin appear on the left side of the other. Examples are hair whorls, birthmarks, and tooth defects. Sometimes opposite handedness is also evident.

Siamese twins are identical twins who are born physically linked. They are formed when the fertilized egg fails to split completely apart. The linkage may be slight, such as at the hips or sides, or it may involve internal organs as well. The original twins, from whom the term Siamese stems, were two brothers, named Chang and Eng. They were born in 1811 to Chinese parents in what was then Siam. They were joined from chest to navel and shared a liver.

Cholla Runnels

2-7
Identical twins are always alike in physical traits and are always the same sex.

Sometimes Siamese twins can be separated so the two persons can live normal lives. The chances for a successful separation are best when no major internal organs are involved.

Multiple Births

Triplets, quadruplets, quintuplets, and even sextuplets have been born. They may be identical, fraternal, or mixed sets. One of the most sensational quintuplet births occurred when five girls were born to the Dionne family in Canada in 1934. What was most amazing was that they were an identical set. The original egg fertilized by one sperm divided and redivided to form quadruplets. Three of these developed into girls, who were named

Yvonne, Annette, and Cecile. The fourth divided again and produced Emilie and Marie. These two girls were frailer and smaller than the others. They manifested mirror imaging. They were more farsighted than the other three. Also, both remained mildly cross-eyed long after the condition disappeared in the other girls.

The Fischer quintuplets, born in South Dakota in 1963, were an example of a three-egg combination. Three identical girls and two fraternal twins, a girl and a boy, made up this set of quintuplets.

A fertility hormone is often used by women who are having difficulty becoming pregnant. This hormone is largely responsible for the increase of multiple births we see occurring today. The hormone stimulates ovulation of more than one egg and increases the chances for multiple deliveries.

Every cell of a woman has two X chromosomes.

Every cell of a man has one X chromosome and one Y chromosome.

Every egg has one X chromosome.

Half the sperm have an X chromosome; half have a Y chromosome.

If a sperm with an X chromosome enters the egg, the result is a person with two X chromosomes—a girl.

If a sperm with a Y chromosome enters the egg, the result is a person with one X and one Y chromosome—a boy.

2-8
The sex chromosome from the sperm determines the sex or gender of the offspring.

Inherited Characteristics

Heredity affects almost every aspect of your life. It controls some traits completely, such as gender (male or female) and eye color. It works with your environment in determining other traits, such as intelligence and longevity. By examining the characteristics you have inherited, you can learn more about your total personality and future potential.

Determination of Sex

Perhaps the most important of all inherited characteristics is that of gender. Of the 23 pairs of chromosomes, 22 are alike in both the male and female. These are called the *autosomes*. The chromosomes of the 23rd pair are the sex chromosomes.

In the male, the pair of sex chromosomes consists of one X chromosome and one Y chromosome. Thus, when the pair of genes splits, one sperm has an X chromosome, and one sperm has a Y chromosome.

In the female, the pair of sex chromosomes consists of two X chromosomes. Thus, each egg contains one X chromosome. If a sperm with an X chromosome combines with an egg, the fertilized egg will have two X chromosomes. It will be female. If a sperm with a Y chromosome combines with an egg, the fertilized egg will have one X chromosome and one Y. It will be male. See 2-8 to review the process of determining gender.

Sex-linked Characteristics

Characteristics that are determined by genes on the X chromosome are called sex-linked characteristics. Examples are color blindness and hemophilia. Color blindness is the inability to distinguish between colors,

usually red and green. About eight percent of the males in the United States are troubled with this to some degree.

Hemophilia is a bleeding disorder in which blood clots very slowly. Even a slight bruise or cut can cause a large loss of blood. With modern methods of treatment and with care, hemophiliacs can live close to a normal life span.

Males have greater tendencies toward sex-linked characteristics than females. This is because a male has only one X chromosome. If it carries the defective gene, the male will have the characteristic. A female has two X chromosomes. She will have the characteristic only if both X chromosomes carry the defective gene.

Intellectual Ability

Your intellectual potential is inherited, though your environment and your response to your environment affect it greatly, 2-9. Generally, parents who are highly intelligent will probably produce intelligent children. However, an intelligent child may also be born to parents of low to average intelligence. Heredity is also responsible for many mental defects.

Any data interpreting intelligence today is based on I.Q. (intelligence quotient) tests. Authorities vary in the importance they attach to I.Q. tests, but they are the only standardized tests available for comparing intelligence. The I.Q. score is obtained by dividing mental age by chronological age. Suppose a child, age eight, has a mental performance of an average 10-year-old. Then 10 would be divided by eight, giving a quotient of 1.25 or an I.Q. of 125. Scores between 90 and 110 are considered "normal." Scores above 140 are considered "genius."

An I.Q. score is only a score, however. It does not reflect the role of personal motivation, interpersonal skills (for example, relat-

Cholla Runnels

2-9
Your potential for intelligence is inherited, but your motivation to learn affects your actual intellectual ability.

ing well to others), and other factors in attaining success. With dedication and hard work, many individuals with I.Q. scores far from the genius level can achieve very highly.

Blood Factors

Two important blood factors are determined by heredity. They are blood type and the Rh factor.

Blood types are divided into four main groups: O, A, B, and AB. A person's specific blood type is determined by genes. About 42 percent of the people in the United States have type O blood. They are known as universal donors because type O blood can be given to anyone. Persons with blood type AB are known as universal receivers because they can receive any type of blood. Only about eight percent of the population has blood type AB. About 40 percent has type A blood, and about 10 percent of the population has type B blood.

The *Rh factor* is a specific blood element. Persons who have inherited the element are called Rh-positive. Persons who have not inherited it are called Rh-negative. About 85 percent of the Caucasian race is Rh-positive. Other races are almost 100 percent Rh-positive.

The Rh factor creates a problem only when an Rh-negative mother is carrying a baby who has received the dominant Rh-positive factor from the father. During pregnancy and childbirth, some of the baby's blood cells may enter the mother's bloodstream. The mother then produces antibodies to counteract this factor. This seldom creates a problem with the first child. However, if the mother carries another Rh-positive baby, her antibodies can enter the baby's system and attack the red blood cells. Anemia, jaundice, and stillbirth are possible results.

Today, a vaccine is available to prevent this problem. An Rh-negative mother is given the Rh vaccine after the birth of each child. It neutralizes any Rh-positive blood cells that have entered her body. This prevents her system from producing antibodies.

Longevity

If your relatives have tended to have long lives, you may inherit that tendency. Within certain limits, the life span of humans seems to be set by heredity. However, environment also plays a major role in determining longevity, 2-10.

Improvements in environment, such as increased medical knowledge, have extended

Cholla Runnels

2-10
The tendency to live a long life is inherited, but environmental factors such as exercise and diet affect it greatly.

people's life spans. The average life expectancy of the early American colonists was about 35 years. Today it is over 70 years. On the other hand, environment sometimes shortens lives. Accidents, wars, and natural catastrophes can negate hereditary potential for long lives.

Another factor in longevity is the tendency for women to live longer than men. More male children are born, but more boys than girls die during childhood. Thus, the number of male and female young adults is about even. More men tend to die at a younger age in adult life, but this is changing. As careers and lifestyles change, men and women are facing similar pressures and hazards. The result is that the gap in life spans is narrowing.

Skin Color

Skin color depends on race and thus on heredity. A race is a large group of people who were separated environmentally from other large groups for a long time. During this time, they experienced different conditions and developed certain genetic traits that distinguish them from members of other races. See 2-11, 2-12, and 2-13. The three major races in the world are:

2-11
A Chinese family represents the Mongoloid race.

David Hopper

2-12
A black family represents the Negroid race.

1. The Mongoloid, or yellow-brown race, which developed in Asia.

2. The Negroid, or black race, which developed in Africa.

3. The Caucasoid, or white race, which developed in Europe.

Hair and Facial Features

As you look through your family album, you probably will notice certain hair and facial features that appear repeatedly in your family. These features are the result of many genes working together.

Look at the spectrum of inherited traits in 2-14. Analyze your features and compare

David Hopper

2-13
A white family represents the Caucasoid race.

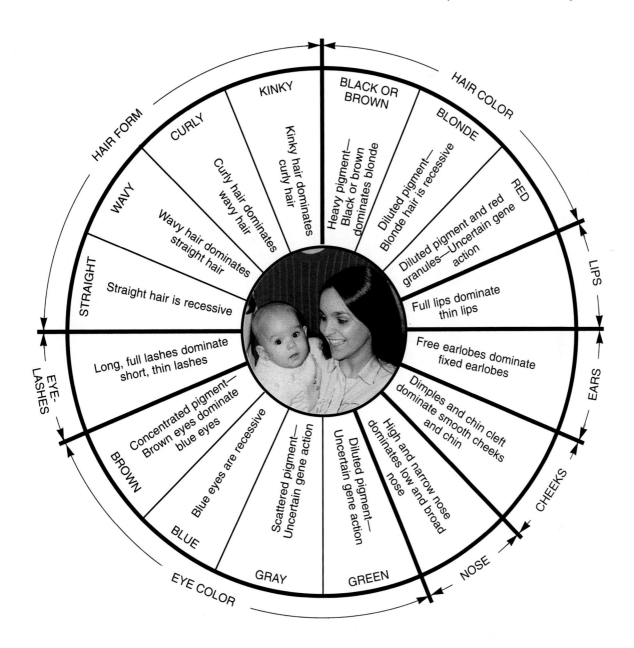

2-14
This spectrum of inherited traits can give you an idea of how certain features are
passed from generation to generation.

them with those of other members of your
family. Which features do you have in common? Are they the result of dominant or recessive genes? Which features will probably
appear in your offspring?

Height and Bone Structure

A person's potentials for height and
bone structure are inherited, 2-15. However,
good health and proper diet (environmental

David Hopper

2-15
These people are similar in age, but they differ widely in height and bone structure.
Heredity is the main cause of the differences, although environmental factors may
also be involved.

factors) also affect these traits. A person's body cannot reach its potential if it lacks sufficient nutrients or if it is diseased.

In our culture today, people are growing taller. College students are over two inches taller than college students 50 years ago. Many basketball teams have five members who are all close to seven feet tall. This increase in height is probably the result of a combination of factors. Because tallness is dominant over shortness, people in some families tend to become taller. Other reasons could include improvements in diet, living conditions, and medical care.

Obesity

Psychological factors, overeating, and lack of exercise are usually the main causes of obesity. In some families, the tendency for obesity is inherited. Heredity can cause differences in the way food is utilized and in the way body heat is lost or conserved. If the tendency to be overweight runs in your family, your health care becomes even more important. A balanced diet and a sensible exercise plan are essential.

Diseases and Defects

Certain diseases and defects are hereditary. Some genes carry the potential for them, as others carry the potential for hair color or height. The list of inherited diseases and defects is long. A few of them are described in 2-16. Genetic roles also have been identified in some forms of cancer (for example, breast and colon), heart disease, amyotrophic lateral sclerosis (Lou Gehrig's

Inherited Defects and Diseases

Disease/Defect	Symptoms	Cause	Treatment
Cleft lip/palate	Noticeable at birth. A cleft lip occurs when the two sides of the upper lip fail to grow together properly. A cleft palate occurs when an opening remains in the roof of the mouth. This creates problems in breathing, talking, hearing, and eating.	Variable; often caused by a number of factors working together.	Corrective surgery and speech therapy.
Cystic fibrosis	A chemical failure affects lungs and pancreas. Thick, sticky mucus forms in the lungs, causing breathing problems. Reduced amounts of digestive juices cause poor digestion of food. An excess amount of salt is excreted in perspiration.	Recessive gene.	Physical therapy, synthetic digestive enzymes, salt tablets, and antibodies can lessen the effect of the symptoms. However, there is no known cure. Patients usually have shorter-than-normal life spans because they are highly susceptible to respiratory diseases.
Diabetes	Metabolic disorders cause high blood sugar. The patient feels thirsty, hungry, and weak and usually loses weight.	A number of factors working together.	The disease can be controlled by insulin injections and careful diet and exercise. It cannot be cured.
Down's syndrome	Distinct physical features are evident. Slanting eyes; large, misshapen forehead; oversized tongue; single crease across palm of each hand; and varying degrees of mental retardation are typical.	Chromosome abnormality. More likely to occur when mother is over age 45.	Special education. Life span may be nearly normal.
Huntington's chorea	The brain and central nervous system gradually deteriorate when the patient is between 30 and 40 years old. This causes involuntary jerking, loss of mental abilities, insanity, depression, and finally death.	Dominant gene.	None.
Hydrocephalus	Extra fluid is trapped in the brain. The patient's head is larger than normal.	A number of factors working together.	Surgical removal of excess fluid. Without treatment, children rarely survive.
Muscular dystrophy	A group of disorders which damage muscles. They cause progressive weakness and finally death.	Often sex-linked.	There is no cure, but therapy and braces offer some relief.
Phenylketonuria (PKU)	An enzyme deficiency makes the patient unable to digest a certain amino acid. The baby appears healthy at birth, but slowly develops mental retardation because the amino acid builds up in the body and causes brain damage.	Recessive gene.	A carefully prescribed diet that balances the enzyme deficiency. The effects of the disease can usually be avoided if treatment begins within the first six weeks of birth.
Sickle-cell anemia	Red blood cells are sickle-shaped rather than round. They cannot carry oxygen efficiently throughout the body. Patients become pale, tired, and short of breath. They have occasional pains and low resistance to infection. Their life span is often shorter than normal.	Recessive gene.	There is no cure. Various treatments relieve some symptoms, and blood transfusions are needed occasionally.

2-16
Inherited diseases and defects have many different causes and effects.

Contemporary Topics *of interest to teens:*
The Genetic Revolution

Personal genetic codes determine a wide range of physical characteristics. These include the likelihood of contracting genetically transmitted diseases. Medical researchers are making remarkable strides in helping doctors detect and prevent many such illnesses. All forms of a disease may not be genetically based. However, those that are genetically transmitted often can be detected through a blood test.

Tests for many diseases (see box) are available now. Researchers expect other tests to be available soon. These include tests for genetically based forms of Alzheimer's disease, breast cancer, and colon cancer.

A person with a strong family history of a particular disease may wish to be tested for it. Testing can provide useful input in personal life decisions such as career choices. For example, if a person knows that a terminal disease is likely to strike in midlife, perhaps he or she will be less likely to choose a career requiring long years of preparation. Perhaps such a person will plan to reach major goals, such as career success or travel, earlier in life.

A positive test result also may alert a person to the importance of a healthy lifestyle and early detection of disease. A person who is a potential "carrier" of a genetically based disease may wish to carefully weigh childbearing decisions.

Often, people who are tested find that genetic counseling is useful in helping them deal with test results. Other individuals would prefer not to know whether or not they have a genetic potential for a disease.

Some Available Genetic Tests

Cystic fibrosis
Down's syndrome
Fragile X syndrome (causes mental retardation)
Hemophilia
Huntington's disease
Lou Gehrig's disease (amyotrophic lateral sclerosis)
Melanoma (skin cancer)
Muscular dystrophy
Myotonic dystrophy (degenerative muscular disease)
Neurofibromatosis (nerve disease)
PKU (phenylketonuria)
Sickle-cell anemia
Tay-Sachs disease (metabolic disorder)

disease), and mental illnesses such as schizophrenia and manic depression.

Some inherited diseases are noticeable at birth; others may not appear until much later in life. Some defects are minor; others can be fatal. Some can be corrected; others are permanent.

Valuing Your Uniqueness ▪ ▪ ▪ ▪ ▪

Of all the human beings who have ever lived, you are uniquely and wonderfully yourself! This in itself is cause for reflection and celebration.

Inborn physical influences play a significant role in who you become. Some traits, such as crooked teeth, can be changed. Other traits, such as height or bone structure, cannot.

People achieve the greatest happiness regarding their perceived "faults" if they learn to change what they can change and to accept that which is beyond their control. You cannot change the hand you have been dealt in life, but you have a great deal of control over how you play the cards you have been given. How each person deals with his or her own unique set of strengths and limitations tells the world how this person has decided to live life.

Some people focus on their faults and use them as an excuse for failure. "I didn't get asked to the prom because my nose is too big" or "No one will ask me out because I'm so tall" are common complaints.

Other people do what they can to either improve or downplay their self-perceived faults and then get on with life. They may decide to focus on developing other physical or emotional aspects of themselves instead of worrying about things that are beyond their control. For example, a short teenage boy may decide to concentrate on developing his interpersonal skills. He may use his friendliness and sense of humor to cope with situations where he would be at a disadvantage (for example, in a bullying situation). People may forget his height because they enjoy being around him. He may go on to use these skills to become highly successful in later life.

Similarly, a teenage girl in a wheelchair may develop an outgoing, cheerful personality. She may learn to forget her self-consciousness by reaching out to others and learning to put them at ease. When others feel challenged in situations of their own, they may look to her for lessons on how to face the ups and downs of life with courage and humor.

Summary ▪ ▪ ▪ ▪ ▪ ▪ ▪ ▪ ▪ ▪ ▪ ▪ ▪ ▪ ▪ ▪

- A study of personality development must look at the whole personality, including hereditary contributions.

- Heredity is a repetitive cycle. Your hereditary potentials were determined by your parents, and through you, these potentials will be passed on to future generations.

- Hereditary information is contained in chromosomes. When a man and woman mate, each gives 23 chromosomes to the offspring.

Together, these 46 chromosomes determine the total hereditary potential of the offspring.

■ The genes in chromosomes are the basic units of heredity. Genes occur in pairs. In mating, only one gene from each pair is passed on to the offspring.

■ The effect of a recessive gene may be masked by that of a dominant gene.

■ Identical twins are formed by a single fertilized egg that divides. Fraternal twins are formed by two eggs fertilized by two sperm. Multiple births may include combinations of identical and fraternal twins.

■ Heredity affects such characteristics as gender, intellectual ability, blood type, longevity, skin color, hair and facial features, height, bone structure, obesity, and certain diseases and defects.

■ Some hereditary traits cannot be changed, and some can.

■ Successful people learn to do what they can with their hereditary limitations and "faults" while developing other aspects of themselves.

To Review ■ ■ ■ ■ ■ ■ ■ ■ ■ ■ ■ ■ ■ ■ ■ ■

1. Humans have ___ pairs of chromosomes in every cell of their bodies.

2. True or False. Traits such as bone structure, musical ability, and certain diseases can be traced through generations of families.

3. Which of the following statements is NOT true?
   a. Genes are strands of thousands of chromosomes.
   b. The gene is the basic unit of heredity.
   c. Genes occur in pairs.
   d. Many pairs of genes work together to form each trait.

4. Will a person with two dominant genes for a particular trait exhibit that trait?

5. Will a person with two recessive genes for a particular trait exhibit that trait?

6. What happens when a person has one dominant gene and one recessive gene?

7. Explain the difference between fraternal and identical twins.

8. True or False. In mating, the sex chromosome of the female determines the sex or gender of the offspring.

9. Which gender has the greater tendency toward inheriting sex-linked characteristics—males or females?

10. Your I.Q. score is obtained by dividing your _____ age by your _____ age.

11. Persons with blood type _____ are known as universal donors.

12. Describe the problem that could occur if an Rh-negative pregnant mother is carrying an Rh-positive fetus.

13. Name four hair or facial features that are controlled by dominant genes. Name four that are controlled by recessive genes.

14. Describe two hereditary diseases or defects.

To Do ■

1. Have several small group discussions and share the results with the rest of the class. For each group, appoint a leader to record responses and report them to the class.

    Group A: Should heredity be an important factor in selecting a mate? Consider potentials for intelligence, beauty, body build, obesity, longevity, and birth defects.

    Group B: Suppose your neighbor fell in love with a person whose heritage included an obvious hereditary defect. What would you advise your neighbor to do?

    Group C: Should people be able to select the gender of their future children? Consider the consequences if all firstborn children were boys, or if all were girls. Consider the impact on business, politics, education, marriage, and families if gender selection were possible.

2. Scientists will soon be able to identify individuals with genetic predispositions toward serious—and sometimes fatal—diseases. The identification will take place through simple procedures such as blood tests. Suppose you knew that a serious disease, such as Huntington's chorea, ran in your family. Would you want to get tested to know whether you were likely to develop the disease later in life? If you were found to have a genetic predisposition toward the disease, would you tell a prospective spouse about it? Would you want your medical insurance company to know about it? Why or why not?

Your
Environment

TXDOC, R. Reynolds

**After studying this chapter,
you will be able to**

- describe environmental influences on your personality development.

- explain the role of the family in the development of the child's personality.

- summarize the role of peers in personality development.

- analyze ways in which education, occupation, religion, changing economic conditions, and the mass media may influence personality development.

Terms to Know

authority figures	sibling rivalry
culture	peer group
role	peer pressure
siblings	telecommuting

Which has the greater effect on human development: heredity or environment? Scholars have debated this question for years. Almost all experts would agree, however, that the effects of your heredity cannot be easily separated from the impact of your environment. You are a product of the interaction between the two. Your hereditary traits affect your functioning within your environment, and your environment affects the development of your inherited traits.

Evidence of this interaction is all around you. Look, for instance, at the highlights that enhance the hair of some of your friends. Those highlights may be achieved by many hours of exposure to the sun's rays or simply by a chemical treatment. In either case, the inherited hair color is changed by environmental factors.

You might also consider your friends' personal appearance. Each friend is born with a set of physical traits (heredity). Your friends modify their appearance to some degree with hairstyles and clothing (environment). Still, it is difficult for them to change their appearance very far beyond the limits set by heredity.

Your personality development is also affected by your surroundings. Environmental factors that influence personality will be studied in this chapter. By looking at 3-1, you can see some of the environmental factors that affect your life now. The influence of these factors will probably shift within the next five years, as shown in 3-2.

Your Family

The family undoubtedly provides the single most important environmental influence on a child's personality development. It is within the family that the infant first learns to love and trust others. This sense of trust is gained in the early years through the love and consistency with which the baby's caregiver

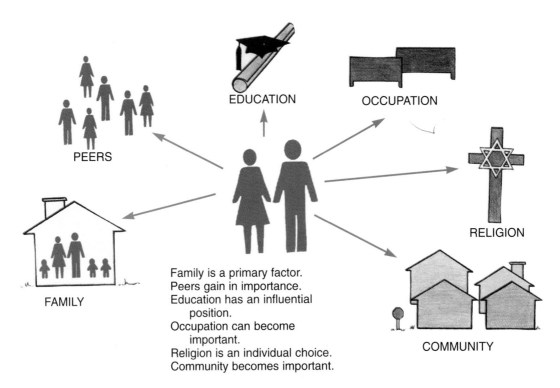

EDUCATION

OCCUPATION

PEERS

RELIGION

FAMILY

Family is a primary factor.
Peers gain in importance.
Education has an influential
    position.
Occupation can become
    important.
Religion is an individual choice.
Community becomes important.

COMMUNITY

3-1
Several environmental factors affect the personality development of high school students.

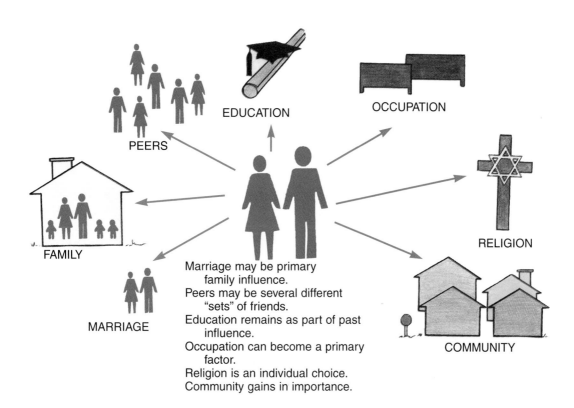

EDUCATION

OCCUPATION

PEERS

FAMILY

MARRIAGE

RELIGION

COMMUNITY

Marriage may be primary
  family influence.
Peers may be several different
  "sets" of friends.
Education remains as part of past
  influence.
Occupation can become a primary
  factor.
Religion is an individual choice.
Community gains in importance.

3-2
Environmental factors shift in importance during the five years after leaving
high school.

responds to the baby's needs. Family members also shape the child's personality development through the values and behaviors they impart to the child.

In a positive and nurturing family environment, children learn that they are loved and valued. As part of this process, they acquire a healthy level of self-esteem. Because they know they are loved, they are able to take the psychological risks necessary to learn new things. They know that the important thing is to try their best, and that if they fail, their family will be there to comfort them and help them try again.

As part of family living, children also are taught the difference between right and wrong. Discipline is administered in a firm but loving, consistent, and fair manner. In this way, children learn healthy ways of relating to *authority figures* (people who make final decisions, such as parents, teachers, and the police). They also learn to respect the limits and boundaries of others.

As children grow, they learn to be sensitive to, and considerate of, the feelings of other family members. They learn to empathize with their brothers and sisters, and to treat others as they themselves would like to be treated. This understanding influences the environment which children later provide as adults for their own children. Thus, positive (or negative) family values and behaviors are often passed from generation to generation.

Cultural Diversity

What do you know about your family background? In what country did your ancestors live? One of the most interesting and enriching parts of life is to look into your past and to see how your ancestors lived their lives. The total social environment of a people or group is called its *culture.*

Our society is culturally diverse. It is made up of families representing many different cultures. Successive generations blend these cultural characteristics into their current way of life. They celebrate their individual cultural backgrounds while also valuing the many things they have in common with the larger human family.

Are you aware of how your cultural background influences your life? Special holiday traditions and foods, heirlooms from "the old country," and colorful ancestral costumes all remind us of our cultural roots, 3-3. We can learn many important lessons from our ancestors. Many of them lived their lives with pride and dignity despite hardship and suffering.

Each family learns its customary values, beliefs, and modes of behavior from its country of origin. These traditions and expressions help to make each family unique. Families can also benefit by learning about the customary values, beliefs, and behaviors of other cultures.

Cholla Runnels

3-3
A young boy demonstrates a dance and the ceremonial dress of his culture.

Family Interactions

Your family provides you with daily experiences no other setting can give you. Each family member interacts with each other member.

Each member of a family fulfills certain roles. A *role* is a socially expected behavior pattern. Your role now is that of a son or daughter. However, you may fill other roles as well. If your grandparents are living, you may also have the role of a grandson or granddaughter. If there are *siblings* (brothers or sisters) in your family, you are also a brother or sister.

By now, you have learned to get along with different members of your family. Your reaction to each is different. The "give and take" of sibling relationships helps your social development. Sometimes you may compete with your brothers and sisters for a parent's love or attention. This is normal. In fact, this sense of competition with your brothers and sisters, called *sibling rivalry,* can even be a good thing. It can give you an understanding of sharing and compromise.

David Hopper

3-4
The companionship of siblings adds to their personality development.

Siblings also offer companionship. See 3-4. This is also true in later life. Although a young child may not seem to have much in common with a sibling who is several years older, the age differences between children seem much less significant when they become adults. Loving family members provide a source of emotional support to one another throughout life.

Influences of Birth Order

Each of your brothers and sisters has a different personality. Some of these personality traits are shaped by the age of each child in relation to the rest of the children.

Oldest-Child Influences

If you were the firstborn, you were the center of your parents' attention until the next child arrived. Because you were first, each of your achievements was new and exciting for your parents. As you mature, you will be the first to be treated as an adult and a friend by your parents.

Firstborn children usually grow up rapidly and have more responsibility than other children, 3-5. Parents may pin high hopes on their first child. Statistics show that the oldest child is the most likely to go to college.

Oldest children usually have the strongest desire to achieve. More is expected of them. They are often asked to take care of their younger siblings and to set an example for them.

Oldest children tend to be comfortable with respect and admiration. They often make good dating and marriage partners. They are usually more independent and may be less outwardly affectionate than other siblings.

A second child who becomes a "middle child" may feel some pressure. The middle child never knows the feeling of being an only child, and has the advantages of being the youngest child only until the next child is born. A middle child may feel less interesting than an older sibling and not as "cute" as a younger sibling.

Middle children tend to be good all-around students. If they feel overshadowed by an older sibling, they may put extra effort into a special skill. Thus, a middle child from an athletic family might turn to music or some other interest for recognition.

Middle children may not like the role of following in their elder sibling's footsteps. However, the middle child's path is often easier. Parents are usually less demanding of middle children than their elder siblings.

Cholla Runnels

3-5
Firstborn children are often given extra responsibilities such as helping their younger siblings.

Cholla Runnels

3-6
A secondborn child has the advantage of companionship with his or her older sibling.

Middle-Child Influences

If you were the second child born in your family, you did not have the advantage of individual attention from parents, but you had the companionship of a sibling, 3-6. The second child often has less responsibility and is less independent than the first child.

Middle children often become particularly good at dealing with the ups and downs of human relationships. They often function as peacemakers. They tend to make calm, even-tempered marriage partners and parents.

Youngest-Child Influences

Youngest children may be given a lot of attention, but they also have more family members telling them what to do. See 3-7. In many families, the youngest child is expected to mature quickly in order to "catch up" with the others. On the other hand, the child may be pampered and indulged. Sometimes parents have difficulty allowing the youngest child to become independent. Youngest children may become confused about whether they really want the responsibilities of growing up.

Some youngest children may become used to getting a lot of attention and being protected. They may seek a partner in marriage who is warm and capable of "taking charge."

Your personality development has been and will continue to be affected by the arrangement of the children in your family with respect to age. Your personality may have been somewhat different if this aspect of your environment had been different.

No matter what position you have in your family, you are contributing to the environment of all family members. The way you interact with other members of your family affects their personality development as well as your own.

Your Peers

The influence of your *peer group* (people about your own age) is one of the strongest forces in your life. Your family will continue to be a strong influence, but your peers will also emerge as an important force. The impact of the two influences will vary as you pass through different developmental stages of your life.

3-7
A youngest child may get a lot of attention, but he or she also gets more "bossing" from siblings.

Peer Influence during Adolescence

At this time of your life, your peers are very important to you, 3-8. You share many experiences with them that contribute to the development of your self-esteem and personality. Your friends can be a source of strength and reinforcement. Such peer influence is natural and even essential in the development of healthy adolescents.

As an adolescent, you are searching for an identity (sense of who you are) and social acceptance. You are particularly vulnerable to peer pressure. *Peer pressure* is the influence exerted by a person's age group. Many young people go along with their peers' choices, thinking that they are asserting their individu-

ality. In reality, they are conforming to (fitting in with) the decisions made by others.

Peer-group pressure is a powerful force in establishing conformity, especially during the adolescent years. Most people want to be accepted and valued by their peers. However, if your choices simply reflect your friends' choices, you will not be reinforcing your own self-esteem. Also, you will not be learning the process of decision making. You may become dependent on others to make your decisions for you. It is important to remember that you can make your own choices. You do not have to conform to choices of your peers just to be accepted by them.

If your friends are influencing you toward behaviors that go against what you think is right, it will be necessary for you to stand

David Hopper

3-8
Peers are a strong influence in the life of almost every teen.

3-9
Good teachers help students develop problem-solving skills that can last a lifetime.

up for what you believe. Those peers who are truly your friends will admire you more for adhering to your convictions.

Loyalties between your friends and you may be tested if they have standards that are unlike yours. If you become aware that your standards are quite different from those of your friends, you may wish to become closer to people with whom you have more in common. The old saying, "You are known by the friends you keep," will continue to apply.

Changes in family structure in our society today have tended to strengthen the influence of peers. As ties in some families grow weaker, peer influence becomes stronger. In today's society, some families are unable to provide the authority and discipline that young people need. There may be no family or close relatives nearby to provide a stabilizing force. Teens may feel "emotionally abandoned" by busy or absent parents.

These young adults are often attracted to peers who are similarly free of strong emo-

tional ties. They may join with one another, sometimes in "gangs," with few restraints imposed on them by their families. In such cases, peer influence becomes so powerful that it can completely overshadow the influence of the family.

Learn to identify and live by your own values. If they are similar to those of your friends, it simply indicates that your ideas and lifestyles are similar. Your choices should be your own, though you can benefit from sharing ideas with others.

Your Education

Your educational environment provides another important influence on your personality development. A positive school environment provides you with information and problem-solving skills, 3-9. It also gives you a sense of yourself as a learner. Whether your individual learning style is fast or slow is of minor significance. The important thing is that you learn to the best of your ability. An appreciation for learning will equip you to seek information to help you solve problems throughout life.

A positive educational environment teaches other useful skills as well. Students learn to relate effectively to authority figures, such as teachers, coaches, and club sponsors. In competitive events, students see the importance of playing by the rules. They observe the role that authority figures play in enforcing the rules fairly. Occasionally, students observe situations in which life isn't fair, and they learn to live with those occurrences, too.

The classroom provides an arena in which you learn both to compete and to cooperate with others. You are also presented with opportunities to develop and test standards of right and wrong, for example, in deciding whether or not to cheat on an exam. All of these experiences and opportunities help you develop your personality. They also provide a valuable training ground for later life.

Your Occupation ▪ ▪ ▪

One of the most influential factors in your environment is your occupation. Many students have part-time jobs. Such jobs offer a number of benefits. They give people a chance to develop their personalities. Part-time work can also contribute to their self-knowledge.

As people perform their jobs, they can evaluate their assets (good points) and their liabilities (negative aspects). As these people are faced later with career choices, their decisions will probably reflect this self-knowledge.

Individuals' occupations contribute to their personalities throughout their lives. A job or career identity is one of the first aspects of personality people reveal to each other. When people are introduced, a career or pre-career label is often used to identify them. They may say, for example, "Mary is an architect" or "Joe is a student teacher."

As you move into the future, new skills will become part of your identity, 3-10. Now you are a student, and your developmental environment is determined largely by your family, your peers, and your school. Your career is in its formative stages, but soon it will expand to consume a major portion of your time. As it gains importance in your life, it will have increasing influence on your lifestyle. Your career will affect the hours you work, the money you make, and the place you live.

3-10
This fashion consultant is analyzing a client's personal wardrobe. Her work role forms a part of her identity.

3-11
Religion is a vital factor in the lives of many people.

Cholla Runnels

It will challenge you to develop new aspects of your personality. Career success can be an important source of self-esteem.

Your Religion

Religion is one of the most personal aspects of your environment. Religion means different things to different people. For many people, religion provides a sense of meaning and purpose for life. They feel that their religious faith offers them security and direction as they strive to reach their goals and to be responsible family and community members.

The freedom to choose a religion is one of the basic freedoms we enjoy in this country. If religion is one of your personal priorities, you will be influenced by it throughout your life.

Religion offers psychological security, which can be helpful in your life. It also broadens the dimensions of your faith in yourself and in others, and may make you a more loving and caring person. People who are religious often are better able to handle personal crises. Trust, tolerance, and humility are often obvious in people who practice a faith.

The importance religion plays in your life is one of the most personal elements in your environment. See 3-11. Many teens uphold the religious beliefs that they learned in their childhood. Others who did not have early childhood training in religion begin investigating religious beliefs during their teenage years.

Your Community and World

The world is constantly changing. The social and economic conditions that affected your grandparents or even your parents have changed. The trends affecting you today may not affect your children or grandchildren. Each generation develops within its own set of environmental conditions.

Influence of Technology

One of the most profound changes in our environment in recent decades has been the shift from an industrial society to an information society. This shift has had a dramatic impact on individuals and families. Rather than just producing commodities, people are now increasingly expected to be "computer literate." They are expected to be able to gather and exchange information using technologically sophisticated equipment such as computers.

Word processors and other types of computers are becoming commonplace in our lives. Computers are found in the workplace, in most schools, and in many homes. Some businesses are even allowing their employees to "telecommute." (*Telecommuting* is the practice of working at home—rather than commuting, or traveling, to work—by using a computer. Completed work is then sent to the office by computer.) This new method of employment allows one or both parents to remain at home with their children. At the same time, parents can generate income for the family.

For children and teenagers, computer games provide a popular source of recreation. Some computer programs help students research and write papers for school assignments. Several hours each day can be spent clicking a mouse and staring at a computer screen. Sometimes, these hours compete with other activities such as family responsibilities, physical exercise, and social events.

New advances also allow people to automate the processes by which they shop, send letters (by fax), engage in banking activities, and pay bills.

Technology has brought about a new awareness of global conditions. With satellite TV, people have a window on the entire world. You can see how others live, and they can see how you live.

Technology enables you to keep in touch with others throughout the day. By simply punching buttons on a telephone, you can communicate with others from your home or car. Videotapes can be exchanged that allow family members and friends to hear and see each other even though they may be miles apart.

These advances in technology provide you with information, convenience, and recreational opportunities that could only have been imagined a few decades ago. Care must be taken, however, to prevent technological devices from replacing valuable one-to-one contact between people. Children as well as adults will increasingly interact with electronic devices instead of with other people. As this occurs, individuals may need to make a greater effort to communicate with each other. Families will need to balance openness to learning about and using new technologies with concern and emotional support for one another.

Changing Economic Conditions

In our country, we witness an ever-changing economy. There are periods of inflation and periods of recession. The economy has a continuing impact on our lives. Learning to live with both affluence and scarcity can help us develop various sides of our personalities.

Because our nation is so large and so diverse, economic conditions may vary from region to region. One region may be prospering while another is depressed. People living in a depressed region may envy people who live where business is booming. People living in prosperous areas may feel moved to assist those who are having hard times.

Many young people today have few worries about their basic needs. The money they have is spent most often for luxuries and recreation. Teens are major consumers of everything from soft drinks and tapes to CD players and cars.

Many teens view spending as an expression of adult behavior. What they do not realize is that truly adult behavior involves spending for necessities and saving for a rainy day as well as paying for recreation. Choosing more adult attitudes toward saving money in times of affluence can be a healthy aspect of teens' personality development.

The teen market is one of the most lucrative in the economy. Teens who have money to spend are establishing new buying habits. Businesses realize this, so they direct much of their advertising to the teen market. They want to encourage teens to establish the habit of buying and using their products, 3-12. Adolescent consumers may be too easily swayed by advertisements for products that hold out the promise of physical attractiveness or popularity. They may need to develop the side of their personality that is reflected in realism, thrift, and sensible spending behavior.

In regions where the economy is weak, teens are likely to feel pressure. The job market for young people entering the work world may be tight. Financial funds for college or training programs may be limited. Such situations may help adolescents appreciate the importance of an education and a steady job. It may also help them develop personal qualities such as determination and willingness to work hard to achieve an objective.

Teens may be able to help their families by getting part-time jobs, 3-13. As they contribute to their families, teens also learn valuable lessons. They learn the significance of managing money wisely. They learn that life isn't always easy. They learn the importance of being able to adapt to changing economic conditions. They also learn that families can pull together to make it through difficult times.

David Hopper

3-12
Businesses are eager to attract teenage customers. They hope the teens will develop a habit of buying their products.

3-13

Cholla Runnels

This young man is applying for a part-time job. If he gets it, he will be able to help with family expenses and learn some valuable lessons. Young people today have more privileges as well as responsibilities.

The Media

Probably one of the most significant influences on your personality development is that of the mass media. Television, movies, magazines, newspapers, compact disks, and videos are only a few examples of such media. It is unrealistic for adults to think that youth can be totally protected from exposure to media influences. However, parents have a responsibility to exert some guidance in this area.

The media are an important source of both information and entertainment. For example, educational programs, news reports, and political analyses keep you informed. The mass media provide ways of learning about the world—good and bad. However, you should make no apology for avoiding programs or other material that can disturb or upset you or that can harm your personality development.

You have a responsibility to protect yourself from the desensitizing effects of viewing too much violence or other unwholesome programming. Some studies indicate that young people exposed to violent television programs have a tendency to exhibit more

Contemporary Concerns *of today's teens:*
TV Violence: Its Cost to Society

By the age of 18, the average American youth has seen 200,000 acts of violence and 40,000 murders portrayed on TV, according to some estimates. Does TV violence promote violent behavior in real life? Many social scientists think so, though others disagree. A recent national survey revealed that a majority of Americans believe that their entertainment TV is too violent and that TV violence is harmful to society.

Television's influence on children starts early. A recent survey revealed that the average preschooler watches more than 27 hours of television per week. Most children at this age have difficulty separating fact from fiction. Therefore, TV violence may be very harmful to their sense of what is normal or acceptable behavior.

To address TV violence, some concerned individuals and officials advocate greater censorship of violent programs. Others fear that increased censorship threatens first amendment ("freedom of speech") rights. One thing is certain: Parents have the right and responsibility to limit children's television viewing to programs that are informative and wholesome.

aggressive behavior in real life. Whether or not this is true in all cases, few would argue that a steady diet of TV or video violence is healthy.

The more violence you see, the less sensitive you may become to your own and others' physical and emotional pain. The less sensitive you are, the less skilled you will be at forming and maintaining close personal relationships.

Similarly, the more antisocial behavior you see on TV, the more you may think that such behavior is to be expected. You may subconsciously begin to view antisocial behavior as the norm rather than as a bad part of an otherwise good society. These are only a few of the many reasons for limiting your exposure to violence. Similar arguments could be made for content glorifying sexual violence, materialism, dishonesty, self-centeredness, and other behavior.

Try to interact with the media material you see rather than passively absorbing it. Ask yourself, What is the message I am supposed to be getting? Do I agree with this message? What kind of society would we have if everyone agreed with this message?

Finally, think about the amount of time you are giving to being entertained and influenced by the mass media. Evaluate this time commitment in light of your overall life goals. Ask yourself, Is this program worth the time it is taking me to watch it? Would I feel better about myself if I were doing something else?

Sometimes it takes will power to turn off the TV or to walk out of a movie. People who do so are often pleasantly surprised at how much they can accomplish toward worthwhile life goals by putting their time to other uses.

Summary ▪ ▪ ▪ ▪ ▪ ▪ ▪ ▪ ▪ ▪ ▪ ▪ ▪ ▪ ▪ ▪

- Personality development is affected by the continuing interaction between hereditary and environmental factors.

- The family is the primary factor in the personality development of most people. A positive, nurturing family produces future parents who will form positive environments for their own children someday.

- People can enrich their lives by celebrating their cultural backgrounds. They can also benefit by learning about the cultural backgrounds of others and about what each person has in common with the larger human family.

- Your birth order in relation to your siblings and the number and ages of your siblings will continue to influence your development.

- Peers are a strong influence in your personality development.

- When families cannot provide the authority and discipline that young people need, the influence of peers can overshadow that of the family.

- A positive educational environment can help children develop a sense of themselves as learners. An appreciation for learning can benefit a person's personality development throughout life.

- Technology is playing an increasing role in people's lives. Families should ensure that use of technology is balanced with one-to-one interaction.

- As the world changes, each generation faces a new set of social and economic conditions.

- Families change as they reflect changes in society. Both affluence and scarcity will influence the development of an individual's personality.

- Religion may be an important aspect of your environment. If religion is one of your personal priorities, it can offer meaning and purpose throughout your life.

- Teens have a responsibility to protect themselves from the negative aspects of the mass media.

To Review ■ ■ ■ ■ ■ ■ ■ ■ ■ ■ ■ ■ ■ ■ ■ ■

1. What is the most influential factor in shaping most people's personalities?

2. What is meant by the phrase "culturally diverse"?

3. List three characteristics that are typical of each of the following age positions.
   a. Oldest child.
   b. Middle child.
   c. Youngest child.

4. How does the influence of peer groups compare with the influence of families during adolescence?

5. How can an appreciation for learning benefit an individual throughout life?

6. How can students' part-time jobs influence their later career choices?

7. Name five traits typical of persons with a deep religious faith.

8. Why do businesses direct much of their advertising to the teen market?

9. What lessons can teens learn as they help their families through tough financial times?

10. Name one positive and one negative influence of mass media on personality development.

To Do ■ ■ ■ ■ ■ ■ ■ ■ ■ ■ ■ ■ ■ ■ ■ ■

1. Summarize television programs or movies that depict various types of environments provided by families. Identify one situation that you believe represents positive family functioning. Identify another situation that you feel represents negative family functioning. Explain the reasons for your choices.

2. Describe a positive family rule, childrearing technique, or way of dealing with a problem situation that you have observed. If you have children someday, will you use the same technique? Why or why not?

3. Ask class members to describe traditional holiday customs reflecting their individual national ancestry or cultural background. What meaning do families find in passing these traditions down from one

generation to the next? What family priorities may be reflected in the traditions?

4. Prepare skits to demonstrate various sibling relationships. Highlight traits of oldest, middle, and youngest children.

5. Discuss the influence of peers on the personality development of teenagers. Contrast positive and negative peer pressure.

6. Research a situation in which religion played an important role in the development of our society. Report your findings to the class. Include your opinion on the strength of religion as an environmental factor in today's society.

7. Debate the positive and negative influences of the media on our society. Should there be more or less censorship?

©Future Homemakers of America

Your environment—all of the conditions, objects, and circumstances that surround you—play a major role in your personality development.

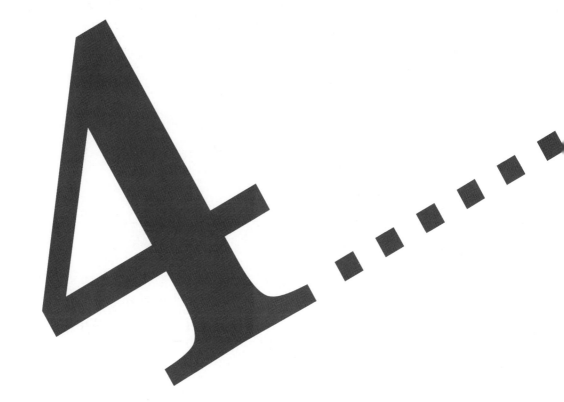

Your
Response to
Your
Environment

David Hopper

Terms to Know

autonomy	scapegoat
initiative	displacement
inferiority	conversion
identity	regression
generativity	idealization
integrity	phobias
self-actualization	introverts
morals	extroverts
defense mechanisms	ambivert
direct attack	attitude
compensation	prejudices
rationalization	bigots
projection	stereotypes

After studying this chapter, you will be able to

- explain the theories of Erikson, Havighurst, Maslow, and Kohlberg concerning personal development.

- describe the use of defense mechanisms in responding to your environment.

- explain various types of personal response patterns.

Your personality is determined by three major factors. Two of the factors are heredity and environment. They provide you with potentials and limitations. The third factor is your response to your environment. It helps you develop the unique qualities of your personality.

How You Respond to Your Environment

Every situation in your life requires you to respond to your environment. You may laugh at a joke. You may shout during an argument. You may study all night to prepare for an exam. No matter what your responses, they work together to help shape your personality.

Many theories have been formed concerning the development of humans and their personalities. Each theory represents a different aspect of personality development. Some of the most famous theories have been developed by Erikson, Havighurst, Maslow, and Kohlberg. By reviewing each of these recognized theories, you will be able to better understand how your personality is shaped in response to your environment.

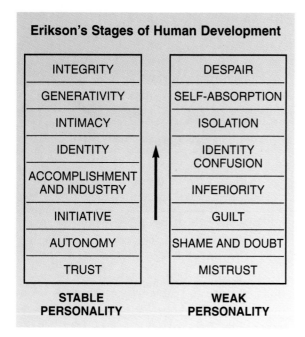

Erikson's Stages of Human Development

INTEGRITY	DESPAIR
GENERATIVITY	SELF-ABSORPTION
INTIMACY	ISOLATION
IDENTITY	IDENTITY CONFUSION
ACCOMPLISHMENT AND INDUSTRY	INFERIORITY
INITIATIVE	GUILT
AUTONOMY	SHAME AND DOUBT
TRUST	MISTRUST
STABLE PERSONALITY	**WEAK PERSONALITY**

4-1
Erikson recognizes eight stages in human development that affect personality development.

Erikson's Stages of Human Development

One of the most respected theories is that of Erik H. Erikson, a noted psychoanalyst and professor of developmental psychology. Erikson's theory is that personality development is affected by each of eight stages in the life cycle, 4-1. In each stage, a person confronts certain crises which must be resolved before moving to the next stage. The successes and failures met in these stages cause personalities to develop and change.

Trust Versus Mistrust

The first stage occurs during infancy and establishes our most basic sense of trust. Children who receive love and attention develop confidence and trust in themselves, in other people, and in their environment. See 4-2. They become secure and optimistic. They have a good foundation for building a healthy personality.

Children who are unloved or who are abused (either physically or emotionally) tend to become insecure and mistrustful. This may affect their personalities throughout life since mistrust is a poor foundation for personality development. Such individuals are likely to mature with deep emotional scars.

Autonomy Versus Shame and Doubt

The second stage occurs between the ages of one and four. During this time, children begin to experience *autonomy* or the freedom of self-direction. With encouragement and support, they develop the confidence to assert themselves. They move out

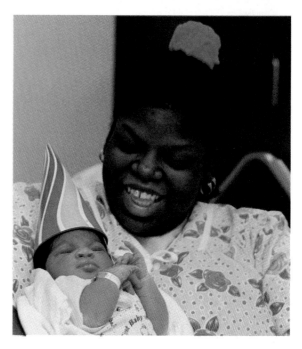

4-2
Infants who receive love and attention establish a sense of trust.

Initiative Versus Guilt

Erikson's third stage of development involves feelings of *initiative* or desires to begin action. Children reach this stage when they are four to five years old. They develop imagination and begin to do things on their own. At the same time, they learn the social skills of cooperating, leading, and following, 4-4. This helps them get along with their peers. To succeed in this stage, children need the freedom to think of new things to do. They should be encouraged to test their activities with peers.

Children who are not allowed to play with peers and develop their own games and

Cholla Runnels

4-3
Children who are encouraged to explore the world around them will be able to establish their autonomy more easily.

into the world with a feeling of security, 4-3. They begin to make decisions, but they sense the need for reasonable limits. Children learn many social lessons and take pride in their accomplishments.

Children who are not allowed to explore the world around them have difficulty establishing their autonomy. If their failures are emphasized rather than their successes, they will feel ashamed and discouraged. They will develop feelings of doubt about their own self-worth.

Evin Thayer

4-4
Preschoolers often follow the leader in exploring and playing new games.

activities may feel guilty and cling to adults. They do not develop good play skills, and they tend to lack imagination.

Accomplishment and Industry Versus Inferiority

From about age six to twelve, children are in the fourth stage of development. During this time, they establish a sense of accomplishment and industry. They learn that work is worthwhile and meaningful, 4-5. They also learn self-discipline and more about getting along with peers. Both school and home environments are important. Ideally, children in this stage are allowed to plan their own projects and activities and to carry them through to completion. Praise for their efforts helps them meet success in this stage.

Children whose efforts are not reinforced by praise may develop a sense of failure. Deep feelings of *inferiority* (of feeling inadequate and unimportant) will dominate their developing personalities. Children may

Cholla Runnels

4-5
A child who plans an activity and works on it until it is completed develops a good sense of industry and accomplishment.

4-6
Learning to accept other people as they are is part of healthy personality development.

passively accept feelings of inferiority, or they may behave in devious and dishonest ways to compensate for their lack of achievement.

Identity Versus Identity Confusion

The fifth stage occurs during adolescence. The central need of this period is to establish a sense of identity. This sense of *identity* means knowing who you are and what your roles are in society. For success in this stage, adolescents need to be guided by good models and inspired by high ideals.

As adolescents gain maturity, they begin to view life and the world around them differently. They experience new feelings, and they have new desires. They need time to sort through these new ideas and emotions and to discover who they are. In addition, they need to develop good relationships with peers and to learn to accept other people as they are, 4-6. Adolescents who succeed in this stage find stable roles to assume in our society.

Adolescents who are not able to establish stable roles for themselves become preoccupied with their identities in the eyes of others. Their self-identities become fragmented and insecure. As a result, they lack self-confidence and self-esteem. They have weak foundations for further personality development.

David Hopper

4-7
Once young adults have accepted themselves as worthwhile persons, they are ready for close, stable relationships.

Intimacy Versus Isolation

Erikson's sixth stage is concerned with being able to establish a sense of intimacy. Young adults who succeed in this stage have accepted themselves as worthwhile persons. They are able to give of themselves to others. They feel a need to establish close, stable relationships, 4-7.

Persons who have difficulty establishing close personal relationships due to a feeling of insecurity feel isolated and alone. Many will continue to live within themselves and may never be able to form effective relationships with others.

Generativity Versus Self-Absorption

In the seventh stage, adults develop a sense of generativity. With *generativity*, people begin to be concerned with others beyond their immediate families and especially with future generations. Generativity is found not only in parents, but in any person who is concerned with the welfare of others, 4-8.

People who fail to establish a sense of generativity may fall into a state of *self-absorption*. Then their only concerns are for their own personal needs and comfort.

Integrity Versus Despair

A sense of integrity develops in people who succeed in the final stage of development. *Integrity* is a state of being complete; the person is satisfied with his or her life. Mature adults are able to look back on their lives

Cholla Runnels

4-8
Generativity, or concern for future generations, is a sign of healthy personality growth in an adult.

David Hopper

4-9
"I made this myself." This woman has developed a sense of integrity. She can look at her past with satisfaction, and she still finds enjoyment in new activities.

with satisfaction. They can look forward to the rest of their lives with confidence. They feel satisfied and secure in themselves, 4-9. A person with a sense of integrity can say, "It's good to be me." This is the goal each of us seeks.

Those who have not achieved integrity are likely to feel despair. They may wish they could have lived totally different lives. People who look back on their lives as a series of missed opportunities and wrong decisions will feel despair. They will never be at peace with themselves.

Havighurst's Developmental Tasks of Adolescence

Personality changes and develops throughout life, as Erikson explained in his stages of human development. Robert J. Havighurst, a well-known educator and behavioral scientist, identified developmental tasks

that people perform as they grow and develop. People may not even be aware of their developmental tasks, but the manner in which they perform these tasks helps determine their overall personalities. Success in these tasks leads to happiness and success in other developmental tasks they will perform later in life. Failure leads to unhappiness, disapproval by society, and difficulty with later developmental tasks.

Havighurst has identified eight developmental tasks of adolescence. These are tasks that people perform as they grow and develop during their teenage years.

Task One

The first of Havighurst's developmental tasks is to achieve new and more mature relations with peers of both sexes. See 4-10. You learn to view girls as women and boys as men. You become an adult among adults. You learn to work with others for a common purpose.

Cholla Runnels

4-10
During adolescence, you form more mature relations with peers. You learn to work well with others in groups.

4-11

In your teen years, you will have many opportunities to learn socially approved masculine or feminine social roles.

Task Two

Adopting socially approved masculine or feminine adult roles is the second task for adolescents. This may be more challenging today than in the past, for roles are no longer preset for you. You must decide for yourself what roles you wish to adopt, 4-11. Your decisions will affect your dating patterns, your career choices, and your overall lifestyle.

Task Three

This developmental task is to accept your physical self and to use your body effectively. During adolescence, your body goes through many changes. You need to accept these changes and become comfortable with your body. You need to learn to care for your body and to keep it healthy. You also need to protect it from physical harm and from abuse of tobacco and drugs, including alcohol.

Task Four

When you fulfill this task, you achieve greater emotional independence. You are able to think critically, review alternatives, and make your own decisions. You develop a new type of affection for your parents on a more adult level. Likewise, you develop respect for other adults without being dependent on them.

Task Five

In completing this task, you develop your personal attitude toward marriage and family living. See 4-12. If you are like most people, you will want to establish a family of your own and raise children. In this case, you

4-12
This young woman is having fun painting children's faces. Working with children will help her develop her personal attitude about parenthood.

Cholla Runnels

will need to obtain knowledge about marriage relationships, home management, and parenthood.

Task Six

Havighurst's sixth task is to select and prepare for an occupation, 4-13. After evaluating your skills, talents, and goals you choose an occupation for which you are suited. You then prepare yourself for that occupation. The first step is to finish high school. Then you may need to take additional on-the-job training or to attend a vocational school, community college, or university. When you complete this task, you will feel better able to make a living.

Evin Thayer

4-13
Studying architectural drawing can help you prepare for a career in many related professions.

David Hopper

4-14
Family unity is important to these people. They enjoy spending time together.

Task Seven

This task is to acquire a set of standards as a guide to behavior. In this task, you need to form a set of personal values concerning what is important to you in life. See 4-14. Your values are patterned by experience in the family and in society. This process of building personal values takes place through your relations with people who are special to you: parents, teachers, other adults, peers. The personal values you develop should help you guide your behavior. When you are faced with a difficult decision, you should be able to rely on your personal values. They should help you choose the alternative that will give you the most satisfaction in life. If you value honesty, for example, you should be able to resist such temptations as shoplifting or cheating.

Task Eight

Havighurst's final task for adolescents is to accept and adopt socially responsible behavior. As an adolescent, you need to learn how society expects responsible people to act. You can incorporate this knowledge into your value system. Society will then accept you, and you will be able to participate in the functions of your community, state, and country.

Maslow's Theory of Human Needs

Because you are a human, you have certain needs. You share these needs with all other humans, but you fulfill them in unique ways. For instance, all people need food, but the food you eat differs from the food eaten

HUMAN NEEDS

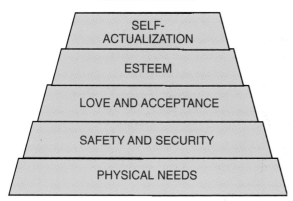

4-15
According to Maslow's theory, human needs can be seen as a hierarchy. Physical needs have first priority and must be at least partially fulfilled before a person can begin to meet any other needs.

by people who lived centuries ago. It also may differ from the food eaten by people who live in foreign countries. The ways you fulfill your needs affect your thoughts and behaviors and therefore your personality.

Abraham Maslow, a noted psychiatrist, devised a system for studying human needs. In his system, he arranged needs in order of their priorities, as shown in 4-15. His theory can help explain the influence of human needs on personality.

Physical Needs

According to Maslow, physical needs have first priority, 4-16. Among these needs are food, water, shelter, clothing, sleep, and to some extent, sex. Fulfillment of physical

Red Cedar Shingle & Shake Bureau

4-16
Shelter—whether a simple hut or an elegant house—is a physical need of humans.

needs is necessary for good health, a state of well-being, and the continuation of life. Typically, a person whose physical needs are not met can think of little else until these needs are at least partially met. For instance, it is difficult to concentrate on studying if you are hungry because you skipped breakfast. Physical needs demand your primary consideration.

Safety and Security

Once you have satisfied your physical needs, you can address other needs, 4-17. You need to feel safe from physical danger. You need to feel secure in daily routines so you know what to expect from life. In addition, you need to know that you are protected against financial troubles.

When you have satisfied these needs, you have the courage to experience more of life and to expand your personality. On the other hand, if your life centers around protecting yourself (whether from wild animals, thieves, bill collectors, or mean classmates), your personality has little chance to develop.

Evin Thayer

4-17
A warm family environment helps satisfy the need for safety and security.

Love and Acceptance

Everyone needs to be needed. This is the basis for Maslow's third level of human need. You need to feel that you are accepted by others. You need to feel secure in your relationships with family members and friends, 4-18. Praise, support, encouragement, and personal warmth will help you fulfill these needs. Then you will have the chance to develop a healthy personality. You, in turn, will be able to accept others and to give them praise, support, and affection.

Esteem

In addition to love and acceptance, you need esteem (respect and admiration). Self-esteem must be established first. You must respect yourself before you can expect others to respect you. Family members can help you establish self-esteem. Friends can help, too. They can help you feel that you are a worthy person who adds an important dimension to their lives.

When you have both self-esteem and the esteem of others, you have the potential for further personality development. You have the confidence to strive for achievement and independence. You become a vital part of your world.

Self-Actualization

Self-actualization is the realization of your full potential. To reach this level, all other levels of needs must be at least partially fulfilled. At this level, you combine concern for self with concern for others, and for society as a whole. You strive to become the very best you can be, 4-19. If your special talents are related to art, you become the best artist you can be. If your talents are related to auto mechanics, you become the best mechanic you can be.

When you reach self-actualization, you believe in yourself. You have the confidence to express your personal beliefs and to reach

4-18
Belonging to a group in which you feel comfortable helps you fulfill your need for love and acceptance.

Cholla Runnels

out to others and offer your support. Your personality is fully developed. However, this does not mean that you stop learning, or that your personality stops changing. On the contrary, you are even more interested in improving yourself. You can continue to strive to become a better person.

Kohlberg's Stages of Moral Development

Lawrence Kohlberg did his research on moral development. Kohlberg believed that people pass through a series of predictable stages in their moral thinking. These stages show how morals develop during childhood

David Hopper

4-19
These young men are meeting their need for self-actualization. They are using their talents to become the best swimmers they can be.

and on into young adulthood. *Morals* are beliefs about right and wrong behavior.

Kohlberg identified three general levels of moral development. He further divided each of these levels into two stages. Thus he describes six stages of moral development. These are listed in 4-20 and described below.

Preconventional Level

At the preconventional level, children make moral decisions based on what the consequences will be. Consequences at this level are in the form of rewards and punishment.

In the first stage, children respond to the threat of punishment as they learn good from bad and right from wrong. If the act is bad, the child is punished. The decision making of children includes little abstract reasoning as to what is right or wrong. Behavior is "wrong" because it leads to punishment. Children learn they can avoid punishment by being good. Those in authority, usually the parents, determine the punishment.

In the second stage, children learn that the correct or right action brings rewards. "I will do this because it is good for me." An attempt at sharing to satisfy mutual needs also brings rewards. "If you are good to me, I will be good to you."

Conventional Level

At the second level, decisions are based on social rules and expectations. The child learns it is important to meet the expectations of the social order in order to gain approval from family and friends, as well as society.

In stage three of the conventional level, children are concerned about the opinions of others. "Good" behavior is that which pleases or helps family members and friends and is approved by them. A friend's approval is sought by "being nice" to that friend.

In the fourth stage, law and order are valued. By obeying laws, all people benefit, not just family and friends. The rights of the

---

Kohlberg's Stages of Moral Development

Preconventional Level: Moral decisions are based on punishment and rewards.

Stage One: Threat of punishment influences decisions.
Stage Two: Desire for rewards influences decisions.

Conventional Level: Moral decisions are based on social rules and expectations.

Stage Three: Opinions of others influence decisions.
Stage Four: Respect for law and order guides behavior.

Postconventional Level: Moral decisions are based on personal ethics concerning what is morally right.

Stage Five: Personal values concerning individual human rights influence decisions.
Stage Six: Self-chosen ethical principles guide decisions.

4-20
According to Kohlberg, moral development occurs in six stages, beginning in early childhood.

individual are protected. People show respect for authority and obey laws for the sake of orderliness in the society, 4-21. People at this stage believe that as long as their behavior is lawful, it is ethically acceptable.

Postconventional Level

In the third level of moral development, decisions are based more on personal ethics concerning what is morally right. People appeal to higher principles. They believe laws can be wrong and may need to be changed through the democratic process. Not all people reach this level in their moral development.

In the fifth stage, personal values are more a factor in decisions concerning moral behavior. The right action is that which respects individual human rights and democratic principles. There is the possibility of making changes in the law to protect the rights of individuals if current laws are wrong.

The sixth stage is the highest stage of moral development. According to Kohlberg, relatively few people ever reach this stage. Personal conscience defines self-chosen ethical principles. Decisions are based on such abstract principles as life, liberty, and equality. At the heart of this is a feeling of respect for the dignity of human beings and their human rights.

Defense Mechanisms ▪ ▪ ▪ ▪ ▪

Each time something happens in your environment to threaten your self-concept, you react. If you have a positive self-concept, you face the threat, analyze it, and respond in a way that promotes growth. Sometimes you may respond in a defensive manner to protect your self-concept. When you react defen-

sively to a problem or threat in your environment, you may use a defense mechanism.

Defense mechanisms are automatic and involuntary ways people react to anxiety-producing events or threats. People are generally unaware that they are using these mechanisms. Their use is often a way of avoiding reality.

Some defense mechanisms are healthy ways of dealing with problems. Others are not. Sometimes the same defense mechanisms can be used in either healthy or unhealthy ways.

Everyone uses different mechanisms in different situations. The following are the most commonly used defense mechanisms.

Direct Attack

When you use *direct attack* in response to a threat to your self-esteem, you attack the source of the threat. This may take the form of "lashing out" at another person. For example, if someone in your class comments, "The

David Hopper

4-21
Laws are established and enforced to protect the rights and safety of all people.

outfit you are wearing is out of style," you may retort, "Who are you to judge? I've seen you wear some pretty weird outfits!" In making this response, you are not really dealing with the question of whether your clothing is out of style. You have not asked yourself honestly whether your critic may be right. Instead, you have used a defense mechanism. You have defended the threat to your self-esteem by attacking the person making the comment.

Some people are able to respond to a verbal attack with a direct attack of their own that is less critical of the other person. This is a healthy use of a defense mechanism. For instance, in the example given above, a person might respond with, "I'm an individualist. I choose my clothes based on what looks best on me—not what others think is in style."

Compensation

Using a substitute method to achieve a desired goal is called *compensation*. Suppose a person wanted to succeed in sports, but was not tall enough or fast enough to succeed in basketball. Other sports, such as golf, swimming, and skiing, may provide this person with opportunities for success. Another example is shown in 4-22.

Whistler, a famous painter, flunked out of West Point and had to give up a military career. To compensate for this, he developed his artistic talent. Compensation allows a person to make up for some real or imaginary deficiency by doing well in something else.

Compensation can be used negatively. For instance, some parents do not spend much time with their children. They may try to compensate by giving their children many material things. The "bullies" at school may be compensating for their own unhappiness by making others unhappy. Boastful people may be trying to compensate for their inferiority feelings.

David Hopper

4-22
If you want to be involved in sports but do not qualify, you can compensate by being the team manager.

Rationalization

When you explain your weaknesses or failures by giving socially acceptable excuses, you are using *rationalization.* An example of rationalization occurs when you say you failed a test because the subject is impractical and not worth knowing. See 4-23. Another rationalization is saying that the reason you received a speeding ticket is that you had other things on your mind.

Rationalization may make you feel better temporarily, but it does not help you solve the real problem. Instead of fooling yourself, you should recognize the real problem and work to solve it. If you failed a test because you did not study well enough, you should admit it and try harder the next time. If you were speeding on a road where you always speed, you should recognize this as a problem. You should allow yourself more traveling time and slow down.

Cholla Runnels

4-23
If you get a low grade on a test, you may try to rationalize it by making excuses.

Projection

When you blame other people or things for your failures, you are using *projection*. This differs from rationalization in that you are actually projecting the blame to someone or something else. You are not just making excuses for your failures.

A small child may blame a pet or a fantasy friend for spilling some milk. Children's first tales may sound cute, but they can develop a habit of projecting blame since they are eager to please others.

As you are driving down a road, someone may pull out in front of you and cause a collision. If the person were to jump out of the car and yell, "Why don't you look where you are going?" that person would be projecting the blame on you. A similar situation could occur in a hallway as shown in 4-24.

Scapegoating is the common term used to describe projection. The person who bears the blame for others is called a *scapegoat*. For instance, Ann, Sue, and Inez might say, "Everything is Mary's fault." In this case, the girls are projecting the blame on Mary. Mary is the scapegoat. For another example, suppose Jack said, "Steve, you said the test would be easy!" Here, Jack is projecting the blame for failing an exam on Steve using Steve as a scapegoat.

Displacement

When you transfer an emotion connected with one person or thing to an unrelated person or thing, you are using

Cholla Runnels

4-24
You may be bumped by someone while walking in the hall. The person may use the defense mechanism of projection and blame you by saying, "Why don't you look where you are going?"

displacement. The key word here is emotion. You can displace hate, aggression, annoyance, or frustration. For instance, if your employer finds fault with you on the job, you may take out your frustration on your family or a friend.

Some people displace the emotion of love. Perhaps you have read accounts of people who show more love to their pets than to their families. People who are concerned about a certain social problem often displace their hatred and aggression. As a result, they may commit crimes against a politician or other well-known person.

Displacement is not a healthy defense mechanism. It does not help you solve the original problem. Rather, it creates more problems with the people involved in your transfer of emotion.

Conversion

With *conversion*, you transfer the energy of a desire you cannot express into a physical symptom or complaint. Children who are nervous about going to school for the first time can actually develop stomachaches. This is sometimes called "school phobia." If you have ever been uneasy about getting up in front of a class to read a report, you may have lost your voice. Conversion can also cause other physical symptoms, such as headaches and clammy hands. Although such symptoms are psychosomatic (physical or mental reactions to mental conflict), they are very real. They can be just as bad as symptoms caused by an infection, virus, or other physical problem.

Regression

Regression is a defense mechanism in which you revert back to a less mature stage of development. The individual who "acts like a baby" to meet a problem is regressing, 4-25. Spouses who run back home to their parents

when they face critical points in their marriages may not be meeting their problems in a mature manner.

Although life may have been simpler when you were younger, you cannot go back. As you grow older, you must accept more responsibilities. Your behavior should be consistent with your age and maturity. Crying, calling names, throwing and breaking things, or trying to escape problems by using drugs are all forms of regression. They are behaviors that should be avoided, since they rarely solve problems. Instead, they often create additional problems.

Cholla Runnels

4-25
Regressing to childish behavior will seldom help you solve your problems.

Idealization

When you value something far more than it is worth, you are using *idealization*. You may idealize yourself and act conceited, 4-26. Persons around you will soon recognize this defense mechanism and will probably choose to ignore you.

Some people idealize another person. They will do almost anything to become that person's friend. They think that by gaining the friendship, all their problems will be solved.

Possessions are idealized by some people. To have fine clothes, a fancy car, or a huge house, they will forfeit many of life's other pleasures.

Daydreaming

People may daydream to accomplish in their imagination what they cannot accomplish in reality. A little daydreaming is not unhealthy. It is a pleasant way to remember the past and to think of future desires. However, if you have frequent daydreams that seem to be real, you are living in a fantasy world. By attempting to escape reality in this manner, you are not facing life as you should. Although you may achieve great things in your fantasy world, constant daydreaming will hinder your efforts to achieve real success.

Giving Up

You may have friends who have simply given up because they are discouraged. They feel the world is against them. They think everyone else has the talents and skills they lack. They feel all their efforts to achieve goals have been blocked. They do not want to face any more situations in which they may fail.

Persons who are giving up on the world need support and encouragement. Before family and friends can help them, however,

Cholla Runnels

4-26
Some people idealize themselves and act conceited.

they must want to help themselves. Then they will be able to build their self-confidence. They will be able to face difficult situations and learn from them. They will be able to develop the talents and skills they feel they lack.

As you review these defense mechanisms, try to remember the times you have used them to counterbalance some action or feeling. At times, you have undoubtedly needed to defend yourself against the world.

Contemporary Topics *of interest to teens:*
Rules! Rules! Rules! Why Do We Need Them?

A *rule* is a regulation governing conduct, actions, procedures, or arrangements. Rules serve several purposes. Some are designed to provide personal protection, enabling people to live together safely. Rules also provide predictability. If there are rules and they are followed, behavior is more predictable. Rules are often designed to protect individual rights and freedoms. Rules influence values and morals, and teach responsibility.

Rules provide structure. They often set limits on or otherwise promote management of behaviors. This structure is designed to prevent problems from occurring.

Do you remember the rules your parents set? "Brush your teeth after you eat." "No hitting your little brother." "Look both ways before you cross the street." Those were important rules when you were little. Your parents set these rules for your health and welfare.

Childhood rules often set boundaries or "fences," which provide a sense of security. Children know what they can and cannot do—and where they can and cannot go. This gives them a feeling of security, along with the sense that someone cares about their well-being.

Now you are a teenager, and instead of fewer rules, it seems as though there are more rules! Your school has all kinds of rules. Did you ever think what would happen if there were no rules at school? You could wander up and down the halls at will, eat where you wanted and when you wanted. You could come and go as you pleased, but would any learning take place? Probably very little. Would young people learn appropriate behavior? Probably not. Would the school be a safe place to be? Maybe not. The school sets rules in order to provide a safe learning environment for every student. This enables you to learn those behaviors that will help you become a self-supporting member of the community.

As you leave school and enter the world of work, you will find there are still rules, but the rules will be different. Your employer will make some of the rules. You may be told when you are to arrive at work and when you can leave, and perhaps how much you should accomplish or how much you should sell. Each job will have different rules. The government also makes rules—traffic rules and tax regulations, to name only two. You will be expected to follow all of these rules in order to function in our society.

Rules! Why do we need them? To make our society a better place for everyone to live.

This is only human nature and not a threat to your personality development. The danger is that some people are constantly using various defenses because they cannot face the realities of daily life.

Personal Response Patterns ▪ ▪ ▪ ▪ ▪

Your responses to your environment affect your personality development in many ways. Through these responses, you have formed certain behavior patterns, attitudes, and prejudices. These have all become a part of your personality.

Anger

One of the ways you respond to your environment is through anger. You will probably become most angry with people you depend on or love. Family members usually love and respect each other enough to withstand occasional angry feelings. However, repeated outbursts of anger are destructive.

Anger is a normal human reaction to a stressful situation. If you repress anger, you may make your own life uncomfortable. You may start biting your nails or grinding your teeth. You may even develop chronic depression. However, when you do express your anger, you should be careful to see that no one is harmed by it.

Anger can be used constructively when it is directed against the forces that have caused a problem. For instance, some students were angry because their friends were injured and killed in an accident caused by a drunk driver. They formed the SADD (Students Against Driving Drunk) program. Across the country, student groups have formed a coalition of student leaders who hold seminars and offer peer counseling.

They also work to provide alternative modes of transportation for students in situations where alcohol is involved.

You, too, can use anger to correct a bad situation. Be sure you know the real cause of the problem so you can attack it directly. Then try to find some people who agree with you and will work with you (like students in SADD). You can learn to express anger in a useful, constructive way. This will bring the best results.

In your relationships with family and friends, you sometimes feel anger and frustration. How do you resolve conflicts when you are angry or frustrated? Look at the chart in 4-27. On a separate sheet of paper, answer the questions it asks. Do your responses follow a pattern? The pattern of responses you follow now may stay the same throughout your life. Are you satisfied with the ways you respond to anger? If not, you will have to make a conscious effort to change your behavior. You will have to think before you act and remind yourself to respond to anger in a better way.

Fear

Fear is a discomfort that may vary from a mild feeling of being unsafe to an intense anxiety about losing your life.

Fears may be the result of unpleasant experiences, especially in childhood. The subconscious mind may retain this trauma of fear and cause behavioral problems.

You may also have fears that have been communicated to you through other persons. Parents can pass on their fears to their children. For instance, if your parents were afraid of thunder and lightning, they might have drawn the shades during a storm and acted nervous. Today, you might find yourself afraid of storms as well.

**How Do You Handle Anger
in Your Daily Life?**

When you are frustrated, do you . . .

go for a walk?
listen to music?
go somewhere to be alone?
talk to a good friend?
throw things or hit things?

*When you have a disagreement with your
family do you . . .*

find information to back up your argument?
ask family members to discuss the problem
    calmly?
ask a third party to discuss the problem with
    you?
refuse to talk to anyone?
argue loudly with family members?
throw things or hit a family member?

*When you have a disagreement with a friend
do you . . .*

find information to back up your argument?
discuss the problem calmly with the friend?
arrange another time to discuss the problem
    calmly?
bring in a third party?
refuse to talk to anyone?
argue loudly, shout, and insult your friend?
throw things, or physically abuse your
    friend?

4-27
Your reactions to anger influence your personality
development.

Fears Can Serve a Purpose

A certain amount of fear can be useful. Small children are taught to be afraid of fire. As people grow older, they learn to fear other dangers that could threaten their well-being and safety.

Fear also can give us the added strength we need in dangerous situations. In sudden danger, the body produces adrenaline. This is a hormone that is released into your bloodstream. This makes the heart beat faster and causes the body to react with increased energy. In extreme cases, people have been known to do seemingly impossible tasks. For instance, one woman lifted a car so her friend who was trapped beneath it could escape.

Fear Can Be Harmful

Fear can be harmful when it prevents you from facing your problems. If allowed to persist, fear can damage mental or physical health. Persons with deep fears may be afraid to face even the simplest demands of daily living.

Overcoming Fear

The first step in overcoming fear is to discover the cause of the fear. Often it can be traced back to some traumatic childhood experience. Once you know the cause of the fear, you can deal with it directly and work to overcome it. Overcoming fears takes inner strength. President Franklin Roosevelt recognized the destructive potential of fear. At the onset of World War II, he cautioned the entire nation, "The only thing we have to fear is fear itself."

If you do not succeed in overcoming your fears, they may develop into phobias. Exaggerated fears of everyday objects or events are called *phobias.*

One common phobia is the fear of being confined in a small space. This is known as *claustrophobia.* Persons with this phobia will not ride in an elevator. They may feel uncomfortable in rooms without windows or in rooms with closed doors. Claustrophobia could affect a person's choice of a job or a home.

Many other phobias also exist. Some of them are listed in 4-28. People whose lives are crippled by phobias should seek professional help. Many phobias can be treated successfully with a combination of medication and counseling.

Phobias

ACROPHOBIA — fear of high places
AGORAPHOBIA — fear of open places
AUTOPHOBIA — fear of being alone
BATHOPHOBIA — fear of depths
CHIONOPHOBIA — fear of snow
DEMOPHOBIA — fear of crowds
HOPTEPHOBIA — fear of being touched
KINESOPHOBIA — fear of movement
MUSOPHOBIA — fear of mice
MYSOPHOBIA — fear of contamination
NYCTOPHOBIA — fear of night and darkness
PEDOPHOBIA — fear of children
PHONOPHOBIA — fear of noise
PHOBOPHOBIA — fear of fear
PSYCHOPHOBIA — fear of cold
PYROPHOBIA — fear of fire
THALASSOPHOBIA — fear of ocean or sea
TOXICOPHOBIA — fear of poison
TREMOPHOBIA — fear of trembling
ZOOPHOBIA — fear of animals

4-28
Many different types of phobias or exaggerated fears have been identified.

Depression

Perhaps you have heard someone say, "The teen years are the happiest years of a person's life." When everything is going along fine, you may agree. You cannot expect, however, to be happy every day of your life. You will experience some low moods. When you do, you may feel that the teen years must surely be the worst years of your life.

Even though teenagers have many exciting and happy times, they also have some very sad moments. Happiness and depression can be viewed as the two ends of a musical keyboard of feelings. The high notes may be associated with happiness, while the low notes may be considered gloomy. The whole range of feelings is needed to make music.

Many teenagers have occasional feelings of inferiority. This adds to their depression. Many teenagers set high goals for themselves and become scared of not reaching them. Some have devastating feelings of loneliness. They struggle with feelings of emptiness and unworthiness. Frustrations, disappointments, and personal losses can make anyone feel gloomy. During the teen years, these feelings may seem even more profound.

You need to distinguish between times when you feel down for the moment and times when you may have more serious problems. Deep depression is an emotional state of dejection. It is exaggerated sadness coupled with pessimism. Depressed persons often feel their sadness will persist forever. They feel that they can't do anything about it. People who are depressed for a prolonged period of time should seek professional help. (See Chapter 21 for more information about serious depression.)

For most people, feeling low is simply a matter of having a bad day. Your feelings of self-worth may be shattered momentarily, but you can do something to renew your self-esteem.

It is important that you give yourself permission to have low feelings, 4-29. Accept the fact that it is okay to feel down in the dumps,

David Hopper

4-29
Feeling down occasionally is okay, but do something about negative feelings before they drag on too long.

but do something about those feelings before they drag on too long. Try to understand what is causing your low feelings. Then put the feelings in proper perspective. Talk to someone with whom you feel comfortable. Let off a little steam. Try to keep a sense of humor and look on the bright side of your life. To regain your self-esteem, concentrate on something you do well. Hand yourself little triumphs. Success in even a minor task will make you feel better.

Time usually heals a common case of the blues. Your emotions are remarkably resilient. Most of you will develop your own ways of handling mood swings. Recognize that depressed moods can be balanced with positive ones. Accept the fact that low feelings will be a part of your life, but they need not control your life. They will exist, but you will have positive and happy times to balance them.

Introverts and Extroverts

One way to classify personalities is according to introvert and extrovert characteristics. *Introverts* are persons who prefer to be alone and to keep their feelings and thoughts to themselves. *Extroverts* are persons who love to be with people and to tell others about their feelings and thoughts, 4-30. Other characteristics of introverts and extroverts are listed in 4-31.

Very few people are true introverts or true extroverts. Most people have characteristics of both and are known as ambiverts. *Ambiverts* behave as either introverts or extroverts depending on the circumstances. All three types of personalities are needed in the world.

Attitudes

An *attitude* is a feeling or mental position about something. An attitude may cause a person to choose one type of behavior in place of another. Your attitudes are formed by your own experiences, by concepts you gather through second-hand experiences, and by accepting the viewpoints of others. Your attitudes, and the manner in which you express them, tell other people a great deal about you.

Negative Attitudes

Occasionally, you may develop negative attitudes toward groups of people or toward life in general. Some of you may develop such attitudes because you think they will please your peers. At times, you may form a negative

Cholla Runnels

4-30

Extroverts are sociable and impulsive. They like excitement and activity.

The Introvert

Is quiet and retiring.
Prefers to be alone or with just a few close
   friends.
Does not crave excitement.
Accepts daily life with seriousness.
Keeps feelings under control.
Prefers thought to action.
Is more likely to expose his or her own true
   feelings to others.
Spends much time thinking and imagining.
May be more fond of books than people.
Is reserved and distant except with close
   friends.
Tends to plan ahead.
Seldom loses his or her temper.

The Extrovert

Values both material and nonmaterial things of
   the world.
Likes parties and is sociable.
Prefers being with people rather than studying
   or reading alone.
Often takes chances and desires excitement.
Is impulsive and fond of practical jokes.
May lose his or her temper quickly.
Changes jobs more frequently.
Is carefree and optimistic.
Prefers action to thought.
Is more prone to accidents.

4-31
These characteristics are typical of introverts and
extroverts.

attitude because you do not know enough
about a subject. Such negative attitudes can
be destructive to yourself and to others.

Positive Attitudes

If you have developed some negative attitudes, they can be changed to positive ones.
The changes may be due to new experiences,
increased knowledge of a subject, a change in
group membership, or direct suggestion
from someone. You can express your new,

more positive attitudes through the enthusiasm you show, the words you speak, and the
actions you take.

Developing positive attitudes toward
yourself and those around you is very important. People often base their entire opinion
of you on the attitudes you express. They may
use an "attitude label" to describe you to
other people. Examples of "attitude labels"
are given in 4-32.

Prejudices

Prejudices are attitudes based on false or
insufficient information. They are usually
negative in nature. Since prejudices are
formed without enough accurate knowledge,
they are likely to be unreliable and harmful.
People who have strong prejudices are called

Attitude Labels

Negative Labels:

- He always puts people down.
- She's always talking about people behind
   their backs.
- He's such a martyr (suffers sacrifices for
   the sake of someone else).
- She always finds something wrong with
   everything we do.
- He never stands up for what he believes
   is right.
- She is so conceited.

Positive Labels:

- He always finds the good in others.
- She can be trusted to keep a secret.
- He tries to remain upbeat even when
   things are going wrong.
- She's a tough competitor.
- He is always willing to stand up for what is
   right.
- She's always so happy.

4-32
People may use attitude labels to describe someone's
personality. Both positive and negative attitude labels
are often used.

bigots. Bigots staunchly support their own group, party, or belief and will not consider the right of others to have varying opinions.

Prejudices have many different causes. Fear, guilt, frustration, or feelings of inferiority are the basis for some prejudices. Others result from attitudes expressed by family, television, and peer groups. Sometimes personal experiences can create prejudices. If you have fun the first time you try surfing, you will probably say you like to surf. If you are flipped off your board and injured, you may develop a prejudice against the sport.

By the time you reach adolescence, many of your prejudices are firmly established. In some cases, your prejudices may dictate your behavior. Since prejudices are based on false assumptions, such behavior could harm you as well as others.

Prejudices can be overcome or avoided altogether. If you realize that you have a prejudice and you want to overcome it, the following guidelines will help. These guidelines will also help prevent new prejudices from forming.

- Before you express a strong opinion, ask yourself whether or not it is based on facts.

- Increase your knowledge. The more you know about a subject, the less prejudiced you will be against it.

- Be aware of the prejudices of a person trying to convince you of something.

- Be wary of statements regarding common areas of strong prejudices, such as religion, politics, and race or ethnic origins.

Stereotypes

Stereotypes are widely held beliefs that all members of a group share the same characteristics. Some members of a group may have these characteristics, but not all members do.

Some common stereotypes involve age, gender, and race. For instance, some people believe the stereotype that old people are always slow. This implies that *all* older people are slow. You have only to view or read news stories of active senior citizens to realize that this is not the case. Similarly, teenagers may be stereotyped as irresponsible by adults when, in fact, most teenagers act responsibly.

Gender or sex-role stereotyping is frequently heard. For instance, men are often labeled as unemotional. People seem surprised when they see men cry or show similar emotions. Women are often stereotyped as indecisive (unable to make decisions). However, there are many businesswomen who have become successful because they could make decisions quickly. Both labels may describe some men and some women, but not *all* men nor *all* women.

Occupational stereotyping is very unfortunate. It causes many young people to rule out certain careers that might interest them because they think of them as women's work or men's work. Career options are open to

David Hopper

4-33
Almost any career field is open to you if you are willing to work at learning the necessary skills.

everyone today. Females are pilots, engineers, and auto mechanics. Males today are nurses, secretaries, nursery school teachers, and beauticians. Almost all careers are open to everyone. You should choose a career on the basis of your interests, aptitudes, and skills, not on old stereotypes, 4-33.

Stereotyping is an attempt to fit people into preconceived pegs. If you believe stereotypes, you are failing to realize every person is unique. You are prejudging people before you ever get to know them.

You may be the victim of a stereotype. People may prejudge you as well. You may be afraid to be yourself for fear of what other people will think of you.

Stereotypes can be overcome by being open to other people. Get to know others and hear their ideas before you judge them. Enjoy meeting men and women with different personalities and people of different races and ages. Everyone has qualities that make them unique. Find those unique qualities. Keep stereotypes out of the picture.

Summary ■ ■ ■ ■ ■ ■ ■ ■ ■ ■ ■ ■ ■ ■ ■ ■

- The way you respond to your environment helps you develop the distinctive qualities of your personality.

- According to Erikson, personality development is affected by each of eight stages in the life cycle.

- Havighurst has identified eight developmental tasks that influence the personality of adolescents.

- Maslow's theory shows how human needs affect personality development.

- Kohlberg believed that everyone passes through a series of predictable stages in their moral thinking from childhood through young adulthood, though not all people attain the highest stages.

- Defense mechanisms are used by people to protect their self-concepts when faced with problems or threats in their environment. Their use may be healthy or unhealthy.

- Anger may be used either constructively or destructively.

- Fear may be the result of an unpleasant experience or conditioning from another person. Some fears can be helpful, but exaggerated fears or phobias can be damaging.

- Low moods and negative feelings must be accepted as part of life, but they can be balanced with happy times and positive feelings.

- Personalities can be classified as extrovert, introvert, or ambivert.

- Negative attitudes can be changed to positive attitudes as the result of new experiences, increased knowledge, a change of group membership, or a direct suggestion from someone.

- Since prejudices are formed without enough accurate knowledge, they are likely to be unreliable and harmful. Prejudices can be overcome or avoided altogether.

- Some common stereotypes involve age, gender, and race. Stereotypes cause people to prejudge others and to fail to recognize that each person is unique.

To Review ■ ■ ■ ■ ■ ■ ■ ■ ■ ■ ■ ■ ■ ■ ■ ■

1. According to Erikson's stages of development, match each positive outcome with its identifying phrase.
    _____ Initiative
    _____ Trust
    _____ Identity
    _____ Autonomy
    _____ Intimacy
    _____ Accomplishment
    _____ Generativity
    _____ Integrity
    a. You develop imagination and begin to think of your own activities.
    b. You feel confident of yourself, other people, and your environment.
    c. You carry your project through to completion and learn that work is meaningful.
    d. You accept yourself and become ready to establish stable relationships.
    e. You experience the freedom of self-direction and have the confidence to assert yourself.
    f. You are satisfied with your past and look forward to your future.
    g. You sort through your thoughts and feelings to discover who you are and to find a stable role for yourself in society.
    h. You express concern for the welfare of young people and the world.

2. Why is it important that each of Havighurst's developmental tasks be performed?

3. According to Maslow, _____ needs have the first priority.

4. Which of the following is NOT included in Maslow's list of human needs?
    a. Safety and security.
    b. Financial success.
    c. Love and acceptance.
    d. Esteem.

5. According to Kohlberg, what guides a child's decision making in the first stage of moral development?

6. True or False. Kohlberg believes that everyone eventually reaches the sixth stage of moral development.

7. Match the following defense mechanisms with their identifying phrases.
    _____ Rationalization
    _____ Direct attack
    _____ Idealization
    _____ Giving up
    _____ Regression
    _____ Projection
    _____ Displacement
    _____ Compensation
    _____ Conversion
    _____ Daydreaming
    a. Attacking the source of a threat.
    b. Using a substitute method to achieve the desired result.
    c. Explaining your weaknesses and failures by using a socially acceptable excuse that does not reflect the real problem.
    d. Transferring an emotion connected with one person or thing to an unrelated person or thing.
    e. Reverting back to a less mature stage of development.
    f. Using imagination to accomplish what you are not accomplishing in reality.
    g. Valuing something far more than its real worth.
    h. Transferring energy into a physical symptom or complaint.
    i. Deciding not to face or resolve problems.
    j. Blaming other people or things for your failures.

8. Give an example of how anger can be used constructively and an example of how it can be used destructively.

9. Give an example of how fear can serve a purpose.

10. A(An) _____ is a feeling or mental position about something.

11. What are prejudices based on?

12. Give an example of a stereotype. Explain how this label could affect or harm a person.

To Do ▪ ▪ ▪ ▪ ▪ ▪ ▪ ▪ ▪ ▪ ▪ ▪ ▪ ▪ ▪ ▪ ▪

1. Working in small groups, look through current magazines and find pictures that illustrate each of Havighurst's developmental tasks of adolescence. Explain your selections to the rest of the class. Display the pictures on a bulletin board.

2. Review the ten defense mechanisms. Recall instances when you or someone you know has used them.

3. Read newspapers to find examples of how various defense mechanisms have been used by people in the news.

4. Keep an anecdotal record for one week of every expression of anger you hear or see. Discuss your findings with classmates.

5. Recall several fears you have had throughout your life. Can you trace the origin of the fears? Do the fears help or hinder you? How can you overcome the negative effects of fear?

6. Research books, stories, poems, movies, and plays to find how fears and phobias have been used in plots. Consider works such as *Jane Eyre, Three Faces of Eve, The Sisters,* etc.

7. Ask a psychologist to come to class and discuss depression. Find out how it is identified and when a person should seek medical help for severe depression.

8. Cite examples of well-known people who are extroverts or introverts.

9. Find examples of stereotypes in advertising or news stories and share with the class. How are these stereotypes harmful?

Assoc. of Handicapped Artists, Inc.

Every situation in life requires you to respond to your environment. How has this artist responded to her enrironment?

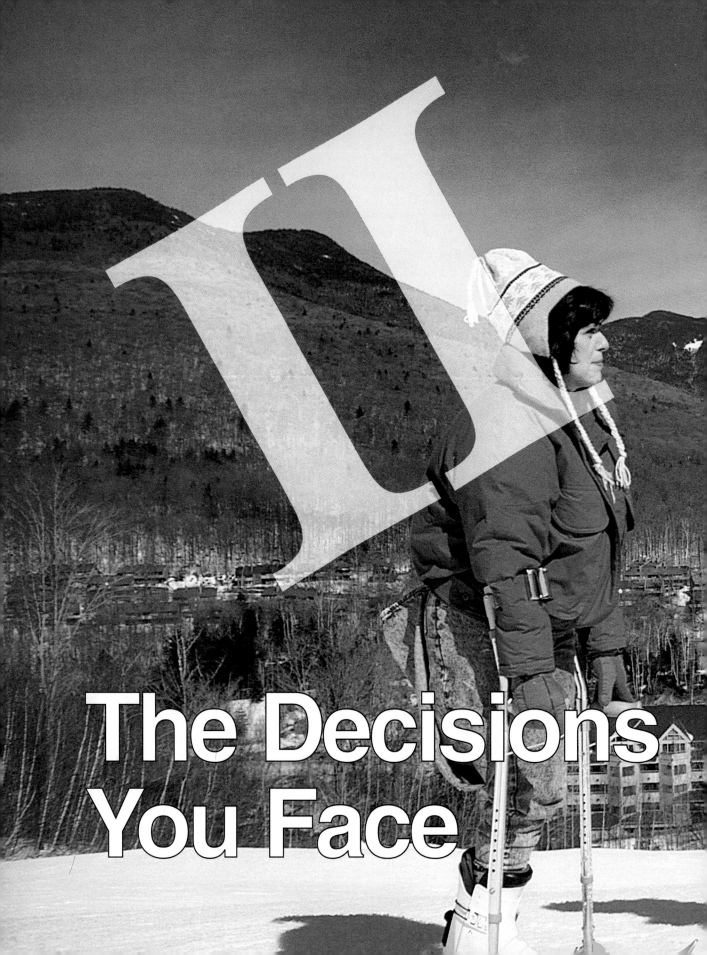

II

The Decisions You Face

It's Your Decision

After studying this chapter, you will be able to

- define values and explain how they influence decisions.

- give examples of short-term and long-term goals.

- plot goals based on the stages of an individual's life cycle using a time/life line.

- identify types of human and nonhuman resources.

- establish standards for measuring goal achievement.

- explain the steps in the decision-making process.

- describe the four stages of dependency in decision making.

Terms to Know

values

short-term goals

long-term goals

resources

human resources

nonhuman resources

standards

decision-making process

Do the following words sound familiar? "It's your decision. You will have to live with it."

As you mature, you gain the privilege and responsibility of making more of your own decisions. You may remember times in your childhood when your parents did not allow you to make decisions. They felt you were not old enough to make the right choices. At those times, you probably wished you could have had your own way.

Now that you are older, you have more chances to make more of your own decisions. Within the next few years, you will have to make some of the most important decisions of your life. These decisions may have a profound influence on your entire life span, 5-1. Some of these decisions will be difficult to make, but they are your decisions. You will have to live with the consequences of the decisions you make.

Values

To make the best decisions, you need to know yourself—especially your values. Your values will influence the decisions you make.

Cholla Runnels

5-1
Within the next few years, you will face many important decisions, such as what career to pursue and where to go for further education.

Your values will also influence the goals and standards you set for your life. Since values play such an important role, this chapter on decisions will begin with a discussion of values.

What Are Values?

Values are the concepts, beliefs, attitudes, activities, and feelings that are most important to you. Your values may include some of the following: love, knowledge, religion, power, health, and friendship. You may feel more strongly about some values than others. Your values become a part of your personality, and they affect your behavior.

How Are Values Formed?

As you read this book and participate in the learning experiences, you will find yourself agreeing and disagreeing. You will accept some ideas and reject others. In any course dealing with human development, you will find some concepts (ideas) that will help you improve your life, some that you have already accepted, and some that do not apply to your situation.

As you evaluate the information, you will be using and perhaps forming values. Creating a priority system for concepts and beliefs that are important to you is a difficult task. Putting "first things first" is not simple, for it forces you to decide what is really most important to you. Once you have made these decisions, however, you can take the needed action.

Many of your values have been forming for years due to the influence of your family. For instance, your parents may have instilled in you and your siblings the belief that family members should care for one another. They may have made it a priority that you all try to be together for the evening meal. You could talk about what happened to each family member during the day and share your concerns. As a result, you may hope to continue this practice when you marry and have children of your own. Other values that you may have acquired from your family might include compassion, loyalty, honesty, and caring. These values will help shape your future choices.

Value choices of your friends may influence your values, 5-2. You may have a very close friend. Many of your value choices will be influenced by this particular friend. Other people you come in contact with may also influence your values. These include teachers, religious leaders, neighbors, and other adults.

You are also influenced by your culture and the traditions you see practiced daily. People who move to other countries may bring certain cultural traditions with them to their new countries. These traditions may continue to be a part of their value system for many years, and even generations, to come.

The environment in which you live will also influence your values. If you live in a rural setting, for instance, you may value the

5-2   David Hopper
Good friends often share the same values.

sense of community you find there. If you live in an urban area, you may value the choices you have for enjoying the arts.

How Values Influence Decisions

You have been making decisions all of your life. Some of your decisions do not require a great deal of time or planning. For example, when it is time for you to go to baseball practice, you may jump on your bike and take off. Your choice to ride your bike includes value judgments. You may hold strongly to the belief that you should take every opportunity to exercise. You may value robust health and believe this is a way to improve it. You may also believe in the concept that the more we use bicycles the less fuel our nation will be using. Without even thinking about it, your values have influenced your decision!

The following examples will illustrate further how values influence decisions. Jodi is very close to his family. He values his relationship with his brothers and sisters. When he had the choice of camping with his family over the weekend or staying with a friend so he wouldn't miss a party, he chose to go with his family. At that time, being with his family meant more to him.

Your values will also influence decisions you make about doing your homework. If you are content with just doing enough to pass, you reveal how you value preparing for your future. You may put a greater value on having a good time and hanging out with your friends. If this value has a higher priority, it may hurt you later when your grades become a factor in getting a job or being accepted into a college.

You may sometimes question certain value choices your friends make. They may place you in a situation requiring you to "test" your values. For example, a friend may ask you to skip a day of school and go to the beach. Your decision would depend on your values. How much do the respect of your teachers and the trust of your parents mean to you? How important are the classes you would miss? How important is a day of companionship with your friend?

Tyra's values were also being tested when she was asked to go along with a group of friends. She knew they were planning a prank that might get them in trouble with the police. Her values helped her to say, "No, I can't go with you." Because she respected the rights (and property) of others, it was easy for her to make this choice.

Some of the most difficult value-related decisions during the teen years involve personal relationships. Kendra was faced with such a decision. Her social life had been limited to group activities. She and her parents had talked about different situations she might find herself in when she started to date. She was thrilled when a new guy in school asked her to the Homecoming dance. After the dance, they stopped off at a friend's house where a party was going on. They danced for a while and were having a good time. Then her date led her to a quiet room where they could be alone. When she pulled back, he said, "Hey, haven't you had a good time?" Kendra replied, "Yes, I've had a great time, and I'd like to keep it that way. Let's go home now." Kendra made a decision based on her values and acted on it. She did not allow another person to make her decisions for her.

During your teen years, you may find yourself more willing to take risks. Knowing your values can help you avoid potentially dangerous situations. Your values will help you weigh the options you have in many areas involving behavior. You will more easily recognize an option that is not in line with your

David Hopper

5-3
Knowing your own values will help you make decisions regarding your personal
behavior.

values, 5-3. Then you will find it easier to say no when you sense your values are being compromised.

Each of you has beliefs, ideals, and concepts that are important to you. These values will help you make more satisfying decisions. Your basic values will be internalized, and you can apply them in many different situations in your life.

Values Change in Priority

Some values, such as honesty, integrity, perseverance, and compassion, may always be a factor in your decisions no matter how old you are. Others, however, will change as the years go by. Your values will vary in importance at different stages of your life. During the teen years, for instance, loyalty to friends may be a top priority. At the same time, the value of an education may be of less importance because you are focusing on your friendships. Toward the end of high school, you may start thinking more about your future. You may decide on a career field that requires further education. Suddenly, getting good grades takes on greater importance. Your values shift in emphasis. You begin to spend more time studying and less time partying.

There may be periods in your life when your career occupies much of your energy and time. You may focus all of your attention on moving up on your job. Family and friends may take a back seat for awhile. Some people value money and the luxuries money can buy. For others, the desire for prestige and power influences value decisions.

During other stages of your life, you may feel the need to give more attention to your family. If and when you marry, you will want to spend more time with your spouse. You and your spouse will probably share similar values that will influence your joint decisions. If you have children, the members of your family unit will take center stage. Loving them and caring for their needs will become an important value for you.

Setting Your Goals ■ ■ ■

As you learned in Chapter 1, a goal is something you want to achieve or obtain. A goal is the direction or end toward which you strive. When you set a goal, you begin to work out a plan for reaching it.

Some of your goals are short term. *Short-term goals* are reachable in the near future—the next hour, day, or week. You may want to get your chores done early so you can go out with your friends Saturday afternoon. You may want to complete your term paper this week, so that you can visit a college campus over spring break. Your sister plans to buy her prom dress this weekend because she has finally saved enough money. These are all examples of short-term goals.

Some of your goals are long term. *Long-term goals* are goals you hope to achieve next year or several years from now. These often include saving money for major purchases, such as a car or vacation. They may include plans for further education beyond high school. Many people set goals for their careers, outlining where they hope to be in one, five, and ten years.

You will probably have multiple goals at the same time. All of your goals will fit together much like a jigsaw puzzle. For instance, right now you may be trying to study for an important test while working on a term paper that's due at the end of the week. You may have a part-time job so you can save money for your first car. You may also have plans for what you intend to do following graduation from high school. Some people have specific career goals in mind. Maybe you intend to open your own child care center some day. As you can see, it is possible to be working toward multiple goals at the same time.

Goals Are Based on Values

You set your goals based on your values, or that which is important to you, 5-4. When you know what your values are, you can plan your goals with greater ease, as Jose did. Some of Jose's values include independence, hard work, a comfortable lifestyle, self-respect, and a sense of accomplishment. His long-term goal was to become a restaurant manager. Jose began working at a local restaurant while he was a senior in high school. He worked hard at his job, but didn't let his grades slip. He maintained a B average in school while working 20 hours a week. He did not miss one day of school or work all year. His boss told him if he continued to perform well on the job, he would be in line for a managerial position within two years. Jose had to turn down a lot of fun times with his friends in order to work toward his goal. Some of his friends couldn't understand why he wanted to work so hard.

After graduation, Jose worked full time at the restaurant. He made many suggestions to management for improving the business. Within two years, he was offered a junior managerial position at a new restaurant the company was opening. Jose was thrilled.

to achieve in the next five years? By the time you are 30? What would you like to be doing by the time you are 55 or 60 years old?

Your Individual Life Cycle and Time/Life Line

Each of you has the same basic unit of time—one life. The number of years in each person's life will vary, but everyone passes through an *individual life cycle.* You travel through stages of birth, infancy, childhood, young adulthood, adulthood, middle age, aging, and death. The exciting challenge of living this life is choosing and achieving goals as you pass through each of these stages. The decisions you make steer you through the life cycle and help you reach your goals.

Setting goals and plotting them on a *time/life line* gives you an idea of how your future goals will fit into your life, 5-5. It also lets you see how decisions you are making today will have an effect on your entire life.

Try to set your goals in a general time frame. It may be difficult for you to imagine

Cholla Runnels

5-4
People's lives are more meaningful when they set goals for themselves that are based on their values.

Jose's values kept him focused on achieving his goal. He worked hard to make a life for himself. He can foresee a comfortable lifestyle. His self-esteem is high due to his sense of accomplishment. His goal now is to make his restaurant one of the most successful in the area.

Jose's goals were long term, and it took him several years to achieve them. He is still plotting goals for his future, and this gives him a focus for his life.

Think about your life now and what you would like to achieve. Do you see a pattern in the events in your life? What would you like

Cholla Runnels

5-5
Plotting your goals on a time/life line can help you relate what you are doing today with where you want to be years from now.

Contemporary Concerns *of today's teens:*

Risk Taking vs. Goal Achievement

You are at a point in your life where many of the decisions you make today can influence your entire life path. At the same time, young people are vulnerable to many risks in our society. You can reduce these risks by setting goals and acting responsibly in order to achieve these goals.

Several goals typical of teens are listed below. Risks teens may face in reaching these goals are listed in the second column. Behaviors that can help reduce or eliminate the risks are described in the third column. Do any of these risks pose problems for you?

Goals	Risks Teenagers May Face	Behaviors That Help Reduce and Eliminate the Risks
To graduate from high school.	Poor attendance in school, poor grades, and dropping out of school.	Keep school attendance a top priority. Get plenty of rest, exercise, and eat nutritious foods to maintain good health. Complete homework and projects on time. Be attentive in class. Seek additional help when needed. Talk with teachers, parents, or a counselor if problems arise.
To develop friendships with peers whose values are similar to yours.	Friends pressure you to participate in activities you question.	Peer pressure may become a problem if friends do not share your values. Know what you value and hold firmly to these values. If your friends don't respect your values, they are probably not the type of friends you would enjoy.
To be responsible and accountable for your behavior.	Your friends become involved in questionable or illegal activities.	If this happens, be assertive in distancing yourself from these people. Instead, choose activities that enable you to build relationships with caring and responsible friends.
To prepare for a future career.	Lack of motivation or optimism for the career goals you can achieve.	Looking ahead to your future can be challenging for teens. Not every teen has the same set of possibilities for their future, but each person can set achievable goals and build on them. There is new technology to investigate, emerging service fields that need young people, and broadening global challenges. You can have a bright and challenging future—catch onto the positive possibilities!

Possible Goal Sequences

High School ➡ College ➡ Career ➡ Marriage ➡ Parenting.

High School ➡ Work ➡ Vocational Training ➡ Career ➡ Marriage ➡ Parenting.

High School ➡ Marriage ➡ Work ➡ Community College ➡ Career ➡ Parenting.

High School ➡ Work ➡ Marriage.

High School ➡ Vocational Training/Work ➡ Career ➡ Marriage ➡ Parenting.

5-6
After high school, you and your friends may choose from these different sequences for reaching your life goals.

what you might be doing when you are 60 years old. However, if you start planning what you would like to do in your life between now and then, it may be easier for you to view a longer life span.

You have many options when deciding on long-term goals. Thus, everyone's time/life line will be different. As you plan your time/life line, keep in mind long-term goals of education, career, marriage, and family. Some goals have definite stopping points, such as graduation from high school or college. Some goals, such as being a parent, continue for a lifetime. Many goals will overlap, such as marriage, parenting, and a career. Life is not either work or marriage or family. These goals, if chosen, have to be combined and balanced.

Many people will have similar goals, but the sequence of achieving these goals will vary. Figure 5-6 shows several possible sequences. Some people want to marry early and have their children while they are relatively young. Later on, they may resume their education. Other people will want to complete their educational goals and become established in their careers before they marry.

In 5-7 you can see how goals can be plotted on a time/life line. The stages of the life cycle are also indicated. These graphs illus-

trate the blocks of time that are devoted to different life goals.

As you plan your goals and plot them on a time/life line, keep the following points in mind:

- View education, work, marriage, and family as interconnected parts of a whole. They are not separate entities.

- Evaluate various careers and try to select the one that will bring you the greatest personal satisfaction.

- Consider the best time to marry. Today, many couples are marrying later, after they have become established in their careers.

- Consider how childrearing will fit into your life plans.

Identify Your Resources

In order to reach your goals, you will need to use various resources. *Resources* include the various ways and means that you have for reaching your goals. The challenge to you is to recognize your resources and to

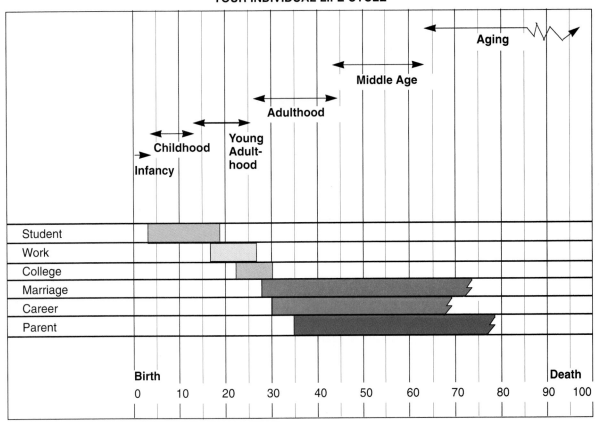

Jesse's goal is to own his own business someday. He plans to finish high school, but he knows his parents cannot afford to send him to college. Therefore, Jesse intends to work full-time while attending community college at night. He hopes to save enough money so he can attend college full-time during his senior year. Marriage will wait until he is in his late 20s. Jesse has been promised a job managing a small machine shop when he graduates from college. The owner will be near retirement age then, and he intends to work out a plan for Jesse to purchase the business within 15 years.

5-7
In plotting his time/life line, Jesse was able to plan for completing his education and owning his own business.

choose the right ones to reach your goals. You are the manager of your resources.

You already have many resources that can help you achieve some of your goals. To reach all of your goals, you may need to seek out new resources. There are two kinds of resources—human resources and nonhuman resources.

Human Resources

Many resources come from within a person. These are known as *human resources*. They come from within yourself and from other people who support you in some way. They include your health, energy, and time. Your personality characteristics and character traits are also important human resources.

Many of your personal characteristics can serve as resources as you make choices and meet new challenges. Most teens are in excellent health and are full of energy. Many teens use these resources to fulfill school, job, and family responsibilities. Time is a resource that may be in limited supply if you have many goals you are trying to reach at the same time.

Certain aspects of your personality may be some of your most valuable human resources. Self-discipline will allow you to assess and fulfill your obligations. "I will take care of it" tells people you are responsible, but you must follow through. Being optimistic can help see you through difficult times. Friendli-

ness and compassion are human resources that will help you in many ways.

Your talents and skills are human resources. You may have skills in creative writing that will be useful to you throughout your life. Some people are quite comfortable using the latest computer technology, 5-8. Others are superb athletes. Musical talent may allow you to contribute to creative productions.

Other people can serve as human resources for you when you need them. Your parents, your siblings, friends, religious leaders, and teachers are just some of the people you can call upon. They can encourage you and advise you as needed or direct you to other resources.

Cholla Runnels

5-8
You may be very good at using a computer. If so, your skill is one of your human resources.

Nonhuman Resources

Nonhuman resources include money, material possessions, and community resources and facilities. These resources are not physically a part of any individual.

Money is a resource people use every day to satisfy certain needs or reach specific goals. Money is used to buy goods and services. You may have some money if you have a job or get an allowance. Your money is a resource if you use it to buy items you need.

You may have possessions that can be used as resources. With a computer, you can research and write papers for school. You may even develop your own computer programs. You could use your family lawn mower to earn extra money mowing neighbors' lawns. Having a means of transportation, whether a bicycle, a truck, or a car, can also be a resource.

You have many nonhuman resources available to you in your community that you share with other citizens. There may be trade schools, community colleges, and perhaps even a college or university in your local community. Colleges are a valuable resource for library research, public-forum programs, sports, and entertainment.

Many facilities in your local community are supported by your tax dollars. Public libraries are an important resource for information and entertainment. Parks and park district programs offer many sports, entertainment, and education opportunities. The recreational facilities in your community provide opportunities for participation in sports activities.

Other government services can be important resources. Various levels of government offer different types of assistance. A look through the community services section of your phone directory will give you an idea of the many services available. There is help for housing, civil rights violations, health care, and crisis situations, to name a few.

You need to use resources to reach your goals. Be sure you are aware of all of your human and nonhuman resources.

Set Your Standards ▪ ▪ ▪ ▪ ▪ ▪

As you set your goals, you will have certain measures that show how you're doing in reaching your goals. These measures are your *standards*, or levels of achievement. These help you determine whether you have achieved your goals.

Standards that you set for yourself are personal standards. What you achieve must be acceptable to you based on your personal standards. For instance, you may want to maintain a certain grade point average in school. This average may be higher or lower than the standards set by other students or your parents, but it will be the personal standard that you feel is right for you. This is the standard you will use to measure your achievement, 5-9.

You may have personal standards regarding your appearance. If you work in a part-time job, you may be very particular about wearing appropriate clothing. Your work supervisor will recognize that you have accepted these standards.

People have standards concerning behavior, too. An athlete may set certain performance standards he or she would like to achieve. It might be scoring a certain number of points during a game or running a mile in so many minutes. Behavior standards also relate to personal behavior. "I will not talk about my friends behind their backs" might reflect a behavior standard of yours. You also may have higher or lower standards of housekeeping, neatness, courtesy, or honesty than others.

Your personal standards may or may not agree with conventional standards—the standards commonly accepted by society. For instance, you may feel no one should be allowed to smoke in restaurants. Others may feel that smokers have a right to smoke wherever they want. One conventional standard is to allow smoking in certain areas only, thus attempting to meet the needs of smokers and nonsmokers alike. These differing standards may cause conflicts in some instances.

Some people accept lower standards in some areas so they can uphold higher standards in others. For example, you may accept a lower standard of excellence in your tennis game so you can spend more time studying. You believe in higher academic standards.

Your standards are related to your values. Consider job-performance standards as an example. If you are satisfied with just putting in your time with little regard for performance, you do not have a strong work ethic. Your job-performance standards may be low. You'll do as little as is needed to keep your job. On the other hand, if your standards are high for any job you do, it reveals your values concerning the work ethic. It also indicates you are willing to put in the kind of effort needed to achieve certain career goals.

5-9   Barrier Free Environments, Raleigh, NC
This student is reaching his academic goals by reading braille.

Making Decisions ■ ■ ■

You have just read about values, goals, resources, and standards and how they relate to one another. These also play an important role in making good decisions. During your high school years, you will be looking ahead to possible options for the future. This will require making many decisions. Your decisions should reflect your values. Your decisions should also be based on your goals. Then you will look at the resources that you have within you and that are available to you from the people around you. These resources will be considered as you make decisions. Finally, many of your decisions will be influenced by

your standards. You can see how your values, goals, resources, and standards all relate to decision making.

You can learn to make good decisions in your life. You first must have a positive self-concept. You must have confidence in your ability to make responsible decisions. Then you can develop critical thinking skills so that you can think through your decisions. You may seek the advice and opinions of other persons, but you need to learn to make your own decisions considering their suggestions. Becoming an adult means accepting the responsibility for making the decisions that will benefit you, your family and friends, and your society.

Making decisions can be fun. It is an exciting learning experience. You should not think of decision making as something to be feared or something that is overwhelming. When you learn to make your own decisions, you will be better able to make the most of your life.

Types of Decisions

When you make a decision, you make a choice or a judgment. You arrive at a solution. You make up your mind.

You make many decisions every day. Many are easy, such as deciding what to wear or what to eat. Many are more difficult, such as deciding which classes to take. Some of your decisions affect just you, but some affect other people, too. The consequences of some decisions may affect the rest of your life.

Ways to Make Decisions

Just as there are many different kinds of decisions, there are also many different ways to make decisions.

Some decisions are simply habits. Perhaps when you roll out of bed in the morning, you head straight for the shower. After getting dressed, you may have a bowl of cereal and a glass of orange juice for breakfast. If you follow the same routine every day, it becomes a habit. You don't even have to think about the decisions you make each morning.

Some people depend on their common sense to make decisions. They think of all the options they have. They consider the consequences for each option—for themselves, for other people, and for society. Then they choose the solution they think will have the best results with the fewest complications. This entire reasoning process may be done so quickly and automatically that people may not even be aware of it. They consider it to be just common sense.

Some people use intuition to solve problems. They follow their instincts or feelings. Sometimes they may just make a guess, but in most cases, their intuition is based on some knowledge of the situation.

Others base their decisions on past experiences. If a person faced a similar problem before and found a good solution, that person will probably make the same decision again. If the solution did not work before, the person will probably make a different decision next time.

Some decisions may be made by applying lessons learned as a result of parental guidance. Beliefs that a person may have gained from parental or religious training can also be a main resource for decision making.

The Decision-Making Process

Another way to make a decision is to follow the *decision-making process*. This method of making decisions and solving problems is a step-by-step process that you can learn. It is a good way to approach a decision you haven't faced before. It can help you organize your thoughts and arrive at the best solution. It is also a good way to make important decisions that will have long-term consequences.

As you begin using the decision-making process, try to write each step on paper. This will help you learn the process and develop a clear thinking pattern. The following are the six steps in the decision-making process. They are also listed in 5-10.

1. Identify the decision to be made.

This step might sound too simple to be important, but it isn't. In fact, this first step is sometimes the most difficult one. You may feel overwhelmed by a situation, but you will not make any progress until you identify the one decision that needs to be made first.

There are times when you would probably like to ignore the fact that you have a decision to make. Putting off decisions does not make them go away. Not making a decision is actually making the decision to let someone or something else take over for you.

If you have a decision to make, focus on the issue. Many times people are confused by the many side issues involved. In order to make a decision, you have to clear your mind of issues that are not a part of the decision. State the decision verbally, or write it down.

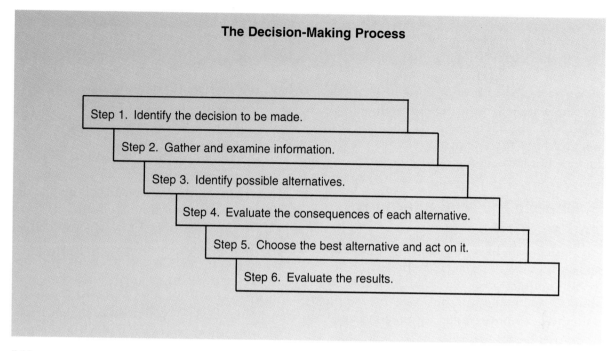

The Decision-Making Process

Step 1. Identify the decision to be made.

Step 2. Gather and examine information.

Step 3. Identify possible alternatives.

Step 4. Evaluate the consequences of each alternative.

Step 5. Choose the best alternative and act on it.

Step 6. Evaluate the results.

5-10
The steps in the decision-making process can be used to make all kinds of decisions.

2. Gather and examine information.

The second step is to gather and examine information. There are many sources of information to help you. Your school counselor may be able to direct you to the most helpful resources. Your parents, religious leader, or friends may be able to provide some information also.

There are constant changes in the information sources and many times you may be unaware that help does exist for your particular concern. Asking for this information is not a sign of a weak person. It is the sign of a knowledgeable person seeking the best possible course of action.

3. Identify possible alternatives.

After you have gathered information, you are ready to identify possible alternatives. There are often several ways to address a problem or find a solution. Use the information you have found in helping you select possible alternatives. Write down the alternatives, 5-11.

4. Evaluate the consequences of each alternative.

Each alternative may pose certain consequences for you or for others. In order to arrive at the best solution, you have to examine the possible consequences for each of the alternatives. There will be both positive and negative consequences, so write these down under the pro and con column. Review these and evaluate them carefully.

Look at each consequence and ask yourself if it would be compatible with your values and your family's values. Family members' needs must be considered. Does this decision recognize these needs? Does the decision live up to your standards? You should also examine each consequence to see if it is socially acceptable in your community.

By honestly critiquing your alternatives and their consequences, you will be able to arrive at the best possible decision. You may eliminate some of your options immediately when you consider the consequences. You may exclude those that have some positive factors, but have more negative factors.

5. Choose the best alternative and act on it.

After you have evaluated the alternatives, your next step will be to choose the best option and act on it. Put your plan into action. All the thoughtful consideration you put into the decision is wasted if you fail to act.

6. Evaluate the results.

In this important step you evaluate the results. You can now see the results of your decision. You see how the results have affected your life and the lives of those around

Cholla Runnels

5-11
After you have listed all possible alternatives, you are ready to evaluate each alternative.

you. Once you recognize the consequences of your decision, you must accept responsibility for them.

If the consequences are good, you will have the satisfaction of knowing you made a good decision. Keep this positive decision-making experience in your memory for future reference.

If the consequences are bad, think about how you can learn from your mistake. Then try to improve the results of the first decision by making another decision.

Do not feel locked into a series of bad situations because of one bad decision. If you find that you made a bad decision, you can start right away to change your direction. "Sticking with it" won't make a bad decision any better. (Even if you make a change, however, you still have responsibility for the previous decision.)

Remember, making no decision is making a decision. It is deciding not to act. It is deciding to accept whatever happens or whatever other people decide for you. It may mean giving up a chance to manage your own life.

During your teens, you make many decisions that involve only one day out of your life. However, many will impact your entire life. This is why it is so important to adopt a workable decision-making system. Knowing the best way to make decisions will help you now and for the rest of your life.

Stages of Dependency in Decision Making ▪ ▪ ▪

As you learn the decision-making process, you gain maturity. You will pass through different stages of dependency as you reach this maturity.

Dependency Stage

When you were a small child, you depended on your parents to make decisions for you. During the *dependency stage* you needed to lean on the strength of others. Without that "block of strength," as pictured in 5-12, you would have felt insecure. During this time of your life, you needed guidance to make your choices.

Counter-Dependency Stage

As you seek your self-identity, you want to make more of your own decisions. You may resist the decisions of authority figures. It is as if one block were pushing against the other, as pictured in 5-13. This is known as the *counter-dependency stage.* It generally occurs during adolescence. In this stage, parents represent a strength that teenagers need, yet teenagers push against this strength as they learn to make their own decisions. They feel

Cholla Runnels

5-13
In the counter-dependency stage, teenagers test their ability to make their own decisions.

Cholla Runnels

5-12
In the dependency stage, children need guidance in making decisions.

the security of their parents' love, but they are testing their ability to make their own decisions. Parents and teenagers alike need to maintain respect and understanding for each other during this important learning process.

In the counter-dependency stage, you may also resist the decisions of peers. Suppose your friend wants you to do something, and you choose not to go along with the suggestion. In this case, you would be questioning the decision of your friend and learning to make your own decisions. If you never question the decisions made by others, you may have a harder time reaching the next stage of independency. The stage of counter-dependency is an important learning step as you gain the maturity to make your own responsible decisions.

Cholla Runnels

5-14
In the independency stage, young adults make their own decisions and feel "in charge."

Cholla Runnels

5-15
In the interdependency stage, adults share decisions while retaining their individual personalities.

Cholla Runnels

5-16
In the codependency state, individuals have difficulty maintaining their self-esteem and relating to others.

Independency Stage

When you have confidence in yourself, then those around you will sense your ability to make responsible decisions. You will feel "in charge." You will be responsible for your own actions. See 5-14. This is the *independency stage.*

Teenagers seek independence and often think this will be the greatest time of their lives. It is a very important stage, but you will discover there is an even greater expansion of dependency in your life. As you form relationships with others, you will discover another stage of dependency.

Interdependency Stage

The *interdependency stage* may bring even greater satisfaction in your life. As you develop relationships with friends and with a future mate, you will recognize that decisions made by both of you are interdependent. This allows you to give to and take from another person, while still retaining your individual personality. As shown in 5-15, the two boxes stand alone but there is mutual give-and-take between them.

Codependency ▪ ▪ ▪ ▪

A term sometimes confused with dependency is codependency. *Codependency* is a term psychologists use to describe people who have difficulty maintaining their self-esteem and relating to others in a healthy way. Co-dependent people often lose touch with their feelings. They may try to control others, or they may let others control them. They often feel powerless to do anything. They may adapt to someone or something in a compulsive way. The individual loses control of the ability to manage his or her own life. This condition often describes the compulsive addiction to drugs. Codependency is an unhealthy emotional or psychological state rather than a healthy stage of normal development. See 5-16.

Summary ▪ ▪ ▪ ▪ ▪ ▪ ▪ ▪ ▪ ▪ ▪ ▪ ▪ ▪

- Your values are the concepts, beliefs, attitudes, activities, and feelings that are most important to you.

- Values are influenced by family members, friends, teachers, religious leaders, and other significant adults. Values are also influenced by your culture and the environment in which you live.

- Your values influence the decisions you make. They may vary in importance at different stages of your life.

- Short-term goals are those that are reachable in the very near future. Long-term goals are those you hope to achieve next year or several years from now.

- You set your goals based on your values. When you know what your values are, you can plan your goals with greater ease.

- The stages of the individual life cycle are the same for everyone, yet each person's life is unique.

- A time/life line gives you a glimpse of what you think your life might include. It helps you set goals and make decisions as you manage your life.

- Human and nonhuman resources are the various ways and means you have for reaching your goals.

- As you set your goals, you will have certain measures that show how you're doing in reaching your goals. These measures are your standards, or levels of achievement.

- When you learn to make your own decisions, you will be better able to make the most of your life.

- There are many different types of decisions and many different ways to make decisions.

- The decision-making process is a series of six steps that can help you make decisions and solve problems.

- Most people pass through four stages of dependency in decision making as they mature.

To Review ■ ■ ■ ■ ■ ■ ■ ■ ■ ■ ■ ■ ■ ■ ■ ■ ■

1. Explain how a person's environment might influence his or her values. Give an example.

2. Explain how values influence decisions and give an example.

3. Give three examples of short-term goals and three examples of long-term goals.

4. What are the eight stages of the individual life cycle?

5. What is the purpose of a time/life line?

6. Name three types of human resources and three types of nonhuman resources.

7. Give two examples of standards set by your school.

8. Name five ways to make decisions.

9. Explain each of the steps in the decision-making process.

10. Explain the statement, "Making no decision is making a decision."

11. Which stage of dependency are you in when you can make your own decisions and are responsible for your actions?

To Do ■ ■ ■ ■ ■ ■ ■ ■ ■ ■ ■ ■ ■ ■ ■ ■ ■ ■

1. Name ten values you think the average high school student in your school would have. Take a random sampling of the values of 30 sophomores, 30 juniors, and 30 seniors. (Do not include their names.) Tally the results. Look for patterns in the responses according to age or sex of the students. Report findings to class.

2. List two beliefs, two ideals, and two concepts that you have. How will they help you describe your values?

3. Form a panel and discuss the following topic: Value choices of friends can influence you both positively and negatively.

4. Write down three short-term goals that you have this day. Write down three long-term goals you have. Do your short-term goals have any bearing on your long-term goals?

5. Draw the individual life cycle on a bulletin board. Find photos representing the different stages and mount them in the appropriate position on the life cycle.

6. Draw a time/life line for yourself, projecting your different goals of education, work/career, marriage, and/or parenthood that you think you may follow. Keep it and refer to it every few months, revising it when necessary. You may also want to keep a journal of your thoughts concerning your time/life line.

7. Think of a real or imaginary decision to be made. Use the decision-making process to make the decision, writing down the six steps as outlined in your text.

8. Working in a small group, follow a fictitious character's development from childhood into adulthood. Write anecdotes describing the character in each of the four main stages of dependency in decision making.

6

Decisions Concerning Your Future Career

©Future Homemakers of America

Terms to Know

aptitude	resume
apprenticeship	cover letter
leadership	networking

**After studying this chapter,
you will be able to**

- identify career decisions that need to be made.

- describe education and training options related to career preparation.

- evaluate the pros and cons of combining work with education.

- explain the importance of developing leadership skills.

- list the steps in a job search.

- describe characteristics necessary for keeping a job.

Choosing a career is one of the major tasks confronting you. When you leave high school, you can expect to live at least 50 more years, on average. A major portion of that time will be spent working. Few of you will choose one career to last your entire lifetime. The average person changes jobs five times. Each job decision you make expands your horizons and contributes to your personal growth and development.

Decisions about work command a great deal of most people's attention. They also have a great deal to do with personal happiness and satisfaction. There are decisions to make about preparing for jobs, finding jobs, succeeding on jobs, and changing jobs.

The "right" job is one that meets two sets of needs. The work must satisfy your needs, and the work you do must satisfy your employer's needs.

To make wise job decisions, you need lots of information. You have to know yourself—your true motives, interests, and abilities. You have to know what you can contribute. You also need to find the answers to questions about the job and the organization.

Cholla Runnels

6-1
School guidance counselors can give you information about various careers and the
training or education needed for them.

Deciding on a Career

You face a variety of choices as you investigate future careers. How can you decide which career to choose and thus what type of education you will need? The task is not an easy one, but it can be interesting, and it must be done.

School counselors can help you sort through the many career options and training programs available, 6-1. Employees working in your field of interest can provide you with information for your career considerations. If you choose to obtain education or training beyond high school, representatives of educational institutions can answer any questions you may have. Your parents, relatives, and family friends can also assist you by providing information about their occupations. They can also provide information on the educational requirements of these occupations.

Factors Affecting Career Choice

A number of factors enter into the choice of a career. These include personal preferences, aptitudes, abilities, knowledge of career alternatives, and the career preparation required.

Personal Preferences

In choosing a career, you begin by asking yourself about your likes and dislikes. Do you like to work with people or do you prefer to work with objects or information? Although any job requires dealing with people, some have more people contact than others. For instance, in sales, teaching, and social work, you would work directly with people. Working with machinery, computers, or scientific formulas would require less contact with people.

How do you react to the conditions in your working environment? Do you prefer dealing with abstract concepts such as time, space, and ideas, or do you prefer working with concrete objects such as motors, power tools, and word processors? The answers to these questions can provide you with important clues as to the type of job you might find satisfying.

Aptitudes and Abilities

Everyone is born with certain **aptitudes** (potential for special talents). You probably have a friend who is great at solving math or computer problems, 6-2. Another of your friends may seem to be a natural when it comes to styling hair. Perhaps your friends compliment you on your ability to play the piano or to work on cars. Learning what your aptitudes are can help you reach your full potential. If you develop your aptitudes wisely, you may be able to put them to use in a successful career.

Think about the types of activities in which you have excelled. Which subjects have been easiest for you in school? These activities and subjects could be the clues to a successful career. You could also ask your school counselor for an aptitude test. Aptitude tests measure your potential abilities and skills. If you have an aptitude for a certain skill, you will be able to learn the skill easily.

Knowledge of Career Alternatives

Learning about the array of possible careers open to you is important. Too many young people drift into jobs that are easy to obtain rather than jobs that they will find fulfilling. Learning about the many career alternatives will help you avoid this situation.

Often, young people may feel almost "lost" in trying to evaluate career alternatives. They may feel that their opportunities to observe people first-hand working in a variety of

6-2
You may have friends who are good at singing and playing their guitars.

occupations is limited. If they live in small towns or rural areas, they may feel that this is especially true.

Some individuals may limit their vocational aspirations to occupations deemed as traditional for their gender. Women may avoid considering jobs in auto repair or plumbing, and men may avoid secretarial work or nursing. Others may limit their educational choices to those of other family members. You may be the first person in your family to want to go to college. You can succeed if you have the ability and are willing to apply yourself to your studies.

Sometimes, well-meaning families try to dictate young people's future occupations. Just because your parent enjoys an occupation doesn't mean that you will. On the other hand, your parents, relatives, and family friends can be excellent sources of information about many aspects of their jobs. It is difficult to imagine yourself in an occupation if you do not personally know anyone engaged in it. Reading about careers and talking to as many workers in as many fields as possible will help address this dilemma.

Career Preparation Requirements

Everyone who plans a career must find an occupation that fits in with his or her aptitudes and abilities. Not everyone who enjoys gazing at stars at night will have the mathematical aptitude to become an astronomer. Not everyone who enjoys discussing legal issues will be able to survive the rigors of law school. Not everyone who is interested in health matters will be able to become a physician.

When you are young, however, you may not know yet what your aptitudes and abilities are. Many people aim too low in their job choices in this and other ways.

Every adult worker you see happily engaged in fulfilling employment once faced the career fears and quandaries you may be facing now, 6-3. Most of them will be willing to help you learn about their occupations if you ask for that help.

Making the Most of Career Opportunities

When you talk to successful adults about their career paths, you often find that those paths were identified by a combination of purposeful activity and happenstance. For example, a person's career with Company A rather than Company B may have begun because Company A was hiring when the person happened to be looking for a job. An important opportunity for an assistant to "grow into" a job may have occurred when a more senior person happened to accept a position elsewhere.

The French scientist Louis Pasteur acknowledged the role of luck in scientific discovery when he wrote, "Chance favors the

Cholla Runnels

6-3
This successful textile designer may have had uncertainties concerning her career when she was a teenager.

prepared mind." A popular advice columnist has stated that "Luck is where preparation meets opportunity." Both adages point up the importance of preparation in improving your odds of success.

Finding a fulfilling job often involves years of patient inquiry, discussion, reflection, and tentative steps toward degrees or jobs that may or may not work out. Circumstances will guide you as you move back and forth between discovering aptitudes, taking coursework, and learning about school and career opportunities. At the same time you will be trying out jobs in the areas of your choice and re-evaluating your career options in light of new information.

You may find a job that pays the bills while you gain education and experience that will advance you toward your "dream job." You may find a job that combines your interest and abilities at a different level from the one you originally considered but which is right for you. If you enjoy the outdoors, you may not become an astronomer, but you can become a forest ranger. If you enjoy legal issues, you can enjoy an interesting career as a paralegal worker even if you do not want to go to law school. If you like the field of medicine, you can find fulfillment as a nurse or other health worker even if you do not become a doctor. Of course, you may indeed become an astronomer, lawyer, or physician. The important thing is to respect yourself at your own level of functioning. There is much that you can contribute to the world at any level.

As you engage in this process of discovery, you can learn much about yourself and about how the working world functions. Most people eventually find a satisfactory job situation that reflects their personal preferences, aptitudes, and career preparation. Keep your eye fixed on your career destination, but try to learn as much as you can while getting there.

Careers Related to Personal and Family Relations

A background in family and consumer sciences can prepare you for a broad range of career options. Specific training in family relations and child development would enable you to find employment in many of the career fields described in 6-4. An added benefit of this training would be its application to your own family roles.

People who choose careers in personal and family relations usually like people and want to help them. Individuals with potential for successful careers tend to be flexible, open to establishing close relationships with others, and comfortable with discussing thoughts and feelings. They appreciate the importance of optimal interpersonal relationships and are motivated to help others become the best individuals and family members they are capable of becoming.

For many family-related careers, your place of employment would be a school, government agency, or private company. Some of these careers, however, could provide you with the opportunity to operate your own business. A business gives you entrepreneurial opportunities. For instance, you could provide child care in your own home or open your own nursery school. As an image consultant, you could operate your own consulting firm. If you have writing skills, you could be a free-lance writer.

A job description is provided in 6-4 for each of the careers listed. Some of the personal characteristics essential for success in each career are also given. All of the careers described require at least a four-year college degree except where noted.

Career	Job Description	Personal Characteristics
Extension Specialist in Family Relations, Child Development, or Family Economics	Conduct educational programs on topics of interest to families. Act as a consultant to industry or community agencies. Provide information to the community through the media.	Able to work with people in a variety of settings; good public relations skills.
Specialist, Family Life Education Programs	Plan, write, and promote family life education programs.	Concern for families; able to communicate information.
Writer on Family Life Topics	Write textbooks, how-to books, newspaper and magazine articles, and TV programs.	Enjoy researching topics; able to present topics clearly in writing.
Recreation Worker	Plan, organize, and direct individual and group leisure events such as arts, crafts, music, drama, and sports events. (Entry-level positions available with high school diploma.)	Good at motivating people and sensitive to their needs; good health.
Guidance Counselor	Help students with education, career, and personal decisions. Meet with parents and teachers. Administer tests. Provide group counseling.	Strong interest in helping others and able to inspire respect, trust, and confidence.
Financial Consultant	Work with families and individuals to solve financial problems. Conduct seminars on money management.	Able to analyze detailed information; tact and good judgment in counseling clients.
Image Consultant and Analyst	Work with individuals and groups to promote a positive professional image. Conduct seminars, give speeches, and write articles on career strategies.	Enjoy working with people; able to keep abreast of fashions and beauty techniques.
Family Life Educator	Teach family life and parenting. Work with junior high, high school, or college students, or adults.	Enjoy working with people and sharing knowledge with others.
Child Development Teacher	Teach parenthood education, early childhood training, and child development.	Good communication skills; able to motivate others.
Social Worker Child Guidance Specialist	Work with family members or teachers, helping individuals with emotional or social problems, and/or assisting with childrearing problems.	Emotionally mature, objective, sensitive, and concerned for people and their problems.

continued

6-4
This is just a sample of the many careers related to family relations and child development.

Career	Job Description	Personal Characteristics
Child Care Worker Teacher's Aide	Help care for children in a home, school, or center. Supervise and entertain children individually or in groups. (Some positions require only a high school diploma.)	Creative, dependable, patient, and competent in handling classroom situations.
Nursery School Teacher Kindergarten or Primary Teacher	Introduce children to basic math, language, science, and social studies concepts. Help children learn to interact well with others.	Strong interest in educational and emotional development of children.

6-4
continued

Decisions about Your Education ■ ■ ■ ■ ■ ■

One of the greatest pressures on adolescents today is the completion of their education. As our society has become more complex, the period of education in preparation for a career has lengthened. More and more students are continuing their educations beyond high school. Scholarships, loans, and grants are available to help students further their education.

Without a doubt, the completion of a high school education is helpful for any job or career you choose. Your choice of subject matter depends on the goal you hope to achieve.

Students who become discouraged and drop out of school usually encounter problems as they attempt to compete in the job market. Although you may think your schooling is confining, it is one of the necessary steps in achieving maturity. If you are eager to enter the world of work, try taking advantage of part-time job opportunities while continuing your education.

Educational Options

Several types of training and education are available starting in high school and continuing beyond high school. If you settle on a career choice early in life, you will be able to determine the type of education you need.

Vocational Training Schools

Vocational schools offer occupational training through coursework at both the secondary and post-secondary levels, 6-5. Public vocational-technical schools are administered by the Department of Education in each state. Individuals who wish to train for a specific trade while still in high school will find these schools best for them. Some technical preparation programs are designed to begin during the last two years of high school and continue for two years following high school graduation. The training is completed in community colleges.

There are many private schools that provide occupational training to high school graduates. When choosing a school, make sure it has up-to-date equipment and facilities as well as excellent instructors.

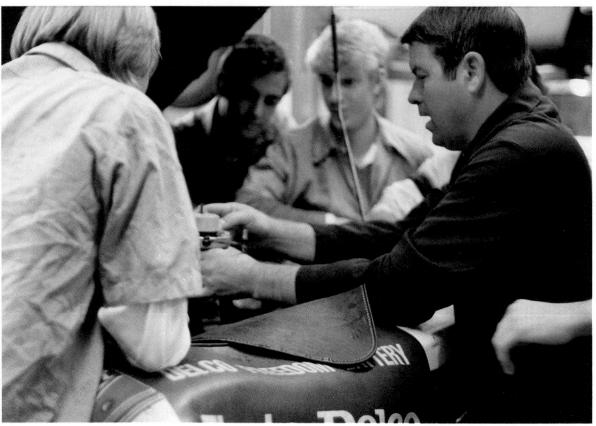

Cholla Runnels

6-5
Vocational-technical schools offer training as part of your coursework.

Community Colleges

Community colleges can provide you with comprehensive training in vocational programs. You may take a combination of liberal arts courses to broaden your background and vocational courses to learn a trade. Many of the classes are scheduled at night or at times convenient for people who are working. Graduates may find employment in companies that are familiar with the program and use it regularly for finding new employees. Some graduates go on to pursue a four-year degree at a college or university.

Apprenticeships

An *apprenticeship* is a formal, registered program for training an individual in a skilled craft or trade. You will have classroom instruction as well as job training under the supervision of a highly skilled tradesperson. You will learn all the skills of a certain craft, and you will have a written agreement with the employer and/or a union. At the end of your training, you will be awarded a certificate as a skilled journeyman. If you are hardworking, are interested in a certain trade, and can handle responsibility, this is a good program for you.

Contemporary Topics *of interest to teens:*
Education Pays Off

Staying in school pays off in dollars and cents throughout life, according to a recent Census Bureau study. On average, a high-school graduate will earn $821,000 over a lifetime. A person with a bachelor's degree can expect lifetime earnings of $1,421,000. Individuals who go on to get a medical or law degree will generate even more earnings over the same time period—an estimated $3,013,000.

However, degrees in themselves are not enough. To survive in today's fast-changing, competitive job market, workers need skills and experience as well. Taking advantage of refresher courses, on-the-job training, and other opportunities to upgrade your skills can prove invaluable in advancing in the workplace.

Formal Employer Training

Training programs set up by companies to teach the skills they need are another possibility. You receive thorough training for the specific skills your employer needs. Company training may be offered through regular class instruction by company instructors. You receive pay while you are learning. If you like the particular job and are willing to learn all you can about it, this is usually an excellent opportunity.

Colleges or Universities

If you desire a college degree, you will want to enroll in a college or university that offers degrees in the field that interests you. Many of your college courses will be designed to give you a well-rounded background. The courses that apply to your major field of study provide you with comprehensive training in that area. Upon graduation, your varied background may enable you to seek a variety of jobs in your field. You may want to continue your education in graduate school. Advanced degrees open even more doors to professional careers. See 6-6.

Combining Work with Education

You may have already faced the decision of whether or not to combine part-time work with your education. The majority of high school students today do work, and still more say they would if they could find a job.

Cholla Runnels

6-6
A college education will require a lot of studying but will give you a well-rounded background as well as specific training.

You may have considered this decision when you planned your four-year high school program. Many students are enrolled in vocational programs that combine their academic school courses with on-the-job training. For many, this is a logical choice. These programs allow students to receive their high school education while gaining work experience in related jobs. See 6-7. Other students carry a full schedule of classes and work in part-time jobs after school or on weekends.

Students who decide to work must judge the relative worth of their jobs in relation to their educations and their long-term goals. Some students' earnings are needed to help meet family expenses. Other students save the money they earn to help pay for further education. However, studies show that most students who work in part-time jobs spend their money to satisfy their personal needs and wants. Many students spend their money for entertainment, gasoline, cars, and trendy clothing.

One crucial factor in determining the effects of part-time jobs is the amount of time spent working. Studies show that teenagers who spend more than 15 to 20 hours a week at work are likely to feel more of the work's negative effects.

Performance in school is a standard that can be used to measure the effects of a part-time job. If you are working so many hours that your schoolwork begins to suffer, you ought to cut back on or eliminate your work hours and find a better balance between work and studying.

Cholla Runnels

6-7
These students are enrolled in a cooperative education program that combines classroom study with on-the-job training.

Some working students find themselves caught in a chain reaction. Long hours of work keep them from taking part in extracurricular activities. As school becomes less enjoyable, they spend less time on their studies.

Activities at home are a second way to measure the effects of a job. Working students may have less time for household chores and family activities.

A third factor to consider is the value of the work experience gained in part-time jobs. Many part-time jobs can be labeled as menial. Students may become cynical about the value of the type of work they do. They may develop poor work habits and negative attitudes as a result.

Working during high school does have benefits, especially for those students who will not go on to college. A job teaches something that academic high school courses cannot teach—survival in today's working world. A part-time job in school provides work experience that usually means better jobs and higher earnings once students are out of school.

Some part-time jobs are challenging. They allow students to learn new skills and practice cognitive skills (like reading, writing, and math) in practical settings. Earning money gives students a chance to learn the basics of money management. Working also offers experiences in interaction with people. This may lead to a greater understanding of the moods, needs, and preferences of others.

If you are considering the possibility of working part-time during high school, apply the decision-making process to help you. See 6-8. If you decide to work, keep a proper balance between school and work. You need to develop both learning skills and job skills to succeed at the next step of your career.

David Hopper

6-8
Workers have to decide whether their work experiences are positive.

Developing Leadership Skills

Choosing a career and making plans to obtain the necessary training for that career are important steps in preparing for your future. In addition, an important skill or trait that employers look for in job applicants is leadership. Those individuals who can show that they have also developed leadership skills as they prepared for their careers will have an edge when they go for important job interviews.

What makes a leader? How can someone develop leadership skills? Will these skills help you reach your goals in your school years and throughout your life?

Leadership is the ability to lead and influence others. Different types of leadership are needed for various roles. A government leader may possess skills that are different from those of a leader of a small social organization. There are, however, some skills that all leaders need.

People exhibit leadership skills when they direct the activities of a group toward a shared goal. Consideration of others' needs is one of the characteristics of good leaders. They recognize the needs of those in their groups. If they are in work-related activities, they also recognize the needs of their employers.

Leaders must also provide structure (clear expectations) for their groups. They must be sure that all group members know what is expected of them and what they can expect of their leaders. In school activities, structure helps groups reach their goals. In the work environment, structure assures efficiency and production control.

Successful leaders speak for members of their groups and defend them when necessary. They also act to advance the groups' interests by being representatives for their groups in various situations, 6-9.

You may recognize other skills of leaders whom you admire. Some of these skills are described in 6-10.

Responsible leadership is always needed. During your school years, you have many opportunities to develop your leadership skills. Class activities, sports teams, school clubs, and community organizations need students to fill leadership roles. In the working world, persons who can exert leadership are needed in every occupation and at every level.

The world needs good leaders and good followers. The secret of success lies in the

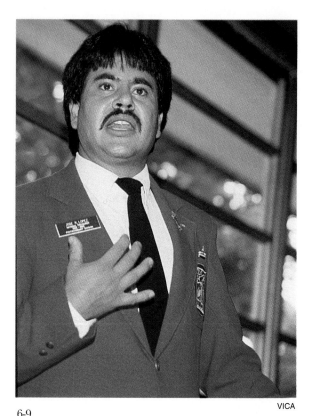

6-9

VICA

This young man is speaking up for the members of his organization.

ability of the leader to balance the needs of individuals, the group, and the community. Good leaders achieve goals and understand that the work is done by people with needs, skills, and feelings.

Developing leadership skills allows you to take charge of your own life. It also allows you to give something back to the group, community, or work place. Many of you have these skills, and you are needed to lead others and achieve goals.

Getting a Job ■ ■ ■ ■ ■

One of life's challenges is that of looking for and finding a job. As in other types of projects, you can enhance your chances of success by engaging in certain behaviors and developing certain skills. You can also polish your skills through rehearsal and practice.

Very few people are handed a job "on a silver platter." Those who do may seem lucky at first. However, they may be missing out on the opportunity to learn skills that they will need to find subsequent jobs. These skills include doing job research, learning about job vacancies, developing contacts, and writing a resume and cover letter. Additional skills include presenting oneself effectively in a job interview and following up on the interview.

Doing Job Research

The first step in researching job possibilities is to develop a list of potential employers. These should be organizations that have entry-level positions in the field in which you have an interest. You probably know of at least a few such organizations. By asking teachers, counselors, and people already working in the field, you can expand your list. If you ask these people for the names of other individuals to contact, you will expand your file of potentially helpful contacts even further.

Your entry for each employing organization should include the organization's name, address, and phone number. Also include the names of personal contacts or other data that you believe may be helpful.

After compiling the basic facts, you are ready to call the companies to request any further information you might like. It is often helpful to start by calling the organization's personnel office. Staff members of this office can provide general information on the company, such as the organization's purpose. They can also provide guidance on company hiring procedures. This might include where and how often job vacancies are advertised and any tests, such as a typing test, that may be required.

When speaking to company representatives, try to be businesslike, courteous, and brief. Keep your voice low, and try to speak clearly. The people with whom you speak may exhibit a range of characteristics, from warm and friendly to distant and cool. Beyond a certain point, you cannot influence how others behave, so do not worry about it. Just try to concentrate on making the best impression you can. After you end the call, make notes on what you have learned and put them in your job research file. Create a system to stay aware of new job vacancies as the company announces them.

Developing Job Contacts

Job contacts are people who can help you find a job. An organization's personnel office may be a good place to start. However,

Leadership Skills

- Having a positive self concept. Leaders believe in themselves.
- Putting the success of the group ahead of personal success.
- Having the empathy to listen to others and recognize their needs and rights.
- Taking a stand and being able to resist unreasonable demands.
- Helping groups.
- Weighing alternatives before making decisions and setting goals.
- Providing the stimulation to move groups toward their goals.
- Having convictions and the courage to follow through on decisions that have been made.
- Delegating responsibility and giving credit to others for their work and efforts.

6-10
People need to develop certain skills to assume roles of leadership.

Tracy Rodriguez
582 Elm St.
White Plains, IL 20201

Objective	Employment in the food service industry.
Education	White Plains High School, White Plains, IL (expected graduation: June 1996). Grade point average: 3.0
Work Experience	
1994-1995	Mercy Hospital, White Plains, IL. Employed part-time as a food service worker. Prepared produce and assisted with cleanup.
Summer 1994	Home Cafeteria, White Plains, IL. Served hot entrees in cafeteria line. Responded to customer requests and replenished supplies as needed.
Summer 1993	Dew Drop Inn. Waited tables and acted as substitute hostess. Described daily specials, responded to customer requests for recommendations, took orders, served food, and totaled checks.
Activities and Honors	Active in high school chorus, 1992-1994. Played on soccer team, 1992. Was voted "Miss Manners" at 4-H Tri-County Summer Camp, 1992.
Other Skills	Am proficient in word processing and am knowledgeable in the QuickAccess word processing software.
References	Available upon request.

6-11
Potential employers will judge you in part by the appearance and content of your resume.

you may increase your chances of being hired if you make a contact with the person who is in a direct position to hire you. A brief letter with a resume followed by a phone call can help this person become acquainted with your qualifications.

It is important that this person not feel that you are pressuring him or her to find you a job immediately. Therefore, when you call, keep the conversation pleasant, brief, and courteous. Tell the person that you would be very interested in any upcoming openings. Also mention that you would equally appreciate any career advice this person may have. If the person seems friendly and helpful, you might ask him or her to evaluate your resume and make suggestions as to how it can be improved. If you listen politely and ask one or two related follow-up questions, the potential employer will be more likely to remember you favorably when a job vacancy occurs.

Again, be sure to record detailed notes on any conversations in your job research file, along with the date the conversation occurred. Few mistakes are more embarrassing than contacting someone you just spoke to a week ago and asking them the same questions!

Writing a Resume and Cover Letter

A *resume* is an information sheet about a person's educational and job background. Your resume (also called a *curriculum vitae* or *c.v.*) is the primary instrument by which potential employers evaluate your suitability for any vacancies, 6-11. At minimum, it should contain your name, address, and telephone number; your educational background; your work experience; and any memberships in work-related associations or organizations. Some job seekers like to include additional information, such as a one-sentence statement of your career objective and a list of areas of expertise (specific skills), with an explanatory paragraph on each.

As you progress in your career, you will find that you gain experience in many different areas. In updating or rewriting your resume, you can select the areas of experience that are most appropriate for the job you are seeking. By customizing your resume to the requirements of individual jobs, you can increase your chances of consideration.

It is important, however, to be very honest about the information you put on your resume. Although there is nothing wrong with "putting your best foot forward," dishonesty is never advisable. At best, you will live with the guilt of knowing you have been dishonest and the fear that your dishonesty will be discovered. At worst, your misstatements will be discovered and your reputation will be damaged. Either way, you will have gained nothing. Honesty is always the best policy.

The file of job contacts yielded by your job research will provide you with a list of persons to whom to send your resume. Some job seekers write only in response to the posting of specific vacancies. Others, especially those seeking entry-level positions, tend to write potential employers regardless of whether a specific vacancy exists.

A *cover letter*, addressed to the appropriate person, is sent with your resume, 6-12. The cover letter is meant to "cover" or introduce the accompanying material. Like the resume, the letter should be neatly typed on a good grade of plain white or ivory stationery. It should be free of erasures, misspellings, grammatical errors, or other mistakes for a positive first impression.

The Job Interview

Even experienced professionals can feel apprehensive about job interviews, 6-13. The feeling that you are being appraised and judged is rarely a comfortable one. However, you can use several strategies to increase the likelihood of a favorable outcome.

First, be sure that you correctly note the time and place of the interview. Estimate the time you think you need to get ready for and travel to the interview. Then build in some "buffer" time in case you get lost, make a wrong turn, have a flat tire, or are otherwise delayed. Unless you are quite sure about how to reach the interview location, it is a good idea to find a map and rehearse your route ahead of time.

If you are delayed and know you will be late, find a phone booth and call the interviewer immediately to reschedule your appointment. The interviewer will appreciate

582 Elm St.
White Plains, IL 20201
May 19, 1994

Ms. Elizabeth Yu
Office of Personnel
Beth Israel Hospital
White Plains, IL 20205

Dear Ms. Yu:

I would like to express my interest in the position of food service worker, as advertised recently in the *White Plains Post-Gazette*.

As the enclosed resume states, my work experience includes responsibilities in several areas of food service, including food preparation, waiting tables, and on-line cafeteria duties. My high school classes in food and nutrition also have been useful in preparing me for food service work.

I expect to graduate from White Plains High School on June 12 of this year and will be available for full-time employment after that date. I would welcome the opportunity to discuss my qualifications with you at your convenience.

Thank you.

Sincerely,

Tracy Rodriguez
Tracy Rodriguez

6-12
A cover letter introduces the material on your resume.

your courtesy. Calling ahead of time is much better than keeping the interviewer waiting and then showing up late with an excuse.

Wear your most businesslike attire and pay attention to your grooming. Because this will probably be your first meeting, the interviewer will have to depend to some extent on external cues in evaluating your employability. You may have a superb array of personal qualities, but most people find it difficult to overcome a poor initial impression based on careless grooming.

It is a good idea to bring a copy of your resume to the interview, as well as any samples of your work that might be appropriate. You should also have a list of people who have agreed to serve as references, along with their addresses and phone numbers. Bring a pen and note pad with which to jot down notes. Also bring a brief list of questions to ask the interviewer.

As your experience with interviews increases, you will find a wide range of interviewer characteristics. Expert interviewers will strike a balance between sharing information about the position and asking questions that give you a chance to express yourself. Other interviewers may become so caught up in telling you about the kind of person they are seeking that the interview becomes a sort of monologue. The allotted time may expire without your having had a sufficient chance to express yourself and to share your ideas and questions about the position.

In cases such as this, your list of questions about the company and the position can come in handy. When you see conversational openings, use them to ask your questions and to briefly provide information about why you think the questions are important.

Be prepared to answer standard interview questions, 6-14. Examples of such ques-

Common Interview Questions

Please tell me about yourself.

What type of work are you seeking?

Why are you interested in this type of work?

What are your long-term career goals?

Why do you think you are qualified for this job?

What are your strengths? Your weaknesses?

Why did you leave your last position?

What salary are you looking for?

When could you start work?

6-14
Be ready to answer your interviewer's questions about your qualifications and vocational goals.

David Hopper

6-13
Even experienced workers can feel nervous at a job interview.

tions include, "Why are you interested in this position?" "Why do you think you are qualified for it?" "What do you envision yourself doing five and ten years from now?" "What do you see as your strengths relative to this position?" "What are your weaknesses?"

As a rule, it is never a good idea to admit true weaknesses in a job interview. If you are hired, your employer will become familiar with your weaknesses soon enough. Successful answers to this type of question tend to center on "weaknesses" that the company probably views as strengths, such as "I tend to get so caught up in my work that I work long hours and cut back on other areas of my life, such as leisure-time activities."

If the interviewer asks what hourly wage or salary you are seeking, it is usually best not to name a figure. If you do name a figure and the interviewer thinks it is too high, it may put you out of the running. If you name a figure that is too low, you may be limiting your earnings. One good response is to ask the interviewer, "What wage (or salary) is usual for this type of position?"

Sometimes the interviewer will ask you why you are interested in leaving your present position. Be careful of how you respond to this question. Discussion of dissatisfaction with your current job almost always works against you. Regardless of the validity of the employee's complaints, the management of one company usually tends to sympathize with the management of other companies. Rather than discussing past job difficulties, try to cast your answer in positive terms. You might say, "I am seeking to grow as a person by taking on additional responsibilities" or "I am interested in contributing to this area of my chosen field."

Usually, near the close of the interview, the interviewer will ask you if you have any additional questions. This is the time to clarify any uncertainties you may have or to request any additional information you need. Job-seekers may ask questions such as, "How soon do you expect to fill this vacancy?" "What is the salary range for this position?" or "What fringe benefits are offered with this position?" It is important, however, to emphasize what you can do for the company rather than what you expect the company to do for you. When the interview is over, thank the interviewer for taking the time to see you and leave promptly.

Following Up

Once the interview is over, it makes a good impression to send the interviewer a brief letter. It should thank him or her for the opportunity to learn more about the company and express your continued interest in the position. Even if the interviewer has concluded that your qualifications are not right for the current position, a letter such as this may position you for consideration for future vacancies.

Keeping a Job

Keeping a job and qualifying for raises and promotions calls forth the best that most people can give. In good employment situations, this means

- doing the work to the best of your ability.

- being punctual, well-groomed, appropriately dressed, and considerate of others.

- treating others in the respectful, courteous manner that you yourself would like to be treated.

In difficult job situations, people are challenged in additional ways. Getting along with others whose values may differ from yours can be harder work than you may think. Learning to relate constructively to a difficult supervisor can call forth all the ingenuity and patience you can muster. The important thing to remember is that you can learn as much from difficult situations as from good ones. By observing the ways in which supervisors and other authority figures operate, you can learn valuable lessons about what tactics are most effective, 6-15. This will be of use to you if you become a supervisor yourself someday. You can also learn a great deal about doing a job well from someone even though you may not care for all of his or her personality traits.

It is also important to learn to appreciate your own shortcomings and to try to remedy them. For many young people, the transition from the classroom to the office is not an easy one. New employees are often better off keeping a low profile until they learn the customs of their new work situation. Each company tends to have its own individual set of expectations and ways of doing things. You can increase the likelihood of job success if you work to adjust to your supervi-

Cholla Runnels

6-15
By observing your supervisor you may learn skills that you can use someday if you become a supervisor yourself.

sor and to the company rather than expecting them to adjust to you.

You can get along best with most supervisors if you exhibit a positive attitude and try hard to do the best job you possibly can. This will mean that you arrive on time; limit personal phone calls (preferably calling during breaks and lunches); limit personal conversations with co-workers; maintain a businesslike, task-oriented attitude; and maintain a respectful, cooperative, helpful demeanor.

Many successful employees believe that it is very important to avoid causing your supervisor inconvenience, especially on short notice. This means requesting personal or medical leave well in advance so that he or she can adjust work schedules accordingly. If you wake up feeling sick, it is important to inform your supervisor as early as possible. This is better than letting your supervisor wonder where you are until you get around to calling. Be sure to call in sick only when you really are ill. It does not take the average supervisor long to figure out which employees are taking advantage of the company's provisions for medical leave.

Sooner or later, everyone makes a work-related mistake and must decide whether and when the supervisor should be informed. Here again, honesty is the best policy. It is far better to give your supervisor advance notice of a potential problem, so he or she can plan for "damage control," rather than waiting until your mistake is discovered.

Strategies for Job Success

It is a basic rule of work life that promotions are earned, not demanded. You will be given additional responsibility (and higher pay) only if the quality of your work warrants it. If you lack *interpersonal skills* (skills in getting along with others), you can be passed over for a promotion even if your work is excellent.

Assuming your work is good and you are getting along well with others, what else can you do to increase the likelihood of advancement? First, you can look the part. Image consultants advise aspiring workers to dress for the job that they would like to have rather than the one they have. Pay close attention to what your supervisor and his or her colleagues are wearing. Follow their example, 6-16.

If you are female, remember that an office is not an appropriate place for heavy makeup; extreme hair styles; gaudy, jangling jewelry; or low-necked, short, tight clothing. Even if your office has no dress code, the way you dress will send a message to your supervisors about your personal standards and your dedication to the job. Be sure that you are a worker who raises—not detracts from—the overall tone of the work place.

A second way to advance on the job is to offer to take on additional responsibility—even if it means putting in extra hours. Your supervisor may then begin to view you as an assistant rather than just another worker. Whether or not you receive an early promotion as a result, you will gain the satisfaction of contributing to your company. You are also likely to gain valuable experience. This experience can be outlined on your resume and will enhance your overall employability.

Third, pursue opportunities for additional education and training related to your

David Hopper

6-16

If you want to be considered for a promotion, observe what supervisors wear at your place of work and dress accordingly.

chosen career. In a competitive job market, the person with the greater preparation usually gets the job.

Fourth, join work-related organizations and associations. These offer job-related educational activities as well as opportunities for *networking* (making professional contacts). Participation in educational activities will help you increase your expertise while learning about job opportunities with other companies. These activities allow you to get to know prospective new employers. Most employers prefer to hire people they know or people who have worked for someone they know rather than strangers.

Finally, always keep your desired next job in the back of your mind. Update your resume and keep your file of job contacts current. Although you do not want your resume to reflect a history of "job hopping," it is a good idea to stay alert to new opportunities. These may be both within and outside of your present situation.

Summary ■ ■ ■ ■ ■ ■ ■ ■ ■ ■ ■ ■ ■ ■ ■

- Sources of career information include your school guidance office, employees already working in your field of interest, representatives of educational institutions, and your parents, relatives, and family friends.

- Factors affecting career choice include personal preferences, aptitudes, and knowledge of career alternatives and career-preparation requirements.

- Finding a fulfilling job situation or career path often involves years of patient inquiry, discussion, reflection, and re-evaluation of prospective career directions.

- Successful workers in personal and family relations careers tend to be flexible, open to others, and comfortable discussing thoughts and feelings.

- Several types of training and education are available beyond high school. The type you choose will depend on your career goals.

- Combining work with education has pros and cons. Students who decide to work must judge the relative worth of their jobs in relation to their education and their long-term goals.

- Leadership is the ability to lead and influence others. Responsible leadership is always needed—in school, in the community, and in the working world.

- A successful job search often includes doing research on prospective employers, making contacts, writing effective resumes and cover letters, and performing effectively in job interviews.

- A variety of characteristics and behaviors increase the chances of job success, including hard work, consideration for one's supervisors, punctuality, good grooming, effective interpersonal skills, appropriate dress, willingness to assume additional responsibility, pursuit of additional educational qualifications, and networking.

To Review ■ ■ ■ ■ ■ ■ ■ ■ ■ ■ ■ ■ ■ ■ ■

1. What two sets of needs are met by the "right" job?

2. Name three careers that people who like to work with others might enjoy. Name three careers people who like to work primarily with objects or information might enjoy.

3. Give an example of an aptitude. Then give an example of a career that might be appropriate for someone with that aptitude.

4. What is the "added benefit" of a career in personal and family relations?

5. Briefly describe an apprenticeship.

6. Name three advantages and three disadvantages of combining work with education.

7. Describe three leadership skills.

8. What is the first step in researching jobs?

9. What items should be included in a resume?

10. List three suggestions for a successful job interview.

11. True or False. If a prospective employer asks you why you wish to leave your present job, it is helpful to express any negative feelings you may have about your current employer.

12. Name three personal characteristics necessary for keeping a job.

To Do ■ ■ ■ ■ ■ ■ ■ ■ ■ ■ ■ ■ ■ ■ ■ ■ ■ ■ ■

1. Study career information resources that are available to you. Choose a career that you think you would enjoy. In a written report, describe the education or training you would need.

2. Hold a class debate about the pros and cons of combining work with education.

3. Make an appointment with your high school counselor to find out what information he or she has about opportunities for further education or training beyond high school.

4. Ask your school guidance counselor to visit the class to discuss various types of tests, such as tests of aptitude and vocational interest or preference, available through the guidance office.

5. Choose a leader with national prominence. (The person can be a leader in any field, not necessarily politics.) Research the person's background and his or her climb to prominence. Prepare a report on this person, focusing on his or her leadership skills. Present the report to the class.

6. Interview adults about work decisions they have made. Ask questions about how they have prepared for and found jobs. Find out whether and why they have changed jobs. Be prepared to share their responses (anonymously) with the class in a discussion.

7. In small groups, observe and interview several adults engaged in various occupations in their respective work places. Share what you have learned with the class.

Decisions Affecting Your Health

After studying this chapter, you will be able to

- choose nutritious foods that promote good health.

- describe the benefits of regular exercise.

- adopt an appropriate exercise program.

- describe causes of stress and ways to deal effectively with stress.

- identify community resources that promote health.

- make informed consumer choices related to health.

Terms to Know

Food Guide Pyramid	unsaturated fat
hemoglobin	anorexia nervosa
osteoporosis	bulimia
Dietary Guidelines for Americans	blood pooling
	stress
cholesterol	biofeedback
saturated fat	support groups

Most people have the good fortune to be born healthy. Heredity causes some limitations, of course. Environmental factors, such as accidents, may also affect one's health, but most people begin life with a healthy body.

Through the years, though, people often become careless with their health.

They think that advanced technology and new cure-alls can save them from their own disregard of basic health rules.

Slowly, however, we are waking up. We are realizing that the key to good health is prevention. Good health is not just a matter of chance. It is making smart decisions. It is taking responsibility for your own well-being. It means modifying your lifestyle—what you eat and how you exercise. It means making wise decisions concerning tobacco and drugs.

Preventive Health Practices

As a teenager, you have several factors working for you. First and most obvious is the fact that your body is young. Second, a wealth of research-based knowledge concerning good health is available to you. Finally, good health is "in style." It is discussed in newspapers, in magazines, and on TV. The nation's attention is focused on ways to promote good health and prevent disease.

Your challenge is to use your teenage years as a springboard for developing a healthy life pattern. It may be hard for you to imagine that your life may someday slow down because of health problems. Your current levels of energy and endurance may seem endless. However, statistics show that many adults who seem healthy suddenly face major health problems. They often find that their health problems can be traced to poor health habits formed during their teenage years.

You cannot know what your future holds. Your smartest move is to do all you can to achieve good health now. At the same time, you need to establish a pattern of living that will help you prevent ill health in the future. Your health is one of the most important resources you have. See 7-1.

To maintain that resource, your pattern of living should include certain health practices. These include

- eating the foods that will meet your nutritional needs and maintain your ideal body weight.

- adopting an appropriate exercise program and getting sufficient sleep.

- managing stress effectively.

Nutrition and Your Health

The way you look and the way you feel has a lot to do with what you eat. Good nutrition means eating a variety of foods that will supply your body with the nutrients needed to keep you healthy. Teens need more nutrients than adults. All teens experience a period of rapid growth during which their energy needs increase. They also need to see that vitamin and mineral requirements are met during this growth spurt.

This is also a time of busy schedules, skipped meals, fast-food stops, and junk-food binges. The pace of some families is so hectic

David Hopper

7-1
The challenge for teens is to use their high levels of energy to achieve good health and to establish a healthy pattern of living.

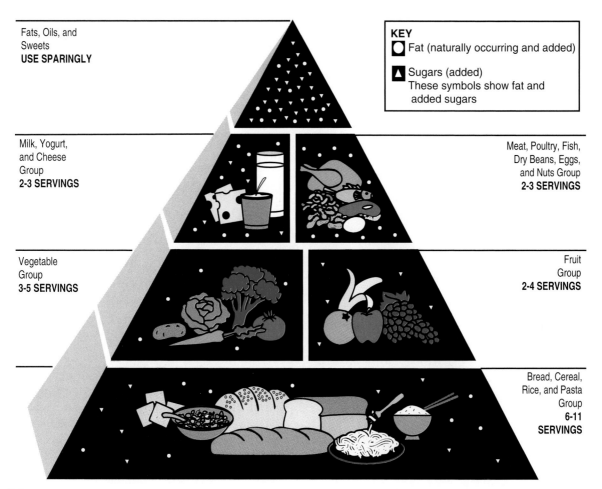

KEY
◯ Fat (naturally occurring and added)
▲ Sugars (added)
These symbols show fat and added sugars

Fats, Oils, and Sweets
USE SPARINGLY

Milk, Yogurt, and Cheese Group
2-3 SERVINGS

Meat, Poultry, Fish, Dry Beans, Eggs, and Nuts Group
2-3 SERVINGS

Vegetable Group
3-5 SERVINGS

Fruit Group
2-4 SERVINGS

Bread, Cereal, Rice, and Pasta Group
6-11 SERVINGS

7-2
The Food Guide Pyramid is a simple guide to good nutrition.

that well-planned family meals are a rarity. There are many dual-career families today in which teen members of the family may work as well. It often becomes the responsibility of each adult and teen family member to attend to his or her own nutritional needs. Teens must be aware of the foods needed in a balanced diet as they make their daily food selections. To simplify the process of choosing foods to fulfill daily nutritional needs, a basic food guide has been designed.

The Food Guide Pyramid

The *Food Guide Pyramid* is a simple guide to good nutrition. This guide works for just about anybody who is not on a special medical diet. Eating the recommended number of servings from each group in the Food Guide Pyramid provides all the nutrients you need each day. See 7-2.

Foods of similar nutritive value are grouped together to form the following groups in the Pyramid:

■ Bread, cereal, rice, and pasta group.

- Fruit group.

- Vegetable group.

- Meat, poultry, fish, dry beans, eggs, and nuts group.

- Milk, yogurt, and cheese group.

- Fats, oils, and sweets group.

The Bread, Cereal, Rice, and Pasta Group

Carbohydrates, B-vitamins, iron, some incomplete protein, and fiber are provided by foods in this group. Carbohydrates are the body's chief source of energy. B-vitamins help the body digest foods efficiently. They also help keep the skin and the nervous system healthy. Iron is needed to make hemoglobin in blood. (**Hemoglobin** is a component of blood that carries oxygen to all the cells of the body.) Six to eleven servings from the breads, cereal, rice, and pasta group are needed daily.

The Fruit Group

Fruits provide vitamins and minerals. They are needed for normal bodily growth and maintenance and for the regulation of body processes. A good source of vitamin C should be included in the diet every day. Examples of good sources include citrus fruits, such as oranges and grapefruit, as well as strawberries and cantaloupe. Two to four servings are recommended each day.

The Vegetable Group

Like fruits, vegetables promote normal bodily growth and maintenance. A good source of vitamin A should be included in the diet several times a week. Examples of good sources include dark green and dark yellow vegetables, such as spinach, green leafy vegetables, carrots, sweet potatoes, and pumpkin. Three to five servings are needed daily.

The Meat, Poultry, Fish, Dry Beans, Eggs, and Nuts Group

Protein is the most important nutrient in this group. It is needed for the growth and repair of body tissues. B-vitamins and iron are also provided by these foods. Two to three servings from this group each day are recommended.

The Milk, Yogurt, and Cheese Group

Calcium is the most important nutrient in milk and milk products. It is needed for healthy bones and teeth. Phosphorus, riboflavin, protein, and vitamins A and D (in whole and fortified milk) are also found in milk and milk products.

Some people think that milk is important just for children. Calcium, however, is needed daily by people of all ages. Years of calcium deficiency may cause a condition called *osteoporosis* later in life. Bone mass is lost, causing bones to weaken. Vertebrae may collapse, causing stooped posture, and bones may break easily. This condition affects more women than men.

The recommended number of daily servings from the milk and milk products group varies.

Children...........................2 or more servings.
Teenagers........................3 or more servings.
Adults..............................2 or more servings.
Pregnant
    and nursing women ....3 or more servings.

The Fats, Oils, and Sweets Group

There is an additional group of foods that are made from fats, oils, sugars, and other food substances. These foods provide energy but little nutritional value. Some of the foods in this group are candy, salad dressings, butter, margarine, jellies, syrups, and soft drinks. These foods are not needed for good health, but add flavor and variety to meals. Because they supply calories but few nutrients, foods from this group should be eaten sparingly.

Dietary Guidelines for Americans

In addition to following the Food Guide Pyramid, there are other eating practices teens need to follow. The federal government has published the following recommendations concerning the foods we eat. These *Dietary Guidelines for Americans* can help you make healthful food choices, 7-3.

1. **Eat a variety of foods.** Selecting foods from a wide array of healthful choices helps ensure that you will get the nutrients you need.

2. **Maintain healthy weight.** People should eat the right amounts of foods to meet their energy needs. Eating more than the body needs for energy can cause weight gain. Eating less can cause a per-

son to be underweight. Being overweight or underweight can lead to health problems.

3. **Choose a diet low in fat, saturated fat, and cholesterol.** In general, high-fat diets are associated with a number of health conditions, including obesity and high blood cholesterol. (*Cholesterol* is a fat-like substance in your blood.) High blood-cholesterol levels are strongly associated with heart disease.

One type of fat, called saturated fat, is a factor in high blood-cholesterol levels. *Saturated fats* (so called because of their chemical structure) tend to be solid at room temperature and to come from animal sources. *Unsaturated fats,* in contrast, tend to be liquid at room temperature and to come from plant sources.

To eat for health, use fats and oils sparingly, and try to choose unsaturated fats from plant sources rather than saturated fats from animal sources. For example, use liquid vegetable oils rather than butter and cream. Select lean meats and eat more fish and poultry. Choose foods that have been steamed, poached, baked, or broiled rather than fried or sautéed.

4. **Choose a diet with plenty of vegetables, fruits, and grain products.** A high-fiber diet is believed to be a significant factor in avoiding obesity, heart disease, and some types of cancer. Good sources of fiber include fruits and vegetables as well as whole-grain breads and cereals.

5. **Use sugars only in moderation.** Watch the amount of sweets in your diet. Eating too much sugar can lead to weight gain, and eating sugar too frequently can cause tooth decay.

6. **Use salt and sodium only in moderation.** Salt (a high-sodium food) is present in

---

Dietary Guidelines for Americans

Eat a variety of foods.

Maintain healthy weight.

Choose a diet low in fat, saturated fat, and cholesterol.

Choose a diet with plenty of vegetables, fruits, and grain products.

Use sugars only in moderation.

Use salt and sodium only in moderation.

Avoid alcoholic beverages (adapted for teenagers).

7-3
The Dietary Guidelines for Americans can help you make healthful food choices.

many beverages and foods that we eat. Processed foods, condiments, sauces, pickled foods, and salty snacks contain high levels of sodium, 7-4. Though sodium is necessary in your diet, high sodium intake can lead to high blood pressure. Most Americans take in much more sodium than they need.

7.　**Avoid alcoholic beverages.** (Adapted for teenagers.) The many serious risks that alcohol use poses for teens are discussed in Chapter 8. Alcohol use contributes calories—but little nutrition—to the diet. Alcoholics whose diet consists mainly of alcohol tend to be malnourished.

Other Tips for Healthy Eating

Teens today eat many of their meals at fast-food restaurants. These meals are quick, convenient, and inexpensive. Most fast-food items provide nutrients, but many are high in fat, sodium, and sugar, and low in vitamins A and C. If low-fat foods are selected following the Food Guide Pyramid, however, your nutritional needs can be met. Watch the "extras" if you're counting calories. Calories in cheese, bacon, and sauces can add up quickly. Shakes and soft drinks also add extra calories. When these foods are eaten, more nutritious foods tend to be ignored.

Snacks can be nutritious and can supply many of the nutrients the body needs daily. If you find you haven't enough time for regular meals, try to substitute low-fat, nutritious snacks for high-fat foods. Select fresh fruits and vegetables, low-fat yogurt, low-fat whole-wheat crackers, and cereal with skim milk, 7-5. Substitute water or naturally sweetened fruit juice for carbonated beverages.

If you are an athlete in training, it is especially important to follow the Food Guide Pyramid. Select foods from each of the food

Cholla Runnels

7-4
Many processed foods, such as those available in vending machines, are high in salt.

groups, but also add more calories for increased energy. Choose carbohydrates, such as breads, cereals, and pastas, that provide the best fuel for muscles. Eat three to four hours before participating in strenuous athletics. Also drink plenty of water or juices to maintain energy production and control body temperature. Avoid beverages containing caffeine, which increase urine production and deplete body fluids.

Weight Control

Many teens want to lose weight. There are others who may wish to gain weight. If teens are seriously underweight or overweight, or if they have health problems, they should see a doctor.

For average, healthy teens who want to shed a few pounds, patience and moderation are the keys. Drastic fad diets seldom work, and they may pose health risks. Many fad

7-5
Fresh fruits and vegetables make nutritious snacks.

diets emphasize one food or food group and eliminate the others. These diets can be extremely dangerous to growing teens. Other diets result in weight loss due to the loss of body fluids. When you go off the diet, you gain back the fluid lost as well as the pounds. Popular fad diets usually aren't designed for teens. No diet of less than 1,800 calories is meant for a growing body.

The principle for weight loss is simple. Your body needs a certain amount of energy (calories) to maintain its weight. To lose weight, you have to use up more energy than you take in through food. This means eating less or exercising more, or some combination of the two. This sounds simple, and it can be. The best weight-loss plan is to use the Food Guide Pyramid and exercise regularly.

People can eat the recommended number of servings from all five groups and still lose weight. They just have to make smart food choices. They can choose skim milk and low-fat yogurt instead of whole milk and ice cream. They can have a bowl of whole-wheat cereal at breakfast instead of fried eggs, sausage, and a buttered biscuit, danish, or croissant. They can save calories by eating steamed broccoli or carrots instead of creamed corn. They can save more calories by eating a grilled, baked, or broiled chicken breast instead of a greasy hamburger. Good nutrition does not have to be high in calories.

Weight that is lost slowly and steadily is more likely to stay off. One pound of body weight is equal to 3,500 calories. Thus, a pound can be lost in seven days by cutting back by 500 calories a day. A pound can also be lost by increasing activity to burn up an extra 500 calories a day. For most people, a combination of decreased calorie intake and increased physical activity works best.

Eating Disorders

Some teens and adults, especially women, suffer from eating disorders. They are obsessed with being slim. Their obsessions may result in malnutrition, serious illness, or even death. Anorexia nervosa and bulimia are the two most common eating disorders.

People who suffer from *anorexia nervosa* have an intense fear of being obese, sometimes described as a "fat phobia." They have distorted images of their bodies. Even when they are sickly thin, they may pinch some skin and complain about how fat they are. As a result, they starve themselves. They refuse to eat, and they may exercise to excess to become even thinner.

People with anorexia nervosa are usually under some kind of emotional stress. Many are perfectionists or overachievers who have feelings of inadequacy and self-doubt. Food becomes one area in which they can assert themselves. They prove their self-control to themselves by refusing to eat even when they are starving.

Bulimia is often associated with anorexia nervosa. *Bulimia* is sometimes described as "desperate overeating" or the "binge-purge syndrome." People with bulimia go on food binges, eating large amounts of high-calorie foods in a short time. Then they feel guilty and purge themselves of the food by vomiting or taking laxatives. They may also go on a strict diet, exercise excessively, and abuse diuretics (water-loss pills) in an effort to lose weight. Then when they go on another food binge (usually in secret), they again react by purging, dieting, and exercising. The cycle may go on and on, causing weight fluctuations of 10 or more pounds.

Like anorexia nervosa, bulimia is often triggered by emotional stress. People with bulimia are often high achievers. They strive for perfection in their appearance and performance. They may have wide mood swings based on their performance. They may feel great when they do well and feel depressed when they fall short of their own expectations.

The sooner eating disorders are treated, the better the chances are of avoiding serious health problems. People with eating disorders may show the following symptoms:

- Refusal to eat or binge eating.

- Excessive exercise.

- Abnormal weight loss or a cycle of weight gains and losses.

- Vomiting with no other signs of illness.

7-6

Cholla Runnels

Many teens are inactive. To reach their full health potential, they need to change their living patterns and exercise regularly.

- Secretive behavior.
- Depression.

Treatment for eating disorders should address both the physical and emotional problems. The first step is usually hospitalization to treat the effects of malnutrition. Once the body is renourished, psychological counseling can help the person understand and cope with his or her problems.

Regular Exercise

Teenagers are often pictured in scenes of constant activity such as dancing, skating, swimming, or jogging. These active scenes accurately portray the lives of many teenagers, yet many other teenagers are inactive. Some spend as much as 50 hours a week sitting in front of the TV screen. See 7-6.

Regular exercise has a big impact on how you look and feel. Vigorous exercise increases muscle strength, stamina, and coordination. Lung capacity is increased and blood circulation improves. Exercise promotes flexibility and improves posture. Weight is more easily managed, and stress, boredom, and depression are less likely to occur.

Even with all of these reasons to exercise, some of you may still find excuses to avoid exercise. You may not like getting hot and sweaty. You may dread the thought of counting push-ups and sit-ups or of running around a track. Perhaps you feel you just don't have the time.

If you don't like feeling sweaty, try to arrange your schedule so you exercise just before your daily bath or shower, or try swimming. If you don't like doing push-ups and sit-ups, try jogging. If you don't like jogging, try bicycling. If you don't like to exercise alone, go to a local YMCA, sign up for an aerobics class, or join a health club. If you decide that good health is one of your goals, you can find a way to exercise.

Adopting an Exercise Program

As high school students, many of you participate in competitive sports programs. You follow carefully designed exercise programs. You use safe equipment and follow proper procedures under the guidance of coaches. You benefit from increased knowledge about sports medicine, 7-7.

However, many of you are unable to participate in school sport programs. Setting up and following an exercise program becomes your own responsibility.

Before you start an exercise program, it is a good idea to have a complete physical examination. Then you need to decide what kinds of exercises you will do and how often.

A good physical fitness program includes two kinds of exercise. It includes exercises that improve respiration and

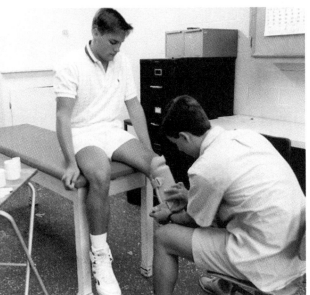

Cholla Runnels

7-7
Students who participate in competitive sports programs have the help of coaches and trainers.

Cholla Runnels

7-8
Several bending and stretching exercises should be included in the warm-up part of
an exercise program.

circulation. (Examples are bicycling, swimming, and running.) It also includes a variety of exercises that develop muscle strength, coordination, and flexibility. (Examples include calisthenics and gymnastics.)

To be most beneficial, exercise should be done regularly. The ideal fitness program includes exercise several times a week. Even a short exercise period has been shown to be beneficial. Most fitness experts suggest 30 minutes of exercise four days a week.

An exercise program should consist of three parts: warm-up exercise, conditioning exercise, and cooldown exercise. Each of these types of exercise serves a special purpose.

Warm-up Exercise

Before conditioning exercises are attempted, the body should be warmed up. The warm-up should begin with a little light exercise to increase respiration, pulse rate, and body temperature. Try walking normally, running in place, or bicycling slowly.

Once you have done the light exercise, your body will be ready for bending and stretching exercises, 7-8. These stretch your muscles and tendons and improve your flexibility. They prepare your body for the more strenuous conditioning exercises you will do later. If done correctly, stretching exercises may help prevent lower back problems. Look through exercise manuals to find a sequence of appropriate warm-up exercises.

Conditioning Exercise

The main part of your exercise program should consist of vigorous activity that you sustain for at least 20 to 30 minutes. The activity should be one that you enjoy and that is convenient for you to do.

Why should conditioning exercise be vigorous, enjoyable, and convenient? It must be vigorous if it is to be of benefit to your health. Only vigorous exercise can help your lungs, heart, circulation, strength, and stamina. An exercise program helps you only as long as you work at it. If you don't enjoy it or if it is inconvenient, you are more likely to quit.

As you exercise, remember that your physical needs are unique. Your friend's endurance level may be different from your own. The guiding rule is that you should feel better, not worse, after exercising. Pain is a warning that the body has been overworked.

Pay close attention to your body for early warning signs of trouble. There are several symptoms that signal the need for prompt medical attention. They include unfamiliar pains in the chest, neck, jaw, arms, shoulders, or upper abdomen that occur during or right after exercise. They also include weakness, shortness of breath, tightness in the chest, or what you might believe to be indigestion.

Cooldown Exercise

As the warm-up is important in preparing the body for vigorous exercise, the cooldown is equally important. It provides a transition to a state of normal activity. Without a gradual decrease in activity, blood pooling can occur. **Blood pooling** is the accumulation of blood in the large muscles of the legs. It causes the heart and brain to be deprived of an adequate blood supply. This, in turn, could result in irregular heartbeat or fainting. To avoid blood pooling, do not stop vigorous exercise abruptly. Instead, slow down gradually. You may even want to repeat some of the light exercises you did in your warm-up.

Rest and Sleep

Along with exercise, the body also needs rest and sleep. Individuals vary in their sleep needs. Some people need ten hours per night; others feel rested after six hours. Overbusy teens who skimp on sleep night after night may build up a "sleep deficit." This can have negative effects on their health, appearance, ability to concentrate on schoolwork, and overall feeling of well-being.

Following a regular program of proper diet, exercise, and rest can help you feel good—physically and mentally. Even more important, it will help you maintain good health throughout your lifetime.

Coping with Stress

Stress is a state of bodily or mental tension resulting from change. Stress is not always bad. In fact, you need some stress in your life. Without it, life would be dull and unexciting. Challenges and changes add spice to your life. Stress can even improve your performance by causing physical changes that lift your body into a higher state of alertness.

On the other hand, too much stress leads to irritability, frustration, and lessened motivation. Unchecked stress can be a major factor in the development of many serious diseases, including heart trouble, high blood pressure, and strokes.

Contemporary Topics *of interest to teens:*
What Happens during Sleep?

The average person spends approximately one-third of his or her life sleeping. However, comparatively little is known about what actually happens during sleep. Some researchers believe that sleep allows the brain cells to restore their chemical balance each night.

A good night's rest involves several sleep stages, including rapid-eye-movement (REM) and non-rapid-eye-movement (NREM) sleep. REM sleep is characterized by rapid eye movement, faster breathing, and a higher heart rate. Most dreaming occurs during REM sleep.

In NREM sleep, an individual's eye movement, blood pressure, and breathing and heart rates decrease. NREM sleep accounts for as much as 80 percent of total sleep time.

People vary widely in their sleep needs. A few feel refreshed after four hours of sleep; others require as much as nine or ten hours. Individuals who regularly get insufficient sleep usually feel drowsy and irritable. Thus, sleep deprivation can have social as well as physical consequences.

Change Causes Stress

Changes such as a death in the family, a serious injury, or being fired from a job are sure to cause stress. However, changes don't have to be that dramatic to be stressful. Moving to a different home, failing an exam, or arguing with a friend can cause stress, 7-9. In fact, even positive changes cause stress. Getting a promotion, starting college, or winning a contest can be stressful events.

Certain changes create more stress than others. Chart 7-10 rates the stress level of various events in life. If several stressful events are occurring in your life, you need to be aware of how they are affecting you. Pay attention to warning signals such as increased fatigue, irritability, or illness.

Learning to Manage Stress

The key to good mental and physical health is learning to manage stress. A healthy lifestyle brings with it a certain amount of

David Hopper

7-9
Stress can occur when you have a disagreement with your boyfriend or girlfriend.

Stress Rating Scale

Note each of the life events listed below that have affected you within the last 24 months. Add up the total points. (Count multiple occurrences of the same life event.)

Life Event	Point Value	Life Event	Point Value
Death of spouse	100	Trouble with in-laws	29
Divorce	73	Outstanding personal achievement	28
Marital separation	65	Begin or end school	26
Jail term	63	Change in living conditions (new house, remodeling, deterioration of home or neighborhood)	25
Death of close family member	63		
Personal injury or illness	53		
Marriage	50	Revision of personal habits (dress, manners, associations)	24
Fired from job	47		
Marital reconciliation	45	Trouble with boss	23
Retirement	45	Change in work hours or conditions	20
Change in health of family member	44	Change in residence	20
Pregnancy	40	Change in schools	20
Gain of new family member (birth, adoption, grandparent moving in, etc.)	39	Change in recreation	19
		Change in church activities	19
Change in financial state (better or worse off than usual)	38	Change in social activities (clubs, dancing, movies)	18
Death of a close friend	37	Change in sleeping habits	16
Change to a different line of work	36	Change in number of family get-togethers	15
Change in number of arguments with spouse	35	Change in eating habits (more or less food, different hours or surroundings)	15
Foreclosure of mortgage or loan	30	Vacation	13
Change in responsibilities at work (promotion or demotion)	29	Christmas	12
Son or daughter leaving home	29	Minor violations of the law (traffic ticket, disturbing the peace)	11

Research has shown that among people with more than 450 stress points within the past two years, about 90 percent will become ill in the near future. With 300 points, the illness rate is 60 percent, and with 150 points, only 33 percent.

Reprinted with permission from Journal of Psychosomatic Research, Vol. II, Holmes, T.H., and Rahe, R.H., The Social Readjustment Rating Scale, Elsevier Science Ltd., Pergamon Imprints, Oxford, England.

7-10
Events in life create varying amounts of stress. Stress can accumulate and set the stage for illness.

stress that adds interest and excitement. However, people must learn to keep negative stress under control. They need to relieve excess stress that could damage their health. Knowing how to manage stress will help you maintain a healthy lifestyle. Guidelines for a low-stress lifestyle are presented in 7-11.

Stress-resilient people are open to change. In other words, when changes occur, they accept them instead of fighting them. They take advantage of whatever opportunities the changes may bring. They feel that they have control of their lives. They say, "I choose to do this," much more often than, "I have to do this." They have the confidence to manage their stress. They don't allow stress to ruin their health and their lives.

To deal effectively with stress, you must become aware of your reactions to stressful events. You must also learn to recognize early

Guidelines for a Low-Stress Lifestyle

1. Develop a positive attitude about life. It is not so much what happens to you, but your perceptions of what happens to you that produce stressful emotions. Thus, a positive attitude helps to prevent stress.
2. Maintain good physical and mental health. Good health protects against the harmful effects of stress.
3. Participate in activities that you enjoy. Concentrate on enjoying the activities themselves rather than on how well you are performing.
4. Turn your attention outward. Care about someone other than yourself. Appreciate the efforts and achievements of others.
5. Learn to recognize your personal limits. Accept your lack of control over some situations, and make the best of the results.
6. Develop a kind, benevolent sense of humor. Most people believe they already possess a good sense of humor. Few really do.
7. Learn to tolerate and forgive both yourself and others. Intolerance of our own frailties leads to stress, tension, and low self-esteem. Intolerance of others leads to blame and anger.
8. Develop friendships. A good talk with a close friend can relieve stress.
9. Strive for a reasonably efficient and well-managed life-style. Laziness, self-indulgence, and sloppiness usually create more stress than they relieve.
10. Stop waiting for the day when "you can relax" or when "your problems will be over." That day will never come. The struggles of life change, but they never end.

7-11
A low-stress lifestyle promotes good mental and physical health.

signs of negative stress. Then you will be able to take positive actions to overcome stress. The following suggestions may help you handle negative stress or stress overload.

- Exercise regularly. Your mind and body work together, so physical exercise can help you to relax and cope with problems.

- Talk to someone. It's important to talk out your problems with a friend, a coworker, or a counselor.

- Know your limits. Set realistic priorities and practical goals for yourself. One thing that contributes to stress is the feeling that you have to do everything perfectly. This may make you nervous and anxious. Learn to recognize your own limitations. Take on only what you know you can accomplish. Also recognize there are some things over which you have no control. Worrying about them will not help. Instead, concentrate on what you can do.

- If you are already under a lot of pressure, try to avoid additional stressful situations. For instance, a time when you are having problems in school might not be a good time to start a new job. You can't avoid stress, but you can learn to manage it.

- Take care of yourself. If you are trying to do too much, slow down. If your stress is the result of boredom, increase your activities. A change of pace can do wonders for your stress level.

- If you feel like crying, go ahead. It's okay to cry. In fact, crying can be a good, healthy way to relieve anxiety or tension.

- Avoid self-medication. Although you may think that alcohol, tobacco, or illegal drugs relieve stress, they do not remove the condition that caused the stress in the first place. In fact, these substances tend to be habit-forming and thus can create far more stress than they take away.

- Learn to relax. Take time out every day for some quiet time for yourself.

Have you ever been told to relax just before an important event? Perhaps you were going to take an exam or try out for the school play. You may have wanted to relax. You may have even told yourself to relax, using the logic that to do your best, you would have to relax. However, relaxation-on-command is easier said than done. See 7-12. Under tension or stress, your body reacts with a "flight or fight" response. Your pulse quickens, your blood pressure rises, and your muscles tense as you prepare to deal with the situation. Even if it's only a test or a tryout, your body reacts to your feelings of apprehension.

Athletes often do their best when they tell themselves, "I'm just going to try my best." Instead, a baseball player might say, "I can't afford to strike out. I've got to get a hit." This causes the player to tense up. He or she is then more likely to strike out. Putting extra pressure on yourself causes tension and undue stress.

Stress Reduction Techniques

Stress is inevitable, so learning stress-reducing techniques makes sense. Authorities who study stress recommend the following techniques to reduce the effects of stress.

David Hopper

7-12
When a person is under stress, relaxing may be difficult.

Try taking some deep breaths. This can interrupt tension and create a relaxing feeling throughout your body. First, make yourself comfortable and close your eyes. Then take a deep, slow breath and inhale all the way, counting "one" to yourself, quietly. Then slowly exhale all the way, counting "two" to yourself. Another inhale is "three," and exhale is "four." Continue to take quiet, slow breaths through the count of 10, and repeat if needed. Taking slow, natural breaths is a simple technique you can do anywhere.

Some people have trouble recognizing what makes them tense and how their bodies react to tension. To locate centers of tension, tense and release muscles in different parts of your body. Begin with your toes and work up to your head. This helps you pinpoint certain areas of the body—neck muscles, for instance—where tension exists.

Biofeedback helps you tell the difference between states of relaxation and tension. It involves "feedback" from "biological" responses. Electronic equipment is used to measure blood pressure, respiration rate, skin temperature, and tension in individual muscles. The equipment does not relax you, but it does provide measurements so that you can monitor stress. After learning to distinguish between feelings of relaxation and tension, you should be able to relax more easily.

Stretching exercises promote relaxation. The focus of attention is on stretching muscles, holding them in a certain position, and then relaxing them. This produces a sense of deep relaxation.

Finally, one of the best ways to reduce stress is to exercise. Doing some kind of physical activity, such as walking, running, playing basketball, or participating in any sport, can help you relax. You'll feel much better, both mentally and physically, when you get up and start moving.

Community Health Resources ▪ ▪ ▪ ▪ ▪

Motivation and self-discipline are very important in forming and practicing good health habits. However, persons striving for optimal health need not go it alone. Support for maintaining health and wellness is often available through a variety of community health organizations. In some cases, such support may be only a phone call away.

Community Facilities

Many communities have parks and recreation centers that offer sports and exercise facilities. Typical facilities include swimming pools, baseball diamonds, and volleyball or tennis courts. These publicly supported resources usually are available free or at low cost. The public library in your area provides sources of information on health and health care topics.

Most communities have hospitals with highly trained doctors, nurses, and other staff who can help you if you have a physical or emotional illness or symptom. Some "storefront" clinics provide services at low or no cost.

Health Education

Many hospitals conduct education programs, not only for patients and their families but for the larger community as well. Examples include seminars to help people quit smoking, deal with an eating disorder, cope with stress, or lower their blood cholesterol levels.

Nutrition programs are also available through several sources. Most county extension offices conduct nutrition education programs. The Women, Infants, and Children

(WIC) program helps low-income mothers learn to plan nutritious meals for their families.

The public health departments of most counties offer a variety of educational programs. Topics may include prenatal care and preventing the spread of sexually transmitted diseases.

Health Screening

Hospitals, public health departments, and other community groups may offer a variety of health screening services. Health screening may be available for such conditions as AIDS/HIV, tuberculosis, glaucoma, high blood cholesterol, high blood pressure, and sickle-cell anemia.

Community health fairs acquaint people with available sources of medical assistance. Some health fairs provide free or low-cost screening services.

Support Groups, Hotlines, and Helplines

Sometimes an illness or other crisis makes special help necessary. *Support groups,* usually made up of people with a common concern, offer emotional help, information, and the benefits of shared experience. Support groups are often sponsored by medical or other community groups and are led by knowledgeable professionals. They are formed to help individuals and their families deal with such conditions as AIDS/HIV, Alzheimer's disease, cancer, and alcoholism. Mental health services are also available to help people cope with emotional and family problems, such as the death of a loved one. See 7-13 for a list of support groups available in most communities.

Phone hotlines and helplines may assist people in getting through a crisis. Examples include an accidental poisoning, snake bite, potential suicide, incidence of child abuse, or rape. Check your telephone directory for the correct telephone number.

Government Programs

Government-supported medical care is available for low-income individuals (through the Medicaid program) and elderly persons (through the Medicare program). Public health departments routinely inspect restaurants and other private establishments to ensure that sanitary procedures (for example, proper food preparation and storage) are being followed.

People with physical or mental disabilities should check with their local government and school system to see what services may be available for them. Some aid may be mandated by law, for example, special school programs for people who are hearing impaired or mentally retarded.

Several sources of help are available to individuals and families who find themselves in trouble. Battered spouses and abused children can often find refuge in community shelters. Persons with very low incomes can apply for welfare benefits and food stamps. Individuals who become homeless may seek lodging in publicly supported shelters for the homeless. Although budgetary constraints and bureaucratic red tape may pose problems, people in serious need of such help should persist in seeking it.

Nonprofit Organizations

Nonprofit organizations, such as the American Cancer Society and the American Heart Association, offer an array of resources to patients and their families. Examples of such resources include informational brochures, support groups, annual meetings

Support Groups for Families

Adult Grief Support Group: for bereaved adults.

AIDS Support Group: for people who have tested positive for HIV.

Al-Anon: for family members and friends of alcoholics.

Alateen: for teens (ages 11-18) affected by another person's alcoholism.

Alcoholics Anonymous: for people who want to stop drinking.

Alliance for the Mentally Ill: for families and friends of persons with severe mental illness.

Alzheimer's Disease Support Group: for family members of people with Alzheimer's disease.

Battered Women's Support Group: for abused women who are victims of domestic violence.

Cancer Support Group: for cancer patients and their families.

Child Find: for parents trying to find missing children and teens.

Cocaine Anonymous: for cocaine addicts who still suffer, but are trying to recover.

Diabetes Support Group: for diabetics and their families.

Down's Syndrome Parent Support Group: for parents of children who have Down's syndrome.

Families Anonymous: for those concerned about drug abuse and behavioral problems of a relative or friend.

Gamblers Anonymous: for people who gamble compulsively.

Make Today Count: for people who face life-threatening illnesses, their families, and friends.

Mended Hearts: for those who have had heart surgery.

Nar-Anon: for family members and friends of drug addicts.

Narcotics Anonymous: for drug addicts who seek to recover from this affliction.

National Center for Missing and Exploited Children: for parents trying to locate missing children or teens.

Parents Anonymous: for the treatment and prevention of child abuse.

Parents Helping Parents: for families who have children with special needs (covers all handicapping conditions).

Parents United: for individuals and families who have experienced child sexual abuse.

Parents Without Partners: for single parents and their children.

Phoenix: for people going through divorce, widowhood, or separation.

Resolve: for infertile couples who are trying to become parents.

Runaway Hotline: for children or teens who have run away.

Share: for parents who have experienced the death of a newborn through miscarriage, stillbirth, or infant death.

Tough Love: for parents whose teenage children are experiencing adjustment/addiction problems.

Visually Impaired Support Group: for the newly blind and those facing blindness.

7-13

Support groups offer help to persons dealing with a serious physical or emotional problem.

7-14
Informed consumer choices can promote health.

with educational sessions, and individual visits by volunteers to patients and their families. Such organizations also may sponsor medical research targeted at specific diseases.

Consumer Choices Related to Health

As discussed in this chapter, your daily choices related to food, exercise, rest, and stress management can have a profound influence on your health. As a health-conscious consumer, you can help shape a society that promotes optimal health for its members.

By demanding and purchasing more healthful foods, consumers have made it cost-effective for the food industry to offer a variety of more healthful items. Examples are seen in the many low-fat, low-sodium, low-cholesterol, reduced-sugar foods now found on grocery shelves. Although these "lite" items are subject to continued government monitoring regarding their health claims, most of them did not even exist 10 years ago. Consumers are making a difference.

Concerned consumers have also made their voices heard in relation to the negative health effects of cigarette smoking. (This subject is discussed in detail in the next chapter.) A few years ago, offices and public spaces that were free of "second-hand" cigarette smoke were rare. Today, however, smoke-free spaces increasingly are becoming the norm. These advances occurred only because consumers asserted their rights to smoke-free space.

An individual's motivation to achieve optimal health is essential to maintaining health and wellness. Healthful foods are available, but you must choose them over less healthful alternatives, 7-14. Exercise opportunities are available to you, but you must take advantage of them in order to gain the health benefits of physical activity. If you believe that your community's exercise facilities should be improved, it is up to you and citizens like you to work to achieve this goal.

Responsibility for maintaining a healthy environment is everyone's business. With enhanced awareness of health and wellness issues, consumers can continue to improve society through the choices they make and the policies they support.

Summary ▪ ▪ ▪ ▪ ▪ ▪ ▪ ▪ ▪ ▪ ▪ ▪ ▪ ▪ ▪

- Many adults' health problems can be traced to poor health habits formed during the teenage years.

- Positive health practices include eating a variety of nutritious foods, exercising regularly, getting sufficient sleep, and managing stress effectively.

- The Food Guide Pyramid and the Dietary Guidelines for Americans provide information on choosing a healthful, nutritious diet.

- By making smart food choices, people can eat the recommended number of servings from the Daily Food Guide and still lose weight. Weight that is lost slowly and steadily is more likely to stay off.

- To lose weight, you have to use up more energy than you take in through food. This means either eating less or exercising more. For most people, a combination of decreased calorie intake and increased physical activity works best.

- Anorexia nervosa and bulimia are eating disorders that may result in malnutrition, serious illness, or even death.

- You must exercise regularly to reach your full health potential. An exercise program should consist of three parts: warm-up, conditioning exercise, and cooldown.

- Stress is a state of bodily or mental tension resulting from change. A healthy lifestyle includes a certain amount of stress to maintain interest and excitement. Yet people must learn to keep negative stress under control.

- Relaxation techniques can help reduce the effects of stress.

- A variety of resources and services are available in your community to help you maintain your health. There are also many services available when health care is needed. Some are free or low cost.

- Consumers can exert an influence in the marketplace by making choices that promote health.

To Review ▪ ▪ ▪ ▪ ▪ ▪ ▪ ▪ ▪ ▪ ▪ ▪ ▪ ▪ ▪

1. Name the six food groups in the Food Guide Pyramid. How many servings should teens have daily from each group?

2. Describe two ways in which saturated and unsaturated fats differ.

3. List the Dietary Guidelines for Americans.

4. True or False. Anorexia nervosa occurs with equal frequency in males and females.

5. List five benefits of regular, vigorous exercise.

6. Which statement is true?
   a. Most fitness experts suggest at least 60 minutes of vigorous exercise six days a week.
   b. A warm-up should begin with aerobic exercises.
   c. The main part of an exercise program should consist of vigorous activity.
   d. Pain, during and after exercise, is a good sign that the exercise is effective.

7. True or False. Healthy people are those who are able to eliminate all sources of stress from their lives.

8. Describe three positive ways to reduce stress.

9. List three examples of community health resources along with an example of a service offered by each.

10. Give two examples of how informed consumer choices can promote health.

To Do ▪ ▪ ▪ ▪ ▪ ▪ ▪ ▪ ▪ ▪ ▪ ▪ ▪ ▪ ▪ ▪

1. Prepare daily eating plans for a teenager for five consecutive days. Be sure to include the recommended number of daily servings from the Food Guide Pyramid.

2. Use a calorie chart to add up the number of calories consumed each day according to the eating plans prepared in Activity 1. Alter the eating plans for someone on a weight-loss diet. Subtract 500 calories a day without sacrificing any of the recommended numbers of servings.

3. In small groups, discuss the symptoms of eating disorders. Discuss what actions you might take if someone you knew had several of the symptoms.

4. Design an exercise program that would work for you.

5. As a class, make a list of sources of stress for students in your school. Make another list of ways to cope with stress. Then design posters about coping with stress and display them in the hallways of your school.

6. When you feel tense and under stress, try various techniques described in this chapter for reducing stress.

7. Keep a record of your sleep over a week's time. How many hours did you get each night of the week? How many hours did you need in order to feel rested and refreshed the next morning?

8. As a class project, put together a file of health resources in your community. Note the type of help, telephone number, and cost of services for each resource.

David Hopper

Exercise contributes to a healthy lifestyle.

Avoiding Harmful Substances

David Hopper

Terms to Know

nicotine

passive smoking

smokeless tobacco

alcoholic

drug

drug use

drug misuse

drug abuse

physical dependence

addiction

psychological
dependence

habituation

designer drugs

narcotics

depressants

stimulants

hallucinogens

marijuana

amotivational
syndrome

inhalants

anabolic steroids

over-the-counter
drugs

prescription drugs

After studying this chapter, you will be able to

- explain the health hazards of smoking.
- describe the consequences of drinking alcohol.
- define various terms related to drug use and abuse.
- describe various kinds of drugs and how they affect the body.
- explain how peer pressure influences behavior.

The discussions in the previous chapter emphasized positive health habits. You learned how to select the foods that will help keep you healthy and well. You learned the importance of exercise in maintaining a healthy body. These are preventive health practices that will help you now and on into your adult years. These health-oriented practices should become a part of your lifestyle.

Many decisions involving your health, however, are based on the use of tobacco, alcohol, and other drugs. If any or all of these substances are used heavily and repeatedly, they pose a significant risk to your health. It is important for you as a young adult to be aware of the effects of substance abuse. You need to know the facts about tobacco, alcohol, misused or abused prescription and over-the-counter drugs, illegal drugs, and inhalants. You may be faced with some very important decisions concerning their use and your health.

Tobacco

Many young people are confronted with a decision about the use of tobacco sometime during their teen years. Their decision can affect them for the rest of their lives. It can also affect other people in their lives.

When high school students who smoke are asked why they started, over 70 percent say they started smoking because their friends smoke. Research also shows that the decision to smoke is made more readily if the person has parents, brothers, or sisters who smoke.

When people of your parents' generation were teens, they began smoking cigarettes for several reasons. It looked grown-up; it was glamorous; it helped them feel sophisticated. Today, however, it is clear that the smart thing to do is to avoid tobacco, 8-1. Now that research has provided conclusive evidence as to the dangers of tobacco, its continued use is an unnecessary and avoidable health risk.

The cigarette industry promotes a glorified image of people who smoke. However, the government has put some limitations on the industry. Television advertising is no longer legal. Printed ads and packages of cigarettes must include warnings, as shown in 8-2. Many state and local governments have passed strict anti-smoking laws. In addition, non-smoking areas have been set aside in restaurants and other public places. Smoking is banned on buses by many bus companies and on the domestic flights of U.S. airlines. Many businesses also restrict smoking in the workplace in an effort to provide workers with a smoke-free environment.

SURGEON GENERAL'S WARNING: Cigarette Smoke Contains Carbon Monoxide.
SURGEON GENERAL'S WARNING: Quitting Smoking Now Greatly Reduces Serious Risks to Your Health.
SURGEON GENERAL'S WARNING: Smoking Causes Lung Cancer, Heart Disease, Emphysema, and May Complicate Pregnancy.
SURGEON GENERAL'S WARNING: Smoking by Pregnant Women May Result in Fetal Injury, Premature Birth, and Low Birth Weight.
WARNING: The Surgeon General Has Determined That Cigarette Smoking is Dangerous to Your Health.

8-2
Warnings must appear in printed cigarette ads and on all packages of cigarettes.

How Smoking Affects Health

Smoking and inhaling "second-hand" smoke can cause several health problems. The chart in 8-3 shows how smoking can affect the health of your body. Cancer, heart disease, emphysema, and other diseases have all been related to smoking. Smoking is a hazard for pregnant women, and it can shorten a person's life span.

David Hopper

8-1
Teens who want to stay healthy choose not to smoke.

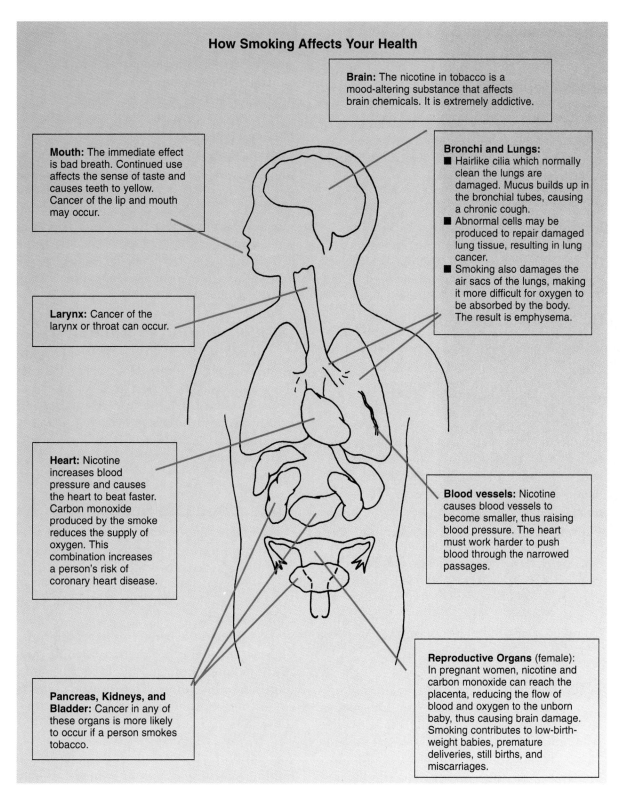

How Smoking Affects Your Health

Brain: The nicotine in tobacco is a mood-altering substance that affects brain chemicals. It is extremely addictive.

Mouth: The immediate effect is bad breath. Continued use affects the sense of taste and causes teeth to yellow. Cancer of the lip and mouth may occur.

Bronchi and Lungs:
- Hairlike cilia which normally clean the lungs are damaged. Mucus builds up in the bronchial tubes, causing a chronic cough.
- Abnormal cells may be produced to repair damaged lung tissue, resulting in lung cancer.
- Smoking also damages the air sacs of the lungs, making it more difficult for oxygen to be absorbed by the body. The result is emphysema.

Larynx: Cancer of the larynx or throat can occur.

Heart: Nicotine increases blood pressure and causes the heart to beat faster. Carbon monoxide produced by the smoke reduces the supply of oxygen. This combination increases a person's risk of coronary heart disease.

Blood vessels: Nicotine causes blood vessels to become smaller, thus raising blood pressure. The heart must work harder to push blood through the narrowed passages.

Pancreas, Kidneys, and Bladder: Cancer in any of these organs is more likely to occur if a person smokes tobacco.

Reproductive Organs (female): In pregnant women, nicotine and carbon monoxide can reach the placenta, reducing the flow of blood and oxygen to the unborn baby, thus causing brain damage. Smoking contributes to low-birth-weight babies, premature deliveries, still births, and miscarriages.

8-3
Tobacco affects the health of the body in many ways.

The Toxic Effect of Smoke

Smoke itself is harmful. It is a mixture of gases, vaporized chemicals, and tiny particles of ash and solids. These are drawn through the nose and throat and into the lungs when smoke is inhaled. Smoke irritates the bronchial tubes leading from the windpipe to the lungs. The result is a chronic cough and spitting up of heavy phlegm.

One of the vaporized chemicals in smoke is *nicotine,* a toxic substance found in tobacco. Nicotine is as lethal as cyanide. A smoker gets more nicotine from cigarettes than from pipes or cigars. If smoke is inhaled, 50 percent of the nicotine is absorbed. Even if the smoker does not inhale the smoke, 25 percent of the nicotine is absorbed.

The fact that nicotine is addictive has been confirmed by recent research. Most smokers find it difficult to stop smoking once they have become addicted to nicotine.

Cancer

Smoking is directly related to lung cancer. The more you smoke, the greater are your chances of developing this disease. The death rate from lung cancer is 10 times greater among smokers than among nonsmokers.

Smokers also have a greater chance of developing other forms of cancer. A Surgeon General's report states, "Cigarette smoking is a major cause of cancers of the lung, larynx, oral cavity, and esophagus. It is also a contributory factor for the development of cancers of the bladder, pancreas, and kidney."

Emphysema

Emphysema is a disease that affects the air sacs of the lungs. Smoking thickens the membranes that line the air passages and blocks them with secretions. In addition, smoking causes the muscles along the air passage walls to contract. This makes them narrower and further reduces air flow. Potentially harmful particles are deposited into the air sacs. When the lung tissue is so badly damaged that it cannot absorb oxygen, emphysema has developed.

Heart Disease

Heart disease is also directly related to smoking. Nicotine stimulates the part of the nervous system that controls the heart and blood vessels and other internal organs that function automatically. As a result, blood vessels constrict, and less blood is carried to the heart, thus causing damage. Smokers die more often from coronary heart disease than do nonsmokers.

Dangers during Pregnancy

Smoking is a hazard for pregnant women and the fetuses they carry. Studies show that smokers have a greater chance of having premature deliveries and smaller, less healthy babies who are at greater risk of developing illnesses. The babies of chain smokers sometimes must undergo withdrawal from nicotine.

Anticipated Life Span

On average, a 25-year-old person who smokes two packs of cigarettes a day will lose roughly eight years of anticipated life span. A cigarette lasts only about six minutes—but enough cigarettes can cut eight years off your life!

The longer a person smokes, the more difficult the habit is to break. People who start smoking early in life tend to smoke more and inhale more. They run a far greater risk of illness, disability, and loss of life than those who start later or never start at all.

If you have developed a smoking habit, you may find it hard to break. Remember that quitting smoking is always beneficial—and the sooner the better.

Passive Smoking

Even if you are a nonsmoker, your health may be at risk. If you spend time in smoke-filled places, you may be seriously affected by inhaling second-hand smoke, or *passive smoking.* Recent studies reveal that children reared in homes in which one or both parents smoke can suffer many of the ill effects of smoking. There can be health problems associated with a smoke-filled workplace. Also, pregnant women need to be particularly careful. Exposure to cigarette smoke for about two hours a day in pregnancy can double a nonsmoker's risk of having an undersize infant.

Smokeless Tobacco

Smokeless tobacco refers to snuff and chewing tobacco. Like tobacco in cigarettes, smokeless tobacco contains nicotine and is habit-forming. Laws have been passed requiring health warning labels on packages of snuff and chewing tobacco. Advertisements of the products are banned on radio and television.

Using smokeless tobacco can lead to a number of health problems. Tobacco juice irritates the inside of the mouth. Eventually, oral cancer may develop. Smokeless tobacco can cause dental problems such as receding gums, increased wear and tear on tooth enamel, and tooth decay. It causes bad breath and discolored teeth. It also lessens the senses of taste and smell.

Ways to Break the Tobacco Habit

There are many reasons for not using tobacco. Many of these are listed in 8-4.

If you do use tobacco and want to quit, you can break the tobacco habit. No one can make you stop smoking, but you have the

Reasons for NOT Using Tobacco

I want to do what is considered the "in" thing to do. The "in" thing now is to NOT use tobacco.

I want to be in control of my life. I do NOT want tobacco to control me. I do not want an addiction to nicotine to interfere with the way I manage my time. I don't want to have to take time to "have a cigarette."

I want to do all I can to promote my health and wellness. I want to be able to exercise and not feel winded. I want to have a complete sense of taste and smell.

I want to live a long, healthy, and productive life. People who continue to smoke can develop serious health problems that can cause death as much as 5 1/2 to 8 1/2 years prior to their normal life spans.

I want to be well groomed and pleasant to be around. Smoking causes bad breath, stained teeth and fingers, and red eyes. In addition, a smoker's hair and clothing smell of smoke.

I want to use my money to achieve creative, recreational, and productive goals. A person who smokes a pack of cigarettes a day might spend as much as $850 per year. This money could be used to purchase needed items or reach financial goals.

I want to live my life within the limits of the law. In most states, young people under the age of 16 cannot purchase cigarettes. In some states, it is illegal for people under the age of 18 to buy cigarettes.

I want to be able to move about freely when I am away from home or at my place of work. Smokers may be restricted to certain areas set aside for smoking or may not be allowed to smoke at all in certain places.

I want to set a good example for my future children and do what I can to protect their health. Studies show that children are more likely to begin smoking if their parents smoke. Children also suffer from passive smoke created by parents who smoke.

8-4

Many teens cite these reasons for not using tobacco.

ability to stop if you really want to stop. How can you accomplish this?

Many individuals who have successfully stopped smoking have done so simply by saying, "This is it. I'm not going to smoke anymore." They eliminate the use of tobacco in one step. They will have some tempting moments when they consider breaking their promise to themselves, but as long as they really want to quit, they can.

For many people, the biggest obstacle is their emotional dependence on tobacco. To overcome it, they try to find substitute activities such as chewing gum. At the times of day they used to enjoy smoking, they make a conscious effort to engage in this substitute activity.

Some people gradually decrease their use of tobacco until they can finally eliminate it. This can be done by smoking fewer cigarettes and by smoking less of each one. It can also be done by following programs that use special commercial products, such as nicotine chewing gums and skin patches. Most of these programs are based on the slow reduction of nicotine in the body.

Other people seek counseling and self-help programs that use individual and group therapy sessions. These are designed to alter smokers' emotional dependence on tobacco and thus change their habit of smoking. Some smokers even use hypnosis to break their habit. Still others heed the advice of their physicians and follow the methods they prescribe. The strategies for quitting listed in 8-5 may be useful.

Alcohol ■ ■ ■ ■ ■ ■ ■

Like every other question that involves human behavior, the question of drinking must be resolved at a personal level. The legal drinking age in all states is 21. Most teens do not drink for this reason. However, after the

---

Tactics for Quitting

Make a list of reasons to quit smoking. Review the list when the need for a cigarette is greatest.

Keep a record of each cigarette smoked. Identify why there was a need to smoke each time. Habits and routines can then be changed to counter the need for a cigarette.

Find a distraction when the urge for a cigarette is greatest. Call someone, go for a walk, run an errand, or do something to keep hands busy.

Participation in a support group or teaming up with a friend can be helpful. Counseling on how to cope with the loss of cigarettes is beneficial.

For severe dependence on nicotine, a temporary replacement, such as a chewing gum containing nicotine to relieve withdrawal symptoms, can be helpful.

Decide on a reward when the goal is reached. The money that would be used to buy cigarettes can be used for a special treat. Also, small rewards can be planned for each day a person goes without smoking.

Be persistent in any attempts to quit. If a person doesn't succeed on the first attempt, try again and again.

8-5
These strategies might help a person who wants to stop using tobacco.

---

age of 21, people choose not to drink for personal reasons, including their health.

As a young adult, you already may have had to make a choice concerning the use of alcohol. If you have not faced that decision yet, you will likely face it in the future. You need to form your own attitudes about the use of alcohol. Your attitudes may differ from those of your friends, or they may be similar. However, it is important that you be prepared to make your own decision about alcohol in your life.

If you decide not to drink, you will not have to make any other decisions about alcohol. Your friends will recognize your decision, and you may, in turn, help friends to reevaluate their decisions about alcohol, 8-6.

Health Consequences of Drinking Alcohol

A person who does decide to drink should be aware of the many consequences of such a decision. Alcohol is a depressant drug. It is absorbed into your bloodstream within two to ten minutes. The rate is determined in part by the amount of food in the stomach.

Alcohol taken without food is absorbed more quickly. The effects of alcohol also vary according to body size. Smaller persons may feel the effects of alcohol more quickly and more strongly.

Since alcohol is a depressant drug, its first effect is a relaxing one. It temporarily eliminates fatigue and nervous tension. It acts on the brain as an anesthetic, putting it "to sleep." It slows the heart and lowers blood pressure. It also reduces inhibitions, self-control, and judgment.

Some people think that alcohol acts more like a stimulant than a depressant. They feel more outgoing after they have been

David Hopper

8-6
Friends may be influenced by the decisions you make.

drinking. This is because the alcohol has reduced their inhibitions, and they are less likely to hold back their feelings and actions. However, they often feel depressed later.

As more alcohol enters the body, it begins to affect muscle coordination, including speech, balance, and breathing. The speed and the degree of the effect will depend on how much is consumed, how fast it is consumed, the amount of food in the stomach, and the total body mass. People have died from alcohol poisoning after drinking one pint of liquor all at once. Their breathing apparatus stopped working because their system was so depressed. Combining alcohol with other depressant drugs such as tranquilizers can have the same result. The bodily processes will slow down to the point that the person will not be able to breathe.

Once alcohol is in the bloodstream, its effects cannot be stopped until the body has burned it up. This happens at a steady rate—about one ounce every two hours. A person cannot speed up the process. The idea that coffee and cold showers can help a person become sober again is a myth.

Frequent consumption of large amounts of alcohol can cause many problems. People who drink in excess may use alcohol as their main food source. Alcohol does not fill their nutritional needs, so they become malnourished. Other health problems that may appear include blackouts, delirium tremens, neuritis, brain damage, cirrhosis of the liver, pancreatitis, and heart problems. The effects of alcohol on the body are summarized in 8-7.

Alcohol Use by Pregnant Women

Consumption of alcohol poses a special danger to pregnant women. A woman who is pregnant needs to be aware that the alcohol she drinks passes from her bloodstream into her unborn baby's bloodstream. Alcohol is present in the fetus for several hours after the mother's blood alcohol level has diminished.

Alcoholic mothers or mothers who drink heavily during pregnancy may give birth to babies with *fetal alcohol syndrome.* Such babies experience mental handicaps as well as heart and joint abnormalities and slower physical growth. Because no level of blood alcohol has been established as safe, most physicians believe that it is best for pregnant women not to drink at all.

Social Consequences of Alcohol Abuse

Alcohol abuse is associated with a number of serious societal ills. These include automobile accidents, on-the-job accidents, domestic abuse, date rape, assault, divorce, and many other social problems. Hundreds of millions of dollars are spent each year addressing the social consequences of alcohol abuse. The costs in terms of human suffering are incalculable.

Alcoholism

The term **alcoholic** refers to a person who suffers from a condition manifested by compulsive, obsessive drinking that is beyond the person's control. An alcoholic has an addictive disease and needs medical attention.

A person does not become a problem drinker with the first decision to drink. However, a person can lose control of his or her use of alcohol after making many decisions to drink a lot and to drink often. Alcohol causes alcoholism. If a person does not drink alcohol, he or she will not become an alcoholic. It is as simple as that.

If a person reaches for a bottle instead of coping with problems, if a person needs a drink to relax, or if alcohol is craved for no particular reason—*beware.* The person may be headed toward dependency on alcohol.

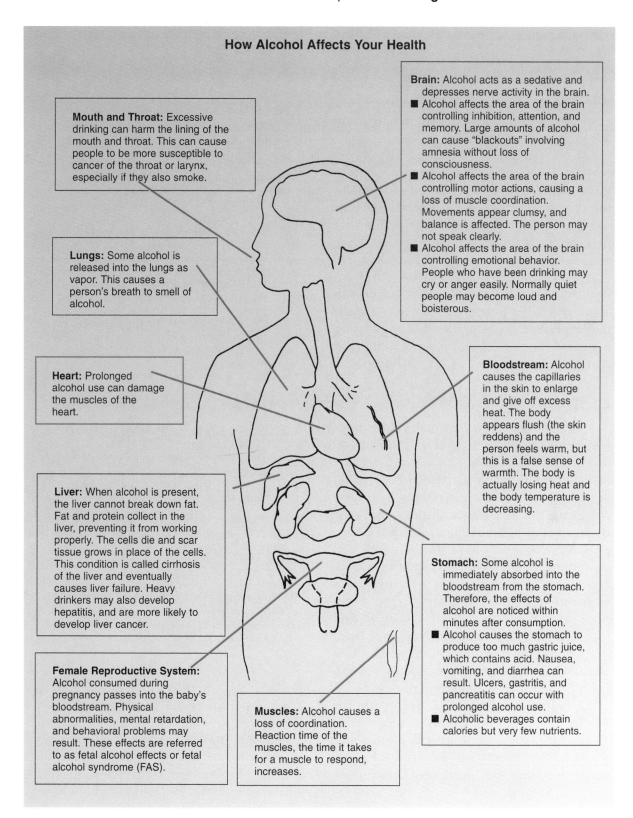

How Alcohol Affects Your Health

Mouth and Throat: Excessive drinking can harm the lining of the mouth and throat. This can cause people to be more susceptible to cancer of the throat or larynx, especially if they also smoke.

Lungs: Some alcohol is released into the lungs as vapor. This causes a person's breath to smell of alcohol.

Heart: Prolonged alcohol use can damage the muscles of the heart.

Liver: When alcohol is present, the liver cannot break down fat. Fat and protein collect in the liver, preventing it from working properly. The cells die and scar tissue grows in place of the cells. This condition is called cirrhosis of the liver and eventually causes liver failure. Heavy drinkers may also develop hepatitis, and are more likely to develop liver cancer.

Female Reproductive System: Alcohol consumed during pregnancy passes into the baby's bloodstream. Physical abnormalities, mental retardation, and behavioral problems may result. These effects are referred to as fetal alcohol effects or fetal alcohol syndrome (FAS).

Brain: Alcohol acts as a sedative and depresses nerve activity in the brain.
■ Alcohol affects the area of the brain controlling inhibition, attention, and memory. Large amounts of alcohol can cause "blackouts" involving amnesia without loss of consciousness.
■ Alcohol affects the area of the brain controlling motor actions, causing a loss of muscle coordination. Movements appear clumsy, and balance is affected. The person may not speak clearly.
■ Alcohol affects the area of the brain controlling emotional behavior. People who have been drinking may cry or anger easily. Normally quiet people may become loud and boisterous.

Bloodstream: Alcohol causes the capillaries in the skin to enlarge and give off excess heat. The body appears flush (the skin reddens) and the person feels warm, but this is a false sense of warmth. The body is actually losing heat and the body temperature is decreasing.

Stomach: Some alcohol is immediately absorbed into the bloodstream from the stomach. Therefore, the effects of alcohol are noticed within minutes after consumption.
■ Alcohol causes the stomach to produce too much gastric juice, which contains acid. Nausea, vomiting, and diarrhea can result. Ulcers, gastritis, and pancreatitis can occur with prolonged alcohol use.
■ Alcoholic beverages contain calories but very few nutrients.

Muscles: Alcohol causes a loss of coordination. Reaction time of the muscles, the time it takes for a muscle to respond, increases.

8-7
When alcohol is consumed, the body is affected in many ways.

A number of questions about alcohol use are listed in 8-8. If a person answers yes to any of them, he or she should review decisions about drinking. There is a fine line between social drinking and dependency on alcohol. A person does not want to end up on the wrong side of that line.

If alcoholics stop drinking, they can recover to some extent. The damage done to their bodies cannot be repaired completely, but they can stop the deteriorating effects of alcohol. Treated alcoholics must realize that they can never drink again, for they can never completely overcome alcoholism. Alcoholics must learn to solve their problems without using alcohol. They must learn to trust themselves and other people. They need to know that there is a life without alcohol and that many people are willing to help them find that life.

Help for the Alcoholic

If a person realizes that a drinking problem has developed and sincerely wants to do something about it, he or she has taken the first step. A few people can overcome a drinking problem completely by themselves. They recognize the problem and know that only they can stop it. Sometimes a crisis makes a person realize a serious problem exists.

Many alcoholics are helped by friends or family members. Their loved ones help them recognize the problem through sincere expressions of concern, understanding, and love. Nagging and accusations will not help, nor will pity or overprotectiveness. The best approach is to accept the fact that they are alcoholics and then seek sources of help.

An increasingly popular technique for helping loved ones is known as *intervention*. This is a technique that forces alcoholics into treatment. A "mini-crisis" is created to persuade them that they need help before their lives are ruined. Celebrity figures such as

Quick Tests to Unmask Alcoholism

- When troubled or under pressure, does the person always drink more heavily than usual?
- Is the person able to handle more liquor than when he or she first began drinking?
- Does the person sometimes feel guilty about drinking?
- Does the person get irritated when family or friends discuss his or her drinking?
- Are memory blackouts increasing in frequency?
- Does the person often wish to continue drinking after friends say they've had enough?
- When sober, does the person often regret things done or said while drinking?
- Does the person usually have a reason for the occasions when he or she drinks heavily?
- Does the person try to avoid family or close friends while drinking?
- Are school or work problems increasing in number?
- Does the person eat very little or irregularly when drinking?
- Has the person recently noticed that he or she cannot drink as much as before?
- Does the person sometimes stay drunk for several days?
- Does the person sometimes feel very depressed and wonder if life is worth living?
- Does the person get terribly frightened after he or she has been drinking heavily?

If the answer to any of the above questions is yes, the person may be a candidate for alcohol abuse problems.

8-8
These questions from the National Council on Alcoholism may help people determine if they or others they know have symptoms of alcoholism.

Betty Ford have publicized the technique, but it must be done with professionally trained counselors.

Every state and many cities have agencies devoted to preventing and treating alcoholism. One well-known group is Alcoholics Anonymous (AA). It is designed to help alcoholics of all ages. About 20 percent of AA members are under the age of 31. An important aspect of the AA program is mutual support. Members can confide in their sponsors and call them whenever they need help.

Alcoholics damage not only their own lives, but also the lives of other people. Family members, friends, and coworkers are all affected. Organizations like Al-Anon and Alateen are designed to help these people.

Alcohol treatment centers are available in most areas, and many have special programs for various ages. They often provide counseling as well as treatment. Social services may provide residential care for short periods of time for people who have lost contact with their families. Career counseling services provide counseling concerning education and work opportunities. Some people whose drinking has involved them with the law have need for legal counseling services.

To find sources of help in your area, look in the yellow pages under "Alcoholism Information and Treatment Centers."

Why Do People Drink?

Most people begin drinking because of social pressure. A friend or someone at a party offers them a drink, so they take it. They feel that drinking will help them "fit in" with the rest of the group.

Some people begin drinking for other reasons. They may use alcohol to help them escape from problems. They may use it to help them relax. Others drink just because they are bored.

Research has shown that there may be other reasons why teens drink. When compared to teenage nondrinkers, teenage alcohol abusers often value independence more than academic achievement. They are often more influenced by peers than by parents. They are usually more aggressive and impulsive. Lower self-esteem and higher anxiety

levels are common. Teen alcohol abusers generally lack a desire to succeed in attaining life goals.

Saying No to Alcohol

Many people choose not to drink. Some of the reasons they give for not drinking are listed in 8-9. Many of these people turn down drinks even in social situations. Refusing al-

Reasons for Not Drinking

- I want to do what is considered the "in" thing to do. More and more young people are choosing NOT to use alcohol.
- I want to be in control of my life. I do NOT want alcohol to control me. A person who becomes addicted to alcohol has a physical and psychological need for alcohol, and these needs take over the person's life.
- I want to live my life within the limits of the law. Drinking is illegal for a person under 21.
- I want to live a long and healthy life. A person who drinks excessively can shorten his or her life by 10 to 12 years.
- I want to feel good and be ready to meet daily challenges. I want to be able to achieve my full potential in life.
- I want to maintain healthy and strong relationships with my family, my friends, and my coworkers. I know I do not need to drink to be popular and well-liked.
- I want to make a positive impression on other people. I want to be in control of my behavior and able to communicate effectively at all times.
- I want to use my money to achieve creative, recreational, and productive goals. Money spent for alcohol could be used to purchase needed items or saved for future goals. Also, an alcoholic risks being laid off or fired from his or her job.
- I want to set a good example for my future children. If I don't drink, my children will not be influenced by the presence of alcohol in my home.

8-9

Young people are choosing not to use alcohol for reasons such as these.

David Hopper

8-10
These teens are enjoying soft drinks at a soda fountain following a "Fifties Party."

cohol has not hurt their friendships, 8-10. They have made a decision, and their friends respect them for that decision.

You can say no to alcohol in many different ways. Some of these ways are listed in 8-11. Read through the list and see if any of the phrases will work for you. Perhaps one of them will help you say no the next time you are offered a drink.

Drugs

The teen years can be difficult ones at best. You are faced with new feelings and relationships. You sometimes find it hard to talk to your parents. There are increased demands on you at school and where you work. Everything can get terribly confusing and difficult. What would you do if someone offered you a drug to "help" you cope? This is a possibility you should consider, so you will be prepared if it happens. You would not want to have to make this kind of decision under pressure. You need to know the facts about all

Ways to Say No

What I would really like is...
   a Coke or Sprite, straight.
   a Horse's Neck (ginger ale with lemon
      peel).
   just a glass of water.

No, thank you...
   I don't really care for any.
   I feel great now, and I don't want to spoil
      this feeling!
   my date couldn't stand me if I felt any
      giddier!

I'd love one, but...
   I'm counting calories.
   It gives me a headache.
   I really don't like the taste.

Not now...
   I'm in training!
   I'm the driver!
   I'm the backseat driver!
   I'm testing my willpower!

Sorry, but...
   I never drink on Fridays (Saturdays, etc.).
   It makes me sleepy.
   I promised myself I wouldn't.
   I just don't want to drink!

8-11
One of these phrases may help you say no the next time someone offers you alcohol.

drugs and the consequences of misuse or abuse of prescription and over-the-counter drugs and illegal drugs.

Drug Terminology

You need to know some drug terminology before you can make informed decisions concerning drug use. The following definitions are from the Food and Drug Administration.

A *drug* is a substance, other than food, that has an effect on one or more systems of the body, especially the central nervous system. Drugs change body chemistry, and different people react differently to the same drugs. *Drug use* is the taking of a drug for its intended purposes, in the appropriate amount, frequency, strength, and manner. *Drug misuse* is taking a substance for its intended purpose but not in the appropriate amount, frequency, strength, or manner. *Drug abuse* is deliberately taking a substance for other than its intended purpose, and in a manner that can result in damage to the person's health or his or her ability to function.

Drug dependence is of two types: physical and psychological. *Physical dependence* occurs when the body chemistry of a user is altered by repeated use of the drug. The user's body develops an actual physical need for the drug. *Addiction* is physical dependence on a drug. An addicted person usually builds up a tolerance to a drug. He or she must have increasing amounts in order to get the same effects.

Psychological dependence on a drug occurs when the user has learned to use the drug as a mental and emotional crutch. The user's need is real, but it is psychological rather than physical. *Habituation* is a term used to describe psychological dependence.

Drugs Have a Wide Variety of Effects

The effects of a drug vary depending on the user's personality, emotional state, expectations, and previous experience with this and other drugs. Because each person is unique, predicting the effects drugs will have on a person is impossible. One person may not be affected by a drug, while another may become seriously ill.

Combining drugs adds a new dimension to the problem. People may think they can handle one drug, such as alcohol, but when they combine their drinking with smoking marijuana, or using another drug, the effects may be deadly. Trying to predict how a drug will affect you is like playing Russian roulette. You may not win.

Using Drugs Means Dealing with the Unknown

Researchers have not yet completed their studies of the psychological and physical effects of drug use. To add to the problem, drugs secured illegally are inconsistent in quality and potency. Diluting or cutting these drugs with less expensive substitutes is a common practice. These substitutes may be damaging, and drug users may have to use more and more to get the desired effect. In some cases, the substitute can be deadly.

Today, new illegal drugs called *designer drugs* are being manufactured. They have slightly altered formulas, but they closely resemble other illegal drugs such as cocaine. Federal laws identify most illegal drugs by their chemical structures. Since the designer drugs are structurally different, they have eluded the laws to control them. People using them are dealing with unknown types of drugs. When they use these drugs, they are guessing what will happen. They are taking a big gamble. If they lose, death may occur.

Types of Drugs

Most drugs fall into four general categories: narcotics, depressants, stimulants, and hallucinogens. Marijuana and inhalants are also frequently abused drugs, as are steroids. Another category of drugs that are sometimes misused or abused is prescription and over-the-counter drugs.

Narcotics

Narcotics are drugs that induce sleep or stupor and relieve pain. They are addicting. Opium, heroin, morphine, codeine, and synthetics such as methadone and Demerol are narcotics.

Heroin, also called scag, smack, junk, or H, is a very powerful narcotic. It belongs to the pain-killer family of opium. It is very addictive. Many people start by sniffing heroin. The body eventually builds up a tolerance, and the user usually progresses to mainlining (injecting into a vein). When heroin is injected, it gives instantaneous, pleasurable feelings. These are quickly followed by a period of drowsiness.

Heroin users can contract HIV/AIDS, hepatitis (a serious, often fatal liver ailment), and other diseases if they share needles with infected individuals. "Shooters" may also experience skin abscesses, collapsed veins, strokes, and heart problems.

For an addict, getting heroin becomes a costly and time-consuming activity. Criminal behavior becomes a by-product in order to meet the high costs of the habit. Treatment consists of total withdrawal or substitution with a manageable drug, such as methadone.

Depressants

Depressants, also called sedatives, slow down the central nervous system. They can cause addiction. Alcohol, barbiturates (sleeping pills), and some tranquilizers such as Valium and Librium are depressants.

Stimulants

Stimulants are drugs that speed up the central nervous system. They accelerate body processes, often to a dangerous degree. They produce a false sense of well-being that may be followed by severe depression. Amphetamines, pep pills, some weight-reduction pills, methamphetamine (speed), and cocaine are stimulants.

Amphetamines are synthetic drugs that act as stimulants. They are similar to cocaine, but are slower acting and have longer effects. These drugs are also known as uppers, ups, and pep pills. *Methamphetamine* is the most potent amphetamine. The powdered form of this drug is called speed, and a smokable form is called ice.

The "high" from these drugs may last as long as 24 hours, but the psychological "crash" is worse. Severe depression and disturbing psychological reactions may last up to 48 hours. A person with a habit will go through cycles of binge and withdrawal, staying awake for days, then crashing (coming off the drug and sleeping) for several days. Speed is highly addictive.

Cocaine was once known as the drug of the rich, but now it is used by people from all backgrounds. Cocaine is typically snorted through the nose. A new, smokable form is called crack, rock, or bait. The effects of crack are far quicker and more intense. It is intensely addictive and greatly multiplies the danger of cocaine use.

Because it is cheaper and easily available on the street and in "crack houses," crack is used by younger people. Young people who are addicted to crack have to develop methods to afford their addiction. They may turn to theft, prostitution, or dealing drugs.

Hallucinogens

Hallucinogens are mind-altering drugs. They cause hallucinations with frightening mental experiences. Examples include LSD, peyote, STP, and PCP.

Lysergic acid diethylamide (LSD) is also known as acid, sunshine, or white lightning. LSD is a very potent hallucinogen. The "trip" starts about 30 minutes after taking the drug.

Effects differ, depending on the personality of the user, previous use of the drug, potency of the drug, and amount used. LSD acts on the nervous system and can cause terrifying experiences. Some individuals on LSD have died after trying to "fly" by jumping out of windows. LSD "trips" may recur spontaneously in "flashbacks."

Phencyclidine hydrochloride, better known as *PCP,* is a deadly drug. Street names include rocket fuel or super joint. Because it is most commonly used in powdered form, it is also called angel dust. The effects of the drug are unpredictable. At its worst, PCP can cause wild hallucinations, physical violence, coma, and death.

Marijuana

Marijuana, also known as pot, grass, tea, or weed, is a product of the hemp plant, cannabis sativa. Hashish, or hash, comes from the same plant. It is more advanced and potent. Marijuana acts as a stimulant, depressant, and hallucinogen, depending on the amount used and the stability of the user.

Short-term panic reactions are sometimes experienced by young pot smokers. Time and space distortion, impairment of judgment, and loss of motor skills may occur during a marijuana "high." Many long-term pot smokers neglect work and adopt a "dropout" personality. This behavior has been labeled *amotivational syndrome* by researchers. Heavy use of marijuana can also cause physical problems. The throat and lungs are damaged, and the user may be more prone to sore throats and bronchial infections.

Inhalants

Some young people have become involved in sniffing inhalants. *Inhalants* are substances that give off fumes that are sniffed for a quick high. Many inhalants are household

Contemporary Concerns *of today's teens:*
Legal Consequences of Marijuana and Alcohol Use

You should consider the legal consequences of using marijuana and alcohol before making decisions about using them. A police record may affect your ability to find a job, to obtain a driver's license, to seek military service, and to take advantage of other opportunities.

Legal penalties for the possession of marijuana vary according to three major factors:

1. The amount possessed.

2. The number of prior convictions for possession.

3. The purpose of possession.

This means that a first offender who has a small amount of marijuana for personal use is likely to receive a comparatively light penalty. A repeat offender who has a large amount of marijuana and is trying to sell it is likely to receive a harsh penalty.

Generally, the possession of marijuana for personal use is a misdemeanor, and the distribution of marijuana is a felony. Each state differs in the exact penalties. They can range from probation to fines, rehabilitation programs, and jail terms. You should know the consequences of the decision to use marijuana.

It is illegal in all states for people under the age of 21 to buy or consume alcohol in public places. Some states, counties, and communities also prohibit the serving of alcohol in homes and other nonpublic places to people under 21. Other regulations concerning the use of alcohol may exist in your community. For instance, people who serve alcohol in their homes may be responsible for their guests. Know the laws that apply to your community and abide by the laws. These laws are for your protection.

Laws against driving while intoxicated (DWI) exist in every state, and the penalties are getting tougher. The concentration of alcohol in the bloodstream can be measured by either a breath test or a blood analysis. In most states, a blood alcohol concentration of 0.10 percent or higher indicates that the driver is incapable of operating a vehicle safely.

DWI laws are for your protection and for the protection of all other people who travel in vehicles. Alcohol is involved in half of all fatal traffic accidents, and traffic accidents are the number one cause of death among teenagers. Most of these accidents involve a driver who has been drinking. Teens are inexperienced drivers. Even small amounts of alcohol can impair their ability to operate vehicles safely. Though the legal consequences of DWI are significant, the lifelong personal anguish a drunk driver will feel if an injury or death occurs will be even more profound.

products such as glue, paint thinner, spray paint, aerosol products, and gasoline. The sniffs of glue or gasoline may produce a sensation comparable to alcohol intoxication.

Inhaling chemicals can be deadly. Inhalants can cause death due to suffocation as the oxygen in the body is replaced with the chemicals. Sniffing inhalants can also cause brain damage, as well as serious damage to the liver or kidneys. Inhaling certain aerosol spray products can kill in seconds by freezing the larynx and respiratory system.

Steroids

Many teens who participate in high school sports have an intense desire to win. This desire has led some athletes to use so-called bodybuilding drugs that they believe will build their muscles. *Anabolic steroids* are synthetic testosterone-like drugs that have tissue-building properties. Doctors prescribe steroids to aid in the treatment of anemia, leukemia, and other conditions.

Though steroids may well build muscle, their use in the large doses that athletes take can lead to damaging side effects. These long-term side effects may include stunted growth, early heart disease, and liver tumors. There also are many possible immediate consequences. These include acne, jaundice, sexual function problems, enlarged breasts in males, and irreversible masculine traits in females. Because of such side effects, national sports organizations have taken a strong stand against the use of steroids. Athletes are tested for steroids and suspended (and sometimes banned) from participation in their sports.

Prescription and Over-the-Counter Drugs

The average American home has a well-stocked medicine cabinet that contains drugs that are used to treat or prevent illness. Many of these drugs, called *over-the-counter (OTC) drugs,* are available without a doctor's prescription.

Other drugs in the home are *prescription drugs*, which are available only with a doctor's recommendation. According to the Federal Food, Drug, and Cosmetic Act, prescription drugs are those that are habit-forming or unsafe for use except under a doctor's supervision. Over-the-counter drugs are considered safe for use if the required label directions and warnings are followed. Studies show that six out of every ten of the medicines in the home are OTC drugs.

Though people are careful to follow the directions given by a doctor for prescribed drugs, they are dangerously careless about the use of OTC drugs. Used properly, OTC drugs are safe and usually very effective. Many, however, have a potential for harm if used over an extended period of time or in combination with other drugs. Some OTC drugs can be very addictive. If people experience any physical or psychological withdrawal symptoms after they stop using OTC drugs, then they are addicted. Some of the OTC drugs that may become habit-forming are sleeping pills, diet pills, stimulants, laxatives, eye drops, and nasal sprays. It is important to read the labels and warnings on OTC drugs and use them with caution.

Why Do People Abuse Drugs or Use Illegal Drugs?

The people who abuse prescription and OTC drugs and those who use illegal drugs come from all age groups, social classes, economic levels, and races. For some, drug use seems an easy way to escape from problems. Others think it is a way to win friends and prestige in group settings. In many cases, people use drugs to express their need for something to give their lives meaning.

Drug abuse and illegal drug use are often the result of a whole chain of events. Many young people get caught up in a series of decisions that lead them to drugs. They begin by letting their "friends" talk them into smoking cigarettes and having a few drinks. Then these same people may introduce marijuana and other drugs. Before they understand what is happening, the young people may be caught up in a culture of drug use. Other drug experiences may be a constant temptation to them.

Drugs Prevent Young People from Learning How to Solve Problems

Everyone has problems, and everyone has to learn how to deal with them. People cannot escape their problems by misusing drugs or using illegal drugs. In fact, using such drugs usually makes problems worse.

Coping with problems is a process individuals learn as they mature. If you can learn to solve each problem as it occurs, you will have more success in life. You will prevent your small problems from becoming big ones.

If you try to escape problems by using drugs, you are not being fair to yourself. If your mind is clouded by drugs, you will not be able to make good decisions.

Drug abuse and illegal drugs can negatively affect your ability to reach maturity. Instead of being more independent, drugs may force you to remain dependent on others to make decisions for you. If you develop a dependence on drugs, you will not be able to make decisions for yourself.

Saying No to Drugs

Why can some people meet the challenges of social pressure and other stresses in life without turning to drugs? These people have the same opportunities for social involvement. They have the same frustrations. They have the same wide range of feelings

David Hopper

8-12
Teens can have good times without using drugs.

from anger to love and from sadness to happiness. As they have matured, they have learned to deal with people, to cope with stress, and to handle their emotions. They don't allow themselves to hide behind the effects of drugs, 8-12.

More and more young people are saying no to drugs. Many of their reasons are listed in 8-13. Make the decision to be free of drugs, not addicted to their use. Allow yourself to be who you are, not someone created by the influence of drugs.

Sources of Help

If you use drugs and want to stop, the first place to look for help is within yourself. You were the one who chose to use drugs, and you must make the decision to stop. Once you have taken this step, you may want to seek the help of your family, a friend, or a professional person such as a physician.

Most communities have many resources to help those who ask for help. Look in the yellow pages under "Drug Abuse and Addiction Information and Treatment." In some areas, you can call a hotline for immediate help. The person who answers your call will help you talk it out or give you information about other resources. School nurses, counselors, or teachers may be able to refer you to professional help. Many churches, community agencies, and hospitals offer programs that can help.

Dealing with Peer Pressure ■ ■ ■ ■ ■ ■

During the school years, teenagers have an intense desire for conformity. While they are striving for more independence from their parents, they are naturally attracted to their peers. Wanting to look the same and act the same is an outgrowth of this desire. Teens

Why Say NO to Drugs

- I want to do what is considered the smart thing to do. That means not abusing drugs or using illegal drugs.
- I want to be in control of my life. I do NOT want to become addicted to any drugs. A person can become physically and psychologically dependent on a drug. The compulsive need for the drug takes over and the person is no longer able to function without the drug.
- I want to live my life within the limits of the law and avoid involvement with illegal drugs.
- I want to do all I can to protect my health and life. I want to avoid unnecessary physical and psychological damage to my well-being. If I give birth, I want my baby to be healthy and free of drug dependency.
- I want to make a positive impression on other people. I want to be able to communicate effectively in my personal and work life. A drug abuser often becomes disinterested in keeping up his or her personal appearance. The ability to communicate is hampered as well.
- I want to be able to perform effectively at school and/or at work. A person using drugs may develop memory loss and lack motivation. Performance suffers due to increased inconsistency in task completion.
- I want to maintain healthy and strong relationships with my family, my friends, and my coworkers. A person who abuses drugs may begin to place more value on the drug dependency than on maintaining meaningful relationships with others.
- I want to use my money to meet my needs for food, clothing, and shelter, and to save for future goals. A drug abuser spends money on drugs that could and should be used for essential items. A drug abuser may have to steal in order to support his or her drug dependency.
- I want to set a good example for my future children by using OTC and prescription drugs wisely.

8-13
Young people have given these reasons for saying no to drugs.

may be swayed to conform to the group if they tend to be shy or if they fear group disapproval, embarrassment, or intimidation.

Peer pressure is being influenced by one or more people who are close to you in age. See 8-14. It can be positive, but often it is negative. Partly, it is due to curiosity. Teenagers' desires to appear grown-up spark interest in experimenting with tobacco, alcohol, and other drugs. Once peer pressure is brought to bear, teens tend to go too far because they are afraid to say no. When teens approach a potentially troublesome situation, they should weigh the pros and cons. They should ask themselves whether the surroundings tempt trouble, and if so, they should leave. It

is better to be overcautious than to risk one's health, reputation, and future.

Perhaps the hardest step in dealing with peer pressure is learning how to say no. Many suggestions for saying no to tobacco, alcohol, and other drugs were given in this chapter. If teens find it difficult to say no, perhaps another technique might work. Some young people overcome this problem with a good sense of humor. They can joke their way out of trouble. Others can often make an excuse or change the subject to avoid problems.

Teenagers want to learn about life through first-hand experiences. Parents want to protect their children from group pressures and physical dangers. These opposing

Cholla Runnels

8-14
This young man is feeling peer pressure. The others want him to get in the truck with them.

desires can create friction within the family. Parents need to understand their teenagers' desire for greater independence. They also need to retain the strength and understanding of loving and caring parents. If teenagers feel secure in their relations with their parents—even when there is conflict—they are more likely to make wise decisions. If there are serious problems in the family relationships, teenagers are more likely to reject family priorities in favor of those of the peer group.

This period can be one in which teenagers gain respect for parents. They can resist negative peer pressure and the possible consequences of conforming. They can make their own decisions and move closer toward responsible adulthood.

Summary

- Smoking causes lung cancer, heart disease, emphysema, and other diseases. Exposure to smoke during pregnancy can result in premature babies and smaller infants who are at greater risk of developing illness.

- Smokeless tobacco, like tobacco in cigarettes, contains nicotine, is habit-forming, and can lead to a number of health problems.

- Most people begin drinking because of social pressure. However, many people choose not to drink.

- Frequent consumption of large amounts of alcohol can cause many health problems. It can lead to malnourishment, blackouts, delirium tremens, neuritis, brain damage, cirrhosis of the liver, pancreatitis, and heart problems.

- Consumption of alcohol during pregnancy can result in birth defects. If a pregnant woman consumes large amounts of alcohol, her baby may be born with a pattern of defects known as fetal alcohol syndrome.

- Alcoholism involves damage to the alcoholic, the alcoholic's family, and society. Treatment and counseling are available for alcoholics and their families.

- Drug abuse is often the result of a chain of events. It usually begins with smoking cigarettes and having a few drinks. It often continues with the smoking of marijuana and then leads to the use of other drugs.

- Drugs cause a wide variety of negative effects and may lead to serious illness or even death.

- Steroid use results in unpleasant and often dangerous side effects.

- Used properly, over-the-counter drugs are generally safe and usually very effective. Many, however, have a potential for harm if used over an extended period of time or in combination with other drugs. Some OTC drugs can be addictive.

■ Peer pressure can be positive, but often it is negative and needs to be resisted.

To Review ■ ■ ■ ■ ■ ■ ■ ■ ■ ■ ■ ■ ■ ■ ■ ■

1. True or False. Research studies have provided conclusive evidence that tobacco is dangerous to your health.

2. Describe five health hazards of smoking.

3. True or False. Smokeless tobacco is a safe alternative to smoking.

4. Describe three methods people use to quit smoking.

5. Which of the following statements are true?
    a.   The legal drinking age in all states is 21.
    b.   Alcohol is a stimulant drug.
    c.   The effects of alcohol may vary according to body size.
    d.   Alcohol reduces inhibitions and self-control.
    e.   When alcohol is combined with a tranquilizer, the effect of the alcohol on bodily systems is lessened.
    f.   Coffee and cold showers help people sober up faster.
    g.   Alcoholism is an addictive disease.

6. Explain the differences between drug use, drug misuse, and drug abuse.

7. How do the effects of crack compare to the effects of cocaine?

8. Describe the behavior of long-term marijuana smokers who have amotivational syndrome.

9. Describe the physical problems that are associated with the use of inhalants.

10. True or False. Athletes who use steroids to enhance their performance may develop heart disease, liver tumors, jaundice, and other problems.

11. Explain how peer pressure can influence a person's behavior.

To Do ▪ ▪ ▪ ▪ ▪ ▪ ▪ ▪ ▪ ▪ ▪ ▪ ▪ ▪ ▪ ▪

1. Poll students about their smoking habits. Ask if they smoke, why they smoke, when they started smoking, and if they have tried to quit smoking. Ask for opinions on school rules concerning smoking and on rules about nonsmoking areas in public places.

2. Use role-playing to practice ways of saying no to tobacco, alcohol, and other drugs.

3. Investigate the possibility of starting a SADD (Students Against Drunk Driving) group or other anti-drinking group in your school or community.

4. Hold a class debate on this statement: Cigarette smoking should be banned in all public places.

5. Choose one of the drugs mentioned in this chapter and do further research on it. Present an oral report to the class about the drug's effects and health hazards.

6. Ask a physician to speak to your class about health problems related to drug misuse and abuse.

7. Ask a law official to speak to your class about legal problems related to drug abuse. Ask about local, state, and federal laws. Compare them with drug laws in foreign countries.

8. Make a file of community resources in your area for people with drug and alcohol problems. Note the type of help, telephone number, address, and cost of each type of assistance.

Lifestyle Options and Consequences

After studying this chapter, you will be able to

■ define lifestyle and identify adult lifestyle options as they exist today.

■ describe reasons and circumstances people cite for choosing a single lifestyle, marriage, childless marriage, or living together.

■ identify an unplanned pregnancy as a lifestyle consequence.

■ evaluate alternative options available when an unplanned pregnancy occurs.

■ identify sexually transmitted diseases and explain the health crises they pose.

■ assess the role of responsible behavior concerning lifestyle options and consequences.

In the previous chapters, you have learned of decisions that affect your health—healthful choices, as well as those that can be damaging to your health. You've also learned about the decisions you need to be making now regarding your career and education options. In this chapter, you will learn of the lifestyle options available to you. The decisions you make regarding your lifestyle can have both positive and negative consequences. To make the best decisions concerning your lifestyle, you need to learn as much as you can about these options and their consequences. Once again, irresponsible decisions concerning lifestyle behavior can affect many aspects of your life. These include your health, your sense of self-esteem, your relationships, and your long-range goals for your life.

Terms to Know

lifestyle	AIDS
toxemia	HIV
anemics	gonorrhea
agency adoption	syphilis
independent adoption	herpes
open adoption	genital warts
closed adoption	chlamydia
sexually transmitted disease (STD)	abstinence

Adult Lifestyle Options

Lifestyle can be defined as a set of behaviors adopted by personal choice. The two key words are *behaviors* and *choice*. Responsible choices concerning behaviors can give you a sense of promise for your future. Irresponsible choices may disrupt your hopes for achieving your long-term goals.

You have choices as you decide how you want to live. Your choices will be influenced by your family, your friends, and your career goals. Even more important, your lifestyle will depend on what you want to do with your life.

As you look around, you will see a variety of lifestyles. You will see pros and cons for each option. Learning about the different lifestyles does not mean you are accepting or rejecting any of them. It just means you are becoming more knowledgeable about them. Your values and goals will help you choose the best lifestyle for you.

Single Life

Single living means one person is living in a household. The number of people living alone is increasing in our country. Currently, about 25 percent of American households consist of just one person.

Most people will experience living as a single person at some time in their lives. Some single living is temporary. Young adults may live alone after they leave the parental home to work full-time or to attend college. Many other people are single due to divorce or the death of their spouses.

Today, one of the main reasons for the increased number of single adults is that young people are delaying marriage. Heightened educational requirements for some jobs may prompt many to delay marriage to complete their education. Even then, many will choose to marry later after they become es-

tablished in their careers. This also means they will be more financially stable when they do marry.

Social pressure to marry early has lessened. The old label of being an "old maid" is no longer used when describing a young unmarried woman advancing in her career. Women are finding they are very capable of making it on their own. The more educated women are, the more likely they are to delay marriage. Many want to prove to themselves that they can pay their own way in life. They want to be sure of themselves before making a commitment to someone. Some women

David Hopper

9-1
Previously married single people have many adjustments to make as they learn to live on their own again.

Cholla Runnels

9-2
Single people have more freedom to spend their time as they wish.

become involved in their careers and find it difficult to commit to a serious relationship.

Sometimes unexpected events bring about a single lifestyle. The death of a spouse leaves a person alone. Separation and divorce means the spouses will live separately. These changes require an emotional adjustment as well as a change in living styles, 9-1.

The choice to remain single permanently is made by those who enjoy the freedoms and challenges of single life. These singles feel they are able to achieve an enjoyable life without having to rely on anyone else. Their self-esteem is dependent on who they are and not on their marriage partner. Some do not want the responsibilities of marriage and parenting. They may decide that living alone is better than being a part of a bad marriage. Others may be responsible for the care of a parent and find that single life for them is the most convenient way to meet those responsibilities.

Pros and Cons of Single Living

Society has accommodated the increasing number of singles with a variety of changes. New regulations provide for more equality for women. Credit is more readily available for single people. Many buy their own homes. Housing developers are building smaller houses and town homes to appeal to the single buyer. Appliance manufacturers market a variety of scaled-down appliances. Food companies package many foods in single serving portions.

Single people have more mobility than married couples. They can move from city to city or job to job more easily to advance their careers. They are more likely to choose careers involving travel.

People living alone have more time to themselves, 9-2. They can also go out when they choose. Many singles feel they can meet many people and form a network of family and friends. If they choose to be very active, they can be. If they wish a more quiet life, they are able to choose this, too.

There are some concerns regarding single living. Singles may have to make a greater effort to have a social life. They may have to overcome some stereotypes. For instance, some singles are labeled as being self-centered. If single people did not choose the single life, they may feel they are missing out on a full life. They may desire to marry and have children, but have not met the right mate. The dating experience is often limited because of few eligible partners.

Marriage

Marriage is a basic lifestyle in our society. Marriage relationships have changed over the years, but marriage is still the choice of most Americans, 9-3. The percentage of married-couple households in the U.S. is decreasing, however.

This lifestyle fulfills the basic need for establishing a bonding relationship between a man and a woman. Two persons joined in marriage share a total commitment. This commitment provides a stable foundation for intimacy and inner security. Marriage partners can communicate their deepest feelings. They can share their thoughts, hopes, and dreams. They can work together to reach their common goals.

The commitment of marriage does not mean entrapment or stagnation. Rather, it can give committed individuals the confidence and freedom they need to grow. Today, more young people are seeking a marriage relationship in which they can grow as indi-

9-3

Jeff Johnston

Marriage continues to be the most popular lifestyle in our society.

viduals and as a couple. Recognizing the need for both individual and mutual growth helps a marriage to be vital and successful.

In many marriages, both husbands and wives have careers outside the home. In these dual-career marriages, both spouses grow individually, and they accept the pressures that this busy lifestyle dictates. If the commitment to the marriage relationship remains the primary goal, these marriages can be healthy and expanding. If either spouse places more importance on individual goals than on their mutual relationship or family goals, the marriage will probably deteriorate.

One of the basic strengths of marriage is the setting it provides for raising children. More couples, however, are now waiting to have children until they are older. They are sharing more of the decisions. Together, the husband and wife decide whether and when they want to have children, how many children they want, and what spacing they want between children. Once the children are born, the couple shares the responsibilities of parenthood as well. See 9-4.

In a dual-career marriage, both spouses often choose to continue their careers after children are born. This means even greater sharing of child care roles by both father and mother.

If parents view the addition of children as a source of enrichment in their lives, their relationship will remain strong. They will look forward to the changes children will bring in their lives.

Childless Marriage

Most couples regard having children as an important part of marriage. However, many couples prefer not to have children.

In the past, couples who chose to remain childless were often viewed as selfish and as ignoring the "natural" purpose of marriage. They received social pressure from par-

David Hopper

9-4
Marriage provides a good setting for raising children.

ents and peers to reproduce. Parents expected the married couple to provide them with grandchildren. Some peers thought that children were necessary in a marriage, and that without children, the couple would be lonely in their old age. These arguments sometimes are still used. However, couples today generally are freer to make their own decisions and to have their decisions accepted by others.

Most couples who choose to have a childless marriage view parenthood as a difficult and demanding task. Many recognize that they are not adequately trained for parenthood. Some feel that they have not handled their own lives well and do not want to be responsible for others' lives. Some couples are disturbed about the rising number of child abuse and child neglect cases. Some recognize the relationship between overpopulation and environmental deterioration. Others are concerned about financial factors. They feel they could not afford to give children all they would want them to have.

Some couples feel their commitment to their careers is greater than their desire to have children. Some admit they prefer to invest all their resources in the husband-wife relationship. They do not want to add the dimension of parenthood. See 9-5.

Today, parenthood is considered by most people to be a privilege, not a duty. This attitude gives couples the chance to decide for themselves whether or not to have children.

The question of having or not having children is a key issue in a marriage. Thus, partners should discuss their feelings and come to an agreement before they get married. They should maintain a certain degree of flexibility, however. Sometimes decisions are changed after marriage. A couple who planned to have children might find that they cannot have children of their own. Another couple may decide they enjoy their husband-wife relationship so much that they don't want to change their lifestyle. Another couple who had planned to have a childless marriage may feel that their relationship is missing something. They may reverse their decision and have one or more children.

Throughout a marriage relationship, partners should feel free to express their thoughts and feelings. If their ideas about having children change after marriage, they should be able to discuss the issue honestly. Together, they should reach a decision that is right for them and their marriage.

Living Together

Living together is a lifestyle that combines aspects of single living and marriage. A person who chooses this lifestyle is legally single, but emotionally committed to a partner.

Surveys indicate that there are three main reasons for living together. They are reducing living expenses; getting to know the person better before marriage; and abandon-ing traditional male/female roles. However, studies have not shown that people who live together are happier than those who choose the more traditional lifestyles of single life or marriage.

Many couples say they live together for financial reasons, yet few of these couples discuss financial arrangements in detail before moving in together. They see the short-term advantage of paying just one rent instead of two, but they fail to consider long-range financial security, 9-6.

Couples often decide to live together with a "let's see" attitude. If the relationship works, they will get married later. The fact that there is no commitment is cited as both a strength and a weakness. Many feel this allows the couple freedom to establish a good relationship. They feel that living together allows them to learn about each other completely, without any restrictions. If the couple

Cholla Rı

9-5
Some couples remain childless because this lifestyle gives them more time to spend with each other.

find they do not get along, they can simply separate.

On the other hand, the lack of commitment can cause feelings of insecurity. Keeping the possibility of a breakup in mind may actually help to cause the breakup. Many authorities feel that more "living together" relationships could be permanent if the partners would enter them with a real determination to succeed. Instead, living together is often a method young people use to avoid responsibility. They find it easier to "play house" rather than to commit themselves to a marriage.

Counselors have another concern about young people living together. They believe that when young people avoid making deep personal commitments, they may be setting themselves up for mediocre relationships. The goal for living together is often expressed as, "Can we avoid splitting up?" They do not ask, "How good can we make this relationship?" Counselors sense that a couple who live together may be settling for too little. They possibly could have a richer, more meaningful relationship if they would accept the commitment of marriage.

Couples who live together may want to abandon traditional male/female roles. However, the division of labor within these households tends to follow traditional patterns, just as it does among married couples. Many women feel that they are being "taken" financially. They share costs equally, but continue to perform most of the household duties.

A person may be at another disadvantage as the years go by. One partner may live with the other in hopes of obtaining a commitment to marriage. If marriage does not occur, the person has lost precious years during which a marital partner may have been sought and found.

Couples who live together usually don't realize the powerful influence of their parents. A man and woman may enter the relationship knowing their parents disapprove,

9-6

Cholla Runnels

In a lifestyle of living together, unmarried partners typically share living expenses and housekeeping chores.

but failing to realize the powerful effect of that disapproval. Visits become awkward, and family relationships are strained. This conflict reduces the couple's chances for a happy and lasting relationship.

Other problems to consider are the legal ones. What constitutes a family? Legally, a family must be bonded by either a common ancestor or a marriage contract. The legal family serves four functions that, according to the judicial system, cannot be served by another lifestyle. These are provisions for the following:

- A protective environment for raising and educating children.

- An economic support system.

- A legal outlet for sexual expression.

- Psychological satisfaction through a structure of social relationships.

Any other form of living together is penalized by our existing laws. Some of the problems the couples face are as follows:

- Social security survivor benefits are denied.

- The right of interspousal protection (not having to testify against a spouse), important in criminal cases, is denied.

- Joint income tax returns cannot be filed.

- When one partner of an unmarried couple leaves or dies, the question of ownership of property arises. Laws related to this question vary. In most cases, the remaining partner has no legal claim to the property. If one partner chooses to walk away from the relationship, he or she may take property. The other partner has little, if any, legal chance of claiming it.

- If an unmarried couple have a child, custody problems arise when and if the partners separate or when one dies. In some states, the children of unwed fathers become wards of the state upon the mother's death. The father has to go to court to seek custody. If the father leaves or dies, custody is often awarded to the mother. Children have no inheritance rights.

Lifestyle Consequences

Responsible behavior concerning lifestyle options can lead to positive consequences. Irresponsible behavior concerning your lifestyle can lead to unplanned consequences, some of which may be negative. Some of these negative consequences may affect your health, your self-esteem, your personal relationships, and your long-term goals.

Deciding on your lifestyle means you have a choice. You make choices regarding your behavior in many areas of your life. If you make irresponsible choices in one area, there is a higher probability you may make poor choices in other areas. Your sexual behavior, for instance, is closely related to your ability to make responsible decisions. Poor choices in the area of drinking or drug use may impair your ability to make wise sexual decisions. You can see how problems can cluster together, magnifying the consequences that impact your life. You may make some poor choices—everyone does. However, you don't want these poor choices to form a pattern.

An Unplanned Pregnancy

One lifestyle consequence that may have a major impact on the lives of the people involved is an unplanned pregnancy. The impact is even greater if the couple are very young and unwed.

Every year in the United States over one million teenage girls become pregnant. One of these girls gives birth every three minutes. This event can spell tragedy for mother, father, and child. In addition, it costs our communities in both human and economic terms.

Most teens make responsible decisions concerning their sexuality. They have a set of values and standards that guides their behavior. They have goals for their lives that would be difficult to achieve if an unplanned pregnancy should occur. They are able to make responsible decisions in the area of sexuality.

Reasons Unplanned Pregnancies Occur

Why, then, do some teens risk getting pregnant? Most pregnant teens did not plan to get pregnant. They say, "It just happened." Teens are prone to risk-taking. They think, "It

Myths about Pregnancy

"It couldn't happen to me; I'm too young to have a baby." There is no way of knowing how young is too young. A girl can get pregnant even if she has never had a menstrual period. A girl can get pregnant the first time she has sexual intercourse.

"It's not that time of the month." It is very difficult for a young girl to know just when she is most likely to get pregnant or most likely to be "safe." Stress, emotional ups and downs, or illness can alter the menstrual cycle. There is a possibility of becoming pregnant at any time of the month, for anyone who is sexually active.

"If we do have sexual intercourse, I can always douche afterward." Sperm move very quickly. Before a woman could douche, the sperm could have already passed through the vaginal tract. Douching is not an effective birth control method.

"I haven't thought about birth control because that would mean that I was planning to have sexual relations. If I do have sex, it will be spontaneous and beautiful. Planning it makes it seem *bad*." Many young people do not know enough about their reproductive abilities and do not want to discuss sex and birth control. However, those who find themselves in relationships that are becoming deeply emotional should stop and think. Discussing what to do about contraception is better than discussing what to do about an unwanted pregnancy.

"If I get pregnant, he'll love me, and he'll marry me." If pregnancy occurs, a young man may well walk out. He may even ask, "How do I know I'm the father?" Studies show the young woman is most often left to face the unplanned pregnancy alone. If they do marry, they are three times more likely to get separated or divorced than couples who have children after age 20. Very few teenage fathers pay child support or help with the financial support of the mother or the baby.

"If I have a baby, at least I will have someone to love and someone who will love me." This is one of the most unfortunate myths concerning teenage pregnancy. A young woman who uses pregnancy to find someone to love her will instead find herself trapped by motherhood. The cuddly baby suddenly becomes a 24-hour responsibility, which she may not be mature enough to handle. She will find that her whole life is full of responsibilities that are difficult to handle.

9-7
Myths regarding pregnancy can hide the true risks of premarital sexual experiences.

will never happen to me." They believe in many of the myths surrounding pregnancy as explained in 9-7.

Some teens lack complete information about the human reproductive system. Even more troubling is the misconception some have that pregnancy cannot occur the first time sexual intercourse takes place. Pregnancy can occur with the first sexual encounter. If a pattern of sexual activity develops, the possibility of pregnancy increases.

Teens are getting mixed messages from the media. They see recording and screen stars having babies without being married. They are led to believe that such pregnancies are acceptable.

Some young women mistakenly think that becoming pregnant will help their self-esteem. One young girl reported, "Before I was pregnant, I was nothing. Now I am somebody—I am a mother."

Other teens honestly think they are in a committed relationship with someone who loves them. They think this person will always be there for them, but this is not very often the case.

Risks Involved with Teen Pregnancies

The pregnant teen and her offspring are at risk physically, educationally, financially, and socially. The young fathers also face certain risks. Often the teen parents have already had difficulty taking care of their own lives. The added pressures of having a baby compound the problems.

Physically, a young teenage girl's body may not be fully developed. The added strain of pregnancy places more stress on her young body. If pregnancy occurs before gynecological maturity is achieved, maturation of the skeletal bones may be affected. The added nutrient demands of pregnancy may jeopardize the teenager's growth potential and increase her risk in pregnancy.

Adolescents who are malnourished prior to pregnancy or are overly concerned about weight gain have an increased incidence of low birth-weight infants or premature babies. Complications such as anemia and toxemia are higher in poorly nourished pregnant teens. *Toxemia* results in fluid retention, causing swelling of fingers and feet, and weight gain. *Anemics* have a low level of hemoglobin in their blood caused by a deficiency of iron in the diet.

Compared to older mothers, teenagers are twice as likely to have low birth-weight babies or premature babies. Either of these consequences may pose serious health risks for the babies and for their continuing health through childhood.

The risk of infant death is twice as high for teenage mothers as it is for older mothers. The risk of the mother's death is 60 percent higher for teens under 15 years of age compared to women in their 20s.

Many teenage girls deny or ignore the fact that they are pregnant as long as possible. They often do not get adequate prenatal care. In some cases, they give birth without medical care, putting themselves and their babies in real danger.

Educationally, the teen mother is at risk. Of pregnant teens, 80 percent never finish high school. The responsibility for caring for a baby while trying to study and attend classes becomes more than most teen mothers can handle. Pregnancy is the number one cause of female high school dropouts. Without a high school diploma, career options are limited.

Socially, teen mothers often feel isolated from their peers. When friends are going out, the young mother is staying home to care for her baby. Getting a baby-sitter is often too expensive, or there is no one available. Being able to experience the social life of a teenager is difficult because there is a child to care for 24 hours a day.

Many teenage mothers seek government welfare to handle their financial needs. Many will continue to rely on welfare, reducing chances to upgrade their lifestyle. Their lives revolve around caring for their babies and making ends meet. They are unable to get jobs because they must take care of their children.

The effect on the young father may also be detrimental to fulfillment of future goals. If he maintains an active role in the life of the child, he may have to drop out of school and find full-time employment. This will lessen his chances for completing an education. With little education, his career options will be limited.

Most teen males do not associate the sex act with pregnancy. They view it as a purely physical experience. They may not even have any emotional commitment to the girl. By the time the pregnancy is confirmed, the boy may disassociate himself from the girl. He may be totally out of the picture by the time the birth takes place.

Contemporary Concerns *of today's teens:*
Paternity Involves Responsibilities

Paternity (fatherhood) brings with it many responsibilities, whether the father marries the mother or not. Many of these are based on laws regarding child support. Do you know the answers to the following questions about paternity issues?

Q: *If the mother is not married to the child's father at the time of birth, is he the legal father?*

A: No. He is the biological father. Unless certain legal steps are taken after the baby is born, he will not be the child's legal father.

Q: *What are these legal steps?*

A: The child's father can voluntarily admit paternity and have an attorney file legal papers. Acknowledgment of paternity entitles the child to medical, veteran's, and social security benefits. It enables the child to inherit from the father's estate. It also gives the child access to a complete medical history.

Q: *What can the mother do if the father refuses to admit that he is the father?*

A: The mother can see an attorney about filing a paternity suit with the court.

Q: *What will happen then?*

A: The court may order him to give a blood sample that will be used to determine paternity.

Q: *If the court decides he is the father, can the baby have his name?*

A: Yes.

Q: *Can the mother collect support from the legal father?*

A: If the court rules that he is the legal father, the court can order him to pay child support.

Q: *If the baby and the mother are living with the mother's parents, will the baby's father have to pay child support?*

A: Where the mother lives usually makes no difference to the court in determining whether the father should pay child support.

Q: *Can the baby's father be made to pay child support if he is only sixteen years old?*

A: Yes. If he has an income, he can be ordered to pay support no matter what his age.

Q: *If the baby's father is living with his parents and not working, can he still be ordered to pay child support?*

A: Yes. Whether he pays support and how much he pays depends upon his resources, including his ability to work and his personal property. The court makes the final decision about how much he can afford to pay.

Q: *If the baby is raised by the father, will the mother have to pay child support?*

A: Both parents are legally obligated to contribute support even if the child lives with someone other than one of the parents, such as a grandparent or foster parent.

Alternatives for the Pregnant Teen

When a teenager discovers she is pregnant, she will no doubt wonder, "What shall I do?" She is probably living in her parents' home when she discovers she is pregnant. Sharing this news with parents can be one of the hardest steps to take.

The decision to have sexual relations is largely a private one. The decision to reveal a pregnancy involves many people. The male partner, parents, friends, school officials, and medical personnel will ultimately have to be consulted.

Because teens are very "present oriented," the long-term reality of a pregnancy will be hard to comprehend. When an unwed teen becomes pregnant, many lives will be affected for years to come. The teen girl and her partner have a very difficult decision to make. What are the alternatives they may consider?

Single Parenting

Slightly less than half of all pregnant teens give birth. Of these, only about 10 percent marry the father. The majority of these mothers choose to keep and rear their babies alone. In a few instances, the father raises the child alone.

A person who chooses this alternative must be willing to assume great responsibilities. Parenting is never an easy task, and being a single parent requires even more time and effort. The consequences of this choice will affect the entire lifetime of both the parent and the child. See 9-8.

Single parents have many decisions to make. They must first decide where they will live. Single teen mothers are most likely to live with their parents. If the parents are supportive and caring, this arrangement will meet her needs. In many instances, however, the teen mother and her parents find it hard to cope with her role as a mother while she is still thought of as their daughter. In some homes the baby will be raised by the grandparents and will be more like a younger brother or sister to the teenager. If the grandparent is a single parent, the added burden may create relationship and financial problems.

Teen mothers may want to continue their education, but they will have to find child care for their infants. Some schools offer child care during the school day for young mothers. The babies are cared for in a child care center while the mothers attend classes.

Money is a big problem for single parents. If the young mother lives with her parents, they may be willing to continue to pay her expenses. However, some families may expect the young mother to pay them something to defray the added costs of an additional family member.

Very few young parents can live alone without financial assistance. The government offers some financial help in the form of AFDC (Aid to Families with Dependent Children), Medicaid, and other programs. However, this makes the teen dependent on welfare assistance and creates a dependent lifestyle for her. She may then find it hard to become independently responsible for herself and her child.

Marriage

Marriage was often the path selected in past years. This became the obvious next step when a teen became pregnant. Parents of teens often forced this decision upon the young people. A forced marriage is seldom recommended. The couple will always ask the question, "Did my spouse marry me only for the sake of the baby?" Today marriage is chosen by only a small number of pregnant teens.

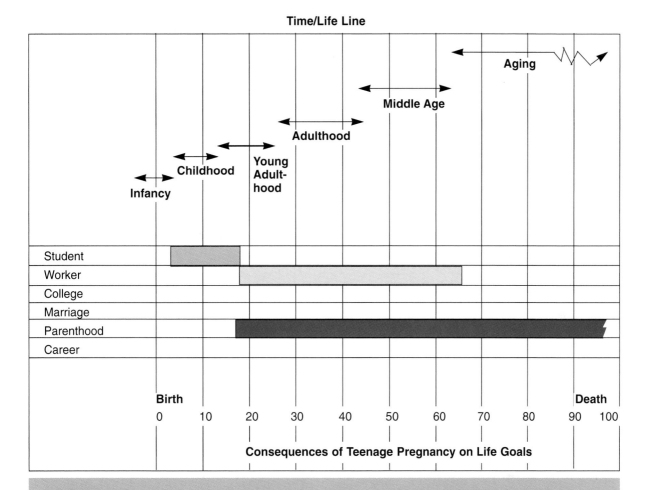

9-8
An unplanned pregnancy will impact lifetime goals, as illustrated in this time/life
line.

Marriage itself requires many adjustments. Learning to live with another person takes patience, understanding, and true love, 9-9. Premarital pregnancies are often the result of immaturity. Marriage will not encourage maturity, nor will marriage encourage the development of true love if it was not present earlier. Instead, a forced marriage places additional burdens on a relationship. The emotional and financial strains on the couple may compound any difficulties they have adjusting to marriage. If the couple faces too many

9-9

José Nieto

Marriage requires many adjustments when a baby is a part of the picture, but many couples make it work.

problems, they may decide to end the marriage. The rate of divorce among young teen couples who are parents is very high.

Teen parents who decide to marry face many of the same problems as the single teen parent. Handling the living and financial arrangements may force the father to drop out of school to get a job. This cuts off his hope for further education and locks him into lower-paying jobs. If the teen mother decides to work, she will have to find child care. This can be expensive.

The couple's relationship is often strained because of the added responsibilities of parenting. The couple sees their peers having fun. They are suddenly not able to be that carefree. Free time is very rare for young parents.

The couple may be forced to live with either set of parents. A place to live is supplied, but blending these two families may create problems. Parents who supply support may feel they have a right to dictate how the cou-

ple spends time and money. Lack of privacy, sharing housework, and caring for the baby may create clashes between the two families. The couple may feel they are still being treated like children themselves.

Adoption

A single woman who is pregnant may wish to have her baby adopted by a couple who are unable to have children of their own. A pregnant woman can work with an adoption agency or arrange for an independent adoption (legal in most states).

In an *agency adoption,* the birthparents (biological mother and father) relinquish their child to the adoption agency rather than directly to adoptive parents. The agency then places the child with a carefully selected adoptive family. A counselor is available to help the mother look at her options and think through her concerns. A counselor will listen and answer questions. The woman will not be forced into any decision that she does not feel is right for her. The counselor can assist the woman in finding a place to live if she does not wish to remain in her family home. She might want to live in a home with other pregnant women, 9-10. She may wish to stay in a private home and earn her board and extra income. The counselor can also advise her on medical care and financial support.

After the baby is born, the birthparents sign a relinquishment paper. This paper releases the baby to the adoption agency. The baby may stay briefly in a foster home until the final papers are signed by both the mother and father, if the father is identified.

In an *independent adoption,* the birthparents go through the legal process of placing their baby directly with adoptive parents. They may actually select the adoptive family. Sometimes the baby is placed with relatives or friends, or a family doctor or lawyer may know a couple wishing to adopt. In this type of adoption, it is important to have a lawyer assist with the legal matters.

Agency and independent adoptions may be either open or closed. In an *open adoption*, the birthparents and adoptive parents meet or know each other. In some cases, arrangements are made for continued contact with the child by the birthparents. In a *closed adoption*, the birthparents do not meet or know the adoptive parents. Laws concerning these types of adoptions vary from state to state.

In most adoption cases, the baby is placed with the adoptive parents soon after birth. The child's original birth certificate is placed under court seal. A new certificate is issued which names the adoptive parents as the child's parents. The birthparents have to sign papers to legalize the adoption. Once the papers are signed, the birthparents cannot ask to have their child returned to them.

Adoption is not an option chosen by many pregnant teens, but this may be due to a lack of information concerning the adoption process.

Some teens criticize their peers as being selfish and uncaring if they consider adoption as an option. They might say, "How could she give her baby away?" However, plac-

9-10

United Way of Houston

Special homes provide single, pregnant women a place to live until their babies are born.

ing a baby in an adoptive home is putting the welfare of the baby first. Sometimes young teens cannot provide the best home for a child at this time in their lives. Choosing a family to parent a child is NOT being selfish and uncaring. It is putting the welfare of the baby above oneself.

The need to find the best answer for loving and caring support of the baby may lead an increasing number of pregnant women to consider adoption. Today less than five percent of pregnant women arrange for an adoption for their babies.

Ending a Pregnancy

Willfully ending a pregnancy is an emotional issue for many people. As a teen, you should be aware of the ethical and legal issues involved as the debate on abortion continues. The following outlines the history of abortion in our society.

A 1973 decision by the U.S. supreme court established a woman's legal right to an abortion. An abortion is the removal of an undeveloped embryo or fetus from a woman's uterus. Abortions are generally performed to end a pregnancy that would harm a woman or a pregnancy in which the embryo is severely damaged.

In 1989, the supreme court gave the individual states the right to set their own regulations. These include parental consent or notification, waiting periods, and certain required medical backup procedures. The ruling opened the way for state legislatures to pass laws that could limit access to abortion in their states. Thus, laws concerning abortion vary from state to state.

Women of various ages, races, religions, and social classes choose abortions. A decision about abortion should be made by the individual only after seeking the best counsel available from religious leaders, parents, doctors, and counselors. Abortion is considered in cases of rape or incest or when the physical or mental health of the woman is in jeopardy. In some cases, the normality of the future child is in doubt. Some women consider abortion because they are unable to care for a child.

Despite its legalization, the topic of abortion is still debated. Those against abortion say that a human life is present from conception and that it should be protected. Those in favor of the right to choose abortion say that an embryo is not yet a human life. They say that a woman has the right to decide what she will do with her body. They also point out that every child born should have the right to be wanted by loving parents.

Before 1973, abortions were illegal, but as many as one million women had abortions each year anyway. Such illegal abortions were often performed under nonsterile conditions and by unskilled persons. As a result, the operations were dangerous. When abortions are legal, they are performed under sterile conditions by skilled physicians.

When an abortion is performed during the first 12 weeks of pregnancy, the operation is usually safe. However, some complications may occur such as infection, hemorrhage, perforation of the uterus, and laceration of the cervix. These complications occur more frequently in young women pregnant for the first time. Serious complications can result in sterility (the inability to reproduce).

Abortions should not be used as a method of birth control. Couples who do not wish a pregnancy should be careful to prevent conception. In making a decision, all aspects of abortion should be considered by the woman.

Sexually Transmitted Diseases

One of the most serious consequences of certain lifestyle decisions can affect not only a person's health, but life itself. For women, the life and well-being of any unborn children may also be affected. This very serious consequence is that of contracting a sexually transmitted disease (STD).

Sexually transmitted diseases are illnesses spread by sexual contact. There are no effective vaccines for immunization against STDs, nor is it true that once you have been cured of an STD you cannot get it again. Some potential sexual partners may not know they have an STD. Others will be reluctant to tell you. Every time you have sexual contact without knowing the health of the other person, you are running the risk of getting an STD.

Most people who contract STDs are between the ages of 15 and 25. Unfortunately, young women, in addition to bearing the major part of the burden associated with an unplanned pregnancy, are also at a biologically greater risk for STDs.

Anyone, at any age, can have one or more STDs. Although there are many kinds of sexually transmitted diseases, AIDS, gonorrhea, syphilis, herpes, genital warts, and chlamydia are the most common.

AIDS (Acquired Immune Deficiency Syndrome)

AIDS stands for Acquired Immune Deficiency Syndrome. This condition is caused by a virus called *HIV* (human immunodeficiency virus). AIDS develops when this virus attacks the immune system of the body, creating a weakness to infections. Many of the diseases that destroy the health of people with AIDS are called *opportunistic infections*. These are infections that would not harm a body with a healthy immune system. The resulting disease takes advantage of the weakness in the body caused by the virus. Even a simple cold could lead to a life-threatening illness.

AIDS is primarily a sexually transmitted disease, but it can be spread in other ways. Many cases can be traced to intravenous (IV) drug use. Some babies contract the disease while in the mother's womb or through breastfeeding by infected mothers. Some early cases of AIDS in the United States resulted from transfusions of contaminated blood. The risk of receiving contaminated blood has been reduced sharply by routine screening procedures for blood and blood donors. However, contaminated blood is still a problem in many less developed countries.

HIV is spread through contact with certain body fluids—primarily semen, blood, and vaginal secretions. The virus has also been detected in saliva and tears. Among intravenous drug users, the virus spreads by the sharing of contaminated equipment.

According to the national Centers for Disease Control and Prevention, there is no evidence that AIDS is spread through the air, by insects, or through casual contact such as hugging or a handshake. A person cannot contract HIV by donating blood.

HIV is contracted by people because of their behaviors. Intravenous drug users are at high risk. Homosexual or bisexual males have a high risk factor. Heterosexuals who have sex with people who have HIV are also at risk.

Infection with HIV is spreading among teenagers. From 1990 to 1992, the number of teens diagnosed with AIDS nearly doubled. Today, people in their 20s account for one out of every five AIDS cases in the United States. Many of these people were infected during their teen years. The HIV virus can exist in the body for years before symptoms of AIDS appear. AIDS may occur anytime from six months to five or more years after infection. This is why teens may mistakenly believe they are not vulnerable.

Blood tests have been developed to detect antibodies to the HIV virus. The immune system creates antibodies to fight viruses such as HIV. These antibodies may not be detected for several months after HIV infection. Researchers believe that all or almost all people who test positive for HIV will actually develop AIDS. AIDS is diagnosed only after a person's immune system has been overwhelmed by another disease. As the disease progresses, the inability of the body to fight the infection, such as tuberculosis or pneumonia, becomes life threatening.

The risk of contracting AIDS is one of the biggest health concerns of our time. The risk is greatest for those who have multiple sexual partners, although one sexual encounter can pass the disease. The more partners a person has and the less he or she knows about their sexual history, the greater the chance of coming into contact with HIV.

There is currently no effective vaccine to prevent AIDS, nor is there a cure for AIDS. The careful use of latex condoms will reduce the possibility of spreading the virus, but condoms are not 100 percent effective. Relying on a condom for protection against a disease that is 100 percent fatal is making a poor choice. No other methods of birth control provide any protection from HIV. The most effective way to avoid contracting AIDS through sexual contact is to abstain from sexual activity outside of marriage.

Gonorrhea

Gonorrhea is commonly called "clap," a "dose," or the "drips." The first symptoms usually occur in the lining of the genital and urinary tracts. Two to eight days after exposure, the infected person may notice a pus discharge or dripping from the sexual organ and may experience pain during urination. However, many women and some men have no noticeable symptoms of early infection.

If a man receives no treatment or insufficient treatment, the urethra (the canal carrying urine outside the body from the bladder) may become blocked. When this happens, the urethra has to be mechanically stretched to permit urination. Gonorrhea may also cause sterility as the infection spreads to the tubes that carry sperm from the testes.

If a woman receives no treatment or insufficient treatment, the bacteria may spread up the reproductive tract and cause a painful infection. Sterility may occur if the infection advances and causes scar tissue to block the tubes that carry eggs from the ovaries to the uterus. Pregnant women with gonorrhea are likely to have spontaneous abortions or babies who are premature or stillborn. If a baby is carried to full term, it may acquire a potentially blinding eye infection as it passes through the infected birth canal of the mother. To prevent this and other eye infections, all babies born in hospitals are treated promptly with medicated eyedrops.

In addition to the symptoms mentioned above, gonorrhea can cause heart disease, crippling arthritis, and blindness in both men and women.

Treatment for gonorrhea consists of injections of specific dosages of penicillin or similar antibiotics. Treatments vary for different forms and stages of the infection. Although gonorrhea can be cured at any stage, the damage that the disease has already done cannot be undone.

Syphilis

Syphilis is sometimes called "siff," "bad blood," or "pox." The first symptom of syphilis appears 10 to 90 days after exposure. A small, firm sore or *chancre* (pronounced

SHANG-ker) develops at the site of infection. The chancre may resemble a bad pimple or cold sore and thus be ignored. The chancre disappears within three to five weeks even without treatment. This leads many to believe the disease is cured, but it is not.

The second stage of syphilis begins 2–12 weeks after the chancre disappears. A rash develops that may cover the entire body or only the hands or feet. The victim may feel tired, lose some hair, and have a fever, headaches, and mouth sores. These symptoms also may be overlooked or diagnosed as something else.

After the second stage of syphilis, some untreated people are spontaneously cured. Some others, although not cured, never have further evidence of disease. The majority of untreated people go through two more stages—latent syphilis and late syphilis.

Latent syphilis begins when all the symptoms of the second stage have disappeared. It continues for an indefinite length of time, sometimes as long as 25 years. During this time, the victim is no longer infectious to others. (An exception is a pregnant woman who may transmit her disease to her unborn child.)

Unfortunately, a sure diagnosis of latent syphilis cannot be made. Eventually, the victim enters the final stage, or *late syphilis.* The bacteria begin to damage the heart, brain, or spinal cord. Mental illness, blindness, paralysis, heart disease, and eventually death may result.

Syphilis can be detected and diagnosed by a blood test during most stages. Injections of antibiotics are used to treat the disease in any of the stages.

Herpes

Herpes occurs in different forms, and not every form is an STD. The form of herpes that is an STD is known by many different names. It may be called herpes simplex virus type 2 (HSV-2), herpes II, or genital herpes. Because this virus has spread across the country so quickly, it has received lots of publicity. New reports that mention "herpes" are usually referring to genital herpes.

Symptoms of genital herpes usually show up 2–20 days after contact. Blisters appear on a man's penis or in and around a woman's vagina. They disappear in a week or two, but they may reappear later. There is no cure for the herpes virus. It stays in the body and typically flares up at irregular intervals. Although there is no cure, people with genital herpes should seek medical attention. Medication can lessen the severity of the first attack and may be helpful for people with frequent outbreaks.

A woman with an active case of genital herpes may infect her baby during delivery. If the infection is severe, the baby may not survive. If the baby does survive, the infection usually causes physical and/or mental damage. The doctor of a woman with genital herpes may recommend a cesarean delivery so the baby does not have to pass through the infected birth canal.

Genital Warts

Genital warts are caused by a virus and spread by sexual contact. The virus has a long incubation period, so the symptoms may appear six weeks to eight months after exposure. They show up as small, flat or raised warts in the genital area. Sometimes the virus is present in normal-looking skin. Sometimes it is hidden from view on a woman's cervix or in the vagina.

Genital warts may enlarge and spread. They are contagious, and they may be transmitted during childbirth. Growing evidence links certain strains of the virus to cancer of the cervix and vulva. Genital warts can be treated and removed, but they may recur.

Chlamydia

One of the most widespread STDs is *chlamydia* (pronounced cla-MID-ee-a). It can be cured with antibiotics when detected, but detection may be difficult. Most of the men and women who are infected do not have any symptoms. They can carry the infection for years without knowing it.

If symptoms appear, they do so from one to five weeks after contact. Men may notice a watery or milky discharge from the penis and painful urination. Women may notice abnormal discharge or bleeding from the vagina, pelvic pain, and fever. Women may also have painful urination, blood in the urine, and a frequent urge to urinate.

Chlamydia is a major cause of urinary tract infections in both men and women. It also infects the male and female reproductive tracts. Women may develop pelvic inflammatory disease (PID), which can lead to infertility. Infants born to mothers with chlamydia may develop serious eye infections and pneumonia. Women who are sexually active should be tested for chlamydia annually.

Sexually transmitted diseases should not be taken lightly. If a person suspects the possibility of having such a disease, he or she should seek help immediately. See a family physician or go to a community health clinic where the treatment is usually free. Under no circumstances should a person try self-diagnosis or self-treatment. If a person is found to be infected, he or she should contact anyone with whom sexual intimacy has occurred so that these former partners can seek medical help. Try to prevent any further spread of the disease.

Responsible Behavior

You learned earlier in this chapter that your lifestyle is the set of behaviors you choose to make your own. Your behavior, as you live your life, identifies your lifestyle. For the most part, you are free to choose your behavior in every aspect of your life. You have not always had a choice concerning the circumstances surrounding your life. However, you do have choices in what you do with your life in the future. You have choices when deciding how responsible you will be for your actions, 9-11.

In this chapter you have read about the various lifestyle options. You have also learned of some lifestyle consequences that you need to be aware of as you make decisions about your life. Responsible behavior on your part can help make the difference between a lifetime of challenges or a lifetime of rewards.

Cholla Runnels

9-11
The majority of teenagers act responsibly in their relationships, controlling their emotions and safeguarding their health.

Abstinence, not having sexual intercourse, is the only guaranteed effective means of preventing an unplanned pregnancy. Other birth control methods are not 100 percent effective. Any woman who is sexually active runs the risk of becoming pregnant.

Abstinence is the most effective means of avoiding sexually transmitted diseases. Teens are given "safe sex" messages promoting the use of condoms. However, using condoms does not guarantee that sex will be safe. A latex condom, used properly, can provide a degree of protection from STDs and is preferable to no protection at all. AIDS is ultimately fatal, often following a period of debilitating illness. You can see the risks of promoting the use of condoms to prevent a disease that kills.

Teens must realize the consequences of sexual activity. By learning to show affection in nonsexual ways, couples can enjoy being together without feeling anxious about their health and life. There is promise for those teens who are willing to accept responsibility for their own behavior choices concerning their lifestyle.

Summary ■ ■ ■ ■ ■ ■ ■ ■ ■ ■ ■ ■ ■ ■ ■

- Decisions you make about your lifestyle can have both positive and negative consequences for your health, your sense of worth, your relationships, and your long-range goals.

- Most people will experience living as a single person at some time in their lives, either by choice or by circumstance.

- Marriage can offer two people a rewarding relationship, fulfilling their needs for love, affection, respect, recognition, and intimacy. One of the basic strengths of marriage is the setting it provides for raising children. However, many couples prefer not to have children.

- Couples who choose the lifestyle of living together are penalized in several ways by existing laws. People choosing this lifestyle should be aware of these problems.

- Irresponsible lifestyle choices may result in an unplanned pregnancy. Reasons given for why such pregnancies occur are a risk-taking attitude, inaccurate information about human reproduction, a pattern of sexual activity, a more accepting attitude toward such pregnancies, and a desire to improve self-esteem.

- Pregnant teens and their offspring are at risk physically, educationally, financially, and socially. Young fathers are at risk educationally, financially, and socially.

- Those faced with a premarital pregnancy may select from the limited alternatives of single parenting, marriage, adoption, or abortion. Alternatives must be carefully considered in making this very difficult decision.

■ Sexually transmitted diseases are a serious consequence of sexual activity. A person's health and life are at risk, as well as the health and life of a woman's offspring.

■ The most common STDs are AIDS, gonorrhea, syphilis, herpes, genital warts, and chlamydia.

■ HIV breaks down the immune system, leaving the body vulnerable to AIDS. The weakened body easily succumbs to opportunistic infections.

■ Abstinence is the only guaranteed effective means of preventing an unplanned pregnancy. It is also the most effective means of avoiding STDs.

To Review ■ ■ ■ ■ ■ ■ ■ ■ ■ ■ ■ ■ ■ ■ ■ ■

1. Lifestyle is defined as a set of _____ adopted by personal _____.

2. Describe three reasons or circumstances why some people live a single lifestyle.

3. True or False. The percentage of married-couple households in the United States is increasing.

4. Cite three reasons why a couple may choose not to have children.

5. Name five ways our existing laws penalize a couple who decide to live together without being married.

6. Describe two physical problems that can occur when teenage girls become pregnant.

7. Describe three decisions a single parent must make.

8. True or False. Today, more pregnant teens choose to marry the father than in past years.

9. Explain the difference between an open and a closed adoption.

10. Why is arranging for an adoption NOT a selfish act for a pregnant teen?

11. True or False. If people use condoms, they will NOT get AIDS.

12. Why are cesarean deliveries sometimes performed on mothers with genital herpes?

13. What can happen in late syphilis if the disease was not treated earlier?

To Do ■ ■ ■ ■ ■ ■ ■ ■ ■ ■ ■ ■ ■ ■ ■ ■

1. Ask three persons representing the single lifestyle to speak to your class about the pros and cons of this lifestyle. Try to select a man in his late 20s, a career woman in her early 30s, a divorced person, and a widow or widower.

2. Accept or reject the following statement: "A lifestyle of marriage provides the most fulfilling relationship between a man and a woman." Support your answer.

3. Ask a family law attorney to come to class and discuss the legalities of living together. Prepare questions in advance concerning financial responsibilities, inheritance rights, property rights, and other legal issues.

4. Ask a social worker to speak to your class about the problem of teenage pregnancy in your area. Have the speaker describe the resources available in your community to assist teen mothers.

5. Have a panel of male students from the class discuss child care and support from a young father's point of view. Ask how they would feel if, as fathers, they were not allowed to be involved in providing for their children.

6. Invite an obstetrician to class to discuss the risks of teenage pregnancy.

7. Ask an adoption agency representative to speak on the topic of adoption as an option for pregnant teens. Ask the speaker to describe a typical adoption plan.

8. Assign students to research the availability of adoption in your community. Cite different resources, types available, and costs.

9. Role-play a situation in which a teenage girl announces that she is pregnant. Consider the emotions of the girl, her mother, her father, her boyfriend, her boyfriend's mother, and her boyfriend's father.

10. Ask a physician to speak to the class about sexually transmitted diseases.

11. Write a paper on how AIDS can impact the life of a young person.

12. Research the resources available to help people who think they may have a sexually transmitted disease.

13. Set up a panel discussion of students to debate the topic of responsible choices concerning lifestyle options.

III

Getting Along with Others

10.....

Communicating with Others

Terms to Know

communication

verbal
 communication

nonverbal
 communication

active listening

feedback

passive listening

empathy

body language

assertive

clique

bullying

conflict resolution

mediator

sexual harassment

**After studying this chapter,
you will be able to**

- recognize the many ways you communicate with others.

- evaluate the importance of good listening skills.

- judge the importance of communicating a positive image of yourself to others.

- identify five levels of communication.

- describe assertive behavior and its effect on communication.

- analyze communication skills that work well with parents.

- describe group behaviors that involve violence.

- define sexual harassment.

Communication is very important in getting along with others. You need to be aware of all of the forms and levels of communication and how best to use them. We all think we know how to communicate, but there are obviously problems. Poor communication accounts for many misunderstandings among friends, among family members, and even among nations.

What Is Communication?

Communication is any means by which you share a message with another person. You may use either words or gestures, or combine them, 10-1. You may choose to write your message.

You are a part of the "communication generation" with access to many new forms of communication technology. For instance, modems allow you to send and receive

Cholla Runnels

10-1
A father and son communicate in many ways. A simple gesture can communicate love and affection.

information through computers. Fax machines can transmit and receive pictures as well as words. Cellular telephones are completely mobile so you can communicate from virtually any location. Even full-color videophones are available. Small new portable devices called personal communicators allow people to make calls, send faxes, take notes, and send handwritten messages using a special pen instead of a keyboard. New technology is changing our means of communicating every day. However, even with all the technology, you have to be able to communicate your message in a clear, concise manner that is easily understood.

Communication involves a sender and a receiver. The *sender* transmits the message in a variety of ways. The *receiver* hears and interprets the message. A message may be hard to understand if the sender does not send clear, accurate, and complete messages. The receiver needs skills in listening and interpreting the message, 10-2.

Forms of Communication ■ ■ ■ ■

There are two ways people communicate. They use either verbal or nonverbal communication. **Verbal communication** uses words to send and receive messages. Any time you use words to communicate, you are using a form of verbal communication. When you write a letter or a term paper, you are using verbal communication. When you speak in front of your class, you are using verbal communication.

Nonverbal communication uses factors other than words, such as gestures, facial expressions, eye contact, and body movements. Nonverbal communication is effective in sending messages even though you do not use words. You may not always be aware of the nonverbal messages you are sending, but those around you may still receive nonverbal messages from you.

Listening

Your skill in listening is as important as your skill in sending messages. Both are equally important.

Cholla Runnels

10-2
For good communication, people must be willing to both send and receive messages.

The way you listen affects the quality of conversation. Listeners can lead others into deeper communication. As a good listener, you can indicate to the sender that you heard the message and you understand. You may nod, smile, or make eye contact that indicates you have received the message. You may even say, "I see." This is *active listening.* It encourages further communication.

Feedback is communicating to the other person how you feel about what was said. The sender knows you listened because you are responding. People feel good when they know you really listened to what they said, even if you disagree.

The opposite of active listening is *passive listening.* A passive listener simply takes in the words and offers no sign of hearing or understanding the message. The sender gets the message that it isn't worth trying to continue the conversation. Further communication is likely to be cut off.

Careless listeners pick out bits and pieces of conversation and don't listen to the rest. This selective listening often causes them to take words out of context. *Narrow listeners*

Cholla Runnels

10-3
Defensive listeners read meanings into what is being said and feel they are being attacked.

hear only what they want to hear. They tune out anything that does not fit in with their preconceived notions. *Defensive listeners* read meanings into what is being said, 10-3. They have negative feelings about conversations because they feel they are being attacked.

Listening is a skill that you can develop. If there seems to be a misunderstanding, it is helpful to repeat what you heard. This allows the sender to clarify the message. It is also important to listen to the entire message and to keep your mind open to all ideas.

Empathy

A key word in good communication skills is empathy. **Empathy** is the process of seeing things from another person's view. When you empathize with someone, you understand how that person feels and why, without sharing those feelings at the same time.

Empathy differs from sympathy, but both have Greek origins. Em (Greek for in) and pathos (Greek for feeling) combine to form the word empathy. This means, "I know how you feel. I have been sad or angry in the past and know what you are going through." Sym (Greek for with) and pathos are the roots for the word sympathy. This means, "I feel as you do. You are sad and I am sad, too. You are angry, and I share your feeling of anger."

Sympathy is sometimes resented: "How can you be sad? I am the one who has lost a brother!" Empathy is more likely to be appreciated and helpful. This assures more open communication and a better understanding of other people.

Nonverbal Communication

Each of you sends messages through your facial expressions, body motions, and the use of the space around you. This is nonverbal communication—sending messages without using words. Pantomimes and silent movies are fun to watch. Even without spoken words, the messages are very clear.

Body Language Communicates

Body language is a form of nonverbal communication. You reveal some of your inner feelings through your use of body lan-

David Hopper

10-4
Some people "steeple" their hands when they feel they are in control of a situation.

guage. For instance, drumming your fingers and swinging your leg may be signs of tension. Smiling and nodding your head may indicate enthusiasm. Steepling your fingers may suggest that you feel you have authority and are in control of a situation, 10-4.

You can express either positive or negative emotions through body movements. If you remain in face-to-face contact with some-

one, you indicate your desire to communicate. If you turn your body, move farther away, or fold your arms across your chest, you may be setting up barriers to communication. See 10-5.

In a group meeting, people often imitate each other so the entire group sits in the same way. A person who wants to assume a higher status may shift to a different position.

The use of hands and arms to emphasize speech allows people to "read" each other

Cholla Runnels

10-5
By crossing your arms, you may set up barriers to continuing communication.

Cholla Runnels

10-6

Gestures may help people communicate their messages more clearly.

more clearly. An example of this is shown in 10-6. Another form of body language is the use of facial expressions. The students in 10-7 are communicating their lack of enthusiasm to their teacher.

Eye contact is yet another way of expressing yourself. Many people claim they can "read" others by eye contact alone. In peak communication, eye contact is maintained continually. Sometimes our eyes expose our true feelings, even when we are saying something else. When we break eye contact, we may be indicating that we want to stop verbal contact as well.

Cholla Runnels

10-7

How would you react, as a teacher, to a classroom full of students with facial expressions like these?

Your Appearance Communicates

People form both first impressions and lasting images of you according to the way you look. This, too, is a form of nonverbal communication. If you want to create a good impression, you should project a positive image, 10-8. This is especially important in job interviews. Not everyone is beautiful or handsome, but everyone can be well-groomed.

Your Grooming

Good grooming habits help you show that you care about yourself and about other people's opinions of you. Clean hair that is properly cut and shaped will enhance your total appearance. Hands that are clean and smooth and fingernails that are neatly trimmed will also help you create a good impression.

Cleanliness and good grooming habits will be essential throughout your life. They will help you achieve success both personally and professionally. Your family and friends judge your appearance now. In the future, your appearance will be judged by your employer, fellow workers, and customers. Employers have the right to demand certain standards of grooming as they evaluate job applicants. They are selling a product or a service, and the people they hire must reflect a positive image.

Your Clothing

There is a saying that "clothes make the person." This is because people often judge you according to the clothes you wear. Different clothes create different impressions. Consider the following—evening gowns, jeans, swimsuits, business suits, and military uniforms. Each type of garment brings a differ-

ent image to mind. Likewise, the clothes you wear help create your image.

Both men and women can enhance their appearance by wearing appropriate clothes for their figure and personality type. This does not mean that they need large, expensive wardrobes. They just need clothes that help them look attractive, make them feel comfortable, and help them express the image they want to portray.

Proper care of clothing is equally important. Even good quality clothes will create a poor impression if they are soiled or wrinkled. Hang or fold garments so they will retain their shape. Use proper laundry and cleaning methods. Press garments well.

David Hopper

10-8
Looking clean, neat, and attractive helps you communicate a positive image of yourself to other people.

Contemporary Topics *of interest to teens:*
Communicating Socially

Have you ever felt uneasy when you were eating dinner in a restaurant or when a friend wanted you to meet his or her parents? Knowing what to do in social situations will help you enjoy them more and can improve your feeling of self-esteem. Feeling comfortable when you are in a new situation, such as a job interview, also helps you communicate more effectively. Rules of etiquette are meant to make situations pleasant for others and for yourself. Using proper etiquette shows you care enough about others to behave in a thoughtful and courteous manner. Using the following rules of etiquette will help you feel comfortable in most social situations.

Introductions

When making introductions, always mention the name of the *key* person first. Key people, or those whom you want to honor, include: women over men, older over younger, host over guest, and senior-level job title over junior-level title. For instance, if you were introducing your parents to your teacher at school, the teacher would be the key person. You would say, "Mrs. Jackson, I would like you to meet my parents, Mr. and Mrs. Ortez." If Mrs. Jackson were visiting your home, your parents would be the key people. You would say, "Mother and Dad, I would like you to meet my teacher, Mrs. Jackson." This simple rule—key person first—will help you make your introductions with ease.

Shaking Hands

Shaking hands is a symbol of friendship today. In years past, it was done to show the person you were greeting that you had no concealed weapon in your hand. A woman usually extends her hand first if she is being introduced. In job interviews, it is a nice gesture to extend your hand and thank the employer for taking the time to interview you. A good, firm (but not crushing) handshake can be a positive gesture that may help you get the job.

Phone Calls

You should limit the length of your calls, especially if you know that other people have to use the phone. If you are calling to ask for a date, make your purpose clear. Don't just ask, "What are you doing Saturday night?" Instead, state the occasion and the time. For instance, you might say, "There is a football game Friday night, and a dance afterward. Would you like to go with me?" This clear communication gives the other person the information needed to respond. It also prevents the guessing game that makes people feel uncomfortable.

At the Table

The placement of flatware (knives, forks, and spoons) confuses some people, but the rules are quite simple. Knives and spoons are on the right of the plate, forks on the left. When you begin eating, use the outside pieces of flatware first. For example, suppose a meal began with soup. You would find the soup spoon at the extreme right. Suppose salad were served next. The salad fork would be at the extreme left. Flatware for the main course would be toward the middle, closer to the plate. Occasionally, dessert silver is placed crosswise at the top of the plate.

Once you have used a piece of flatware, do not place it back on the tablecloth. Place it on the plate instead. Napkins are usually placed to the left of the forks, unless they have been folded and placed in a special manner. Napkins should not be tucked into your collar unless a special type of service is being used, such as for lobster or barbecued foods. When finished, fold the napkin loosely and place it on the table to the left of the plate.

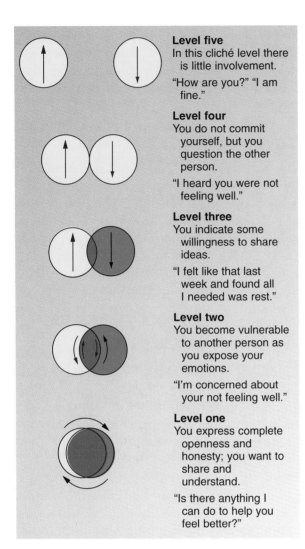

Level five
In this cliché level there is little involvement.

"How are you?" "I am fine."

Level four
You do not commit yourself, but you question the other person.

"I heard you were not feeling well."

Level three
You indicate some willingness to share ideas.

"I felt like that last week and found all I needed was rest."

Level two
You become vulnerable to another person as you expose your emotions.

"I'm concerned about your not feeling well."

Level one
You express complete openness and honesty; you want to share and understand.

"Is there anything I can do to help you feel better?"

10-9
Levels of communication vary according to how openly you reveal your inner self.

Teens today like to express themselves in the clothing they choose. They also like to "fit in," so they often choose the same clothing styles that everyone else seems to be wearing. These items may not always be considered appropriate by parents and school officials.

Some schools have established dress codes to discourage the wearing of certain items of clothing. An item of clothing may not be allowed in a school if it causes a substantial disruption in the work and discipline of the school. The school environment is a place for learning, and offensive clothing can create problems and unnecessary distractions. Teens like to express their feelings, but the feelings of others need to be considered also.

Clothing selection is one way to create an image of who you are. Ideally, you will want that image to be pleasing to yourself as well as to others.

Your Posture

Your posture is a clue to your personality. If you slump your shoulders, bow your head, and keep your eyes on the floor, you give the impression of wanting to go unnoticed. If you lift your chin, square your shoulders, and walk with pride, others will see that you are full of vitality.

Posture in movement, as well as in sitting and standing, can communicate your self-confidence. When you are walking down the hall at school, when you are dating, or when you are on an interview, your posture gives others an insight into your character. If you appear self-confident, you will feel more self-confident, and you will communicate that feeling to others.

Levels of Communication

Communication can be achieved on five different levels as shown in 10-9. Each level varies with your desire to expose yourself to another person. Few people reach peak communication with many different people.

Level Five

The weakest level of communication is level five. It is often called the cliché level. You often communicate words with little meaning behind them. You do not allow yourself to become very involved. A common exchange at this level is, "How are you?" "I am fine."

Level Four

In level four, you draw out very little from others or from yourself. You may be willing to tell what others have said or done, but you will not invest any of yourself in the conversation. You may say, "I heard you were not feeling well," but you add nothing about your concern for the person.

Level Three

You show some willingness in level three to share your ideas or judgments with another person. Usually you reveal some of your ideas, but you carefully restrict them until you test the reactions of the listener. If you sense any doubt, you refuse to expose yourself further. You may say, "I felt like that last week, and I found that all I needed was rest." If the other person says, "That's all right for some, but I can't rest," you will probably not involve yourself any further. However, the person may respond by asking, "Did the rest really help you?" In that case, you might be willing to go into more depth.

Level Two

In level two, you are becoming increasingly open to another person as you expose more of your feelings and emotions. You have a strong desire to let someone else know how you think and feel. You are completely honest; you do not judge the other person. The statements, "I think physical fitness is impor-tant for everyone. I'd like to start an exercise club in my neighborhood," may reveal a great deal about you. Such statements may also open the door to further and deeper communication.

Level One

On level one, complete openness and honesty exist between two people, 10-10. They accept each other for what they really are. They have the courage to reveal their deepest thoughts and feelings to each other. Each wants to understand how the other person feels and why. This is the real sharing that is needed for total communication.

Assertiveness in Communication ■ ■ ■ ■

To be *assertive* means to express your feelings directly, to ask for what you want, and to refuse what you don't want. When you are assertive, you are sure and confident. You re-

David Hopper

10-10
Level one is peak communication, in which both communicators desire complete sharing and understanding of feelings and emotions.

spect yourself and others. You treat the people around you fairly and honestly.

Assertiveness is not the same as aggressiveness. Aggressive behavior is forceful, hostile, or destructive. It involves putting another person down. Assertiveness is positive. Aggression is negative.

Passive behavior is simply observing and not becoming emotionally involved. It is literally doing nothing. Passive behavior can be negative as well.

Learning to be assertive helps teenagers communicate effectively. It helps them relate to other people in positive ways. It helps them reach their goals and thus to feel good about themselves.

When you learn to be assertive, you will be able to

- express your feelings honestly.

- say no without feeling guilty or apologetic.

- stand up for your own beliefs without attacking the beliefs of others.

10-11
If you are assertive, you make your wishes known to the group in a respectful manner.

- express yourself without trying to put others down.

- admit your anger and express it directly to the appropriate person—without physical or verbal abuse.

If you are assertive, you will be able to work actively and openly to get what you want, 10-11. You will be straightforward and yet show respect to others. Your peers, your family, and those with whom you work will feel that they have been treated fairly and honestly.

Using I-messages, You-messages, and We-messages

When you communicate with others it is important to send clear messages. "I-messages" help. I-messages are not accusing or belittling. By using an I-message, you take responsibility for how you feel. Such messages are less threatening and help keep communication open between people. You will discover your communication with others will improve when you start your message with "I." You are stating how you feel, and not blaming someone else for how you feel.

"You-messages" are often used, but they tend to be more negative than I-messages. You-messages may actually create an adversarial confrontation when you didn't mean to do so at all. You-messages are accusing and belittling. They criticize the other person, and they place blame on others for how you feel. For instance, suppose you are sharing a room with a brother or sister who refuses to help keep it clean. Using a you-message, you might say, "You are so messy. You never pick anything up!" With an I-message, you might say instead, "I'm upset because you have not

You-messages	I-messages
Ordering, commanding "You have to help me."	**Seeking cooperation** "I would appreciate your help."
Warning, threatening "You had better do it this way or else."	**Suggesting** "I would suggest that you do it this way."
Judging "You are always late."	**Praising** "I know you will be on time because it is important to you."
Accusing "You lied to me!"	**Advising** "I feel there is a misunderstanding."
Demanding "You have to be there on time."	**Persuading** "I would like you to be there on time."
Blaming "You didn't get up in time—that is why you were late."	**Reassuring** "I realize it will be difficult, but I know you will try to be there on time."

10-12

You can see from this comparison how I-messages are more likely to bring about
positive feelings and actions than you-messages.

picked up your things like you agreed to do." Using I-messages allows you to state your feelings and the reasons for your feelings. You are likely to get more cooperation using this approach. I-messages and you-messages are compared in 10-12.

As a teen, you can learn to use I-statements in your relationships with your parents. You may help communication in your family if you use I-statements. For instance, you may wish your parents would trust you by extending more privileges to you. Your parents may feel the rules they have set should stay in place. If you use a you-statement, you would be blaming your parents for being too rigid. "You are too rigid. You have a rule for everything!" If you use an I-statement, you are stating how you feel and why. "I feel as though you don't trust me because there are so many rules. I am not given a chance to show that I can act responsibly." Using this approach, your parents are more likely to listen to your concerns.

"We-statements" offer a further step in improving communication, particularly in families. We-statements define the problem as one that is of mutual concern to several people. An I-statement indicates that an individual has a problem. We-statements indicate that the problem exists in a group or a relationship, such as the family. Two or more people are jointly involved in the situation.

We-statements minimize the individualistic aspects of the problem and emphasize the togetherness aspects. These statements give everyone in the group equal responsibility for solving the problem. One person does not have more responsibility than another. They communicate, "We're in this together." For instance, a family might use the following we-statement: "We need to decide what we are going to do over the holidays." Each family member may have different ideas as to how the problem should be solved, but all members' wishes should be considered in the final decision.

I- and we-messages can help people improve their communication patterns with their friends, family members, or dating partners. Most people are not very cooperative when they feel they are being criticized or accused. Since I- and we-messages are less threatening than you-messages, they help keep communication lines open for further discussion.

Communicating with Parents

Communication problems between teens and their parents are widely publicized. Some families have more problems than others. When conflicts do occur, they are often the result of teens trying to establish independence and parents expressing concern for their children's welfare.

Communication Problems of Teens and Parents

Many young people complain, "My parents don't trust me. They won't let me do anything." This lack of trust may have resulted from their failure to fulfill small responsibilities. If teens have demonstrated that they cannot be trusted to fulfill minor tasks, parents will doubt their ability to handle larger responsibilities. Trust is a privilege that must be earned. When teens show their parents they can be trusted, they will win their parents' encouragement and support, 10-13.

Some parents say, "I'll never understand young people today!" Their children reply, "My parents don't understand the problems I face!"

Parents often enter parenthood with very little understanding of what is required to develop and maintain good relationships with their children. To make the problem worse, attitudes are changing quickly in today's fast-paced world. There may be large differences between the attitudes of parents and their children. Some parents even notice differences between the attitudes of their older and younger children who may be separated by only a few years. As culture and attitudes change, the need for good communication between parents and teens grows even greater.

Privacy is a basic need for teenagers, but sometimes the way they communicate this need creates problems in families. If you want more privacy, show your family that you deserve it. One way to do this is to stay out of trouble and to be as upfront with your parents as you can be. Another way is to accept the responsibilities that come with the privilege of privacy. This means you don't have the right to set your own lifestyle and

David Hopper

10-13
Young people earn the trust of family members by showing that they can be responsible.

10-14

David Hopper

Everyone needs some privacy to relax, to read, to listen to music, or just to think.

schedule, independent of everyone else in the family. Each family member shares parts of his or her life with others in the family. You may like to sit in your room by yourself, with music playing and the door shut. That's fine, if you aren't disturbing others.

Sometimes you have to find your own privacy. If you share a room with a sibling, you may have to find another place where your privacy will be honored. See 10-14. Remember that your parents and siblings need some privacy, too.

Solving Family Communication Problems

Good communication is important for families. It can help prevent barriers from getting in the way of family and individual goals. The following suggestions may help you solve communication problems with your parents.

Problem: You can't find a good time to talk with your parents. In many families, discussions started in the hour before dinner are more likely to flare up into problems. At this time

of day, roles are shifting, and family members are tired and hungry. The psychological strain creates a poor atmosphere for thoughtful discussions.

Try to approach your parents at a time when they seem to be the most relaxed and free from pressure. Get up 15 minutes early and talk with your parents before breakfast, or bring up the subject after dinner, 10-15. If they cannot talk then, tell them you need to talk with them, and ask them to schedule a time.

Each family handles discussions in its own way. Some families have brief, casual discussions while sharing family chores. Other families prefer the structured atmosphere of a family council. If a heated discussion is apparent, some families stop whatever they are doing to talk it over. Others settle problems by scheduling a discussion at a later time, when they can give their full attention to the issue.

Problem: Your parents ask too many questions. If you resent their probing at certain times, try to understand why they need to ask

Cholla Runnels

10-15

In many families, the best time to discuss important issues is in the kitchen after dinner.

questions. Have you effectively communicated your needs to your parents? Have you reassured them by telling them what you want to do and why? If you remember that they are deeply concerned about your welfare, you will understand that they want to know how you feel, what you need, and what you are doing. Perhaps then you will understand how they feel and the reasons for their questions.

Problem: You are not sure how to approach your parents about a problem you have. You may want to talk first to a third party. This should be a person whom you respect and with whom you can talk freely. Sometimes a family friend, a minister, a school counselor, or a teacher can help you sort out your thoughts. Then when you are ready to talk to your parents, this person may help you open the doors.

You should not feel embarrassed to ask a person you respect for help in reaching a parent. Likewise, parents should not be upset when their child seeks help from a respected third party. If this three-way process can reestablish communication, it will be worth the effort. It also will indicate maturity on your part in working out a method for establishing communication.

A mended line of communication is better than a broken one. You may discover that your parents felt that you were wrestling with some problems, but they were waiting for you to take the first step in seeking their help. Every family can experience voids in communication. A stable family can recover from these voids and reopen communication lines.

Problem: Your parents are upset about your friends. Perhaps your parents have not had a chance to get to know your friends, 10-16. Have you provided your parents with as much information as you can about them? Have you asked if you could bring your friends to your home or tried to arrange a meeting somewhere else? When they have been in

your home, have they respected the wishes of your parents? If you are sincere in your efforts to establish an understanding between your friends and your parents, your parents will probably act favorably.

Most parents realize that it is beneficial for you to evaluate your friends in familiar surroundings. They know that forcing you to make these judgments in secrecy or under strained conditions would be unwise. In your home, or in the company of your parents, you will be able to determine if the friendships really mean a lot to you.

If your parents continue to be negative about a friendship, you should ask yourself if they are right. With their added experience, they may be better judges of character than

David Hopper

10-16
If your parents are unhappy with your choice of friends, maybe they just need a chance to get to know them better.

you are. It is true that the best way to learn is often by experience. However, if there is a good chance that you are moving toward a disastrous situation, your parents would be helping by warning you.

Time helps to settle many conflicts about friends. Given time, either your parents or you may have a change of attitude. If neither side gives in, time will prove who was right, and both sides will learn from the experience.

Problem: You want to be given more control over your life. During the teen years, control is gradually shifting from almost complete control by parents to increasing control by the young adult. During this shift in control, negotiation can be an effective tool. For instance, you may want permission to go somewhere, and your parents are reluctant to grant permission. Negotiation can often resolve the matter. The following steps can be used:

1.   Ask for permission.

2.   If your parents deny you permission, find out their objections.

3.   Propose a compromise that might overcome their objections.

Sheena used this approach with her parents. She wanted permission to attend a party a classmate was having. Sheena's parents said she could not go, so she asked why. Her parents were afraid the party would not be chaperoned. Sheena decided to propose a compromise. She called the friend who was giving the party to make sure it would be chaperoned. She further told her parents that if the party began to get out of hand, Sheena would leave immediately. With this information, Sheena's parents decided to let her attend the party. Sheena was given some control, as well as the chance to prove that she can be responsible for making good decisions.

Further tips for improving family communication are described in 10-17.

How to Improve Family Communication

■   Build a "trust fund." Earn your parents' trust by keeping promises, honoring commitments, and fulfilling responsibilities.

■   Pick a good time to begin a discussion. Parents and teenagers alike have busy schedules, but if you all try, you can find time for a good talk.

■   Indicate your honest wish to talk. Parents may not be aware that you want to talk until you tell them so.

■   Retain a pleasant tone of voice, and avoid critical or sarcastic remarks. Nothing is gained by raising your voice or speaking harshly.

■   Use I-messages rather than you-messages.

■   Know when and how to "throw in the towel." It's important to know when to give up a lost cause and put an end to an argument. You can't expect to get your way all the time.

■   Sometimes it's best to suggest dropping the issue for the time being.

10-17
If your family has good communication patterns, do all you can to maintain them. If they need to be improved, take the initiative to do so.

Group Communication Patterns ■ ■ ■ ■ ■

Most teens enjoy being a part of a group. In fact, some of your fondest memories of your friendships thus far are likely to be connected with group activities. Communicating in a group gives you opportunities for individual expression and group sharing. These

David Hopper

10-18
Young people enjoy group activities during the teen years.

experiences provide for individual growth, and they also give you chances to communicate with a variety of people.

In the teen years, many group activities are centered around social activities. In every school, students sometimes form loosely organized groups just to enjoy being together, 10-18. Good communication enhances the social interactions within any group.

Cliques

Group interaction can be fun when you are in the group. If you are on the outside, wanting to be "in," you may have some sad experiences concerning groups. A *clique* is a narrow, exclusive group of people held together by common interests, views, and purposes. Being excluded from a clique can be a very painful experience.

Wanting to be in a group is a natural part of growing up. Groups can be helpful because they provide support and security, and they give teens a sense of identity. Cliques, however, can often cause hurt feelings. Unfortunately, clique members have a hard time accepting differences among people, and they sometimes go too far in expressing their dislikes. Some snub and criticize anyone who fails to meet all of their predetermined qualifications. Cliques often put pressure on teens to pretend they are something they're not. Often teens think they have to belong to one particular group or their whole life will be worthless.

Wanting to interact with others is normal. However, before joining a group, young people should be sure of what the group has to offer and what it will demand. Young people should concentrate on their own interests and strengths, such as music, art, or sports. By doing so, they will naturally fall into groups that share those interests. Joining a group or a clique may not be the answer for you. For some teens, having one or two close friends is more rewarding. Other teens like to belong to several groups, developing friendships with all types of people. Still other teens are naturally loners who do not enjoy group interaction.

What is important is to retain your own identity—whether you are in a group or not. You can do this by pursuing your interests and following your instincts about how to act. If you are true to yourself, you will like yourself. When you like yourself, others will like you, too.

Group Behaviors Involving Violence ■ ■ ■

One of the most important needs of teenagers is that of belonging. Friendships are important, but belonging to a group gives a teen a sense of even greater acceptance. Socially oriented groups help teens develop qualities that they can carry through to adulthood.

Banding together may also produce other, less healthy results. Some groups condone violence. In some schools and neighborhoods, violence seems to be erupting everywhere. Violent behavior by some group members has created an atmosphere of fear. This behavior often begins with bullying and becomes progressively worse. Gangs may use violence as their primary form of communication.

Bullying

Bullying refers to the infliction of physical, verbal, or emotional abuse on another person. Bullying is a form of violence. It comes in many intimidating and hurtful forms, including name calling, theft, extortion of money, physical intimidation, harsh pranks, and imposed territorial bases.

Bullying can happen to anyone in any place and at any time. In school, bullies may "tax" students so they can pass through a hall or sit in a special place at school events. Bullies may demand lunch money or clothing. They threaten the student with physical harm if he or she objects. Students walking home from school may be assaulted.

Gangs

Gangs are groups of bullies working together. Gang members usually group together to achieve a sense of power. Gang behavior is negative and hostile. Gang members wear identifiable clothing, symbols, or colors to designate membership. Gang members are not always just guys. There is an increasing number of girls who join the male gangs, or form gangs of their own.

Gangs are sometimes referred to as "hoods," "posses," or "crews." Female gang members may be called "queens." Boys have rigid initiation rites, but they feel this is an important rite of passage. If they survive, they know the gang will take care of them. Initiation for female gang members may consist of fighting several gang members at one time. This is called being "jumped in."

Many male gang members do not have an adult male role model in their families. The gang becomes their family. Teens join gangs seeking structure and discipline, which they think is a sign of power. They find that both the structure and discipline are extremely rigid, making it hard to get out of a gang. Loyalty to the gang is demanded, causing some gang members to live in fear.

Gang violence can erupt over the smallest action, such as a bump in a hallway. A simple misunderstanding in one area prompts a violent reaction, and this fuels further violence. Instead of using any form of peaceful problem solving, the violent behavior escalates and spreads. Gang members seek revenge on other gang members.

Gang members target people who stand out in some way—either in appearance or temperament—or who are weaker or smaller than themselves. Victims don't always reveal that they are victims. They may be threatened if they report being victimized. Thus, violent behavior holds the school or neighborhood in fear.

What Can Teens and Adults Do to Stop the Violence?

Across the country, teens and parents are seeking answers to the problem of gang violence. Meeting the problem of violence in your school and community will take everyone's cooperation.

First of all, teens need to be informed about what they can do to avoid being targets

Avoid Being a Victim

- Try to stay away from areas frequented by gangs.

- Don't wear clothing that resembles gang symbols. You will be giving the gang an excuse to harass you.

- Try not to let bullies or gang members scare you. This is what they want. If possible, ignore them and walk away.

- Don't get into a fight. Stand up for yourself without being hostile. Getting into a fight is acting like the bully or gang member.

- Get help from your friends. Ask your friends to stay around you and to be there to support you.

- Keep a written record. If you are confronted by a bully or gang, write down everything that happened so you will have specific information to take to the school authorities.

- If an incident occurs, tell your parents as well as school authorities immediately. Don't wait to be attacked again. This is not "ratting" or "tattling." It's helping yourself and other teens, too.

10-19
These suggestions will help prevent teens from being victims of bullies and gangs.

of bullying and gang violence. The suggestions given in 10-19 will help.

Further, there are positive steps that can be taken to stop the pattern of violent behavior. Violence is negative communication that is a learned behavior. Bullies and gang members have learned that anger, aggression, and intimidation are tools for solving problems. They communicate their feelings through anger and violent action. Actions can be taken to turn this negative form of communication into positive communication.

Using Conflict Resolution or Mediation

Teens involved with violence need help by learning new skills for handling conflict in their lives. *Conflict resolution,* or mediation, is a skill that is being used in schools and communities across the country as a means of resolving conflict in a positive way.

What are the steps in conflict resolution? Those using violence, as well as the victims of violence, have to be a part of the process. Both have to feel they have a fair chance to reach an acceptable conclusion. Sometimes it is necessary to have a third party help in resolving the conflict. The person who has this role is called a *mediator.* The mediator may be a peer. The mediator does not take sides, but can help with the following steps:

Step 1. Gather information. Each party is allowed to tell the story of what is causing the conflict. Ground rules of active listening and risk-free communication are understood. Only the people involved in the conflict should be present.

Step 2. Define the problem(s). The mediator restates the facts and issues that were presented by each party. After summarizing these facts and issues, the mediator asks each party if they understand them.

Step 3. Identify alternative solutions. Both parties can propose solutions.

Step 4. Identify a possible solution. The mediator revises possible solutions, based on the feelings of both parties. Negotiation is used to provide both parties with some of what they want.

Step 5. Reach an agreement. The mediator helps each party accept an agreement that would work for both parties. The agreement should then be written down and both parties should sign the agreement. The parties should also discuss what will happen if either of them breaks the agreement. Finally, ask the participants to tell their friends that the conflict has been solved to prevent rumors from spreading.

Schools and communities that have used conflict resolution techniques have found them to be successful in many cases. If the conflict is not resolved, legal steps may have to be taken to achieve peaceful coexistence.

Sexual Harassment

Another form of negative communication that happens all too often is sexual harassment. It happens not only in the workplace, but also in our schools. A lot of students, both boys and girls, have suffered as victims of sexual harassment. In one recent study, four out of five students reported experiencing some form of sexual harassment in school.

Many young people are not sure what sexual harassment includes. *Sexual harassment* is defined as unwelcome sexual advances, requests for sexual favors, or other verbal or physical conduct of a sexual nature. Sexual harassment includes, but is not limited to

- comments about a person's body, clothing, looks, or sexual activity.

- obscene jokes, pictures, or stories.

- sexual remarks, suggestions, or name calling.

- pressures for sexual intimacy.

- suggestive sounds or obscene gestures.

- leering or staring at someone's body.

- touching, grabbing, massaging, pinching, or brushing up against someone's body in a sexually offensive manner.

When sexual harassment occurs, the victims often feel completely helpless. They feel they are powerless to stop the behavior, and they often don't know who to turn to for help. They don't want to cause problems, and they fear that others will think they are making a big deal out of nothing. Therefore, they often say and do nothing while continuing to suffer. They feel such emotions as anger, fear, shame, guilt, confusion, embarrassment, and depression. It can all be very frightening to a teenager, especially if the person doing the harassing is an adult.

Sometimes it is hard to tell when someone is just flirting with you or teasing you and when the behavior is really sexual harassment. The key point is how it makes you feel. If you welcome the comment or action, it is okay. If you are hurt, insulted, or want it to stop, then you are probably being sexually harassed.

Boys sometimes misinterpret girls' behavior as sexual even though this is not intended. Girls have to be aware that they may send strong nonverbal messages about their sexuality with their posture, tone of voice, clothing, gestures, or eye contact.

What can you do if you are experiencing sexual harassment at school or work? The following suggestions may help:

- Talk to someone, such as a friend, parent, or trusted adult. It is important to confide in someone.

- Avoid being alone with the harasser.

- Say no so that others around you know what is happening.

- Know your rights. Under the Civil Rights Act, sexual harassment is against the law.

- Keep a dated, written record of all incidents.

- Find out if others have been harassed and might be willing to come forward to confront the harasser.

Sexual harassment policies are in place in many schools and places of employment. You might want to find out if such a policy exists in your school.

Summary ■ ■ ■ ■ ■ ■ ■ ■ ■ ■ ■ ■ ■ ■

- Communication takes place whenever someone shares a message with another person, either verbally or nonverbally.

- Listening skills can promote or detract from the communication process.

- You transmit many messages through your use of body language.

- Your appearance, including your grooming, your clothing, and your posture, communicate your self-image to others.

- People relate to one another on five levels. Level one represents peak communication, in which there is complete openness and honesty.

- Assertive people express their feelings directly in a nonaggressive manner.

■ I-messages and we-messages state how you feel and why. They are less threatening than you-messages and are more likely to bring about cooperation.

■ Communication problems between teens and their parents are often the result of teens trying to establish independence and parents expressing concern for their children's welfare. Negotiation can often resolve conflicts.

■ Group effectiveness depends on good communication and commitment to mutual goals.

■ Violence as exhibited by bullies and gang members is a negative communication tool.

■ Bullies inflict physical, verbal, or emotional abuse on others. Gangs are groups of bullies who exhibit hostile and violent behavior.

■ Teens involved with violence need help in learning conflict resolution skills.

■ Victims of sexual harassment at school or work need to know how to bring an end to the harassing behavior.

To Review ■ ■ ■ ■ ■ ■ ■ ■ ■ ■ ■ ■ ■ ■ ■

1. Give three examples of ways people communicate.

2. Match the following terms with their definitions.

     _____ Passive listeners
     _____ Feedback
     _____ Active listening
     _____ Careless listeners
     _____ Defensive listeners
     _____ Narrow listeners
   a. Read meanings into what is being said because they feel they are being attacked.
   b. Pick out bits and pieces of conversation and don't listen to the rest.
   c. Hear only what they want to hear and tune out other information.
   d. Tells the other person how the listener feels about what is being said.
   e. Take in words but offer no indication   they hear or understand.
   f. Smiling, nodding, or making eye contact.

3. Differentiate between empathy and sympathy.

4. Describe three ways to communicate using body language.

5. Explain how posture, grooming, and clothing help you communicate.

6. Briefly describe the five levels of communication.

7. True or False. When you are assertive, you build your self-esteem by putting other people down.

8. Give an example of an I-message and then reword it as a you-message. Which is more likely to improve communication?

9. List three steps you can use in negotiating with your parents.

10. List the types of behaviors commonly used by bullies.

11. Briefly describe the steps used in conflict resolution.

12. What is sexual harassment?

To Do ■ ■ ■ ■ ■ ■ ■ ■ ■ ■ ■ ■ ■ ■ ■ ■ ■ ■ ■

1. Make a list of every method of communication you have used since you awoke this morning. Compare your list with those of your classmates.

2. Complete each of the following statements:
   a. The best way to make a favorable impression on others is...
   b. My biggest complaint about the way people communicate is...
   c. The personal traits I think are most important for good communication are...
   d. The most important rule of etiquette is...
   e. An assertive person is...

3. Divide into groups. Identify communication problems that could arise in each of the following situations and list possible solutions. Share with the class.
   a. In club or activity meetings.
   b. When dating.
   c. In classrooms.
   d. At home.

4. Form groups and role-play the following interaction situations. Afterward, discuss the use of verbal and nonverbal communication and the problems that can arise when messages are misinterpreted.
   a. A boy and girl who have gone together for over a year are having problems in their relationship. They wonder if they should break up now, one week before senior prom, which they had planned to attend together.

      b. A couple plans to go to dinner and a show. The boy wants to make this a special evening and has saved money for several weeks. The girl seems completely indifferent to the plans.

      c. A teenager wants permission from his or her parents to use the family car to go to a rock concert with a friend.

5. Ask a police officer to speak to your class about gang activity. Ask what students can do to help solve the problem of increasing violence.

6. Role-play a situation in which conflict resolution is used to end a conflict between two groups. One person should act as the mediator.

7. If appropriate, write up a proposal for a student forum to address the problem of violence in your school. Write this with the assistance of your teacher and present it to the school administration for consideration.

David Hopper

Your appearance can communicate a positive image of yourself to others.

Developing Close Relationships

Cholla Runnels

Terms to Know

group dating   ambivalence

steady dating   infatuation

intimacy   rape

love   acquaintance rape

After studying this chapter, you will be able to

- identify friendships that involve important, close relationships.

- describe the informal and formal dating choices of teens.

- describe the qualities that characterize a serious relationship with a member of the opposite sex.

- discuss the issues involved in ending a relationship.

- recognize the many different types of love.

- differentiate between love, infatuation, and sexual gratification.

- analyze the issues involved in sexual decision making.

- practice techniques for saying no to sexual relations.

- define acquaintance rape and identify ways to prevent it.

During your teen years, you will form many new relationships. These friendships can be valuable learning experiences for you, 11-1. Being able to establish meaningful relationships with others is an important skill for teens to develop. Friends can help you learn more about yourself and more about other people. The knowledge you gain will help you determine what you want in a serious relationship that may lead to marriage.

Friendship

What is friendship? Would you agree with the following descriptions of a friend?

- A friend often knows how you feel about certain things without being told.

Cholla Runnels

11-1
Friendships formed during the teen years will help you learn more about yourself.

- A friend is someone who shares many of your viewpoints, especially on subjects you consider important.

- A friend is someone who never talks about you behind your back.

- A friend is someone you can share your most important secrets with and not worry that anyone else will be told.

Friendship requires communication, and this is the channel that connects you to others, 11-2. Friendships provide you with a network that connects you to what is happening around you. With a friend, you have someone to share your thoughts, your hopes, and your dreams. Some of the most important qualities in a friend are loyalty, trust, affection, and supportiveness.

Friends can be important for several reasons, including the following:

- Friends provide emotional support. They help you believe that you are a worthwhile person.

- Friends help you to expand your knowledge, ideas, and perspectives.

- Friends are willing to help you meet your needs and reach your personal goals.

During your teen years, you will form many new friendships. You will probably keep

Ways to Promote Friendship through Communication

- If you are interested in someone, find out what his or her interests are. Promote communication by asking questions the other person likes to answer. Then be an attentive listener. This is one of the best ways to build a friendship.

- A good way to open communication is to say something nice. Begin by letting the other person know how important the friendship is to you.

- Rehearse what you want to say. Acting out an anxiety-provoking situation is a good way to build your self-confidence while practicing your communication skills. You will have a better chance of pinpointing conversation weaknesses and improving them.

- Tune out any self-defeating messages and replace them with positive thoughts. If you think the other person will not want to listen to you, try to think more positively. Tell yourself, "He probably feels just as confused as I do." Then you both can learn something by talking.

- Remember that your thoughts, feelings, and opinions are just as valid as anyone else's. You don't have to hide them, or change them. On the other hand, try not to get upset just because someone disagrees with something you've said. Don't take it as a personal rejection. No two people can ever think exactly alike.

- Remember that the thoughts, feelings, and opinions of others are just as valid as yours.

- Listening is just as important in building a friendship as talking. Concentrate on what the other person is saying before you answer.

11-2
Good friendships depend on good communication.

in touch with a few of your high school friends during most of your life. You may later have college friends, friends where you work, neighborhood friends, and friends you meet as you participate in sports or community activities.

You will have different types of friends. There may be some friends you call when you want to do something. You probably have certain friends who enjoy skating and others you might call when you want to go to the mall. Friendships are based on people talking to each other and sharing thoughts, feelings, and ideas. You may have a special friend with whom you share your hopes, concerns, and ambitions.

Your friendships will vary through the years. As you change, your friendships will change. During your teen years, you may feel possessive of your friends. You may regard a friendship as an exclusive relationship. You may say, "She can't be your best friend. She's my best friend."

As you mature, you will understand the need for each of you to grow. You can communicate this feeling without fearing the friend will no longer be your friend. You will be able to trust each other's independence. It is a sign of true friendship to allow someone to grow.

A close friendship with a person of the opposite sex is not uncommon during the teen years. Sharing a "just friends" relationship can be a positive experience. These opposite-sex friendships can be a testing ground for the honesty, truth, respect, and communication that is critical to any lasting male-female relationship. This type of friendship may remain as a very special relationship for your entire life. The friendship may also grow into a more serious emotional relationship later on because the basis for mutual understanding has been established.

Dating Patterns ▪ ▪ ▪ ▪

Dating is a part of our culture. As people date, they not only have fun, they also learn about interpersonal relationships. This helps them prepare for adulthood and marriage.

Dating encourages good peer relationships and helps you learn to evaluate personalities. You become better able to discover those personality traits that appeal to you and those that do not. Dating experiences make you aware of the demands and restrictions involved in getting along with members of the opposite sex. People who have these experiences are likely to be more successful marriage partners.

Dating relationships vary among generations, among regions of the country, and among individuals. However, many relationships follow a pattern that starts with informal group dating and ends with engagement.

Informal Group Dating

Most young people begin dating in informal group settings. Many prefer "just being with people" rather than having structured dates. There is more emphasis on groups of people than on couples. This is called *group dating.* Today's teens may refer to this form of group dating as "hanging out."

Group activities are often planned jointly by males and females. Many times everyone just meets at some popular spot with no actual planning. A group of teens can get together on the spur of the moment to enjoy many activities. This may be a game of touch football or a trip to the beach. Teens enjoy doing things in groups that they might not do alone. The activities may involve any number of people from just a few to a group of ten or more. Everyone can socialize and enjoy the company of others. This gives teens an opportunity to learn about a lot of different personalities.

11-3
Many mixed groups form during school-related activities.

Being part of a mixed group of males and females prepares teens for one-to-one relationships with the opposite sex, 11-3. Cross-gender friendships are often an important part of group activities. As teens participate in different activities in the group, some members may start to pair off for certain activities. A person may pair off with different people for different events. Young people can enjoy being with members of the opposite sex without the pressures of dating.

These informal group experiences allow you to form your own ideas about people and about life. You can share thoughts and feelings while relating to a person as a friend rather than as a prospective mate. Meeting many different people and having a variety of experiences will prepare you for making decisions later in life.

Formal Pair Dating

As you spend time with friends in group settings, you will probably discover one person you really like. You may begin to "see each other." As you begin dating this special person, you may not date anyone else. If you continue to date this same person and only this person for a period of time, friends will say that you are "going out." This is also called *steady dating.* At some point during your dating years, you will probably form this type of special relationship with one person.

Dating helps you discover yourself and to learn about other people in a variety of settings. Some people prefer dates where they watch others perform, as in a play or an athletic event. Others prefer dates in which the couple is involved in the activity. Many times, however, couples will simply strike out for a day or evening of fun with little detailed planning. Your dating activities will revolve around the interests you and your date share.

As you date one person more and more, you will feel that this person really understands you and cares about you. You enjoy being special to someone. You find that you can have a great time just being together. It is a nice feeling being on comfortable terms with one person, 11-4.

An important change in recent years is the greater concern for one another as individuals. This has been accompanied by an in-

Cholla Runnels

11-5
A relationship can begin with just a smile.

creased understanding in relationships. Dating is more a meeting of equals who do not need to fool each other about their feelings. Couples can share in decision making, witness honest reactions to stress and joy, and develop good communication patterns.

Young people today are marrying at a later age. This gives them time to develop more friendships. Then when they are ready, they can move from friendship to a caring and committed relationship. They will be ready to offer closeness, loyalty, understanding, open communication, and a special sense of intimacy.

Developing Relationships ▪ ▪ ▪ ▪

Boy meets girl, 11-5. They are attracted to each other. They share many interests. Their values and goals seem to be very similar. Their relationship deepens. This appears to be a magic formula, but developing a lasting relationship between two people is not that easy. There is a great deal that takes

Cholla Runnels

11-4
As you date one person more and more, you feel comfortable just being together.

place between the first meeting and the final relationship that develops.

Relationships develop step by step. As you communicate over time, you learn more and more about each other. You also realize that you are learning more about yourself and your reactions to the other person. You will have pleasant times and you will have times when one or both of you are sad. You are moving toward a more serious relationship. Carl Sandburg, a poet, was describing this process when he said, "People are like onions. You uncover them a layer at a time, and sometimes you cry."

What Qualities Characterize a Serious Relationship?

Several characteristics are often found in relationships that become "serious." *Trust* is very important when two people are building a relationship. Trust is needed between friends. It is even more important between two people who hope to build a committed relationship. Being able to trust a person means you feel that person would not betray you or cause you any harm. A relationship built on trust is caring and responsible.

Self-disclosure means sharing significant information about yourself with the other person. In a serious relationship, partners feel free to talk about their deepest concerns and feelings. They also are not afraid to reveal their idiosyncrasies (tendencies, characteristics, or modes of expression peculiar to an individual). Your ability to disclose information to a person you trust and care for is healthy. Self-disclosure is a sign of trust. However, there is a certain amount of vulnerability (openness to pain or loss) when you become this close. When you open yourself to another person, you take some risk that he or she might ridicule you, reject you, or betray your confidences.

A relationship must have *communication* to grow. The couple need to express their beliefs, values, goals, and concerns. They need to recognize the differences they have and share what they have in common. With good communication, couples can learn to give and take. Sometimes one person may have to give a little more than the other, but the next time it will be the other way around. If good communication does not exist, the relationship cannot grow.

One of the important aspects of a developing relationship is the feeling of intimacy. *Intimacy* is a sense of familiarity that develops over a long and close association, 11-6. It is a feeling of warm friendship. Intimacy means you accept another human being as he or she is. You feel free to communicate your thoughts and feelings honestly and openly. You are able to share your life while still retaining your own individuality. "I feel good when I am with you" is a common expression.

Intimacy does not necessarily mean sexual intimacy. Intimacy can develop between two people with no sexual expression involved. In your teen years, it is important that you realize the real meaning and significance

Cholla Runnels

11-6
Intimacy develops between two people over a period of time.

of personal intimacy. A feeling of intimacy should be the foundation for any expression of love.

Ending a Relationship ▪ ▪ ▪ ▪

Dating forms a cycle: informal dating—dating a special person—breaking up. This cycle may be repeated many times, but with each cycle a relationship ends.

Ending a relationship is hard to do. It usually hurts both people. When you are a teen, you may think it is the worst thing that can happen to you. It is hard when someone tells you breaking up is normal because at the time you may not feel very normal.

Signs That a Relationship Should End

There are times when it is better to break off a relationship than to keep it going. How can you tell when a relationship is going wrong and needs to end? Watch for the following signs:

Conflicting values. When a couple differs on personal values, it can lead to many conflicts. Your values reflect what you consider important in life. If your dating partner does not have similar values, you are bound to have repeated disagreements.

Withdrawal from other friendships. When couples withdraw from their other friendships to spend time only with each other, personal growth is limited. A healthy relationship should make both of you more secure, understanding people—when you are with each other and when you are with others.

Overemphasis on physical involvement. With some couples, the total relationship revolves around sexual gratification. Sexual involvement sometimes masks problems in the relationship. If this is the total focus of the relationship, the couple may not share other interests. These relationships are more likely to eventually end.

Frequent arguments and fights. Every couple will have misunderstandings, but arguing and fighting should rarely occur. If arguments are frequent and the fights outnumber the peaceful times, it is time to call it quits.

How Not to Break Up

When you want to end a relationship, you want to stop seeing someone. Your intent should not be to cause pain or embarrassment for the other person. Therefore, when breaking up try to avoid the following:

- Do not "tell the other person off." This serves no purpose. It only makes the other person feel unworthy and unlikable.

- Do not begin dating someone else right away. Appearing immediately with a new person at your side may be an attempt at revenge, but again it serves no purpose. It is not a good idea to seek another serious relationship immediately.

- Do not break off a relationship without an explanation. The relationship meant something to both of you at one time. You began as friends. Friends talk to each other. Leave the lines of communication open between you so you can continue to be friends.

- Do not lead the other person on. Being nice one minute and nasty the next is not fair. This hot and cold treatment will only leave bad feelings.

Breaking Up without Pain

Even though a breakup is likely to hurt one person more than the other, it can be done gently. Breaking up usually hurts because one person feels rejected. There are ways to break up that can ease the hurt and sense of rejection. Then you both can move on to new relationships.

■ Choose an appropriate time and place to break up. Breakups are a private matter and should not be done in front of others or in a public place. Respect the feelings of the other person.

■ Try to remember the good times you spent together. There must have been some for you both to have become emotionally involved. Compliment each other on some good qualities.

■ Share the responsibility for the failure of the relationship. Don't put all the blame on the other person. There obviously is blame on both sides. If things went wrong, sort them out and learn from your mistakes.

■ Recognize that just because two personalities don't mesh perfectly doesn't mean that either person is inadequate. Lasting relationships are rather like a lock and a key. Just because a key does not fit a particular lock doesn't mean there is anything "wrong" with either one. The same is true of dating partners.

■ Be honest about the reason for the break up. Most people would rather know the reason even though it might hurt to find out. You may not fully realize how each of you feel about the reasons.

Believe it or not, there is life after a breakup. You may not feel ready for another relationship right away, but you will have opportunities again. The breakup of one relationship will not ruin chances for establishing others. What you have learned in one relationship can be applied to enhance the next relationship. You will probably look back on this experience as one of the best things to happen to you at the time. You will survive. The suggestions in 11-7 will help.

Communication of Love ■ ■ ■ ■ ■ ■ ■

Love has many forms, and each is expressed differently. The love between parents and children is different from the love between brother and sister, 11-8. The love between family members is different from the love between friends. The love between friends is different from the love between dating partners. The love between dating part-

---

How to Survive a Breakup

■ Don't be ashamed to feel sad. A breakup is the end of a relationship that meant a great deal to you. You will feel unhappy for awhile.

■ Talk with a good friend or relative. Sharing your feelings with someone close to you can help you through this difficult time.

■ Give yourself time to heal before entering a new relationship. Then date several people rather than just one.

■ Learn from the experience. Take a look at yourself and the strengths you do have. Then look at the mistakes you might have made and learn from them.

■ Keep busy. Get involved in new activities that interest you.

■ Put reminders of the relationship, such as pictures and mementos, out of sight until you have had time to heal.

11-7
These suggestions will help you recover from a breakup.

ners is different from the love between husbands and wives.

Sometimes feelings of love can be confusing. By gaining insight into yourself and your emotions, you can learn to judge the depth of a relationship. Then you can know what the love means to you and how to deal with your feelings.

What Does Love Mean?

Love can be defined as a strong feeling of personal attachment between friends or family members. It can also be defined as tender and compassionate affection shared between two people.

When you love someone, you respond emotionally to that person's needs. You help each other so that your lives are better when you are together than when you are apart. Love in this sense grows as your personality develops. It is capable of continually becoming deeper, richer, and stronger throughout your life.

Some people say that to know love, you must experience it. You have experienced some forms of love already in your life, 11-9. You will experience more as you grow emo-

Cholla Runnels

11-9
You have already experienced some forms of love such as the love between grandparents, parents, and children.

tionally and socially. The more relationships you have with people, the more meanings the word love will have for you.

Types of Love

Both positive and negative feelings are closely related to the emotion of love. Songs, poems, and books have been written about the good and bad effects of love. They show the power that love can have to either improve or harm a person's life.

Cholla Runnels

11-8
Parents and children share a special form of love.

Cholla Runnels

11-10
True love involves total communication and commitment between two people.

Positive Types of Love

Positive types of love add richness and fullness to life. They help people feel good about themselves, about others, and about life in general.

True love involves total communication and commitment between two people. It means sharing what one has and what one is when with another person. With true love, people strive toward shared thoughts, feelings, attitudes, ambitions, hopes, and interests. While maintaining their individuality, partners tend to think and plan in terms of "we"—what "we" want, how "we" feel, what "we" will do. See 11-10.

True love motivates two people to help each other grow and improve. They want each other to have the best life possible. Their love gives them energy to work together to reach their goals.

True love is realistic; it does not expect perfection. With true love, a person accepts the faults and weaknesses of the loved one. The two people are willing to work together to overcome any obstacles and to make the relationship as good as it can be. The realism of true love also allows people to express their true feelings. They can show their joy, anger, or sorrow without fear of losing the love and respect of the other person.

Time is a good test of true love. If a relationship endures varying emotional climates, developing interests, and deepening feelings, it will probably continue to grow as long as the people do.

Tender love is happy and satisfying, 11-11. It is not only beautiful in itself, but it increases the loveliness of the people involved.

David Hopper

11-11
Tender love makes people feel warm and happy.

Tender love makes people feel warm, secure, and cheerful. As people mature, tender love becomes an increasingly familiar and satisfying part of relationships.

Friendly love grows through the years. It is neither passionate and consuming nor hostile and hurting. Friends are kept together with feelings of mutual respect and understanding. They are rarely shocked by the actions of one another. Friendly love is usually the basis for friendships, 11-12. Sometimes a true love relationship can be built upon a foundation of friendly love.

Negative Types of Love

Just as positive love can strengthen and deepen relationships, negative love can damage them. Love is usually considered "good," but you should be familiar with the "bad" effects love can have on relationships.

Jealous love is a possessive love. The jealous lover holds the other person so tightly that the person is cut off from other people. Jealousy is almost always a mark of immaturity and insecurity. As lovers grow confident of their love and of their loved ones, feelings of jealousy fade. They have faith that their love

Cholla Runnels

11-12
Friendly love is sturdy and faithful. Partners express feelings of mutual respect and understanding.

will last. They realize they do not have to cling desperately to it.

Passionate love is vigorous, insistent, and urgent. It centers on the sexual relationships of men and women. It is driven by nature's desire for biological fulfillment, and it often operates without reason.

Passion alone can be painful. It can also be selfish, with little concern for the other. By itself, this kind of love is tempestuous and exhausting. Blended with other love forms, it can be exhilarating and fulfilling.

Hostile love frequently raises its voice in anger against the loved one. The emotions of love and hate are closely related. When you love someone, you may occasionally have real feelings of hostility toward them. This tendency to hate those you love involves a feeling of **ambivalence**—being attracted to and repelled by someone at the same time. It can be explained by recognizing that although some characteristics of a person are good, others may be irritating. If you love someone too narrowly to accept the person's limitations, you become annoyed when that person does anything that displeases you. Then your love may take on a hostile quality as you become critical of the other's behavior.

Unreturned love is frustrating because it is unfulfilled love. When you realize your love is not being returned, you may react with feelings of pain, sorrow, and hopelessness. Unreturned love can go on indefinitely. The saying, "He still carries a torch for her," describes a man experiencing unrequited love. In its worst form, unreturned love can become a form of harassment, as the person persists in forcing unwanted expressions of love on another. More often, however, this type of love is forgotten as the person focuses energy on attaining happiness in a more rewarding way.

Love Versus Infatuation

Infatuation is often mistaken for love. A young person who has not experienced either feeling may have difficulty distinguishing between the two.

Definitions of love mention strength and lasting qualities. Definitions of infatuation mention foolish, extreme attractions that do not last. Love takes time to grow and develop. Infatuation begins quickly, and may end as quickly as it began. Love is relatively steady and secure. Infatuation is hasty and changeable. It gives thrills, but they are accompanied by doubts and jealousy.

Love inspires ambition and cooperation in working to achieve goals. Infatuation inspires only selfish thoughts and actions. Physical attraction may be a part of love, but it often is the only basis for infatuation.

You need to understand the emotions related to love and infatuation so you know how to handle relationships. Emotions and expressions related to seeking physical satisfaction may appear along with either love or infatuation. You also need to know how to deal with these feelings. Chart 11-13 can help you learn to distinguish between love, infatuation, and the desire for sexual gratification.

Physical Expressions of Affection

Physical attraction is one part of love, and physical expressions can help people communicate deep feelings. However, physical expressions are just one method of communicating affection, and they should be combined with other methods. By themselves, physical expressions cannot communicate all the ideas and feelings couples need to share.

Too much dependence on physical expressions can cause problems in a relation-

Comparison of Love, Infatuation, and Sexual Gratification

Love	Infatuation	Sexual Gratification
Feeling of strong personal attachment.	Engulfing, selfish feelings.	Sensuous feelings.
Concerned for the welfare of other person.	Concern for your own welfare.	Concern for own sexual gratification.
Grows slowly and steadily.	Emotions flow at a fast, accelerating pace.	Immediate physical urgency is felt and quickly spent.
Continues to grow and encompasses more of personality.	Initial attraction is quickly consumed and grows no further.	Ends abruptly with little feeling of responsibility.
Makes one feel proud, confident, and ambitious.	Tends to destroy purpose and ambition.	Promotes feelings of guilt.
Physical attraction is only one part of the relationship.	Physical attraction often is the major factor in the relationship.	Physical desires are the only basis for the relationship.
Aware of other person's faults, but accepts them as part of total personality.	Overlooks undesirable traits and pretends they do not exist.	Unconcerned with personality traits.
Both partners give of themselves generously.	Each partner seeks rewards but gives little in return.	Each partner demands fulfillment with little thought of the effect on other person.
Exhibits a "we" feeling and indicates that "I care about how you feel."	Exhibits an "I" feeling and indicates concern only for "How do I feel?"	Exhibits a possessive feeling and indicates "You are mine!"
Increases ability to relate to many friends.	Has only a few friends, and tends to be moody and indifferent.	Prefers isolation.
Unselfish in actions.	Very selfish in actions.	Possessive and demanding in actions.
Trust, openness, and acceptance of others.	Distrustful and slow to accept others.	Frequently jealous when ego needs are not met.

11-13
Relationships based on love, infatuation, or sexual gratification differ in many ways.

ship. Some people seek physical expressions of affection from another person just to prove their femininity or masculinity. In such relationships, one or both people may be using the other. These relationships are full of problems and rarely last.

Physical expressions of affection are a healthy part of a love relationship. A kiss and an embrace are part of a normal relationship, but with continued repetition or prolonged embraces one partner may interpret the sensual feelings of the other as sexual urgency. Unless the couple have firm beliefs about sexual relations, they may let their emotions take over. They may become more involved than they had planned. Once a couple become sexually involved, they are forced to assume responsibility for making decisions involving themselves and others. These decisions will affect the couple's future goals and views of marriage.

A couple who are truly committed to each other and to what they hope to have in the future should think ahead. The two people can talk about how they feel and set limits with which they are mutually comfortable.

Before entering into a sexual relationship, you need to understand your developing sexuality. You should carefully consider the responsibilities you will be assuming. Some people, especially teens, may find that they are not yet ready to accept them, 11-14.

Understanding Your Developing Sexuality

New feelings concerning sexuality may occur during adolescence because of dramatic hormonal and body changes. These feelings can cause confusion when you are ex-

11-14
Many teens feel they are not yet ready to assume the responsibilities of a sexual relationship.

Cholla Runnels

periencing new social relationships. However, these feelings are a normal part of maturation.

Differences between the Sexes

It is natural when you have been dating someone for awhile to want to express your affection for each other. It is also true that these expressions and feelings of affection may differ between the sexes. The following statements may be true of young people in their early relationships. "Girls play at sex, for which they are not ready, because they want love." "Boys play at love, for which they are not ready, because they want sex."

Many people feel there is still a "double standard" in our society. This is the belief that boys will always behave differently from girls in sexual matters. Boys may feel it is up to them to make the first move and to pressure their partners for more. Girls may feel they are the ones to set limits and to say "no." This attitude may be changing as girls are taking more initiative and boys are realizing the responsibilities they have.

Some girls like to tease and flirt with their dates. They think boys will magically know when to stop. A girl may be surprised when her playfulness leads a boy to pressure her for more physical expression. A boy may interpret any initiative the girl takes as a sign that she wants to go farther.

Sexual Decision Making

Many teens are not prepared to handle their new feelings. They are confused about what to do in situations involving emotional expression. They may not know the facts about sexual behavior. They may not have correct information concerning their own sexual development. They may be confused by what they hear and see. The media tell them that sex is romantic and exciting. At the same time, the message they receive from parents and authorities is to say no to these feelings.

The responsibility for making decisions concerning your own sexuality is yours. Sexual decisions involve making value judgments about how you feel you should behave. Your values are based on parental guidance, your religious beliefs, and your own developing morality. Your parents may advise you, but you will be on your own when you are actually faced with a decision. You are responsible for your decisions about your life. If you make careless choices or give in to pressures, you are likely to be hurt. Your life goals will be shortchanged, and your health may be jeopardized. These are high prices to pay.

To make wise decisions and manage your life responsibly, you need to be informed. See 11-15. Your life is too precious to leave to chance. Your health is too important to risk because of lack of knowledge.

Teenagers obtain most of their information about their sexuality from their peers and the media. This information usually is not factual, and much of it is misleading. Many teenagers are seriously misinformed about the risks of pregnancy and disease and about ways to prevent them.

Teenagers are also influenced by friends. You know how demanding pressure from peers can be. You have probably felt uncomfortable when people your own age have told you to do things that you really didn't think were right. Teenagers don't want to feel different, and they don't want to be left out. Teenagers who wish to resist sexual involvement often do not know what to say or do when confronted with peer pressure.

Sexual decision making requires maturity and knowledge. Your sexuality is a part of your total personality. Any sexual experience you have becomes a part of you. You have to accept the physical and emotional responsibilities that go with this experience. Any deci-

sion you make has consequences—good and bad—for you and your partner. Both of you will be influenced by your decision for the rest of your lives. Saying no to sexual expressions during your teens is delaying this important part of your life until you are better able to make a responsible decision.

Young people who say, "I'll just wait until I have to make a choice," often find themselves making that choice under great emotional pressure. Because of this pressure, they may make decisions that they will regret later.

Because sexual experiences affect your self-concept and personality, they should not be taken lightly. Sex should not be used as an attempt to enhance your popularity or to keep a boyfriend or girlfriend interested. It should not be used to defy your parents, to counter loneliness, or to prove your maturity. Sex should not be used in order to be one of the crowd or to avoid hurting someone's feelings.

Some people feel that contraception allows anyone to have sexual intercourse freely because pregnancy can be prevented. Young

Cholla Runnels

11-15
Factual information about sexuality from class lectures, textbooks, and other reliable sources can help you learn to manage your life responsibly.

people, however, have the right and responsibility to express their own wishes concerning intercourse. They know they have the right to choose. Many say, "I choose not to have sex before I am married." Their choice reflects the way they assess their worth as individuals. It also indicates their feelings of responsibility toward themselves, their possible sexual partners, and their future marriage partners.

Some people argue that having sex helps a person choose a future husband or wife. However, it more often confuses the relationship. After having sex, many people feel obligated to continue the relationship. They may marry the partner even if true love is not present in the relationship. Such marriages usually end in divorce.

The argument that having sex helps people to improve techniques is unfounded. Most experiences in premarital sex take place in less than ideal settings. The possible guilt, the danger of being discovered, and the fear of rejection by one's partner inhibit feelings of relaxation and enjoyment. The security of marriage allows freer expression of love. Sexual experiences between spouses are usually more satisfying.

"If you love me, you will prove it." This line has been used often, but it is a poor reason for having premarital sex. "Making love" and "being in love" are two different things. True love does not have to be proven. Partners in true love respect each other and do not put one another under pressure. Sexual decisions should not be forced, 11-16.

Some people use sex as a bartering position. "I gave you a nice time, now what are you going to give me?" Sex is not an item to trade off or to use as payment.

The most common reason people give for having had premarital sex is, "We thought we were in love and that we were meant for each other." At the time, and under the circumstances, both of them thought they had found true love. Each of them may have fought against going all the way at different times, but they finally gave in to their impulses. Later, many couples discover that instead of strengthening their relationship, the experience caused them to doubt themselves, their relationship, and their love.

How to Prepare Yourself for Sexual Decision Making

How can you prepare yourself to make the right decision? Know yourself, accept yourself, and believe in yourself. Develop a healthy self-concept and learn to deal with your strengths and weaknesses. Refine your

Cholla Runnels

11-16
Sexual decisions should not be forced. True love does not have to be proven.

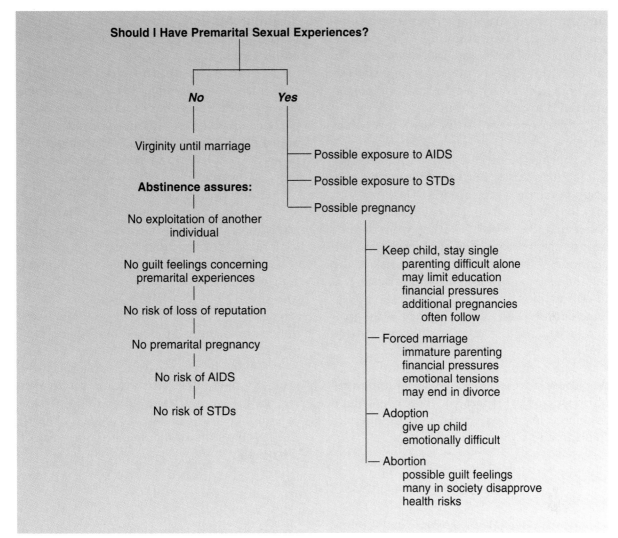

11-17
Single people have decisions to make about premarital sexual experiences.

decision-making skills. Recognize your values, and set goals for your future. Learn to communicate honestly with others. Think ahead about what you will do if you are with someone who is pressuring you. Think also about how you can communicate your feelings for someone without getting involved sexually. Then you will be able to develop sound relationships with the people around you and possibly with a special friend.

Consequences of Your Decisions

Why do decisions concerning your sexuality have such an impact on your life and the life of others? A decision-making model is shown in 11-17. It shows the possible consequences of decisions concerning sexual relations. Two of the obvious consequences were discussed in Chapter 9. Unplanned pregnancies and sexually transmitted diseases can impact a person's entire lifetime. They also affect the lives of both families and the possible life of a child. There are other less obvious consequences as well. For instance, a person may develop a callous attitude towards sex if experiences as a teen are less than satisfying.

During the teen years, you may choose to take many risks. Performing on a balance beam is taking a risk. Asking a popular person to be your date for the homecoming dance may be a risk. Getting your driver's license involves some risk. You face risks each and every day of your life. Healthy risk taking that helps you grow and learn is necessary. It is critical, however, that you see the difference between risk taking that helps you grow and risk taking that may harm you or someone else.

The sexual part of your life can be wonderful when experienced in a committed relationship like marriage. If experienced prematurely, it may involve consequences that can affect your entire life.

Saying No to Sexual Relations

Abstinence from sexual intercourse means saying no. It is not always easy to say no, especially when you are being pressured by someone else to go farther. It also is not easy to control your own emotions. Sexual urgency can interfere with your ability to think rationally about how you will feel the next day and the risks you might be taking. However, there are ways to make it easier for both of you to practice abstinence.

First, prepare for those times when you might go too far. If you have thought about how you will handle a situation, it will be easier to put on the brakes before you go too far.

Second, know what your limits are. Discuss these limits with your date. Talk about how you both feel. Knowing your limits can help you both stop before things get out of hand, 11-18.

Third, avoid situations that may be difficult for you to handle. Don't spend time alone together in either of your homes when parents or siblings are not present. Avoid being alone in a parked car for any length of time. Some places and some situations are more likely to lead to a loss of control.

Limit the amount of time you spend alone together. Perhaps several shorter dates are better than all-day dates where you spend long periods of time together.

Avoid the use of drugs that would impair your ability to make good decisions. People who drink alcohol or abuse drugs are not always able to think clearly. They are less likely to be able to control their emotions and their actions.

Finally, let your partner know that you value yourself and that you care about your life. If you let your date know this and that you value him or her too, you are less likely to do anything that would damage your sense of self-worth.

Cholla Runnels

11-18
Talk to each other about your limits before you go too far.

How to Say No

When you must say no to sexual pressures, do so firmly, but with respect. Keep the other person's self-esteem in mind. Saying no doesn't have to be done in an angry voice.

There is no need to offer excuses, and you don't have to give reasons. You do not have to try to convince your partner—you only have to say what you will and will not do. Refuse to argue. State your position and stand firm.

Finally, get away from the situation as soon as you can. This is the best way to avoid any further pressure. Ask to be driven home, or go home on your own. If necessary, you may need to ask someone else to drive you home, or you can call your parents or a friend. See 11-19 for additional ways to help you say no.

Ways to Help You Say No

- Give your partner a compliment—and mean it. "I appreciate your wanting me, but I'm not ready for that kind of relationship."
- Say in a light-hearted manner, "Hey, not so fast."
- Change the setting by saying, "I'm starved. Let's go get something to eat."
- Tell your date, "You really are special to me. I like you, and I want to keep it that way."
- Use I-statements, such as, "I feel really uncomfortable right now. I'm not ready for this. I'm afraid it might damage our relationship and I might lose respect for you and for me."
- Tell a joke. Sometimes humor can get you out of a difficult situation.

11-19

It's not always easy to say no to sexual pressures. These ideas may help you.

Date or Acquaintance Rake

Rape is any sexual intimacy forced on one person by another. Though rape is usually thought to be committed by strangers, it is often committed by someone the victim knows. *Acquaintance rape* or "date rape" is committed by a dating partner, friend, someone the person just met, or someone known at school or work. In other words, the rapist is an acquaintance, and therefore a trusted person, who forces or pressures the victim into non-consenting intercourse. Statistics reveal that over half of all reported sexual assaults and rapes of teens are committed by people they know. In these instances teens feel they can trust their assailants because they know them. The rapists are not the strangers about whom the teens have been warned. A rape can occur even if the person is known to the victim.

Rape is forcing someone to have sexual intercourse without his or her consent. Consent is based on choice. Being deceived is not giving consent. Some males wrongly think that young women just need to be persuaded—that their no doesn't always mean no. This callous attitude on the part of males has led some to be prosecuted for rape.

Many people are reluctant to report a rape by someone they know. Many teens don't even tell their parents about sexual assaults. They are afraid of upsetting their parents. They may have been breaking a rule when the act occurred, so they think they will be in even greater trouble if they tell their parents. Some victims feel they may have been partly to blame for what happened. Perhaps they feel they could have prevented the incident.

Parents often feel that teens are less likely to be victimized if they go to parties or on group dates instead of single dates. Parties

Myths Vs. Realities of Rape

Many young people are confused about rape—what it is and is not. The following statements are commonly held myths about rape. The responses to these myths will help you become more knowledgeable about rape.

Myth
The primary motive for rape is sexual.

Reality
The primary motive for rape is power—to overpower, control, humiliate, or dominate another person.

Myth
Rape occurs between strangers.

Reality
The majority of rapes involve persons who move in the same social circle. Acquaintance rape occurs when the victim and the perpetrator are acquainted (friends, dormmates, classmates, etc.). Date rape occurs when the two are seeing one another in a dating relationship.

Myth
Giving in to the rapist is the same as consenting to sexual relations.

Reality
Consent is based on choice. Consent is active, not passive. Giving in out of fear is not giving consent. Being deceived is not giving consent.

Myth
A sexual attack is provoked by the victim.

Reality
This mistaken belief holds that women "ask to be raped" through their actions or dress. This takes the criminal action away from the rapist and shifts the blame to the victim.

Myth
If the male is "led on" by the female, he cannot be charged with rape.

Reality
A male may be charged with rape even if he thought he was doing what the girl wanted.

Myth
Women often lie about being raped.

Reality
People often think there is a great deal of false reporting. In fact, only about two percent of rape calls turn out to be false reports, which is the same false-report rate as for other felonies.

and groups have their own dangers. Both male and female teens need to be aware of these dangers. If there is drinking, which is often the case, the ability to make good decisions is jeopardized. The people involved may not realize what is happening to them.

Some people may be more likely to victimize others when they are in a crowd. This may be because they think they can blame someone else. These people may later feel ashamed of their actions although they did not think about the consequences at the time. Peer pressure can make going against the crowd difficult, even when teens know what they are doing is wrong.

How to Avoid Date Rape

How can you, as a young person, protect yourself from date or acquaintance rape?

First of all, respect the limits set by your parents or those in authority. Family ground rules are one of the best ways parents have to protect their children. When invited to a party, know where it is and who will be there. Make sure that parents will be present.

Before you get involved in a difficult situation, you need to set your own personal limits. You need to decide how you feel about particular issues. Then you can decide how you will handle these problems should they arise.

Learn how to recognize trouble situations and be alert to circumstances that might get out of control. Maintain your options for leaving a situation if this should happen.

Learn how to say no and mean it. You don't need to come up with apologies, excuses, or reasons. You do need to let the other person or persons know through your facial expressions and body language that you mean what you say. Be assertive in expressing what you think is right for you.

At a party, stay out of bedrooms and other isolated areas. If drinking or drug use is going on, the best thing to do is to leave. If your date will not leave with you, get a friend to take you home. If that is not possible, call your parents. Always take enough change with you to make a few phone calls.

Practice responses to use when you feel someone is taking advantage of you. Your date may say, "If you love me, show me." Your reply might be, "If you really loved me, then we can wait for our relationship to grow even more." Someone who won't take no for an answer might say, "You can't say 'no.' I just spent lots of money on you." You could reply by saying, "I've done a lot of things for you, too, but I've never asked for repayment."

If someone makes you feel uncomfortable you should know it is all right to decide you don't like that person. Everyone experiences times when standing up for what you believe is uncomfortable and perhaps even scary. This is particularly true when your friends are doing something you think is wrong. When you feel uncomfortable, it is time to leave regardless of what others do. If you need help, appeal to a friend or call for someone to come for you.

What to Do if a Rape Occurs

If acquaintance rape does occur, teens need to realize they should report the incident. Reporting will help them get needed medical care and counseling. Counseling following the incident speeds up the recovery process. Without such counseling, emotional damage to one's self-esteem can have long-term repercussions. Victims may fear any close personal ties to others for they feel their trust has been violated. Counseling can help victims work through the emotional trauma and learn once again to develop a sense of closeness and trust. Victims also need to know they are still loved and valued.

Summary ■ ■ ■ ■ ■ ■ ■ ■ ■ ■ ■ ■ ■ ■ ■ ■

- Teens will have many new and different types of friends. Friendships will vary through the years.

- Dating helps young people learn about interpersonal relationships. This helps them prepare for adulthood and marriage.

- Today's dating patterns of teens are less structured and more informal. There is more emphasis on groups of people than on couples.

- Qualities of trust, self-disclosure, comfort, communication, and intimacy are important in building a serious relationship.

- Breaking up a relationship may be hard to do for a teen. The intent, however, should be to avoid undue pain or embarrassment for the other person.

- True love, tender love, and friendly love are positive types of love. Jealous love, passionate love, hostile love, and unreturned love are negative types of love.

- Love is stronger and more secure than infatuation. Love is less selfish and more patient than the desire for sexual gratification.

- Physical expressions are one method of communicating affection. They should be combined with other methods in a good relationship.

- Sexual decision making requires maturity and knowledge. Any sexual experience you have becomes a part of you. You have to accept the physical and emotional responsibilities and consequences that go with this experience.

- Abstinence is saying no to sexual intercourse and the possible consequences that might have resulted.

- There are techniques teens can use to help resist sexual pressure.

- Teens can easily become victims of acquaintance rape because they tend to trust the people they know.

To Review ■ ■ ■ ■ ■ ■ ■ ■ ■ ■ ■ ■ ■ ■ ■ ■

1. Explain how dating can prepare you for adulthood and marriage.

2. Describe how teens can benefit from informal group dating.

3. Dating only one person for a long period of time is called "going _____" or _____ dating.

4. List and briefly describe four qualities that characterize a serious relationship.

5. List four signs that indicate a relationship is having problems and should end.

6. List four ways to break up that can ease hurt and a sense of rejection.

7. Match the following terms with their descriptions.
   _____ Passionate love
   _____ Infatuation
   _____ Hostile love
   _____ Unreturned love
   _____ Friendly love
   _____ Jealous love
   _____ True love
   a. Involves total communication and commitment between two people.
   b. May form the foundation for true love to build on.
   c. Possessive love.
   d. Is vigorous, insistent, and urgent.
   e. Raises its voice in anger against the loved one.
   f. Is frustrating because it is unfulfilled love.
   g. Foolish, extreme attractions that do not last.

8. Name five ways to prepare yourself to make the right decisions concerning sexual relationships.

9. Explain how to effectively say no to sexual pressures.

10. Compare the terms *rape* and *acquaintance rape*.

11. Describe four things you can do to protect yourself from acquaintance rape.

To Do ▪ ▪ ▪ ▪ ▪ ▪ ▪ ▪ ▪ ▪ ▪ ▪ ▪ ▪ ▪ ▪

1. Accept or reject the statement, "All relationships begin as friendships." Discuss the reasons for your opinion.

2. Interview teens and adults about their friendships. Ask each person to describe a friendship that is (or was) important to him or her. Find out how and when the friendship began, how long it lasted, and what the person gained from it.

3. Form a panel of guys and girls from the class to discuss current dating patterns in your community. Have them cite the most popular dating activities.

4. Prepare a list of characteristics of dating partners such as, "gossips about friends" or "always on time." List these under two columns: Negative Traits and Positive Traits. Then place a check mark in front of the characteristics you think describe yourself. Review your list and make an effort to improve yourself.

5. Role-play a situation in which a couple is breaking up and each is very hurt in the process. Then role-play the same situation using methods that will keep hurt and rejection to a minimum. Compare and discuss the two.

6. Make a collage of magazine pictures, words, or cartoons that depict the different types of love. Explain your selections to the class.

7. Write a paper titled, "Why abstinence is the best choice for teens."

8. In small groups, discuss the best ways to say no to sexual pressure.

9. Discuss the problem of acquaintance rape in your community. Ask two college students to join the discussion and to give their views of the problem on college campuses.

David Hopper

Dating relationships often begin when you meet someone in school that you really like.

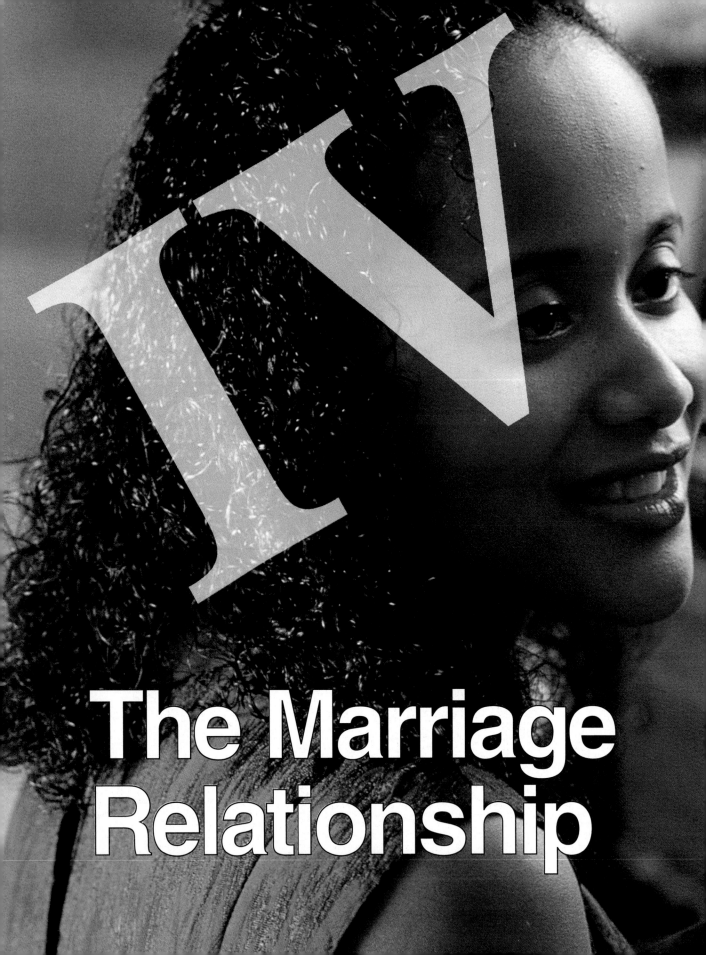

IV
The Marriage Relationship

12...

Choosing to Marry

Cholla Runnels

After studying this chapter, you will be able to

- list social and psychological forces involved in choosing a spouse.

- describe other personal factors people use to evaluate possible spouses.

- identify issues related to mixed marriages.

How do people go about choosing a spouse? Is it true that opposites attract, or do people tend to marry people like themselves? What factors may increase or decrease a person's chances of marital happiness? This chapter explores some forces that influence people's marital choices. It also examines the implications of these choices for marital happiness.

Forces Affecting Mate Selection

The process of choosing a husband or wife in our culture may seem haphazard, especially as it compares to that of other cultures. However, the mate selection process is guided by certain forces. These forces are social and psychological, and partners may or may not be aware of them.

Terms to Know

parent image

proximity

complementary
 needs

mixed marriage

theist

atheist

Similarity

The first guiding force in choosing a spouse is the tendency to marry someone much like yourself. People tend to choose spouses from their own race, religion, ethnic background, and social class. Men and women who have never married tend to marry other never-married people.

People from similar groups usually have similar attitudes about many aspects of their lives. They can share their ideas and feelings easily with each other. Thus they are more likely to form lasting relationships.

Parent Image

Have you ever heard the old song that contains the line, "I want a girl, just like the girl, that married dear old Dad"? Spouse selection based on the *parent image* theory holds that a man looks for a wife similar to his mother. Likewise, a woman looks for a husband similar to her father.

You may be influenced more than you realize by the images you have of your parents. If you have been raised to value high ethical standards, you will probably look for a spouse who shares these standards. If your parents are warm and understanding, you will probably look for these qualities in the person you choose to marry.

Proximity

Another force at work in choosing a spouse is physical *proximity,* or nearness. A person is more likely to form a meaningful relationship with someone who lives or works nearby, 12-1. Our mobile society has broadened our personal contacts, but you are still likely to marry someone you meet near your home.

David Hopper

12-1
Many relationships begin with friendships you form at school during your teen years.

Complementary Needs

The force of *complementary needs* leads you to seek a partner who is strong in areas in which you are weak. For instance, suppose you are a dominant person and a leader. You may be attracted to someone who is easygoing and a follower. Likewise, one partner who likes to help and care for people may be attracted to someone who needs care and attention. Couples may or may not be aware of the complementary needs they share. As partners mature, they may gain skills and confidence in areas in which they previously depended on their spouse.

Role Expectations

Every person expects a spouse to perform certain roles in marriage. Wage earning and taking care of the children are examples of such roles.

In today's society, roles are becoming more varied than they tended to be in the past. In many families with children, both the husband and wife work outside the home. In these families, spouses may expect to share many roles—for example, wage earner, cook, housekeeper, and gardener. Both may be involved with caring for the children. In other families, spouses may decide to split the roles of wage earner and homemaker, 12-2. Dating partners should discuss their future roles before they get married. Then they will know each other's expectations and be better able to fulfill them.

Choosing a Partner: Other Factors

The forces just discussed are social and psychological in nature. They may subconsciously guide the choice of a spouse. Other factors in choosing a partner, which will be discussed now, are more easily recognized and consciously judged.

Values

The force involving values simply means that you will tend to marry someone who has values that are similar to yours. This is logical since you tend to choose people with similar values for friends, and you will probably choose your spouse from your circle of friends.

Having similar values is very important in marriage. It gives the partners a common ground for the sharing of ideas, feelings, and goals. Because of this common ground, the partners are likely to communicate with greater understanding.

Personality Traits

Every person is unique and has a set of traits that work together to form a personality. That set of traits may favorably impress some people, yet "turn off" others.

The personality traits that a group of students said they would want in a mate are

listed in 12-3. How does this list compare with your ideas?

Thinking about the traits that are important to you will help you evaluate people throughout your life. You may even wish to list all the personality traits that you consider important and then try to find a spouse who has all of them! Such a strategy is unlikely to work. If this were possible, we could use computers to match people for successful marriages. Computer dating has been tried, but no machine can match whole personalities.

Cholla Runnels

12-2
Some couples split roles. One is the wage earner, and one is the homemaker.

Desirable Characteristics in a Mate

Ability to show affection
Understanding
Trustworthiness
Honesty
Concern for others
Good physical appearance
Pleasing personality
Sense of humor
Faithfulness
Good educational background
Positive self-image
Emotional maturity
Desire to have children
Desire not to have children
Self-confidence
Ability to communicate well
Acceptance of constructive criticism
Empathy
Ability to handle money

12-3
High school students developed this list. Which personality traits would you want a spouse to have?

Family Background

The statement, "Happiness runs in families," is often true. If your parents have a happy marriage, you will have a greater chance of having a happy marriage. This is because you are learning how spouses who love and respect one another behave in a marriage relationship. Also, a child raised in a happy home is more likely to be emotionally secure and to be able to build fulfilling relationships. See 12-4.

On the other hand, children brought up in a home full of hostility tend to feel less secure in their relationships. This does not mean that if your home is unhappy you are doomed to marital failure, however. People raised to expect constant happiness or to believe that life is always easy may not be willing to work at a marriage. This may be why some marriages fail even when the couple seem to have everything going for them.

Also, if the partners have experienced the instability of an unhappy home, they may have more motivation to make their marriage work. They may be more willing to do everything possible to establish a happy home. This means learning healthy ways of relating to one another based on mutual love and respect. It may also mean unlearning patterns of interaction that are destructive to close, loving relationships.

Parent Approval

Another factor related to family background is parental approval of the partner. If parents approve of the partner and the marriage, the new couple will have a greater chance for success.

If parental approval is lacking, the couple would be wise to proceed slowly. A marriage that takes place without parental approval may face three potential problem situations.

12-4
Children raised in a happy home tend to be emotionally secure. They have a good chance for marital happiness.

■ In most cases, parents have good reasons for opposing the marriage. These reasons may become apparent to the couple as they try to adjust to married life. If the couple refuse to listen to the parents' reasoning and to take advantage of the parents' experience, the couple may not realize their mistake until it is too late.

■ When parental disapproval exists, justified or not, the young couple are likely to feel tense whenever they are with the parents. As a result, they may try to ignore the parents, saying that they married each other, not each other's family. The truth is that they have married into two families. The families' approval or disapproval will be a constant factor in the happiness of the marriage.

■ If disapproval is a factor, the new husband or wife may be quick to say, "My parents were right," when the first conflicts arise. The partners may give up easily instead of working to improve the relationship. In some cases, they may even subconsciously use this as an excuse to get out of the marriage.

Health Factors

Poor health may not destroy a marriage, but good health can help it, 12-5. All marriages meet occasional stresses, and people who are healthy can resolve them more easily.

Mental and emotional health are just as important as physical health—maybe even more so. If a partner is emotionally stable, he or she will be able to meet the demanding responsibilities of marriage.

Leisure-Time Activities

Today's world offers many people more leisure time than they had in the past. A couple can use this leisure time to improve their

Miracles Portrait, Cedar Rapids, IA

12-5
Good health—both physical and mental—makes marriage easier and more enjoyable.

relationship. Generally, spouses who share many interests have a good chance for happiness in marriage, 12-6. Those who enjoy being together have more opportunities for living creative and abundant lives.

Leisure-time activities vary widely. They may occur inside or outside the home. They may be couple-oriented or shared with other people. Some provide an escape from the demanding world of work. Some allow people to grow and improve themselves. Others simply provide companionship among friends and family members.

By sharing leisure time, partners can release tensions and discuss frustrations and ac-

Evin Thayer

12-6
A shared interest in gardening brings this couple closer together.

complishments. When they become parents, their children will be able to share their companionship. When they retire, they will still find life meaningful and satisfying.

Leisure time can add a dimension of sharing and appreciation to a relationship. Partners should discuss their social and recreational interests before marriage. They need to know each other's expectations. Then they will be better able to balance their work roles, free time, and financial resources.

Education

Differences in the educational levels of two people are sometimes a factor in their relationship. Generally, a couple who have had about the same amount of education can share and communicate more easily than those who have not, 12-7. If their educational levels vary widely, they are more likely to have problems.

Wide differences in educational levels occur less often today than in the past. This is because men and women have become more similar in their career goals and opportunities.

Age

The younger you are when you marry, the more likely you are to divorce. This is because marriage requires maturity, and maturity usually increases with age.

Cholla Runnels

12-7
People with similar levels of education can usually communicate more easily with each other.

Contemporary Topics *of interest to teens:*
Age at Marriage: How Much Does It Matter?

Research suggests that a couple's age at marriage is one of the most important factors in marital success. The older the couple is, the less is the likelihood that they will divorce.

According to the National Center for Health Statistics, the chances that a couple will divorce are

- about 40 percent for couples under age 20.

- 26-30 percent for couples age 20-24.

- 25 percent for couples age 25-44.

- less than 14 percent for couples who do not marry until age 45.

People who wait until they are older to marry are more likely to have the emotional, social, and financial stability that often comes with age. These qualities can contribute significantly to marital success.

Although some people are ready for marriage before others, studies show that many teenage marriages fail. Teens may not have the emotional maturity needed to handle all the responsibilities of marriage. Another problem of most teenage marriages is money, 12-8. Money may remain a problem for a couple, especially if they had to quit school in order to marry. Couples who do this usually limit their earning potential for the rest of their lives.

The number of high school marriages is decreasing. Few boys marry while still in high school. Most of the girls who marry at that time have husbands who are older or who have dropped out of school. Sometimes the marriage is a way to escape from an unpleasant home environment. Some marriages take place because the woman is pregnant and the couple wishes to avoid an out-of-wedlock birth.

Though teenage marriages still take place, more and more young people are

12-8
David Hopper
Financial problems may occur in teenage marriages.

choosing to delay marriage. Most express the desire to be sure of themselves and their goals before they marry. Many want to complete their education and begin a career before committing themselves to another person, 12-9.

Fewer college students are marrying today than in the past couple of decades. Those who do marry while in college face several challenges. Two major challenges relate to money and social life.

Most couples have to work to support themselves. Long work hours, combined with long study hours, leave little time for social activities. To improve their financial position, one of the spouses may decide to quit school and work full-time. Authorities discourage this decision. They feel that both spouses should continue their college educations, even if they have to reduce their course loads and take an extra year or more to graduate. A marriage is usually healthier if the educational levels of the spouses are as equal as possible. This tends to promote greater similarities in other areas of the marriage (such as career goals) as well.

Mixed Marriages

A *mixed marriage* is one involving persons of different countries, races, or religious faiths. These marriages have greater potential for problems because of significant differences, but many succeed. Partners considering a mixed marriage should be

12-9
Many young people wish to visit other countries before they commit to marriage.

aware of the many adjustments they will have to face. Some couples delay talking about their differences for fear of destroying the feelings they share. However, if the relationship is strong, honest talk will add to its strength. If the couple have differences that cannot be settled, they would be wise to realize this before the relationship grows too serious.

International Marriages

International marriages involve people from different countries. These marriages occur more often as our society becomes more mobile and cosmopolitan. (A *cosmopolitan* society is one composed of people from a variety of countries around the world.) Many of these marriages work, but couples should realize the challenges involved. The partners will have to blend different cultural backgrounds and traditions. They may have to reconcile different beliefs—for example, beliefs about the role of women in society.

Interracial Marriages

Of all the types of mixed marriages, interracial marriages are often the most challenging. In many cases, families may tolerate the marriages, but they may do little to promote good relations.

An interracial couple may feel that they do not "fit" comfortably with either spouse's family or racial group. This feeling, as well as other social conflicts, may become even stronger when children are born. However, much adversity can be overcome with love, patience, empathy, and understanding on all sides.

David Hopper

12-10
The biggest problem of an interfaith marriage is often deciding on the religious training of the children.

Interfaith Marriages

A person's religion is a major factor to consider before marriage. Sometimes young people underrate the importance of religion in their lives. In such cases, they may not realize the potential problems of marrying someone of a different faith. People who are raised in a religious home are constantly influenced by the beliefs and practices of their religion. Such influences cannot be ignored. They affect people's thoughts, feelings, and actions in everyday life. If either partner is religiously oriented, each should be aware of the other's feelings and respect them.

The biggest problem facing any interfaith marriage is the question of raising the children in a religious faith. See 12-10. Other potential problems concern the acceptance of holiday and festive customs and views on birth control, abortion, and divorce. All of these issues should be discussed before the marriage.

Catholic-Protestant Marriages

Attempts have been made in recent years to point out that Catholics and Protestants have much in common. However, they also have some differences.

The Catholic faith holds that marriage is indissoluble, and it does not recommend divorce. Remarriage after divorce is permissible only if the church grants an annulment of the first marriage. Neither abortion nor "artificial" means of birth control (contraception) is acceptable.

These teachings should be considered carefully by a non-Catholic contemplating marriage to a Catholic. Both partners would be wise to meet with one or more local spiritual leaders before making any binding commitment. Many Catholic churches offer instructional classes to help non-Catholics become familiar with the faith.

Jewish-Gentile Marriages

Marriages between Jews and Gentiles (non-Jews) are increasing in number. Recent research suggests that as many as one-half of all Jews who marry are now choosing non-Jewish spouses.

Judaism represents a culture as well as a religion. The non-Jewish person can help make the relationship work by learning about both the culture and the faith.

Customs followed during holidays and other days of special religious observance can complicate or enrich the lives of Jewish-Gentile families, depending on their attitudes. The parents of each partner may expect their child to uphold the parents' beliefs and customs in the new home. If the young couple do not, parents with rigid attitudes may reject their child's spouse and their own child as well.

Perhaps the most painful conflicts arise when the couple has its first child. In which faith should the child be raised? Potential conflicts should be explored and resolved well before the wedding ceremony.

Although both families in an interfaith marriage experience many challenges, people who maintain open minds can find much to appreciate in each other's religious traditions. Many couples express this appreciation by observing the holidays of both faiths. With kindness and tolerance, many potential conflicts in such marriages can be resolved amicably.

Theist-Atheist Marriages

Religion plays an important role in the lives of many people. If a *theist* (one who believes a god exists) marries an *atheist* (one who denies the existence of a god), they may have problems. They may disagree about the time, money, and effort the religious spouse devotes to religious concerns. They may react differently to conflicts and stress in their lives. They may confuse their children by teaching them different beliefs and values.

A couple should discuss the importance of religion in their lives before they marry. Then they can make decisions that will prevent future problems.

Alternatives for Church or Synagogue Attendance

Church or synagogue attendance may be a problem for people in an interfaith marriage. This issue should be discussed, and a decision made, so it will not cause an argument each week. There are four basic alternatives.

- Each may attend his or her own church or synagogue and retain membership in his or her own congregation. This calls for accommodation on the part of each spouse. As long as the two of them are in accord, a stable relationship can be maintained. Some spouses enjoy accompanying one another to religious services for reasons of companionship and personal enrichment.

However, the problem usually arises again when children are born. Some parents deny their children religious instruction in either faith in the hope that the children will choose their own faith later, as adults. However, many spiritual leaders believe that raising children in one faith or the other is preferable to this alternative. Children raised without religious instruction may end up choosing no faith at all.

■ One may adopt the religion of the other. This alternative has the advantage of allowing the couple to share their religious experiences. However, neither partner should have to give up a religion unwillingly.

■ Both may drop their religions, or one may drop it while the other continues to practice it. Sometimes this happens gradually. If problems persist, one or both partners may feel it is not worth the trouble to continually raise the issue.

■ Both may drop their religions and accept a new religion. This very rare compromise may be made by couples who feel that neither partner should be asked to do more than the other. An intense study of the new religion occasionally lays the foundation for a stronger faith than either partner previously had. Each spouse's parents and family, however, may have difficulty accepting this decision.

Summary ■ ■ ■ ■ ■ ■ ■ ■ ■ ■ ■ ■ ■ ■ ■ ■

■ Several forces affect spouse selection. They include similarity, parent image, proximity, complementary needs, and role expectations.

■ Several additional factors in spouse selection are more obvious. They include values, personality traits, family background, parental approval, health factors, leisure-time activities, education, and age.

■ Reasons for the failure of many teenage marriages include financial problems and lack of emotional maturity.

■ A mixed marriage is one involving partners of different cultures, races, or religious faiths.

■ Partners who choose an international, interracial, or interfaith marriage should take a realistic look at the adjustments they will have to make.

To Review ■ ■ ■ ■ ■ ■ ■ ■ ■ ■ ■ ■ ■ ■ ■

1. Match each of the following factors affecting spouse selection with its description.

   _____ Proximity
   _____ Complementary needs
   _____ Parent image
   _____ Similarity
   _____ Role expectations

   a. A man will tend to marry someone who is much like his mother.
   b. You will tend to marry someone who lives fairly close to you.
   c. You will tend to marry someone who will behave the way you expect a spouse to behave.
   d. You will tend to marry someone who is strong in areas where you are weak.
   e. You will tend to marry someone who is much like yourself.

2. Explain why people raised in happy homes tend to have an easier time establishing happy marriages.

3. Which of the following statements are true?
   a. More and more people are choosing to delay marriage.
   b. A couple who have had about the same amount of education are likely to communicate more easily than a couple with very different levels of education.
   c. The younger you marry, the more likely you are to divorce.
   d. Mixed marriages never work.

4. Explain how shared leisure-time activities can benefit a marriage.

5. List two things a couple can do to prepare for a Catholic-Protestant marriage.

6. Describe two challenges faced by Jewish-Gentile couples.

7. Name two problems that may arise in a theist-atheist marriage.

To Do ■ ■ ■ ■ ■ ■ ■ ■ ■ ■ ■ ■ ■ ■ ■

1. Write a paper entitled "The Ideal Spouse."

2. Working in small groups, research the leisure-time activities that are available in your area for couples and for families. Report group findings to the class.

3. Accept or reject the following statement: "Teenage marriage is a poor idea." Support your answer.

4. Research one type of mixed marriage. Prepare a written report explaining its strengths and its potential problems.

Engagement
and Marriage

After studying this chapter, you will be able to

- describe the purpose of the engagement period.

- identify issues for you and your future spouse to discuss prior to marriage.

- recognize your legal and moral commitments in beginning a marriage relationship.

- assess wedding plans as they affect your total commitments and goals in marriage.

For most couples, becoming engaged is a fulfilling and often exciting experience. There is the thrill of announcing your love to the outside world and showing off an engagement ring. Planning a wedding and thinking about your first apartment is exciting. However, there is a serious side to engagement, too. It is the prelude to one of the most important steps of your life—marriage.

A loving marriage can bring some of the deepest happiness and fulfillment that two human beings can experience. There is the joy of loving and being loved, and the satisfaction of building a life and often a family together. There is also the security of knowing that you are part of a mutual support system—emotionally, financially, and in many other ways. Ideally, this support system will last throughout your life.

Terms to Know

monogamous

polygamous

bigamy

consanguineous marriage

marriages of affinity

common-law marriage

officiate

civil weddings

ceremonial wedding

The happiness brought by a good marriage does not just happen. It is the result of hard work, patience, communication, and understanding. It also benefits from the maturity and perspective that only the passing years can bring. Hard work and maturity, however, are no guarantee of marital happiness if you have made a poor marital choice in the first place. That is why it is so important to think carefully about whether your relationship is likely to be a successful one.

Engagement

The engagement period represents both an end to courtship and a start of plans for married life, 13-1. In the past, engagement was considered to be a legally binding contract. If the partners both wanted to end the engagement, the contract was canceled. However, if just one partner (for instance, the man) wanted to break the engagement, he could be sued for *breach of promise*. The woman could force him to marry her or to pay for damages. Such damages could in-

clude reimbursement for her actual monetary losses, for her humiliation, and for the loss of financial gain she would have derived from the marriage. Many fraudulent breach-of-promise suits were brought against men. As a result, many states have put severe limits on these suits or banned them completely.

Today, engagement is usually viewed as a sign of a couple's intentions to marry—not as a legal contract. The purpose of the engagement period is three-fold:

- It serves as an announcement to family, friends, and society of a couple's intentions to marry.

- It is a testing period during which the couple can evaluate their relationship and make plans for their future.

- It gives the couple time to plan the wedding ceremony.

Customs and rules of etiquette concerning engagement vary among families, communities, and regions of the country. Activities that take place during engagement should reflect the desires of the couple as they look ahead to their marriage. Too often the wedding becomes a way of repaying social obligations and is managed by the parents of the couple. It becomes a spectacle, competing with similar events organized by other families. Although wedding plans are important, the couple should keep the deeper meaning of the engagement in mind.

Testing Process of the Engagement Period

The testing and planning process is the most important function of the engagement. As you look ahead to your future life together, you will want to talk about your values and goals, 13-2. You may find that you do not agree on matters of everyday living. You may take a more critical look at each other in

13-1
Dennis Hopper

Engagement represents an end to courtship and a beginning of plans for the future as husband and wife.

Cholla Runnels

13-2
Engagement is a testing period during which a couple should discuss important
issues and take a critical look at each other.

areas such as grooming, irritating habits, inconsistent money management, or casual concern for family courtesies. Although engagement is not the same as marriage, it is a testing period that should be viewed as realistically as possible.

Many counselors feel that engagement offers a chance to improve a future marriage, or to expose differences that would make marriage unwise. This, then, is a crucial period for you. If you look honestly at your relationship at this time, you may be reassured that your future together will be a happy one. On the other hand, taking an honest look at your relationship during engagement may help you prevent future problems. If you see patterns of serious conflict, if you feel less committed to your love as you realize what marriage involves, and if you can openly admit those feelings to yourself, you may be able to prevent a bad marriage. At that point, you would be wise to break the engagement. A broken engagement is better than a broken marriage.

Communication during Engagement ■ ■ ■ ■ ■

What can you do to make the most of the engagement period? How can you use it as a foundation for building an even deeper relationship? How can you be honest with yourself, and with each other, if you feel conflict or doubts about your relationship? Perhaps one of the best starting points is to review what most authorities believe should be discussed during engagement.

Personality Traits

The dating relationship before an engagement is somewhat unrealistic. It rarely prepares you to accept your mate as a "whole" person. You have undoubtedly become aware of the personality traits that you like, but have you accepted or learned to tolerate the traits that you do not like? When you plan to marry someone, you must be prepared to accept the person as he or she is. A wedding ceremony does not change a person's character, personality, or habits.

To evaluate your relationship, each of you might ask yourself the following questions:

- Do I like and respect myself? Do I have pride in my fiancé, and do I respect him or her? Can we feel confident in accepting our future together?

- Do I value my individuality? Can my fiancé and I allow our individual personalities to grow and yet accept the ties of married life?

- Can we empathize with each other's feelings? Can we recognize and understand each other's needs and emotions while still maintaining our own personalities?

David Hopper

13-3
Some careers, such as law enforcement, place extra pressures on marriages. Spouses must be able to accept these pressures and to offer support when needed.

- Do I have any "leftover" negative feelings from childhood? Can we absorb or "work through" any such negative feelings and make our future life together a positive one?

- Am I trustworthy? Can we feel completely secure in the trust we have for each other and use this trust as a foundation for our marriage?

- Am I moody and indifferent at times? Can we accept each other's right to privacy, and yet share moments of sorrow, anger, joy, and contentment?

- Am I able to communicate verbally and nonverbally? Can we share our affection through words, looks, and touch?

- Can I accept constructive criticism? Will we both feel secure in our love when negative, as well as positive, statements are made?

- Do I have a sense of humor? Will we be able to laugh with each other and not at each other?

- Am I able to communicate my expectations to my fiancé? Can we accept each other's expectations, knowing that we may or may not be able to live up to all of these expectations?

Setting up a "formula" for a successful marriage is impossible. However, if you can answer most of these questions positively, your future relationship probably has much positive potential. If you find that many of your responses are negative, you should review your total relationship in greater depth. Marriage does not mean that you have to agree on everything. It does mean that you need to share the space between your two viewpoints and work together to achieve happiness.

Career Goals in Marriage

You should ask yourselves how you plan to balance your career and family goals. Some professions are more demanding than others. People who want to succeed in certain professions must accept the demands they impose. Their spouses also have to accept the demands and must be ready to lend support during times of pressure. See 13-3.

People who choose careers in social services must recognize the demands of emotional involvement with others. Religious leaders, as well as their families, have to be ready to share their lives with entire congregations. Skilled laborers are under competitive pressure to maintain their skills and to update their technological knowledge. Business executives have to learn to balance their ups and downs in financial matters as well as other emotional stresses.

Some people like to own their own businesses. Others feel best working under the guidance and direction of supervisors. Some people prefer relatively free work environments controlled only by their desire to produce. Others choose to work within the structure of huge corporations. Whatever type of career you choose, it will affect your marriage and family life.

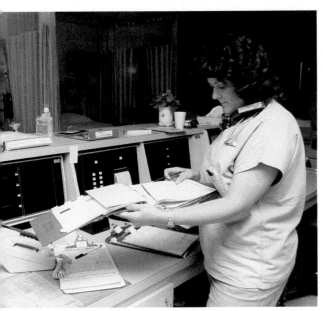

David Hopper

13-4
A nurse may have a rotating schedule that includes some night shifts. This possibility and its consequences should be discussed before marriage.

If you, your future spouse, or both of you choose careers that involve unusual demands, you should discuss this before marriage, 13-4. A career is more than a means of financial support for your family. Your career identity affects your whole life and thus the lives of all your family members. Combining the career role with those of spouse and parent can be difficult. You will need each other's help and support.

You might ask yourselves the following questions:

- Do I want a career that requires a college degree? Will we be willing to work to achieve this goal?

- Do I want to choose a training program for a skilled craft? Will we be able to adapt to irregular schedules, overtime hours, or weekend work, if necessary?

- Do I want a career that will require involvement with other people, such as medicine, social work, or theology? Will I be able to maintain my commitment to my spouse as I meet the demands resulting from this choice?

- Will I feel satisfied in my career? Will we be able to accept our career identities as a positive factor in our personal and family lives?

- Will I accept a dual-career marriage? Will we recognize the advantages and disadvantages of a dual-career marriage? Will we be able to balance our lives to reach our goals?

Discussing Sexual and Reproductive Expectations

During engagement, the two of you will need to discuss many aspects of your future life together, including sexual and reproductive matters. Discussion of feelings about having children—how many and when—is very

13-5

Cholla Runnels

Does your future mate like children? Would you like to have children? These are good questions to answer during engagement.

important, 13-5. If one person does not want to have children, the other partner must be aware of this.

Engaged couples should also discuss their sexual expectations for marriage. They should be aware of one another's expectations regarding sexual relations. Attitudes toward various types of birth control and toward abortion under various circumstances (including detection of fetal abnormalities) should also be shared. If partners do not discuss these matters, they may experience disappointment and conflict after marriage.

If discussing sexual relations is difficult for a couple, they may want to start by reading factual books about sex together. They may want to ask for help from a professional such as a doctor, counselor, or religious leader.

Sexual adjustment in marriage is interrelated with all other areas of adjustment. Like your love, a mutually satisfying sexual relationship can grow and develop with time if you have realistic expectations.

Sex is only one of many areas for discussion during your engagement. The important point to remember is that the two of you should try to communicate honestly about everything in your life during this important time.

Medical Counseling

Premarital medical counseling should be done early in the engagement period, rather than immediately before the wedding. There are several reasons for medical counseling and a physical examination. These include the following:

- Based on the results of your physical examination, the doctor will be able to determine your general state of health.

- The doctor will discuss your partner's and your medical histories, including previous illnesses. The doctor will also review your family backgrounds and warn you of any hereditary conditions that may cause problems if you decide to have children.

- You and your partner will have the chance to ask questions concerning your sexual roles in your future marriage.

- If you desire, you will have the chance to ask about contraception.

- Premarital counseling and a physical examination establish a doctor-patient relationship, which might be helpful later. If the couple develops any problems in the future, the doctor will be better able to counsel them.

Future In-laws

By the time the engagement takes place, many couples are on good terms with their future in-laws. If the engagement has the ap-proval of both sets of parents, the couple may not have any in-law problems. In fact, the parents may give them support and encouragement. A couple and their in-laws often become good friends.

Other couples are not as fortunate. A discussion of wedding plans may reveal that the values of the two families differ. One family may want to handle all the plans for a large, formal wedding. The other family may resent all the plans and prefer a simple ceremony. Family traditions that seem important to one may seem irrelevant to the other. The main concern should be the wishes of the bride and groom. If they find themselves

Cholla Runnels

13-6
Try to keep a positive attitude toward your in-laws and to appreciate their interests and hobbies.

divided at this time because of family pressures, it may be a sign of their inability to make their own decisions as a couple.

As you look ahead to your marriage, you should try to keep a positive attitude toward your in-laws. See 13-6. "Giving up" their son or daughter may be difficult for them. Patience and tact, as well as a good sense of humor, are needed in handling in-law situations. Some suggestions are given in 13-7.

Suggestions for Good In-law Relationships

- Your first loyalty is to your mate.
- Live apart from your in-laws. This will allow you to establish your own marital system.
- Authorities find that "Mother" and "Dad" are the labels preferred by most parents. This denotes equality and shows respect. Some parents will offer their own suggestions instead, such as, "Just call me Frank."
- Treat in-laws with the same respect you show to your friends.
- Do not use a parent as a model for your spouse to follow.
- When visiting in-laws, be thoughtful and courteous. Do not expect to be treated as a guest; offer to assist with household chores. Try to keep your visits fairly short.
- Give advice to in-laws only when they ask for it.
- If your in-laws give advice, accept it graciously. If the advice is not good for your marriage, do not follow it.
- Discuss the faults of your spouse only with your spouse—not with your family. They may bring up traits they dislike and make the problem worse.
- Do not try to change your in-laws; accept them as they are. You love their child, so you should try to appreciate them.

13-7
Patience, tact, and a good sense of humor will help settle most in-law difficulties.

The most common complaint about in-laws is that they are meddling or interfering. It may be hard for parents to stand by and see their married sons and daughters struggle with some of life's problems. Thus, their first reaction may be to give assistance immediately. In most cases, they would be wiser to wait until their help is actually sought. When in-laws do offer help, whether it was sought or not, the young couple should thank them for the offer. However, they should accept it only if they think it is good for their marriage.

Studies show that the second most common problem with in-laws (after meddling) is indifference, thoughtlessness, or lack of appreciation. The ideal relationship would seem to be one in which the in-laws show affection and concern, but provide help only when asked.

Money Management

Another important area to be discussed is money management. Money is a major factor in your relationship, both before and after marriage. Spending habits developed prior to marriage will carry over into your marriage. Financial decisions will influence your wedding plans and will affect your married lifestyle.

During the engagement period, you and your future spouse need to talk candidly about money management. If income sources and amounts are known, you would be wise to plan a budget for the first months of your marriage. This will allow you to learn about each other's financial priorities. If you find your priorities differ widely, it is best to know this before marriage.

A spouse who looks forward to home ownership may be willing to forgo certain luxuries to save for this goal. If the other person places a higher value on entertainment and recreation, this difference should be understood. The couple should work to reach a compromise before the wedding. Studies show that couples who have similar financial priorities have greater chances for happiness in marriage.

Future Living Arrangements

The engagement period gives you time to plan your future living arrangements. Your choice of a home will depend primarily on your job location and financial situation.

Your home should be a place where you both find comfort and contentment. This is why the furnishings should reflect the tastes of both husband and wife. See 13-8.

You probably will not be able to afford a fully furnished apartment or house when you are first married. Therefore, it is usually best to add pieces of furniture as you can afford them. In this way, you do not have to go into debt.

Begin with a few basic pieces. You may be able to get some from friends and relatives. Secondhand stores and neighborhood garage sales are also good places to look.

Once you are in your new home, you will have a better idea of what pieces of furniture you need. You and your mate may enjoy planning each purchase as you can afford it. You can shop together and make joint decisions. Later, you may find that each piece of furniture in your home has a happy memory behind it.

Religious Commitments

Planning a wedding often involves religious decisions. Where the wedding will be held and who will perform the ceremony, for instance, are decisions that need to be made. You may wish to talk about your future religious commitments as well. If you do not discuss the matter of religion at this time, an adjustment may be more difficult later in

13-8

With the courtesy of IKEA

Furnishings should satisfy both the husband and wife, so they can both feel comfortable in their home.

your marriage. This issue will become especially important if you have children and face decisions about their religious training.

If you both have been reared in a religious faith, you may share a commitment to a religion. If you are of the same faith, you may continue in this faith. If you have different religious backgrounds, you will have to decide if each will retain his or her faith. Sometimes, one will change to the faith of the other partner, or they will both change to a new, third faith.

Counselors report that couples may experience adjustment problems if one partner wants to establish a religious commitment, but the other partner is totally against such involvement. The important thing is that a couple begin to resolve any conflicts involving religious commitments before they marry.

Assessing Friendships

The engagement period is a good time to assess friendships more closely, 13-9. The friends of your future spouse may soon

David Hopper

13-9
The engagement period gives you time to get to know each other's friends well.

become your friends, too. Likewise, your friends may become your spouse's friends. These friendships can have a significant impact on your future marriage. If the relationships are positive, they can add variety to your lives and broaden your range of experience. They can also provide you with sources of support in times of need.

On the other hand, friends may cause conflicts if they expect you to continue to be their friend without considering that you are now part of a couple. Marriage will change your availability and responsibilities. Your friends should be able to accept this.

If you find that a particular friend of your future spouse disturbs you, you should mention this before marriage. You are expecting a lot if you demand that your future mate end a long-term friendship. However, your first step in reaching a solution is to admit that the friendship upsets you. If you do not care for the values on which the friendship is based, this could be a warning sign for future marital conflict.

Revealing the Past

What information about your past should be revealed during the engagement period? The answer to this question varies with each couple. However, some items should definitely be revealed. These are

- a previous marriage and any obligations it entails.

- hereditary problems or other defects that would prevent the couple from having children or indicate that children might be born with abnormalities.

- a history of heart disease, sexually transmitted disease, or other health problems.

- a criminal or prison record.

- debts or similar obligations that might handicap the marriage.

Should you also reveal past relationships that may have meant a great deal to you at the time and may have involved sexual intimacy? Authorities disagree on the extent to which people should discuss previous intimate relationships. Some prospective spouses have trouble accepting too many revelations. Others may not.

Engagement offers the unique opportunity to work out problems together in the context of "us." Each couple must find the level of openness that suits them best. The two of you can ask, "What will be best for us and our future marriage?" Certainly, direct questions deserve an honest response.

Attitudes toward Marriage Counseling

Most engaged couples do not anticipate serious problems in their marriage. However, these expectations are not borne out by current divorce statistics. During the engagement period, partners may wish to become aware of each other's attitudes toward marriage counseling. Although these attitudes can change, it may be of interest to know whether your partner is willing to go with you to a marriage counselor if your relationship develops significant problems.

Breaking Engagements

For most people, engagement is a happy time. They are looking forward to a new life that they believe will be happy and satisfying. For others, the testing period of engagement causes many doubts to emerge. If either partner decides that the marriage would probably not work, the couple would be wiser to break the engagement than to go ahead with the wedding. See 13-10. Divorced couples often admit that patterns of conflict or poor communication appeared during their engagement. If they had heeded the warning signs then, they might have been able to avoid the trauma of divorce.

The process of planning a future life together may reveal differences that cannot be resolved. If a partner feels that a true "we" quality is not a part of this planning and that either partner is still more interested in "I," any further planning should be questioned. A person who feels exploited or ignored should realize that a future marriage would probably not succeed.

Although planning a wedding can become a time-consuming activity, the major goal of the engagement should be to prepare the couple for marriage. Disagreements will exist between engaged people just as they do between married people. Such disagreements provide the couple with opportunities for problem solving. A couple will never agree on every issue, but if a pattern develops showing irreversible problems in a certain area, they may want to seek premarital coun-

seling. Any and all possible problems are best settled before marriage.

If both partners find that they are really not suited for each other, they should make a mutual decision to break their engagement. See 13-11. When this must be done, it is better if both accept it rather than creating problems for one another. Acting immaturely—with careless disregard for the feelings of the partner, or even with a deliberate attempt to hurt the partner—makes the situation even worse. It is difficult enough to have to face

Cholla Runnels

13-10

If you decide your future marriage would probably fail, you would be wise to call off the wedding. A broken engagement is better than a broken marriage.

Reasons for Breaking an Engagement

- Acknowledgment of strong feelings of incompatibility—not just doubts.
- Realization that the engagement was made originally under pressure from relatives or circumstances.
- Recognition that either of the pair is emotionally dependent on parents or friends and too immature to withstand the demands of marriage.
- Changes in the planned future of the couple due to a serious accident, health problem, or similar disaster affecting the ability to earn a living and raise children.

13-11
There are several valid reasons for breaking an engagement.

friends and family with the announcement that the engagement has been broken.

Sometimes the one most hurt may regress to an immature level of behavior to try to hold the unwilling partner. Threats of violence or suicide may be made in an attempt to regain attention. Such actions may only confirm the wisdom of the decision to break the engagement.

A form of revenge that some disappointed lovers use is a quick marriage to someone else. This is called "marrying on the rebound." Marriage for spite has little chance for success, and the innocent spouse in the rebound marriage deserves better.

Marriage Laws ▪ ▪ ▪ ▪

Marriage is one of the most successful legal arrangements in our country, 13-12. Even with the high divorce rate, more business contracts are broken than marriage contracts.

The state views itself as the third party in any marriage. The family that is established at marriage must accept the responsibilities dictated by state laws. Marriage laws vary among states, so people planning to marry should check the laws of their particular state.

Monogamy

The laws concerning marriage recognize only a *monogamous* (one wife, one husband) relationship. Any person who is already married cannot legally remarry. Remarriage is possible only if the first spouse has died or the marriage has been dissolved by annulment or divorce.

Some people with certain religious views have allowed *polygamous* marriages (those with more than two spouses). For instance, when the Mormons settled in Utah, they declared polygamy to be legal. This was mainly an attempt to populate their sparse communities. Polygamy is no longer legal anywhere in the United States. A person who enters a second marriage before the first one is dissolved can be charged with *bigamy*. The crime of bigamy is classified as a felony.

Physical and Mental Qualifications

Each state has its own laws concerning physical and mental qualifications for marriage. Some of the laws, such as the age requirement, are affected by broader federal laws.

Age

As a result of federal action, all states allow persons 18 years of age or older to marry without parental consent. Most states will allow younger people (as young as age 13) to marry if they have parental consent. In some cases, persons under age 18 need both a court order and parental consent to obtain a marriage license.

Blood Test

Most states require people wanting a marriage license to present a physician's statement. This statement must declare that both the man and woman are free of certain communicable diseases, particularly some sexually transmitted diseases. A few states require more complete examinations. The physician's statement must be signed within a certain time period before obtaining the license. The time period varies, depending on state law. Another test would be needed if the couple did not obtain the marriage license during this period.

Sound Mind

Most states have laws concerning the marriage of people who are mentally disabled or who are unable to understand the act of getting married. Such lack of understanding at the time of marriage is sometimes used as grounds for annulment or divorce later.

Prohibited Relationships

Consanguineous marriages, or marriages of people related by blood, run the risk of producing defective children. If faulty genes exist in a family, a consanguineous union allows a greater chance for them to combine and create a child with disabilities. Most states prohibit marriage of blood relatives such as brothers and sisters, fathers and daughters, mothers and sons, grandfathers and granddaughters, grandmothers and grandsons, uncles and nieces, or aunts and nephews. Marriages between first cousins and between second cousins are also prohibited in many states.

David Hopper

13-12
Marriage is one of the most long-lasting and successful legal arrangements in our country.

Marriages of affinity, or marriages of people related by marriage, are often prohibited. The most common interpretation prohibits stepparents from marrying stepchildren. State laws differ concerning marriages of affinity. Some states prohibit them on the basis that such relationships are less stable and have less chance of success.

Common-law Marriage

Common-law marriages are one of the outgrowths of our early history. If a couple wanted to marry, but did not want to wait for a circuit judge or minister to travel to their community, they simply started living together as husband and wife. These marriages are still recognized as valid in some states.

The distinguishing trait between common-law marriages and relationships involving living together is the intent behind them. If a couple intend to be husband and wife and present themselves in public as such,

13-13
Many couples choose to be married by a religious leader.

they have a common-law marriage. They are considered legally married. Property and inheritance rights apply as in legal marriage, and children of the couple are legitimate. In some cases, the couple choose to appear in court and make a declaration of informal marriage in which they state their intention to be husband and wife. In other cases, they simply present themselves as husband and wife and are considered married. If the couple choose to dissolve this union, they must go through legal divorce procedures. They cannot simply move apart and consider themselves legally separated or divorced.

In states where common-law marriages are legal, any plan to live together should be considered carefully by both persons. Once the couple present themselves in public as husband and wife, one partner may declare the relationship to be a common-law marriage. If this should happen, a legal divorce would be required to terminate the marriage.

Obtaining a License

To get married, you must apply for and obtain a marriage license from the clerk of the city or county in which you live. Most states have laws that dictate the length of time people must wait to marry after applying for a license. Many states have a three- to five-day waiting period between the time a couple applies for and obtains a license. Some states require a one- to five-day waiting period between the time the license is issued and the wedding. In addition, most states limit the time that the license remains valid. This period varies from three weeks to one year.

The Marriage Officiate

A marriage *officiate* is a person who can legally marry a couple. *Civil weddings* may be performed by certain judicial officials and, in some states, by certain public officials. These officiates are chosen by couples who elope or who do not choose to have a religious ceremony. The most common of these officiates are judges, justices of the peace, magistrates, and mayors.

Many couples choose to be married by a minister, rabbi, or priest in a *ceremonial wedding.* See 13-13. Couples who choose ceremonial weddings tend to be those who value the customs traditionally associated with their religious and cultural beliefs.

In the Quaker ceremony, the couple is married without an officiate. The congregation signs the certificate as witnesses, and the couple literally marry themselves. The law waives the usual legalities associated with the wedding to accommodate people of this faith.

Some couples choose to write their own marriage vows and marriage contract. To do this, they must consult the officiate who will marry them. Some officiates do not wish to deviate from traditional ceremonies. Others realize the value of individualizing the ceremony for the particular couple and will cooperate with the changes. Marriage contracts drawn up by the couple cannot, however, replace the legal marriage license.

Changing Your Name

Most women take the last name of their husbands when they marry. However, this is a custom, not a law. Today, more couples are choosing to ignore this custom. Some women keep their own last names. Some couples join their last names with a hyphen, such as Smith-Jones. When children are born, decisions must be made about the last name they will have.

Weddings ▪ ▪ ▪ ▪ ▪

A wedding serves three important functions, as follows:

- It signifies the start of the couple's new life together.

- It announces the marriage to the public.

- It satisfies the legal requirements of the state.

13-14
A traditional, ceremonial wedding is chosen by the majority of people who marry.

Contemporary Topics *of interest to teens:*
Your Wedding Budget

How much should a wedding cost? Each couple needs to decide this question for themselves, perhaps in consultation with their families. This is especially so if one or both families are paying for the event. Couples may choose from a range of possibilities. They might choose a very simple ceremony or a large wedding with many attendants and guests, a reception and sit-down dinner, a band, and a limousine.

As the average age at marriage increases, more couples are sharing wedding costs with their parents or are financing their weddings themselves. Couples tempted by the glamour of a lavish wedding may wish to consider the event in the larger perspective of their lives together. Would their lives be enhanced, for example, if some resources were reserved for higher education, a down payment on a home, furniture, travel, or other items?

Couples who opt for a large wedding may wish to budget for items such as the following:

- Wedding consultant

- Stationary and postage (invitations, reply cards, guest book, thank-you notes)

- Flowers (bridal bouquet, attendants' bouquets and boutonnieres, corsages, arrangements) and other decorations

- Music (organist, soloist, orchestra)

- Wedding gown and tuxedo

- Food (rehearsal dinner, wedding cake, refreshments, and/or wedding dinner)

- Fees for officiate and others

- Gifts for attendants

- Favors for guests (rice packets, groom's cake)

- Security, valet parking, coat check, restroom attendants

- Photography

- Wedding trip

Any legal wedding ceremony fulfills these three functions. The emphasis you place on your wedding is up to you and your future spouse. It can be simple or elaborate. Your age and religious beliefs are likely to affect the type of ceremony you choose. The city, state, and country in which you live will also affect it.

The traditional ceremonial wedding is still chosen by the majority of people who marry, 13-14. Ceremonial weddings may enhance the stability of the marriage relationship. Most cultures and religious groups cling to traditions surrounding weddings.

On the other hand, many people prefer simple civil weddings. They feel that ceremonial weddings have become highly commercialized affairs. They feel that the real commitment that should evolve between the two persons is shrouded in the pageantry of some ceremonial weddings.

Some couples choose to elope. This choice is usually made because of parental objection to the marriage. Elopement bypasses the important function of the engagement period. It also may alienate friends and in-laws.

Wedding Plans

Wedding plans begin when the couple informs both sets of parents of the engagement and sets the wedding date. The date should be chosen with the couple's education and career responsibilities as well as the parents' wishes in mind. Space in churches and synagogues needs to be reserved in advance. Attendants of the bride and groom are usually chosen with their availability in mind. Saturday is the most popular day for weddings. June, August, and December are the most popular months.

A couple should talk frankly with their parents concerning wedding costs. Both sets of parents should be consulted, for the re-

Responsibilities of the Bride and Her Family

Groom's wedding ring.
Bridal gown and trousseau.
Invitations, announcements, and postage.
Floral arrangements for decoration.
Bridal attendants' bouquets.
Organist and soloist charges.
Reception costs.
Engagement and wedding photographs.
Transportation for bridal attendants.
Bridesmaid luncheon.
Gifts for bridal attendants.
Personal gift to groom.

Responsibilities of the Groom and His Family

Engagement ring.
Bride's wedding ring.
Clergy's fee.
Marriage license.
Rehearsal dinner.
Bridal bouquet and going-away corsage.
Mothers' and grandmothers' corsages.
Boutonnieres for groom's attendants.
Personal gift to the bride.
Honeymoon.

13-15
Traditionally, families have divided the wedding responsibilities in this manner.

sponsibilities of both families can be sizable. See 13-15.

Once the wedding budget is made, the couple should set their priorities. Some couples prefer to put more of their money into photography because this is the most lasting aspect of the occasion. Others prefer to invite lots of friends and relatives and to spend most of their money for the reception. The wedding should reflect the honest wishes of the bride and groom, within the boundaries of financial limitations. See 13-16.

David Hopper

13-16
Although wedding plans should reflect the wishes of the bride and groom, parents of the couple may have helpful suggestions.

When planning a religious ceremony, a couple may find that their pastor, priest, or rabbi has restrictions on music, liturgy, video-taping, or photographs. The couple may wish to deviate from established religious cere-monies. They may want to add their own per-sonal touches in music, setting, or vows. They may even choose to write their own cere-mony, though some clergy may discourage these changes.

Plans for the reception may need to be made early. They can be very time-consum-ing, complicated, and costly, depending on the type of reception. Arrangements may need to be made for rings, flowers, cake, clothes for the wedding party, and gifts for the attendants. A couple also may wish to plan a wedding trip.

The organist, soloist, photographer, and anyone else who will have a special function at the wedding will have to be contacted. In-vitation lists should be made by both families, keeping in mind any necessary limitations. Invitations should be sent four to six weeks before the wedding date.

Legal requirements, such as having blood tests and obtaining the marriage li-cense, must be met. As the date for the wed-ding draws near, the couple should double-check all the arrangements and make any necessary final decisions. Complete and efficient plans will help the wedding day go smoothly so that everyone can enjoy it.

The Honeymoon

The honeymoon or wedding trip allows the bride and groom time for intimacy and relaxation following the busy schedule of their wedding. See 13-17. This can be an important time for the couple if they have the necessary resources of time and money. The location chosen should reflect the wishes of both spouses. A relaxed schedule that includes activities with other people as well as periods of privacy is best. A long, extended honeymoon is not often recommended by counselors. Most suggest a brief honeymoon, with a longer vacation planned about six months later.

Expectations for complete personal satisfaction are often not achieved during the honeymoon. This time is the beginning of a couple's life together. It represents a transition from single life to married life. Remnants of fears that you may not please each other may affect your ability to be completely relaxed.

Switching your behavior from restraint to complete intimacy may not be easy in a few short days. Even those who have shared sexual intimacies before marriage may find that the honeymoon does not fulfill their expectations. Our culture has built so many fantasies around honeymoons that the reality may be disappointing.

How can you make your honeymoon fulfilling? You should both be knowledgeable concerning your sexual roles in marriage. You should be aware of your expectations for

13-17
For many couples, a honeymoon is a chance to travel. It is also a time to relax and to begin adjusting to the new roles of husband and wife.

satisfaction as well as those of your mate. A climate of trust and complete sharing will allow you to communicate with each other, verbally and nonverbally.

The sharing of your future life together is just beginning on your wedding trip. You should look forward eagerly to all you can learn and experience together. Any inhibitions you may have concerning living with your new spouse can be overcome through sharing, understanding, and a deep commitment to one another.

The wedding represents the start of a new life full of meaning. The honeymoon gives you and your spouse time to become intimately acquainted. Together, the wedding and honeymoon can establish a foundation upon which you can build an abundant and meaningful life.

Summary ■ ■ ■ ■ ■ ■ ■ ■ ■ ■ ■ ■

- The engagement period allows the couple time to announce the intended marriage, complete wedding plans, and test their relationship.

- The engagement period gives the couple time to review personality traits and future career goals, to prepare for their sexual roles as husband and wife, and to receive medical counseling. It also gives them a chance to establish good relationships with future in-laws, to discuss money management and future living arrangements, and to assess their friendships.

- Honest communication during engagement can reveal important differences or patterns of conflict. If these are serious, breaking the engagement could prevent a later divorce.

- Marriage is one of the most successful contractual arrangements in our country.

- Marriage laws concerning age, health, marriage of relatives, and wedding officiates vary from state to state.

- The marriage ceremony may be civil or ceremonial. A majority of people choose ceremonial weddings.

- A wedding signifies the start of a couple's new life together, announces the marriage to the public, and satisfies legal requirements.

- Wedding plans should reflect the wishes of the bride and groom within the boundaries of financial limitations.

- The honeymoon gives the bride and groom time to become acquainted intimately and to adjust to their new life together.

To Review ■ ▨ ▨ ▨ ■ ▨ ▨ ■ ▨ ▨ ■ ▨ ▨ ■ ▨

1. True or False. Since a career is just a means of financial support, it seldom affects a person's marriage and family life.

2. List four reasons why a couple should have premarital medical counseling.

3. List two suggestions for maintaining good relationships with in-laws.

4. Describe one positive and one negative influence of friendships outside of marriage.

5. What five items should definitely be revealed about your past during the engagement?

6. True or False. If patterns of conflict emerge during engagement, the couple should ignore them and hope that they will get along better once they are married.

7. Give one example of a consanguineous marriage and one example of a marriage of affinity.

8. Who officiates at civil weddings? Who officiates at ceremonial weddings?

9. True or False. According to law, a married couple must share the same last name.

10. True or False. Most counselors feel that a short honeymoon is preferable to a long one.

To Do ■ ■ ■ ■ ■ ■ ■ ■ ■ ■ ■ ■ ■ ■ ■ ■ ■

1. Role-play the following situations concerning engagement.
   a. A couple who have known each other six months and have been engaged a week are planning to marry next month. Both sets of parents are against the hasty plans.
   b. An engaged couple have differing views concerning career goals. They wonder if this will create problems in their marriage.
   c. A couple attending college are debating whether to get married during the semester break or to wait until the end of the year when they will both graduate.
   d. A couple who want to marry as soon as they graduate from high school both have low-paying jobs. Both sets of parents favor the marriage, but question the couple's financial capabilities and advise them to further their education before marrying.

2. Ask a panel of husbands and wives to discuss problems of career involvement in marriage. Ask them to point out both trivial and major conflicts.

3. Discuss the statement: A broken engagement is better than a broken marriage.

4. Review the marriage laws in your state. Check on the physical, mental, age, and time qualifications.

5. Discuss reasons for choosing ceremonial weddings and civil weddings.

6. Research marriage vows that have been written by couples themselves. Compare them to traditional vows from a variety of religions, and to the vows from a civil wedding.

7. Write a calendar of events that could be followed to prepare for a wedding, including all the necessary details.

8. Research wedding costs such as invitations, flowers, reception, photographs, and honeymoon.

Building a Marriage

Terms to Know

intermittency

compromise

accommodation

concession

martyrdom

ongoing hostility

productive
  quarreling

negotiation

destructive
  quarreling

**After studying this chapter,
you will be able to**

- recognize factors related to happiness
  and success in marriage.

- analyze five techniques for handling
  marital disagreements.

- distinguish between productive and
  destructive quarreling.

- recognize the normalcy and function
  of conflict in marriage.

- assess the resources available to help
  couples resolve conflict.

The moment you become a husband or
wife, you will undoubtedly feel that your marriage will be the best one of all time. This is
as it should be, for it is important that you
feel that your marriage is special. Every couple hopes their marriage will succeed and
last forever.

Happiness in Marriage

Happiness is a normal expectation of
marriage. However, continuous happiness is
not a realistic goal. Happiness is a fringe benefit. It is the side effect you feel as you strive
for contentment. Some couples feel happy
when they share affection, when they agree
on issues, when they realize they are not
lonely, and when they share common interests. It is important that a couple have a
sense of commitment and sharing. Then
happiness will be a natural by-product.
Nathaniel Hawthorne wrote many years ago:

Happiness is like a butterfly.
The more you chase it, the more it will elude
  you.
But if you turn your attention to other things,
It comes and sits softly on your shoulder.

14-1

Cholla Runnels

Affection is the primary emotion in a happy marriage. Something as simple as a good-bye hug or kiss in the morning can make the whole day better.

What brings happiness to one marriage may not work for another. However, a couple will have a better chance of being happy if they enter marriage with realistic expectations, good communication patterns, a sense of humor, and trust in one another.

Realistic Expectations

When you enter marriage, you should have realistic expectations. You will naturally hope for a full and satisfying life together. However, you cannot expect to have a fairy-tale life in which you "live happily ever after." No one's life is perfectly happy all the time.

Affection is the primary emotion couples hope to feel and show in marriage, 14-1. The high value placed on affection helps explain why the onset of disillusionment in a marriage can be so devastating. (*Disillusionment* is the shattering of illusions or unrealistic ideas.) The first instance of lack of affection often causes spouses to mistakenly conclude that they are no longer loved.

If and when disillusionment occurs, the partners should be ready and able to accept each other on a regular basis, taking the bad with the good. It is not wrong to have high ex-

What you are.

What you think you are.

What your husband thinks you are.

What you are.

What you think you are.

What your wife thinks you are.

14-2

Each person brings three personalities into a marriage relationship.

Contemporary Topics *of interest to teens:*
Marital Happiness: Do Children Make the Difference?

Childless young couples enjoying their relationship and their respective careers may wonder whether having children would add to their marriage. It is undeniable that many couples find childrearing a deeply meaningful, satisfying, and enriching experience.

Studies of married couples over time, however, suggest that children may represent a source of marital stress as well as marital satisfaction. There are a number of reasons for this. Often, one spouse puts a career on hold to devote time and energy to rearing children, with loss of wages, career identity, and career standing. Husband and wife may disagree over childrearing issues such as discipline, freedom, and actions that constitute "spoiling" a child. Raising and educating children may strain financial and other resources.

Many couples report that their marriages were happiest before the arrival of their first child and after the departure of their last one. Childless couples, on average, report higher marital satisfaction than couples with children.

What do these studies mean for a young couple thinking about having children? Some couples enjoy parenting more than others. All major life decisions—especially one as important as the decision to parent—require careful consideration.

pectations for marriage, but they must be within the bounds of reality.

Some people expect to feel happier as a married partner than they did when they were single. A marriage relationship can be only as stable as the two people who comprise the union. If one, or both, bring significant insecurities into the marriage, the couple will have problems.

Disappointment is a strange emotion which people rarely reveal openly. It may be hard for you to admit disillusionment with your marriage. For example, you may think you need a new color television. When your spouse objects to spending the money, you may become upset. You may not be as disturbed about not having a new television as you are disappointed that your spouse objects

to buying it. Your spouse may be just as upset, feeling that you want to sacrifice the financial stability of your marriage for unnecessary luxuries.

You may also fail to understand the different aspects of your mate's personality. Each of you takes three different personalities into marriage—what you are, what you think you are, and what your mate thinks you are. See 14-2. Thus, marriage relationships deal with six different personalities! They can be confusing and can cause much frustration, especially if you fail to recognize each of them.

One of the good points of more casual dating today is that young people have the chance to meet many different persons. They have learned to get along with many different types of people. They are better able to understand each other. They are more likely to accept each other as humans—with both strengths and weaknesses.

No matter how understanding you are, you cannot know what to expect of marriage before you live together as husband and wife. The best way you can prepare yourself is to accept the fact that problems will arise. Then you need to be willing to face them one at a time with the help of your mate. If you can do this, your relationship will have a good foundation.

Importance of Self-Esteem

One of the most basic needs in marriage is the genuine acceptance of your own self.

Self-esteem is very different from selfishness. If you have self-esteem, you have confidence in yourself. You do not need to seek constant attention and approval from your mate. You are able to focus on the "we" feeling rather than only on the "I" feeling.

The emotions of love and anger are closely related. When you love someone, you care deeply about how the person thinks and acts. Thus, you are more likely to feel angry when the person fails to meet your expectations.

Anger is a healthy emotion, and it will occasionally arise in a marriage. If two people feel secure in their self-esteem, each can better withstand the other's anger and deal with it effectively. The secret to stopping the "love-anger cycle" is first to recognize the anger and try to step back from it. Then you can work on the issue that caused the anger. To say "I'm sorry" is often a step in the right direction. If you have self-esteem, saying "I'm sorry" will not hurt your pride. You will be able to say it and to go on and find a solution to the problem.

Intermittency of Love

Sometimes love seems to fade and then reappear. This is what is meant by the **intermittency** of love. It is a hard lesson for anyone to learn. When you love someone, you cannot possibly love the person all the time, in exactly the same way. Your love will have periods of growth where it attains great heights. It will also have periods where it reaches a plateau and simply sustains itself.

This lesson of intermittency, as it concerns your love and happiness, may be hard for you to accept. However, if you demand a constant high level of happiness, you may drain the relationship. You should try to be in tune with your own feelings and with those of your mate. Be aware of the ebb and flow of love. Happiness in marriage is much like the waves on a beach. A feeling of complete happiness will surge over you at times. Then there will be periods of quiet expectancy. If you have a good relationship, happiness will come again, like the waves, if you do not turn and walk away from it.

Communication Is Vital

Communication is needed to achieve happiness. Communication is more than words. It is the sharing of feelings and thoughts. People communicate in many ways: by body movements, words, tone of voice, and even silence. The intimacy of marriage allows total communication, which can add depth to a relationship. This intimacy makes any communication, in any form, even more meaningful.

Empathy is an essential ingredient of communication in marriage. Empathy allows you to understand how your partner feels without necessarily sharing those same feelings at the same moment. Empathy as a part of your communication allows you to understand your partner even when the two of you do not agree.

Cholla Runnels

14-3
Communication about trivial matters, as well as about major issues, helps a couple
keep in touch with each other's feelings and thoughts.

Another vital aspect of communication in marriage is keeping in touch with each other's changing feelings and thoughts. See 14-3. One way to do this is to recount the day's events to each other each evening. In this way, you can share the hours you are apart. Some stories may seem trivial, but they help you stay aware of how each of you is changing and growing. This will help you grow together, so you become closer rather than farther apart.

Marriage partners also need to share their "ups" and "downs" in mood. Everyone has changes in mood. Through experience, you have learned how to deal with your own. When you marry, you have to learn how to deal with your partner's as well. You and your partner can help each other through the

down periods by offering love and understanding. Good communication in a healthy marriage means that neither spouse should feel like saying, "What's the use of bringing it up?" Instead, both spouses should feel free to look to their mates for support and guidance.

When you marry, you may find that some of your personality traits differ from those of your spouse. In order to blend them in a fulfilling marriage, you need to discuss them openly. For instance, you may be a morning person, while your mate is a night person. The process of adjusting to this can be fun, or it can be extremely difficult. Communication makes the difference.

One frustrating aspect of communication is sensing that the other person is not really listening. Many times this is a signal that

14-4

Cholla Runnels

Prolonged silence due to anger can harm a relationship.

a marriage is having problems. Our human weaknesses often hamper our ability to be good listeners. You may tend to listen selectively, picking out the bits and pieces that interest you. You may twist the meaning of what is said to fit your own needs. Poor listening blocks effective communication. To keep the lines open, you need to talk honestly and listen carefully.

Sharing words is indeed important, but good communication also recognizes the value of unexpressed words. There will be glorious moments in your marriage when feelings and expressions surge over you. There will also be times when you have warm

14-5

You may have to go more than halfway when you plan a vacation. If your spouse enjoys fishing, you may find yourself near water. You can both have fun if you read or learn to fish rather than pouting.

feelings of quiet understanding and support. A good climate of communication allows both periods of talking and of silence. Sometimes a few moments of quiet understanding can be the most comforting kind of communication. A smile across a crowded room of people or a gentle nudge can be as meaningful as spoken words. However, if the silence is due to anger or resentment, problems can arise. Someone must reopen communication in a situation such as this to prevent a prolonged stalemate, 14-4.

As you live together, you may increase your ability to "read" each other. You may sense when something is wrong and when your partner does not feel like talking. One wife stated, "I can tell when Bill walks in the door if he has had a good day." Another couple, at the start of their marriage, established a sign to show each other when one had had a bad day. Each placed a small figurine on a table just inside the front door. Turning it backward was a sign to the other partner that peace and quiet were needed. They soon found, as do many couples, that they did not need such a sign, for they learned to sense each other's moods.

An inability to sense moods, however, is not the same as lack of love. A common mistake is to expect your mate to be able to read your mind. One young wife told her husband, "If you loved me, you would know how I feel." Such an expectation is unrealistic. Each mate is responsible for expressing thoughts and feelings to the other.

Give and Take of Marriage

Marriage is a give and take relationship, but it is not always a 50-50 proposition. Many people wrongly assume that if they have gone halfway, they have done their part in solving marital problems. Many times you may have to give much more than half in order to reach a solution. You may give 70 or even 80 percent while your spouse appears to be giving very little. The willingness to go more than halfway to reach a solution is the catalyst needed to bring happiness. See 14-5. If you always give only 50 percent, your marriage may be in for stalemates and unresolved issues. Flexibility and willingness to adjust are among the most important factors in achieving a good marriage relationship.

A Sense of Humor

A sense of humor is a good quality to incorporate into your marriage. Laughter makes life easier and more enjoyable. While gloom is deadly to a household, laughter brings happiness and liveliness. If you and your mate have a healthy sense of humor, you will have fun times to share and remember. See 14-6. Mark Twain said, "Humans are the only animals that laugh—or need to."

It can be fun to laugh with your mate, but you should not laugh at your mate. Jokes pointed at your mate are not funny. Sarcasm and ridicule—either when you are alone to-

David Hopper

14-6
Can you laugh with each other and recognize how important a sense of humor is in your relationship?

14-7
Everyone needs to be appreciated, and a spontaneous hug or kiss can be very reassuring.

gether or with others—should be avoided. They can be extremely damaging to a person's self-esteem. Some television personalities may use ridicule to create audience laughter, but it is a poor method of communication to use in your marriage relationship.

Trust

Trust is a secure foundation for any relationship. It is especially needed in marriage. A relationship built on trust is caring and responsible. It contains no anxiety or apprehension, nor does it need power or force to hold it together.

As your marriage grows, so will trust. When you trust each other, your marriage re-

lationship will endure the gravest of pressures. You will feel happy and secure as you live your lives together.

Appreciation

All humans need to know that they are appreciated. As a small child, you may have received small rewards or "gold stars" when you did a task well. In school, your efforts are rewarded by good report cards and honors. On a job, you are recognized for your work through praise, bonuses, raises, and promotions.

In marriage, too, you need to know you are appreciated, 14-7. You do not want to be taken for granted. Sincere compliments, praise, and thoughtfulness are methods of showing appreciation. Often all you may want is a simple thank you, or to be gathered into your mate's arms. Presents are not necessary. Money is not needed to express appreciation. The wife who feels misunderstood is probably just looking for a sign of appreciation from her husband. The husband who feels neglected may only need a word of understanding and approval from his wife.

Adjustments in Marriage

No two people are so perfectly compatible that they can live together without any conflict. A certain amount of disagreement is to be expected in marriage. Some marriages require greater emphasis on making adjustments because these marriages have more conflict. It is not the amount of conflict, but the success in reaching satisfactory adjustments that determines the degree of happiness in the relationship.

Whenever two people try to live together peaceably and pleasantly, adjustments have to be made. They may have realized they had areas of disagreement while they were dating. Until they were married, it was possible to ignore or dismiss these points of disagreement. However, when spouses settle down to the everyday business of living, these points of disagreement cannot be ignored.

There are five basic ways to make marital adjustments when disagreements arise. These are described in 14-8 and the discussion that follows. Some of these ways of making adjustments are healthy, and others are destructive. You will not always use the same form of adjustment. Different situations will require you to use different techniques.

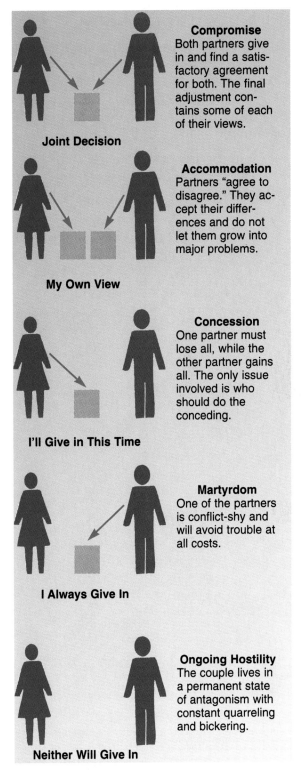

Joint Decision

Compromise
Both partners give in and find a satisfactory agreement for both. The final adjustment contains some of each of their views.

My Own View

Accommodation
Partners "agree to disagree." They accept their differences and do not let them grow into major problems.

I'll Give in This Time

Concession
One partner must lose all, while the other partner gains all. The only issue involved is who should do the conceding.

I Always Give In

Martyrdom
One of the partners is conflict-shy and will avoid trouble at all costs.

Neither Will Give In

Ongoing Hostility
The couple lives in a permanent state of antagonism with constant quarreling and bickering.

14-8
Your choice of a form of adjustment will depend on the situation and your personalities.

Compromise

In a *compromise,* both partners give in and find a satisfactory agreement for both. It is the most common and, in many respects, the most desirable form of marital adjustment. The distinguishing characteristics of compromise include the following:

- Neither partner has to make a great sacrifice in giving in to the wishes of the other.

- The solution lies somewhere in between the partners' preferences, and it contains some elements of both.

Cholla Runnels

14-9
Compromise is a good way to settle the question of who should clean the garage. If both give in a little and agree to work together, the task will be easier.

- More companionship is maintained.

- No one wins or loses. Both partners share in the adjustment.

Compromise can be chosen in most decision areas in marriage. See 14-9. It is the best way to settle issues when both the husband and wife desire to have some say in the decision. Compromise does not foster indifference, for both participate in finding a solution. Neither partner wins all, but neither partner loses all. A "we" feeling is maintained. Compromise encourages further communication and helps feelings of security and trust to grow.

How can compromise be used to solve the following problems?

Tiffany and Jamal are discussing what to do on Friday night. They plan to go out to dinner and to a movie. Jamal wants to see a mystery movie, but Tiffany wants to see a comedy. Jamal likes Mexican food, but Tiffany prefers Chinese dishes. They could compromise by allowing one to choose the movie and the other to choose the restaurant.

Juanita and Carlos may use compromise to solve the problem of where they will live. Juanita is a school teacher. Her job is in an elementary school in a suburb on the west side of the city. Carlos' job is with a computer industry on the city's industrial east side. Both would like to live close to their jobs, but they decide to live in the area between their jobs. In this way, each will have to travel about the same distance. They select a townhouse near the freeway interchange that will be convenient for both of them.

Compromise often works, but it is not suited to all problems. For instance, in deciding when to decorate a Christmas tree, compromise may not work. Suppose Nan wants to decorate the tree two weeks before Christmas to usher in the season. Suppose Josh wants to decorate it on Christmas Eve, as his family has always done. Compromise may not be possible. Splitting the tree and decorating half to meet the wishes of each is not a logical choice. In this situation, they may have to seek another form of adjustment.

Accommodation

Marriage partners may hold some seriously opposing viewpoints. In these cases, the couple may consider the adjustment form of *accommodation,* where the partners "agree to disagree." The distinguishing characteristics are the following:

- Each recognizes the right of the other to have a different belief.

- Differences continue to exist, but they do not hinder the relationship.

- The couple maintain a sense of proportion about what will be good for their total relationship.

No two humans have identical interests. In every marriage, some differences will arise. Accommodation allows a couple to work around these differences. They recognize that certain issues are not important enough to cause trouble in their relationship. See 14-10.

Accommodation is often used by couples who have widely divergent viewpoints in areas such as religion or politics. They realize that their relationship is strong enough to survive these differing viewpoints. They each respect the other's right to a differing opinion or belief.

Accommodation can be used to prevent minor issues from becoming major ones. In one marriage, the husband enjoyed bowling as a form of recreational exercise, but the wife preferred aerobic dancing. An accommodation was reached when the husband joined the bowling team at work. Now he

bowls one night a week, and stays home with the children another night while his wife attends aerobics class.

In another marriage, a political issue caused extreme disruption during an election year. The wife was a Democrat and openly argued with her husband who was a Republican. The couple settled their differences by using accommodation. The husband stayed with their baby so the wife could work in the local Democratic headquarters. The wife accepted the fact that her husband would be active in the Republican party. They

Cholla Runnels

14-10
You can use accommodation to solve big issues as well as trivial issues such as different brands of toothpaste.

went to the polls together, knowing that they would "cancel" each other's vote. They agreed to disagree and recognized each other's right to freedom of choice in politics.

Concession

Concession is a form of adjustment in which one must win and one must lose. The only question is who should give in or concede. Concession has the following distinguishing characteristics:

- It allows a partner to win certain issues.

- The partners communicate and bargain with each other.

- Both partners must be willing to live with the possible resentment of the loser and the impact of this resentment on the relationship.

- The winner is happy, and the loser must accept the loss. However, the loser can look forward to winning at another time.

David Hopper

14-11
If one partner does most of the cooking, the other partner would probably concede to the cook the final choice of a microwave oven.

A couple may arrive at concession in a number of different ways. The concession may be voluntary. One mate may simply say, "I will agree to do it your way." Perhaps it involves a simple choice such as the selection of a movie. It may be a larger decision such as, "I am willing to go to Iowa and visit your parents at Thanksgiving."

Sometimes the decision to concede may be forced. This will not promote an ideal adjustment. If a domineering husband wants to maintain financial control, he may force his wife to accept a tight budget, even if they have plenty of money. She, in turn, may quietly try to find ways to "get revenge." When forced concessions are used too often, a spouse may feel that he or she is being treated as a child rather than as an equal partner. Resulting problems may lead a couple to divorce.

Often one mate is more knowledgeable in the area under consideration. Then the other mate may be willing to concede final choices to him or her after some discussion. For instance, a spouse who works as an insurance agent would probably make the final decision about the couple's insurance policies. The spouse who does most of the cooking would probably choose most of the kitchen appliances. See 14-11.

There are times when a simple flip of the coin may be used to arrive at a solution. This approach may lessen tensions and allow the partners to realize the simplicity of the choice. Heated discussions can arise when a couple try to choose a place to go for a vacation. Flipping a coin may set the stage for an enjoyable vacation. It allows the couple to use a childlike approach to make a decision about a pleasant time.

Taking turns may be another way to achieve a concession. If a stalemate seems to be developing, one partner may bargain. "We'll choose your way this time, but next time it will be my turn!" This will renew communication. The wins and losses can be equalized.

A different approach may have to be used when the couple is unable to arrive at a decision. In order to avoid a stalemate, a third party might be consulted. The third party should be someone whom both spouses respect. He or she should also be free from emotional involvement in the decision. This approach is sometimes necessary for serious problems. Perhaps aging parents need care. Spouses may have to decide whether the parent should move into their home or into a nursing home. A counselor or physician could help the couple make the best decision. Someone who is not emotionally involved may be able to see all the alternatives and implications more clearly.

Concession will be used at times in every marriage. It can be a good way to settle conflict. As long as most of the concessions are voluntary ones, they can help spouses make many satisfactory decisions.

Martyrdom

The fourth form of adjustment could really be called a form of non-adjustment. *Martyrdom* results when one partner avoids trouble at all costs. The distinguishing characteristics of martyrdom are the following:

- One partner always gives in, so the other always wins.

- The relationship deteriorates.

- Respect is lost for the person who always gives in.

- Adjustments are not satisfying to either.

Martyrdom is a sign of a weak relationship, 14-12. The person giving in seems to become less of a person. Those who choose to play the role of a martyr lose respect from all involved, including themselves.

Wm. E. Barnhart

14-12
A wife who uses martyrdom will pick up after her husband because she wants to avoid conflict at any cost.

Ongoing Hostility

In the fifth type of adjustment, *ongoing hostility,* the couple never really settle their conflicts. The distinguishing characteristics are as follows:

- Quarreling and bickering are continuous.

- Tension and antagonism occur frequently and are expressed destructively.

- The marriage relationship deteriorates.

- No decisions and adjustments are made because hostility continues.

- Hostility in one area will spread to most other areas.

- Other people are uncomfortable in the company of the couple.

A relationship can hardly survive on a daily diet of hostility. Once the hostility begins in one area, it probably will expand and affect most other areas of the relationship,

14-13. The couple will be unable to cope with their hostility and will tear down any remaining mutual respect. Loud arguing, cutting sarcasm, or complete indifference may characterize their relationship. Friends of the hostile couple will feel uncomfortable in their presence and may discontinue further communication with them.

Children who are subject to ongoing hostility in the home tend either to grow resentful or to feel guilty and somehow responsible for it. The insecurity they feel in their home as children may become a permanent part of their personalities. As adults, their marriages may also suffer from unresolved conflicts.

Adjustments need to be made in all marriages. If a couple boasts that they never have problems and never argue, perhaps no "meshing" of emotions and needs is taking place. The relationship may exist only on the surface, without real feelings of involvement with one another.

David Hopper

14-13

If a couple cannot agree on money management, even after a serious discussion, their hostility might spread to other areas of their relationship.

No one method of adjustment can be used all the time, for no method would suit every couple on every issue. You need to recognize that you will have to make adjustments. Then you will have to try to select the best adjustment forms for the conflicts you will face. The important thing is to be honest with yourself and your mate about your true feelings and to work at finding the best ways to resolve issues as they arise. If you can do this, then your relationship is likely to remain strong and healthy.

Time as a Factor in Making Adjustments

Adjustments will be necessary throughout married life, but they are easier to make early in marriage. There are several reasons why this is true.

First, each spouse is anxious in early marriage to please the other and to make the marriage succeed. Willingness to admit, "I am wrong," is easier when you are starting out.

Second, youth may make adjusting easier. Maturity is needed to make adjustments, but youth allows a person to accept changes and to adapt to a new situation.

Third, marriage habits have not yet been formed, and the relationship is still quite flexible. There are many new behaviors to be learned when you first marry. Many routines are established in the early months. If something your partner does upsets you, it is easier to mention this early in the marriage when you can still admit that you find certain habits annoying. Many adjustment problems occur during the first year of marriage.

Usually the trivial, day-to-day behaviors are the ones that cause friction when two people start living together. One may even criticize the way the other squeezes the tube of toothpaste. Most days, these little annoyances are overlooked. When tension exists because of other issues, the little annoyances can build up and become major problems. When two people who have lived alone suddenly live together, it is normal that each will have a few habits that irritate the other.

As you live together, new aggravations may continue to appear. You will need patience and understanding as you make adjustments throughout your married life, 14-14.

14-14

Evin Thayer

Love, patience, and understanding can help a couple as they adjust to married life.

Functions of Conflict ▪ ▪

Every marriage is to some degree a mixed marriage. Even if you married the girl or boy next door, you would discover that you have many differences. Conflict is normal because each of you brings your unique personality into the marriage. A great deal of conflict will, of course, have a negative effect on the marriage. However, some conflict can actually be helpful.

Conflict Can Lead to Problem Solving

A problem must be faced before it can be solved. Conflict helps bring troubles out in the open where couples can deal with them. Thus, conflict can help solve problems.

There are two schools of thought concerning expressions of conflict in families. Some people feel that open conflict can be damaging to the relationship and to children. On the other hand, many authorities feel if conflicting feelings are not expressed, the real solution to the problem may never be found. When conflict exists, children are usually aware that something is wrong. It may be more damaging for them to wonder what is wrong than to realize that all families have problems that sometimes cause conflict. Family relationships can continue to function even when conflict exists. Ideally, the family will recognize the problem and solve it for the benefit of all concerned.

Conflict Can Release Tensions

Conflict produces tensions, but as conflict is resolved, these tensions are released. If the conflict is not openly expressed, it can only increase in volume and intensity. The "explosion" of tensions then might be more damaging. When tensions are building, you might be wise to "count to 10." This gives you time to see things in perspective and to think how best to express your feelings constructively.

Most authorities agree with the saying, "Don't let the sun go down on your wrath." Others point out that some conflicts between tired spouses seem more solvable after a

Productive and Destructive Quarreling
Productive:
Quarreling is limited to the issue.
Issue may be redefined.
All available information is used to find a solution.
A solution can be reached without hurting anyone's feelings.
Marriage is made stronger.
Destructive:
Quarrel often extends beyond the original issue.
Individuals become defensive as their egos are attacked.
Arguments are often emotional and irrational.
Tension and irritation are increased.
Marriage relationship is damaged.

14-15
Productive quarreling resolves conflict. Destructive quarreling creates even more conflict.

night's rest. The thing to remember is that conflicts have a way of multiplying if no attempt is made to resolve them.

Conflict can be a resource for your marriage, for it indicates willingness to bring a disagreement into the open. Acknowledging conflict is the first step in reaching a solution. If the problem is not brought into the open, the conflict will smolder beneath the surface of daily living. It may erupt later in a big fight as a result of an incident not even related to the real problem.

Productive Quarreling

There is an art to quarreling. Quarrels may either be productive or destructive. See 14-15. *Productive quarrels* can actually strengthen a marriage as they often clarify is-

sues so that couples realize their viewpoints are not so different. Perhaps you have noticed this during a quarrel with a friend or parent.

A productive quarrel sticks to the issue, 14-16. It does not wander off into other topics. It involves honest expressions of feelings and careful listening on both sides. It does not involve attacks on the self-esteem of either partner. Sentences begin with phrases such as "I feel" (hurt, unimportant, etc.) rather than "You are" (insensitive, rude, etc.). If the issue is not clear, the couple may attempt to redefine it. In this way, both will be able to understand and agree, at least, on the reason for the quarrel.

Once the issue is clear, the couple can work on finding a solution. Through *negotiation,* they can confer with one another and arrive at a settlement of the matter. The problem can be solved with a minimum of hard feelings. Productive quarrels make the marriage stronger.

Cholla Runnels

14-16
Identifying relevant information can help you settle a quarrel constructively.

Destructive Quarreling

Destructive quarreling attacks the self-esteem of the persons involved. It is devastating to the marriage and accomplishes nothing as far as problem solving is concerned. It succeeds only in harming the self-esteem of the people involved.

Destructive quarreling is often full of tension and irritation. The partners use personal attacks to hurt each other's feelings. As a result, both become defensive in order to protect their own self-esteem. Statements are made that cause emotional pain rather than clarify issues. In many cases, the quarrel extends beyond the original issue. Each person may add verbal attacks on relatives, cherished values, or prized possessions.

Quarreling is a part of most relationships. If you can stick with productive quarreling, your marriage will be stronger. A review of conflict resolution techniques that can be used by married couples is presented in 14-17. These negotiation techniques can help couples resolve conflicts.

Marriage Counseling

In a sense, there is no such thing as a "successful marriage." There are only marriages that are succeeding or failing. As people and situations change, new adjustments are required within marriage.

As this discussion of adjustments and conflicts has shown, marriages can become troubled. Often the frustration and anxiety are so great that the help of a qualified marriage counselor is needed. This step requires the commitment of both spouses to the relationship. Both must be willing to make

A Review of Conflict Resolution in Marriage

- Establish a climate in the relationship for open expression of both positive and negative feelings.
- Recognize that conflict is normal and that it can serve a constructive function in your marriage.
- Be aware that people handle conflict differently. Some people are slow to anger; others are quick to anger.
- Weigh the degree of conflict. Many mountains are made out of molehills. Look to see if the problem has been blown out of proportion.
- Quarreling can be destructive if it is allowed to attack a person's self-esteem. It can be productive if it sticks to the issue.
- Pinpoint the real issue. Do not allow old animosities to surface again. Don't choose a "safe" issue rather than revealing what you are really angry about.
- Use specific rather than general language. Confrontation is most effective when it is specific and timely. Use I-messages to state how you feel.
- Seek and find areas of agreement. Acknowledge where you agree—then the conflict will not tend to widen as easily. You may find you agree on more than you thought possible.
- Accept the fact that there may be more than one solution to a problem. Productive quarreling can produce alternative answers. Explore them together. Don't get stuck on one or two choices.
- Be willing to say no if you are not satisfied with the suggested solution.
- Try to arrive at the best possible solution. Recognize that both of you may have lost something, but both may also have gained something in return.
- Give each other credit for caring enough to engage in respectful conflict. This is crucial. Don't end the negotiation without giving each other credit.
- If your efforts at negotiation do not succeed, consider seeking professional counseling.

14-17
Your approach to resolving conflict will have a great effect upon the overall atmosphere of your marriage.

changes within themselves for the sake of their marriage. They also must be honest and open-minded enough to reveal their true emotions and to accept counseling.

Finding a Marriage Counselor

Once a couple decide they need marriage counseling, they then have to decide where to find it. Some couples may turn to friends and relatives. However, these people are rarely good sources of marital advice. They become emotionally involved and often take sides. This tends to cause even more problems. In addition, a friend or relative who was against the marriage in the first place may not want to help. Instead, the couple may simply hear, "I told you so."

A couple seeking marital advice should beware of counselors who are incompetent and unqualified. They can do irreparable damage to an already unstable relationship. Only a few states recognize marriage counseling as a legal and independent profession. In many states, almost anyone can profess to be a counselor.

Counselors need to be trained to deal with more than just husband and wife problems. They should be skilled in the whole realm of family relationships that may include husband, wife, children, and in-laws. They should be able to counsel people with child, adolescent, pre-marriage, marriage, pre-divorce, post-divorce, and aging problems.

Many ministers, educators, psychologists, psychiatrists, social workers, and physicians provide marriage counseling as part of their work. Some have had good training and are highly skilled. Others may mean well, but without adequate training, they may do more harm than good. However, those who recognize their own lack of expertise can often refer you to a good counseling service.

A growing number of businesses provide qualified counselors as part of employee-assistance programs. These businesses recognize that people who have problems need high-quality counseling. They are aware that their employees will be more productive if they can get good counseling when it is needed. If it is readily available to them, employees will lose less time on the job.

If you are interested in finding a qualified counselor, you might contact one of the following:

- The American Association for Marriage and Family Therapy.

- Family Service America.

- United Way agencies in your area, including family service bureaus, child welfare agencies, county welfare agencies, and mental health organizations.

What Does the Counselor Provide?

Counselors rarely tell their clients what to do. They try to help people develop their own solutions. They help spouses see how their personal problems may be affecting the deeper level of feelings in their marriage.

Techniques used by counselors are varied, but most are designed to re-establish communication between marital partners. First, the partners have to want help. All the counseling in the world will not help them if they do not want to help themselves. The spouses have to be willing to talk and to listen to each other. Sometimes this is the only problem—neither has heard what the other was saying. A good communication experience often draws them closer together. They may ask, "Why didn't you ever say that to me before?"

Counselors sometimes suggest creating lists to reopen communication lines. Partners may be asked to list each other's faults. This list can reveal small, irritating habits as well as major problems. It may be the first time that a partner realizes that a certain behavior irritates the other. Similarly, a list of good points can help a spouse who feels undervalued realize that he or she is appreciated.

Counselors also use checklists of personality traits and of wants and needs to get the couple to communicate. Open-ended questions like, "What would you do if..." can stimulate good discussions. Role-playing techniques in which one partner takes the role of the other can help the couple develop empathy and understanding.

The counselor may wish to see the partners alone at some meetings and together at other meetings. Seeing them as a couple allows the counselor to observe patterns of interaction. The counselor can note behaviors that add to the couple's continuing problems. Sometimes group sessions or weekend retreats may be helpful. This allows couples to listen to other couples who have relationship problems. Often some simple communication or conflict resolution technique used by one couple will help another couple.

In some troubled marriages, one partner wishes to see a counselor and the other refuses. In such cases, the partner who wishes counseling can often benefit from individual sessions with a qualified professional.

When spouses have conflicts that remain unresolved, they may begin thinking about separation and divorce. Divorce conversation can be destructive. Divorce is a word full of meaning to both partners. It has the power to pull apart a marriage that might have succeeded. Once spouses begin to talk about di-

Cholla Runnels

14-18
Marriage counseling can help a couple rediscover the love they thought they had lost.

vorce, they may think their marriage is hopeless. They may give up trying to strengthen and renew their relationship.

Marriage counseling can aid a marriage relationship when conflict seems to be unresolvable. A counselor can help a couple take a fresh look at their relationship. The couple can then evaluate the growth of their marriage and their own growth as individuals. After doing this and reopening lines of communication, the couple will have a good start toward renewing their relationship, 14-18.

Summary ■ ■ ■ ■ ■ ■ ■ ■ ■ ■ ■ ■ ■ ■ ■ ■

- It is good to have high expectations for marriage, but they should be realistic.

- Positive self-esteem is basic to the success of a marriage.

- Feelings of intense love and happiness will be intermittent and will not be maintained on a constant level.

- Good communication, both verbal and nonverbal, is an essential part of a happy marriage relationship.

- Marriage is a give-and-take relationship, but it is not a 50-50 proposition in every situation.

- A sense of humor, trust, and mutual appreciation make marriage more enjoyable and secure.

- Five forms of adjustment are used in marriage: compromise, accommodation, concession, martyrdom, and ongoing hostility.

- Adjustments may be more easily made early in marriage.

- Conflict is normal, and it can be used as a positive communication device to strengthen a relationship.

- Productive quarreling sticks to the issue and helps settle a conflict. Destructive quarreling attacks the partner's self-esteem and makes the conflict even worse.

- When marriage partners cannot resolve their conflicts, they may want to find a qualified marriage counselor to help them.

- A marriage counselor does not usually tell husbands and wives what to do. The counselor simply guides the partners as they analyze their problems and work out possible solutions.

To Review ■ ■ ■ ■ ■ ■ ■ ■ ■ ■ ■ ■ ■ ■ ■ ■

1. The important point to remember about achieving happiness in marriage is:
    a. Couples who cannot express any negative feelings are more likely to be happy than couples who can.
    b. Happiness can never really be achieved in marriage.
    c. Happiness is a by-product as you strive for contentment.
    d. What brings happiness to one marriage will work for any other marriage.

2. Select the true statement concerning communication in marriage.
   a. A contented silence is a sign of poor communication.
   b. Empathy means that you are able to feel exactly as your partner feels at the moment your partner communicates his or her feelings.
   c. Good communication includes the verbal and nonverbal sharing of feelings and thoughts.
   d. It is best not to bring up negative feelings.

3. True or False. If you have gone halfway, you have done your part in solving marital problems.

4. Name the adjustment form described in each of the following statements.
   a. The couple agree to disagree.
   b. One partner gives in constantly.
   c. Tension and antagonism occur frequently and are expressed destructively.
   d. The solution lies somewhere between the partners' preferences and contains some elements of both.
   e. Both partners must be willing to live with the resentment of the person who "lost."
   f. Respect is lost for the person who always gives in.

5. Explain how conflict can be helpful in a marriage.

6. Name two good and two questionable sources of marital counseling.

7. Describe two methods counselors use to reopen lines of communication between spouses.

To Do ▪ ▪ ▪ ▪ ▪ ▪ ▪ ▪ ▪ ▪ ▪ ▪ ▪ ▪ ▪ ▪ ▪

1. Arrange chairs in a circle so that all students are a part of that circle. Ask each to respond to the following statements.
   a. The most important characteristic I think a future spouse could possess is . . .
   b. One of the most irritating characteristics of a future mate would be . . .
   c. The conflict that I think would be the hardest to solve if it occurred in a future marriage would be . . .

2. Role-play the following situations. Use each of the five forms of adjustment to settle each conflict.

a. Where should they go for the holidays? Jason and Tracy live in Dallas. Tracy's parents live in Chicago, and Jason's parents live in Los Angeles. They have five days of vacation. They can go to only one place, but they do have money for the trip.

b. Teresa and David have received an income-tax refund check. Teresa wants to put it in a savings account, and David wants to use it to purchase a video recorder.

c. Eduardo and Julie married in college and have not made any decisions concerning their church membership. Julie wants Eduardo to join her church, but Eduardo is reluctant to do so.

3. Research resources available in your area for marriages that need help, such as marriage enrichment labs, church groups, private counseling workshops, etc. Report your findings to the class.

Flexibility and willingness to adjust are among the most important factors in achieving a good marriage relationship.

V

Dimensions
of Families

15

Family Life
Today

Terms to Know

family

given role

chosen role

functional family

dysfunctional family

two-parent family
system

single-parent family
system

blended family
system

extended kinship
family system

foster parenting

family life cycle

**After studying this chapter,
you will be able to**

- analyze the factors contributing to the
changing family.

- identify the three functions of the
family.

- explain the relationship between
family roles and responsibilities.

- list characteristics of strong families.

- identify six common family systems.

- describe the five stages of the family
life cycle.

Your family is probably the most influential factor in shaping your personality. Almost everything you do is guided and
affected by the relationships within your family, 15-1. In this chapter you will learn more
about family life and how it has changed
through the years.

15-1
From the moment of birth, a child's personality is affected by relationships within
the family.

What Is a Family? ■ ■ ■

Family may be defined in many ways. Some definitions emphasize an emotional tie, while others stress the ancestry of the individuals. According to the U.S. Census Bureau, the term *family* means a group of two or more persons, related by blood, marriage, or adoption, who reside together in a household.

Families are as varied as people themselves. A family consisting of a father, mother, and children is only one type. Variations are caused not only by the different relationships within families, but also by different economic and social needs. Variations also occur because of a family's cultural heritage.

The Changing Family ■ ■ ■ ■ ■ ■ ■

Many of you have heard grandparents and parents describe their childhood years. Their stories may seem unfamiliar. Many family activities and functions that they describe are no longer typical of the family today.

In early history, the family hunted and gathered food in order to survive. Family members filled roles that allowed the family to live off the land and to be protected from predatory animals. Permanent communities were not possible as the family groups continually moved to find food. This ability to adapt to changing needs is a characteristic that has been important to families throughout the ages.

As agriculture evolved, families set up permanent homes and acquired land. Each family was independent and able to meet its own needs by assigning a variety of tasks to family members.

The industrial revolution brought new pressures on society and the family. Families moved from rural areas to urban areas. Family members no longer worked solely for the survival of their own family. Instead, they took jobs that served a larger group, but provided income to purchase food and clothing for family members. Families thus became dependent on other families and adopted the role of consumers. Urban centers grew in population, while the number of people living in rural areas declined. The father was the main provider. His parenting role was limited to the short time he was home from his job. The mother, who was the full-time homemaker, provided the main care for the children. Marriages were based on meeting people's needs as well as on love. The government took over some of the family functions, such as providing for the education of the children.

The technological age that followed continues to affect families today. More jobs became available in a variety of businesses. Rural areas continued to decline in population, and urban areas grew as they attracted those seeking careers in emerging technological fields. Household care was made easier with new equipment. Women began to join the workforce in greater numbers. Child care needs were met by child care providers in the home, in nursery schools, or in child care centers.

In today's society, families are adapting to change. New careers are attracting both men and women. People of both genders are seeking higher education and aspiring to responsible careers. Marriages are based more on love and affection than on the necessity of providing care for one another. Men and women are sharing the wage-earner role and sharing in child care and household tasks, 15-2. Parents are beginning to value time as highly as money. Employers are finding ways to help families meet the needs of both work and family.

Throughout history, families have had to adapt to varying economic and social pressures. Today's families are developing strengths to meet contemporary pressures. Most Americans, however, will continue to live in families. Though families may vary in form, they still offer the most stable environment for personal growth. Families are here to stay in one form or another.

Functions of the Family

Though families take many forms, they still perform the same basic functions. The three basic functions of the family are the following:

- To provide for the physical needs of family members.

David Hopper

15-2

In families today, fathers are spending more time with their children.

Contemporary Topics *of interest to teens:*
The Boomerang Age

Prior to World War II, leaving home before marriage was almost unheard of. Young adults lived with their parents even after they finished school, contributing to the family's resources until they married. After World War II, young adults began leaving home to marry at an earlier age.

Today, however, this trend has reversed once more as young adults are delaying marriage and living with their parents longer. There are several reasons for this change:

- More young people are continuing their education beyond high school. They know that most well-paying jobs now require either post-secondary training or a college degree.

- College costs are higher today and career tracks are more complex, causing young adults to take longer to finish school.

- Full-time college students are more likely to live with their parents or other relatives to save money while they complete their schooling.

- Local community colleges are expanding their programs, enabling more young adults to live with their parents while getting their degrees.

Even after their education is complete, young people may return home for awhile. Many young adults just entering the workforce have to live with their parents because their starting salaries are low. They cannot initially afford to live on their own. These young people continue to live with their parents until they are financially able to live independently.

For those people who do marry before the age of 25, over half of the men and more than two-thirds of the women get divorced. Teenage marriages in particular have a high rate of failure. If young adults divorce shortly after they marry, they are more likely to return to their parental home. Some return with their young children in tow. They may stay with their parents for a short while until they are able to make arrangements to live on their own again.

All of these trends have caused social scientists to label this the boomerang age. Some adult children may leave and then return home, often several times, before they leave their parental home for good.

Adult family members are responsible for the care and protection of all family members. Food, clothing, health care, and shelter are the main physical needs that must be met. Many of these needs are met by adult family members performing tasks within the home. Such tasks include preparing meals, keeping the house clean, and doing the laundry. One or more adult family members is likely to work outside the home to provide the income to meet many physical needs.

- To provide for the socialization of children.

The family provides the environment for nurturing the social skills of children,

15-3. This equips them to move out into the world. The family guides children as they learn right from wrong. Children learn about the culture of the society in which they live. Families teach by example what is acceptable behavior and what is unacceptable behavior, so that children can take their places as productive members of society.

- To provide for the psychological well-being of all family members.

An important family function is to provide an emotional "safe haven" for family members. Family members seek out this safe place, where they know they are loved and accepted. At the same time, family members learn the give and take of living together in a close relationship. Family members learn to live in harmony with each other while at the same time encouraging individual growth. Successful individuation (becoming a unique individual) of children is the result. Families

Cholla Runnels

15-3
Children learn how to interact with others from the nurturing they receive within the family.

who have a belief in the self-worth of each individual fill these needs for their family members.

Roles and Responsibilities of Family Members

Members of families have certain roles. Your role as a son or daughter is a ***given role*** that you acquired when you were born into the family. You may also have the given role of brother or sister. When you marry, you will assume a ***chosen role*** as husband or wife. You may also choose to assume another chosen role—that of father or mother. These and other family roles will overlap throughout your life. The emphasis you give to each particular role will change from time to time. If there is a major change in your family, such as a severe illness, divorce, or death, roles may change.

Roles are defined by responsibilities. How people fulfill these responsibilities determines to a large extent how well they perform their roles. In many families, mothers have major responsibility for the care and nurturance of children. Even if the mother works outside the home, the responsibility for care and supervision of the children usually continues to be her role. As children grow older, mothers' responsibilities may include volunteering at their children's school and supervising neighborhood play activities. Mothers often arrange for their children to participate in a variety of activities and sports. If the mother is employed, many of these responsibilities are shared with the father.

Providing the income to buy food, clothing, and housing for family members has traditionally been the responsibility of the father. Today this responsibility is often shared by both father and mother. Today's fathers are also sharing more of the child care responsibilities and often are seen in grocery stores doing the shopping for the family. Care of the yard and outside chores have traditionally been the responsibility of fathers, but today the entire family may share in these tasks. If the mother works, the father may be the one to take the children to school or serve as coach for sports teams. Guiding children is a shared responsibility in many of today's families. Fathers are finding they enjoy the nurturing role, and that mothers enjoy sharing the provider role. As they share these roles, they offer encouragement and support to each other.

Your role expectations for your future family are likely to be influenced by the roles played in your family today. For instance, if both parents work outside the home, their children will be more likely to share nurturing and provider roles in their future families. The career you choose will influence your future family role responsibilities. Changes in the economy and the stability of our society can also affect your future family roles.

In all relationships, it is important to understand people's role expectations. If you decide to marry someone with different role expectations, the two of you will need to decide how you will share responsibilities. Each of you may need to alter your views in order to meet the needs of all family members.

Functional and Dysfunctional Families

Families operate as a system or team. In a *functional family,* all family members fulfill their roles and responsibilities. If one family member does not fulfill his or her responsibility, the system is out of balance, or may become *dysfunctional.* A father who leaves the family with no thought for their ability to function on their own throws the family sys-

tem out of balance. A teen who rebels and refuses to cooperate can create problems for the entire family. When family members fulfill each others' needs and treat each other with affection and respect, the family will sustain its functioning base.

Characteristics of Strong Families

Strong families are crucial to our nation's well-being. Parents have a primary obligation to raise their children to be responsible, caring, and contributing members of the community. The community, in turn, has the responsibility to help support families. Families do not exist in a vacuum.

Strong, healthy families have many characteristics in common. In today's strong families, members communicate and listen to each other, 15-4. They listen responsively. They pay attention to nonverbal communication, particularly when there is silence. Family members may express disagreements, but they recognize the importance of respectful communication.

Members of strong families support one another. They offer affirmation to each other and thus contribute to heightened self-esteem. They also respect the individual uniqueness of each person, recognizing both strengths and weaknesses. Healthy families value the contribution each member can make.

Trust is evident in many aspects of family living. Spouses trust one another. Parents trust their children with responsibilities that help them learn. This helps children feel a sense of worth and value in the family. Children trust their parents and feel secure and loved in the family setting.

The healthy family has a sense of play and humor. Family members laugh with each other, and get-togethers become a time of fun and mutual relaxation. Members of strong families pay attention to signs of stress and use humor as well as empathy to diffuse tensions or explosive situations.

Members of strong families exhibit a sense of shared responsibility. They also realize the importance of individual responsibility on the part of each member.

Strong families recognize right and wrong. They guide children in choosing behavior that is acceptable to the family and to society. They assess the consequences when any member does something wrong as well as the responsibility that must be assumed. They guide children in critical thinking and in considering decision-making alternatives.

Strong families believe in upholding family traditions. They also may create new traditions that become very meaningful for the family. They respect the cultural and ethnic traditions of other families.

Strong families realize the importance of healthy interaction among members. They respect the desire for privacy at times, yet foster conversation and sharing at other times.

Strong families share a belief in the importance of a religious or philosophical foundation. They recognize the stability this provides for the children as they grow to adulthood and establish families of their own.

Strong families believe in the contribution they can make to their communities. Such families work together for a good balance between emphasis on individual rights and acceptance of responsibilities to the community.

David Hopper

15-4
Family members listen and respect each other's wishes as they make plans for a family vacation.

Family Systems ▪ ▪ ▪

As society changes, new family systems emerge. Today there are many different family systems. There is no one best system as long as the family is performing its functions and members are fulfilling their roles. The six common systems in our society today are the two-parent, single-parent, blended, extended kinship, foster family, and adoptive family system.

The Two-Parent Family System

The *two-parent family system* is made up of a married couple and their biological children, 15-5. One or both parents may work outside the home. If one parent does not work, he or she will usually care for the home and the children. Social activities often center around the family. The two-parent family is sometimes called the nuclear family. A little over one-third of American families consist of married couples with children.

The Single-Parent Family System

A *single-parent family system* occurs as the result of divorce, separation, death, or having children outside of marriage. See 15-6. The single-parent family is growing faster than any other family form. About one-eighth of all families are currently single-parent families. About half of all children born in the 1980s will live in single-parent families sometime during their childhood.

Most single parents did not plan to be single parents. They have had to face an unexpected stress—the death, divorce, or desertion of a spouse or an out-of-wedlock pregnancy. The first stress may have created other problems that continue to affect the

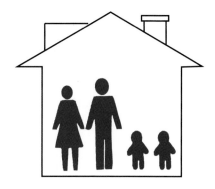

15-5
The two-parent family system is made up of a married couple and their biological children.

family. A single parent faces the strain of being the sole head of the household. Like all parents, single parents must provide supervision, care, and financial security for their families. Time, energy, and money may be in short supply. Single parents have the additional burden of compensating for the missing parent. In some instances, an absent parent may create tensions.

Parents Who Are Single As a Result of Desertion, Divorce, or Death

People who have been deserted or have divorced may begin single parenthood on a foundation of uncertainty. Such parents have the challenge of reshaping their own lives and the lives of their children under difficult circumstances. Time, effort, and the cooperation of all family members are needed to reestablish a secure family unit.

Death forces some people to accept the responsibilities of single parenting. The finality of the loss may be hard for these people to accept, but the needs of their children may help them overcome the feelings of personal loss. The surviving family members need to offer each other support in the readjustment period. A main concern of these single parents is to prevent themselves from growing too dependent on their children. They must allow their children to grow and to become independent and responsible adults.

Unwed Parents

Today, many unwed mothers are choosing to keep their babies rather than arranging for an adoption. A woman who keeps her baby should recognize her true reasons for doing so. Her reasons affect the way she behaves as a mother. If she keeps her baby just to have someone to love her, she will expect too much from the child. If she is trying to escape from an unhappy home life, she will probably find her new life even more disappointing. If she keeps her baby because she truly wants to raise her child, and if she is willing to accept all the responsibilities, she and her child can have full and satisfying lives.

Occasionally an unwed father raises his child. A man who wishes to do this should claim paternity while the woman is still pregnant. He should show his sincere interest and involvement in the approaching birth. In addition, he should show his concern for his parenting responsibilities once the child is born. In some cases and in some states, a man who shows his concern in this way can be awarded custody of his child.

Single Parents by Adoption

Sometimes a single man or woman seeks to adopt a child. As in any adoption, the background of the prospective parent is investigated thoroughly. In single-parent adoptions, the reasons for wanting to accept parenting responsibilities are especially questioned. In addition, the person must be able to provide the child with adult contacts of the opposite sex. For instance, a woman would have to have male relatives and friends who would spend time with the child. A man would have to have female relatives and friends who would spend time with the child. Thus, the child would grow up with both male and female influences.

Support for the Single Parent

With the increase in the number of single-parent families, more sources of emotional support may be sought. Friends and other family members may supply support and serve as role models for the children. Businesses, churches, governments, and community organizations offer support and services. They may provide child care programs or services such as Big Brothers and Big Sisters.

A single-parent family system can provide a happy and positive setting in which children feel loved and secure. See 15-7. As in any family system, children in a single-parent family can grow up to be cooperative, friendly, and responsible individuals.

The Blended Family System

Blended families have become another major family system in our society. In a *blended family system,* either or both spouses

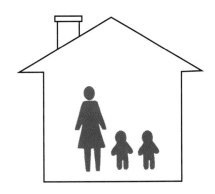

15-6
The single-parent family system is made up of one parent living with his or her children.

15-7

David Hopper

Members of a single-parent family can share many enjoyable activities, such as baseball games.

have been married before and have one or more children from the previous marriage. If both spouses had been previously married, the blended system consists of two former two-parent systems. The couple may or may not add to the family by having children of their own. See 15-8.

Relationships in blended families may be complicated. For instance, one blended family may include natural parents, brothers and sisters, stepparents and stepchildren, and half sisters and half brothers. Add to this relatives outside the immediate family. Children may have four sets of grandparents.

There may be increased financial concerns in the blended family. A larger household may create more financial burdens. Alimony, child support, or debts from previous marriages may also drain a blended family's financial resources.

When two families combine, their lifestyles have to be blended into one. Space, time, and energy resources must be allocated carefully. Needs and wants of individual members may have to give way to new family

priorities. Each family member needs to be dedicated to making the new family system work.

Blended families can be happy and successful, 15-9. They can provide rich new experiences for all family members. When the strengths of all the family members are combined, the result is a powerful family system, full of resources and potential. With time, and with cooperation and understanding, more and more positive interactions take place. Those positive interactions help to increase feelings of self-esteem for each member and for the family as a whole.

The Extended Kinship Family System

In the *extended kinship family system,* several generations of a family live together, 15-10. A mixture of grandparents, parents, children, aunts, uncles, and cousins can be found living in one dwelling. Family needs in everyday living, as well as in crisis situations, are met by family members. In many foreign countries, the extended kinship family is

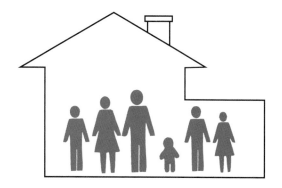

15-8

In a blended family, either or both spouses may have been married before and have one or more children. The couple may or may not add children of their own to the family.

David Hopper

15-9
Life in a blended family can be happy, busy, and complicated!

15-10
In an extended kinship family, several generations live together.

more common. Many who immigrate to our country bring members of their extended family with them and set up this system in this country.

An advantage of the extended kinship family system is the interaction between family members of all age groups. Aging members are likely to have an honored position in the family. Children can learn to respect and appreciate them. Elderly members, in turn, offer experience that can be helpful in raising children.

In some cases, extended kinship families control the family activities. For instance, senior members may choose marriage partners and careers for the children. In some other families, kinship activities are controlled but marriage and career choices are made independently.

Many extended kinship families are formed for a short period of time. For instance, a family member may marry and the couple will live with a parental family until they can afford a separate living space. A divorced family member with children may temporarily move back into a parental home, 15-11. Other examples are young adults who find they can't afford to live on their own. They may have to "return to the nest" while establishing their careers.

Sometimes the needs of aging parents have to be met. A grandparent may move in with an adult child's family. This may be temporary or it may become permanent, de-

Cholla Runnels

15-11
In this extended kinship family, three generations live together, sharing a home and daily activities as well as special occasions.

pending on the health of the aging family member.

In spite of these examples, the extended kinship family is not likely to become a major family system in our country. Most families want to live independently.

The Foster Family System

Foster parenting provides children with substitute families while their parents are unable to care for them. This may be for a short period of time or for many years.

Some children are placed in foster homes because they and their parents do not get along. Others are placed in foster homes because their parents cannot give them adequate care. In other cases, the parents have, in effect, abandoned their children, but the children cannot be adopted because of legal restrictions.

Foster family homes are evaluated and licensed according to state requirements. Foster parents give their time, effort, and love. They are reimbursed only for the children's expenses. The payments vary with each child, family, and state.

Foster parents experience the joy of helping children grow and develop. They receive the reward of making important contributions to the lives of children who need parental models. On the other hand, foster parents face some special challenges. Children come to them from many different backgrounds. The children are often bewildered, angry, frightened, and resentful. They may be hesitant about living with strangers. They need time, love, and understanding to adjust to their foster homes. Once the adjustments are made, foster families may become very close. If a child has to leave a foster home at a later time, both the child and the parents may have difficulty saying good-bye, 15-12.

Cholla Runnels

15-12
One of the hardest tasks of foster parents and grandparents is to say good-bye.

The Adoptive Family System

When a couple chooses to adopt a child it means they become the legal parents of the child they bring into their home. Adoptive parenting is a rich and fulfilling way to realize the joys of parenthood. If the couple have been unable to have their own children, they will eagerly look forward to giving love and care to their adopted child, 15-13.

Most couples prefer to adopt newborn babies. Then they can experience all the joys

The Gladney Adoption Center, Ft. Worth, TX

15-13

When a couple adopts a child, grandparents experience a new excitement in their lives as well.

of raising the children from infancy to adulthood.

Adopting older children is often more challenging. The children may feel guilty or depressed about the loss of their biological parents. They may withhold affection from their adoptive parents while hoping that their biological parents will return. Some adoptive children may even go through a stage of testing the love of the new parents. They may intentionally misbehave to find out if the adoptive parents will love them when they are "bad" as well as when they are "good." Eventually, most children come to accept and appreciate their adoptive parents. When this occurs, the family unit can grow stronger, and a loving and caring environment develops.

Stages of the Family Life Cycle

Beginning Stage	Expanding Stage	Developing Stage	Launching Stage	Aging Stage
Major focus:	Major focus:	Major focus:	Major focus:	Major focus:
Adjustment to married life.	Birth of children.	Reorganization of the family around school-age children.	Children leave home.	Retirement.
Adjust to separation from parents.	Focus on needs of children.	Parents recognize individual needs of each child while sharing family goals.	Children leave for college, careers, and marriages.	Break away from work.
Establish feeling of interdependence.	New responsibilities.		Parents refocus on their relationship.	Focus on friendships, hobbies, interests, and travel.
Both spouses may have careers.	Interpersonal relationships expand in family.	Parents involved in children's activities.	Parents relate to sons and daughters as adults.	Grandparenting continues.
	Role conflicts may occur.	Teens seek more independence.	Parents may become grandparents.	

15-14

The number of years involved in the different stages of the family life cycle depends on the number and spacing of children. In many families, the stages overlap.

Cholla Runnels

15-15
During the establishment stage, a couple adjust to living together as husband and wife.

The Family Life Cycle

One of young people's fondest dreams is the establishment of their own families. Young couples' expectations are high as they look ahead. Your family will be uniquely yours, but your *family life cycle* may consist of five stages that begin with marriage and end with aging. See 15-14.

Beginning Stage

The first stage of the family life cycle begins with the establishment of a family unit when the couple marries. During this stage, the main goal is adjustment to married life. Newlyweds must adjust to the separation from their parents. They need to achieve a feeling of comfort with each other. They also need to establish a feeling of interdependence. This means that each must learn to give and take from the other person while still maintaining his or her own individuality.

During this stage, each spouse must adjust to life with another person, 15-15. Each one has to learn to consider the other per-

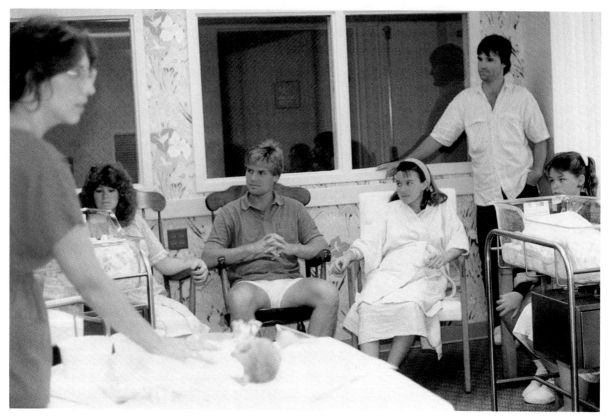

15-16
Even before first-time parents leave the hospital after the birth of their baby, they begin to learn how much care their newborn will require.

son's needs. Gradually, a couple works out acceptable patterns for everyday activities. Morning routines are settled, and household responsibilities are divided. Often in this stage, both spouses have careers. Further adjustments may be needed as spouses learn to support each other in their work as well as in their marriage.

The length of this stage varies. Some couples shorten this stage and enter the expanding stage right away. Other couples may stay in this first stage and bypass the stages involving parenthood. Many will simply lengthen this stage as they postpone parenthood.

Expanding Stage

The second stage begins with expectant parenthood, when the couple's focus is on the coming birth. Pregnancy is considered to be a time of transformation. The couple prepares for a new family member and begins to realize that nothing will ever be the same again.

When the first child is born, the focus of the couple suddenly shifts, 15-16. Primary attention is given to the needs of the infant. New responsibilities, new demands on time and energy, new limitations on freedom, and new expenses occur. The new roles of father and mother are added to the roles of husband and wife.

Parenthood can bring a couple closer together, or it can increase conflict. If parents want the child and have realistic expectations, a child can bring a sense of fulfillment. If one or both did not want a child, parenthood may be viewed as limiting and confining.

As a couple have additional children, the number of interpersonal relationships within the family expands. Children's roles also change. Sons become brothers. Daughters become sisters. The family experiences new levels of sharing and growing. Each additional child brings more challenges and responsibilities, but also more possibilities for love.

Parents with young children often experience role conflicts. They have to decide how to balance being a spouse with being a parent. One or both will also have the role of wage earner. Marriage partners have to communicate and make mutual decisions about how to handle their many responsibilities.

Developing Stage

The main goal in this stage is reorganization of the family to fit the expanding world of school-age children. Parents need to recognize the individual needs of each child. Blending these individual needs and sharing family goals can bring both joys and pressures.

Children also become involved in many activities outside the home. Parents spend much of their time taking children to school, lessons, practices, and social events.

Parenthood during the adolescent years calls for increasing parental flexibility as children become more independent. A major family goal is to provide children with increased freedom and responsibility as they mature.

Learning how to blend assignment of responsibilities with teenagers' growing needs for independence is a challenge for parents, 15-17. At the same time, parents may be experiencing new stresses in their lives. Career demands often reach a peak at this time. Some parents may fear losing their authority or control.

Launching Stage

During the launching years, children leave the family home to pursue education and career goals or to establish families of their own. Thus, the major family goal is reorganization of the family as members leave (and perhaps return temporarily).

As each child leaves, a void is felt. When the youngest child leaves, the parents are alone again. This is a big adjustment for parents. Their "on-the-job" parenting role may

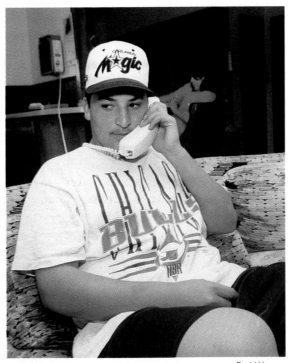

David Hopper

15-17
Teens and their parents may have to negotiate use of the family phone during the developing stage.

be over, but they feel continuing involvement with their children's lives. Parents have to learn to relate to their sons and daughters as adults.

This stage offers still another opportunity for growth. As husband and wife refocus on their marriage, they find renewed needs for communication and sharing. The couple learn to let their children live their own lives. Parents have more leisure time and can pursue new interests.

The couple's relationship often brings them increased satisfaction. If they maintain their friends, hobbies, and other interests, these are years of continuing growth. If they withdraw from friendships and activities, they may feel isolated and bored.

Post-parental years may overlap with grandparenting. Grandparenting creates new relationships. Grandparents and grandchildren often form close bonds.

At this point in the family life cycle, some couples face the dual responsibility of caring for both their children and their parents. Elderly parents may need financial help or health care. Caring for elderly relatives requires a family to make adjustments. Coping with their deaths may be difficult as well.

Aging Stage

For most people, the aging stage begins at the time of retirement. Couples enter this stage at varying ages. Some take early retirement, but many continue their careers as long as they are physically able to do so.

The retirement years mean breaking away from work and focusing on hobbies and interests. Travel and friendships can add enjoyment in the retirement years. Grandparenting roles continue to expand as grandchildren mature.

Summary ■ ■ ■ ■ ■ ■ ■ ■ ■ ■ ■ ■ ■ ■

- Family roles and functions have changed throughout history in order to meet the changing needs of family members.

- Families perform three basic functions: to provide for the physical needs of all family members, to provide for the socialization of the children, and to provide for the psychological well-being of all family members.

- Family members have both given roles and chosen roles. Each of these roles include certain responsibilities, though the specific responsibilities will vary among families.

- When all family members fulfill their roles and responsibilities, communicate clearly, and treat each other with affection and respect, they contribute to a functional family system. When responsibilities are not fulfilled and interpersonal relationships deteriorate, the family may become dysfunctional.

- A number of characteristics appear to be common among strong families.

- The six most common family systems are the two-parent, single-parent, blended, extended kinship, foster family, and adoptive family systems.

- The five stages in the family life cycle vary in length and may overlap. These stages are the beginning, expanding, developing, launching, and aging stages.

To Review ■ ■ ■ ■ ■ ■ ■ ■ ■ ■ ■ ■ ■ ■ ■

1. Define family according to the Census Bureau. Then write a brief definition of what the word "family" means to you.

2. Name four factors in our society that have caused families to change through the years.

3. How do families provide for the socialization of the children?

4. Explain the difference between a given role and a chosen role.

5. Explain the difference between a functional family and a dysfunctional family.

6. List four characteristics often found in strong, healthy families.

7. Match the following family systems with the correct identifying phrase.
   _____ Extended kinship
   _____ Single-parent family
   _____ Foster family
   _____ Two-parent family
   _____ Blended family
   _____ Adoptive family
   a. A family system made up of a married couple and their biological children.
   b. A couple become the legal parents of a child that is not their biological child.
   c. A family temporarily cares for children while their parents are unable to care for them.
   d. Either or both spouses have been married before and have one or more children from a previous marriage.
   e. Family system that occurs following divorce, separation, death, or birth of out-of-wedlock child.
   f. Several generations of a family live together.

8. What is the main focus of the developing family?

9. Name three key adjustments that a married couple must make during the launching stage.

To Do ■ ■ ■ ■ ■ ■ ■ ■ ■ ■ ■ ■ ■ ■ ■ ■ ■

1. Research family functions and roles in our country and compare them with family functions and roles in other cultures. Note similarities, differences, strengths, and weaknesses. Present an oral report to class.

2. Interview a grandparent or elderly neighbor. Find out how family roles and responsibilities have changed since their youth.

3. Make a list of characteristics of strong families. What role do teens play in each of these?

4. Create a bulletin board depicting the six different family systems.

5. Cite TV shows or movies that depict various family systems. Also cite shows or movies that feature families in various stages of the life cycle. Discuss how these families differ.

6. Discuss the changes that occur in roles, major goals, length of stage, number of relationships, and special problems in each of the stages of the family life cycle.

7. Role-play each stage of the family life cycle, setting up a typical family as it moves through the five stages.

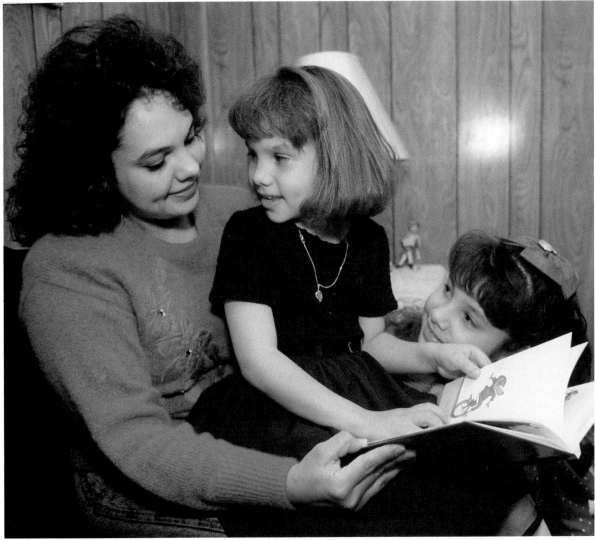

David Hopper

A single-parent family system can provide a happy and positive setting in which children feel loved and secure.

16 .....

The Parenting Decision

David Hopper

After studying this chapter, you will be able to

- describe the roles and responsibilities of parenthood.

- describe the sharing of parenting responsibilities in families today.

- identify several factors involved in the decision to become parents.

- explain the human reproduction process in females and males.

- describe methods of planning or preventing pregnancy.

- recognize alternatives available when a couple cannot achieve a pregnancy.

- assess the importance of genetic counseling and testing.

Terms to Know

artificial
  insemination

in vitro fertilization

genetic counseling

amniocentesis

ultrasound
  examination

When two people marry, they often have preconceived ideas regarding their roles as husband and wife. They usually discuss their thoughts about household tasks and money management. They probably know about the biological aspects of conception and pregnancy. However, they may not be familiar with their options concerning parenthood. The decision-making process regarding if and when to have children is often overlooked. Before such a decision is made, a couple should carefully consider all that is involved in parenting.

Parental Roles and Responsibilities ■ ■ ■ ■

Young husbands and wives today have more responsibilities, more career opportunities, and more choices. One of these choices is when and whether to become parents. This change in roles involves much more than a change from husband to father or wife to mother. Taking on a parental role means both are willing to make a lifetime commitment to the child. Both must understand what that commitment means in terms of time, energy, financial resources, and love. If the couple wants a child and they are ready to be parents, their parenting responsibilities will be easier to fulfill. See 16-1.

Parenting responsibilities are constantly changing to meet the changing needs of the child. Every child is a unique individual with his or her own special needs and potential. This is what makes the parental role an exciting and fulfilling endeavor.

The most important responsibility of parenting is the nurturing of the personality of each child. Children need lots of unconditional love, and they need to be shown that they are loved. They must feel that they can count on their parents' love throughout their lifetime. There may be times when parents don't like what their children are doing, but parents must assure them they will always love them.

Parenting Responsibilities Include . . .

To provide unconditional love. Children need to be loved and to be shown that they are loved. They must feel that they can count on your love.

To provide for children's physical needs. Food, clothing, shelter, and medical care must be provided.

To provide for children's intellectual needs. Mental stimulation, instilling a desire to learn, should begin at an early age.

To provide for children's social needs. Opportunities for social interaction, both within and beyond the family, are necessary for learning socially approved roles.

To instill positive character traits and encourage mutual respect. Such traits as honesty, responsibility, loyalty, and courtesy, for instance, should be emphasized.

To encourage independence when maturity is reached. Parents will have fulfilled their responsibilities when their children become self-sufficient adults.

16-1
Before deciding to become parents, a couple should consider the responsibilities that come with the parenting role.

Parents need to be sure the physical needs of the children are met. These include shelter, food, clothing, and medical care. Nutritious food in adequate amounts is important at every age as the child matures. Clothing should be appropriate for both temperature and aesthetic needs. The health needs of well children as well as ill children are the responsibility of parents.

Parents need to fulfill the intellectual needs of their children. Parents' attitude toward learning can influence their children's motivation to learn. Many teachable moments occur in the home as part of everyday living. Parents can use these moments to expand the child's love for learning.

Parents need to give their children opportunities for social growth. Opportunities for social interaction, both within and beyond the family, are necessary for learning socially approved roles. Through these interactions, children will learn valuable lessons in sharing, communicating, and compromising.

The virtues of honesty, responsibility, trust, loyalty, courtesy, and mutual respect need to be instilled in children by the example and guidance of parents. These character traits will be internalized by the children as they see their parents react to day-to-day stresses and joys. As children mature, their ability to make responsible decisions will be enhanced.

One of the basic responsibilities of parents is to encourage their children's independence when maturity is reached. Parents will have fulfilled their responsibilities when their children become self-sufficient adults who accept responsibility for their own decisions.

Sharing Parenting Responsibilities ▪ ▪ ▪ ▪

In earlier times, a mother had the main responsibility of caring for children. The father's role was primarily that of provider. Children spent most of their waking hours in the care of their mother. The mother fed, clothed, and disciplined the children. The threat, "Wait until your father gets home," was used as a last resort when children misbehaved. A father had less time for his children because he was busy making sure the family's needs were met.

Spousal roles have undergone many changes compared to those of only a generation ago. Many of these changes are due to the employment of wives outside the home,

16-2. When the wife is employed, a shift in responsibilities usually occurs. For instance, wives learn that if they are going to drive a car to work, they have to take care of it. Likewise, husbands learn that if they need a suit cleaned for an important meeting, it is their responsibility to take it to the cleaners. Both also learn that when their baby cries in the middle of the night, either of them may have to comfort the child. If both have to go to work in the morning, they learn to take turns soothing a restless baby.

Fathers today have become much more involved in parenting their children from the very beginning. Couples mutually agree on when they are ready to start a family. Once pregnancy occurs, fathers-to-be often become involved in preparing for the baby. They may

David Hopper

16-2

When wives work outside the home, parenting responsibilities need to be shared by the spouses.

participate in birthing classes and be present during the birth of their child. The father's role has expanded to include changing diapers, giving baths, and taking the child to preschool. Fathers are seen more often in grocery stores with babies and children in tow. More fathers are seen in parks with their children. Fathers are more involved with the care and guidance of their children throughout their growing years, 16-3. Mothers continue to be nurturing and caring, but they are also supportive of fathers who share the caregiving role.

Today's fast-paced world demands compromise and cooperation in the redistribution of family roles. Children benefit when they see that dads can fix meals and help with homework. They also benefit when they see that mom has an important role in the world of work.

Parenthood Is a Choice ▪ ▪ ▪ ▪ ▪ ▪

Issues of family planning involve the attitudes and desires of each individual, as well as the mutual desires of the couple. Each individual must ask, "Do I want to be a parent?"

16-3
Many fathers are spending more time with their children.

David Hopper

Parenthood is first an individual choice. As you look ahead to your future life, you will have many goals. Deciding whether or not to include parenthood as a goal is a decision you will have to make.

Parenthood is also a mutual choice. Becoming parents is a future goal for many young couples. As they marry and look forward to their life together, they will consider their future goal of becoming parents. They will make choices as to when they wish to start their family and how many children they desire.

As you looked at your time/life line in Chapter 5, you may have had many alternatives as you considered your future goals. Your decisions about education and career goals can be based on information that describes alternatives and consequences. You can even try certain courses in school based on the major of your choice. If you find you don't enjoy them, you can change your major. If you go to work and decide you are in the wrong job, you can look for a different one. Your education and career decisions are not necessarily final.

Once you choose parenting as a goal, or if you "just happen" to become a parent, you cannot change your mind. When you have a child, you can't go back and decide you really didn't want to be a parent. Parenthood is one decision in your life that is irreversible. It will change your life forever. You can't "try out" a child. Parenthood is real.

Parenthood As a Personal Choice

In order to consider parenthood as a personal choice, you first need to accept yourself. You need to recognize your strengths and your weaknesses. You have to know yourself and like yourself. Once you have accepted yourself as you are, you are more likely to form successful relationships

16-4
Since parenthood is a lifetime commitment, it must be a mutual decision.

David Hopper

with other people. You are also better able to see yourself as the guiding force in a child's life. If you want to be a parent, you need to like yourself and feel that you have a lot to offer as a parent.

You have to ask yourself, "Do I honestly like children?" As you interact with children, you can evaluate how you feel. You also need to consider how you feel with children under less than ideal conditions. Can you soothe a frightened child? Can you clean up a mess resulting from a toddler's temper tantrum without losing your own temper? If you want to be a parent, you should enjoy being with children.

Parenthood As a Mutual Choice

Parenthood must be a mutual choice for both you and your spouse, 16-4. You may feel you want to have children, but find that your

partner does not share your feelings. It is important for you and your spouse to consider goals for your life together, including parenting goals. As you compare your individual goals, you will be able to talk about your mutual parenting goals. The two of you should consider if you both want a family. Think about how you like to spend your leisure time, and how career goals may affect family goals. If one seems unsure of parenthood, it would be wise to delay or forgo having a child.

The stability of your marriage will affect your parenting decision. You should feel secure in your roles as husband and wife and be ready to accept the roles of mother and father. Before you decide to become parents, you should be prepared to handle multiple role commitments.

Your emotional maturity as a couple is also important, 16-5. Ideally, your mutual commitment to parenthood will be based on a sense of complete sharing. As a couple, you also have to realize that your lifestyle will change. If you say yes to parenthood, you will be saying no to other options. Your social life

Cholla Runnels

16-5
When marriage partners are emotionally mature and make a mutual commitment to parenthood, a baby adds to their feelings of sharing.

Common Reasons for Having Children	
Individual Decision	**Joint Decision**
I want to experience the delight and wonder that children will provide.	We want to share our beliefs with children.
I want to share my love with a child.	We feel children would add another dimension to our marriage.
I want the warmth and closeness of a family.	We want our love to expand and to include children.
I want to have the experience of being a parent.	We want children so we can enjoy being grandparents.
I want someone to carry on my family name.	We want to have a family lifestyle that includes children.
I feel my life would not be complete without having a child.	We want to teach and nurture children.
I think children will expand my life.	Having children is a true expression of our love.
Having a child completes my feeling as being female or male.	We feel children will deepen and strengthen our relationship.

16-6
People want to have children for many different reasons.

may be limited and confined. A view of parenthood as enriching and fulfilling can help you adapt your lifestyle to the changing demands of parenthood.

You both need to have some knowledge about children's growth and development. You can study child development, and you can find opportunities to interact with children. Knowing the basic principles of child development and basic parenting techniques will help you prepare for parenthood. You will never be able to predict exactly what your own child will be like. However, the more knowledge you have about children, the better able you will be to make a wise decision about parenthood.

Some common reasons for having children are listed in 16-6. Some common reasons for not having children are listed in 16-7. Review the lists and evaluate your feelings concerning parenthood.

Other Factors to Consider in the Parenting Decision

Taking responsibility for a new life is awesome. It is a decision that will affect you for the rest of your life. There are other factors to keep in mind as the parenting decision is made.

Age of the Woman

The best time for a woman to have children is when she is in excellent physical health. Today, many couples are choosing to start their families later in their marriages. As long as the physical health of the woman is good, delaying parenthood should not be a problem. Pregnancy during the teen years may pose some health risks if the woman's body has not yet physically matured. The key

Common Reasons for Not Having Children

Individual Decision	Joint Decision
I was not happy as a child, so I do not want to give birth to a child who might also be unhappy.	We want to devote our time and energy to each other and our marriage relationship.
I value my personal freedom and feel that children would be confining.	We are both devoted to our careers.
Children are expensive. I don't feel financially secure enough to have children.	We both feel there are too many problems in the world.
I don't want the responsibility of caring for children.	We do not feel our relationship is stable enough for children.
I want to travel, and children would make traveling difficult or impossible.	We want to be free to travel, and children would tie us down.
I want to do my part in controlling population growth.	My partner does not want a child.
I want to be able to maintain my privacy.	Neither of us feels comfortable with children.
I don't want to bring a child into a world with so many problems.	It would be wrong to give my partner the added responsibility of children.

16-7

People give many reasons for choosing not to have children.

factor is good prenatal care for very young mothers as well as older moms.

Women over 35 may have some complications if they have not maintained good health. When the couple does choose to delay pregnancy until their thirties, they should realize their parenting responsibilities will extend into middle age.

Career Considerations

Another factor for a couple to consider is career goals. Studies show that most people need successful and satisfying jobs even though both men and women consider family to be more important than work. A husband and wife should discuss their career goals and the ways in which those goals would

be affected by parenthood. If both have careers, they should discuss how they feel about raising children in a dual-career family.

Financial Considerations

Having a baby costs money. Medical expenses for childbirth continue to rise. In addition, babies require food, clothing, furniture, blankets, and toys, 16-8. As children grow, their needs grow, too. An average child will cost middle-class parents tens or even hundreds of thousands of dollars before the age of 18. See 16-9. Many parents continue to support their children beyond this age. College expenses can raise the total costs even further. This may be a factor in deciding how many children you will have, as well as

David Hopper

16-8
Baby supplies can be expensive. Financial considerations are an important part of planning a family.

the spacing of these children. Parents who have more than one child in college at the same time will have double the education costs during these years. These costs may be hard for a couple to handle if they have not saved for this purpose.

Couples who have their children soon after marriage are likely to find themselves under great financial pressure. If they need two incomes to handle their expenses, starting their family may mean loss of the wife's income at the same time their expenses are increasing.

Another financial factor to consider is child care. Child care provided by others can be expensive. On the other hand, if an employed parent quits a job to stay home with the child, the family loses income. As spouses plan for a pregnancy, all of these financial factors must be taken into consideration.

What It Costs to Raise a Child

Health Care

During the months of pregnancy and at the time of delivery, parents will suddenly realize the costs of having a baby. These initial costs of pregnancy and delivery are only the beginning. During the first two years of life, the American Academy of Pediatrics estimates that a baby will make about 10 trips to the pediatrician. The number of visits will decrease over the next few years, but the average child will require about $500 each year for various medical expenses. During the teen years, the major expenses may be orthodontia (braces) and check-ups. This could cost $2,000 or more.

Food and Clothing

These essential items will take one of the biggest bites out of the budget. If the baby is breast fed, the added nutritional needs of the mother need to be considered. If the baby is bottle fed, formula will cost $2.00 or more per quart. At six months, the addition of solid food will add about $150 to the grocery bill.

The cost of baby clothes will vary, but the cost for diapers adds a substantial amount. Disposable diapers can cost at least $700 a year. Babies grow fast, and too-small clothes have to be replaced with new clothing. Baby shoes are outgrown about every three months when the baby is young.

Housing

New parents and a new baby can get along very nicely in a cozy apartment or small house. However, as parents decide they need more room, the cost of renting an apartment with more bedroom space will increase the rent charge. Parents may choose to move to an upgraded home with more room.

Transportation

A stroller and a good car seat are about all that is needed to move a young child around. If a second car is needed to meet increased needs of getting children to school and other activities, this will create additional costs. The urban dweller may be able to use mass transit facilities, but suburban and rural families will need additional transportation.

Other Expenses

Providing necessities are not the only costs of raising a child. Music lessons, camp, and entertainment for children can be very costly. The Toy Manufacturers of America estimate that the average parent spends about $250 annually on toys for each child. Regardless of income level, parents tend to spend as much as they can on their children's activities.

Education

This is the biggest variable. Providing children with a college education is expensive. College costs vary greatly depending upon whether a state university or a private college is chosen. On average, four years at a state university will cost $17,000 to $20,000. Private college costs may run $40,000 to $50,000 or even more. These costs will be much higher by the time your children consider college.

16-9
Raising a child from birth to adulthood includes expenses that add up to many thousands of dollars.

Contemporary Topics *of interest to teens:*
"Onlies" Are OK!

Many myths used to exist about families with only one child. Parents of "onlies" were often criticized for denying their offspring the companionship of siblings and real-life lessons about sharing. An only child was often pictured as being spoiled, lonely, and uncooperative.

The current thinking of psychologists, however, is just the opposite. They now agree that onlies are as cooperative as other children and are often leaders. Only children learn to negotiate with those who are older and younger, not simply their peers. As adults, onlies differ little from others. The type of parenting children receive has more influence on their personalities than does the presence of siblings.

Psychologists believe that earlier attitudes about only children were often based on economic and health-related issues. For example, before the Depression, farms needed extra hands—which spurred families to have several children. Now, for economic, social, and medical reasons, couples are having fewer children. Many women postpone childbirth until they have established careers, a time which often coincides with a slow-down in their fertility. Moreover, women who become pregnant after age 35 are at increased risk of developing health complications and of delivering babies with abnormalities.

Many adults deliberately make the decision to have just one child. They cite the advantages of greater independence and closer relationships with their own parents and other relatives. Parents of only children also recognize they have more resources in time and money to devote to their child.

Evin Thayer

16-10
An only child has more opportunities to receive the attention of parents.

Number and Spacing of Children

The number of children and the spacing between them affect both the marriage and the entire family.

Some couples have just one child. Only children have the educational benefits of accompanying adults more often, 16-10. They have more contact with the vocabulary and ideas of the adult world. Such intellectual stimulation gives many only children a higher motivation to succeed.

Most couples plan to have more than one child. Siblings provide companionship for one another, 16-11. They also help one another learn the important lessons of sharing and getting along with others. In addition, their presence may allow parents to have more time for themselves.

Spacing children three or four years apart is recommended if possible. This allows parents to have greater interaction with each child. Children born closer together have less parent contact, and in some cases, the younger child becomes too dependent on the older sibling.

Spacing children a few years apart helps the mother to maintain better health. Physically, her body has time to return to normal after each pregnancy. Psychologically, this time span assures her greater stability.

Another advantage of three to four years of spacing is that the financial impact of the children can be spread over a longer period of time. Income has a greater chance to increase, and the impact of major child-raising costs is not as abrupt.

Spacing children a few years apart lessens the chances of sibling rivalry due to competition. These children will be able to establish themselves at their own developmental levels. Thus, they will be less likely to compete with each other.

Planning Pregnancy ▪ ▪ ▪ ▪ ▪

Planning pregnancy can be a major part of family planning. Some couples plan to achieve pregnancy. Others wish to prevent pregnancy. Their plans should be based on the goals they have set for their families.

Couples who want to plan their families need to know the basics of the human reproductive system. With this knowledge, they can avoid being misled by false information. They will be able to make wiser decisions and to feel confident in their marital relations.

The Female Reproductive System

A woman has two ovaries. The *ovaries* store and mature eggs, and they produce hormones. Ovaries are solid, with an uneven surface. Each measures about 1½ by ¾ inches.

The *uterus* is a pear-shaped organ a little smaller than a fist. It is hollow and has thick walls. When a woman is pregnant, the fetus is

16-11
Wisconsin Tourism Dev.
Siblings can be fun playmates.

held and nourished in the uterus until birth. As the fetus grows, the walls of the uterus stretch and become thin. After birth, the walls shrink back to their original size and shape.

The *cervix*, or neck of the uterus, dips down into the vagina. The cervix has a tiny opening through which menstrual flow can pass to the vagina and through which sperm can enter the uterus.

On either side of the uterus are thread-like tubes called *fallopian tubes*. The tubes are four to five inches long and have fringed ends. Mature eggs pass through the fallopian tubes on their way from the ovaries to the uterus.

The *vagina* is the canal between the vaginal opening and the cervix. The walls of the relaxed vagina have many small folds of membrane. When the vagina is expanded, as in childbirth, the folds disappear, and the vaginal walls appear smooth.

Once every *menstrual cycle*, or about once a month, a mature egg is released from an ovary of an adult female. This is called *ovulation* and is regulated by a hormone. Each month, a different hormone causes the inner lining of the uterus, the *endometrium,* to grow rapidly. This lining becomes thick and spongy and ready to accept a fertilized egg.

Once the egg has been released from an ovary, it enters a fallopian tube on its way to the uterus. If the egg is not fertilized by a sperm in the tube, it will deteriorate and pass out of the uterus in the menstrual flow. If it is fertilized, it will implant in the endometrium and develop into a fetus.

The Male Reproductive System

The man has two testes. The *testes* produce sperm and the male sex hormones. The testes are oval and are about 1½ inches long.

The testes are contained in the *scrotum,* the skin pouch beneath the penis. The testes are located outside the body because sperm production requires a temperature lower than that inside the body. Next to each teste is an elongated structure called an *epididymis.* Here, the sperm are matured and stored.

The *vas deferens* are long tubes that are attached to the epididymis and lead inside the body. They meet to form the *ejaculatory ducts.* These ducts are about one inch long. They both lead directly into the *urethra,* or urinary duct. The urethra extends through the penis and transports the sperm out of the body.

At the time of sexual excitement, sperm move from the epididymis through the vas deferens, the ejaculatory ducts, and the urethra. As they move through these organs, secretions from three sets of glands are added to them. The secretions form a thick, milky substance that helps the sperm on their journey to fertilize an egg. Together, the sperm and these secretions are called *semen.* On ejaculation, which occurs during intercourse, about one teaspoon of semen is released. It contains about 300 million sperm.

The erectile tissue in the penis fills with blood during sexual excitement. Pressure builds and causes the penis to become larger and firmer. The erect penis can then penetrate the vagina and expel the sperm near the cervix. From there, the sperm travel up through the uterus and into the fallopian tubes. If the timing is right, millions of sperm will meet the mature egg. They will crowd around it until one is permitted to penetrate and enter. At once, a chemical barrier will form and shut out all other sperm. The nucleus of the sperm will join the nucleus of the egg. *Conception,* or *fertilization,* will have occurred.

Methods for Planning or Preventing Pregnancy

Couples who want to plan or prevent pregnancy should investigate the methods that are available, 16-12. They should choose the one that will be morally acceptable and most effective for them. Though abstinence is the only sure way of preventing pregnancy, the following are the most common methods of birth control.

The *rhythm method* is based on abstinence during the period of the female reproductive cycle when the egg is available for fertilization. The woman determines when she ovulates and has no sexual intercourse for a few days before and after this occurs. If a woman is perfectly regular (on a 28-day cycle), she will ovulate at the midpoint of her cycle, or on day 14. Unfortunately, the woman's cycle is not always that regular. Her cycle is affected by stress, by general health conditions, and by changes in environmental temperature. Therefore, ovulation does not always occur on the fourteenth day.

Natural family planning involves the careful observation of signs and symptoms of fertile and infertile periods. First, the woman can note the consistency of her mucus. During the fertile period, mucus usually flows for about three to five days. Its consistency becomes like that of a raw egg white as ovulation approaches. When this change in mucus is noted, the fertile period begins and

16-12
An engaged couple should discuss family planning during the engagement period.

abstinence should follow for a period of 8 to 10 days. A woman also can take her body temperature daily during this time. When it rises, the fertile period will likely end in three or four days. The effectiveness rate of natural family planning methods may be comparatively low unless practiced correctly and consistently. There are no side effects.

Spermicidal vaginal preparations contain a chemical that immobilizes or kills sperm on contact. Spermicides are available as creams, foams, or jellies and may be purchased without a prescription. The preparation is deposited in the upper vaginal canal a short time before intercourse. Spermicidal preparations used without barrier contraceptives (such as a condom or diaphragm) have a comparatively low rate of effectiveness in preventing pregnancy.

A *diaphragm* is a shallow cup of soft rubber that fits over the cervix. A similar device, called the *cervical cap,* is smaller than a diaphragm and is shaped like a thimble. Both the diaphragm and cervical cap cover the cervix and act as a mechanical barrier to sperm, preventing them from entering the uterus. Spermicidal cream or jelly should be used with these devices. The diaphragm and cervical cap must be prescribed by a physician. They are comparatively effective in preventing pregnancy when used correctly and regularly. After childbirth or a large weight change, the devices must be refitted by a doctor.

The *condom* is a male contraceptive that fits over the erect penis and traps semen so no sperm enter the vagina. If it is defective, slips off, or ruptures, however, it provides no protection. Condoms are available at a minimal cost. They are effective if used properly, and especially if used together with a spermicide. An added advantage of the latex condom is that it provides some protection against sexually transmitted diseases. This is because it serves as a barrier between the penis and the vagina. The condom has been highly promoted as a method of preventing the spread of AIDS. However, AIDS is a fatal disease, and relying only on a condom for protection is still very risky. The best protection against contracting the HIV virus that leads to AIDS is to practice abstinence.

Intrauterine devices (IUDs) are small plastic or metal devices that come in a variety of shapes. An IUD is inserted into the uterus by a physician. Once inserted, it can remain in place for months or even years and effectively prevent pregnancy. IUDs can cause side effects including heavy menstrual periods and severe cramping. They can sometimes lead to pelvic inflammatory disease and infertility. Because of lawsuits brought by women who developed infections or other problems using IUDs, few manufacturers are making these devices today.

Taken regularly, an *oral contraceptive,* often called *the pill,* is a highly effective method of birth control. It prevents ovulation by use of synthetic hormones. Since no egg is released from the ovaries, fertilization cannot occur. The pill is simple to use and may be taken at a time independent from the sex act. For most women, merely stopping its use restores fertility. It is prescribed only after a careful examination by a physician. The most dangerous side effect is an increased tendency for some women to form blood clots. The risk of side effects increases for smokers, especially those over age 35. Regular checkups can reveal any problems.

A fairly new method of birth control that is being used more often now is *Depo-Provera.* Depo-Provera is a contraceptive injection (shot) that is given in the buttock or upper arm that prevents pregnancy for three months. It is one of the most reliable methods of birth control. Depo-Provera contains a synthetic hormone that prevents a woman's egg cells from ripening and being released (ovulation). The most common side effect is a change in the normal menstrual cycle, causing irregular and unpredictable bleeding. The menstrual cycle generally returns to normal when usage stops.

Norplant is also a relatively new method of birth control. Norplant consists of six rubber capsules, each about the size of a matchstick. Using a local anesthetic, the capsules are placed under the skin of the upper arm in a fan-like pattern. The capsules contain a hormone that makes the female body think that it is pregnant so that an egg is not released each month. The capsules continuously secrete the hormone for a period of five years. After the fifth year, if the woman wants to continue this method, the capsules are replaced. Norplant is extremely effective. Though it is initially more expensive, it is effective for five years so the cost is spread over a long period of time.

Withdrawal refers to the removal of the penis from the vagina before ejaculation. Some people mistakenly believe that this prevents conception. Actually, some sperm may be released into the vagina before ejaculation occurs. The effectiveness rate is very low since any semen deposited in the vagina can cause fertilization to occur.

Permanent Methods

Sterilization brings a complete end to fertility. Methods are available for both men and women. Although research is being done to find ways of reversing sterilization, these methods must be considered permanent measures. Couples who decide their family is complete may choose either the *vasectomy* for the male or *tubal ligation* for the female.

A vasectomy does not destroy a man's sexual desire or performance. The procedure is simple and quick. A tiny cut is made on either side of the scrotum. Each vas deferens tube is tied or cut and sealed. The sperm are prevented from traveling the route of the vas deferens at ejaculation. This procedure does not affect any of the other secretions of the male reproductive tract.

Tubal ligation is the most common operation for female sterilization. A small cut is made below the navel, exposing the fallopian tubes. These are tied or cut and sealed. Although there are many variations to this procedure, the result is always the same. The fallopian tubes are blocked, preventing the egg from traveling to the uterus. Sterilization does not decrease a woman's femininity or sexuality. Ovulation and menstruation continue, but the eggs cannot reach the uterus.

If a Couple Cannot Have Children

Some couples who desire children cannot have them. About 10 percent of all marriages are infertile. Many cases of infertility are psychological rather than physiological and can sometimes be cured by reducing tension. Other cases of infertility are due to hormonal factors, blocked fallopian tubes, blocked vas deferens, or a low concentration of sperm in the semen. These require medical help. If a couple believe they are infertile, they should see a doctor to determine the cause of infertility and to learn of possible treatments.

For couples who have not been able to conceive, there are two ways they can possibly achieve pregnancy. These include artificial insemination and in vitro fertilization. If these two methods cannot be used, couples can become parents by adopting a child.

Artificial Insemination

Through a process called *artificial insemination,* a physician places sperm directly in the upper part of the woman's uterus or in the fallopian tubes. This increases the chances for fertilization. If possible, the husband's sperm are used. If his sperm cannot fertilize an egg, the sperm of a donor can be used, providing the husband and wife both agree. The donor is unknown, but he is chosen carefully so that physical hereditary traits will be similar to those of the husband. If artificial insemination is chosen, legal papers are signed indicating that the husband will accept responsibility as the father of the child.

In Vitro Fertilization

Advanced technology in human reproduction has developed the technique of *in vitro fertilization.* In this process, an egg is removed from a woman's ovary and fertilized in a glass dish (not a test tube). After the fertilized egg has begun cell division, it is implanted into the uterus. Babies born as a result of this technique are sometimes called "test-tube babies."

This process presents an alternative answer for couples who want children but cannot achieve pregnancy. An increasing number of fertility clinics across the country are offering this service, though it costs thousands of dollars.

Adoption

If the couple cannot have children, or if their hereditary backgrounds are such that they have been counseled against it, they may choose to adopt children, 16-13. Adopting a baby requires careful study. Both husband and wife should be equally in favor of the adoption. Refer to Chapters 9 and 15 for information concerning the adoption process.

Genetic Counseling ▪ ▪

Genetic counseling is advice given by a physician to prospective parents on matters of heredity. The doctor studies the medical histories of both prospective parents'

16-13

Herman Hospital

Adopting a baby can bring genuine contentment to a couple who cannot have children by any other means.

families. The doctor may also examine the prospective parents for possible disease conditions. If the risk of hereditary defects is high, the couple may want to consider adoption instead of childbirth.

The best time to seek genetic counseling is before conception. However, if a pregnant woman believes the baby may be born with a heredity defect, she may choose to undergo tests.

Two common tests used to identify potential genetic defects in the fetuses of pregnant women are amniocentesis and ultrasound examinations.

In *amniocentesis,* a long, thin needle is inserted into the uterus. Part of the fluid surrounding the fetus is drawn out and analyzed for abnormalities.

Ultrasound examinations use sound waves to provide an outline or "picture" of the fetus inside the mother, 16-14. It can show whether the fetus is growing normally. The test can provide evidence of such problems as an intestinal obstruction, kidney disease, brain abnormalities, or missing arms and legs.

Pregnant women who are over age 35, who have a family history of hereditary disease, or who have previously given birth to a

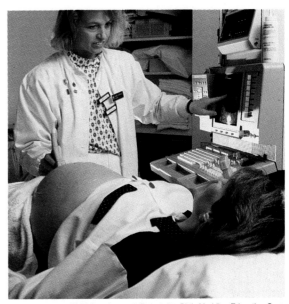

Child Development: Prenatal to Birth, Meridian Education Corp.

16-14
A pregnant woman may wish to have an ultrasound examination to detect any possible hereditary defects.

physically challenged child may be especially interested in genetic tests and counseling. Couples who receive genetic counseling can then make their parenting decisions armed with all the facts available to them.

Summary ■ ■ ■ ■ ■ ■ ■ ■ ■ ■ ■ ■ ■ ■ ■

- The most important responsibility of parenting is the nurturing of the personality of each child. Children need lots of unconditional love and they need to be shown that they are loved.

- Spousal roles have undergone many changes compared to those of only a generation ago. Many of these changes are due to the employment of wives outside the home. Couples are now sharing more parenting responsibilities.

- Once you become a parent, you cannot reverse your decision.

- Parenthood is both a personal choice and a mutual choice.

- Factors to be considered in the parenting decision include the goals of the wife and husband, the age of the woman, career and financial considerations, the desired number of children, and the desired spacing of children.

■ Basic knowledge of the human reproductive system can help couples plan their families.

■ Couples who want to choose when to have a child and the spacing of future children may choose different methods of birth control that are available to them. They should choose the one that will be morally acceptable and most effective for them.

■ Couples who desire children but cannot achieve a pregnancy need to seek medical counsel to determine the cause of infertility and to learn of possible treatments.

■ Couples who cannot have children, or whose hereditary backgrounds are such that they have been counseled against having children, may choose to adopt.

■ Genetic counseling is advice given by a physician to prospective parents on matters of heredity. Examples of tests that can identify genetic defects in fetuses are amniocentesis and ultrasound examinations.

To Review ■ ■ ■ ■ ■ ■ ■ ■ ■ ■ ■ ■ ■ ■ ■

1. Describe three parenting responsibilities.

2. Briefly explain how traditional spousal roles have changed in recent years.

3. Explain how parenthood is a personal choice as well as a mutual choice.

4. List three benefits of spacing children three to four years apart.

5. Match the following reproductive organs with the correct identifying phrase.
    _____ Uterus
    _____ Epididymis
    _____ Fallopian tube
    _____ Semen
    _____ Cervix
    _____ Vas deferens
    _____ Ovaries
    _____ Testes
    a. Stores and matures female eggs.
    b. Thread-like tubes connected to the uterus.

    c.   Pear-shaped organ that holds the developing fetus.

    d.   The neck of the uterus.

    e.   Organ in the male that produces the sperm.

    f.   Thick, milky secretion containing the sperm.

    g.   Long tubes leading from testes to the ejaculatory ducts.

    h.   Elongated structures next to the testes.

6.   The only sure way of preventing pregnancy is _____.

7.   Describe the rhythm method of birth control.

8.   _____ is a birth control method in which six capsules containing a hormone are inserted in the upper arm.

9.   A _____ is a sterilization method for men.

10.   _____ _____ is the most common sterilization method for women.

11.   Name two technological alternatives for couples who have not been able to achieve a pregnancy through sexual intercourse.

12.   What is included in genetic counseling?

To Do ▪ ▪ ▪ ▪ ▪ ▪ ▪ ▪ ▪ ▪ ▪ ▪ ▪ ▪ ▪ ▪

1.   Make a list of parenting responsibilities. Discuss whether most teens are ready to handle these responsibilities.

2.   Ask two married couples to come to class to discuss how they share their parenting responsibilities.

3.   Find pictures and cartoons that depict parenting roles. Discuss the differences and similarities of the roles and how they have changed from the past. Post on the bulletin board.

4.   Collect several articles from newspapers and magazines concerning family planning. Also look for articles describing new methods of family planning. Write a brief summary of each.

5.   Have several small-group discussions on the topics below and share the results with the rest of the class. For each group, appoint a leader to record responses and report them to the class.

    Group A—Genetic counseling. Suppose your neighbor fell in love with a person whose heritage included an obvious hereditary defect. Should the couple consider genetic counseling? What traits, characteristics, or defects might prompt them to seek genetic counseling?

    Group B—Selecting the sex of a child. Should people be able to select the gender of their future children? Consider the consequences if all firstborn children were boys, or if all were girls. Consider the impact on business, politics, education, marriage, and families if gender selection were possible.

Group C—Control of families and population. Some sociologists have proposed that family size be controlled by the government. Should people have to "apply to the government" in order to have their first child? What about their twelfth? If persons in your group have read *Future Shock* by Alvin Toffler, discuss the implications of world population growth for the future.

David Hopper

Spending time with a friend's baby may help you make the parenting decision.

17

A Baby Is Born

After studying this chapter, you will be able to

- identify signs of pregnancy.

- describe the changes that occur during pregnancy.

- summarize important health practices for pregnant women.

- explain the process of childbirth.

- describe methods of childbirth.

When a couple is told that they are going to be parents, it is an emotional time. Emotions can range from excitement and delight to fear and doubt. The announcement may be long awaited or come as a complete surprise. It may be welcomed or, in some cases, it may cause concern. Whichever the case, the months of pregnancy may seem to last forever, but the moment of birth lasts only an instant. The birth of a baby is an emotional experience for new parents, 17-1.

Evidence of Pregnancy

The majority of married couples want children and are able to have them. Out of every 100 married women of childbearing age who have normal marital relations, 80 will become pregnant within a year. (This statistic assumes that no form of birth control is used.)

When a woman suspects she is pregnant, she has three sources of evidence to confirm it. These are her own observations of symptoms of pregnancy, the physician's observations, and laboratory tests.

Terms to Know

areola
colostrum
quickening
conception
endometrium
placenta
amnio-chorionic membrane
amniotic fluid
lunar months
embryo
fetus
fetal alcohol syndrome

miscarriage
lightening
umbilical cord
Lamaze method of childbirth
Leboyer method of childbirth
family centered childbirth
cesarean section
bonding
postpartum period
lactation

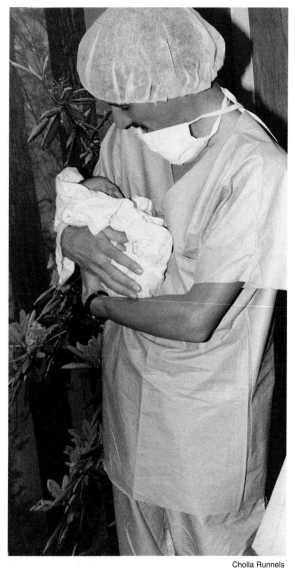

Cholla Runnels

17-1
The birth of a child is a joyful event.

The Woman's Observations

The woman will become aware of several symptoms of pregnancy. When she suspects pregnancy, she should make an appointment with her doctor so that these symptoms may be confirmed.

Cessation of Menstruation

When an expected period of menstruation is missed by more than 10 days, under normal circumstances, pregnancy is likely. When the second period is also missed, the probability becomes stronger. There are times, however, when a woman might delay or miss her period for other reasons such as the following:

■ Emotions can affect a woman's physiological functioning. In some cases, a woman might want a baby so much that she may skip her period or actually manifest other signs of pregnancy. On the other hand, she may be so afraid of an unwanted pregnancy that her period is delayed.

■ A change of climate may cause temporary changes in the cycle.

■ Exposure to cold may affect the cycle.

■ Chronic disease, such as anemia, or other conditions that impair health can cause changes in the menstrual cycle.

Breast Changes

These changes may be one of the first symptoms noted by the woman. When pregnancy begins, changes in the breasts occur simultaneously. (Most women note temporary fullness in the breasts prior to their menstrual periods. Some even feel changes at ovulation.) During pregnancy, the following breast changes occur:

■ The breasts become larger, fuller, and more tender with a sensation of stretching. This is often accompanied by a tingling feeling in the breast and nipple.

■ The *areola,* the pigmented area around the nipple, becomes darker in color, widens in diameter, and becomes puffy.

- *Colostrum,* the sticky precursor of milk, may be expressed from the nipple as early as the fourth month. This is the substance that the baby will receive when nursing until the third day after birth. Then milk comes into the breast.

Frequency of Urination

Frequent urination is another symptom of pregnancy. The growing uterus stretches the base of the bladder. This causes the bladder to feel heavy. As pregnancy progresses, the uterus stretches and rises out of the pelvis, so the frequency of urination lessens. However, it increases again when the fetus becomes larger and actually presses against the bladder.

Nausea

About one-third of pregnant women suffer no nausea at all. Another one-third experience waves of nausea for a few hours. In the remaining third, it will actually cause vomiting. This "morning sickness" may begin about two weeks after the first missed menstrual period. It usually ends after a month or six weeks, and almost always by the end of the third month.

Quickening

Later in pregnancy, the woman may feel active movements of the fetus. These first movements are referred to as *quickening.* This usually occurs at the end of the fifth month as a flutter low in the abdomen. The first stirring of the baby is faint, but as time goes on, the movements grow stronger. They may occasionally disturb the mother's sleep during the later weeks.

Abdominal Changes

During the first three to four months, abdominal changes are not noticeable. See 17-2. As early as the third month, the woman may be able to feel a lump just above the pubic bone, but it is not noticeable to others. It gradually enlarges to reach the navel by the fifth month. By this time it begins to show.

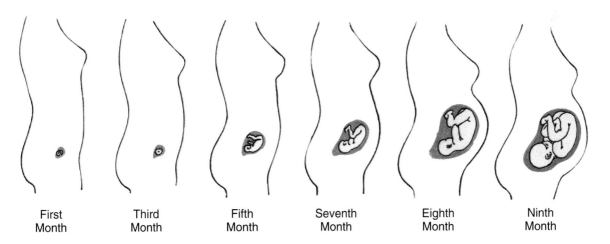

| First Month | Third Month | Fifth Month | Seventh Month | Eighth Month | Ninth Month |

17-2
Noticeable abdominal changes occur in the latter half of pregnancy.

During the last half of pregnancy, pinkish streaks may appear over the woman's abdomen. These represent small breaks in the lower layer of skin, which is less elastic than the upper layer. These "stretch marks" can be prevented by massaging the skin with a good lubricant. It also helps to keep weight gain under control.

The Physician's Observations

During a woman's first visit to confirm pregnancy, the physician will give her a thorough examination. The physician will run lab tests and question her about her medical history.

The physician will usually begin with an examination of the breasts. Any change in color of the areola, enlargement of the areola, and "heaviness" of the increased breast size will be noted. The physician will also give the woman a pelvic examination. He or she will study the woman's reproductive organs and note any changes that would indicate pregnancy. Her blood pressure will be taken, and samples of blood and urine will be sent to a lab for tests.

Next, the woman will be asked for a complete medical history. She will be questioned about any hereditary defects, her history of communicable diseases (such as sexually transmitted diseases), and her menstrual history.

If pregnancy is confirmed, the physician will tell the woman what to expect. A possible birth date will be determined based on a formula, 17-3. During later visits, the physician will check the growth of the fetus and watch for abnormalities. The physician will advise the woman as needed and answer any questions she may have.

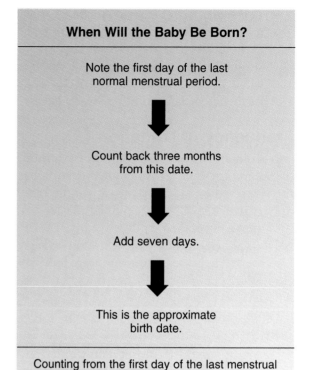

When Will the Baby Be Born?

Note the first day of the last normal menstrual period.

⬇

Count back three months from this date.

⬇

Add seven days.

⬇

This is the approximate birth date.

Counting from the first day of the last menstrual period, the average duration is 10 lunar months, or 40 weeks, or 280 days. This is about nine calendar months.

17-3
This formula can be used to estimate the birth date of a baby.

Laboratory Tests

For most women, confirmation of suspected pregnancy is done during a visit to a doctor eight to 10 weeks after conception (as previously described). However, a woman may want to know earlier than this for either medical or psychological reasons. She may be able to find out as early as one week after her missed menstrual period. She can go to her family doctor, an obstetrician (physician specializing in pregnancy), a medical lab, or a health clinic for a laboratory test. Kits are also available in stores for home tests.

The most common test is an examination of a urine specimen. The presence of certain hormones in the urine confirms pregnancy.

The Developing Baby

Within about nine calendar months, one single cell can develop into a human being. This process follows a precise series of events, beginning at conception and ending at birth.

Conception

The instant a sperm and egg unite, *conception* or fertilization takes place, and pregnancy begins. Within hours, the fertilized egg begins to divide into two cells, then four, then eight, and so forth. It continues to grow rapidly as it moves down the fallopian tube, a trip that takes about four days. By the time the egg reaches the uterus, it has become a hollow ball of cells that implants in the *endometrium* or inner lining of the uterus.

Then the placenta forms between the endometrium and the hollow ball of cells. The *placenta* is a special organ that functions as an interchange between the developing fetus and the mother. It allows food, oxygen, and water to reach the fetus, and the fetus' waste products to be passed to the mother.

Forming around the developing cells are two membranes. The outer membrane, or *chorion*, slips against the inner bag, or *amnion*. Together they form the *amnio-chorionic membrane* or "bag of waters." Inside the amnio-chorionic membrane is *amniotic fluid* that completely surrounds the fetus. This fluid has the following important functions:

- To maintain the fetus at an even temperature.

- To cushion the fetus against possible injury.

- To provide a medium in which the fetus can move around easily.

- To assist in the birth of the baby.

Lunar Month Development

The development of a baby can be studied in periods called *lunar months*. They are more specific than calendar months. Each lunar month is exactly 28 days, or four weeks long.

End of First Lunar Month

At this stage, the developing baby is called an *embryo*. It is about ¼ inch in length. Its heart resembles a bulging gland and is pulsating and sending blood through microscopic arteries. The backbone and spinal column are forming, as well as the digestive system and lungs. Buds that will become arms and legs have formed.

End of Second Lunar Month

The embryo is about 1 1/8 inches in length and weighs about 1/30 of an ounce. The face and features are forming, and eyelids are fused. The limbs show distinct elbows, hands, knees, and feet. The internal organs are developing.

End of Third Lunar Month

The developing child is now called a *fetus*. The fetus is about 3 inches in length and weighs about 1 ounce. The arms, hands, fingers, legs, feet, and toes are fully formed, as well as the fingernails and toenails. Ears are present. Tooth sockets and buds for teeth are forming in jawbones. Eyes are almost fully developed, but lids are still fused.

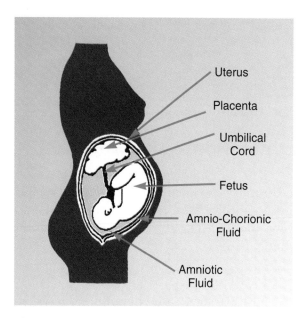

17-4
This fully developed fetus is ready to be born.

End of Fourth Lunar Month

The fetus is about 6½ inches in length and weighs about 4 ounces. Fine, downy hair appears over the skin. The skin is transparent and thin. The fingerprint has formed. There is a strong heart beat, fair digestion, and active muscles. Eyebrows now appear.

End of Fifth Lunar Month

The fetus is 10 to 12 inches in length and weighs ½ to 1 pound. The internal organs are maturing quickly, but the lungs are insufficiently developed to cope with conditions outside the uterus. The skin is less transparent. Some hair is present on the head. Eyelids are still completely fused.

End of Sixth Lunar Month

The fetus measures 12 to 14 inches and weighs 1¼ to 1½ pounds. The skin is very wrinkled, with no fat layers visible beneath it.

Skin is covered by a fatty secretion. Eyelids finally separate, and eyelashes are formed.

End of Seventh Lunar Month

The fetus measures about 15 inches in length and weighs about 2 to 2½ pounds. The skin is still wrinkled with little fat under the surface. If the fetus is born at seven months, it has a good chance of survival if cared for by skilled physicians.

End of Eighth Lunar Month

The fetus measures about 16½ inches and weighs about 4 pounds. The fetus is putting on more weight, and its internal organs are continuing to develop.

End of Ninth Lunar Month

The fetus measures about 19 inches in length and weighs about 6 pounds. The fine, downy hair that had covered the skin has disappeared. The fingernails may protrude over the end of the fingers. The skin is pink and still coated with the protective fatty secretion.

Middle of the Tenth Lunar Month

Full term has now been reached, 17-4. The fetus is ready to be born. Its length is about 20 inches. The average weight is 6½ to 7½ pounds for a girl and 7½ to 8 pounds for a boy.

Care of the Mother

The health of the developing baby is directly related to the health of the mother during pregnancy. Her history of health before conception can also affect the baby.

Cholla Runnels

17-5
Nutrition is especially important during pregnancy. Fresh fruits such as apples are good snack foods.

Diet and Nutrition

During pregnancy, a woman needs to be especially careful about the foods she eats, 17-5. Her diet affects not only her own health, but also the health of her unborn child. She needs a well-balanced diet that includes a variety of nutritious foods.

If the woman has followed a well-balanced diet throughout her life, she will not need to make many changes during pregnancy. Her doctor may recommend adding some foods to her diet or taking a few dietary supplements such as vitamins and iron. It is recommended that pregnant women consume three servings of milk or milk products daily.

If the woman is poorly nourished, the stress of pregnancy may make her nutritional deficiencies more apparent. See 17-6. Unless she changes her eating habits and pays strict attention to her diet, she and her baby may develop health problems. This is especially evident in teenage pregnancies. Besides possibly being underdeveloped, many teens are undernourished and unprepared for the physical stress of pregnancy. Research has shown that babies of undernourished teens have a greater chance of being born premature or with birth defects. These babies may also lack adequate nutrient reserves to protect them through birth and the first two months of life.

Cholla Runnels

17-6
Undernourishment during pregnancy can cause health problems for both the mother and the unborn baby.

Weight Control

Weight gain in pregnancy is very important, 17-7. The doctor will set guidelines for the woman and help her gain the right amount of weight. A total gain of between 20 and 30 pounds is recommended.

During the first three months of pregnancy, the woman's weight should remain

Cholla Runnels

17-7
Weight gain during pregnancy should be carefully controlled.

fairly constant. Some women gain a little, and some even lose a little. During the next six months, the woman should gain slightly less than 1 pound a week. A sudden large weight gain might be due to excess fluid in the body tissues rather than a normal growth of the fetus. Thus, any spurt in weight gain should be mentioned to the doctor so possible problems can be avoided.

Gaining too much weight usually means the woman is eating the wrong foods. Extra weight adds a burden to the woman's back and legs and may make delivery more difficult. Today, doctors are just as concerned about women who gain too little weight. Babies who are too small may have more health problems during the first months of life.

Just before delivery, an average fetus weighs 7½ pounds. The placenta, amniotic fluid, uterus growth, and breast growth account for about 8 pounds. The extra blood and fluid in the woman's tissues weigh about 3½ pounds. Within a week after delivery, the woman will have lost 18 to 20 pounds. She should return to her pre-pregnancy weight within three months.

Teeth

A woman should not plan on having complicated dental work done during pregnancy. However, her teeth should be checked early in pregnancy, and any necessary work should be done then. The dentist should be told of the pregnancy so special precautions can be taken if anesthesia or x-rays of teeth are needed.

Exercise

Pregnant women are not invalids. On the contrary, continued exercise is beneficial to their general good health, 17-8. Walking is especially good since it aids digestion and circulation.

17-8
Moderate exercise is beneficial to the health of most pregnant women.

David Hopper

Each woman should consult her physician about exercise during pregnancy. Most doctors agree that, in general, healthy pregnant women can continue the types of exercise they were doing before pregnancy, if the exercise is done in moderation. However, exercise that involves lying on one's back is not recommended after the early stages of pregnancy. Such exercise may interrupt the flow of blood to the fetus. The doctor may also advise against horseback riding, diving, or any other strenuous exercise. Women may be advised to work out more slowly and to rest a few minutes several times a day.

Marital Relations

Only a generation ago, some physicians advised that sexual intercourse be avoided throughout pregnancy. Most physicians today see no reason to avoid intercourse until the last month of pregnancy.

Travel

A woman with an uncomplicated pregnancy can travel as she pleases. On long trips by plane, train, or bus, she should get up and move around often. When traveling by car, she should stop every 100 miles and walk for a while. This will promote better circulation. Late in pregnancy, most doctors advise their patients not to take any long trips.

Employment

Many women continue to work when they become pregnant. If a woman is in good health and if her job is not too tiring, she may work almost until the due date for her baby. In each case, the woman's doctor should be consulted for advice.

Smoking

Smoking is not healthy for anyone. This is especially true for pregnant women. Smoking is detrimental to the health of the developing baby. Mothers who smoke heavily increase the risk of miscarriage or premature delivery. They also tend to have smaller babies. Smaller babies are more likely to develop health problems early in infancy than babies of normal weight. These children may also have learning problems in school. If ever a woman wanted to stop smoking, this would be a good time to do it.

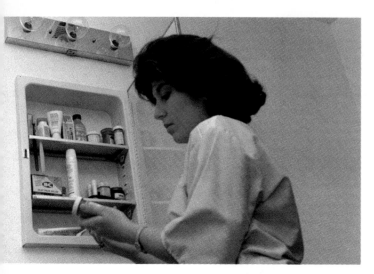

17-9
The total effect of drugs and medications taken during pregnancy is still unknown. A woman should use only those that are recommended by her physician.

Alcohol and Illegal Drugs

Alcohol passes through the placenta quickly. The unborn baby feels a drink as quickly as the mother does. Drinking during pregnancy is not advised. Research in this area is still being done. However, studies have shown that children of alcoholic mothers are sometimes born with a pattern of defects known as *fetal alcohol syndrome*. Common defects are growth deficiencies and limited mental capacities. The children usually have narrow eyes, low nasal bridges, and short up-turned noses. Many are jittery and poorly co-ordinated, with short attention spans and behavioral problems. The National Founda-tion—March of Dimes suggests, "If you are pregnant, don't drink. If you drink heavily, don't become pregnant."

"Street drugs," such as heroin, cocaine, marijuana, and amphetamines, can damage anyone's health and can be especially harm-ful to an unborn baby. The child of a drug ad-dict may actually be an addict at birth.

Use of Medications and Exposure to X Rays

Whenever an expectant mother is feel-ing ill, she should consult her physician. She should never take any over-the-counter or prescription medications unless they are rec-ommended by her physician. This includes aspirin, vitamins, stomach remedies, laxa-tives, antibiotics, and sleeping pills. The total effect of drugs taken during pregnancy is un-known, but a "better safe than sorry" ap-proach is best, 17-9.

Around 1960 a drug called thalidomide caused many birth defects. Almost all of these cases were reported in Europe. The drug had not passed enough tests to be marketed in the United States. The drug was used in a very effective sleeping pill and tranquilizer. It was also used as a cure for nausea.

The effect of the thalidomide was horri-ble. It interfered with the development of the fetus' limbs. Babies were born with no arms or legs, or with very short ones. In some cases, babies were born with hands sprouting di-rectly from their shoulders. Other physical defects affecting the face, ears, and internal organs also occurred. Most of the children are normal in their mental development, but their physical impairments will affect their entire lives. The thalidomide example is ex-treme, but it shows the effect a drug can have on a fetus.

Exposure to radiation from X rays also poses risks to the fetus. If a woman is preg-nant or if there is even a small possibility she is pregnant, she should be sure to let her physician know.

Miscarriage ▪ ▪ ▪ ▪ ▪ ▪

Miscarriage refers to the birth of the baby before it has developed enough to live in the outside world. This usually means before the sixth month. (Physicians refer to this as "spontaneous abortion.") Miscarriages are not rare. In fact, medical authorities estimate that as many as half of fertilizations end in miscarriage. Most of these occur in the first three months of pregnancy. Often, the woman miscarries before she is aware that she is pregnant.

Most miscarriages occur as nature tries to get rid of an imperfect embryo. More than half of all miscarriages are thought to be traceable to imperfect embryos. Thus, one miscarriage should not discourage a woman from becoming pregnant again.

Other miscarriages are caused by maternal conditions or diseases. Anemia (lack of iron) may cause a woman's body to reject any further burden. Lack of vitamin B may cause her to be incapable of carrying the fetus to full term. If she has a tumor, a tilted uterus, or abnormal hormone secretions, miscarriage may follow.

Time for Delivery ▪ ▪ ▪

When the time for delivery arrives, the couple will be excited. Delivery is the climax of long months of anticipation and planning. It is a time that is full of activity, but it is not a time to panic. The doctor will have told the couple what to expect and what to do when the time for delivery arrives.

Lightening

Towards the end of pregnancy, the uterus sinks downward and forward. This is called *lightening* because it relieves abdominal pressure and makes breathing easier. Lightening is the result of the passage of the baby's head into the pelvic cavity and is actually the first step in the birth of the baby. It is often followed by feelings of greater pressure. The woman may have pains in her legs and may notice an increase in vaginal discharge. For women having their first baby, lightening can occur at any time during the last month. For women who have had previous babies, lightening is more likely to occur after labor begins.

The Onset of Labor

The onset of labor is heralded by one or more of three signs:

- Painful, recurrent contractions of the uterus (labor pains).

- Passage of a small amount of blood-tinged mucous (the "show").

- Passage of liquid from the vagina (rupture of the amnio-chorionic membrane or "bag of waters").

At the onset, labor pains are usually located in the small of the back. After a few hours, they move to the front. They begin as a slight twinge, build in intensity, reach a peak that is maintained for a few seconds, and then diminish gradually.

The pains are caused by contractions of the uterus. They are spaced evenly and return in a rhythmic pattern. The time between contractions is entirely free from pain. As labor progresses, the contractions become closer together. They continue rhythmically, and they continually increase in severity.

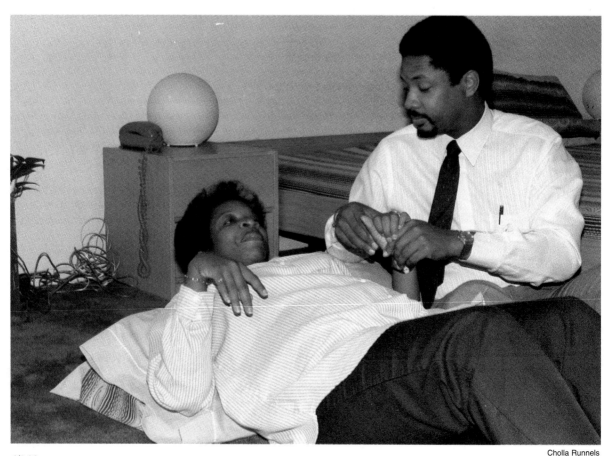

Cholla Runnels

17-10
If a woman feels that she may be in labor, it is best that she go to the hospital.

Some women mistake true labor for "false labor." The intensity of false labor pains remains equal from the outset and does not increase with time. They occur at irregular intervals and are not rhythmical.

Many women make "false runs" to the hospital. Doctors prefer that they come to the hospital if they think they are in labor rather than to take the chance of delivering at home, 17-10.

The Three Stages of Labor

The birth of a child follows a precise pattern and is divided into three stages. The stages of labor vary in length and in intensity of pain.

Dilation Stage

The first stage of labor is the dilation stage. It begins with the first uterine contraction and ends when the baby's head is in the vagina or birth canal. It may last as long as 12 to 18 hours for a first delivery. It may be as short as two to three hours for subsequent

Contemporary Concerns *of today's teens:*

Pregnancy Myths and Facts

Responsible care of children begins *before* birth. There are many myths concerning the pregnancy period, including:

Myth: "It really doesn't matter what a pregnant woman eats—the baby will take whatever it needs from the mother."

Fact: Nature simply doesn't work the way this myth claims it does. Proper nutrition is essential to life. The quality of the mother's diet makes an immense difference in the health of the newborn.

Myth: "A pregnant woman should not gain too much weight."

Fact: In previous years, toxemia (a metabolic disorder that affects blood) was thought to be caused by a large weight gain. However, toxemia more likely occurs in women underweight at conception, especially if they fail to gain adequate weight during pregnancy. Gaining adequate weight is associated with a baby of higher birthweight. Babies of higher birthweight are generally healthier and have fewer problems during the first year of life.

Myth: "Since a pregnant woman is eating for two, she should eat twice as much as usual."

Fact: Pregnancy can be thought of as an energy equation. A woman needs about 80,000 extra calories during pregnancy, and these calories should come from eating extra foods. This averages out to about 300 extra calories a day. However, the nutrients contained in these foods are more important than the calories. Pregnancy is tissue-building time. A new human being is being created. The nutrients in greatest need are protein, vitamins, and minerals.

Myth: "You can make up for a haphazard diet before pregnancy by eating well for the next nine months."

Fact: The mother's health and well-being before pregnancy may be as important as how she eats during her pregnancy. When pregnancy occurs, cell division and development occur immediately. Vital organs are developed and functioning by the end of the first lunar month. This development depends on healthful contributions from the mother. Good nutrition during pregnancy is very important, but it cannot make up for poor nutrition before pregnancy.

Myth: "A woman can have babies close together with no risk to her or her infants' health."

Fact: Women should wait at least nine months between pregnancies to improve the chances of producing healthy, full-term infants. Women need to pause between pregnancies so they can build up the nutritional reserves necessary for a growing fetus. From a psychological standpoint, child development professionals advise spacing children at least two years apart. Proper birth spacing avoids undue emotional stress, both on parents and on children.

babies. The average duration is about nine hours.

The pains at the beginning are slight and far apart. Pain relief is not necessary at first, but it is sometimes given toward the end of this stage. The cervix must dilate (open up) before the infant can be expelled from the uterus. Each contraction of the uterus dilates the cervix slightly. Often the amnio-chorionic membrane will rupture toward the end of this stage.

Expulsion Stage

The second stage of labor, the expulsion stage, begins when the cervix is fully dilated and the baby's head is in the birth canal. It ends with the birth of the baby. This stage is much shorter than the first stage, averaging five to 45 minutes. The uterine contractions continue to push out the baby. The pains are the most severe at this point, but the woman can be anesthetized now, for there is no danger of stopping labor.

As the baby's head moves down the birth canal, the amnio-chorionic membrane breaks if it has not already broken in the first stage. The doctor can see the baby's head. This event is known as "crowning." At this point, an *episiotomy* is performed. An incision (cut) is made in the tissues next to the opening of the birth canal. This allows more room for the passage of the baby and prevents any tearing of these tissues.

After the head is born, the doctor gently turns the baby's head so the shoulders can be born with greater ease. When the baby is born, the second stage of labor is over. The baby is helped to breathe, and the **umbilical cord** (which links the baby to the placenta) is cut. The baby is examined thoroughly and weighed.

Afterbirth Stage

The third stage of labor, the afterbirth stage, usually lasts only about 10 to 15 minutes. The uterine contractions continue and cause the placenta to separate from the uterine wall. When the placenta is expelled, it is examined to be sure that none of the tissues have torn and remained in the uterus.

Methods of Childbirth

Today, couples have options about how their children will be born. If a couple want a certain method, they should discuss their wishes with their doctor.

Traditional Method

This method of childbirth is used in most hospitals. It is very protective of both the mother and baby. The mother is given local or general anesthetics as needed to reduce discomfort. Monitoring equipment checks the baby's progress. Husbands may or may not be in the labor and delivery rooms. After birth, the woman is taken to a recovery room, and the baby is taken to a nursery.

Lamaze Method

This method of childbirth was developed in France. The **Lamaze method of childbirth** is based on the theory that the pain of childbirth can be controlled by the woman. The pain cannot be eliminated, but it can be tolerated so the woman can enjoy the childbearing experience.

During the last two months of pregnancy, the couple attend several Lamaze training sessions. They prepare themselves for working as a team during the birth process. The woman learns exercises in breathing and muscle control that will help her control her body during labor. Instead of becoming tense when a contraction begins, she will be able to relax her muscles and focus her attention on her breathing. In the

Lamaze method, the husband acts as a "labor coach." He encourages his wife to relax and breathe properly. In most cases, he is allowed to be with her in the delivery room. He helps her during the actual childbirth just as he has helped her during the training sessions.

Generally, women who have had Lamaze training need less medication during labor than women who have not had this training. In fact, some Lamaze-trained women receive no medication at all.

Leboyer Method

The *Leboyer method of childbirth* focuses on the birth experience of the baby. Its goal is to make the birth process less shocking and more comforting for the baby.

Before birth, the fetus is used to being in a curled position, surrounded by fluid. The environment of the fetus is dark, warm, and quiet. In the Leboyer method of childbirth, a similar environment is provided, so the baby's adjustment to life outside the uterus is gradual. The lights of the delivery room are dimmed. Soft music is played, and everyone in the delivery room speaks in low voices. Immediately after birth, the baby is placed directly on the mother's warm, soft abdomen. The link to the mother (the umbilical cord) is not cut until it has stopped pulsating, several minutes after birth. When the baby is first separated from skin-to-skin contact with the mother, he or she is placed in warm water. In this comforting environment, the baby can start exploring and adjusting to his or her new world.

The Leboyer method is accepted in varying degrees. Some hospitals and doctors accept all of it. Others accept only certain parts of the method. For instance, physicians may agree with the need for low voices and immediate skin-to-skin contact. However, they may say that bright light is needed to examine the baby properly.

Family-Centered Childbirth

Family-centered childbirth is based on the belief that birth affects the family as a unit as well as each individual family member. Some hospitals have "birthing rooms" where a woman can have her baby in a homelike setting and still have access to any medical facilities she may need.

The father is encouraged to remain with the mother throughout labor and delivery. Other support people may be present during labor and delivery if the mother so desires and the physician approves. The mother, father, and all support people who plan to witness the birth must first attend childbirth classes. These classes prepare them for what will take place in the delivery room.

The mother and father participate in the labor and delivery as they have learned in their childbirth classes. An obstetrical nurse or certified nurse-midwife is usually with them throughout labor and delivery. A physician may be present for the delivery or may just be on call if complications arise. The medical personnel encourage and support the natural forces of labor, interfering as little as possible. They try to make sure that the birth goes well while respecting the family's wishes to share this important experience.

After the birth, the baby, mother, and father may spend as much time together as they wish. Brothers and sisters may visit throughout the day. In some hospitals, the mother and baby are released within 24 hours of birth.

Cesarean Section

Sometimes a surgical procedure must be performed for a birth to occur. In a *cesarean section,* the walls of the abdomen and uterus are cut, and the baby is lifted out of the uterus. The operation is faster than a normal delivery. However, it is a major operation, and the recovery period of the mother is longer. Also, there are more chances for complications.

There are several reasons for performing a cesarean section. One is that the mother's pelvic cage may be too small to permit the baby to pass through. Some cesarean sections are performed to end a prolonged or difficult labor due to the size, position, or condition of the baby. Also, once a woman has had a cesarean section, other babies may need to be born this way.

After the Baby Is Born

Bonding begins from the moment of birth, 17-11. *Bonding* is the beginning of the formation of close emotional ties between the mother and her baby. Both have been through the stress of birth. The baby needs to be comforted and the mother needs to relax. She needs to have a few moments to hold and caress her newborn. If the father has been

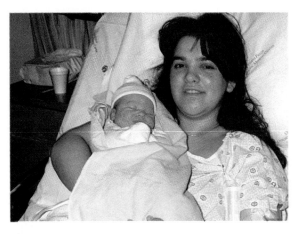

17-11
For bonding to begin, it is important for mother and baby to be together as much as possible from the moment of birth.

present during the delivery, he can be a part of this early bonding, too. The bonding should continue as much as possible during the hospital stay.

A woman will probably stay in the hospital for a few days after delivery. Some go home after 24 hours if the mother and baby are doing well.

The *postpartum period* is the period of time following the delivery of the baby. During this time, the mother should try to get all the rest she can. Her body has been through a lot, and she needs to recuperate. She must make both physical and emotional adjustments as she returns to her "normal" state.

A period of six to eight weeks is required after childbirth for the uterus and other pelvic structures to return to their former condition. Most women feel quite well during this period if their deliveries were normal.

Lactation

All during pregnancy, the breasts have been undergoing many changes in preparation for providing milk for the baby. These changes will continue for three days after birth. At that time, the breasts will be enlarged and filled with milk. The secretion of milk from the breasts is called *lactation.*

Most babies will be put to the breast about eight hours after delivery, even though the milk is not yet ready. The baby will receive colostrum, the precursor of milk. Colostrum has a higher content of protein, antibodies, vitamins, and minerals than milk. It has a lower content of sugars and fats. Colostrum provides the infant with heightened immunity to certain illnesses. It also helps the intestinal tract begin to function.

The breasts become even fuller by the third day, and the baby will probably not be able to use all the milk that is ready. The woman's body will adjust to the demands of her child.

Herman Hospital

17-12
Breast-feeding is economical and convenient. It supplies the baby with human milk, the ideal food for newborns.

Women choose to breast-feed their babies for several reasons, 17-12. Breast-feeding is more economical than bottle-feeding. For some women, breast-feeding is more convenient. Another advantage of breast-feeding is that it supplies human milk, which is the ideal food for newborns. It contains most of the nutrients necessary for maintenance, growth, and development during the first months of life. Human milk is sweeter than cows' milk, and the proteins are easier to digest.

Some people feel that breast-feeding causes women and their children to grow emotionally closer. However, this has not been proved. All babies should be cuddled a great deal regardless of the way they are fed. The cuddling has a much greater effect on the children's emotional health than the method of feeding.

Some mothers cannot breast-feed their babies, and some choose not to do so. One advantage of bottle-feeding is that the husband and wife can share the experience of feeding their child, 17-13. Another is that the formula is consistent in composition, and there is always enough to satisfy the baby's needs.

Bottle-feeding is less tiring to the mother, and she may feel she has an easier time controlling her recovery. In addition, bottle-feeding makes it easier for an employed mother to return to work.

David Hopper

17-13
Bottle-feeding allows the father to share the experience of feeding his child.

Summary ■ ■ ■ ■ ■ ■ ■ ■ ■ ■ ■ ■ ■ ■ ■

- The majority of couples who want children are able to have them.

- Evidence of pregnancy can be confirmed by the woman's observations, by a physician's observations, and, if necessary, by pregnancy testing.

- Conception occurs the instant a sperm and egg unite. This is followed by a specific pattern of development until birth, which occurs about 10 lunar months or nine calendar months later.

- The health of the developing baby is directly related to the health of the mother during pregnancy as well as her history of health before conception.

- Most miscarriages occur as nature tries to get rid of an imperfect embryo.

- The three stages of labor are the dilation stage, the expulsion stage, and the afterbirth stage.

- There are several methods of childbirth: traditional, Lamaze, Leboyer, family-centered childbirth, and cesarean section.

- Babies may be either breast-fed or bottle-fed. Both methods have certain advantages.

To Review ■ ■ ■ ■ ■ ■ ■ ■ ■ ■ ■ ■ ■ ■ ■

1. List three evidences of pregnancy that the woman can observe.

2. _____ refers to the active movements of the fetus.

3. List four functions of the amniotic fluid.

4. After the _____ lunar month and until birth, the developing baby is called a fetus.

5. What is the recommended weight gain for an average woman during pregnancy?

6. What is fetal alcohol syndrome?

7. How can a woman tell true labor pains from false labor pains?

8. Which method of childbirth is based on the theory that although the pain of childbirth cannot be eliminated, it can be tolerated so the woman can enjoy the childbearing experience?

9. The emotional tie that begins to form between mother and baby immediately after birth is called _____.

10. Name two advantages of breast-feeding and two advantages of bottle-feeding.

To Do ■ ■ ■ ■ ■ ■ ■ ■ ■ ■ ■ ■ ■ ■ ■ ■ ■

1. Ask an obstetrician or an obstetric nurse to talk to your class about the care of a mother during pregnancy, about fetal development, and about labor and delivery.

2. Invite several parents to tell your class about their experiences during pregnancy and childbirth.

3. Refer to nutrition charts and compare the dietary needs of pregnant and nonpregnant women. Plan a week's diet for a pregnant woman.

4. Investigate the hospitals in your area. Ask about the available methods of childbirth, the costs involved, the average length of stay, etc. Report back to class.

18

Your New Baby

Cholla Runnels

After studying this chapter, you will be able to

- describe how parenthood changes the roles of husband and wife.

- identify characteristics and abilities of newborns.

- describe scheduling, feeding, bath, and clothing needs of infants.

- summarize the physical, intellectual, social, and emotional growth and development of children during the first year.

- recognize the special needs of children with physical or mental disabilities.

The birth of your first baby will probably be one of the proudest moments of your life. It is a joyful occasion.

Parenthood gives you an even deeper appreciation of your mate. Together you realize a sense of completion as you reflect on the pregnancy period. You feel anticipation as you look ahead to new plans for your family. Throughout parenthood, you need to offer each other support. This strengthens your husband-wife relationship and adds to

Terms to Know

fontanels

tonic neck reflex

rooting reflex

grasp reflex

startle reflex

Babinski reflex

large muscle development

small muscle development

mitten grasp

pincer grip

intellectual development

social development

separation anxiety

the feeling of security for the child. The best possible environment for your family is one in which your love for each other grows along with your love for your child.

Parenthood Brings New Roles

Your new roles as parents will be both exciting and tiring. You will have many joys as well as worries. You will face new demands as you realize the complete dependence of your new baby on you as parents. As you watch your child pass through the developmental phases of childhood, you will be developing your parenthood skills.

As parents, you may experience a change in your freedom to schedule activities. You may not be able to spontaneously decide to see a late movie or go visit friends. Parenthood causes changes. If you look upon these changes only as depriving you of freedoms, you may grow to resent your new baby. If you focus your thoughts on the positive factors of parenthood, you can truly enjoy this new dimension of your life. You can be a proud parent watching a school play or enjoying a walk in the park with your child. Being a parent is demanding, but it does have rich rewards.

The Newborn

Almost all babies are cute—after a few weeks. Immediately after birth, however, babies' bodies may look out of proportion, and their heads may have an odd shape, 18-1. Their skin is wrinkled and blotchy.

Average newborns are 20 to 21 inches in length, and they weigh about 7½ pounds. Boys are generally longer and heavier than girls.

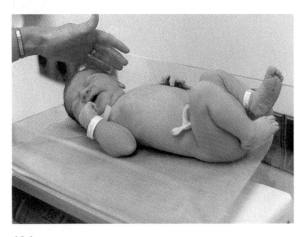

18-1
Newborns look quite different from babies who are two or three months old.

The heads of newborns look large compared to the rest of their bodies. Their heads account for one-fourth of their total length. (Adults' heads account for only one-seventh of their total height.)

A newborn has open spaces or *fontanels* between the bones of his or her head. Fontanels allow the bones of the baby's skull to move together and make birth easier. Because the bones of the baby's skull move together during birth, the head may have an elongated shape. However, the shape of the head will become normal before long, and the skull bones will grow together.

Newborns have fat cheeks; short, flat noses; and receding chins. These features are useful for sucking because their noses and chins do not get in the way. Newborns may have quite a bit of hair, or they may be bald. Eyebrows and lashes are hardly noticeable. The eyes of the newborns are smoky blue. Their true eye color will not develop for several weeks.

Newborns have almost no neck. They have narrow chests, sloping shoulders, and large, protruding abdomens. Their arms and legs look short and thin in proportion to their bodies. Their hands and feet are tiny.

The bones of newborns are mostly cartilage, so they are soft and flexible. Newborns' muscles are soft, small, and uncontrolled. Their skin may be bruised from the pressure of birth.

What Can Newborns Do?

Newborns have many "skills." They can breathe, cry, cough, hiccup, sneeze, blink, yawn, and stretch. They can swallow, digest food, and eliminate waste products. They can see, hear, feel, smell, and taste, although their senses will become more refined.

Most of the actions of newborns are general ones. Anything they do sets their whole bodies in motion. Even when they cry, they wave their arms and kick their legs.

Babies are born with certain reflexes. One of their reflexes is the *tonic neck reflex.* When babies lie on their backs, they turn their heads to one side. If they turn to the right, their right hands extend outward, and their left arms extend upward. If they turn to the left, their left hands extend outward, and their right arms extend upward.

When newborns are touched on one of their cheeks, the *rooting reflex* causes them to turn their heads in that direction and open their mouths. This is how they prepare themselves for feeding.

Newborns have three other reflexes that disappear within a few months after birth. The *grasp reflex* causes them to close their hands tightly when their palms are touched. Newborns use this reflex when they grasp your finger or a baby rattle that is put in their palms. The reflex disappears when the nervous system has developed to the point where the babies can voluntarily grasp objects.

When newborns are tapped on their abdomens or when their support is suddenly removed, they respond with the *startle reflex.*

They spread their arms apart and then bring them together again in a bow. They perform the same motions with their legs. This reflex disappears when the babies are about three months old.

The *Babinski reflex* causes newborns to extend their toes when the soles of their feet are touched. Later, they will contract their toes when the soles of their feet are touched.

Planning a Schedule

Babies need sleep, food, and exercise. Planning a schedule around these needs takes time and patience. A schedule should fulfill the needs of your developing baby and enable you to achieve a sense of fulfillment.

When they first come home from the hospital, most babies sleep for about 18 to 20 hours a day. They have six feedings a day, or one every four hours. The little time that is left is spent crying, exercising, and playing with family members.

Babies are individuals with unique needs. Some babies sleep for longer periods of time and need fewer feedings. Others take shorter naps and need more feedings. Your baby will tell you what is needed, 18-2. He or she will refuse food when full and will cry when hungry. You should not hesitate to respond to your baby's cries. A newborn has not yet learned to use crying to get attention. A newborn cries only when something needs to be done.

By the time your baby is a month old, you probably will have established a workable schedule. It may be similar to the one shown in 18-3. It will allow you to plan your daily activities. However, no schedule is perfect. You will have to use your common sense about altering the schedule to meet day-to-day demands.

David Hopper

18-2
Your baby will let you know when he or she is either hungry or full.

Feeding Your Baby

Mealtimes should be enjoyable experiences for you and your baby. Providing your baby with food is one of the first ways to help your baby feel secure. If you cuddle your baby during feeding, your baby will sense your love and support. Thus, mealtimes can satisfy emotional needs as well as physical needs.

Your physician will suggest any dietary supplements your baby may need, such as vitamins. Your physician will also suggest when you should begin giving your baby solid foods. Cereal, fruit, vegetables, and meat are usually introduced at intervals of two or three weeks. Some parents buy commercially prepared baby foods. Others prefer to prepare the food for their babies themselves. Electric blenders or food processors help reduce the food to a suitable texture.

A Typical Schedule for a Baby

6:00 a.m.
Feeding.

6:30 a.m.
After feeding, be sure the bed is dry and clean and put the baby back to bed.

9:30 a.m.
Bath time.

10:00 a.m.
Feeding.

10:30 a.m.
Nap time. Try to establish this as the main nap period of the day.

2:00 p.m.
Feeding.

2:30 to 5:00 p.m.
Nap time. Take the baby outside for a nap if possible.

5:00 p.m.
Exercise period. This is a good time to play and talk with the baby.

6:00 p.m.
Feeding.

6:30 p.m.
Put the baby to bed for the night.

10:00 p.m.
Feeding. Some parents wake up the baby for this, just before they retire for the night.

10:30 p.m.
Put the baby back to bed.

2:00 a.m.
This feeding will be required for about three to six weeks. The baby will sleep through this feeding when it is no longer needed. Do not awaken the baby for this feeding.

18-3
A schedule is a good guideline to follow, but daily adjustments will have to be made.

18-4
When you give your baby a new food, try to make the experience enjoyable.

When you first give your baby solid food, the texture and taste will be a surprise. Your baby may not know what to do with it, and it may come oozing out of the baby's mouth. Be patient and scoop it back into the mouth. Your baby will soon learn how to swallow it.

Introducing new foods can be frustrating, but try to make the experience enjoyable. Smile and talk to your baby in a reassuring tone of voice, 18-4. When you introduce a food, give the baby just a taste. Gradually work up to several spoonfuls. Introduce only one new food at a time. If your baby dislikes a certain food, wait a few days or weeks before you try it again.

Bathing Your Baby

You can bathe your baby at any time of the day that is convenient for you. You should try to do it at about the same time each day. Before a feeding is a good time, but do not wait until the baby is hungry.

Bath time should be uninterrupted and unhurried. It is a time not only to bathe your baby, but also for socializing. Both you and your baby will enjoy this time together, 18-5.

The room should be warm and free from drafts. Have all your supplies ready and within reach before you start giving the bath. *Never,* under any circumstances, leave your baby alone on a table or in a tub. Continually hold your baby with a firm grip.

Sponge Baths

Your baby's navel area should remain dry until the stump of the umbilical cord has healed. Until that time, you will need to give your baby sponge baths. You can give sponge baths on a bathroom counter or kitchen table. A large folded towel can serve as padding, and a small plastic tub can hold the water you will need.

Wash the baby's face with a soft washcloth, using only plain water. Pat the baby's

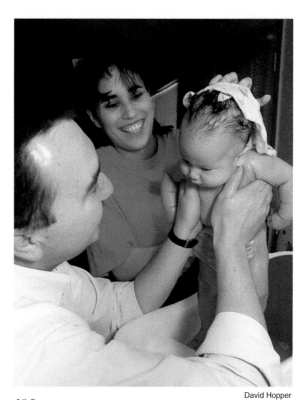

David Hopper
18-5
Bath time can be an enjoyable time for both babies and parents.

face dry. Next, shampoo the baby's scalp. To do this, hold the baby's head back so water will run off at the back, not down the baby's face. Squeeze plain water from the washcloth onto the baby's scalp. Then wash the head with soap and rinse the suds away with fresh water.

Soap the rest of the baby's body (avoiding the navel area). Gently cleanse all body crevices, but never put anything into the baby's ear canal. Rinse away suds and pat dry.

Tub Baths

As soon as the navel and the circumcision (if one has been performed) are healed, you can give your baby tub baths. Fill a tub or large dishpan with about 3 inches of warm water. Test the temperature of the water with your elbow. It should feel comfortably warm. A towel on the bottom of the tub will prevent the baby from slipping. Begin by cleaning the baby's face and scalp as if you were giving a sponge bath. Then lower the baby into the tub, feet first. Hold the baby with a firm grip and rinse the soap off the head.

Soap the baby's body well and rinse. Lift the baby onto a warm, dry surface. Cover the baby with a towel and pat the baby dry.

Clothing Your Baby

Diapers are the major article of clothing for your baby. You may choose to use disposable diapers, cloth diapers, or diapers from a diaper service.

Disposable diapers offer convenience and ease of care, 18-6. They are prefolded and do not require pins. A disposable diaper has three layers. The inner layer, next to the baby, is made from a material that helps keep moisture away from the baby's skin and passes it through to the middle layer. The middle layer is made from a very absorbent material. The outer layer is a waterproof plas-

tic film. Generally, disposable diapers are soft and absorbent. They may even help prevent diaper rash if you keep your baby clean and dry. However, using disposable diapers usually costs a little more than using cloth diapers. Some parents also are concerned about the environmental issues posed by disposable diapers.

Cloth diapers are usually made of cotton. They are reusable and soft. They can be folded in a number of ways to accommodate the growing baby. Contour diapers are also available. They may be purchased according to the weight of the baby.

Diaper liners are often used with cloth diapers. Liners permit moisture to pass through to the diaper, so the baby stays drier and more comfortable. At the same time, liners prevent the cloth from becoming soiled and stained, making the diapers easier to launder.

Even with liners, cloth diapers require quite a bit of work. Soiled diapers must be

Cholla Runnels

18-6
Convenience is the major advantage of disposable diapers.

rinsed, stored in a covered container, and laundered daily. Then the diapers must be dried thoroughly and folded. Another disadvantage is that babies using cloth diapers often need the additional protection of plastic diaper covers, which can irritate babies' skin.

Diaper services are available in some areas. These services furnish you with cloth diapers. They pick up soiled diapers and deliver clean ones twice a week. The diapers are laundered under highly sanitary conditions, so cleanliness and convenience are the plus factors. The drawback is the expense, for this service costs more than buying and laundering diapers yourself.

In addition to diapers, your baby wears other clothes, which should be chosen with care. The primary consideration should be the baby's comfort. See 18-7. Choose clothes that are loose so the baby can move about freely. Look for garments that are easy to put on and take off. For instance, neck openings should be large enough to allow the garment to slip over the baby's head quickly and easily.

Fabrics used for baby clothes should be soft, absorbent, and easy to launder. Cotton fabrics are the most desirable because they meet all these requirements. Blends of polyester and cotton work well for some outer garments.

Before you buy sleepwear for your baby, check the labels. It is important to be sure the fabrics have met the government regulations for flammability.

Do not overdress your baby. Babies have more skin surface in relation to their body weight than adults have. Therefore, they warm up and cool off faster than adults do.

18-7
Comfort is the most important feature of children's clothing.

Discomforts and Problems

When your baby is uncomfortable or ill, he or she will tell you about it by crying. Before long, you will learn to recognize different types of cries.

You will have three clues to help you recognize a hunger cry. First, it is the cry you will hear most often. Second, it usually begins shortly before feeding time. Third, your baby is likely to work up to a hunger cry gradually.

A cry that occurs shortly after feeding is probably an indigestion cry. Try burping your baby again. If your baby has frequent problems with digestion, consult your physician.

Another common cry announces wet or soiled diapers. Diapers should be changed as

Signs and Symptoms of Illness

General behavior
Unusually quiet or irritable; drowsy or restless; any extreme in behavior.

Appetite
May refuse more than one feeding.

Vomiting
All or part of feeding vomited; vomiting forcefully as opposed to the usual spitting up.

Bowel movements and urine
Sudden increase or decrease in number of stools; stools unusual in color, odor, or consistency.

Fever
Rectal temperature of 101° F or above.

Color
Unusually flushed or pale complexion.

Skin
Dry or hot skin; excess perspiration.

Breathing
Hoarseness; continued sneezing or coughing; labored or slow breathing.

Eyes
Red; irritated; especially sensitive to light.

Bodily movements
Twitching or shaking; stiffness or immobility.

Pain
Sharp screaming; head-rolling; ear-rubbing.

18-8
A dramatic change in a baby's behavior or appearance may be a sign of illness.

often as needed to help keep your baby comfortable.

Occasionally, you may hear a different kind of cry from your baby. This cry may be your baby's way of telling you of an illness. A sick cry may alert you to other symptoms, as listed in 18-8. If you suspect that your baby is ill, write down your observations as accurately as possible. Then consult your physician and describe what you have observed. Never give your baby any medication or treatment that has not been recommended by your physician.

Growth and Development during the First Year ■ ■ ■ ■ ■ ■

Children grow and develop according to a patterned sequence. This same sequence is followed by all children, everywhere. As a parent, you need to understand this sequence of development as well as other developmental principles. By knowing the principles of child development, you will be better prepared to care for your children. You will be able to help your children proceed smoothly through the various stages of development.

Your baby's growth and development will follow the same general pattern that all babies follow. However, within this general pattern, there will be some differences. Your baby is a unique person who will not develop exactly like anyone else.

The growth and development of children occur in four main areas: physical, intellectual, social, and emotional. Children pass through many different stages within each of these areas. Each stage builds upon another, so what children learn in one stage helps them in the next stages.

Examining how development proceeds within the four main areas makes learning about children easier. However, you should not expect to see clear-cut stages in the development of your child. Children do not suddenly leave one stage and enter another. Their growth is gradual and continuous.

Physical Development

The most noticeable growth in infants during the first year is in the area of physical growth. Stages of physical growth and development during the first year are described in 18-9.

Your baby's physical growth will depend on both hereditary and environmental fac-

Physical Development

Physical development is the controlled development of physical abilities including motor coordination, which controls and balances the movement of body parts.

Birth to Three Months

Tonic neck reflex, grasp reflex, rooting reflex, startle reflex, and Babinski reflex present.
Head is wobbly and tends to be turned to one side
Whole body twitches when crying.
Tear ducts are not refined, so baby cries no tears.
Can follow large moving object with eyes.

Blinks when objects move close to eyes.
Reaches out to hit objects but may miss them.
May raise chest and head high when placed on tummy.
Kicks legs in air.
Can roll from side to back.

Three to Six Months

Holds head erect.
Back still rounded when placed in sitting position; cannot sit alone.
Can roll from one side to the other side.
Notices hand and may follow movement of own hand.
Hands are not so predominantly fisted.
Turns head purposefully and fixes eyes on objects that are interesting.

Studies and plays with fingers and hands.
Shows eagerness to touch and moves body to try to reach for objects.
Reaches out to grasp, but cannot voluntarily release grasped article.
Uses hand to brush aside a tissue or cloth placed on face when playing peekaboo.
Will double birth weight by five months.

Six to Nine Months

Can pull up to sitting position.
Can stay in sitting position without support for a short time.
Can roll over from stomach to back or from back to stomach.
Likes to creep and crawl when placed on floor.
Stepping reflex when held with feet resting on floor.
Transfers object from one hand to another.
Coordinates hands in inspecting articles.

Discovers feet, may study them for periods of time.
Thumb and forefinger work together in pincer movement.
Can pick up small objects with finger and thumb.
Able to use pincer movement to grasp food, but has difficulty finding mouth.
Likes to drag things.
Likes to bang things together and drop them.
First tooth appears.

Nine to Twelve Months

Can sit alone.
Crawls well.
Stands without holding on.
Can stand and bounce in one position.
Toddles by holding onto assisting hands.
May walk independently, varies with each child.

No longer enjoys lying down; wants to be up as soon as awakened.
Enjoys playing with large blocks.
Can grasp a cup by its handle.
May exhibit handedness preferences.
May have two to eight of the 20 baby or temporary teeth.

18-9
As children grow, they pass through many stages of physical development, but there is no exact time when a child leaves one stage and enters another. The stages described are approximate.

18-10
Before babies can feed themselves, they have to learn to grasp food using their small muscles.

tors, but it will follow a definite sequence. Growth progresses from the trunk outward and from the head downward. Control of large muscles comes before small muscle control.

Large muscle development involves skills that use the large muscles of the body, such as those of the trunk, neck, legs, and arms. Large muscle control helps babies learn to roll over. They learn to control leg and arm muscles as they kick and reach for objects. Still later, babies gain control of their hands and feet, and finally their fingers and thumbs, 18-10. *Small muscle development* refers to actions that use the small muscles, such as those of the hands, fingers, feet, and toes.

Babies' large muscle development provides them with mobility while their small muscle development proceeds more slowly. At first they reach for mobiles and crib toys. They notice their hands and spend much time tracking their hand movements. They grab with a *mitten grasp,* using the palm and fingers opposing the thumb. They love to transfer objects from one hand to another. Slowly they are able to handle objects with the *pincer grip,* using just their thumb and index finger. They love to point and poke fingers into holes.

Parents will be amazed at the speed of physical development during the first year, 18-11. Babies can wave their arms and kick their legs so vigorously parents may have difficulty changing diapers. By six months, babies enjoy sitting up with slight support. When they are placed on the floor, they may try to get up on their hands and knees. They will practice rocking and balancing themselves in this position for some time. Then suddenly they start to crawl.

Babies are born with an instinct to achieve an upright position. By six to nine months, they will start to pull themselves up to a sitting position. Standing becomes a favorite activity for babies by the end of the first year. Some babies enjoy this so much they

18-11
Babies may grow 10 inches in length in the first year.

Intellectual Development

Intellectual development includes the development of abilities in perception, attention, association, and other aspects of the mind at work.

Birth to Three Months

Crying is the primary form of communication.
Learns to respond to perceptions of the five senses.
Learns to bring hand to mouth and to suck on fingers or thumb.

Discovers fingers and hands and may watch movement of hands.
Indicates recognition of person by cooing or becoming excited.

Three to Six Months

Each new activity is the result of mental growth.
Voluntary actions are possible because certain brain cells have matured.

Studies and plays with fingers and hands.
Uses hands to reach for desired objects.
Does not search for object when it disappears.
Recognizes mother and father.
Laughs aloud to express delight.

Six to Nine Months

Talks to self in mirror and registers recognition of mirror reflection.
Able to change facial expressions.
Likes to drop objects to explore disappearance and reappearance.
Uses hands to reach, grasp, crumble, bang, and splash.
Inspects objects held in hand very attentively.
Reaches for spoon when being fed.

Perceives depth.
Can distinguish between angry and friendly tones of voice.
Likes to mimic simple adult sounds.
Recognizes own name.
Crawls or propels self to reach certain destination.
Shows understanding of spatial relations; can detour around objects.

Nine to Twelve Months

Mimics sounds, adds facial expressions to aid communication.
Can say very simple words.
Verbalizes dada and mama.
Can wave good-bye.
Loves to play pointing game such as "Where's your nose?"
Enjoys locomotive behavior to investigate space.

Learns by trial and error.
Tries to produce new events; develops curiosity.
May look for disappearing object where it disappeared instead of place where it was last found.
Can reach and manipulate objects with good control.
Enjoys filling boxes with many items.

18-12
Intellectual development can be observed during the first year. Remember that these are approximate stages and ages.

may not actually start walking for another month or so. Others will seem to be ready to learn to walk so they will practice walking around furniture.

Intellectual Development

Changes in physical development may be easier to see, but advances in intellectual development are equally as amazing. *Intellectual development* refers to development in the areas of perception, attention, association, and other aspects of the mind. As parents watch their babies develop, they can almost see their minds at work. Intellectual development advances in an orderly way, but there are no definite timetables. See 18-12.

Babies learn about the world using their five senses: seeing, hearing, feeling, smelling, and tasting, 18-13. At about three months,

18-13
Babies learn by using all of their senses. They enjoy seeing the beach, hearing the waves, and feeling the sand.

babies begin to coordinate their hand and eye movements. At this time, you can note the interest they take in watching their hands move across their field of vision. Gradually their vision improves, so they can watch moving objects. Loud noises startle young babies, and the sound of their parents' voices reassures them. They may become quiet when they hear a noise or a familiar voice. Infants like to be hugged, and they like the feel of cuddly toys. Babies like the taste of some foods, but they dislike the taste of other foods. Everything babies learn as they respond to their environment helps their intellectual development.

Babies are learning about themselves. They learn to recognize and respond to their own names. They smile at themselves in mirrors. They try to mimic sounds. The game of peekaboo intrigues them as they learn that the person who disappears will reappear. They develop their own games of dropping objects off their highchairs. Once babies learn to crawl, they become very inquisitive and like to pull open doors and drawers.

Babies make their first deliberate sounds at about three months. They begin cooing one-syllable vowel-like sounds, such as ooh, ah, aw. As early as the ninth month, babies learn the meaning of a few specific words such as "no." Toward the end of the first year, they may be able to say mama or dada. They like to learn labeling words. When prompted by words and gestures, they can learn to point to their nose, eyes, and other features.

Social Development

Social development is the process of learning to relate to other people. It is shaped by how other people affect the baby and how the baby affects other people. Infants are not social at birth, but by the end of the first year they begin to interact actively with others. See 18-14.

Their social development begins as they listen to human voices and turn to focus on their faces. When they make eye contact, they often become quiet. They seem to be staring as they study faces. When they smile for the first time, parents are thrilled.

Babies love attention and show their delight and excitement by waving their arms and cooing. They also learn that if they fuss or cry, someone will come. They reach with their arms to signal, "Pick me up."

Social Development

Social development is the developmental process children experience in learning to adapt to the world around them.

Birth to Three Months

Interest centers on parents.
Responds to being picked up and held.
Stops crying when sees parent or hears approaching footsteps.
Responds to a human face; smiles.
Gurgles and coos spontaneously.

Enjoys being cuddled by a loving adult.
Feels contentment when cared for by calm and loving parents.
Responds to bathtime with either a positive or negative reaction.

Three Months to Six Months

Begins to interact with people.
Enjoys a playful peekaboo game.
Laughs when nudged or tickled.
Smiles at familiar people.
Stares solemnly at strangers.
Likes to watch people move around in room.
Likes attention.

Will play alone but prefers to be with people when awake.
Likes to hear people talk or sing.
Shows growing interest in all family members.
Learns that parents will return after they have been out for a while.
Begins learning love.

Six to Nine Months

Stranger anxiety exhibited (attachment to familiar person and fear of strangers).
Highly responsive to parents' moods and emotions.
Likes to talk to image of self in mirror.
Loves company and attention.

May begin to creep to investigate surroundings.
Enjoys imitating parents.
Invents new ways to communicate with adults.
Enjoys being sung to and talked to.
Enjoys social games such as "This Little Piggy" and "Where's Baby?"
Enjoys "riding" on parent's knee.

Nine to Twelve Months

Cooperates when being dressed.
Recognizes self in mirror; plays with reflection.
Waves good-bye.
Crawls and follows parents as they move throughout house.
Loves being "chased" by sibling.
Loves an audience.
Enjoys applause.
Likes to show off.

Will repeat performances that elicit response, especially laughter.
Loves to imitate.
Enjoys rhymes.
Capable of communicating jealousy, affection, and sympathy to another person.
One parent can often soothe baby when the other has tried and failed.

18-14
As children grow, they pass through these approximate stages of social development. Because development is gradual and continuous, some of the stages overlap.

Cholla Runnels

18-15
Babies enjoy being with other people.

Babies need social contact, 18-15. They love to play games of interaction, such as peekaboo. Babies learn to babble, and find parents will talk back to them. They like to make funny faces and have people laugh. They learn to laugh themselves.

Babies become so social by the end of the first year that they may not want to go to bed. Since babies like routines, a routine of bedtime activities can help to smooth the transition from playtime to bedtime.

By the end of the first year, babies may indicate a preference for certain people. *Separation anxiety* is shown by babies when adults they love leave them for a short time. This often occurs when a parent leaves an almost

Emotional Development

Emotional development is exhibited as a continuing refinement of emotions or mental states that causes an individual to act in a certain way.

One to Three Months

Shows affection by looking at person while kicking, waving arms, and smiling.
Responds to continuous warmth and affection.
Gurgles and coos when responding.
Responds to human face.
Shows no fear of strange face.
Responds to comforts of bathing and feeding.

Very content when nursed or fed.
Reflects emotional state of person providing care.
Develops sense of trust when feels loved and secure.
Becomes unresponsive if left alone most of waking hours.

Three to Six Months

Smiles, laughs aloud, coos, gurgles, and chortles to show delight.
Cries, kicks, and waves arms to show distress.
Desires attention.
Expects to be held.
May cry lustily, but will stop abruptly when picked up.

Moves excitedly when sees food coming.
Smiles at familiar people and stares solemnly at strangers.
Initial reaction to being startled is crying, screaming, stiffening body, holding breath.

Six to Nine Months

Highly responsive to other persons' moods.
Enjoys games of imitation.
Does not like to be held in a restricted position.
Anger is not directed toward any one person or object; just registers general anger.
Shows anxiety when with strangers.

Reacts with shyness or withdrawal as reaction to fear.
Sensitive child may be overly aggressive or overly timid.
Quiet, placid child may be very congenial.
Aggressive child is highly active and exhibits extreme responses.

Nine to Twelve Months

Will show affection for others or for toys by hugging.
Still prefers to receive, rather than give, affection.
Wants to be held by a loved one.
Bangs toys excitedly on chair or floor.
May shriek with delight.
Likes to feel, grab, and pull hair.

Baby's whole body conveys feelings of pleasure.
Anger is directed against a specific object or person.
Child learns to recognize attitudes of parents.
Learns that positive behavior will win parental approval.
Learns that negative behavior may promote punishment.

18-16
Children pass through several stages of emotional development during their first year of life.

one-year-old with a babysitter. Babies fear their parents will not return. By the second year, this anxiety usually passes.

Emotional Development

Emotions (feelings) play an important role in the development of the child. Emotions reflect children's mental states and are expressed in their behavior. Babies readily exhibit emotions ranging from happiness to frustration. Knowing the pattern of emotional development can help parents in dealing with the emotional changes in their children. The stages of emotional development are described in 18-16.

A climate of love in the home lays the foundation for feelings of affection and trust.

Withholding love from babies and children can be damaging, for they need to know they are loved. Loved children feel secure and are able to show affection to others, 18-17. Babies who feel insecure will cry more often and show their restlessness. Parents who think they might spoil a baby if they respond to the baby's cries need not worry. Most authorities believe it is practically impossible to spoil a baby. When babies' needs are reasonably met, they seldom display stress and frustration.

Fear as an emotion begins around six months. Babies begin to realize that they can be hurt. They may be fearful of the unknown or of experiences that they have learned can hurt them. For instance, they may learn to fear the doctor after they have received a painful injection. As babies become more mobile, more fears may develop. They may be frightened by loud noises, such as the noise of the vacuum cleaner. Parents can reassure their babies by allowing them to touch and examine frightening objects to show them there is nothing to fear.

By the end of the first year, babies also are capable of showing anger when they are frustrated. Babies may become frustrated by toys that may be too advanced for their physical development. They may also become frustrated in their early attempts to walk. Most of the time, however, babies are happy and responsive.

Children with Special Needs

When a child is born with a mental or physical disability, parents will have an even greater need to show caring and love. Parents may have feelings of self-pity, fear, and even guilt, but the care of the child is of first importance. Parents must understand the nature of the disability and then find the best possible way to care for the child.

Children with Physical Disabilities

A child with a physical disability has an abnormality of body structure, function, or metabolism that interferes with the child's ability to walk, lift, hear, or learn. The cause may be either hereditary or environmental.

Some physical disabilities are present at birth. Others do not occur until later in life, sometimes as the result of an illness or injury. Often, corrective surgery can be done, and the child can live a normal life. In other cases, nothing can be done to remedy the dis-

David Hopper

18-17
A baby will respond to continuous warmth and affection shown by parents.

Contemporary Concerns *of today's teens:*
Relating to Children with Disabilities

According to the National Center for Health Statistics, about 9.6 million children in this country have chronic conditions that restrict their activities or cause them pain. People often use the term "disabled children"—which puts their disability at the forefront—rather than using the more appropriate phrase, "children with disabilities." The National Easter Seal Society offers the following hints to help you relate to children and adults with physical disabilities:

- It's okay to offer your help to someone, but ask first. You can also wait for someone to ask you for your help.

- It's okay to ask people about their disabilities, and it's also okay for them not to talk about it.

- Remember, just because people use wheelchairs doesn't mean they are sick. Many are healthy and strong.

- When you're talking with people who use wheelchairs, sit down so their necks won't get sore looking up at you.

- It's okay to use words such as *see, hear, walk,* and *run* when you're talking with friends who have disabilities.

- It's okay to ask people who have speech problems to repeat what they said if you didn't understand the first time.

- If an interpreter is helping you speak with a person who is deaf, make sure you talk to the person who is deaf, not the interpreter.

- Don't talk loudly to blind people. They usually can hear quite well.

- Never pet or play with Seeing Eye dogs. They can't be distracted from the job they are doing.

- Invite friends with disabilities to come to your home. Think about ways to make sure that they can be included in your activities.

- Don't let drivers you are with park in places reserved for people with disabilities.

- When you go to restaurants and shopping malls, see if a friend with a disability could be there with you. If not, ask the manager to put in ramps, get raised numbers for the elevators, or have braille menus printed.

- Treat a person with a disability the way you like to be treated.

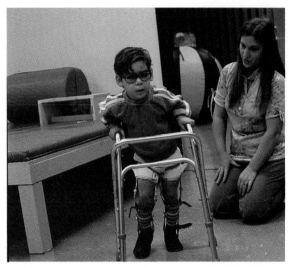

18-18

United Way of Houston

Physical therapy sessions may be needed by children who are physically disabled and living at home.

ability. The parents will have to decide what is best for the welfare of the child and the entire family. If the child can receive adequate care at home, this is probably the best solution. If the child requires constant attention and special care, the child may be placed in a residential facility geared to handle these needs. Parents have a responsibility to the disabled child, to their other children, and to themselves. Their decision about the care of the child with a disability must be made with the welfare of everyone in mind.

Parents who decide to keep the child at home should research all available resources so that the child will receive the best possible care. See 18-18. Schools have special programs for children with mental disabilities. Also, many day care programs offer assistance to parents for care during the day. This relieves the parents from direct responsibility for total care and also provides training and therapy for the child. If parents need to place the child in a residential facility, their physician can help them find an appropriate one.

Children with Mental Disabilities

Children with mental disabilities are usually divided into the following three groups for educational purposes:

- Those who are educable.

- Those who are trainable.

- Those who have severe/profound mental disabilities.

Children who are educable can be taught to function as citizens in the normal pattern of living. They simply need more individualized instruction and special teaching methods, 18-19.

Children who are trainable can be taught certain skills and tasks. They can learn to be productive in a sheltered workshop setting, but they cannot get along by themselves in a community setting.

Children who have severe/profound mental disabilities have very limited mental

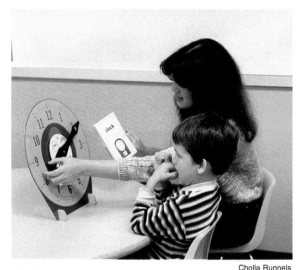

18-19

Cholla Runnels

Children who are educable can learn if special teaching methods are used.

abilities and may need to live in a residential facility. They need complete care, which parents in a typical home setting may not be able to provide. Today, day care services make it possible for parents to keep such children at home. During the day, the children receive special care and therapy. This provides a break for parents and at the same time gives the children the care that can help them.

Parents of a child who is mentally disabled should treat the child as normally as possible, especially in the areas of discipline and love. The child should not be regarded as a source of shame, embarrassment, or hardship for other members of the family. In fact, the presence of a child who is mentally disabled may become a source of positive feelings and cooperation in the family.

Most communities have several sources of help for people who are mentally disabled. Some are funded privately, and some are funded by the government. Parents should investigate all sources of help available for their child.

Summary

- Parenthood brings many changes in roles as husbands become fathers and wives become mothers.

- Immediately after birth, babies tend to have wrinkled, blotchy skin and other characteristics associated with newborns.

- Babies are born with several reflexes, including the tonic neck reflex, rooting reflex, grasp reflex, startle reflex, and Babinski reflex.

- Mealtimes should be enjoyable experiences for you and your baby. If you cuddle your baby during feeding, your baby will sense your love and support, thus both physical and emotional needs will be satisfied.

- When bathing or dressing your baby or changing your baby's diapers, never leave him or her alone for even an instant.

- Children grow and develop according to a patterned sequence. All children follow this same sequence with slight variations. Their growth is gradual and continuous.

- The four main areas of development are physical, intellectual, social, and emotional.

- When a child is born with a mental or physical disability, parents will have an even greater need to express love and caring.

To Review ■ ■ ■ ■ ■ ■ ■ ■ ■ ■ ■ ■ ■ ■ ■

1. Describe the appearance of a newborn.

2. When newborns are touched on one of their cheeks, they turn their heads in that direction and open their mouths. This behavior is known as the:
   a. Tonic neck reflex.
   b. Rooting reflex.
   c. Startle reflex.
   d. Babinski reflex.

3. Why should newborns be given sponge baths instead of tub baths?

4. Why are cotton fabrics more desirable for baby clothes?

5. List three common reasons for newborns to cry.

6. True or False. Children learn large muscle control before they learn small muscle control.

7. How do babies learn about their new world?

8. What do babies learn through the game of peekaboo?

9. What is separation anxiety?

10. What are the three classifications for the education of children who are mentally disabled?

To Do ■ ■ ■ ■ ■ ■ ■ ■ ■ ■ ■ ■ ■ ■ ■

1. Ask several young parents to come to class to discuss changes that a first child makes in the life of a married couple.

2. Ask a pediatrician to speak to your class about the abilities of the newborn and how they change through the first year of life.

3. Investigate the feeding, bathing, and clothing needs of babies. Ask class members to look for magazine articles discussing these needs. Organize the information into a file that will be available to everyone.

4. Divide the class into four groups. Ask each group to prepare a bulletin board display on one of the four areas of development.

5. Research the varying costs of disposable diapers, cloth diapers, and diaper services in your area.

6. Ask a mother to bring her baby and bathing equipment to class to demonstrate bathing a baby.

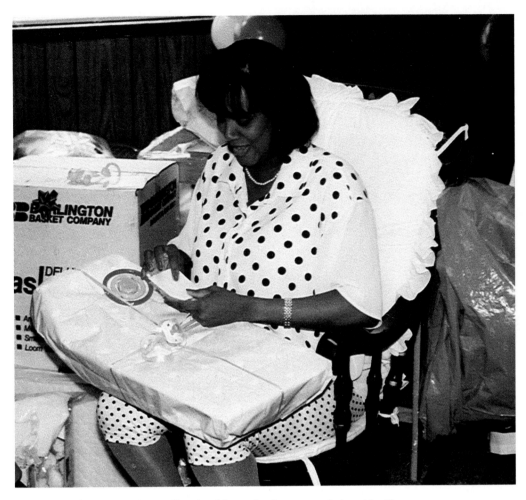

Friends and family members will enjoy "showering" your new baby with gifts.

19

Helping Children Grow and Develop

David Hopper

After studying this chapter, you will be able to

- describe a nurturing, healthy, and safe environment for children.

- summarize the physical, intellectual, social, and emotional growth and development of children from ages one through five years.

- explain parenting concerns related to the preschool years.

- evaluate different types of substitute child care.

- explain parenting concerns related to the school-age years.

An important responsibility of parenting is to nurture your child from infancy to adulthood. *Nurturance* means affectionate care and attention. To nurture means to supply with nourishment. Parenting a child means not only supplying the nourishment

Terms to Know

nurturance

motor development

parallel play

cooperative play

discipline

temper tantrum

leisure time

allowance

latchkey children or
   children in self-care

that comes from food, but the emotional nourishment that comes from love and affection. Nurturing a child is to love the child and to show this love and affection. Without love, a child may not develop normally. For example, a condition known as "failure to thrive" has been found in some infants. These infants are below average in height and weight and do not respond normally to people, though they were normal and healthy at birth. Sometimes there is a medical cause, but often a lack of emotional interaction with parents or other caregivers is identified as the cause of this condition.

fine line, however, between encouraging children and pushing them to do things they either cannot do or do not want to do. Parents who have realistic expectations for their children know that a three-year-old cannot accomplish what a five-year-old can. If you help your children to accomplish reasonable tasks, they can feel successful. When children learn they can succeed, they will look forward to new challenges. When they do succeed, they welcome your praise.

Guiding your children in a positive way will help them become responsible and effective members of their family, community, and

Creating a Nurturing Environment for Your Child ■ ■ ■ ■ ■ ■ ■

From the very beginning of life and continuing throughout their development, children need to hear, feel, and experience love. Children need to know they can always count on their parents' love, even if they may disappoint them from time to time. They need to be told again and again that they are loved.

Young children can sense this love when, as a parent, you cuddle and hold them, 19-1. A simple touch goes a long way in saying "I love you." Getting down on their level or picking them up and talking with them assures them of your love. As children grow older, lots of hugs and looks of reassurance can help to satisfy their emotional needs. Teens can also feel assured when parents actively listen to their concerns. Assuring children that you are there for them and willing to help them whenever necessary is an important part of nurturing. Feeling loved and valued is the goal of nurturance.

Another part of nurturing children is encouraging them to do their best. There is a

Cholla Runnels

19-1
Children need to be reassured of your love again and again.

society. Children learn best by parental example. Children imitate the behavior of "models" they admire, particularly their parents. If this behavior is rewarded with praise, the behavior will be repeated. Modeling has a profound influence on children's perception of how they should behave. Children pick up behavior traits when they see parents act and react to day-to-day situations. Children learn valuable lessons in how to relate to others, how to make decisions, and how to control their emotions. Virtues of honesty, perseverance, and loyalty are best learned by example. When children see these virtues modeled in their parents, their character development will be strengthened.

Creating a Safe and Healthy Environment for Your Child

Providing a safe and healthy environment is another responsibility of parents. Parents must provide nutritious food for their children and see that they get adequate sleep. They must make sure children receive the necessary medical care throughout the growing years. Children also need to be protected from accidental injury and other risks to their safety.

Parents are responsible for providing nutritious food for their children. Nutritional needs change throughout the growing years. Small children need small amounts of food several times a day. Older children will need larger amounts of food but will eat less often. The Food Guide Pyramid provides guidelines to follow in planning meals for your child. Meals must be balanced with a variety of nutritious foods in adequate amounts.

Toddlers and preschoolers need 10 or more hours of sleep a night. The amount of sleep that older children need will vary with the child. Generally at least eight hours of sleep are needed during the growing years.

Parents are responsible for preventive health practices involving their children. Regular visits to the pediatrician during the early years are very important. The pediatrician will outline a series of immunizations that all children need. The pediatrician will check to see that the child is growing and developing properly.

Parents need to watch for signs of illness in their children. When children are ill, parents may need to take them to see a doctor. Parents need to know when an illness requires medical care.

Children must be provided with a safe environment. As soon as a young child begins to crawl, parents need to make a safety check of possible hazards that exist within the home. Accidents are the main cause of death for young children. Most of them could be prevented.

Little children love to explore, and they are inquisitive about doors and drawers. In the home, safety latches on cupboard doors can prevent children from finding objects or substances that might harm them. See 19-2. Poisonous substances should be kept out of reach, and medicines should be capped with safety caps. Plastic bags should be kept out of reach of children. A child can suffocate if a plastic bag is placed over the head. Hot liquids or pots with hot food should be kept out of children's reach and the handles turned away from the edge of the counter. Water heaters should be set for no more than 125° F so bath water will not burn a child. Children should never be left alone in the bathtub.

Young children like to investigate open windows and doors, and neither should be left open without an adult present. Young children love to climb up on tables and counters using chairs or stools. Sometimes they cannot get down without help.

19-2
A child safety latch on cabinet doors allows these toddlers to play freely and safely.

Parents need to supervise children when they are outside and teach them the danger of streets. Parents need to set rules for safety on crossing streets or climbing into unattended cars. Parents should warn their children about accepting any favors, including rides in a car, from strangers.

When in the car, children should be placed in child safety seats with the proper harness system. As they grow older they need to continue to be buckled into car safety belts.

When riding their bikes, children need helmets. They also need to be taught the rules of proper signals and safety precautions. When using in-line roller skates, knee pads, elbow pads, and helmets can prevent serious injuries.

Monitoring children is a responsibility parents need to keep in mind at all times. Teaching safety is an ongoing process. Parents first need to be aware of providing a safe environment in their home and yard. This responsibility expands to include the child's total environment, including school safety, water safety, traffic safety, and safety in public areas. Parents need to keep children with them as they shop in the malls and visit public parks, 19-3. They should explain boundaries and limits that protect the child. All warnings should be explained, and then parents need to insist on obedience.

Growth and Development during the Preschool Years ▪ ▪ ▪ ▪

After the first year of a child's life, physical growth slows down, but significant advances in the areas of intellectual, emotional, and social development occur.

Physical Development

Motor development is significant as infants become toddlers. *Motor development* is the achievement of control over movement of different parts of the body. Motor ability involves the ability of muscles and nerves to work together. As motor ability develops, children will learn to crawl, then to pull themselves up, and eventually to walk. Learning to walk is a significant step in physical development. Failure to achieve motor ability in the earlier stages often results in slower overall development.

Parents who are not familiar with developmental principles often expect far too much from their child too soon. They may be overly anxious for their first child to reach certain stages of physical development such as walking and being toilet trained. Their anxiety may cause emotional problems and frustrations for their child.

On the other hand, knowing when to expect a child to develop certain motor skills can reduce frustration for you and your child. You will not ask your child to do something which the child is incapable of doing. Rather, you will encourage the development of skills that are possible for your child to accomplish.

The physical changes outlined in 19-4 will help you to know what to expect during the preschool years.

Large muscle skills still dominate in the toddler years. Muscle strength increases as children pass through the preschool years. Body proportions change, bringing about improved coordination. Improved walking and running soon expand to include hopping, skipping, and jumping as preschoolers become more coordinated. They use these new

19-3
Small children need to be supervised so they don't get themselves in dangerous situations.

Physical Development from One to Five

The One-Year-Old

Prefers walking to creeping when walking is achieved.

Walks with feet spread wide apart.

Likes to climb stairs, and can be taught to back down by 18 months.

Indicates strong motor drive, of wanting to move all the time.

May exhibit handedness.

Likes to fill small boxes with objects.

Likes to feed self, at first with fingers, then with a spoon.

Can help turn pages of books.

Averages six teeth by one year of age and eight by 18 months.

The Two-Year-Old

Still does not walk erect because knees and elbows are slightly bent.

Spine strengthens and back straightens.

Development of legs, arms, feet, and hands is refined, which helps balance.

Likes to run but cannot measure sudden stops.

Likes to go up and down stairs; may alter feet or go down one step at a time.

Able to throw ball overhead without aiming.

Eye-hand coordination shows improvement.

Likes to fit one object inside another.

Likes to lift everything, lug objects around.

Able to crudely remove wrapping from candy and gum.

Likes to poke fingers into holes.

Has 12 to 16 teeth by two years of age.

The Three-Year-Old

Average toddler is about 3 feet tall and weighs 31 to 33 pounds.

Body assumes more adult shape—less chubby, more upright, longer legs, broader chest.

Increase in muscle growth.

Can run better and maneuver sharper turns.

Eye-hand coordination improves.

Can string large beads, draw with large crayons.

Drawing movements are mostly up and down.

Has full set (20) of baby teeth.

Better coordination in physical skills.

Gets dressed with little help.

The Four-Year-Old

Arms and legs grow proportionately more than trunk of body.

Enjoys vigorous outdoor play.

Likes to climb on play equipment.

Catches and throws ball fairly well.

Can skip in unison to music.

Can hop on one foot, skip rope in simple pattern.

Can pour from small pitcher into glass.

Can place blocks horizontally on floor and stack blocks vertically.

Can stay in lines when coloring.

Forms crude objects with clay.

Can do finger plays.

Can fold paper.

Can use small scissors with difficulty.

The Five-Year-Old

Performs more gracefully, with fewer wasted motions.

Motor activities are accomplished with much greater skill and dexterity.

Has better coordination in throwing balls, building blocks, etc.

Can ride a bicycle that is small enough to balance.

Uses much energy so appetite may increase.

Is independent in toilet habits.

Can draw and paint recognizable pictures.

Can copy designs, letters, and numbers.

Handedness definitely exhibited by physical choice.

Able to bathe self.

Shows definite likes and dislikes in clothing and able to dress self more easily.

Can tie shoelaces and fasten buttons.

19-4
Physical development from the age of one to the age of five is outlined in this chart.

19-5
Children may amaze you with their physical skills during the preschool years.

skills as they try new stunts of climbing, balancing, turning somersaults, and hanging upside-down, 19-5. They enjoy pedal toys, and their speed and strength improve quickly.

Preschoolers' skills of drawing, putting things together, and even working with simple tools often amaze parents, 19-6. By the time they reach five years of age, children are learning life skills such as tying their own shoes and dressing themselves completely.

Intellectual Development

The intellectual development of your child is fascinating to observe. The stages of intellectual development for one- to five-year-olds are outlined in 19-7. Try not to be too concerned with perfection or with comparing your child to your friends' children. You may miss the fun of watching your child make intellectual progress.

Children's intellectual development is related to their interaction with the environment. In the first two years of life, children are interested in objects. They like to explore their environment. They need to have objects they can touch, bang, pile, and carry. Most children like to use familiar household objects and investigate what they can do with them.

Between the ages of two and seven, children think mostly about themselves. They tend to be egocentric, or concerned only with their own well-being. They cannot understand an adult's point of view and cannot put themselves in the position of an adult.

Children like to imitate and pretend, but their knowledge is not yet systematized.

19-6
Improved eye-hand coordination allows this two-year-old to stack many objects.

Intellectual Development from One to Five

The One-Year-Old

Able to find mental solutions to problems, instead of using trial and error.

Likes labeling words, and points when the word is spoken.

Uses gestures along with verbal noises.

Loves to throw things now that releasing objects is understood and mastered.

Knows where things are and where they belong.

Responds to verbal directions.

Enjoys sound patterns of nursery rhymes and TV commercials.

Likes to imitate and pretend.

Enjoys books and colored pictures.

Cannot think from any point of view except own.

Vocabulary of several words by end of year.

The Two-Year-Old

Single words are being replaced by sentences.

Likes to talk to self.

Repeats words to name things.

Applies words to familiar objects.

Can solve problems by imitating past action.

Child thinks mostly from own point of view.

Has a good memory. Can deliver simple message from one parent to another.

Enjoys stories of families sharing experiences.

Can differentiate "before" and "after."

Begins to use imagination and is able to create a make-believe world.

Can assume some responsibility for simple cleanup.

Can take simple things apart and put them back together.

Imitates vertical and horizontal strokes with crayon.

Verbalizes toilet needs fairly consistently.

Recalls events of previous day.

Can repeat parts of favorite stories.

The Three-Year-Old

Is attentive to words.

Likes to repeat words.

Responds to adult suggestions if made in a positive way.

Likes to talk with adults.

Can paste objects to form scene in crude fashion.

Likes stories that answer questions about self.

Knows his or her own age.

Can remember fright caused by one experience and compares it with another experience.

Can play follow the leader.

Can name some colors.

May count to 10 or more.

May compare two objects.

Can recognize different sizes.

Matches puzzle forms: square, circle, or triangle.

Enjoys praise and uses more words.

Can draw a recognizable man or house.

May use symbols in thought, but not yet able to apply rules.

Can remember simple commands.

Asks questions often, "What's this?" "Why?" "What makes it go?"

Knows a few rhymes.

The Four-Year-Old

Sentences become longer.

Likes to experiment with words.

Likes new words and long words and tries to repeat them.

Notices shock value of some words and tries to repeat them.

Makes up words.

Can draw a vertical line and then cross it with a horizontal line.

Interested in death and asks questions about it.

Learns to distinguish fact from fantasy.

Enjoys dramatic and imaginative play.

Tends to think things which change in shape also change in quantity (as when pouring from tall jar to short jar).

Asks "Why?" and "How?"

Likes to have explanations of many things.

Can draw a square, rectangle, and circle.

(continued)

19-7

Children continue to develop intellectually throughout the preschool years as they relate to their environment.

The Five-Year-Old	
I.Q. is relatively stable by school age. Knows full name, address, age, and birthday. Counts to at least 20. Can give and follow simple directions. Can retell a story, following sequence of events. Can create a story about a picture. Enjoys looking at books and listening to stories. Likes stories of unusual situations.	Sees the likes and differences in objects, pictures, and letters. Can draw a recognizable figure. Can draw some alphabet letters. Pays attention, and is able to do a simple reasoning problem. Can tie shoelaces. Appreciates humorous situations. Knows several finger plays, rhymes, and poems.

19-7 *(continued)*

They are influenced primarily by what they see and hear at the moment. Because children at this stage cannot comprehend abstract concepts, they learn best by playing with objects and by being with people. See 19-8 through 19-10.

In this area of development, you can do much to either encourage or frustrate your child. Each accomplishment, no matter how small, should be praised. It is a stepping stone for your child. If your child is sure of your love and support, accomplishments and failures alike will be easier to handle. If your child is not afraid of failing and disappointing you, he or she will have more courage to try new things. By trying more, your child will learn more.

Cholla Runnels

19-8
Children learn about shapes by putting simple puzzles together.

Cholla Runnels

19-9
Children first "read" books by looking at the pictures and turning the pages while listening to a recording of the words.

19-10
Cholla Runnels

Weighing flour on a balance helps children learn basic math concepts such as less, more, and equal.

Social Development

As children develop socially, they learn how to get along with other people. Stages of social development for preschoolers are described in 19-11.

Children's self-esteem will have much to do with their socialization. If they feel threat- ened, they may resort to defense mechanisms and display negative behavior. The family provides the first model for socialization. If children sense optimistic, positive attitudes within their families, they will usually be able to move securely in other social situations.

How children adapt to the world around them affects the degree of cooperation and responsibility they will display as adults. As children move through different stages of social growth, many of their actions are the result of watching and imitating adults, 19-12 and 19-13.

Play is very important in the social development of children. As children grow, their play changes in form. Young children are self-centered and play by themselves. As they grow older, they may prefer *parallel play.* In this form of play, children like to play next to their peers, but they do not play with their peers, 19-14. They watch what others are doing and may copy their actions, but they do not interact. This onlooker behavior prepares them for the next form of play.

In *cooperative play,* children choose to interact with one or more people. At first, most children will choose different playmates each day, but they may eventually choose "best friends."

Preschools and neighborhood play groups give young children opportunities to expand their social skills. These opportunities help children prepare for their next major new social situation—the school environment. Children who have had experience in earlier social situations will feel more secure when they enter school.

Emotional Development

As emotional development continues, the interactions within families are reflected in the emotions displayed by children. Children learn acceptable patterns of emotional response through the interactions within the

Social Development from One to Five

The One-Year-Old

Enjoys talking to adults with simple sounds.

Enjoys playing with pet.

May be easily frustrated when someone says no.

Ability to walk and talk allows child to gain some independence from adults.

Enjoys playing simple games with siblings.

Likes to run from adult in chasing game.

Learns to express affection for persons other than family.

Is constantly on the move, looking for something to do.

Wants to be independent, yet likes to be near parent or sibling.

Likes to listen to music and "dance."

Benefits from being with other children.

The Two-Year-Old

Enjoys watching people.

Enjoys opportunity to use large muscles and participate in climbing activities.

Likes to play near other children rather than with them (parallel play).

Begins learning masculine and feminine social roles.

Becomes a "grabber" and will try to snatch desired objects.

Does not like to share toys.

May pull hair or bite before giving up a prized possession.

May give up a possession more easily when offered a substitute.

Has not learned to say please, but often desires toys held by other children.

The Three-Year-Old

Child is able to play with other children in cooperative play.

Very sensitive about being watched.

Tries to please and conform.

Asks many questions.

Likes simple guessing games.

Enjoys playing dress up.

Loves dirt, water, mud; may play in mud even against parents' instructions.

Needs some group experiences and social play with friends.

Can go places without parents and feel comfortable leaving them.

May enjoy going to nursery school.

May awaken at night and want to be taken into parents' bed.

Parents should comfort the child and fulfill his or her need for security, but the child should not be taken into bed.

May cry when parents leave, but parents should leave, reassuring child of their return. Then they should return on time.

May exhibit direct aggressive feelings by saying, "I hate you." When this happens, parents should not withhold their love, but instead show the child their love can be counted on under all circumstances.

The Four-Year-Old

Gets along better with adults and peers and is capable of cooperative play.

Loves to play dress up and imitate adult roles.

Enjoys parties and anticipates going to them.

Talks about not inviting someone to a party to show dislike of them.

Tries to gain favor of someone by talking about some interesting experience.

Asks many questions of everyone.

Does not hesitate to talk to anyone who comes into house—repair persons, etc.

May pick up "dirty" words and enjoy shocking a parent by saying them.

Learns to obey rules at school and may sometimes rebel at following them.

The Five-Year-Old

Gets along reasonably well with other children and takes part in games and other activities.

Acts courteously in certain situations.

Waits for turn to talk.

Says please and thank you.

Participates in singing.

May choose special friends for the first time.

Can be silly with friends.

Likes to telephone friends, but does not say much when on the phone.

May not like organized games, but prefers to make up own games and play activities.

Enjoys being left alone while at play.

May like to find hiding places and ask friend to share the hiding place.

19-11
This chart outlines the stages of social development during the preschool years.

David Hopper

19-12
Children enjoy dressing up and imitating the
behaviors of adults they have watched.

Cholla Runnels

19-13
Imitating adult roles helps the social development of children.

Cholla Runnels

19-14
In parallel play, children enjoy playing next to each other, but they have little interaction.

family. They learn to manage such emotions as fear, anger, jealousy, and anxiety. Parents can help their children learn acceptable emotional responses by providing good examples in their own behavior. Parents can also recognize and encourage desirable behavior patterns in their children. The stages of emotional development during the preschool years are described in 19-15.

The emotional climate in a home can do much to foster healthy, well-adjusted chil-

dren. A climate of love in the home lays the foundation for affection and trust. Withholding love can be damaging, for children need to know they are loved all the time—not just when they are "good." Loved children feel secure and are able to show affection to others. They gain self-esteem and thus will be better able to develop self-discipline and independence.

Negative behavior patterns are sometimes displayed in families, and in turn, by

Emotional Development from One to Five

The One-Year-Old

Is very self-centered.
Emotionally unpredictable; may respond in different ways.
Capable of indicating affection.
Likes to be near people.
May respond to commands in the opposite manner.

Negativism may be apparent, but it is normal.
May have favorite toy; carries it at all times.
Displays fear of high places, strangers, loud noises, and insecure footing.
May hug pet too hard while showing love and cause injury to animal.

The Two-Year-Old

Enjoys expressing love and affection.
Responds to praise and wants to please parents.
May choose a security toy or blanket.
Needs firm and consistent guidance.
Does not respond readily to commands.
Unable to make confusing choices.
Punishment aggravates frustration.
Emotions are "brittle" and feelings are easily hurt.
Exhibits little patience and is easily frustrated.
Anger is directed at person responsible for frustration.

Jealousy is a recognizable emotion.
Fear of dark may develop; needs soothing and reassurance.
May resent new foods.
May dawdle while eating.
Has little sense of time; hurrying a child often makes him or her stubborn.
Sensitive about being bossed or helped.
May exhibit contrariness (negativism).
Toilet training success depends on feelings of emotional security and whether or not child indicates readiness.

The Three-Year-Old

Is more cooperative and considerate.
Able to show self-control.
Is able to share and wait for a turn.
Praise and affection are eagerly sought.
Intent on seeking status from peers.
Takes pride in tasks performed for others.
Very proud of self-made items and anxious to show parents.
Likes to be praised for efforts.
Needs an understanding, affectionate, orderly environment.
Learns more socially acceptable ways of displaying feelings.

Temper outbursts become less frequent.
Anger is found more frequently in an anxious, insecure child.
Capable of lasting hostility; may try to get even with offender.
Sympathy is displayed by attempting to comfort or help a friend.
Emotional experiences of the day may upset sleep of child at night.
Shame or harsh actions promote fears.
Displays fear of the dark, animals, and storms.

The Four-Year-Old

May say, "I love you," one minute and then say, "I hate you," the next minute.
May use silly names.
Tells tall tales to see their effect on other person.
Likes to boast that they are bigger and better than others.
May over-exaggerate about anything.
May become more selfish and impatient.
May fight, boast, and boss as they change from toddler to child role.
Concerned with imaginary dangers.

Has a strong sense of family and home.
Becomes interested in rules of games.
Is willing to take turns.
Able to plan ahead with adults.
Is learning to accept limits.
Runs ahead when walking with others, but then waits for them.
Acts silly when tired.
Angers last longer and child may want to hurt person or object causing anger.

(Continued)

19-15
Emotions play an important role in the development of the preschooler.

The Five-Year-Old

May be embarrassed when showing affection.	Shows sympathy.
Wants to be with favorite people.	Feels guilty when knows thoughts are "wrong."
Is proud of parents.	Has longer attention span.
Is more protective of siblings.	Is more practical in approach to problems.
Shows more willingness to conform.	Likes to take responsibility in helping with duties.
Is learning to take responsibility for own actions.	Expresses ideas through dramatic play.
Accepts instruction and supervision.	Displays jealousy by tattling, belittling, or lying.
Asks permission to do things.	Anger is promoted more by differences with age
Is more patient and generous.	situations.

19-15 *(continued)*

children, 19-16. If children feel insecure, their feelings may be displayed in over-aggressive behavior, temper tantrums, nervous habits, speech problems, or fretful sleep. If children frequently display such behavior patterns, try to determine what might be causing the problem, 19-17. If the behavior is persistent, professional help should be sought.

Pam Ryder

19-16
Sometimes a disagreement will have to be settled with the help of an adult.

The Preschool Years ▪ ▪ ▪ ▪ ▪ ▪ ▪

Parenting involves many joys as well as responsibilities. During your child's preschool years, the days will be full of activity. You will marvel at the boundless energy of a preschooler, and you may sometimes breathe a sigh of relief when you tuck your child into bed at night.

Every family faces unique challenges as children develop. As parents, you will find yourself filling a variety of roles. The important goals are to enjoy the preschool years with your child and to assure your child of your love.

Discipline

It may be hard for you to think in terms of "discipline" as you hold your one-year-old. However, to be effective, discipline should begin in early childhood. *Discipline* is the use of different methods and techniques to teach children self-control and limits. The goal is for children to develop behavior patterns that are acceptable to society.

Discipline should be based on love and understanding. It should involve respect, sup-

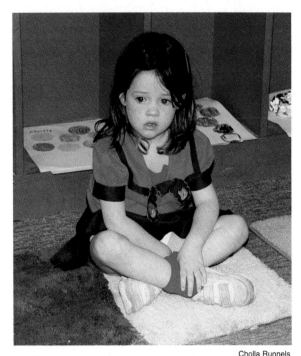

Cholla Runnels

19-17
Children may learn to control their emotions, but they do not hide their emotions well.

port, and encouragement, as well as communication of limitations. Children want and need you to set limits for them. Limits give children a feeling of security, for limits help them define and understand the environment. See 19-18.

Discipline is often equated with punishment. Punishment is one of many forms of discipline. There are many other forms of discipline that are more effective in guiding children's behavior, such as modeling and setting limits.

Discipline should be as normal a part of daily life as eating or sleeping. Children at any age should be able to count on it. Children will still try to get around some rules, but discipline will help them feel loved and secure.

Discipline must be consistent. Children have to be able to count on the "no's" as well as the "yes's." When a bed time is established, children need to know that their whines or tantrums will not force parents to relent. Parents should try to agree on matters of discipline. If they don't, children will soon learn that one parent can be played against the other to get what is wanted.

Cholla Runnels

19-18
When discipline is based on love and understanding, it helps children learn their limits.

Cholla Runnels

19-19
Children's fears are very real to them.

Understanding how to become caring parents is a challenge. If you base your actions on love and understanding, you will help your child establish the basic foundation of trust that is so important in life.

Anxiety and Fears

Although every person experiences fears, the fears of childhood often seem overwhelming, 19-19. It is not uncommon for children to have fears. When fear affects children's ability to accept the daily demands of living, then they need help to overcome it. The most common childhood fears are of the unexpected, the dark, loud noises, strange persons, and being left alone.

Fears can be handed down from parents to children. Parents who are frightened by storms may pull down window shades so they do not have to look outside. The children may learn to fear storms, too.

Often the anxiety of a small child remains unknown to the parent. A small boy who sees his mother going to the hospital to give birth to a baby may remember that his grandmother went to the hospital and never came back.

Parents need to help their children separate fantasy from truth. Sometimes they can simply say that they are going to read a "pretend" story and then explain what pretend means.

Fears can be useful in the lives of children, 19-20. Understanding that fires burn and that knives cut can protect children from

Pam Ryder

19-20
Some fears will keep children from hurting themselves by playing on equipment that is meant for older children.

harm. However, fears that prevent a child from meeting life normally can produce damaging habits and actions. Such negative responses to fear may create long-lasting problems.

When you introduce a new experience to children, try to anticipate any fears they might have. Offer them extra encouragement. Give them time to work through the experience in their own minds. Show them how to do it. Do not force them to accept a new experience because this could cause fear. Never shame or laugh at children for being cautious. Let them know the security they seek from you is always there.

As parents, try to recognize the fears of your children and the causes of those fears. Then help your children dispel the fears with reassurance, security, and love.

Anger

Children are humans, and like all humans, they sometimes become angry. If a child says, "I hate you," you may feel hurt at the time. You need to understand that a child who feels that way may be anxious or frustrated. Simply talking with the child in a calm manner may dispel the child's anger.

A parent or caregiver can help by making a sincere effort to understand and empathize with an upset child. In many cases, children can "let go of" their anger when a new activity is suggested such as a game of "follow the leader."

Some children need to vent their anger, but it should be done in a way that will not be harmful. They could "wear out" their anger through physical activities such as throwing a ball or punching a pillow.

A *temper tantrum,* a violent outburst of anger, is typical in young children. Such a tantrum should be ignored, as long as the child is not harming anyone or anything. Giv-

ing in to children's demands in order to end a tantrum will only tend to encourage such behavior in the future.

Temper is not inherited through genes, but your child may learn to imitate your displays of temper. If you can help your child handle frustration and anger constructively, you will be teaching your child skills that will be helpful throughout his or her life.

Preparing for Another Child

If you plan to have more than one child, be sure to prepare your first child to accept a brother or sister. If the event is a total surprise to the child, it may be very upsetting. If the child believes that the new baby will add to the pleasure of all family members, the child will look forward to the birth. See 19-21.

David Hopper

19-21
This sibling's parents prepared her for the birth of another child. As a result, she is eager to hold her new sister.

Some jealousy is natural, but it will be minimal if the child is allowed to help prepare for the new baby.

Once the baby is born, try to be even more generous in giving love and attention to your older child. Help him or her feel secure in the role of an older sibling. Your child will learn that you cannot always give children equal amounts of attention, but that you love the children equally and will always be fair. The new baby will need more of your attention, and the older child may even enjoy helping you care for the baby. If the child can see all the care the baby needs, the child may understand why you spend so much time with the baby.

Substitute Child Care

The "ideal environment" for a child, according to most authorities, is in the home with loving and caring parents. They believe that a child should have a parent as the primary caregiver for at least the first three years of life. In today's society, this is not always possible. Child care provided by others is a fact of life in many families.

As a parent, you will want to provide the best environment possible to help your child achieve his or her full potential. This environment may include child care provided by others. Parents should discuss their opinions about substitute child care before children are born. In fact, they should be discussed even before marriage.

When making decisions about child care, parents need to review their goals for rearing children. They also need to review alternatives for meeting those goals. Parents who decide to use substitute child care should put some time and effort into the se-

Points to Check When Comparing Substitute Child Care

1. Is the center licensed? Is the license displayed?
2. Do the people who care for the children have training in child development and child care?
3. Is the center clean and sanitary? Does it meet requirements for fire protection and sanitation in food and toilet facilities?
4. Are the surroundings pleasant?
5. Are the children's routines structured, but not rigid?
6. Is the health of the children well protected and regulated?
7. If food is served, is it nutritious? Is it served under sanitary conditions?
8. Are the children divided into age groups with adequate supervision for each age group?
9. Are the groups small enough to facilitate interaction?
10. Is the play equipment safe and appropriate for children of all ages?
11. Have precautions been taken in case of emergency? Are phone numbers listed next to the phone? Are evacuation plans practiced?
12. Are records kept on the progress of each child? Are these records available to the parents?

19-22
If you are considering substitute child care, you should thoroughly investigate the options available to you.

lection, 19-22. Children's development is greatly influenced by their environment and their caregivers.

There are several options for substitute child care. These include in-home care, family day care, and child care centers.

Contemporary Topics *of interest to teens:*
Evaluating Child Care: What to Look For

Child caregiving staff and facilities vary widely in cost and quality. Before entrusting staff with the care of your child, take some time to visit and evaluate several facilities. Spend enough time to gain a real sense of the facility's physical and psychological atmosphere, rather than just its superficial aspects.

Pay special attention to:

■ Safety, health, and cleanliness. Look for environments that are not only educationally stimulating but free of furniture with sharp corners, hazardous electrical appliances, and other sources of potential accidents. Meals and snacks should consist of nutritious items rather than "junk food." Care givers should supervise children in developing basic health habits, such as hand washing before meals and after bathroom use.

■ Caregivers' openness to interacting with parents. Look for a care giver who seems genuinely interested in being your partner in helping your child develop. Such a person will be open to discussing everything from the cause of your child's scraped knee to how the child is interacting with the other children.

■ Caregivers' willingness to interact positively with your child. Look for kind, intelligent, affectionate staff members who will interact with your child rather than encouraging him or her to sit in front of the TV all day. A positive staff-to-preschooler ratio will increase the chances that your child will receive individual attention.

■ Constructive disciplinary methods. Caregivers with a philosophy of discipline based on physical or verbal abuse should be avoided at all cost. Also, pay attention to the actions the caregiver feels are deserving of punishment. For example, if a child is humiliated or punished for accidentally spilling a glass of milk, look for a different facility.

■ Opportunities for both activity and rest. Children need to be able to take "time out" from active play and constant interaction during the day. A good facility allows for a child's need to follow his or her own rhythms of active engagement and quiet time for self.

Finding the right child care setting may not be easy. However, taking the time to search for the best available environment will give parents peace of mind. They will have the satisfaction of knowing that their child is spending each day in a caring, constructive environment.

In-Home Care

In many cases, the most desirable type of substitute child care is care given in the child's home. This is especially true if the caregiver has experience with children and has values much like those of the parents. If the caregiver is a warm and loving person who enjoys children, the quality of the care is likely to be good. Often the caregiver is a grandparent or other relative.

Parents who hire a caregiver to work in their home should check the person's references. They should discuss methods of discipline and theories about rearing children. They should also be sure the person interacts well with their children. After a period of adjustment, parents should review the arrangement. If the child seems unhappy or the parents feel uneasy, alternative arrangements should be made.

In-home child care often costs more than other types of care. The government does not regulate or license such care, so parents are responsible for seeing that their children's developmental needs are met.

Family Child Care

The most common type of substitute child care is that provided in the home of the caregiver. This arrangement provides an atmosphere similar to the child's own home with a small group of children. It is often available within the child's neighborhood.

People who care for children in their homes are often parents themselves. While they stay at home with their own children, they also care for other children. Ideal caregivers in these situations are people who truly love and enjoy children. They have had experience working with children and maintain discipline with gentleness as well as firmness.

Before placing a child in a caregiver's home, parents should visit the home a few times. They should watch the children interact with each other and with the caregiver. Parents should also ask for references and check them thoroughly.

In most states, child care homes are registered but not licensed. Certain restrictions exist, such as limits on the number of children allowed in each home. Parents have to judge the care their children receive, for these homes are not inspected on a routine basis.

Child Care Centers

If child care is not available in a home setting, a child care center may be an option, 19-23. There are advantages to this type of setting. In a child care center, staff are more likely to have received formal training in child care. There may be more opportunities for social interaction among children in a center. More facilities for learning, as well as for play, may be available in a center than in a home. There may be a more organized program of activities to help children learn.

JoAnn Macander

19-23
Children in child care centers learn to interact with other children their age.

On the other hand, your child may not receive as much personal attention. The atmosphere will be more institutional and less "homey." A large group of children may be overwhelming to your child.

There are many different kinds of child care centers from which to choose. All may not be available in your community, however. Costs and programs will vary considerably.

Nationally Franchised Child Care Centers

Child care centers that are part of a national chain offer uniformity in child care. The equipment and overall programming are much the same from center to center. These centers generally have good, safe equipment and well-developed programs designed and supervised by trained personnel. Meals and snacks are usually available. Extended hours allow flexibility in parents' schedules. These centers generally maintain high-quality programs for medium-range fees.

Privately Owned Child Care Centers

Some child care centers are privately owned. Most of these centers have excellent programs run by well-qualified staff members. The good centers have plenty of safe play equipment and a variety of supervised activities. Costs vary according to the services and quality of care provided. Tuition must cover all operating expenses.

Church-Linked Child Care

Some churches sponsor child care programs. Most church-linked programs have high standards and are run by well-qualified staff members. Fees may be charged to cover expenses, but they are usually low. Many of these programs operate a limited number of hours and days. A few offer full-time, daily child care.

University-Linked Child Care

Child care programs are a part of many colleges and universities. They are often called *laboratory schools*. They offer care for the children of faculty, students, and the general public. They also offer educational opportunities for university students studying child development. Children receive excellent care and guidance, and the fees are generally low. Most have a highly qualified staff, a well-planned curriculum, and excellent equipment, 19-24. These programs are so popular among parents that they usually have waiting lists.

Publicly Sponsored Child Care

Head Start, Home Start, and entitlement programs are sponsored by the government. They are available to families who qualify for free or low-cost child care. These programs must comply with strict guidelines in order to be licensed. They are usually excellent programs, but they are not available to everyone. Most of the expenses for the program are funded through grants received from the federal government.

Cooperative Child Care

In many communities, parents have started cooperative child care centers. In these centers, parents provide many of the services for which other centers would have to pay. This lowers the tuition fees. Parents also serve on the board of directors, hiring teachers and managing finances. Maintenance may be provided at "work parties" or on an assigned basis. In this type of child care, parents are able to participate with their children and with other parents. The sharing of experiences between parents and their children and the support system among parents are special advantages of cooperative child care.

19-24
Landscape Structures, Inc.
Laboratory schools usually have well-equipped centers.

Employer-Sponsored Child Care

Business managers know that many of their employees are parents. They know that these employees are concerned about their children's welfare. As a result, businesses are becoming more involved in child care. They have found that it often helps their companies to attract and keep good employees.

Some businesses provide on-site child care for employees' children. This allows parents to be close at hand if their children need them. It also allows parents and children to spend time together as they go to and from work and perhaps during lunch breaks.

Some businesses offer company-paid child care as a fringe benefit. Others offer flexible schedules so employees can coordinate their working hours with their child care responsibilities. Still others offer *job-sharing* where two employees share one full-time job. This allows each employee to work shorter hours.

Some businesses offer child care as a fringe benefit. Those parents who have children may choose the child care facility they want for their child, and the employer will cover some of the tuition costs.

Day Care for Children Who Are Ill

Across the country, there is an increasing demand for day care for sick children whose parents are unable to stay home with them. Children in child care centers and schools are exposed to many illnesses. Special child care facilities allow children who are ill to get well in a center designed exclusively for sick children.

Pediatricians and parents have long felt a need for day care for ailing children. In several communities, an empty hospital wing has been converted to a sick child care facility. Working parents can drop off ailing youngsters and be assured they will receive adequate care. Children with contagious illnesses are cared for in isolated rooms. Nurses are on duty, and doctors are available if needed. The cost is high, but working parents who feel they cannot stay home with sick children find the service worth the fee.

Some communities also have services available that provide in-home care for sick children. Individuals trained in basic home health care are on call to care for sick children in their own homes. Often these persons are senior citizens.

19-25
Parents and children become closer when they enjoy leisure activities together.

The School Years ■ ■ ■

Most parents think they are busy when their children are babies. When their children enter the school years, however, parents may find themselves even busier. School years include car pooling, dropping off and picking up children from after-school activities, watching school plays, serving food at picnics, and nursing childhood diseases. For parents, the demands of the school years can be exhausting, yet exciting. You need to get involved in your child's activities in order to share these important developmental years.

Time for Family

It is important that family members find time to be together as a family during the school years. *Leisure time* is the time you have free from your work and other duties. Leisure time should not be filled with activities that take each member of the family off in a different direction doing his or her own thing. At the same time, your free time should not be spent just taking children to various lessons and activities. Instead, the family should spend some part of their leisure time doing activities together. In busy families, this time may have to be scheduled. A certain time each week can be designated as family time. No other activities should be scheduled at this time. Family members can decide together how they wish to spend this time each week, or members can take turns choosing an activity.

Shared leisure time is important for the health and well-being of the family, 19-25. Participating together in recreational activities helps to pull families together. Communication is sometimes easier when family members are enjoying relaxing activities. Parents and children who find recreational activities that they all enjoy are drawn together because of their mutual interest and enjoyment. As children enter their teen years, this mutual interest can help to sustain a bond that will keep teens from drawing away from their parents.

Your Children's Friends

Once your child starts school, do not be surprised if he or she begins to bring home a continuing array of friends. They will be important to your child and will help your child develop feelings of security and self-esteem, 19-26. How you react to your child's friends may have a lasting effect on the continuing relationship of trust and respect between you and your child.

19-26
Friends are important to the school-age child.

Sometimes you may sense that certain friends are undesirable. This presents a problem, and you should act. Child authorities recognize the tremendous influence of friends, and if the friends are undesirable, you would be wise to try to ease away the involvement. The following situations warrant concern:

- The children are involved in disturbing sex play.

- The friend's behavior is violent.

- The children engage in lawless behavior when together.

Sexual curiosity is natural as your child develops, and friendship may offer opportunities for this curiosity to be satisfied. The important thing is to be aware of what is happening and to tactfully intervene if necessary. School children tend to seek out special friends. It is natural for their play to include tickling and wrestling. They are aware of differences in sexes, and they may vaguely sense that they are doing something wrong. This may attract them even more.

As a parent you may wonder, "What do I do now?" If you degrade your child's friends or if you become horribly shocked, you are probably doing more harm. Instead, try to guide them into other activities without expressing shock or anger. As soon as you are alone with your child, talk with him or her about appropriate behavior. It might be the ideal time to talk about what sexuality means to your child. Such conversation could also open communication for further questions later.

Children need friends, but they need friends who will increase their self-confidence and self-esteem. If your child knows that his or her friends are welcome in your home, you will have a greater chance of controlling who the friends are. Having friends visit your home also allows your child to judge the friends in a familiar setting. Your child may see the differences and realize that the friendship is not a good one.

Tall Tales and Lying

Tall tales are an exaggeration of something real, a story of an imaginary experience, or even a kind of bragging. School-age children have a need to be bigger, stronger, or braver than anyone else, so they tell tall tales.

Children sometimes tell lies to fulfill their needs. For instance, they may be so eager for parental approval that they will tell lies just to get approval.

Children witness adults getting by with lies. When adults use false excuses to decline invitations or to cut phone conversations short, children notice the lies and may imitate them.

Children use tall tales and lies to discover reality through trial and error. If you let them know you are aware of their lies, they will gradually have fewer reasons to lie. However, do not be too stern, for many children pass through a stage of lying in their pattern of development.

Reward children for telling the truth. Help them accept the fact that all people make mistakes. Let them know that they will not be severely punished for making mistakes. Punishment may make children even more skillful liars if they find that they can protect themselves from punishment by lying.

Developing Responsibility

Developing responsibility in your child is a worthy goal, but before it can be achieved, you will experience many ups and downs. At times, you will feel frustrated.

19-27
Children become more responsible when you praise them for a job well done.

David Hopper

There will also be times when you say, "I am so proud of you."

Responsibility involves consideration for others and fulfillment of obligations. Your child can learn to be responsible with your guidance, 19-27. Your child should be encouraged to think, "Let's see what I can do about this problem." As a parent, you can help your child realize that he or she can solve problems. Praise your child when he or she has shown responsibility, and provide opportunities to be responsible again.

Your child can learn to take care of personal property. Present your child with tasks he or she can handle. Such tasks could include picking up toys, making the bed, setting the table, or caring for a pet. As your child performs these tasks, he or she will develop responsibility. Children show an amazing willingness to help out when a real problem or need exists. They like to feel needed.

If your child has trouble meeting responsibilities, take time to explain tasks clearly and completely. Be sure your child is capable of doing the tasks you assign. Then remember to praise your child when the tasks are completed.

If you can help your child develop responsibility at home, your child is likely to be responsible at school and throughout his or her entire life. See 19-28.

Money and Children

It does not take long for children to realize that money plays an important part in life. How can you help your child develop healthy values concerning money?

Most authorities feel the practice of giving an allowance is still the best method of teaching children money management. An *allowance* is money given by parents to children for their personal needs. The object is

19-28
A part of being responsible is taking care of personal hygiene without being told.

Barrier Free Environments, Inc., Raleigh, NC

to help children become self-reliant and capable of handling money.

Under an allowance system, children are given a certain sum at regular intervals, often each week. Several factors are considered when deciding on an amount. The children's needs are a major factor. The income of the family and the needs of other family members should also be considered. Children have to realize that they are part of a family and that every member has needs. Another factor to consider is the amount that other children their age are getting. Children in the same community often have similar needs.

The allowance should include a small amount more than is really needed. This extra amount is what really gives your children the most experience. How will they handle this extra money? Some will waste it. Some will give it away. Some will save it. However, most will eventually learn that they can have what they need and some of what they want if they successfully control their spending. They can learn how to set and achieve financial goals.

Allowances should be paid regularly. They should not be held back as punishment. If the wrongdoing had no connection with money, then the allowance should not be withheld. Likewise, allowances should not be given in advance, as a rule. If children spend or lose their money, they will have to learn to live with the consequences.

If the allowance system is not used, what other methods are available? You may assign a value to all household and yard tasks and pay for each job done. Parents who like this method feel it teaches children the value of work as well as the value of money. Opponents feel that it places a price on tasks that should be a part of family duties and that it teaches children to work only when they will be paid.

Some parents think a combination is good. They give an allowance for regular needs and pay by the job for special tasks. In this way they combine the good points of both methods, 19-29.

Some parents simply hand out money when children need it. This can promote good communication between parents and children. If it is not overdone, it can successfully meet the needs of all family members. Some children do not like to ask for money all the time, so they prefer other methods.

Money is an important part of everyone's life. If you can teach your children to use good spending and saving habits, your children will benefit from them all their lives.

After-School Child Care

When a child reaches school age, parents may have a need for after-school child care. Many working parents need supervision

Cholla Runnels

19-29
If parents pay children for special tasks, they will be more likely to appreciate the money they earn.

for their children between the time their children leave school and a parent returns home. Communities realize this growing need and are developing programs to meet this need. These programs may be offered in extended-day programs in schools, in community centers, in churches, and in existing child care centers. Many school districts are extending half-day kindergarten to full days, often to accommodate working parents.

Latchkey Children or Children in Self-Care

Latchkey children or *children in self-care* are children who are regularly left without direct adult supervision before or after school. Across our country, a growing number of children arrive home from school and enter an empty house to wait for their parents.

Studies of children in self-care reveal the following. Children who are left to care for themselves during nonschool hours have more academic and social problems than their peers who receive adult supervision. Children who are alone tend to be more fearful, lonely, and bored than children who are supervised. The primary fear of these children is that someone will break into their home while they are alone and hurt them.

Many specialists argue that latchkey children are expected to assume too much responsibility too early in life. They agree, however, that for some children, self-care experiences have not been all bad. Self-care has fostered such positive outcomes as increased self-confidence and greater independence. Many children are happy and comfortable with these arrangements.

Much depends on the attitude of self-responsibility and security instilled in the children by their parents. The age of the child is also an important consideration. Parents need to assess the needs of their children, their own responsibilities to their work schedules, and the neighborhood in which they live.

Latchkey children need to be trained in the skills of self-sufficiency and safety. Parents need to establish a safe environment for their children when they are home alone. They need to establish guidelines for the use of appliances and equipment. Emergency telephone numbers should be easy to find. There should be ground rules for allowing other children or acquaintances into the home. Safety precautions concerning strangers should be discussed with the children. Proper use of the telephone should also be covered.

Communities and government agencies are investigating the particular needs of children in self-care. Many communities have designed support services to help children in their homes. Telephone programs offer reassurance for children who are home alone. Children can call for help in emergencies, to report problems, or just to talk.

After-school child care is a concern that is being addressed. However, parents will continue to have the major responsibility for the well-being of their children should they need to be left alone.

Summary ■ ■ ■ ■ ■ ■ ■ ■ ■ ■ ■ ■ ■ ■ ■

- An important responsibility of parenting is to nurture your child from infancy to adulthood. Nurturing a child means loving the child and showing this love and affection.

- Providing a safe and healthy environment is another responsibility of parents. Parents must provide nutritious food for their children and see that they get adequate sleep. They must make sure children receive the necessary medical care throughout the growing years. Children also need to be protected from accidental injury and other risks to their safety.

- Physical growth and development slow down after the first year of life, but refinement of physical capabilities increases.

- Children's intellectual development is related to their interaction with the environment. In the first two years of life, children are interested in objects. They like to explore their environment. Between the ages of two and seven, children think mostly about themselves. They cannot understand an adult's point of view.

- Play is an important part of the developing child's social development. As children grow, their play changes in form.

- The emotional climate in the home can do much to foster healthy, well-adjusted children.

- Discipline that is based on love and understanding helps children learn self-control and self-discipline.

- Fear and anger are normal emotions of all humans, but children may need help handling these emotions.

- Parents who decide to use substitute child care should evaluate the many different types of care available.

- During the school years, parents can help their children establish good friendships, develop responsibility, and learn to handle money.

To Review ■ ■ ■ ■ ■ ■ ■ ■ ■ ■ ■ ■ ■ ■ ■

1. Briefly describe how parents can provide a nurturing environment for their children.

2. Give an example of how modeling could influence a child's behavior.

3. List five safety precautions parents need to take to keep their children safe.

4. True or False. Children learn large muscle control before they learn fine muscle control.

5. Describe the three stages of children's play.

6. Explain the difference between discipline and punishment.

7. Explain how some fears can be useful and others can be damaging to children.

8. Briefly describe four types of substitute child care.

9. How can shared leisure time improve the well-being of the family?

10. How can you help children learn not to lie?

11. Describe three methods parents can use to help children develop values concerning money.

12. What can parents do to help assure the safety of a child in self-care?

To Do ■ ■ ■ ■ ■ ■ ■ ■ ■ ■ ■ ■ ■ ■ ■ ■ ■ ■ ■

1. Accept or reject the statement: There is a fine line between encouragement and pushing children. Explain and give examples to support your response.

2. Divide the class into several groups. Assign each group a different area of the child's environment, such as the home, the neighborhood, shopping areas, cars, parks, etc. Develop a list of rules, limitations, and safety precautions parents should provide in each of these areas. Share the lists with the class, and post them on the bulletin board. Try to find pictures in magazines that depict some of these points to create an informative display.

3. Role-play a variety of situations in which parents are trying to teach their children self-control and responsibility. Situations might include picking up toys, sharing with another child, displaying anger, or learning how to manage money. Present your conclusions to the class and discuss.

4. Write a report on various methods of discipline.

5. Investigate types of substitute child care in your area. Compare their facilities, staff, programs, and costs.

6. Observe a child either in a child care center or in your neighborhood. Using the developmental charts in this chapter, compare this child's abilities to the abilities of an average child of the same age.

7. Ask a child psychologist to speak to the class about children's fears, citing the most common types of fear, how parents influence children's fears, how fears can hamper or help a child's development, and steps parents can take to help children overcome their fears.

8. Investigate programs that provide after-school care for children in your community. Prepare a pamphlet describing available resources.

Doing homework assignments can be a family affair during the school-age years.

VI

Families Face Change

20

Balancing Family and Work Concerns

David Hopper

Terms to Know

dual-worker families

dual-career families

part-time workers

displaced
  homemakers

alimony

rehabilitative
  alimony

cost-effective

Family and Medical
  Leave Act

on-site child care

flextime

block scheduling

job sharing

employee-assistance
  programs (EAP)

quality time

**After studying this chapter,
you will be able to**

- explain reasons why people work.

- evaluate various types of work and
  family arrangements and patterns.

- summarize the impact of work on
  families.

- describe ways that families are
  influencing the workplace.

- identify techniques for balancing
  family and work demands.

Two of life's greatest satisfactions are experiencing a satisfying family life and fulfilling a life's calling—usually through paid or unpaid work.

Both family life and work take time and effort. Sometimes one area can be going well while the other needs special attention. It is easy to get over-involved with one area at the expense of the other. Dealing with the joys and challenges of both is a lifelong adventure.

Why Work?

Most people in our country work during most of their adult lives. Most men and unmarried women have traditionally held full-time jobs. In recent decades, more married women and women with children have also been employed outside the home.

About half of all married women with children under age six are currently employed, 20-1. About two out of three women with children under age 18 are in the labor force.

Why do people work? Working provides opportunities for self-expression, personal growth, and satisfying interaction with other workers. Paid employment also provides the means by which the family supports itself.

In three out of five marriages in our country, both the husband and wife have jobs. Working couples often find that the added dimensions of outside contacts and interests can enhance their marriage. Employed spouses can share interesting work-related experiences with each other. They can also better help each other deal with job pressures.

Working for pay has other benefits as well. An additional income contributes to greater financial security and purchasing power for the family. If one spouse becomes jobless, the other spouse's income will help make ends meet.

Financial self-sufficiency gives people greater independence and more life choices. Although many marriages are very happy, others end in divorce. Some family situations involve emotional or physical abuse. Financial self-sufficiency can make it easier for the abused spouse to leave and start a new life.

Changing Attitudes

In many areas of society, the terms "men's work" and "women's work" have lost their meaning. Most people no longer think that a person's *gender* (whether one is male or female) should determine the type of work one does.

At home, more women can be found taking care of the car, and more men cooking meals. In the working world, more men are becoming nurses, and more women are becoming police officers. It is illegal for an employer to refuse to hire someone because of gender.

Types of Work and Family Arrangements

Which is better, for a mother to be employed or to stay home with the children? Is it okay for a father to stay home to raise the children? What if both the mother and father want (or need) to work full-time? What if

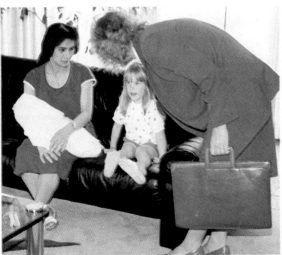

20-1
Many mothers with small children are employed outside the home.

Cholla Runnels

there is no father around? Families in our society have a variety of needs, values, preferences, and opportunities related to work and family roles. Each family must find the way of managing these roles that suits it best.

Dual-Worker Families

In some families, both the husband and the wife are employed. These are called *dual-worker* or *dual-career families.* If both spouses are committed to their jobs, they must work out ways to divide up household tasks fairly. They must also make time for satisfying family life.

Dual-worker families often find that finding high-quality care for children is a major concern. Often there are other family members, such as elderly or ill grandparents, who also require care. Two incomes may allow couples to purchase more services, including child and elder care, rather than doing everything themselves, 20-2.

Families with Part-Time Workers

Many families find that it works out well to have one spouse working full-time and the other part-time. *Part-time workers* work less than a full work week and thus have more time to focus on raising the children and managing the household.

In addition to childrearing, typical responsibilities include such things as food shopping; cooking and cleaning up after meals; keeping the family's clothing clean and in good repair; providing a clean, safe, pleasant home environment; managing family finances; and caring for ill family members. The part-time worker usually cannot take on all the responsibility for all of these tasks. However, part-time work does free up some time that can be devoted to homemaking.

Families with Full-Time Homemakers

Only one family in ten now fits the traditional pattern of husband as full-time breadwinner, wife as full-time homemaker, and children at home. However, full-time homemaking is a legitimate, responsible, worthwhile career for either husbands or wives.

A spouse who stays home today is not rewarded with paychecks or job promotions. Instead, the homemaker finds pride and satisfaction in caring for the family, 20-3. Family members should show their appreciation for this work.

Homemakers provide many services that would otherwise have to be purchased or pro-

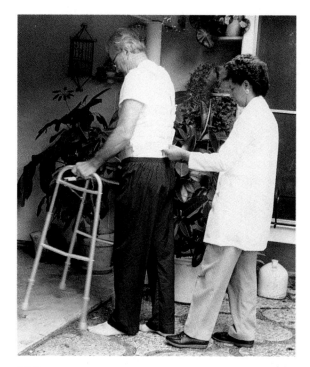

20-2
With two incomes, spouses in dual-career families may be able to hire a physical therapist to help an elderly parent.

David Hopper

20-3
A full-time homemaker may find pride and satisfaction in caring for family members.

vided by other family members. These services typically include such things as child care (and sometimes elder care), meals, laundry, housework, furnishing and decorating the home, family financial management, driving children to medical appointments and after-school activities, caring for ill family members, and many other tasks. To avoid exhaustion, homemakers must establish priorities and make choices based on them.

Wage-earning spouses face challenges, too. They may feel the pressure of being the sole source of the family's support. Often, wage earners feel that they have little free time to spend with their families.

Displaced Homemakers

A full-time homemaker who is supported by a spouse may feel financially vulnerable in the event of divorce. *Displaced homemakers* are longtime homemakers whose husbands have left or remarried and whose children have grown. After a divorce, home-

makers may lose financial support, medical insurance coverage, and other sources of financial security that had been provided by their spouses. Displaced homemakers may find themselves unexpectedly dependent on their own resources for these things.

The financial situation of the displaced homemaker is of special concern in the later years of life. Some homemakers rely solely on Social Security benefits provided through their ex-husband's contributions. However, they usually find it difficult to make ends meet. Worse, some homemakers find that their marriage did not last long enough to qualify them for any lifelong Social Security benefits at all.

Some homemakers expect to receive *alimony*—financial support from the breadwinning spouse—after a marriage breaks up. However, the current trend is for courts to award only *rehabilitative alimony*—financial support for job retraining—rather than lifelong support.

Homemakers who drop out of the workforce for long periods of time are at risk of becoming displaced homemakers. They can protect themselves to some degree by obtaining as much education and job training as possible.

Single-Parent Families

The single parent faces the double challenge of trying to be both mother and father to the children in addition to providing for the family's support. The challenge is even greater if the parent lacks sufficient education or training to get a job that will make ends meet.

More than six out of ten teenage mothers have not completed high school by the time they have had their first child. Some will go on to receive a high school diploma, and a few may even go to college. However, women who bear children in their teens are less likely to complete their educations. Until they do, they will find it more difficult to get a job and support their families. They are at risk of living in poverty.

Although some single parents receive child support, many receive only partial payments or none at all. Congress has passed several laws designed to improve the rate of child support payment. Improved enforcement of child support will probably ease—but not eliminate—the problem of women and children living in poverty.

Members of single-parent families have a special responsibility to pitch in with household tasks. Often, the older children can help out by looking out for and taking care of the younger ones.

Each of the above work and family arrangements involves sacrifices as well as rewards for each member of the family. Each family member needs to recognize and appreciate the pressures faced by the others. Still, family members all have each other. Together, they can work toward a satisfying and fulfilling lifestyle.

Patterns of Work and Childbearing

If a career-oriented couple want to have children, when is the best time to have their first child? Soon after marriage? Or after they have finished their educations and acquired some job experience? How many children should they have? Is it necessary for every couple to have a child?

Most women today, compared to previous generations, are marrying later, having fewer children, and having children at a later age. Since 1960, the average age at first marriage for women has risen from 20.3 years to 23.9 years. For men, it has risen from 22.8 years to 26.1 years.

On average, women are having about two children today, compared with 3.7 children in the late 1950s. Couples are also choosing to have their first child later in life. Today, on average, a child is born within 27 months of the parents' wedding. In the late 1950s and early 1960s, couples on average had their first child within only 15 months of their wedding.

Many women are currently waiting even longer—until they are over age 30—to have a baby. At present, nearly one birth in three in our country is to a mother over 30.

Delaying childbearing for a reasonable time has many advantages. A couple can establish healthy patterns of work and family life without the added complications of children. Spouses can finish their educations and get started on their careers, 20-4. They can also gain a sense of themselves and each other as wage earners.

Cholla Runnels

20-4
Many couples are delaying childrearing until they have completed their educations.

Also, one spouse may choose later in life to become a part-time or full-time homemaker. Then the other spouse will remember a time when the homemaking spouse was a respected wage earner in the outside world. The homemaker will be less likely to be viewed as a "servant." If the homemaking spouse later decides to return to work, a reliable work history will help in finding a job. This is especially true if the homemaker's job skills have been kept current.

The drawbacks of delaying childbearing are mainly those associated with older parenthood. Women over 30 are at somewhat higher risk for complications during pregnancy than younger women. Also, keeping up with high-energy toddlers is easier when parents are younger themselves.

Is it okay to have only one child or to remain childless? Today, more women than in previous generations are choosing these options. Nearly one woman in five in her late thirties currently has not yet had a child. Another one woman in five has had only one child. Such choices are legitimate lifestyle options.

Impact of Work on Families

Have you ever had a bad day at school and later been out-of-sorts with your family? Maybe you have had trouble concentrating at school because of an argument you had earlier at home. Similar events happen once you enter the working world. What happens to workers at home affects their job performance, and what happens to workers on the job affects their family life.

Employment means many positive things to most families. It provides them with a means of support and often with other benefits such as Social Security and health insurance. Working fathers and mothers can serve as good role models for their children. They can teach them good work habits and ways of interacting effectively with others.

However, work makes demands on families, too. Workers have less time available to spend with their families and friends. They also have less time for community activities.

In dual-worker families, quality child and elder care often must be found. Somehow, household tasks must also get done. Balancing work and family demands becomes especially challenging during illness and times of family crisis. An example of a family crisis is a serious illness of another family member. Such a crisis, stressful in itself, can be even more stressful for someone trying to hold down a job.

Working parents with a young child in day care may miss some memorable moments in their child's life. They are likely to feel disappointment if the caregiver—not the parent—is the one who witnesses the child's first step or first word. If the parents have chosen a good caregiver, however, they will find comfort in knowing that the child is in good hands.

Before a couple commits to marriage and a family, they should discuss each other's expectations regarding children. If a child becomes ill, does one spouse expect the other to always be the one to miss work to care for the child? What about the sharing of household chores? See 20-5. Having a clear understanding about such matters before marriage can save much stress later on.

As you have seen, career and family have a direct effect on each other. Employees who are satisfied at home tend to be more productive at work. On the other hand, if work and family roles are not managed effectively, work performance suffers and family relations may become strained. As families learn to balance both roles, all members can reach their full potential. An attitude of empathy and cooperation can go a long way toward making even the most difficult day bearable.

How Families Are Influencing the Workplace

Legislators and many business executives are recognizing the new realities of family and work patterns discussed above. They are putting policies in place to help workers meet their family responsibilities. Employers are finding that such measures can be workable and *cost-effective* (economical in terms of benefits yielded by money invested).

Family and Medical Leave Act

The *Family and Medical Leave Act* of 1991 entitles workers to 12 weeks of unpaid leave per year following the birth or adoption of a child. This time can also be used to care for a seriously ill relative or to take care of a serious personal health condition. At the end of the leave period, a worker has the right to get his or her former job—or a comparable one—back.

Under the Act, an employer may require that the worker use up some vacation or personal time for part of the time the worker is gone. Benefits may be more extensive in some states. (For information on benefits in your state, contact your state attorney general's office.)

The Family and Medical Leave Act applies only to businesses with 50 or more employees. Sixty-six percent of U.S. workers are covered under this law. Smaller businesses are exempt, though they may have leave policies of their own.

Employer-Sponsored Child Care

Offering parental leave is just one of a number of ways businesses have reacted to the need for child care. Some businesses provide on-site child care. An *on-site child care facility* is one that is provided by the employer at or near the job site. This allows parents to be near their children. They may even share lunch times.

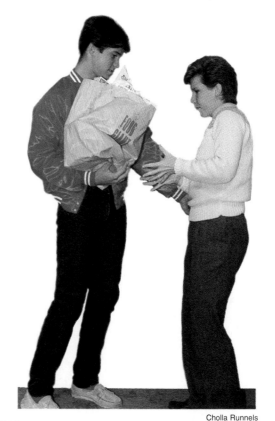

Cholla Runnels

20-5
Before they are married, couples should discuss how they will share household chores.

Some companies offer to pay for all or part of the child care costs in place of other benefits. Parents may receive a voucher or coupon worth a certain amount of money from the company. Parents can then select their own form of child care. Other companies provide flexible work schedules that allow parents to work at times when good substitute child care is available. With flexible work schedules, some parents can arrange to have one parent with their children at all times.

Flexible Work Schedules

Many companies now offer employees the option of varying their work schedules to accommodate family responsibilities.

Flextime

One option, called *flextime,* allows the worker to choose his or her own working hours, subject to certain rules. Under flextime, firms require their employees to put in part of their hours during a specified time each day, for example, from 10:00 a.m. to 3:00 p.m. The employee puts in the remainder of his or her hours either before or after that period of time.

Flextime offers employees greater flexibility in coordinating work and family schedules. For example, employees who can come to work early may be finished with their day's work in time to pick up their children from school, 20-6.

Block Scheduling

Another option offering flexibility is block scheduling. *Block scheduling* allows employees to work 40 hours (a typical work week) in three or four days. This way, workers can have at least one weekday available for family responsibilities.

David Hopper

20-6
Flextime allows this couple to have a parent with the children at all times, saving child care costs.

Job Sharing

With *job sharing,* companies allow two employees to share one full-time job. Together with their supervisor, the two employees find mutually agreeable ways of fulfilling the functions of the job. Frequent communication between the two workers and with the supervisor is key to making job sharing a success.

Employee-Assistance Programs

Another way that some companies are offering support to workers and their families is through *employee-assistance programs (EAPs).* EAP staff can counsel employees faced with problems such as alcoholism or other substance abuse, family illness, financial debt, or finding child or elder care. If necessary, EAP staff can refer employees to outside services.

Some workers hesitate to share personal problems with EAP staff out of fear that their confidentiality will not be respected. Employees may find it helpful to talk with co-workers who have used these services before deciding whether to participate.

Legislators' and companies' efforts to help employees meet family responsibilities involve complex issues. However, progress is being made as the challenges of balancing family and work demands become apparent throughout society. Many policymakers and companies are looking at what other countries are doing to learn how best to help workers. See 20-7.

The Swedish Institute

Child Care in Sweden

Sweden has established an extensive system of government-supported child care for children of workers. About 60 percent of preschool children attend child care centers, usually municipally operated and financed by the municipal and national governments as well as by parent fees. Other small children receive home care, half of them from a parent who is being paid by the parental insurance system. The Swedish government also guarantees that women who take time off to have children will have a job when they come back to work. Parents are provided up to 12 months of maternity or paternity leave at 80 percent of full pay. In addition, parents may take up to 120 days of leave per year, at 80 percent of full pay, to care for a sick child age 12 or younger. Opponents of this type of government involvement point out the high personal income tax paid by Swedish citizens.

20-7
The government of Sweden provides many family-related benefits for workers.

Realities of the Workplace ▪ ▪ ▪ ▪ ▪ ▪

Both men and women may sometimes face challenging situations at work that occur simply because of their gender. For instance, it is illegal for a company to ask prospective employees if they are married or how they intend to handle their child care. However, some people are faced with such questions in job interviews.

Women may also be discriminated against when they become pregnant. The Pregnancy Discrimination Act of 1978 requires that pregnant employees be treated the same as employees with temporary disabilities. This law applies to all employers who provide disability insurance or paid sick leave.

Sexual harassment—making off-color remarks and jokes or making sexual overtures toward employees—is also illegal. Men as well as women may be victims of this type of behavior. Sometimes, a worker may be able to discourage inappropriate behavior such as this by maintaining a businesslike attitude. In serious cases of sexual harassment, victims may need to seek counseling from the companies' personnel office. They may even need to seek outside legal help.

Women have made great advances toward equal treatment at home and in the workplace in recent decades, 20-8. However, many challenges remain. Today, women make on average only 70 cents for every dollar made by a man in a comparable job. At home, many dual-worker husbands do not yet share equally in the child care and household tasks. Sensitivity to such issues throughout society is needed for full equality to be achieved.

Techniques for Managing Family and Work ▪ ▪ ▪ ▪ ▪ ▪ ▪

As you have seen, a dual-worker lifestyle gives spouses many opportunities for sharing. They share financial burdens, and they share home and family tasks. However, sharing does not necessarily mean a 50-50 split on each and every task.

Although older children can help out with home chores, they must still be given time to do their schoolwork. They may also be involved in extracurricular activities. Each

David Hopper

20-8
More women are employed outside the home, but they earn less pay than men in comparable jobs.

family must work out its own plan, according to each member's abilities, preferences, and school or work schedule.

Getting Organized

Organization is absolutely essential to juggling the demands of marriage, children, and a job. Being organized means wearing different "hats" at different times, setting priorities and standards, and planning ahead. It also means learning to schedule, to delegate tasks, and to communicate effectively.

Fulfilling Multiple Roles

Many adults feel torn about the many roles they must play. Sometimes, they may wonder, "Am I a worker who happens to have a spouse and children or am I a spouse and parent who happens to work?"

Both work and family roles are important. Most people find that when they are at work, they wear an imaginary hat labeled "worker." When they leave the workplace, they put on an imaginary hat labeled "family member."

Sometimes, of course, it's not so simple. You may be absorbed in the work at your desk when the phone rings and the caregiver informs you that your child is seriously ill. Maybe you are looking forward to a weekend with the family when the boss asks you to work on a report over the weekend. In situations such as these, flexibility, a supportive spouse, and a positive attitude can help you cope.

Setting Priorities and Standards

Setting priorities means deciding which of a day's tasks are "must do's," which are "nice-to-do's," and which can be put off until a later time. Priorities are influenced by values—ideas about what is important. Most workers find that making lists of tasks is helpful. They then rank the tasks according to priority, scratching them off the list as completed. Setting priorities helps workers get the important tasks done each day.

Setting standards for how well a job needs to be done is important, too. For example, some families set a high standard for how a bedroom should look before family members leave for work or school. They believe the bed should be made very neatly. Other families have lower standards of neatness. The neatness of a bedroom is not a matter of right and wrong, but rather of the individual family's preference.

Most families have high standards in some areas, and lower standards in others. To hold standards of perfection in all areas sets the family up for feelings of frustration, stress, and failure. Having lower standards in areas that are less important can free up time and energy to focus on more important areas.

Scheduling and Planning Ahead

Many busy working parents find that a calendar with space for recording appointments is a valuable aid in keeping track of after-school activities and other commitments. A calendar can also help parents avoid scheduling conflicts. For instance, you would not want to make a dental appointment at the same time you have committed to take your ten-year-old to baseball practice.

Planning ahead means thinking about how tasks can best be accomplished in the time allotted. It also means saving money and vacation days for use in emergencies. For example, you may use up all your vacation time and then get a phone call informing you that your elderly mother has fallen and broken her hip. In order to help her in this crisis, you may have to take leave without pay.

Saving part of family paychecks for unexpected expenses is also important. Sometimes, money can be substituted for time if time is more valuable. For example, let's say you are planning to leave work early to bake

Contemporary Concerns *of today's teens:*
Sharing Household Chores: What's Fair?

Despite the increase in dual-worker households, studies show that married women on average spend much more time on household chores than their husbands. Perhaps because of their traditional roles as full-time homemakers, employed women may feel more responsible for planning and doing more of the housework. As a result, many women are unable to put in the extra on-the-job hours needed to advance in their careers.

Husbands are doing more housework today than they were several decades ago. However, those husbands who see themselves as primary breadwinners are less likely to share equally in household tasks than other husbands. Men who believe that their wife's income is essential to the family's well-being are more likely to put in more hours working around the house.

For a happy marriage and a smoothly running household, each couple must arrive at its own housework-sharing arrangements. The arrangements must be viewed as fair by both spouses and should reflect each spouse's time, skills, and preferences. Some couples like to rotate work responsibilities; others do not. Some couples prefer to lower their standards so that fewer hours of housework are necessary each week. Others opt to pay for outside help. The best solution is the one that works best for the individual couple.

a birthday cake for your child. However, just before you leave, the boss asks you to stay late and work on a project. If money is available, you can stay late at work and buy a birthday cake at the bakery on your way home.

The family member who plans ahead can make each day of the week go more smoothly. Some workers pack family sack lunches on the weekends, when they have more time, and stow them in the freezer for the week ahead. Parents with young children may wish to assemble the child's clothing, including socks and underwear, for each day of the week on a separate closet hanger. This technique may make dressing the child go faster on weekday mornings, when time is short.

Delegating Tasks Effectively

Delegating—or assigning—tasks is one way to maintain a fair distribution of household work among family members. Tasks should be assigned with the abilities, preferences, and schedules of family members in mind. If the task is new, clear instructions should be given. Even if results are less than perfect at first, family members should be praised and encouraged, 20-9.

Family members should try to be kind and patient with one another while new skills are being learned. Some women complain that their husbands don't help with cooking, but ridicule their husbands' efforts when they do attempt to cook.

Husbands, too, may be impatient with their wives in teaching them a household fix-it job. They may give them hurried, unclear directions and then brush their wives aside, sighing, "Never mind, I'll do it myself."

Learning new home and work skills is a lifelong process. Family members can contribute a great deal to each other's development if they can maintain a loving, encouraging attitude at these times.

Communicating

Good communication between family members is very important to balancing work and family demands successfully. The family member coordinating the household tasks needs to give and receive information regularly to keep things on track.

At home, family members can use phone calls, notes posted on the refrigerator, and other ways to keep each other informed. At work, an employee can use a break or part of the lunch hour to keep in touch. A quick phone call can make a big difference to an elderly family member facing a lonely day, a teenager who has come home from school to an empty house, or a spouse facing a stressful business meeting.

Spending Quality Time

Quality time refers to time you spend giving your full attention to another person or persons. Working parents who find quality time for children and each other usually have a more satisfying family life.

When you were young, do you remember how important it was to tell Mom or Dad

David Hopper

20-9
Each family member can contribute to a smoothly running household.

of the day's events when you came home from school? Maybe it is still important. Many parents find that their children need them most when they first see each other after work. In their quality time together, parents can pay special attention to their children. They can listen to their stories about the day's events and provide guidance and affection. It may also be the time to read them a story or to enjoy a recreational activity together. See 20-10.

At the heart of all successful family life are values of love, sharing, support, communication, forgiveness, and appreciation. There is also the simple enjoyment of belonging to a family circle. Management techniques such as setting priorities and making lists are meant to be tools to enhance family life—not ends in themselves.

There are times when even the most careful plans just don't work out. A patient, problem-solving attitude at such times can make a big difference in the life of each member of your family.

When children become adults, they are more likely to value and remember the emotional quality of their family life together than the spotlessness of the house. It will be more important that their parents found time for them than that the parents got everything on their lists accomplished each day.

The time that family members share nourishes lifelong bonds. These ties are based on love, affection, and memories of shared experiences. The love that family members feel for one another will endure throughout life—long after one's working days are over.

David Hopper

20-10
These working parents find the time to give their children loving attention at the end of a busy day.

Summary ▪ ▪ ▪ ▪ ▪ ▪ ▪ ▪ ▪ ▪ ▪ ▪ ▪ ▪ ▪

- In our country, most adults—both women and men—are employed for major portions of their lives.

- Working outside the home provides the family with financial security as well as opportunities for self-expression, personal growth, and satisfying relationships with co-workers.

- In recent decades, society has become more supportive of nontraditional, non-gender-based roles at home and at work.

- Types of work and family arrangements include dual-worker families; families in which one spouse works part-time in order to devote more time to homemaking; families with full-time homemakers; and working single-parent families.

- Although full-time homemaking is a legitimate career choice, the homemaker is financially vulnerable if the wage earner's income is lost. Full-time homemakers can protect themselves to some degree by acquiring as much education and job training as possible.

- Today, more U.S. women are balancing the responsibilities of child-rearing and paid work than ever before.

- Compared with earlier periods in this century, women are marrying later, having children later, and having fewer children. Many women are choosing to finish their educations and establish themselves in careers before having children.

- Because contented family members make more productive employees, many companies are searching for ways to help their employees meet family responsibilities.

- Increasing numbers of companies are offering family and medical leave, employer-sponsored child care, flexible work schedules, and employee-assistance programs.

- Although it is illegal, workers are sometimes subjected to discriminatory gender-based hiring and promotion practices as well as sexual harassment in the workplace.

- Techniques for balancing family and work demands include: switching roles or wearing different "hats" at different times; setting priorities and standards based on values; scheduling and planning ahead; delegating tasks effectively; and communicating.

- Spending quality time with family members is important to preserving a close and loving relationship.

To Review ■ ■ ■ ■ ■ ■ ■ ■ ■ ■ ■ ■ ■ ■

1. List three reasons for wanting to be employed.

2. Name four basic types of work and family arrangements, and describe one advantage and one disadvantage of each type.

3. What is a displaced homemaker?

4. Why are more married couples today having children later in life compared to 30 years ago?

5. Briefly summarize the impact of work on families.

6. Explain the basic provisions of the Family and Medical Leave Act.

7. Match each of the following with its descriptive phrase.
    _____ Block scheduling
    _____ Job sharing
    _____ Employer-sponsored child care
    _____ Flextime
    _____ Employee-assistance programs
    a. Child care provided at the workplace, or care provided elsewhere and paid for by the company for whom the employee works.
    b. Compressing the hours in a full work week into fewer days.
    c. Assistance on personal problems provided by the company for whom the employee works.
    d. An arrangement in which two workers carry out the functions of one job.
    e. An arrangement that allows workers to come to work early or stay late as long as they are present during a certain specified range of time each day.

8. True or False. Women—but not men—can experience gender-based discrimination in the workplace.

9. Describe how setting priorities can help family life run more smoothly.

10. Define quality time and explain its importance in family life.

To Do ■ ■ ■ ■ ■ ■ ■ ■ ■ ■ ■ ■ ■ ■ ■ ■

1. Research and evaluate the personnel policies of three companies in your area. How "family friendly" are their policies? How could their policies be improved?

2. Identify a recent family television program illustrating the balancing of work and family life. What type of work and family arrangement does the family have? What conflicts arise, and how are they resolved? Present your findings to the class in an oral report.

3. Interview a family friend or relative who had her first child after age 30. Did her wish to build a career influence her decision about when to have a child? Is she happy with her decision? Why or why not? Does she believe that there are any drawbacks to waiting until after age 30 to have a child? Summarize the interview in a confidential written report.

4. Role play an exhausted working mom enlisting the cooperation of her teenage son and daughter in sharing more of the household chores. Who ends up doing what? Is the type and level of work assigned to each family member fair? Why or why not?

5. List 10 common household tasks. Rank them in order of priority based on your personal value system. Then indicate the standard of quality you hold for each task by writing "high," "medium," or "low" beside each item. What if your future spouse has different priorities and standards? Discuss methods of resolving such conflicts.

6. Discuss the following statements:
   a. Women workers should feel flattered when male co-workers comment on their physical attractiveness.
   b. Workers should feel free to call other workers of the opposite sex "dear" and "honey" to express their affection.
   c. Women who "flirt" with their male bosses are more likely to get a promotion.
   d. Men who "flirt" with their female bosses are more likely to get a promotion.

21

Dealing with Family Crises

After studying this chapter, you will be able to

- identify resources that can help people handle crises.

- explain how to cope with crises.

- describe specific types of family crises.

All people have problems, but the ways people handle problems differ greatly. Some people magnify unimportant matters into gigantic problems. Other people absorb serious problems and maintain happy, successful lives. What is the nature of crises, and why do people meet crises so differently?

A *crisis* can be defined as a crucial time or event that causes a change in a person's life. A crisis situation is one that has no ready solution. Time is needed for adjustments to be made.

To some people, a crisis is the end to happiness and achievement. They live the rest of their lives wishing to relive their pasts and dreading their futures. To others, a crisis serves as an incentive to achieve new and different goals, 21-1.

Terms to Know

crisis

shelters

telephone hotlines

intervention

enabler

codependency

compulsive gambler

chasing

bailout

depression

violence

domestic violence

child abuse and neglect

physical abuse

physical neglect

sexual abuse

incest

emotional abuse

emotional neglect

halfway houses

21-1

Crises give some people even greater incentives to live productive lives.

Resources to Help Withstand Crises ■ ■ ■

Why do some people manage to survive a crisis while others seem to "fall apart?" One difference is that those who handle crises well have incorporated resources for handling crises into their lives. Through the years, they have prepared themselves for the unexpected. They have mental, physical, financial, and social resources that can help them through crisis situations. They also know what community resources are available to them.

Mental Resources

Mental resources allow people to cope with the complexities and unpredictable elements of a crisis. Mental resources are the internal props that help people withstand external pressures.

In some crisis situations, people need courage to make changes and to follow new plans of action. A crisis may actually improve a person's life if the person reacts positively and makes the best of the situation.

In other crisis situations, people need courage to accept what cannot be changed. Accepting the finality of a crisis can be difficult. Sometimes the only way to make a situation tolerable is to change your attitude. For instance, parents who learn that their newborn has a congenital disability may have difficulty accepting this fact. Because this type of crisis may be irreversible, they will have to change their attitudes and accept reality. Endlessly going over reasons why the crisis happened delays acceptance. When they can accept it, they will find the strength to go on. Some people find the strength to meet crises within themselves. Others find the strength in their religious beliefs, 21-2.

Physical Health

Most people feel that if they have good physical health, they can handle anything. See 21-3. Good health is a rich resource that people can use to meet the demands of crisis situations.

An interesting aspect of physical health is that people can demonstrate unusual phys-

21-2

Some people find the strength to handle crises in their religious beliefs.

ical strength during a crisis. Under stress, the human body produces the hormone adrenaline which makes the heart beat faster and causes the body to react with increased energy. Adrenaline provides the strength to move extremely heavy objects to free persons trapped under them. Adrenaline also gives parents increased energy to get help when their children are injured. Pediatricians can cite many cases in which a parent somehow gets a child to a hospital even though the parent is also injured. Once the parent knows the child is receiving good care, then the parent may collapse from his or her own injuries.

Wm. E. Barnhart

21-4
A crisis usually involves a large amount of money.

Cholla Runnels

21-3
Good health gives people the confidence to feel they can meet any challenge.

Financial Resources

Many crises involve increases in spending, 21-4. Many times the spending demands of a crisis become so great that they cause financial instability—another crisis.

The majority of personal bankruptcies result from sudden, large monetary needs caused by illness or injury. This is why insurance protection is so important. Car, property, health, and life insurance can help people meet the high cost of a crisis.

Savings that are easily accessible are helpful. It is also beneficial if both spouses are completely knowledgeable concerning the financial affairs of the family.

Family Relationships

In most marriage vows, husbands and wives promise to support each other in both good times and bad times. The partnership may be easier during the good times, but it is more important during the bad times.

Particularly in a crisis situation, the relationships within the family must remain strong, 21-5. The problem causing the crisis should not become more important than the family itself. Families that successfully meet crises are those in which family members love and care for each other. Together, the members adapt to the changes that must be made.

Some of the changes made during crises are changes in the roles of family members. The role changes may be either temporary or permanent. During a severe illness, a child may require the care of a nurse and therapist. A family member who learns to massage and exercise the child's muscles may help the child recuperate. By taking on the roles of nurse and therapist during the crisis period, the family member helps the entire family. Imagine another crisis situation in which the wage earner for a family has a heart attack and is unable to work. The spouse may have to take on the role of wage earner for the family. A refusal to accept role changes in ei-

ther of these situations would mean greater problems for the family.

Parents should allow their children to help the family adapt to a crisis. If children are not allowed to become a part of the family's struggle, they may feel they are a part of the problem. Children can sense when something is wrong. If they are told that nothing is wrong, they begin to question themselves. In some instances, they may feel they caused the crisis. This can create greater problems for the family. Children need to feel they are needed. Parents may be pleasantly surprised by the help their children want to give during a crisis. When all is well, children may not offer much help. In a crisis, their sense of involvement becomes greater, and they want to help.

Sometimes a crisis may actually pull a family together. The drug involvement of a teenager may shake a family out of its complacency. The teenager may be able to solve his or her problem when the whole family is supportive. Once family members begin to work together on one problem, they are likely to continue to function as a unit.

Support of Friends

The emotional support of relatives, friends, and neighbors helps families face emergencies. If you have ever witnessed the outpouring of support to a family during a crisis, you realize how important this help can be.

Relatives, friends, and neighbors will help in emergency situations. However, any long-term assistance may be difficult because they are involved with their own families' needs. The family can then turn to community resources.

Cholla Runnels

21-5
Strong family relationships can help people withstand a crisis such as unexpected bad news.

Community Resources

Individuals and families are primarily responsible for their own well-being. However, in a crisis situation, these same people may need help from other sources. Many community resources provide services to individuals and families. In previous generations, a network of extended family members may have helped. Today, with more family members living apart, the role of community agencies has become more important.

Various community resources are described in 21-6. Some of the resources listed are national organizations that might have local chapters. If a phone number for an organization is not listed in the white pages of your phone directory, contact your public library. A librarian can help you find the address and phone number for the national office.

If your community is small, the available resources may be limited. In large urban areas, there may be many community resources. Often, however, individuals and families are not familiar with their services. Try to become familiar with the community resources that are available in your area.

Shelters

Shelters are establishments that offer food and housing for people who have nowhere else to go. Most communities have realized the need to provide help for those individuals and families who are in need of food, clothing, and shelter. Some shelters are specifically planned to provide protection for people who are victims of domestic violence or sexual abuse.

Many people find themselves in crisis situations where they need protection immediately. Battered women, often with their children, need to escape their abusive environments. Shelters for battered women provide housing, child care, and emotional support, as well as counseling and legal services. Shelter staff help find permanent housing for victims as their lives become more stable. Phone numbers for Battered Women's Centers are usually listed in the community services sections in the front of phone books. Police departments and hospitals can also refer people to these shelters.

Hotlines

Telephone hotlines offer an immediate source of information for individuals who need help in a crisis. Most are toll-free 800 numbers. Some hotlines are managed locally and can be reached with a local number. Many hotlines can be used at any hour of the day or night. A person familiar with the particular crisis situation will answer the phone, offer guidance, and refer callers to local services.

Hotlines are typically available for those seeking information about child abuse, drug abuse, AIDS, STDs, and missing children. A runaway can call a runaway hotline that will contact the child's parents to assure them that the child is okay. If young people do not want to reveal their location, the phone call can at least reassure parents of their well-being. See the white pages of your phone directory for a listing of hotlines available in your community.

Intervention

Sometimes the person in a crisis has lost the ability to handle or control the situation. Through intervention, an outside professional trained in handling such a crisis can bring about changes that might not otherwise occur.

Intervention is a means of forcing a person to look at his or her behavior without the mask of denial. The aim of intervention is to convince the individual, such as an addict or alcoholic, that he or she needs help before he

Community Resources

Resource	Clientele	Services
Alcoholics Anonymous	Alcoholics.	Free, local, self-help groups that follow rules of strict anonymity in overcoming alcoholism.
Al-Anon and Alateen	Families of victims of alcoholism.	Local support groups for parents, children, and friends of alcoholic victims.
American Red Cross	Provides services to families in the community.	Provides food, shelter, and other essentials to disaster victims and families in emergencies. Promotes health and safety awareness.
Battered Women's Center	Provides help for victims of family violence.	Offers shelter, counseling, public education, and advocacy for victims. Centers provide shelter, food, and clothing for victims and their children.
Big Brothers and Big Sisters	Provides adult companionship for children from single-parent families.	One-to-one relationship between adult volunteers and children, ages 7 to 15, from one-parent families. Adult provides guidance, social contact, and academic enrichment through regular weekly contacts.
Aid to Families with Dependent Children	Families with children in need of assistance.	A government program that provides cash payments to families with needy children deprived of parental support because of death, absence, or incapacity of one or both parents.
Children's Protective Services (Agency name may vary)	Children who are in need of protection due to abuse, neglect, abandonment, or sexual exploitation.	This government agency assigns social workers to supervise families against whom there have been complaints of abuse and/or neglect. In severe cases, the agency will remove children from the home and provide substitute care, supervision, and related services for the children.
Family Counseling Center	Individuals, families, and groups needing counseling.	Family, marital, parent-child, and individual counseling are provided. Efforts are made to improve interpersonal relationships and family living.
YMCA YWCA	The general public.	Programs include child care, camping, health and fitness groups, informal education, older youth programs, parent-child programs, senior citizen programs, and other related services.

21-6
These are just some of the many community resources available to help families in crises.

United Way of Houston

21-7
Support groups can help young people as they battle their addictions.

or she "hits bottom." This is done by bringing together family members and other important people in the person's life. These people speak truthfully, out of love, confronting the addict with specific details of his or her problem. The outcome in successful intervention is that the person admits the problem and voluntarily enters treatment. Intervention is direct and forceful, but it may bring about the change that is necessary for the well-being of the entire family.

Support Groups

Support groups may be available in your community to help individuals or families through specific crisis situations. Support

groups are usually made up of persons or family members who have experienced a similar crisis situation. Because they have gone through the same situation, the persons in the group can offer first-hand information and advice. They can offer empathy, give advice for using different resources, and recommend specific persons or services. Listening to other people who have gone through similar situations can help a person sustain a positive attitude through a very difficult time. See 21-7.

Individuals and families experience many different crises. In most communities, a variety of support groups can be found. Those individuals or families who have a crisis created by drug abuse may be able to find a support group such as Al-Anon and Ala-teen. Parents with children suffering from severe illnesses may find support from other parents whose children have cystic fibrosis, diabetes, multiple sclerosis, or other health concerns. Families with persons suffering from severe mental health problems may find support in groups such as Helping Hands, Covenant House, and Recovery, Inc. Local churches and synagogues often sponsor various support groups. (See Chapter 7 for a list of support groups.)

Coping with Crises ■ ▪

You may believe that the strongest and healthiest families are those that have never had to cope with a crisis. In fact, the strongest families are probably those who have experienced a crisis and have been able to come through it.

Crises are inevitable. They can occur at different stages of life and in different degrees of severity. As you look ahead to your life, you will benefit from establishing the resources just described. You will still need to know the four steps to follow in coping with a crisis.

Recognize the Existence of a Crisis

The first step in coping with a crisis is to recognize that a crisis does exist. In some situations, the crisis is undeniable, such as when a death occurs or a person loses a job. Even in these situations, however, a person may respond with disbelief, denial, or total shock. In other cases, a crisis might not be immediately recognizable. A person who has an alcohol problem may not realize that he or she has become an alcoholic. The problem develops over time and the alcoholic may deny that

there is a crisis. Family members may need to seek intervention before the alcoholic will recognize the existence of a crisis.

Seek Alternative Solutions to the Crisis

The second step in coping with a crisis is to identify alternative solutions to the crisis. Solutions that will benefit all family members with the least possible negative effects should be sought. If the family has established a good foundation of resources, the solution may be found within the family unit itself. Adequate financial resources and the support of friends and other family members may be sufficient to withstand the crisis. Available community resources may need to be identified.

Even though the primary impact of the crisis may affect only one person, the entire family needs to recognize how the crisis will change the lives of every family member. If the crisis is a serious illness, this means that family members will not be able to function in their normal roles for a period of time. If the ill person is the main wage earner, others may have to help out either by seeking employment or by reducing spending. In most families, both of these have to be initiated. Care for the ill person will have to be supplied either by family members or by hiring a home health-care aide. Schedules may need to be adjusted and obligations outside the home reduced.

When evaluating alternatives, all family members whose lives are affected should be a part of the decision-making process. Underlying these decisions is the importance of communication among family members, including small children who may need help in understanding what is happening.

Once the alternatives have been reviewed and the family has decided on a direction to take, everyone can focus on resolving the crisis. Having a plan can help family members to focus on positive outcomes rather than living in dread of what lies ahead. Family members can begin to get on with their lives.

Look to Each Other for Support

When a crisis occurs, family members should look to each other for support. Some family members may be overwhelmed by the crisis and become emotionally distraught. They may not know what to do or where to turn, 21-8. These family members need help in coping with the crisis. This help can come from other members of the family or close personal friends.

Offer encouragement to those who need it. Be there to listen, and encourage the sharing of personal concerns and feelings. Knowing that there are people who love them and understand the difficulties they face can help family members through the most trying crises.

Resume Efforts to Achieve Personal and Family Goals

Most crisis situations eventually come to an end. Adjustments are made, health is restored, or a solution is found. Life begins to return to normal. Family members can resume efforts to achieve personal and family goals.

Due to the crisis, however, the means of achieving certain goals may need to be adjusted. For instance, a teenage family member may have been counting on going to college. If the family's savings have been depleted as a result of the crisis, the teen may have to attend a local community college the first year or two. Another alternative would be to take a year off from school to work full-

Cholla Runnels

21-8
Some people do not know where to turn for help during a crisis. They need the support of family members and friends.

time and build up a college savings fund. It is important that personal and family goals be maintained—they may just take a little longer to achieve.

Seeking Stability in Crisis

The rest of this chapter examines various types of crises. You will not be faced with all of the crises discussed here, for not every family encounters every crisis. However, as you study the following crises, try to determine how you would react to each one. Someday, you may be able to use this information as a frame of reference. Most people say that one of the worst aspects of a crisis is the element of the unknown. If through this study you become familiar with these crises, the impact of a future related crisis in your life may be lessened.

Unemployment ■ ■ ■ ■

Unemployment occurs both in times of recession and in times of prosperity. In a recession, unemployment is more common, and many will share the same fate. During prosperity, the unemployed are surrounded by the sights and sounds of prosperity, and their isolation and despair may increase.

The threat of unemployment may force people to retrain themselves for other occupations. If their skills are no longer in demand, they should investigate what jobs are available and what skills are needed for those jobs. Many industries offer training programs. Community colleges and vocational schools also offer programs that teach valuable skills.

What happens in families when unemployment becomes a reality? The first and most important step is for family members to be supportive of the unemployed person. See 21-9. If people are out of work, the attitudes of their families can make the difference between financial failure or a comeback. Without their family's support, the crisis of unemployment may be too much for them to handle. Jobless people may turn to alcohol or drugs. They may abandon their families and be content to live on welfare. Some may even become so discouraged that they consider suicide. A positive attitude is the best resource for avoiding disaster and overcoming the crisis of unemployment.

Financial Decisions Related to Unemployment

When a family faces the crisis of unemployment, a program of financial "first aid" must be followed. The family members should sit down and work together as a unit. They should assess all their obligations and make a family budget. The situation may be less serious than they first thought once they find out just where they stand.

The family's next step is to talk to their creditors. If they go to the creditors with a logical repayment program and obvious good intentions, the creditors may accept smaller monthly payments.

The whole family should be aware of the crisis. Children want to take part in the family's efforts and plans. They may offer to help by reducing their spending or by doing odd jobs in the neighborhood. No budget is workable until all members of the family understand it and agree to stick to it.

Unemployment can cause massive changes in the lives of family members. Savings are depleted, and feelings of security are

Cholla Runnels

21-9
The support and encouragement of family members can help a person overcome the crisis of unemployment.

replaced by fears and tensions. The family may need to call on all of their resources to pull through the crisis.

Frequent Moves

The average family in the United States moves several times. Some businesses demand many relocations. People who accept jobs in such businesses expect to move as their careers develop.

What happens when family members are told they will have to move? They may feel a loss of power. When the security of their home is threatened, a feeling of vulnerability surrounds the entire family. They are not sure what the future will hold. They may be hesitant to leave their familiar surroundings.

Children may be especially upset if the move means leaving special friends. This loss is hard to compensate, but parents can help by involving the children in the move, 21-10. If possible, children should be allowed to help select the new home. They can help make plans for decorating. Then they will feel more a part of the move and view it in a positive way.

Once the family has moved, members still may refer to their old residence as "home." Refusing to accept the new residence may cause everyone in the family to be homesick. After the move, the family would be wiser to remember the former home as just that—a place where they used to live. The new residence deserves a chance to be called "home."

Some couples view frequent moves as opportunities to learn about different parts of the country. Other couples resent every move they have to make, and some may simply refuse to move. They decide the move is not worth the stress it causes their family.

If a move becomes a reality in your life, try to look at the positive aspects. Develop an

Cholla Runnels

21-10
Children will have a more positive attitude about moving if they are allowed to participate in the packing.

attitude of acceptance and anticipation. Make the most of the positive contributions the move can make in your life.

Addictions to Alcohol and Other Drugs

Drug addiction is one of the most far-reaching family crises. People addicted to alcohol or other drugs harm not only their own lives, but the lives of many people around them. Family members, friends, neighbors, and coworkers are all affected.

Addiction is the abuse of any drug that results in a physical or psychological need for the drug. The user has taken enough of the drug to cause the body and brain to need the drug to feel normal. If use of the drug is suddenly stopped, symptoms of withdrawal occur. The addicted person has lost control over his or her drinking or drug use. The drug is in control. The user's tolerance for the drug increases, requiring the user to take increasing amounts of the drug in order to feel its effects. When addicted, the user becomes preoccupied with obtaining the drug. (Refer to Chapter 8 for more information about alcoholism and the abuse of other drugs.)

What Causes a Person to Become Addicted to Alcohol or Other Drugs?

Alcohol causes alcoholism, the addiction to alcohol. If people do not drink, they do not become alcoholics. This is a simple answer to the question of cause, but it is true. The decision to drink or not to drink is an individual decision.

We live in a drinking society, and drinking alcoholic beverages is generally accepted. Some people drink responsibly, while others let their drinking get out of control. Many people who drink say that social pressure caused them to begin drinking, but other reasons compel people to drink beyond their capacity for control. The two most common reasons are job stress and family problems, but when alcohol takes control of a person's life, problems increase in these two areas, 21-11.

The use of other drugs has also increased in our society. Unlike alcohol, however, most of the abused drugs are illegal. Those who begin using drugs usually start with marijuana. As with alcohol, they are often introduced to the drug by friends in a social setting. The person experiments with the drug for "fun." Once people start using illegal drugs, they find additional reasons for continuing their use. They may use drugs in an attempt to escape their problems or to relax. They may feel drugs will give them an extra kick to help with a challenging task. Gradually they begin using more and more of the same drug, or trying new drugs, as their tolerance level changes. The drug is used regularly to cope with normal events. As side effects become more and more uncomfortable, alcohol and tranquilizers are used to try to calm the shakiness and unpleasant side effects. Users become preoccupied with obtaining drugs. Financial resources may be depleted, and work and home life are adversely affected. The user loses control of his or her drug use. The drug has taken control of the person's life.

How Do Alcoholism and Other Drug Addictions Affect Families?

Whenever a person becomes addicted to alcohol or any other drug, he or she can no longer behave in a completely responsible manner. The addicted person will suffer physically, emotionally, socially, and intellectually. If that person is a family member, the family will suffer as well. The drug abuser behaves in ways that hurt the very people he or she loves the most.

Small children do not understand why their mother is "sick" all the time or why their father acts "funny." Older children may realize what is happening and blame themselves for the problem. Teens avoid bringing friends home, and they try to hide the problem from others. Children of all ages tend to do poorly in school. These children may complain about their physical health in an attempt to receive the attention they are not getting at home. Mates learn not to count on

Cholla Runnels

21-11
Many alcoholics use alcohol to escape from family problems or job stress. Once professional counselors help alcoholics understand why they drink, the alcoholics have a better chance of quitting.

their addicted spouses, just as children learn not to count on their addicted parents.

Unfortunately, family members sometimes become "enablers" for the addict. An *enabler* is someone who unknowingly acts in ways that contribute to the addict's drug use. The significant people around addicts become enablers because they want to help the alcoholic or drug addict with his or her problem. In reality, they are destroying the ability of the addicted person to do for himself or herself. When an enabler sees that someone is in trouble and is not acting responsibly, the enabler tries to fill these needs. They actually take on responsibilities that the other person should be fulfilling.

All family members may become involved in helping the addicted person cover up his or her problem by denying that there is a problem. They may act to "rescue" the addict by lying for him or her. For instance, they might call and lie to an employer if the family member is too drunk to go to work. Instead of helping the person, the net effect is to perpetuate the addiction.

The enablers of drug-dependent persons may be victims of codependency. Codependency is a condition that often follows when a family member has a compulsive disorder, such as alcoholism or drug addiction. *Codependency* is a set of unhealthy behaviors learned by family members in order to survive in a family that is experiencing great emotional pain and stress.

The family members around the addicted person get caught up in the deceit that is practiced to cover up the problem. Ultimately, the emotional health of everyone is adversely affected. Financial pressures increase, and the safety of the entire family is at stake.

Since the addict has lost control, family members often must take the first step toward breaking the cycle. They will need to stop their enabling behaviors and get professional help. Intervention (described earlier in this chapter) is often a first step.

How Can the Crisis Be Overcome?

Alcoholics and drug addicts must want to help themselves before anyone else can help them. They must be able to admit they have a problem. They then must decide for themselves to stop drinking or using drugs. No one else can make the decision for them.

Once this major step is taken, the recovery period can begin. It will not be easy. Alcoholics and drug addicts need professional help as well as the support of family members and friends. See 21-12.

Professional help is available from the National Council on Alcoholism, family service agencies, community health centers, detoxification centers, and hospitals. Also contact self-help groups such as Alcoholics Anonymous, Narcotics Anonymous, or Cocaine Anonymous. To find sources of help in your area, look in the white pages of your phone book under "alcoholism" or "drug abuse."

**What Can the Mate
of an Alcoholic or a Drug Addict Do?**

1. Learn the facts about alcoholism and drug addiction. Be open-minded in admitting the problem that exists in the family.
2. Realize that alcoholism and drug addiction are learned behaviors and that treatment can be given to change the behavior.
3. Accept the fact that a person can stop drinking or using drugs only if he or she wants to stop.
4. Confront the spouse or family member with the results of his or her drinking or drug use. This may humiliate the user, but it may motivate him or her to seek help.
5. Realize that the spouse cannot be protected from being tempted by alcohol or other drugs. The alcoholic or drug abuser has to learn to turn down drinks or drugs.
6. Seek help for the rest of the family. Many private and community resources exist. When the spouse sees the family seeking help, he or she may seek help, too.
7. Avoid "home treatment" methods. Secure the help of professionals and follow their suggestions.
8. Avoid lecturing, nagging, and begging. Also avoid developing a martyr-like attitude. All of these will make an alcoholic or drug abuser use even more.
9. Do not argue with an alcoholic or drug abuser when he or she is under the influence of the alcohol or drug. It will be futile at this point.
10. Be direct in calling the drinking "alcoholism" or "drug addiction," but do not force your mate to admit he or she is an alcoholic or drug abuser.
11. Do not threaten, "If you love me...." An alcoholic or drug abuser can love people and still be an alcoholic or drug abuser.
12. Do not make deals or promises. Alcoholics or drug abusers have to quit because they want to quit. They cannot be bribed.
13. Do not expect an immediate cure, and do not expect all the family's problems to disappear when the spouse starts getting help.
14. Try to develop a more thoughtful, caring attitude toward the spouse.
15. Talk to someone other than relatives about the problem. Relatives are often reluctant to admit their kin could be an alcoholic or drug abuser. They may blame the other family members for the problem.

21-12
These suggestions can help a person deal with an alcoholic or drug-addicted mate.

Compulsive Gambling ■ ■ ■ ■ ■ ■

When a family member has a gambling problem, the stakes are high for the whole family. Money that was intended to be used for food, clothing, and housing is often gambled and lost. A gambler can go through the family savings account, leaving nothing for the future, such as a new house or a college education for the children. Therefore, family members—often children—must do without and usually become dependent upon welfare. Compulsive gambling often jeopardizes family relationships, education, and career opportunities.

A *compulsive gambler* is someone who loses control over gambling and continues to gamble despite the harmful consequences. The compulsive gambler is addicted to gambling much as the drug abuser is addicted to alcohol or other drugs. Compulsive gambling has been recognized as a serious problem with many of the same consequences faced by people with drug or alcohol abuse problems.

Gambling is a growing problem among adults as well as teens. Many states have expanded gambling opportunities through lotteries, riverboat casinos, and horse and dog racetracks. People often begin gambling as an escape from problems or for the thrill of winning.

The compulsive gambler often goes through four phases. These are: (1) winning, (2) losing, (3) desperation, and (4) hopelessness.

■ Winning. Everyone likes to win. This gives a person the feeling of power and control, 21-13. This is often how the beginning gambler becomes hooked. Usually, all it takes is one big win to make a person feel good about himself or herself. This is almost like the "high" obtained from using drugs. The person begins to crave this winning feeling again and again, so more and more money is wagered. This is when the losing phase often begins.

■ Losing. Once the gambler begins losing, he or she attempts to get back what was lost. This is called *chasing*. The gambler uses money set aside in savings. This money, which should be going toward family necessities or future plans, is spent trying to win back losses. The gambler often discovers that chasing the losses does not work. This is when desperation occurs.

■ Desperation. It is at this point when a gambler, in a desperate financial situation, may turn to family or friends for a *bailout* (money to finance gambling debts). By bailing out the gambler, the well-meaning family member or friend has not helped the gambler. The money often only enables the gambler to chase more losses, creating even more gambling debts. The gambler ends up even deeper in debt—and even more

21-13
A win can be exciting for the gambler, and this is how a person can get hooked.

desperate. The gambler feels guilty and is ashamed to face the people who have bailed him or her out. This is when illegal means of obtaining money may be sought. Compulsive gambling often leads people to engage in illegal activity such as forgery, fraud, or theft in order to pay debts and finance their gambling.

■ Hopelessness. During the hopelessness phase, compulsive gamblers realize that they will never be able to pay off debts or escape the problems they have created. Compulsive gamblers are prone to develop stress-related problems such as high blood pressure, heart disease, and depression. Sometimes they may even turn to drugs or suicide as a way to escape their problems.

Only two states, Utah and Hawaii, now ban all gambling. Seventy years ago, it was banned everywhere. Legal betting is one of today's fastest-growing industries. In many states, gambling has become legalized in order to increase state revenues. These increased opportunities to gamble are actually having the opposite effect. Many gamblers become bankrupt and turn to state welfare to support themselves and their families. Also, crime increases as gamblers seek illegal ways to pay back debts. States then must spend money to fight crime and support prison inmates.

Self-help groups such as Gamblers Anonymous are available to help compulsive gamblers deal with their problems. These groups can be located in phone books or through local hospitals or mental health agencies. A hotline on compulsive gambling is available in most communities.

Depression ■ ■ ■ ■ ■

Depression is a significant health problem in this country, affecting 10 million Americans every year. It affects people of all ages, including up to five percent of teenagers. One person in five will suffer from depression at some time in his or her life. Depressive illnesses often interfere with normal functioning. They can affect family life as well as the life of the ill person.

Depression is a "whole-body" illness, involving the body, mood, and thoughts. It can affect behavior, physical health and appearance, and the way people handle decisions. Everyone feels "down" from time to time, but when the mood lasts for more than a couple of weeks and includes other symptoms, medical help should be sought.

There are three main types of depression. *Major* or *clinical depression* has a beginning, a middle, and an end. It often lasts for months and may recur several times in a lifetime. *Chronic depression (dysthymia)* is a less severe type of depression, but it can last for years. People suffering from dysthymia may never really feel good. The third type of depression is called *bipolar disorder* (formerly called manic depression). In this form, the individual experiences days or weeks of elation (mania) followed by an unpredictable downward mood swing. This cycle is often repeated.

There are many symptoms of depression. These symptoms may not all be experienced by one person, and they may vary in severity. The most common symptoms are sleeping problems, loss of appetite, decline in energy, feelings of worthlessness, and a general feeling of hopelessness. Often people do not recognize their own symptoms and may need your help. See 21-14.

All of the causes of depression are not yet known. Some types of depression run in families. People who have difficulty handling

Symptoms of Depression

People who are depressed often have a hard time thinking clearly or recognizing their own symptoms. They may need your help if you notice several of these symptoms lasting longer than two weeks.

Do they express feelings of
- sadness or "emptiness"?
- hopelessness, pessimism, or guilt?
- helplessness or worthlessness?

Do they seem
- unable to make decisions?
- unable to concentrate and remember?
- to have lost interest or pleasure in ordinary activities—like sports or band or talking on the phone?
- to have more problems with school and family?

Do they complain of
- loss of energy and drive—so they seem "slowed down"?
- trouble falling asleep, staying asleep, or getting up?
- appetite problems? Are they losing or gaining weight?
- headaches, stomach aches, or backaches?
- chronic aches and pains in joints and muscles?

Has their behavior changed suddenly so that
- they are restless or more irritable?
- they want to be alone most of the time?
- they've started cutting classes or dropped hobbies and activities?
- you think they may be drinking heavily or taking drugs?

Have they talked about
- death?
- suicide—or have they attempted suicide?

National Institute of Mental Health

21-14
If you suspect that a friend may be suffering from depression, check these symptoms.

stress, have low self-esteem, and are generally pessimistic may be more at risk. Crisis situations, such as the loss of a loved one, can bring on depression. Research has also shown that certain brain cells may not be communicating properly in people who are depressed.

Untreated, a major depressive episode can last months or even years. Many people do not seek help because they view depression as a sign of personal weakness rather than a medical problem. Others fail to recognize the symptoms or think they will eventually get better on their own. However, depression is treatable and most people can be helped.

When depression is suspected, a family doctor or mental health specialist should be consulted for diagnosis and treatment. A combination of medication and psychological therapy is usually recommended. Treatment can lessen both the severity and the duration (length) of the illness.

Suicide

Suicide is a major concern across the United States. In the last 25 years, the rate of suicide among teenagers and young adults has increased dramatically. It is one of the leading causes of death among young people. Reasons for committing suicide are varied, but the two most common are love conflicts and the feeling that life is not worth living. Suicide often is linked to depression.

There are four general patterns of suicide. Perhaps the impulsive suicides are the hardest to comprehend. Highly successful business executives or seemingly happy individuals suddenly shock families and friends by taking their own lives. They seldom give any signs that they are considering suicide. However, diaries or letters they leave behind often reveal deep feelings of loss regarding some aspect of their lives.

The second group includes people who give many signs of their depression. They tell their friends and family that they feel life is not worthwhile. They can find nothing good about themselves or their lives. They may complain so much and so often that their friends no longer listen to them. Then they attempt suicide.

Contemporary Concerns *of today's teens:*
Worried about a Friend?
How You Can Help

Everyone can have a bad day, but maybe you know someone who seems to be down most of the time. How can you help a friend who appears to be heading toward severe depression and even self-destruction?

First, watch for clues, such as those listed elsewhere in this chapter. They can be the first indication of a problem. Be alert if a friend shows prolonged despondency, leading to talk of not caring about anything—the future, family, or even life itself. Moodiness is typical of teens, but severe mood swings and dramatic changes in activities often signal depression.

If you ask your friend, "What's wrong?" don't give up if he or she answers, "Nothing." Young people have to be convinced that someone is really concerned about them. Be direct, and tell your friend exactly how you feel—that you care and that you are worried. This is a time when honesty and directness are needed. Let your friend know how deeply you care about his or her welfare. Do not minimize problems with comments such as, "It will be better tomorrow."

Really listen to what your friend is saying (or not saying). Try to listen without making judgments or giving advice. Be supportive and empathetic. Be alert to words and phrases that suggest severe depression, hopelessness, or self-destruction. Statements such as "I can't take it anymore" or "I'd rather leave than go back to school" indicate your friend is struggling with a serious problem.

Your friend may be very reluctant to get professional help. He or she may be concerned that the school will put this on his or her record, or that everyone in school will find out. Some young people may be afraid to talk to relatives because they want their feelings to remain private. You may be able to help your friend by offering to go with him or her for help. Even if your friend is reluctant to tell anyone else, it is crucial to enlarge the circle of support and get others involved.

You may feel that you can't help your friend, but you can seek out other trusted persons who may be able to supply the kind of help needed. Your friend's future—perhaps even his or her life— may be in the balance. Do seek help yourself when you don't know what to do for a friend.

The third group includes people who have suffered from illness or who suddenly find out about a serious illness. This can push some people to take their own lives because they do not want to exist in poor health.

The last group includes people who are extremely depressed over lost loved ones. Love conflicts, broken engagements, or divorces drive them to suicide. Sometimes they make a weak attempt at suicide with the hope of winning the other person back. If they fail to regain the lost love, they may make another, more serious suicide attempt.

If a family member or friend has hinted about suicide or has openly talked about it, do not ignore the remarks. Suicide talk should not be taken lightly. If a person hints of committing suicide, express your concern to the person directly. Take a firm stand against any suggestions of suicide. The friend will probably be grateful that you cared enough to say, "No, don't do it." Let your friend talk about his or her problems, but suggest that the person see a professional counselor.

If you feel so depressed that you begin to think of ending your own life, it is important to talk with someone, 21-15. Try to talk to a family member or close friend. If you feel you cannot talk to them, see a school counselor or favorite teacher. If this is not possible, call a suicide hotline. Trained counselors will listen to you and can suggest where you can go for help with your problems. No matter how painful your life may be, there is always a way out.

Many community resources are available today. There are more than 200 suicide prevention centers across the United States. By contacting one of these or your own family physician, you can be referred to a professional agency or hospital in your area.

Criminal Attack ▪ ▪ ▪ ▪

One of the negative aspects of living in a complex society is the high number of criminal attacks. Urban areas report the most attacks, but rural and suburban areas are not immune.

Criminal attacks do not have "average" or "typical" victims. Anyone is vulnerable, at any time and any place. Although some crimes are well planned, many are spontaneous reactions to tempting situations. Alertness and common sense are your best guards against attack.

In Your Home

What can you do to protect yourself and your family in your home? A few simple precautions are described in the following paragraphs.

Keep doors and windows locked when you are home as well as when you are gone. Use secure locks such as dead-bolt locks. Solid wood or metal doors offer more resistance to forced entry.

When people come to your door, ask them to identify themselves before you open your door. If you have a peephole in your

Cholla Runnels

21-15
If you begin to feel that life is not worth living, find someone who can help you with your problems. Help is available.

door, you can see the callers. If you have a chain guard, you can open the door enough to see and still have protection. If it is a service person, ask to see proper identification.

If you leave your home, even for a short time, lock the door. Never leave a note on the door explaining that you will be back by a certain time. This tells a burglar the exact amount of time he or she has to do the job.

If, when you return to your home, you find your door open or unlocked, do not go in alone. By entering under these circumstances, you may find an intruder inside. If you surprise the intruder, he or she is more likely to overreact with violence. A better plan is to go to a neighbor's home and call the police. Have them look through your home before you enter. If you are leaving and must leave a key, do not place it in an obvious place, such as under the door mat or on top of the door jamb. Place the key in a small jar and hide it in a flower bed or some other unlikely place.

If you go out at night, it is best to leave and return with another person. If you have to walk to your front door alone, keep this area well lit. Have your key ready, and go inside quickly, 21-16. If you have been with friends, call them when you are safely inside.

If a person you do not know telephones your home, never indicate that you are alone. Tell the caller that your parent or your spouse cannot come to the phone at this time. Also keep emergency telephone numbers near your phone at all times.

In Your Car or As You Walk

Keep your car full of gas and in good repair so you will not be stalled and need to ask for help. If you can't start your car in a parking lot, call a service station for help. Do not accept help from a stranger. (In one major city, a man would spot a lone woman driver. When she left her car to go shopping, he

Cholla Runnels

21-16
Have your key ready so you can open your door and enter quickly.

would fix her car so it would not start. When the woman returned and found that she could not start her car, he would approach her and offer help. After fixing her car, he would ask her to drive him to his car on the other side of the lot. Once in her car, he would force her to do what he wanted.)

Have your keys ready when you leave your house or a store, 21-17. Go to your car quickly, get inside, and lock your door immediately. Do not leave a purse on the seat beside you. If you stop at a traffic signal, someone can quickly smash your window and grab your purse.

If your car stalls, turn on the flashing hazard lights and wait for help. When someone comes, ask the person to phone for help, but do not open your door. You are safer in the car. Once you leave it, you run the risk of attack. More people are installing car phones so they can call for help in emergencies.

If you are driving and you sense someone is following you, drive to a police station or someplace where you are sure to find people. Do not drive to your home.

When traveling in a car and another vehicle bumps you from the rear, be cautious in

21-17
When you leave your home or a store, have your car keys ready so you can get inside your car quickly.

Cholla Runnels

getting out of your car. The car ahead of you may stop abruptly, causing you to bump it. These acts may be done deliberately in order to collect from your insurance. If you suspect this may be the case, do not get out of your car. Instead, drive to the nearest police station.

When you leave your car with parking attendants or service persons, remove your house key. They could find out your address and have a duplicate key made. They could use this key to burglarize your home.

Rape

Rape is any sexual intimacy forced on one person by another. It can happen anywhere and at any time. It can occur in crowded shopping centers, at schools or parks, or even at parties. Public areas are often places where assaults and abductions take place. If the precautions discussed in the previous section are followed, such assaults are less likely to occur.

Sexual offenders can be of any age, and come from all social, economic, ethnic, or religious groups. They usually appear quite normal so there is no way to "spot" a rapist.

According to a recent Justice Department study, girls under age 18 are victims in more than half of all rapes reported to the police. Younger victims are more often raped by relatives or acquaintances.

There are two kinds of rapists. In the first, hostility is a primary factor. Such emotions as rage, hatred, contempt, and humiliation are the primary goals. Sexual gratification is secondary to brutality. The rapist wishes to overpower, humiliate, and harm the woman.

In the second kind of rape, sexual gratification is the primary motivation. The rapist will not go so far as to brutalize the woman to gain what he wants, but he will use threats and overpowering force. In his own mind, this kind of a rapist may feel he has not raped the woman. He may even feel she brought the situation on herself by her own actions. He feels he is not humiliating the woman, he is simply taking advantage of her.

Rape by a stranger is more likely to be violent in nature. The rapist is not so much wanting sexual intimacy as he is wanting to inflict violence on the woman. Acquaintance rape was discussed in Chapter 11. This type of rape is committed by someone known to the victim.

If you are the victim of a rape, first get to a safe place. Then call someone you trust to be with you. Most cities have a Rape Crisis Center operated by people who are trained to help in this type of emergency. They can give you advice and support and can call the police for you. It is important to report the rape to the police department.

Violent Behavior in Families ■ ■ ■ ■ ■ ■

A family is a collection of individuals whose beliefs and behaviors can differ in many ways. Sometimes the differences are insignificant. At other times, the differences are so important that they can lead to conflicts, 21-18. If a conflict cannot be resolved, it may escalate into violence. The true test of family members' commitment to one another is not in the avoidance of conflict, but how they respond to conflict.

Violence is any harmful physical contact that results in injury or death. *Domestic violence* is violence between family members or intimate friends. Spouse or partner abuse, elder abuse, and child abuse are types of domestic violence.

The Incidence of Violence in Families

The incidence of domestic violence is increasing in our society. Newspapers and the media daily report cases involving violent behavior within families. Every year, more than four million women in the United States are battered, and 1,500 die as a result of domestic abuse.

Domestic violence involves people from every ethnic, religious, educational, and economic background. The abusers are of both sexes.

A recent survey disclosed that women and men were physically abusing other family members in roughly equal numbers. Half of spousal murders had been committed by wives. The survey also found that 54 percent of all violence termed "severe" was by women. Mothers abuse their children at a rate approaching twice that of fathers, according to a survey of state child-protective service agencies.

If children are the victims of abuse, they are three times more likely to abuse their own children. Sons of battered mothers are three times more likely to become wife abusers.

Experts also agree that violence at home can lead children to "act out" violently outside the home. Children learn that violence is an acceptable way to get what they want.

Reasons People Use Violence

Anger is often the emotion that forms the core of domestic violence. It is an emotional reaction to frustration. The frustration can come from many factors. Often abusers are having problems at work, are unhappy with their jobs, or are unemployed. They feel they've lost control over a part of their lives. They may feel isolated from the community and lack support. Stress over money prob-

Cholla Runnels

21-18
Conflicts need to be resolved before they lead to violence.

lems or how to rear the children can cause anger and frustration.

Some people use violence to get back at others when they feel angry and frustrated. Abusers tend to be filled with anger, resentment, suspicion, and tension. They may feel insecure and have poor self-images. They may resort to violence to give vent to the bad feelings they have about themselves or what's happening to them. They may resort to violence at home to prove they can control at least some part of their lives. They can't express anger at their bosses, so they take out their frustration on family members. Weaker family members become targets of vengeance.

Forms of Violence

Violence can take many forms. It may begin with psychological violence—threats, intimidation, controlling behavior, jealousy, and verbal abuse. Verbal abuse can consist of stinging put-downs, name calling, swearing, and sarcastic remarks. Attempts may be made to isolate the victim from his or her support

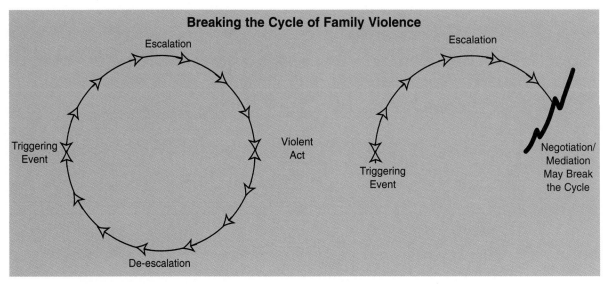

21-19
Mediation may de-escalate family tension and break the cycle of violence.

system, such as other family members and friends. Some family members physically throw things or may punch a door or a wall. This is called property violence. Eventually, the violence becomes physical—pushing, hitting, slapping, punching, or kicking a person.

The Cycle of Family Violence

Because one form of violence often leads to another, many psychologists speak of a "cycle of violence." See 21-19. The cycle of violence starts with some triggering event. This can be a minor misunderstanding or frustration, or it can be a major problem with a particular family member. Tension builds, and accusations related to other issues may be thrown in to add to the conflict. Mounting verbal exchanges may escalate the conflict. If the family members are unable to end this escalation of anger, there is a greater chance for a violent act to occur.

If, before a violent act occurs, a third party can intervene, steps toward conflict res-olution could help de-escalate the tension. (Conflict resolution is discussed in Chapter 10.) Someone acting as mediator may be able to defuse the violence and mediate a win/win solution to the problem. If this movement is made, the immediate conflict will have been resolved. However, unless the family members get professional counseling, the problem may recur.

Legal Action in Domestic Abuse

If the violent behavior is not stopped, a pattern of abuse may result. Family members may not be able to control the violence, and legal recourse will have to be sought. In recent years, almost every state has passed legislation to provide help for abused family members. Laws have been passed that strengthen both civil protection and criminal penalties. See 21-20. Legal remedies are available to protect and assist victims of domestic violence.

Legal Rights of Victims of Domestic Violence

Civil Court

Civil courts settle disputes that are noncriminal. They make decisions about legal relationships such as marriage. The victim can receive legal protection from the abuser without filing criminal charges. In most cases the victim will need to hire an attorney, but free legal assistance may be available for those who have low incomes. The following actions can be taken by a civil court:

An *Order of Protection,* also called a restraining order, is a written court order, signed by a judge, that requires an abuser to change his or her conduct. The judge will specify the conduct that is or is not allowed. For instance, the order may require that the abuser refrain from abuse of any household member, move out of a residence shared with the victim, provide alternate housing for the victim, pay for the support of the victim and any minor children, and pay any medical expenses of the victim.

Rules may vary from state to state. Some states will offer protection orders on behalf of anyone abused by a spouse, former spouse, family member, household member, or former household member. Some states will only issue a protection order to a woman married to her abuser. In other states, protection orders are available only to married women who have filed for separation or divorce.

A permanent restraining order requires a court hearing at which both parties are given an opportunity to testify. A temporary or emergency restraining order may be issued within a few hours or a few days of the time it is requested. A temporary order may be issued with only the victim present in court. This order remains in effect until a full hearing can be held. It may be issued if "immediate and present danger of abuse" is shown.

If a spouse wishes to terminate a marriage because of the abuse, he or she can file for separation and divorce. Some abusers, however, become more violent when victims separate from them. It may be important for a victim to get a protection order when separation or divorce proceedings are started.

Criminal Court

If a victim wants to charge the abuser with aggravated battery, he or she must do so in a criminal court. Every state has laws prohibiting physical assault. Conduct that may violate state criminal laws includes hitting or other physical assault, sexual assault, or harassment or threat of physical assault. In addition, any act causing the death of another, destruction of private property, kidnapping or confining another against his or her will, or violation of the terms of a protection order can be grounds for criminal charges.

The police can make an arrest when responding to a call. After an arrest is made, a criminal charge is filed either by the police or by the prosecutor's office. The victim can also sign a complaint. A complaint is a paper filed with the court that describes the abusive incident. After the complaint is filed, the prosecutor's office will conduct an investigation and decide whether charges should be filed. If charges are filed, the court will issue a warrant for the arrest of the abuser and set a date for the trial.

An attorney from the state's attorney's office will prosecute the charges against the abuser. The victim will not have to hire a private lawyer. The filing of the criminal charge does not necessarily mean that there will be a trial. The charge may be disposed of by other means. If the abuser pleads innocent, he or she will be tried on the offenses charged. If convicted, the abuser may be jailed, fined, or placed on probation.

21-20
Presently, there are several forms of legal protection available for battered family members. These are available through the civil courts and criminal courts.

Spouse or Partner Abuse

Spouse or partner abuse is one kind of family violence that happens far too often. It is believed that one-fourth of all relationships include violence. In most cases, it involves the man beating the woman. The term "battered wife" is often used to describe these victims. In rarer instances, the man is the one that is physically abused.

The spouse who suffers from physical abuse is often a person who was abused as a child, or who witnessed the abuse of one parent by the other. He or she feels violence is a normal part of domestic life. Now, as an adult victim of abuse, the person feels terrified, and trapped within his or her own home.

Victims of spouse abuse may attempt to leave following a violent act, but they often are persuaded to return. They are led to be-lieve that the battering will stop. Instead, a three-phase cycle repeats itself, 21-21. In phase one, tension builds over a series of small incidents that displease the abuser. The tension becomes explosive and the abuser loses control. This results in a violent incident (phase two) involving physical abuse. Following the incident, the abuser realizes he or she has overreacted and is very sorry, often asking for forgiveness. This is phase three, called the "honeymoon" stage. The abuser believes he or she will never hurt the victim again, but often the cycle is repeated over and over.

The first step an abused person should take is to get away. There are places to go to for help. For immediate assistance, there are special homes for battered women and their children in many communities. These homes provide refuge, counseling, and legal advice. Civil protection is available through the courts. A judge can issue a restraining order to the abuser to abstain from abuse, move out of the house shared with the victim, and pay support. A victim may need to also apply for public assistance. These remedies and others may give the victim of abuse the strength to end a violent relationship.

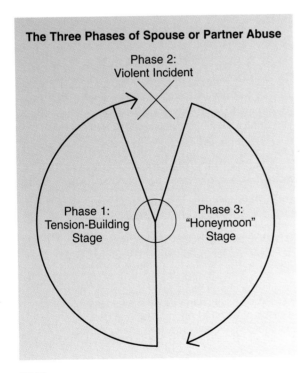

The Three Phases of Spouse or Partner Abuse

Phase 2:
Violent Incident

Phase 1:
Tension-Building
Stage

Phase 3:
"Honeymoon"
Stage

21-21
Spouse abuse typically follows three phases, which are repeated with each episode of violence.

Elder Abuse

Elder abuse is emerging as a growing, largely hidden, problem in our society. Many victims remain silent out of fear of being moved to a nursing home. The declining birth rate in our country means there are fewer adult caregivers. The middle age group, often called the "sandwich generation," must care for both dependent children and dependent parents. They may feel caught in the middle.

Elder abuse may involve psychological violence. Insults and threats of stronger action may be used against them. Elder abuse may be physical, such as slapping and kicking, or denying adequate food or other basic needs. It can be economic, such as withholding or diverting money. In other cases, overmedication may be used, particularly when the elder person is placed in a nursing home.

In small communities, victims of elder abuse might contact a minister, priest, or rabbi for assistance. A family doctor may also be able to provide help. In larger urban areas, many agencies exist that can intervene. Religious organizations, civic organizations, and county and state agencies can all provide help. The phone numbers may be found in the white pages of most phone books under "Social Service Agencies."

Child Abuse and Neglect

Child abuse and neglect can be defined as the physical or mental injury, sexual abuse, negligent treatment, or maltreatment of a child under the age of 18 by a person who is responsible for the child's welfare. Abused children range in age from infants to adolescents. About half are six years of age or younger.

News stories often focus on the tragic realities of child abuse and neglect. These aspects of family crisis demand the attention of individuals, families, and entire communities.

There are several forms of child abuse and neglect. *Physical abuse* is the infliction of physical injury upon a child. This may range from one strong slap to repeated beatings. When a child is hit, slapped, or kicked, severe bruising and bleeding can result, and bones can be broken. In most cases, an abusing parent will make sure the child receives medical attention, but the parent is careful to use different hospitals and physicians. The parent will usually blame the injuries on falls or accidents.

Physical neglect is the failure to provide sufficient food, clothing, shelter, medical care, education, guidance, and supervision for a child. A case of physical neglect may be detected by neighbors or school officials who notice the condition of the child's appearance, lack of alertness, or even episodes of stealing. Authorities may help the parents acquire the resources necessary to provide adequate care for the child. The child may be placed in a welfare institution or foster home until the parents are able to provide adequate care.

Sexual abuse is forcing a child to engage in sexual activities. This abuse leaves long-lasting emotional scars.

Child sexual abusers seldom use physical force. Instead, they gain the child's cooperation through bribes, threats, or use of their position of authority. In a large majority of the cases, the abuser is known to the victim. In many cases, incest is involved. *Incest* is sexual activity between persons who are closely related. Parents also need to be aware of substitute child care situations that may indicate sexual abuse. If children seem frightened, or if they become withdrawn and behave differently after their child care experiences, parents should investigate.

Emotional abuse occurs when parents continually make demands that their children are not capable of meeting. The abuse continues when parents criticize and humiliate the children for not living up to the demands. Continued emotional abuse destroys children's sense of self-respect. It makes them feel inferior and guilty.

Emotional neglect is the failure to provide children with love and affection. Even children who receive excellent physical care may be emotionally neglected. Children need constant assurance that they are loved. Without this assurance, children may lack self-confidence and self-esteem. They may have trouble accepting themselves as worthy individuals. They may also have trouble relating to other people.

Emotional neglect is difficult to measure and prove. The real results of emotional neglect may not be revealed until years later. The child then gets into trouble with authorities or fails to function as a productive member of society.

Understanding the Problem

Child abuse and neglect are not planned. They are the results of constant frustration that has no outlet.

Child abusers are most often immature parents who are looking to their children for the very support and love they should be giving. These parents feel their needs are not met by spouses, friends, or society. They have only one hope left—that their children will give them love and comfort. This is a role reversal that places unfair demands on the children.

Many child abusers were abused as children. This cycling effect is a frightening phenomenon in our society. If children are abused or neglected, they develop a poor self-image, and they may even dislike themselves. They may take out their hostilities on their children years later, and a pattern of child abuse occurs.

In a two-parent family, there cannot be just one abusive parent. One parent may be the active abuser, but the other parent becomes the passive abuser. Passive abusers usually remain silent for two reasons. They are ashamed of the way their spouses abuse their children, and they fear the consequences of telling authorities of the problem.

Why do older abused children accept abuse? In most cases, they are very confused about what they can do. They may fear the parents and expect even more punishment if they try to do anything about it. The children may actually feel guilty about causing the parents to become so angry.

What Can Be Done?

The problems of child abuse and neglect can be approached in several ways. One way is to encourage people to have parenthood education, 21-22. This education helps people learn about stages of children's development and growth. Adults need to realize, for instance, that children cannot be expected to even begin toilet training until about two or two and one-half years of age. After that, they will need to wear diapers at night and will still have accidents. Some days children may not feel like finishing their meals, or they may allow their curiosity to get

David Hopper

21-22
Young adults who take parenting classes learn about children's development and behavior as they work with children. Such knowledge may be helpful in preventing child abuse.

them in trouble. Adults should do all they can to acquaint themselves with what to expect of children. Then they will be able to understand and appreciate children's behavior.

Individual citizens, social workers, physicians, and police can work together to try to protect children from abuse and neglect. See 21-23. Their immediate goal is to give the children help and treatment. Their long-range goal is to change the parents' behavior. The total personalities of abusive parents need attention.

Many therapy programs are available to child abusers. They may be sponsored by private organizations, religious groups, or the government. Parents Anonymous is an organization for child abusers that is based on the self-help theory of Alcoholic Anonymous. Members of Parents Anonymous can meet together and work out methods of coping with their frustrations. They can call each other for help if they sense they are on the verge of abusing a child.

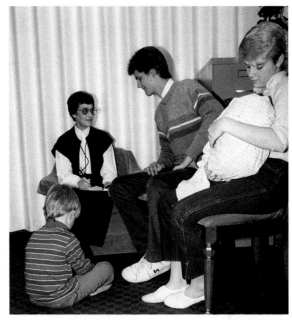

Cholla Runnels

21-23
People from child welfare agencies investigate reports of child abuse and neglect.

Missing Children

No one knows exactly how many missing children there are, but more than one and one-half million are reported each year. Investigators say that runaways or children who leave home claiming to have been abused account for most of the missing. Abductions by parents in divorce cases account for many of the other missing children. Contrary to public belief, the smallest number are abducted by strangers.

Authorities stress that it is not just the stranger that should be feared, but also the situation. Very few child molesters break into homes to abduct children. More often the children are lured by acquaintances or people the children do not regard as strangers. These people make contact with children through youth groups, sports groups, and recreational organizations. Parents whose children belong to these groups have a responsibility to monitor their activities to be sure they are legitimate.

Children should be taught certain precautions to take. They should know how to use the telephone for emergencies and should be warned against giving too much information to unknown callers. They should be told not to tell callers they are home alone or when their parents will return. Not only should they be taught not to ride with strangers, but they should also be warned of some of the stories they might be told. For instance, a stranger might tell them their mother has been in an accident and is in the hospital.

Today's parents are practicing more caution, and communities are attempting to provide more security in public areas and in schools. Community fingerprinting drives are

Tips to Prevent the Crisis of Missing Children

1. Know where your child is at all times.
2. Do not leave your child alone in a car, a store, or other public areas.
3. Teach your child how to use the telephone. Make sure the child knows your home number, including the area code. Also make sure the child knows how to call the police in an emergency.
4. Do not write your child's name on his or her clothes or books. An abductor could see it and begin talking to the child on a first-name basis.
5. Choose a secret code word that you and your child can use for identification in case of an emergency. Tell your child never to go with anyone who does not know the code word.
6. Teach your child not to talk to strangers, ride with strangers, or get involved with strangers in any way. Be sure the child understands the meaning of the word stranger.
7. Teach your child to beware of people who appear to be friendly and who suggest the child go with them.
8. Ask the school to notify you at once if your child does not report to school.
9. Fingerprint your child. Keep a copy of the prints on hand for identification purposes.
10. Cooperate with your neighbors. Let children know which homes are "safe homes" where they can go if they need help. Also, ask neighbors to keep an eye on children when they play outside and to watch for suspicious adults.

21-24
These tips may help parents prevent the crisis of a missing child.

providing parents with records of their children for identification purposes. Photos of missing children are distributed through the mail and are seen in many public locations.

As a result of incidents such as the abduction and murder of Adam Walsh, a 6-year-old boy in Florida, the Missing Children Act of 1982 was passed. The law authorizes the FBI to enter descriptions of missing children in the National Crime Information Computer. It also allows parents of missing children access to the system.

The best assurance that a child will not become a missing child still lies with parents and caregivers. They must be alert and do what they can to prevent child abductions. Tips for parents and caregivers are given in 21-24.

Runaways

Runaways are a nationwide problem, 21-25. Young people from all backgrounds are affected. In most cases, a breakdown of family communications is cited as the cause.

Cholla Runnels

21-25
The average age of runaways in the U.S. is 15 years old.

The breakdown usually involves disagreements between parents and teens on issues such as curfews, drug use, choice of friends, and performance in school. Divorce and remarriage may also create problems that drive teenagers away from home.

Some teens run away toward a vision of an independent life or an alternate lifestyle. Some leave to escape from abusive situations—physical, emotional, or sexual. Some leave their homes because they are forced out.

Runaways can find refuge in several places across the country, but the shelter they get is not always ideal. To improve the situation, many programs have been started. They vary from one area to another. Some local governments have funded *halfway houses,* or centers where runaways can receive care as well as counseling. A telephone program called "Operation Peace of Mind" was started as a result of mass murders of teenage boys in Houston, Texas. Families who had a son missing feared that their son might be one of the victims. An effort was made to encourage all runaways to contact their parents. They still could keep their whereabouts secret, but they could reassure their parents that they were alive and well.

Teenagers live with many pressures, and lack of communication in the family does not help relieve these pressures. However, the problem causing the stress will not disappear by running away from it. In most cases, running away just makes the problem worse. As young people mature, they must learn to cope with their problems instead of running away from them. If they can't cope by themselves, a respected counselor may be able to refer them to professional help.

Summary ■ ■ ■ ■ ■ ■ ■ ■ ■ ■ ■ ■ ■ ■

- A crisis is a crucial time or event that causes a change in a person's life. There is usually no ready solution to the crisis, and adjustments often need to be made.

- Resources that help people handle crises include mental health, religious beliefs, physical health, strong family relationships, financial resources, and the support of friends. Community resources include shelters, hotlines, intervention services, and support groups.

- The strongest families probably include those who have experienced a crisis and have been able to come through it.

- Unemployment is a crisis that affects all family members and forces financial decisions to be made.

- Moving is a crisis that may be viewed either positively or negatively.

- The crisis of drug addiction affects not only the life of the addict, but also the lives of family members, friends, and coworkers.

- The compulsive gambler often goes through four phases. These are winning, losing, desperation, and hopelessness.

- Depression is an illness that involves the body, mood, and thoughts. It can affect behavior, physical health and appearance, and the way people handle decisions.

- Severe depression can lead to suicide. Suicide is one of the leading causes of death among young people.

- Anyone is vulnerable to criminal attack, at any time and any place. The best defenses are alertness and common sense.

- Violent behavior in families includes spouse or partner abuse, elder abuse, and child abuse. Anger is often the emotion on which domestic violence is based. It is often an emotional reaction to frustration.

- Domestic violence takes many forms, including psychological violence, property violence, and physical violence.

- Cases of child abuse and neglect occur in all segments of society and demand the attention of individuals, families, and communities.

- Parents, caregivers, and community officials are working with children to prevent the crisis of missing children and runaways.

To Review ■ ■ ■ ■ ■ ■ ■ ■ ■ ■ ■ ■ ■ ■ ■ ■

1. True or False. If a crisis occurs, such as the loss of a job, children should not be told that anything is wrong.

2. Explain how intervention is used in a crisis situation.

3. List the four steps to follow in coping with a crisis.

4. Why might family members sense a loss of power when they are told they will have to move?

5. Explain the stages that lead to addiction to illegal drugs.

6. Give an example of how an enabler might unknowingly perpetuate a drug addiction problem.

7. For the compulsive gambler, what does the term "chasing" mean?

8. What are the most common symptoms of depression?

9. Name the four general types of people who commit suicide.

10. List three precautions to take in your home to protect yourself from criminal attack.

11. Describe the three phases of spouse or partner abuse.

12. The failure to provide sufficient food, clothing, shelter, medical care, education, guidance, and supervision for a child is called _____ _____.

13. True or False. Most missing children are abducted by strangers.

14. What is the most common cause of child runaway situations?

To Do ■ ■ ■ ■ ■ ■ ■ ■ ■ ■ ■ ■ ■ ■ ■ ■ ■

1. Name seven situations you would consider crises. Rank them according to the effects you think they would have on your life.

2. Write a fictional story about one of the crises listed below. In the story, mention the cause of the crisis, who is involved, resources available, adjustments required by family members, and financial demands.
   a. Sudden unemployment.
   b. Move to another state.
   c. Alcoholic spouse.
   d. Suicide of a sibling.
   e. Criminal attack on a family member.
   f. Disappearance of a younger brother or sister.

3. Working in groups, investigate your community's resources for helping people withstand various types of crises. Each group will fill out index cards with key information such as type of crisis; name, address, and phone number of organization; and key person contacted. Combine the index cards of the groups in a class file. Also prepare an oral report. Use slides, graphs, tapes, or other audiovisual aids if possible.

4. Role-play situations that might occur in families who face the crisis of drug addiction or child abuse.

5. Arrange chairs in a circle for a round-robin discussion. Select a particular crisis. Each class member will make one statement concerning the crisis.

6. Conduct a survey of students in your school concerning gambling. Find out how many have gambled and on what. How many have family members who gamble? Tally the results of the survey and write a report for the school paper.

7. As a class, make a list of reasons why children run away from home. Then make another list of ways to solve problems other than running away.

Divorce and Remarriage

After studying this chapter, you will be able to

- explain possible reasons for the high rate of divorce in the United States.

- summarize the differences between annulment, legal separation, and divorce.

- list the basic procedures, grounds, defenses, and terms of agreement typically used in divorce proceedings.

- explain the adjustments faced by divorced persons.

- describe the challenges faced by blended families.

Divorce is one of the most emotionally charged crises of life. Perhaps some of you have witnessed the divorce of parents, relatives, or neighbors. If so, you have seen and felt the effects of divorce.

Terms to Know

annulment

divorce

legal separation

desertion

contested divorce

non-contested divorce

no-fault divorce

Enoch Arden divorce

condonation

connivance

collusion

custody

visitation rights

child support

community property

separate property

Divorce Trends and Issues ■ ■ ■ ■ ■ ■

Statistics concerning divorce are not encouraging for young people considering marriage. There is one divorce for every two marriages in the United States. The rate of divorce has more than doubled since the 1960s. Similar trends have occurred in other industrialized countries.

Many authorities believe that high divorce rates may be here to stay. Some view divorce as evidence of moral decay and the breakdown of family values in our society. Others point to broad social and economic trends as primary factors.

In the early part of this century, the family served as an economic unit as well as a source of personal fulfillment. When the U.S. population was largely rural, family members had to work together to make the family farm a successful enterprise. Career opportunities for women were limited, and society viewed women's primary role as that of a full-time homemaker. Divorce was comparatively rare and carried significant social disapproval. Thus, personal happiness was viewed as only one factor among many in assessing the strength of a marriage.

In recent decades, however, this picture has changed. Although the family is still viewed as an economic unit, the nation has become more industrialized. Very few families now make their livelihood from the family farm, 22-1. Most family members earn wages individually rather than as part of a family enterprise. Marriage and family life are now valued more for the personal fulfillment they can offer than as an economic enterprise.

Opportunities for women have also changed. More and more women are working full-time outside the home, although employed women's earnings still lag behind men's. American women have greater freedom of career choice today. Because most women can support themselves, they may no longer feel compelled to stay in an unhappy marriage solely for financial reasons. This is especially true for married women with no children or women whose children have grown up and left home.

Pam Ryder

22-1
Today, most family members earn wages individually rather than as part of a family.

Along with increased emphasis on personal happiness has come a decrease in the social stigma attached to divorce. Surveys indicate that although most Americans view marriage as a lifelong commitment, they do not feel that it is wrong for unhappily married couples to divorce.

Your attitude toward marriage may be affected by your attitude toward divorce. Many experts who study marriage and divorce feel that if people were better informed about divorce, they might better understand the commitments of marriage. Some people go into marriage thinking, "If it doesn't work out, we can always get a divorce." With this kind of attitude, it is doubtful if the couple will really try to make their marriage work.

As you learn about legal termination of marriage, keep in mind the commitments involved for you, your future mate, and any children you may have.

Legal Termination of Marriage

A marriage can be legally terminated in the following two ways:

- By *annulment,* which is a court order that states that a legal marriage never took place.

- By *divorce,* which is a legal dissolution of the marriage contract.

A *legal separation* allows a couple to live in separate households but does not end their marriage. It is often, though not always, followed by divorce.

Some people attempt to dissolve their marriages by *desertion,* abandoning the marital partner. In the past, the husband was usually the one who deserted. However, runaway wives account for a growing number of desertions today. Although desertion is not a legal means of terminating a marriage, it can be used as grounds for divorce in most states.

Annulment

When a marriage is annulled, the court rules that the couple were never legally married. The annulment decree reaches back to the time of the marriage and says that it never occurred. It restores both persons to single status. Their legal rights are settled as of the time of the marriage that legally never took place.

The reasoning behind annulment is that a marriage contract that resulted from fraud was not a legal contract. Therefore, it can be set aside if fraud is proved.

Rules concerning annulment vary from state to state. However, some of the most common types of fraud that may lead to annulment are as follows:

- Concealment of a previous marriage or divorce.

- Use of threats or force to induce a mate to enter marriage.

- Financial misrepresentation.

- Misrepresentation of pregnancy (when the woman claims to be pregnant but is not).

- Concealment of pregnancy (when the child is not the husband's).

- Concealment of disease.

- Marriage for ulterior motives (such as to obtain the property of another, to become an American citizen, or to legitimize an unborn child).

- Marriage entered into when under the influence of alcohol or drugs.

Many states have broadened their rules concerning annulments to include certain post-marital developments. Some of these are:

- Insanity of either spouse.

- Inability of either spouse to engage in normal sexual intercourse.

- Sterility of either spouse discovered after marriage, unless it was caused by a post-marital accident or disease.

- Refusal of a spouse to abide by a pre-marital agreement to change religions or to raise the children in a certain religion.

Annulment proceedings must be begun within a reasonable time after marriage. The length of a "reasonable" time depends on the nature of the fraud or complaint. For instance, a woman who learns of her husband's disease immediately after marriage cannot live with him for two years and then expect to have their marriage annulled.

Annulment gives the partners the right to remarry. Each spouse regains his or her property, and joint property is divided between them. The court decides the custody of the children. In some states, the children of annulled marriages may, under some circumstances, be considered legally illegitimate and may lose their right to inheritance.

Legal Separation

A separation does not end a marriage, but it does end a marriage relationship. A couple who are separated no longer live together, 22-2. This recourse is sometimes used if religious beliefs discourage divorce, but the couple do not want to live as husband and wife.

In an *informal separation,* one of the spouses moves to a separate residence. None of the marital rights and obligations is

David Hopper

22-2
Sometimes a couple decide they can no longer live together, so they file for a legal separation.

changed. In a *legal separation,* the partners make a legal agreement to live apart, to divide their property, and to provide for their children.

Sometimes one partner, usually the woman, uses a legal separation suit for financial reasons. The court can award her *separate maintenance.* This means the husband would have to continue to provide for her financial support just as if they were living together. However, if it were proved that the wife was guilty of any marital misbehavior, this maintenance would not be granted.

Legal separation does not give the partners the right to remarry, for they are still legally married. Thus, some people view legal separation as a limited divorce. Terms of the separation agreement (such as custody of children, division of property, financial support, and visitation rights) may later become the basis for the terms of a divorce settlement.

Divorce

Divorce is the most widely used method of ending a marriage. In spite of the growing number of divorces, a divorce is still an emotional and legal crisis. Even if both parties want a divorce, ending the marriage relationship is not easy. The marriage contract must be honored, and the couple must go through legal divorce procedures before the contract can be terminated.

Divorce is much more complicated than the average person suspects. This is why people need to be aware of all aspects of divorce, even before they marry. When they become aware of all the commitments marriage involves and how difficult breaking those commitments can be, they may be more cautious in committing to a marriage.

Three Stages of Divorce

The process of marital conflict that ends in divorce has three distinct stages. The first stage is *emotional divorce*. Some couples in this stage have periods of emotional outbursts and repression. Others just grow farther and farther apart, causing their marriage to die slowly and quietly. During this time, the spouses are living together, but they begin to realize that their relationship is no longer based on close emotional feelings and love.

Emotional divorce may not occur for both partners at the same time. Sometimes one spouse wants to leave the marriage and the other wants to try to save it. It may take a long time for one of the partners to accept that the marriage is over, to detach emotionally, and to move on.

Physical divorce occurs when the spouses actually separate, and one moves out of the home. See 22-3. At this point, family and friends become aware of the breakup. This may add to the spouses' feelings of guilt, insecurity, and failure. However, separation can

22-3
Physical divorce occurs when one spouse moves out of the home.

also bring feelings of relief, especially if the marriage has been physically or emotionally abusive.

Legal divorce is the final stage. The spouses typically consult lawyers and go through the legal issues of deciding property settlements and child custody. The finality of a divorce decree may leave the spouses feeling emotionally drained. Legal divorce is often emotionally shattering, even for couples who have fairly friendly divorces. However, it may be the best course if a relationship has deteriorated beyond repair.

Divorce Proceedings

To obtain a divorce in any state, you must be a resident of that state. Residency laws vary among states. In some states, you can become a resident after living there only six weeks. Other states require that you live there for as long as five years.

A divorce action starts with the filing of a summons and complaint. The *summons,* which is received by the defendant, informs the spouse that a divorce action has been brought against him or her. It also orders the defendant to appear in court to answer charges in the complaint. The *complaint* states the other spouse's reasons for wanting a divorce, such as adultery, desertion, or cruelty.

In a **contested divorce,** a defendant who wants to fight the divorce files an answer and tries to prove that no grounds exist. In some cases, the defendant may file a summons and complaint against the other spouse. Contested divorces usually include difficult questions of child custody and property settlements. They require complicated court-room action. They are usually settled by a judge, though some cases are settled by a jury.

A large majority of divorces are **non-contested.** The spouses agree to the divorce. Together, they decide which one shall bring the action against the other and what type of action will be brought. Non-contested divorces are less complicated and expensive than contested ones. They are settled quickly before a judge.

No-fault divorces or no-fault grounds for divorce are now common in the United States. The details vary among states, but all **no-fault divorce** laws eliminate the need for proving one partner guilty. They allow the couple to end the marriage by mutual agreement. This makes the divorce less bitter and less expensive.

If a married person disappears for a stated period of time, the spouse is entitled to freedom from the marriage through an **Enoch Arden divorce.** The average time of absence is five to seven years, though this varies in different states. The law also states that some effort should be made to locate the missing spouse. Persons who remarry without getting a legal Enoch Arden divorce run the risk of having their mates come back and charge them with bigamy.

Grounds for Divorce

Divorce laws differ among states. The number of grounds (legal reasons) for divorce and their interpretations vary widely.

Incompatibility is used as grounds for divorce in many states. This means that the two mates are unable to live together peaceably or in harmony.

In some states, the term *insupportability* is used to indicate that the personalities are no longer able to support a continuing relationship of marriage. It should not be confused with financial support.

Other grounds that are often used are cruelty (mental or physical), desertion, impotence, insanity, alcohol or drug addiction, adultery, separation (living apart), and non-support (willful neglect).

Defenses to Divorce

Defenses may be used by individuals or courts to prevent a divorce. These laws place restrictions on the ease of getting a divorce in order to protect the rights of individuals and states. However, such laws are seldom used. Few spouses resist divorce when their mates desire it.

Condonation means that once the "guilty" party has been condoned or forgiven for a certain action, that action cannot be the grounds for divorce. For instance, suppose a wife finds out that her husband is having an affair. She files for divorce and then allows him to move back in with her. Once he is back, he can use condonation as his defense against the divorce suit if he wishes to avoid divorce.

Connivance can be used as a defense when one person is guilty of scheming to cause the condition used as grounds for the divorce. For example, if Mr. Brown asked his friend to seduce Mrs. Brown so Mr. Brown could charge adultery, Mrs. Brown could charge connivance.

Collusion occurs when a couple want a divorce but have no legal grounds, so they set up necessary grounds for divorce. They work together to plan a scheme that would make one partner appear guilty of something such as desertion or adultery. Collusion represents a fraud committed against the court, and the court can refuse to grant the couple a divorce.

Terms of Divorce

Through divorce laws, the state can regulate the property distribution and child-rearing activities of its citizens. The following terms of divorce are covered in most state laws.

Alimony. Alimony is the financial support provided by the primary wage earner to the other marriage partner during and after divorce. (In some states, alimony is called maintenance.)

The traditional awarding of alimony was established by English courts, which allowed only partial divorce. The husband and wife could live apart, but they were not free from the marital bond. The husband was forced to continue to support his wife. He also controlled all the marriage property. The courts gave him total responsibility for the family's finances. Husbands and wives were not allowed to make private contracts that would limit the husband's responsibility.

In theory, most states still hold the primary wage earner liable for alimony. However, alimony is actually awarded in only a small percentage of divorce cases, 22-4.

When alimony is granted, the amount is set by the court. It is usually based on the following three factors:

- The primary wage earner's income.

- The couple's standard of living.

- The degree to which the defendant was proved guilty.

DeVry

22-4
Alimony is awarded in only a small percentage of divorce cases. Occasionally, rehabilitative alimony is awarded to help a spouse upgrade his or her job skills.

In some cases, *rehabilitative alimony* is awarded. This type of alimony is paid to enable a spouse to update or upgrade his or her job skills and ability to earn a living. For example, one spouse may provide funds for the other to finish a college degree or to take paralegal or word-processing training. Rehabilitative alimony is limited in amount and duration.

Many alimony agreements remain in force until they are adjusted in court or until the recipient dies or remarries. Because alimony is a state matter, the recipient may have difficulty collecting the payments if the former mate moves to another state.

Child custody. In a divorce, one or both parents are awarded custody of the children. *Custody* refers to the right to raise the child in the home and to make decisions about the child's care, upbringing, and overall welfare. Women are awarded custody of children in about 90 percent of divorce cases. Most mothers desire custody, even though this often places the greater (if not the total) financial burden of child care on them, 22-5.

Visitation rights for the non-custodial parent are also awarded by the court. A parent with visitation rights can arrange with the custodial parent to see the child during specified times (for example, weekends or summers).

There are several types of custody arrangements. Under *one-parent custody,* one parent has sole responsibility for the upbringing of the child. Under *joint custody,* however, parents share this responsibility. Joint-custody arrangements work best if the divorced parents live in the same area, get along reasonably well, and are willing to work together for the well-being of the child.

Divorced parents with *split-custody* arrangements "split" the children between them. For instance, one parent may have custody of the boys, whereas the other parent has the girls. Alternatively, one parent may

Cholla Runnels

22-5
In most divorces, mothers are awarded custody of their children.

have custody of the older children while the other parent has the younger ones. This alternative "breaks up" siblings in a family, which may not be in the best interest of the children.

Third-party custody is awarded when the court judges neither parent to be fit or otherwise able to assume custody of the children. In such cases, the children may be raised by relatives or foster parents as determined by a judge.

Child support. Parents—divorced or not—are legally responsible for the financial support of their children until the children are 18 years old. Just as traditional laws place the responsibility of family child care on the wife, they place the responsibility of family finances on the husband.

Child support payments—by law—are directed to the financial support of the children. In many cases, the non-custodial parent (usually the father) is required to pay child support, even if alimony is not ordered. The amount paid is determined by his income and the children's needs. The custodial parent is not paid for the labor involved in caring for the children.

Unfortunately, many fathers stop payments after a number of years. Some states, however, have passed legislation whereby the person charged to pay child support may be arrested for failure to do so. Other states have instituted other ways of collecting child support, for example, by withholding state income-tax refunds from parents who are behind in their payments.

Property division. Arrangements for property division are a major feature of divorce settlements. Some states, called *community property* states, view any property acquired through the labors of either spouse during their marriage as community property (owned equally by both spouses). If the couple divorce, each partner receives one-half of the property they have acquired. *Separate property* exists only when it can be positively shown that such property was owned prior to marriage or acquired during marriage by gift or inheritance and retained as separate property.

Adjusting to the Consequences of Divorce

Once the divorce is final, the consequences must be accepted. One of the consequences of divorce is that the living standards of everyone concerned typically decline. Each former spouse must set up a separate household. Each needs a place to live, furniture, and possibly a car. This financial stress often adds to their bitterness.

If there are children, the parent who is awarded custody must meet the additional costs of the children's food, clothing, and special needs as they grow up. The other parent may be responsible for child support or alimony (maintenance). However, as noted earlier, these payments are not always made

regularly. The parent who has custody of the children may take the other parent to court, but may become tired of fighting to get the money.

Divorce creates consequences for children, too. When they hear discussions about the settlements and payments, they worry about who will take care of them. Younger children may wonder what will happen to their allowance and to their lunch money. Children need to be reassured that their parents still love them and will still provide for them, 22-6. The parents need to talk with their children honestly. They should let their children know what to expect during the divorce process, immediately after the divorce, and in the future. The parents should reassure the children that the divorce is not the children's fault.

Child visitation may create friction. The parent with custody of the children may want to place certain conditions on the visiting privileges of the other parent. Children may become pawns in the negotiations. The visiting parent may use the time with the children to "pump" them for information about the former spouse. When the children return

22-6
Children from broken homes may need special reassurance from their parents.

home, they may be asked again for information. They may be asked, "What did you do? Who was with you? How does the other home look?" Children may become confused. They would rather not choose sides, but they may feel pressured to do so.

Emotional Aftermath of Divorce

After a divorce, people may go through a variety of emotions. They may feel lonely, depressed, resentful, bitter, and guilty. They may even regret getting the divorce. The parent who has custody of the children may resent the freedom of the other parent who is no longer responsible for the daily care of the children.

Divorce is never "fair," and the final settlements may be the final blow. However, spending painful hours questioning "why" will only throw a person deeper into emotional turmoil. Instead, divorced individuals need to begin thinking of how they will live their new lives as single people.

Divorced persons have to make many adjustments. They have to stop thinking of themselves as spouses and begin thinking of themselves as single. In reality, they can never erase their past marital experiences—good or bad. They can only resolve to learn from the past as much as possible and to go on with their lives.

Divorced persons who have children certainly cannot change the fact that they are parents. Their children will continue to be one of their most pressing concerns. Finding ways to maintain close parent-child relationships may not be easy, 22-7.

Divorced persons must continue to live productive lives. They must also achieve an inner security so they can find peace of mind. They must be able to adapt to changes, accept new roles, rebuild self-esteem, and develop new, fulfilling relationships.

Some persons find help in building a new life by seeing a mental health profes-

sional. A good therapist can help the client sort out what happened in the marriage and to process feelings such as grief, guilt, and regret. The counselor can also help the client become more emotionally independent of the former spouse and to develop healthy new relationships. If destructive behavior was a cause of the failed marriage, it is important for the client to work with the counselor to identify this behavior. The individual can then learn to avoid repeating it in new relationships.

The children of divorced parents also have adjustments to make. They must learn to accept their parents' decision to divorce. They must resist the impulse to feel that they somehow "caused" the divorce. They must remind themselves that in almost all cases, the

Cholla Runnels

22-7
It is important for both parents to make a special effort to spend time with their children.

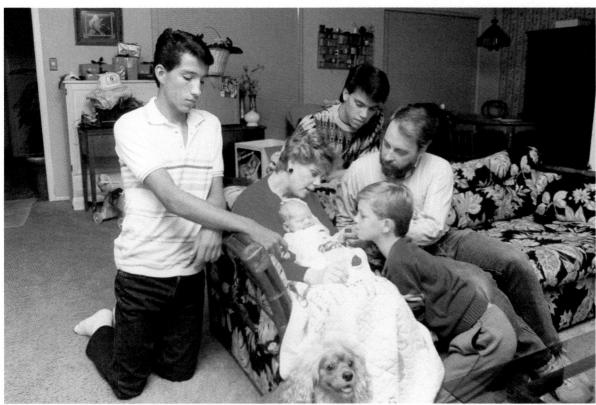

David Hopper

22-8
The blended family makes up a large segment of our society today because of the high rate of divorce and remarriage.

parent who has left the home still loves them very much.

Children of broken homes are asked to accept a difficult situation that is not of their making. If they try to maintain a positive attitude toward themselves and their parents, they will learn a lesson in dealing with change that will help them throughout their lives.

Remarriage

Although persons who seek divorce do so to "get out" of marriage, four out of five divorced persons marry again. Most people who remarry do so fairly soon—within less than three years, on average.

Remarriage rates are affected by many factors, such as age and the presence of children. Women divorced after age 40 are much less likely to remarry than younger women. Divorced women with children at home are also less likely to remarry. In the final decades of life, longevity (length of life) becomes a factor. Recent estimates indicate that for every 100 older unmarried women in this country, there are only 29 unmarried men.

Remarriage after divorce has created a whole new type of family—the blended family. See 22-8. In a blended family, either or both spouses may have been married before and may have one or more children. The couple may or may not add to the family by having children of their own.

Contemporary Concerns *of today's teens:*
Do Remarriages Succeed?

Some divorced persons are reluctant to risk another try at marriage. Some may fear that they will repeat the mistakes that contributed to the end of their earlier marriage. Others may think, "I'm just not cut out for marriage." What are the chances of success for remarried couples?

Couples who have been married before are somewhat less likely to divorce than couples marrying for the first time. A recent study of 87,000 couples found that 29 percent of first marriages had ended in divorce 16 years after the wedding. In contrast, 25.5 percent of couples in remarriages had divorced during the same 16-year period.

The lower divorce rate for remarriages may be due to spouses' more realistic expectations of marriage. The maturity that often comes with age probably is also a stabilizing factor.

Role stress is often magnified in blended families because most children of divorced persons retain relationships with their natural parents. These relationships are permanent links between the first and second marriages. Past and present family relationships become complex. A child in a blended family may have four parent figures in addition to eight grandparents and a variety of siblings, half-siblings, and step-siblings. As a result, family members' expectations of one another may be unclear and confusing.

Financial problems are common in blended families. The multiple obligations to former and present children and households stretch the financial resources.

The parent-child relationships in blended families are sometimes strained. Parents are expected to love their stepchildren as much as their own. At the same time, they may not have equal parental discipline and control. See 22-9. New roles and expectations based on mutual respect need to be established.

Siblings in blended families must also adjust to one another. In many cases, they have been raised with different values, standards, and rules for behavior. They may feel awkward as they try to get used to their new brothers or sisters and may feel that they have

Cholla Runnels

22-9
Discipline can be a problem in blended families because of confusion about a stepparent's degree of authority.

little in common with them. Siblings should watch for opportunities to try to help each other. In a few years, the children will grow up and be on their own. In the meantime, kindness and patience can smooth the way.

In spite of challenges such as these, most blended families are successful. Their members are aware of the obstacles they face, and they work together to overcome these obstacles. With the passage of time, many of the early misgivings that the new families experience will disappear. They will probably be replaced with positive feelings. The new family will build its own set of traditions and memories as the events of life—both happy and sad—unfold.

Summary ■ ■ ■ ■ ■ ■ ■ ■ ■ ■ ■ ■ ■ ■ ■

- It has been estimated that there is a divorce for every two marriages in the United States.

- Marriages may be terminated in two ways: annulment and divorce. Legal separation allows the couple to live in separate households but does not end their marriage.

- Divorce laws differ from state to state.

- Grounds commonly used for divorce include incompatibility, cruelty (mental or physical), desertion, impotence, insanity, alcohol or drug addiction, adultery, separation, and nonsupport (willful neglect). States commonly have no-fault divorce laws that eliminate the need to prove one partner guilty.

- Examples of defenses in a divorce proceeding include condonation, connivance, and collusion.

- The terms of a divorce settlement usually include provision for child support and division of property and may occasionally include alimony or rehabilitative alimony.

- One common consequence of divorce is a decline in the financial well-being of both spouses.

- Adults and children must both make psychological adjustments in the aftermath of divorce.

- Blended families are families in which either or both spouses may have been married before and may have one or more children. The couple may or may not add to the family by having children of their own.

- With patience and understanding, blended families can overcome obstacles to make positive, successful adjustments.

To Review ■ ■ ■ ■ ■ ■ ■ ■ ■ ■ ■ ■ ■ ■ ■

1. Describe the two methods of legally terminating a marriage relationship.

2. Name five possible reasons for the high U.S. divorce rate.

3. Which of the following are legal grounds for the annulment of a marriage?
    a. Concealment of disease.
    b. Financial misrepresentation.
    c. Wishing to marry someone new.
    d. Use of threats or force to induce a mate to enter marriage.
    e. Falling "out of love."

4. Explain how legal separation differs from divorce.

5. Explain what a no-fault divorce is.

6. Match the following grounds for divorce.
    _____ Drug or alcohol addiction
    _____ Separation
    _____ Cruelty
    _____ Incompatibility
    a. Spouses are unable to live together peaceably or in harmony.
    b. Spouses have been living apart for a significant period of time.
    c. One spouse engages in abusive psychological or physical behavior toward the other spouse.
    d. Prolonged and habitual substance abuse.

7. List and explain three examples of defenses in a divorce proceeding.

8. Explain the difference between alimony and child support.

9. Explain why divorce usually results in a decline of financial well-being for both spouses.

10. Describe two special challenges that blended families may face.

To Do ■ ■ ■ ■ ■ ■ ■ ■ ■ ■ ■ ■ ■ ■ ■

1. Research the divorce laws in your state, naming the legal grounds for divorce, conditions that must be met, defenses to divorce action, and terms of divorce.

2. Invite a respected mental health professional from your community to make a class presentation entitled, "Getting Past Divorce: How Counseling Can Help."

3. Research the problems involved in divorce and remarriage and summarize them in a report. Cite challenges faced by blended families, including problems of finances, emotional pressures, the disciplining of children, etc.

4. Ask a panel of respected adult community members who grew up in successful blended families to make a panel presentation to your class. Ask them about the challenges they faced in adjusting to their new families and how they met these challenges.

5. View a television situation comedy concerned with a blended family. What challenges are presented in the program? Did the family members address the challenges successfully? Why or why not?

23

Aging, Fulfillment of Life, and Death

Cholla Runnels

Terms to Know

sandwich generation

intergenerational caregiving

empty nest syndrome

menopause

climacteric

hospice

stages of dying

stages of grieving

autopsy

living will

organ bank

will

beneficiaries

intestate

After studying this chapter, you will be able to

■ recognize the fact that our society, as a whole, is growing older.

■ describe the middle-age stage and the added responsibilities of intergenerational caregiving during this stage.

■ summarize the emotional, physical, and financial aspects of aging.

■ describe various types of housing for the elderly.

■ explain hospice care.

■ list the stages of dying and the stages of grieving.

■ identify the problems of the survivors.

■ define terms related to the legal issues of death.

Aging begins at birth and continues throughout life. People grow older each day.

Middle age begins at 45, and old age begins at 65. The average life span in the United States today is about 76 years. Thus, the average person spends almost half a lifetime as a middle-aged or elderly person.

People's attitudes about aging vary. Some people dread old age. They view it as a time of life that they want to avoid. Other people view aging with the same zest for living they have always displayed. They are glad to have the chance to experience a new aspect of life. They accept the changes that aging brings and take advantage of the new opportunities it presents. See 23-1.

Cholla Runnels

23-1
Some people enjoy old age and take advantage of the new opportunities aging brings.

Middle Age ▪ ▪ ▪ ▪ ▪

Middle age includes the ages between 45 and 65. These years are perhaps the most misunderstood years of people's lives. They are also busy years involving a wide variety of activities.

Four out of five people survive to age 60. Most parents have their children before they are 35, and the children leave home by the time the parents are 48 to 55. With increased life expectancy, the parents may live 20 to 30 years longer. They may spend this time as wage earners, as independent singles, or in renewed companionship with their spouses. See 23-2.

The frantic rush of middle age sees many people reaching a top level in their careers, perhaps sending their children to col-

23-2
During middle age, a couple's children mature and often leave home. Spouses have more time to spend with each other and for travel.

lege and seeing them marry, and meeting new expenses. These years are not all easy, but they are busy!

The Sandwich Generation and Intergenerational Caregiving

Middle age has taken on a new image in recent years, reflective of the changes in our society. Some sociologists have labeled today's middle-aged couples as the *sandwich generation.* The couple is often "sandwiched" between caring for their children and caring for their parents at a time when they would really like more time for themselves. Care provided for both older and younger generations by the middle generation is an example of *intergenerational caregiving.* This term refers to the provision of care to members of one generation by members of another. More families today may engage in intergenerational caregiving due to the needs of young adult children and elderly parents.

Why do today's young adult children require more help from their middle-aged parents? First, young adults face increasingly complex choices today and have more options to investigate before they can settle into adult life. This phenomenon often creates added burdens and responsibilities for parents. Adult children who may have left home to attend college return home following graduation and often remain until they find employment. Even after they begin working, many find they cannot afford to live on their own. Instead, they live with their parents to ease their own financial burdens. Some get jobs, but quit and move back in with their parents if the jobs don't meet their expectations. In other instances, adult children who have married and divorced find their way back to the parental home because they need help in reestablishing their lives. Often these adult children have children of their own who accompany them to the parental home.

Care for elderly parents is another factor increasing the complexities of the sandwich generation. The lengthened life span of people today means that many middle-aged couples find they must provide care for their elderly parents. There are various options for such care, including having the elderly parents move in with them. This adds to the many responsibilities of the middle generation.

Intergenerational caregiving requires many adjustments. Finances may have to be stretched to provide for more members of the household. Space may be a problem in trying to provide comfortable living arrangements for several generations of people. Time will be at a premium if extra care is required for either an elderly parent or a grandchild.

For intergenerational caregiving to succeed, everyone needs to help out. House cleaning, meal preparation, and laundry are activities that need to be divided among those persons in the household who are able to participate. Available income will have to be carefully budgeted to meet critical needs. Additional medical care costs may affect the budget. Child care will need to be provided for very young members of the household. School-age children may be involved in many activities, and someone will need to help them get to where they need to be. This help could be provided by any member of the family who can drive.

Many middle-aged persons suffer from guilt if they don't feel they are adequately meeting their children's or parents' needs. They may think they are not doing enough for their parents, their children, or their grandchildren. Sometimes the desire to provide total care for an elderly parent causes the son or daughter to have health problems of his or her own. A few dependent parents add to the problem by encouraging their adult children to feel ashamed for not taking good enough care of them.

Families caught in the pressures of intergenerational caregiving should look at the resources available in their community. Many communities have community-based day care for the elderly as well as for children. Home health care services may be available through social service agencies. These services allow elderly people to remain in their own homes. Nurses or aides visit them to provide help. If necessary, nursing homes can provide constant care for elderly residents. These options can be considered by middle-aged couples who may need to find care for their elderly parents.

Old Age

As a whole, our society is growing older. About 23 million people in the United States today are at least 65 years old. This is one out of every nine persons, or 11 percent of the population. Today, the number of people over 65 exceeds those under 25. Every day, more than 1,000 people reach age 65. By the year 2000, 30 million people will be at least 65 years old. By the year 2025, 45 million people, or 14 percent of the population, will be in this age group.

Perhaps most startling is the fact that in the next 50 years, the population over age 65 will increase two and one-half times. As a whole, the older population has been growing at a rate much faster than the general population. By the year 2050, there are expected to be as many as 16 million Americans over age 85, or one person in 20 at that time.

Impact of the Growing Population of Older Adults

The increased proportion of older adults will have a major impact on our society. There are fears that a shrinking workforce of younger people may someday be hard pressed to pay for programs that support an ever-growing older population. The sheer number of persons 85 years and older will be substantial enough to have a major impact on the health care and social service systems in our society.

With fewer young people in the workforce, some companies have turned to older workers to round out their ranks of part-time and full-time workers. What older people may lack in agility and physical endurance, they tend to make up for in reliability and a strong work ethic.

Elderly people are generally politically active. Their numbers are sometimes powerful enough to swing elections. As their numbers increase, their influence will be even greater.

The elderly face significant problems. Over time, inflation seriously erodes their incomes. Older people living on fixed incomes worry about medical costs and other costs associated with increasing infirmity.

Aspects of Aging

Every stage of life has its changes. At each stage, some things are lost, but other things are gained. Aging persons may lose some strength or physical vigor. However, they may gain new leisure-time interests and more meaningful relationships with families and friends.

When asked, many elderly persons list finances as their biggest concern. Their other major concerns are crime, poor health, and loneliness. Not all older people have all these

Cholla Runnels

23-3
Many people reach the peak of their careers during middle age and receive awards for their work.

problems. Some are financially secure and in good health. Some have cultivated many friendships and have maintained close family ties. Each person is unique as a child, a youth, a young adult, a middle-aged adult, and a senior citizen.

Emotional Aspects

Emotionally, people may experience some identity problems in redefining their roles as they age. Parents who have stayed at home to raise their children may exhibit the *empty nest syndrome.* They may feel useless and depressed after their children have left home. People who have followed a career often reach the peak of career achievement in middle age, 23-3. This causes some to plunge themselves even further into their work. Others are able to slow down, but they may have difficulty using their leisure time to develop new areas of companionship with their spouses.

On the positive side, middle-aged and elderly people have access to a whole new world. They can begin new recreational and leisure-time activities, 23-4. They can consider moving to a new home that requires less upkeep. They can enjoy visiting with their children, who may now seem more like friends and less like dependents.

Middle-aged or aging couples can profit from broadening and deepening intimacies in their relationships. These intimacies may vary in form. Creative intimacy allows a couple to share appreciation for the arts, music, or hobbies. Intellectual intimacy allows a couple to share a closeness in discussing politics, books, plays, or speeches. Recreational

23-4
This middle-aged woman has developed a hobby that she will enjoy throughout her lifetime.

Contemporary Concerns *of today's teens:*

Accidents and Aging

Accidents at any age seldom "just happen." As a person ages, accidental injuries occur more frequently and are often more serious. Many result in death. The National Safety Council reports that each year about 24,000 persons over the age of 65 die from accidental injuries. This amounts to 23 percent of all accidental deaths, even though older people constitute only about 11 percent of the population. At least 800,000 others sustain injuries severe enough to disable them for at least one day.

Why are elderly persons more accident prone? Poor eyesight and hearing may decrease awareness of hazards. Impaired coordination and balance can sometimes make an older person unsteady. Many suffer from arthritis, an inflammation of the joints, which often makes normal movement difficult and painful. Women, in particular, have more brittle bones as they age. Thus, a minor fall may result in broken bones. Accidental injuries in older persons tend to heal more slowly.

Preventing accidents is the best course of action. Following are suggestions for preventing the most common accidents. If you know an elderly person, you may want to share these safety precautions with them.

Falls are the most common cause of serious and fatal injuries in the aged. The following suggestions can help prevent falls:

- Illuminate all stairways and provide light switches at both the bottom and top of stairs.

- Provide night-lights or bedside remote-control light switches.

- Install sturdy handrails on both sides of stairways.

- Use nonskid pads under loose rugs, and tack down carpeting on stairs.

- Install grab bars on bathroom walls, and place nonskid mats in the bathtub.

- Rearrange furniture and other objects so they are not obstacles.

The following suggestions will help prevent accidental burns:

- Discourage an older person from smoking in bed or when drowsy.

- Discourage an older person from wearing loose-fitting, flammable clothing when cooking because it may touch the flame or source of heat.

- Check water heater thermostats so that tap water does not cause burns.

- Be sure the aging person knows which exits to use in case of a fire or other emergency.

- Don't install multiple door locks that will be hard to open in an emergency. Install one good lock that can be opened quickly from the inside.

intimacy offers a couple companionship on the golf course, at the bowling alley, or during a long walk. Sexual intimacy allows a couple to share themselves completely with each other. Parenting intimacy allows mates to share their dreams through their children and grandchildren.

Together a middle-aged couple can build a new identity. Their success will depend on two factors: their ability to adjust to new situations, and their ability to find new meaning in life. Their success in establishing a middle-aged identity will influence their success in coping with retirement and old age.

Physical Aspects

Physically, a human matures in about 25 years. At this time, the body's framework reaches its maximum size and strength. Then, at an extremely slow pace, the body begins to deteriorate. Some parts of the body age more rapidly than others. Individuals' bodily changes take place at different rates of speed. Aging becomes a different experience for each person.

Persons who eat balanced meals, exercise regularly, have regular medical checkups, and maintain a positive attitude about life are likely to feel the effects of aging more slowly than others. See 23-5.

Eventually, all people show signs of aging. One of the earliest visible signs is noticed in the skin. Loss of elasticity results in wrinkling.

Bones change little in size, but they do change in chemical composition. Bones become weaker and more fragile. Many elderly women suffer from *osteoporosis*—a bone disease caused by insufficient calcium in the diet.

The heart muscles may become less efficient, and blood vessels may become narrower. As a result, circulation problems may

develop. The supply of blood to the legs and the brain may be reduced.

Sensory problems most often begin with a hearing loss. Loss of vision may follow and add to an elderly person's frustrations. The inability to focus on printed material interferes with the ability to read.

Aging persons need to pay special attention to their diets. If their diets improve, their overall psychological and physical health can

David Hopper

23-5
Regular exercise is an important factor in maintaining good health throughout life.

improve. Nutritional needs vary for each person, but certain generalizations can be made. Most older persons need to reduce the total number of calories they consume, but the need for most nutrients does not decrease. They need a well-balanced diet that includes a variety of foods. They should try to cut down on fats and sweets that have many calories. Individuals with constipation problems should be sure to eat plenty of foods that are high in fiber. Examples include fresh fruits and vegetables and whole-grain cereals.

The nutritional problems of elderly persons are sometimes associated with loneliness, 23-6. Some persons do not eat regularly because they do not enjoy eating alone. Mealtime in a family is a social time. When people live alone, they may skip meals because they do not have anyone with whom to dine. This problem can partially be solved by utilizing community centers that offer meals for older persons.

Sexual Aspects

Both women and men experience a "change of life" in middle age. The period of time when this change occurs in women is known as menopause. In men, it is referred to as the climacteric.

Menopause

During *menopause,* biological changes occur that trigger both psychological and emotional changes in women.

Cholla Runnels

23-6
Mealtime may be more enjoyable when it is shared with others.

When a woman is about 50 years old, the production of the sex hormone slows down. As a result, her ovaries cease to produce a ripened egg regularly each month. Eventually the menstrual periods cease.

The imbalance of hormones in a woman's body during menopause may cause her to have *hot flashes.* These are sudden, brief feelings of heat that occur as the blood vessels dilate and fill with blood.

Irregularity in hormone production and menstrual periods can be emotionally disturbing to a woman. Nervousness and irritability, as well as increased fatigue, may result. Well-balanced diets, regular exercise, and an active interest in life can help a woman get through menopause with a minimum of discomfort. Women who have been able to adjust well to various situations throughout life usually do not experience overwhelming problems. They look upon menopause as a stage in their lives which will pass. They maintain a positive view of the future.

Climacteric

The climacteric in men is a much less pronounced change than menopause in women. Production of the male sex hormone peaks at about age 20. The level of production is usually maintained until the man is in his 50's. Then it decreases steadily until age 80, when very little is produced.

During the *climacteric,* a diminishing supply of hormone production in the man results in changes in moods and emotions. The changes are similar to those of a woman during menopause. The man's general state of health, his attitude toward life, and his self-image will determine how he adjusts to these changes.

Both husband and wife should maintain a positive attitude toward this time of their lives and emphasize the positive aspects that the years ahead can bring.

Financial Aspects

Many older persons list finances as their greatest worry. Financial resources will affect adjustments in all other areas of aging. Social Security benefits alone will not meet living costs. Medicaid and Medicare—government-sponsored programs that help pay medical expenses—may not be adequate. Many pension plans have not been able to meet the increased financial needs caused by inflation.

Financial planning must be started early in life to build up savings and investments for the aging years. People should take advantage of all the information available to them as they plan ahead for their financial security. Many types of investment programs are available. They meet different needs for different individuals and families.

As people reach an older age, they should reevaluate their investments. A very elderly person may want to turn the management of his or her financial affairs over to someone else, completely or partially. This step can be taken voluntarily, or in some instances, it may be decided by a court. A relative or friend with an interest in the person's welfare can ask the court to declare the person incompetent (unable to manage financial affairs). An older person would be wise to make arrangements for assistance in financial management while he or she is still capable of making sound decisions.

People work hard all their lives to reach security in their old age. Just as wise money management is crucial in the early years of family life, it is also essential in later life. The way a person manages, saves, and invests his or her money throughout life will be important in acquiring peace of mind in old age.

Housing Arrangements

Where people live is a major factor in their lives. Many elderly people decide to continue living where they have lived for

United Way of Houston

23-7

Many older people want to remain in their homes. This is a good plan if the necessary adjustments, such as a wheelchair ramp, can be made.

and the liveliness of teenagers. Many people find they still prefer a typical neighborhood made up of a variety of people rather than a specific community of all older people.

If elderly persons move in with their children, they may have to accept a secondary role. The adult children should clearly define their own roles without offending their parents. The older persons should be able to feel that they are a useful and active part of the family even though the adult children make the major family decisions.

About five percent of people over the age of 65 in the United States live in nursing homes. However, for people age 85 and over, the percentage increases to 22 percent. When

years. That is the most secure plan, if the housing is convenient, safe, comfortable, and easy to maintain. See 23-7. Moving older persons from familiar surroundings can be a devastating blow to their feelings of security.

Sometimes a move has to be made. If low-cost housing is needed, public housing facilities may provide special units for the elderly. Housing facilities for older persons with low or moderate incomes sometimes are sponsored by churches and other nonprofit groups with federal aid. Some have private units, and some offer services such as meals and recreation.

There are many leisure villages, retirement communities, and condominiums available to older people. Many of these are designed exclusively for elderly residents and do not allow children or younger people, except as visitors. Social activities, complete health care, and shopping facilities are often available. Such areas should be thoroughly investigated before a commitment is made to them. Some people enjoy these environments, but others have been disappointed. They dislike being surrounded completely by older people. They miss a small child's play

How to Select a Nursing Home

1. Ask for advice from physicians and people who have already chosen nursing homes.

2. Look only at those nursing homes which are near enough to allow frequent visits by family and friends.

3. Visit the home during mealtime. Is the kitchen clean and free of insects and rodents? Do the people preparing the food use sanitary practices? Does the food look appetizing? Are adequate amounts of food served? Are snacks available between meals?

4. Look at the physical condition of the building. Is it well-maintained and free of offensive odors?

5. Observe the staff. Do they treat the patients with kindness and respect?

6. Observe the patients. Do they seem happy? Are their clothes neat and clean? Are they well-groomed?

7. Ask about the opportunities for recreation. What facilities are available for recreation? Are activities regularly scheduled?

23-8

These suggestions can help you choose a good nursing home for an elderly person.

23-9
This grandmother is looking forward to spending time with her granddaughter as she grows up.

nursing home care is needed, the facility should be chosen carefully. Factors to consider when making a choice are listed in 23-8.

New Horizons in Aging

Your overall attitude toward living will determine how you approach the last stages of life. Middle age and old age are no better or worse than other stages. You will give up some things as you approach each stage, and you will gain some others. As you experience the last stages of your life, two events may stand apart from the rest. If you have had children who have married and had children of their own, you will gain the new role of grandparent. If you have been employed, you will look forward to retirement.

Grandparenting

Most couples have their children when they are in their 20's or early 30's. Thus, people may become grandparents when they are middle-aged. They will continue this role throughout their lives.

The family systems in our society currently focus on independence. As a result, ties between grandparents and grandchildren are not as strong as in former generations. This is a loss since children can gain a great deal by being close to older people, by loving them, and by understanding their needs. In many families, however, the grandparents do keep in close touch with their grandchildren, 23-9. They may act as babysitters, or they may even help raise their grandchildren in times of crisis.

Grandparents today have more independence than in the past. They are freer to travel, to enjoy new leisure-time activities, and to be friends with their children. They can share their experiences from the past with their grandchildren. Many grandparents find they can enjoy new types of social contact with their grandchildren and their children. Grandparenting is a role that many older persons enjoy, 23-10.

23-10
Children benefit in many ways from spending time with their grandparents.

Retirement

Whenever retirement occurs, it creates change. If a person can adjust to change easily, retirement will not be a problem. Almost everyone at one time or another has said, "Just wait till I retire!" Retirement can be a pleasant stage of life, or it can produce frustration and loneliness. It is more likely to be pleasant if you look ahead to it with positive plans and goals.

Retirement is a process—not just one event. People should start planning for retirement long before they actually reach this stage of their lives. They should investigate pre-retirement programs that are available to them. In addition to financial matters, they should consider health programs, legal matters, and housing possibilities. See 23-11. They should also develop some outside interests or leisure-time activities so they will have

23-11
You can plan ahead for your retirement and perhaps even work on a retirement home.

Cholla Runnels

23-12
Retirement is more enjoyable when old friendships are maintained and new friendships are developed.

something to do during retirement. Some people even turn a hobby into a second career.

Retirement causes changes in a couple's daily schedule. These changes may be difficult for the husband and wife to suddenly accept. If they have planned ahead of time for these changes, they can make better adjustments. The best plan is to give themselves time to adjust to the new abundance of free time that retirement offers. Married couples should work to develop common areas of interest. They should also try to maintain close relationships with their friends, 23-12.

In all communities, there are human needs that need to be met. Many organizations eagerly accept the volunteer help of elderly persons, 23-13. These organizations can be identified by contacting local hospitals, religious groups, community centers, or the National Center for Voluntary Action.

Accepting Death As a Reality of Life ▪ ▪ ▪ ▪

If we are to study living, we must study dying, for it represents the final stage of development. Death is as much a part of the human life cycle as birth is. You must learn to accept it as a reality of your life

Accepting death may be difficult, for we have created a death-denying culture. Medical achievements have led us to believe that it is possible to conquer nature. We can prolong life, but we cannot deny the inevitability of death.

Hospice Care

When a family member or friend is dying, many people turn to hospice programs for help. The term *hospice* refers to a medical facility designed for people who have only a

few months or weeks to live. Hospices provide a more homelike atmosphere than that of a hospital. Emphasis is placed on pain management and maintenance of a peaceful, supportive environment. Hospice-type care can also be provided in the home by family members and friends with the assistance of hospice health professionals and volunteers.

Hospice care or hospice-type home care appeals to those who, given a choice, would prefer to die in a peaceful environment with family members nearby. If an illness is terminal, and death is only a matter of time, some people prefer this alternative. On the other hand, some terminally ill people wish to remain hospitalized. They prefer to fight their illnesses to the very end with the most aggressive medical resources a hospital can offer. This choice is available to terminally ill individuals and their families.

Ingalls Memorial Hospital

23-13
Elderly volunteers fulfill others' needs for help.

Stages of Dying

Death can come at any time to persons of any age. Those who know that death is near pass through clearly defined stages in the acceptance of death called the *stages of dying*. These stages have been identified by Dr. Elisabeth Kubler-Ross, who has studied the needs of dying people.

- Stage One—Denial. When a patient first learns that he or she is terminally ill, the typical reaction is, "No, not me." The denial stage is important and necessary. It helps cushion the impact of the patient's awareness that death is inevitable.

- Stage Two—Anger. In this stage, the patient resents the fact that others will remain healthy and alive while he or she must die. God is regarded as imposing the death sentence, and thus is a special target for anger.

- Stage Three—Bargaining. During stage three, patients accept the fate of death, but they try to bargain for more time. They usually bargain with God. Even people who are not religious will bargain at this time. They promise to be good, or to do something special in exchange for another week or month or year of life. Sometimes a special future family event, such as a wedding or graduation, is used in their bargaining. "Just let me see my grandson be married," a person may say, or "I want to be there when my daughter graduates."

- Stage Four—Depression. In this stage, the person at first will mourn past losses, things not done, and wrongs committed. Then the person enters a state of preparatory grief. He or she grows quiet and wants no visitors. This indicates the person feels ready to die and will be able to go peacefully.

- Stage Five—Acceptance. This is the final stage. The patient knows that death is close and is ready for it. This stage is neither happy nor unhappy. It is simply the calm acceptance of reality, 23-14.

Knowledge of these stages can help family members and friends understand what the dying person is feeling. This can help the person achieve the kind of death he or she wants.

A person can usually sense when death is near. You should not let a dying person feel that he or she is being given up on. However, you should not try to help the person hang on to false hope. The best approach in most cases is to be caring, honest, and responsive as the person prepares for death.

Those Left Behind ■ ■ ■

The death of a loved one is painful to survivors. When someone you love dies, thoughts of what might have been enter your mind. You may feel guilty about apologies not made or injuries inflicted. You may even resent the dead person for dying and leaving you behind.

Stages of Grieving

Those left behind when a loved one dies eventually adjust to the loss. However, the grieving process of the survivors generally follows a series of stages similar to the stages of dying presented above. These may be thought of as the *stages of grieving*.

- Stage One—Denial. If the death is sudden, the survivors experience a strong sense of disbelief. They might say, "This can't be true." However, if the person had a lingering illness, few people are capable of accepting death without questioning, "Why?"

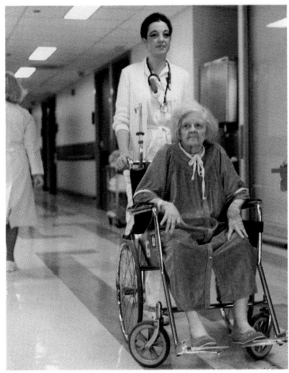

23-14
In the final stage of accepting death, a person finds inner peace and calmly accepts the fact that death is near.

Cholla Runnels

- Stage Two—Anger. The anger may be directed toward the deceased: "Why did you leave me like this?" The survivor takes on the role of the victim because the deceased died and left him or her behind.

- Stage Three—Bargaining. If the person is still alive, the future survivor may seek a bargaining posture, trying to prolong the person's life. The person may say, "Please let him live. I will be good to him." As the survivor recognizes the futility of bargaining, he or she moves to the next stage.

- Stage Four—Depression. This carries with it feelings of loneliness and isolation. "What will I do now?" There is a sense of great loss. Depression involves facing reality, but it leaves a person feeling helpless.

- Stage Five—Acceptance. Finally, the stage of acceptance begins as the person realizes that the death is a fact and cannot be changed. The survivor starts to look at the loss in a constructive way. He or she begins to think about what has to be done now to get on with living. This is the stage of healing and recovery.

The death of someone close to you is one of life's most shocking, and often shattering, experiences. Understanding the stages of grief can help prepare you to cope with the death of someone you love. It will also help you to understand what others may be going through when a death occurs in their lives. The survivors need understanding and comfort from their friends and family members. They need to talk to others about their feelings and about the one who died. Do not be afraid to talk to bereaved persons. They often need and want to talk.

The passage of time will help ease the pain of death. The following suggestions may help you during the grieving process:

- Allow yourself to work through your grief. Try to recognize the full reality of what has happened. View the body and discuss the death with friends and relatives so you can begin to accept the permanence of the loss.

- Accept the comradeship of your friends and relatives as a source of comfort.

- Talk out your grief and cry. This is a normal part of grieving, and you should not be ashamed of it.

- Remember the good times you had with the deceased. This will help you understand the time spent together is worth the grief.

- Delay any major decisions until you have sought proper advice and can think clearly.

Telling Children about Death

Suppressing or denying grief can have a damaging effect on anyone, especially on a child. Psychiatrists believe that children who experience the death of a loved one should complete the task of mourning at that time. If they don't, they may be overwhelmed by their feelings of grief in later years.

There are several expressions to avoid when telling children about death.

Do not say, "Mother has gone on a long journey." This is untrue, and the child will learn you have lied. The child may even interpret this to mean the mother has chosen to desert the family without even saying good-bye.

Do not say, "Grandmother died because she was sick," unless the child is able to understand that all illnesses do not lead to death.

Do not say, "Mother has just gone to the hospital." When anyone has to go to the hospital in the future, the child will expect the person not to come back. This can be very frightening to a child.

The simplest way to talk to a child about death is to talk about how flowers and pets die. If you explain that death is a normal part of life, the child will be able to accept it.

Widows and Widowers

Statistics show that more marriages end by death than by divorce. The widow is more often the survivor. (A *widow* is a woman whose husband has died. A *widower* is a man whose wife has died.) In the average community, there are twice as many widows as widowers. By 85 years of age, 85 percent of wives are widows.

The death of a spouse creates many crises for a person. Widows and widowers must adjust to a single lifestyle. They have to learn how to deal with their loneliness, 23-15. They must also learn to accept total responsibility for their homes. Activities that used to be shared, such as handling financial matters, cooking, cleaning, filling leisure time, and entertaining, must all be done by the survivor. See 23-16.

Cholla Runnels

23-15
A widow may look for letters from relatives and friends to help fight her loneliness.

23-16
Cholla Runnels

Widowed individuals find that mealtimes previously shared with a spouse are now spent alone.

Legal Issues of Death ■ ■ ■ ■ ■ ■ ■

All states have laws dealing with the legal issues of death. They all require that a physician or coroner examine the dead body and issue a certificate that states the time, place, and cause of death. If the cause of death is doubtful, an autopsy may be performed. An *autopsy* is a detailed physical examination of a dead body.

Living Will

A *living will* allows people to choose whether or not they want to be kept alive when there is apparently no hope for them to recover. With this legal document, people usually indicate their desire that no extreme measures by taken to prolong life. Cases in which persons have been maintained for long periods on life support systems prompt people to make living wills so their wishes will be known.

Organ Banks

Some persons make arrangements so that when they die all or parts of their bodies are donated to medical science or placed in an *organ bank* until a need arises. These people believe that in this way they are contributing to the continuation of life.

Funeral Arrangements

A *funeral* is a ceremony that honors the person who has died. Funeral services allow people to express concern and support for the survivors. A funeral causes people to confront the reality of death and helps them prepare to say a final good-bye to the dead person.

Some people make the arrangements for their own funerals while they are still living. They may even pay for their funerals in advance. Preplanning eases the minds of these individuals and of the people who will be the survivors.

If the funeral has not been preplanned, the family will choose a funeral director shortly after the death. The funeral director will make all the necessary arrangements in consultation with the family. The family should be careful to avoid letting the funeral director talk them into a more expensive funeral than they can afford.

The deceased may have expressed wishes concerning disposal of the body. If so, these wishes should be followed, 23-17. If the deceased did not express any wishes, the family will have to decide if the body should be buried or *cremated* (reduced to ashes by burning).

The family will need to make decisions about a wake and the funeral service. A *wake* is a watch held over the body of a dead person before burial. It gives people a chance to pay their last respects and to offer emotional support to the survivors.

23-17
A person may have made arrangements to be buried in his or her family's cemetery plot. If so, the person's wishes should be followed.

The Legal Will

A *will* is a legal declaration of a person's wishes concerning the way his or her property will be distributed after death. The will names the *beneficiaries,* or those who will receive the property. It states how much property each beneficiary will receive and the conditions under which they will receive it. Wills can also name legal guardians for minor children. This is one of the most important reasons for young parents to be sure to have a will.

Dying *intestate* (without a will) creates problems for survivors. They will have the inconvenience and expense of extra attorney services and court procedures. Without a will, the estate taxation will be heavier, and the property may simply be distributed according to the laws of the state. Only with a will can a person be sure the best interests of loved ones will be met.

There are different methods of making a will. Do-it-yourself forms are available, but they are not generally recommended. A *holographic will* is written completely in the handwriting of the person making the will. A *nuncupative will* is an oral will. This type of will needs one or more witnesses, and even then it may be unacceptable. The safest type of will is one that is written by a lawyer in consultation with the client. Two witnesses are required to sign the will in addition to the client.

A person should keep a copy of his or her will in a safe-deposit box. The lawyer will usually keep another copy. The will should be kept up-to-date. Additions or changes may be needed if the person's financial matters, state of residence, or family responsibilities change. If a new will is made, all copies of the old will should be destroyed to prevent confusion.

Summary ▪ ▪ ▪ ▪ ▪ ▪ ▪ ▪ ▪ ▪ ▪ ▪ ▪ ▪

- Aging is a process that begins at birth and continues throughout life.

- Intergenerational caregiving is often required of middle-age couples who may have to provide for both adult children who return home and elderly parents who need care.

- Middle age and old age bring new emotional, physical, sexual, and financial aspects to one's life.

- Persons who eat balanced meals, exercise regularly, have regular medical check-ups, and maintain a positive attitude about life are likely to feel the effects of aging more slowly than others.

- Many older persons list finances as their greatest worry.

- Housing for aging persons should provide safety and comfort as well as socializing opportunities.

- Grandparents can enjoy new types of social contacts with their grandchildren and their adult children.

- Retirement is generally more pleasant for those who begin planning for it early in life and develop interests and activities that they can pursue.

- Death is a part of the human life cycle and must be accepted as a reality of life.

- The dying person will generally pass through these stages: denial, anger, bargaining, depression, and acceptance.

- People in the grieving process will pass through similar stages as they learn to adjust to the loss of a loved one.

- More marriages end by death than by divorce, and there are more widows than widowers.

- A funeral helps people confront the reality of death.

- Having a legal will enables a person to designate how property will be distributed after his or her death.

To Review ■ ■ ■ ■ ■ ■ ■ ■ ■ ■ ■ ■ ■ ■ ■ ■

1. What is the average life span of people in the United States?

2. Briefly describe what is meant by the "sandwich generation."

3. Why has intergenerational caregiving become a factor in the lives of many middle-aged couples?

4. Which of the following statements is true?
   a. All humans age uniformly.
   b. Humans begin to age physically at the age of 50.
   c. Skin wrinkles as it loses its elasticity.
   d. Bones change in length and chemical composition as a person ages.

5. Explain why loneliness may be a factor in the nutritional problems of elderly persons.

6. The sexual "change of life" is known as _____ for women and the _____ for men.

7. Name four general factors to consider when planning retirement.

8. What is a hospice? Describe hospice care.

9. In which stage of dying does the patient resent the fact that others will remain healthy and alive while he or she must die?

10. In which stage of grieving does the survivor begin to make plans for his or her life without the deceased?

11. True or False. When someone you love dies, you should try to forget about the person and the times you shared.

12. True or False. The explanation, "Mother has gone on a long journey," is a good way to tell a child that his or her mother has died.

13. A _____ _____ is a legal document which states whether or not a person wishes to be kept alive by life support systems when there is apparently no hope for recovery.

14. Why should a person have a legal will?

To Do ■ ■ ■ ■ ■ ■ ■ ■ ■ ■ ■ ■ ■ ■ ■ ■

1. Write a short paper entitled, "What I will be doing 50 years from today." Be sure to mention physical health, career goals, financial status, leisure-time activities, and family relationships.

2. Discuss changes in our society that have created new responsibilities for middle-aged parents.

3. Make a list of five steps you can take now to help plan for your retirement.

4. Work in groups to design collages on the following concerns of elderly people: recreational activities, family ties, physical health, types of housing.

5. Role-play scenes depicting aging individuals. Include both positive and negative aspects of aging.

6. On a separate sheet of paper, write five adjectives that come to your mind when you think about death. Compare your list with those of your classmates.

7. Write a short skit in which a child is told about the death of a grandparent. Perform the skit in class.

8. Identify the stages that people go through when they are mourning the death of a loved one. How do these stages compare with the stages of dying?

9. Investigate the costs of various types of funerals and various methods for disposing of bodies.

10. Have a class discussion about why people use "soft" words and phrases when talking about death. (Examples include: "passed away" instead of died and "resting place" instead of grave.)

VII

Managing Family Living

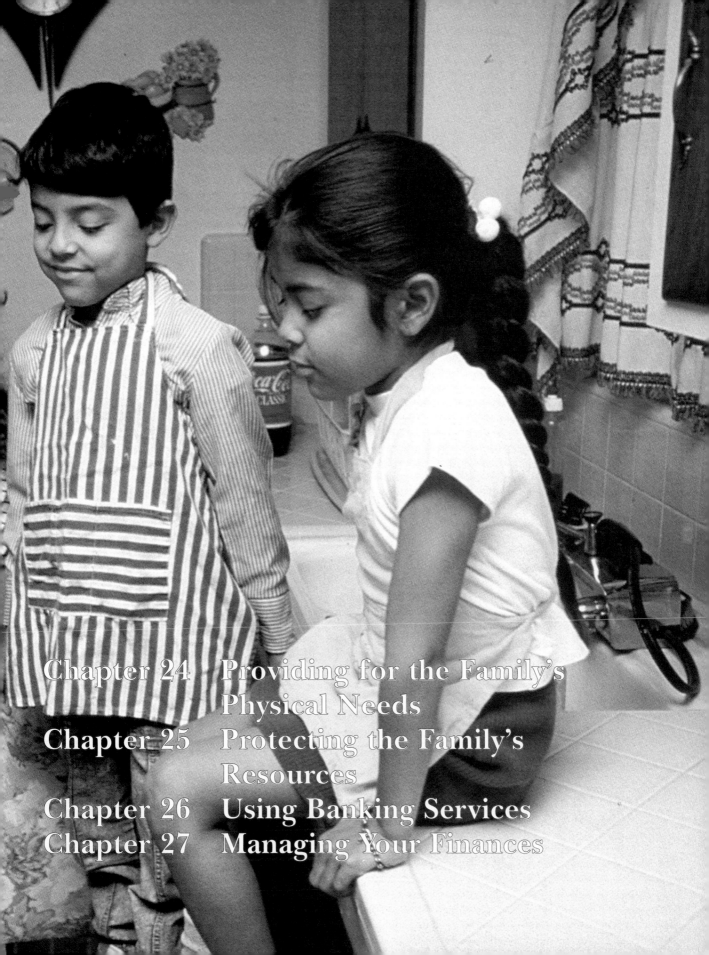

Providing for the Family's Physical Needs

TxDOT

After studying this chapter, you will be able to

- list factors affecting consumer decisions.

- recognize wise consumer choices.

- interpret information provided on food labels.

- evaluate the pros and cons of renting or buying a home.

- identify transportation alternatives.

- describe the costs of buying and maintaining a car.

- list ways in which leisure-time activities can add to family life.

The next few years of your life will be exciting ones. During these years, you will make decisions that may change the pattern of your whole life. You will decide how much education you need and what career you will begin. You will establish buying patterns for necessities such as food and clothing. Choosing a place to live will be a major decision for you. You may decide to marry and begin a family. Each of these decisions brings greater

Terms to Know

needs	biodegradable
consumer	convenience foods
advertising	natural fibers
bait-and-switch	synthetic or manufactured fibers
puffery advertising	
pseudo-truths	net income
subliminal advertising	lease
caveat emptor	assign a lease
caveat venditor	sublet
natural resources	security deposit
environmental responsibility	condominium
recycled	mortgage
	down payment

responsibilities. Therefore, these decisions deserve your careful study and thought.

You and your future family will be setting goals based on your personal values and standards. You will be evaluating your resources to determine how best to reach your goals. You will utilize your decision-making skills many times as you use resources to reach your goals.

What Needs Must Be Met?

You and your future family will have many individual and family needs that must be satisfied. *Needs* are those items or conditions that people must have in order to survive. These include both *psychological needs* (for example, the needs for love and acceptance) and *physical needs*. The physical needs are for food, water, air, rest, and protection.

Cholla Runnels

24-1
Once you establish the habit of stopping at a certain fast-food restaurant, you will probably continue to do so.

These needs are met through your choices of food, clothing, and shelter and your use of resources.

Unfortunately, you do not have unlimited resources. Human resources, such as time and energy, as well as nonhuman resources, such as money, are all limited. Many resources, however, go unrecognized. Family members may have skills and abilities that are never used. Other human resources may be waiting to be developed. You and your family will need to identify all of the resources that are available to you. You can then decide how best to use your resources to satisfy your family's needs and reach its goals.

Factors Affecting Consumer Decisions

A *consumer* is someone who buys goods and services. Your consumer choices influence, and are influenced by, market conditions and marketing priorities. The purpose of this market is to produce goods and services to satisfy consumers. Thus, your buying practices have a great deal to do with our economy.

Teenagers have a tremendous impact on our economy. Each year, teenagers in the United States spend millions of dollars. Manufacturers and advertisers are aware of teens' buying potential. They want to capture a part of this potential for two reasons. One reason is, of course, immediate financial gain. The second reason is that they want teens to establish the habit of buying their products. Habit is the largest single motivator for buying, 24-1. Studies show that buying habits established during youth will probably continue throughout a person's life.

24-2
Eye-catching words are used in advertising to convince you to stop, shop, and buy.

Advertising

Advertisers try to stimulate sales of goods and services by giving consumers *advertising*—information to influence their behavior. Studies show that the average consumer comes in contact with hundreds of advertisements each day. They are seen by way of television, radio, magazines, newspapers, billboards, posters, and direct mail. Wherever you go, you see words such as "sale," "markdown," and "special buy" that are used to influence your purchases, 24-2.

Advertising itself is a big business. Billions of dollars are spent each year to convince you to buy everything from toothpaste to cars. This money is not spent haphazardly. Even the most boring or insulting ad has been carefully designed and produced.

Advertisers conduct motivational research to discover the psychological reasons people buy certain products. They learn which "hidden needs" consumers are uncon-

sciously satisfying when they make purchases, 24-3. The results of this research are used as a basis for selling strategy. For instance, advertisers know that men often buy colognes they hope will enhance their masculinity and sex appeal. Thus, most ads for men's colognes are based on this hidden need. The ads show rugged men such as sailors and sports stars who fit some people's ideas of masculinity and sex appeal.

Advertising can fool you if you are not an alert consumer. In *bait-and-switch*, an item (the "bait") is offered at a very low price to get you to come into the store. Once there, the store owner may try to redirect ("switch") your attention to other more expensive items.

Puffery advertising makes an exaggerated claim that attracts the reader or listener. An ad may suggest, for example, that if a woman uses a certain hand cream, she is sure to become a bride soon.

Pseudo-truths are false statements made to sound as if they were true. No proof is offered to substantiate them. In fact, the statements are not even meant to be believed. Advertising that shows a white tornado sweeping through a kitchen and cleaning it could

---

Hidden Needs

Creating personal image of masculinity.
Creating personal image of femininity.
Calming feelings of anxiety or frustration.
Fulfilling need of security.
Fulfilling need of self-esteem.
Achieving a status symbol.
Receiving a feeling of youth.
Receiving a feeling of maturity and
    sophistication.

24-3
Consumers often base their purchases on a "hidden need."

not literally be true. However, it might attract your attention to a certain brand of kitchen cleanser.

Subliminal advertising is designed to stimulate your subconscious mind. Flashes of suggestive advertising are repeatedly shown on a television or movie screen. Your conscious mind may not notice the few frames of a picture of a soft drink, but your subconscious mind picks up the message. You become thirsty, so you go and get a soft drink. This type of advertising is now illegal because it had the potential of controlling a mass audience without anyone being aware of what was happening.

Advertising is not all bad. In fact, it has several important functions. Through advertising, consumers learn about available products and services, 24-4. Advertising can bring new and better products to the consumer. It helps producers market their goods and services efficiently. In addition, it expands the consumption of goods and the circulation of wealth, thus helping the economy grow.

Welbilt

24-4
Attractive photos of new products available to consumers encourage them to buy. Advertising copy can also be informative.

Caveat Emptor, Caveat Venditor

Our marketplace has been characterized by the *caveat emptor* attitude. This means "Let the buyer beware." It gives the consumer the responsibility of choosing good products. Consumers who make poor choices are expected to blame only themselves.

In recent decades, an opposite attitude has emerged. The *caveat venditor* or "Let the seller beware" attitude gives merchants the responsibility of selling good products. With this attitude, consumers who buy poor products can blame the merchants for selling them. Thus, merchants have had to recall products that were not safe and retract false advertising claims for fear of being sued by dissatisfied consumers.

Ideally, consumers and merchants should work together to make sure consumers receive good and safe products. Merchants should be honest enough to tell consumers exactly what they are buying. Consumers should be informed enough to compare products and choose the ones that best fit their needs. In addition, consumers should be willing to accept responsibility for using products as they were intended to be used. When they work together, consumers should be happy and satisfied, and merchants should make a profit.

Consumer Protection

The United States has over 300 consumer protection agencies at the state, county, and city levels. Every state has at least one. Many of these agencies are associated with the office of the state attorney general or district attorney. Agency staff are familiar with local consumer laws and can answer any questions you may have. They can also act as mediators between consumers and businesses.

Some consumer protection agencies function at the federal level. They rarely become directly involved in specific cases, but they can still help you. Sometimes just threatening to contact them will make a business listen to you more carefully. Sometimes the informal opinion of a representative of a federal agency is all you need to win your argument.

Three major federal agencies offer help and protection to consumers. The *Food and Drug Administration (FDA)* investigates complaints about the safety of food, drugs, and cosmetics.

The *Consumer Product Safety Commission (CPSC)* watches for hazardous products such as malfunctioning appliances. They can tell you whether or not a certain product has been recalled. They can also tell you how to get the repair, replacement, or refund the manufacturer is offering.

The *Federal Trade Commission (FTC)* protects consumers from unfair trade practices and false advertising. It enforces mail-order regulations, warranty legislation, and fair credit and billing laws.

Most large cities have a *Better Business Bureau (BBB)*. This agency promotes advertising and selling practices that are fair to both businesses and consumers. The BBB guards against frauds and misrepresentations. It provides consumers with free informational brochures. Consumers can ask the BBB questions through the mail, by telephone, or in person.

Many industries have established associations or councils to handle consumer questions and complaints in their fields. Examples are the Major Appliance Consumer Action Panel (MACAP), the American Hotel and Motel Association, the Automobile Consumer Action Panel (AutoCAP), and Toy Manufacturers of America.

Environmental Responsibility

In recent years, the responsible use of *natural resources* (such as air, water, and soil) and the preservation of environmental quality have received increased attention worldwide. Americans have become more conscious of themselves as not only users of natural resources, but as protectors of them, 24-5.

Many people have a heightened sense of *environmental responsibility* (feeling of personal accountability for protecting the environment). This, combined with the wish to

State of New Hampshire, David Brownell, Photog.

24-5
Protecting environmental quality is of concern to increasing numbers of Americans.

reduce energy expenses, makes it important to understand how to use energy resources wisely.

Your Energy Costs

Energy costs are becoming an increasingly important budget item for most families. Fuel costs, both gas and electric, account for a large portion of living expenses. To save energy and keep your budget under control, you need to make wise use of your energy dollars. The following tips may help you.

Keep your heating and cooling system running efficiently. Have them checked by a competent service representative. Keep filters clean and replace them when needed.

A great deal of energy is wasted by heat leakage out of your home in cold weather and into your home in hot weather. Insulate the walls and attic and use weather stripping on doors and windows. Close blinds and draperies to block out extreme cold or intense sunlight.

Set your thermostat at the most efficient setting to keep your home comfortable. For every degree you lower the thermostat in the winter, fuel usage is reduced by two to three percent. The reverse is true for air conditioning. An exterior exhaust fan will help eliminate hot air in the attic during summer.

Use your appliances efficiently. Save energy by using small appliances for small jobs.

Environmentally Responsible Consumption

Consumers who are environmentally aware can save energy and contribute toward environmental quality in other ways, too. One important practice involves buying items that are safe for—or minimize damage to—the environment. The other practice is to sort items so that they can be *recycled* (used again to produce new products).

When buying an item, ask yourself, "How will I dispose of this when I am finished using it?" It is easy to think, "That's easy. I will simply throw it away." Environmentalists, however, point out that there is no "away." See 24-6. Once an item exists on this planet it is here to stay—whether it exists on your cupboard shelf, in a city dump, or on a barge in an off-shore landfill. The only exceptions occur if the item is *biodegradable* (decomposes by natural biological processes) or if it can be recycled to make new products.

Try to buy products that are either biodegradable or recyclable. Most paper products, for example, are biodegradable under normal circumstances whereas plastic, aluminum, and glass are not. If a product is not biodegradable, it may be recyclable. Try to purchase products that are labeled "post-consumer recycled." These products are made from items that a consumer once bought and then turned in for recycling. Be aware, however, that some manufacturers use the term "recycled" on products that use scrap left over from the manufacturing process—a standard business practice.

GE Plastics

24-6

Students in this school use refillable plastic milk bottles to reduce lunchroom trash by 60 percent.

Contemporary Concerns *of today's teens:*
Thinking Environmentally: Ten Tips

As concerns over environmental quality increase, many Americans are asking, "What can I do to help preserve the environment?" Here are some tips:

■ Use car pools or public transportation rather than your own car to commute to work or school.

■ To avoid automobile-based pollution, keep your car well tuned and recycle used antifreeze and motor oil after tune-ups.

■ Avoid purchasing disposable items unless they can be recycled.

■ When you go grocery shopping, bring your own tote bag or other container. This reduces the use of paper or plastic bags supplied by the store.

■ Use cloth rags rather than paper towels for clean-up jobs.

■ Wash and reuse plastic dishes and utensils whenever possible.

■ Pack sandwiches in reusable plastic containers rather than disposable plastic bags.

■ To reduce use of packaging materials, buy food in bulk rather than in individual packages.

■ Be sure to recycle items that are recyclable.

■ Look for the recycled and recyclable symbols on consumer items (see below).

The **recycled** symbol identifies items made solely or mostly from recycled materials.

The **recyclable** symbol identifies materials that can be recycled.

The **plastic recycling** symbol is usually found on the bottom of plastic containers. The numbers and letters will vary according to the type of plastic used.

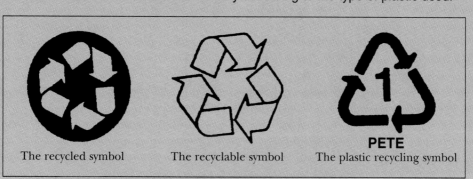

The recycled symbol   The recyclable symbol   The plastic recycling symbol

Recycling

Glass bottles, aluminum soda cans, and plastic foam containers are examples of consumer items that will not biodegrade in your lifetime or in many lifetimes. However, they can all be recycled and made into new products that may themselves be recyclable.

The key to successful recycling is simply to make a habit of it. Separating glass, plastic, aluminum, and paper products for recycling should become as routine a household practice as cleaning up the kitchen after a meal, 24-7. Taking these items to the recycling center or other repository should become a regular practice. Today, many communities pick up recyclable materials from your home at the same time as they pick up the trash.

David Hopper

24-7
Many families make a habit of collecting their aluminum products for recycling.

Food Decisions ▪ ▪ ▪ ▪

The person who takes responsibility for planning and shopping for the family's meals has an important job indeed. The decisions you make are essential to the diets of your family and therefore to their physical health. Your purchasing decisions can also affect the financial "health" of your budget.

Planning Meals

Most people like to plan and shop for meals on a weekly basis. Even experienced meal planners usually use a shopping list rather than trusting their memories. Using a shopping list helps you make sure you have everything and also curbs "impulse buying," 24-8. Buying on impulse can be expensive and result in unbalanced, haphazard menus.

It is a good idea, especially when you are first planning meals, to write out the week's menus for the family. This allows you to plan around meals eaten away from home and to plan special meals (for example, a birthday dinner). It also helps you make sure you have thought about each meal and that your menus meet the nutritional needs of each family member.

Planning for Nutrition

To make sure you are planning well-balanced meals, keep a copy of the Food Guide Pyramid at hand. For each day's menus, select foods from each of the five food groups: (1) breads, cereals, rice, and pasta; (2) fruits; (3) vegetables; (4) meats, poultry, fish, dry beans and peas, eggs, and nuts; and (5) milk, yogurt, and cheese. Because people's needs differ, check to make sure that each family member will get the necessary number of servings from each food group.

24-8
Shopping for the family's meals is an important responsibility.

Planning for Appeal

Most people consider the food that constitutes the major protein source to be the centerpiece of the meal. They then plan the remainder of the meal to complement and harmonize with this dish. Most people prefer meals that include a variety of colors and shapes. For example, a plate of baked fish with carrots and broccoli will have more color and therefore more visual appeal than baked fish with mashed potatoes and cauliflower. A plate of roast turkey with sweet potatoes and green beans presents a more interesting variety of shapes than a plate of macaroni and cheese, hash browns, and hominy.

Try to incorporate a variety of flavors and textures, with not too many sauces poured over various foods. A plate of sliced ham with sweet potatoes and crisp vegetables, for example, has more varied flavors and textures than a plate of fish, potatoes, and cooked vegetables, all covered in cream sauce.

Planning within Time Constraints

Preparation time is another major consideration in meal planning. In today's fast-paced world, most families cannot afford to devote large amounts of time to meal preparation. Although exceptions may be made for holiday or other special meals, most people prefer meals to consist of a few simply prepared dishes. The menu should require little clean-up so that time can be devoted to other activities.

Often the cook has less than an hour to prepare a meal from the moment he or she returns from work until dinnertime. How does dinner get made when time is this short? Some cooks make heavy use of *convenience foods,* which have been partially or fully prepared in order to save time. Examples of convenience foods are frozen dinners, muffin mixes, and brown-and-serve rolls. Other cooks prepare food during the weekends, freeze it, and then reheat it at dinnertime. Still others get food partially ready before leaving for work. Then they ask a teenage family member to put the dish in the oven when he or she comes home from school. Each family works out the methods that suit it best.

It is an unwritten rule in many families that if one member cooks, others take care of the clean-up. This practice distributes the workload more evenly. It helps the cook avoid exhaustion and the feeling that he or she is having to do all the work.

Cooking responsibilities can also be rotated or shared, depending on the family's preference and skills. Some cooks feel overburdened by food preparation chores and would like others to share them. Cooking methods can be learned by most family members. A positive emotional climate should be provided for the new cook or cooks, 24-9.

If you are trying to help others learn to cook, provide a calm, pleasant atmosphere in which the other person can learn. Try not to get impatient, or to elbow him or her out of the way and say, "Here, let me do it." Be generous with both guidance and praise. Try to be very careful not to ridicule or "put down" the new cook's efforts. Unless issues of food or personal safety are involved, the family kitchen is a place for encouragement and learning rather than perfectionism.

Cooks whose actions send the hostile message, "My kitchen is my castle," should not be surprised if offers of help are infrequent. However, cooks who share their knowledge of cooking with other family members may find that they are helping others learn an important, creative new skill.

Shopping for Food

Once you have decided on your week's menus, you are ready to develop your shopping list. Grouping similar items together on your list will result in quicker, more efficient shopping.

In deciding on a food store, balance the lower prices to be found in larger supermarkets with the convenience of neighborhood grocery stores. Many people prefer to shop for their major food items in supermarkets. They use convenience stores, where prices are generally higher, only for occasional or unexpected needs.

Understanding Food Labels

Before you buy a food item, read the label on the item to be sure of what you are getting. Much information can be obtained by studying the list of ingredients. The first item indicates the major ingredient, with subsequent items appearing in decreasing order of quantity. For example, you may wish to compare two dried beef soup mixes. In reading the labels, you may find that "hydrogenated vegetable fat" is the second ingredient listed on one label, and the seventh on the other. If you are watching calories and cholesterol—as most Americans should—you will want to purchase the product with the least hydrogenated fat.

Recent legislation requires that specific types of nutritional information appear on food labels. Under the heading *Nutrition Facts*, labels must now include the standard serving size and the number of servings in the container. Labels must also include total calories and number of calories derived from fat as well as total fat, saturated fat, cholesterol, sodium, total carbohydrate, dietary

24-9
Helping other family members learn to cook can be a positive experience.

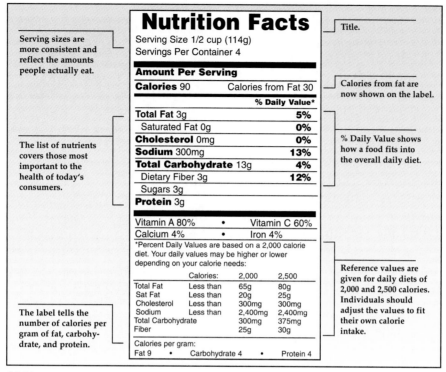

Nutrition Facts
Serving Size 1/2 cup (114g)
Servings Per Container 4

Amount Per Serving

Calories 90   Calories from Fat 30

                                    % Daily Value*

Total Fat 3g	**5%**
Saturated Fat 0g	**0%**
Cholesterol 0mg	**0%**
Sodium 300mg	**13%**
Total Carbohydrate 13g	**4%**
Dietary Fiber 3g	**12%**
Sugars 3g	
Protein 3g	

Vitamin A 80%	•	Vitamin C 60%	
Calcium 4%	•	Iron 4%	

*Percent Daily Values are based on a 2,000 calorie diet. Your daily values may be higher or lower depending on your calorie needs:

		Calories:	2,000	2,500
Total Fat	Less than		65g	80g
Sat Fat	Less than		20g	25g
Cholesterol	Less than		300mg	300mg
Sodium	Less than		2,400mg	2,400mg
Total Carbohydrate			300mg	375mg
Fiber			25g	30g

Calories per gram:
Fat 9   •   Carbohydrate 4   •   Protein 4

Labels (callouts):
- Serving sizes are more consistent and reflect the amounts people actually eat.
- The list of nutrients covers those most important to the health of today's consumers.
- The label tells the number of calories per gram of fat, carbohydrate, and protein.
- Title.
- Calories from fat are now shown on the label.
- % Daily Value shows how a food fits into the overall daily diet.
- Reference values are given for daily diets of 2,000 and 2,500 calories. Individuals should adjust the values to fit their own calorie intake.

24-10
The food label contains much nutritional information that the consumer can use to evaluate the product and eat a healthful diet.

fiber, sugars, protein, vitamin A, vitamin C, calcium, and iron, 24-10. Manufacturers may voluntarily include information on other nutrients as well.

Another part of the new food label centers on the term *Daily Value.* Daily Values are reference figures on food labels that help consumers see how the food products fit into a total daily diet. The label specifies the percent of a nutrient, such as protein, that consumption of a standard serving of the product contributes to the total day's recommended intake.

The reference of Daily Values given at the bottom of the nutrition label indicates the greatest amount of fat, saturated fat, cholesterol, and sodium people should consume each day. It also shows the smallest amount of total carbohydrate and dietary fiber people should consume. The percent Daily Values given are based on a 2,000 calorie diet, which

is recommended for most women and teenage girls and for some inactive men. Daily Values for a diet of 2,500 calories are also provided on the label. This diet is nearer to the recommended caloric intake of active men and women and teenage boys.

The guide must be adjusted according to the caloric intake required by each individual. Some persons, such as elderly people, inactive women, and children, need a daily diet of fewer than 2,000 calories. Because the nutrient percentages are based on a 2,000 calorie diet, these individuals would want their percentages of Daily Values to total less than 100 percent. By using the food label, you can add up the percentages of the nutrients you consume each day to make sure you do not exceed the recommended amount.

Many consumers use the food label to identify products that are low in fat and saturated fat and to monitor their daily fat intake.

Your daily diet should contain no more than 30 percent of calories from fat, and no more than 10 percent of calories from saturated fat. (Persons with some health conditions are advised to consume less in each category.)

Some food labels contain terms implying healthfulness, such as "light" or "lite." Recent legislation sets specific criteria for the lawful use of these terms and others such as "free," "good source of," "high," "less," "more," and "reduced." Specific terms for the designations of "lean" and "extra lean" have now become available for fish, game, meat, and poultry.

Controlling Food Costs

As you become more experienced at shopping, you will develop your own techniques for making the most of your food dollars. Some of the following tips may help you.

Allow extra money in your food budget for nonfood items. Paper products, cleaning aids, cosmetics, and grooming supplies can

24-11
Buy nutritious food that you know your family likes.

David Hopper

David Hopper

24-12
Compare store brands with nationally advertised brands. You may be able to get equal quality at less cost.

add up to 25 percent or more of your "food" dollars.

Plan for part of your food budget to be spent on meals eaten away from home. The amount will depend on your lifestyle.

Plan at least "skeleton" menus as you make your grocery list. Check newspapers for advertised food specials. Take advantage of these when planning your meals.

Buy nutritious food that you know your family likes, 24-11. New items are fun to try occasionally, but they are sometimes wasted if your family doesn't like them.

You will usually come out ahead if you shop at one store rather than going to several different stores. Make your list with the layout of this one store in mind. This will help you shop faster and avoid backtracking.

Buy the correct size for your use. Giant sizes may be the most economical for large families. Generally, larger sizes are priced less

The Dial Corporation

24-13
Healthful restaurant eating is possible if diners make sensible choices.

per unit of measure. However, if you live alone or have limited storage space, giant boxes of items may not be practical.

Buy the right grade and the right pack for your use. If you are planning to make chili, for example, buy stewed tomatoes rather than expensive fancy whole tomatoes.

Compare brands, 24-12. Often, a store's brand is as good in quality as a nationally advertised brand and costs less.

Know the nutritional value of foods. Try to get the most nutrition for your food dollar. For instance, sources of protein that usually cost less than meat include eggs, poultry, beans, and legumes.

Beware of fake specials. Check to see how much the price has actually been reduced. Also check the expiration date, and make sure the item is in good condition.

Clip and use coupons for items you need, but do not get carried away. Buying something just because you have a coupon reflects poor logic. If you can develop good food-shopping skills, you will be able to enjoy the best use of your food dollars.

Eating in Restaurants

Dining out in restaurants is becoming more common as dual-worker families become more typical. Many couples coming home after long hours at work find dining out an attractive option. In doing so, however, they must watch their spending as well as their intake of fat, cholesterol, sugar, and salt.

In choosing and preparing menu items, restaurateurs may or may not have your good health in mind. Large portions of high-calorie items prepared in high-calorie ways appeal to many people and therefore bring in the highest sales. Although it is usually possible to eat healthfully in restaurants, a good deal of self-control is needed, 24-13. Most restaurants, however, do offer healthy items on their menus, and may feature these foods.

24-14
Visit a variety of different types of stores to compare prices and services offered.

Dining out is usually more expensive than cooking and eating at home. Many budget-conscious couples go out to eat only as a "special treat" every week or two. Others choose to do so during especially busy periods when time to prepare meals is at a premium.

Clothing Decisions

You wear clothes for modesty, comfort, and protection from the elements. Clothes also help you look attractive, and they help you tell others about yourself. Clothes provide clues to your personality, self-image, status, gender, and age.

Different clothes work in different situations. For instance, you could wear jeans to a picnic and feel great. However, if you wear jeans to a job interview, you may remain unemployed!

Methods for Acquiring Clothing

There are many sources of clothing. In some families, clothing is handed down from one child to another as the children "grow into" and "grow out of" clothing. Other families stress home sewing and the cost savings that may be realized in an outfit that is handmade.

Most people, however, buy most or all of their clothes. Types, size ranges, and prices of clothing vary widely from store to store. Examples of places from which to buy clothes include department stores, specialty stores, factory outlets, discount stores, used-clothing stores, and mail-order businesses. If you visit a variety of clothing stores, you will get a better sense of what types of clothing are available at what cost, 24-14.

Department stores carry clothes and accessories in various styles, sizes, qualities, and price ranges. In addition, they usually provide many customer services.

Specialty stores limit their merchandise to specific items such as handbags or shoes. Their prices are generally in the medium to high range. If they carry the kind of items you like, they can make shopping easier, saving you time and energy.

Factory outlet stores offer items that represent extra merchandise from normal production. Some items may contain flaws—some of which are barely visible. Such clothing may be available at reduced prices.

Discount stores generally offer lower-quality goods at low prices, with few customer services. However, alert consumers can sometimes find good-quality items at bargain prices.

Consumers wishing low prices may also frequent used-clothing stores, which are also called thrift shops. The range of styles, colors, and sizes at these stores tends to be limited. However, they can be a source of bargains as well as of "antique" or "funky" clothing from another fashion era.

Mail-order businesses provide convenience for people who prefer to shop at home or who lack access to certain kinds of stores. Catalogs let you shop at your leisure, but you cannot try on garments or shoes before you buy them. Some people find it expensive and time-consuming to return items that do not fit or that look different from the catalog depiction.

Whatever the clothing sources you choose, be sure to understand each store's policies on alterations, returns, and delivery charges. The best choice of store is the one that meets your needs best at a price you can afford.

Clothing Selection

Because clothes are so important, you will want to plan your wardrobe carefully. Here are some tips to help you.

Take a wardrobe inventory of the clothes you have. Make a list. Decide which garments you can keep and which ones need to be replaced. Then make a list of items you would like to add.

Try new combinations of old clothes to create new outfits. Also try to create new outfits by adding a few new accessories.

When you are shopping for clothes, you may wish to wear or bring the shoes you are planning to wear with your new outfit. When trying on clothes, be sure you see yourself in a three-way mirror if possible. This way you can spot problems with fit or quality and can see yourself as others will. The garment should fit you without any wrinkles, sags, or puckers.

Be sure to pay attention to quality characteristics, 24-15. Seams should be flat and even in width. Stitches should be short, straight, continuous, and securely fastened at the ends of the seams. If the fabric ravels, the seams should be finished in some way. Hems should lie flat. They should be even in width and invisible on the right side. Trimmings, buttons, snaps, and hooks and eyes should be firmly attached and properly spaced.

Some garments such as suit jackets and skirts usually need linings. These give the garments body and help them keep their shape.

Garment durability is important in clothing and accessories that you will wear often and perhaps over a number of years, such as coats and handbags. If you choose classic styles that will not go out of style, it often pays to purchase top-quality items.

Durability, however, is not as important in a fad item that may be out of style before you will wear it out. People who frequently buy fad items may find themselves with a wardrobe of "gimmicky" clothes and little money for longer-wearing ones.

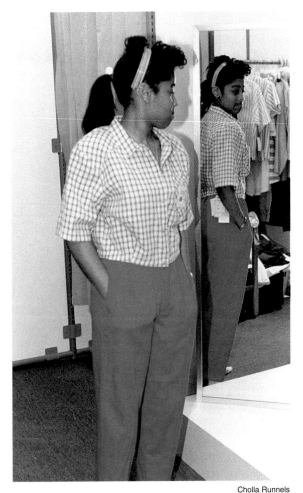

Cholla Runnels

24-15
Check a garment's fit and points of quality
construction before you buy it.

Your Clothing Costs

To stretch your clothing dollar, try to
build your wardrobe around one or two basic
color groups, such as black, brown, or navy
blue. To make your wardrobe seem larger
than it really is, use mix-and-match separates
that can be combined in a variety of ways. Accessories, such as scarves, can also change the
look of an outfit.

If you are looking for a coordinating
item, carry color samples with you when

shopping. If you bring a newly purchased
item with you, be sure you have proof of purchase so you are not accused of shoplifting it.

Buy accessories that you can wear with
several different outfits. Black shoes and
handbag, for example, can be used throughout the year.

Look for versatile garments, 24-16.
Choose basic styles that can be dressed up or
down with jewelry, scarves, or other acces-

24-16
Choose basic garments that can be dressed up or
down with different accessories.

sories, depending on the occasion. Also choose garments in colors and fabrics that can be worn year-round.

Significant cost savings can be obtained by waiting until an item goes on sale before purchasing it. However, be sure you buy only sale items that you really need.

Understanding Clothing Labels

All clothing made in the United States must bear a label that provides information on the fiber or fibers used in the garment as well as the proper care of the item. Fibers fall into two basic categories: natural and synthetic (manufactured). *Natural fibers,* such as cotton and wool, are made from sources found in nature such as the cotton plant or sheep. *Synthetic or manufactured fibers,* in contrast, are made from non-natural sources. Examples of such fibers include nylon, rayon, acetate, and polyester.

Sometimes, natural and synthetic fibers are used together in a fabric in order to take advantage of the best characteristics of each type. For example, a shirt or blouse may be made of a cotton/polyester blend. This garment combines the comfort and absorbency of cotton with the wrinkle resistance of polyester.

Always check the care label before you buy a piece of clothing. If the garment must be dry cleaned, keep this extra cost in mind. If the garment must be hand washed, be sure you will have the time to do this. Before buying a garment, also consider other costs that the purchase will involve, such as new accessories or undergarments.

Clothing Care

Proper care of clothing is important. Your clothes will look better and last longer if you take care of them. When you change clothes, take an extra minute or two to hang up your clothes. Check each garment for stains, ripped seams, tears, or missing buttons. Stains come out more quickly if you treat them early. Similarly, small mending jobs take only a short time if you attend to them promptly. In clothes care, the old adage "A stitch in time saves nine" is often true.

Housing Decisions

Housing will be one of your largest expenses. Your housing decisions will greatly affect your financial well-being. At some point in your life, you will probably have to choose between buying and renting. The following questions may help you clarify your thoughts and priorities on housing:

- How much do you value home ownership?

- How much of a housing payment can you handle?

- How much time will you spend at home?

- Will children be affected by either choice?

- Do you want to invest money in a home?

Housing Costs

Housing costs vary from region to region just as other living costs do. Housing costs include more than just rent or mortgage payments. They include costs for utilities, maintenance, and repairs.

As a rough guide, you should try to keep your monthly housing costs to no more than one-third of your monthly net income. *Net income* is the money you receive after social security, income tax, and other deductions have been taken from your paycheck. Deductions vary from job to job and from state to state.

This guideline is not absolute. The amount you can afford to spend for housing depends on your situation. If housing is your top priority, you may want to spend more on housing and less on cars, clothes, and entertainment. If you expect your salary to grow, you may be able to spend more. If you have many debts or if housing is a low priority, you will not want to spend as much.

Renting a Home

Most young people rent their first homes. See 24-17. The main advantage of renting is flexibility. Renters can move from place to place fairly easily. Another major advantage is that renters do not need a large sum of money. They pay for their housing in monthly installments.

Renters also have the advantage of knowing just how much their housing will cost. They do not have to worry about hidden costs such as new plumbing or heating systems. Others are responsible for any needed repairs. Since renters do not own their homes, they can easily resist spending money on home improvements.

If you decide to rent, you will have many questions to answer. Do you want to rent a

David Hopper

24-18
When looking for a place to rent, follow up on leads in newspapers. Check the conditions, features, and leases of several different places.

Cholla Runnels

24-17
Many single persons and young married couples rent their homes.

house, a townhouse, or an apartment? Do you need to live near a bus or subway line? Do you need to live close to school or close to your job? Do you want to be near your family or friends? Do you want a furnished or unfurnished apartment? How much can you afford to pay for rent and utilities?

Once you have answered these questions, you are ready to start hunting for housing, 24-18. Always visit an apartment before you rent it. Take some time to check the condition of the apartment. Turn on the shower and flush the toilet. Open and close doors, closets, and windows. See if any repairs are needed. Ask about the maintenance service, security measures, pest-control services, and laundry facilities. Ask whether rodents, cockroaches, or other pests are a problem. If the previous owner had a pet, you may inherit a problem with fleas. Take notes so you will be able to compare the apartments you see.

The Lease

Once you decide on the place you want to rent, you will have to consider lease arrangements. A *lease* is a written, legally binding rental agreement. Most leases are for one year. Be sure the lease includes the specific address of the rental unit, the date of occupation, the length of time covered by the lease, and the cost of the rent. It should also include a statement concerning who is responsible for such expenses as water, electricity, gas, lawn care, and repairs.

If the landlord promises to make repairs or improvements, ask him or her to write it in the lease. Any such additions to a lease should be dated and signed. That way, you will be able to take legal action if the repairs or improvements are not made.

A lease may include several demands and restrictions. Be sure to read the entire lease carefully. Understand everything in it before you sign it.

Beware of an automatic renewal clause in your lease. Under this clause, you must tell the landlord if you plan to move when your lease is up. According to the terms of your lease, you may have to give this notice 30 or even 60 days before the lease expires. If you don't do this, the landlord can hold you responsible for another year's rent.

Watch out for a clause that prevents you from letting someone else move in with you. A lease may say that only the persons whose names are on the lease can live there. This doesn't mean you can't have overnight guests, but it could cause problems if you decide to have a roommate.

A lease may have restrictions on children, pets, and excessive noise. Be prepared to live with such restrictions if you sign the lease.

Look for a clause that allows assigning the lease or subletting the rental unit. It may come in handy if you want to move out early. To *assign the lease,* you transfer the entire un-expired portion of the lease to someone else. Once that is done, you can no longer be held responsible for the lease. To *sublet* the property, you let someone else rent it for a period of time. Both you and the other person would be responsible for all terms of the lease.

The Security Deposit

A lease should include a statement concerning the *security deposit.* This is a sum of money, usually one month's rent, that you pay the landlord before moving into the rental unit. It insures the landlord against financial loss in case you damage the unit or fail to pay the rent.

Before you sign a lease, you should know how the security deposit will be handled. Some landlords see this as money they can use for "cleaning." Most simply return the money to you after you have moved out if you left the apartment in good shape.

Most states have regulations about security deposits. Several states require landlords to put security deposits in separate bank accounts and pay tenants yearly interest on the money. Be sure your landlord's explanation is the same as the words written in the lease. If you have a problem, check with local tenants' organizations or look into the possibility of using small claims court.

Tenants' Rights

There is no single, national source of information on tenants' rights. However, progress is being made. Many states have passed a Uniform Residential Landlord and Tenant Act (URLTA). It spells out the rights and obligations of both parties and provides legal solutions for tenants with less-than-perfect landlords. A majority of states have passed laws stating that you don't have to pay rent for an apartment that isn't fit to live in. The landlord must meet a certain standard of "habitability."

Buying a Home

For some people, home ownership is the fulfillment of a dream, 24-19. It gives them a sense of independence, security, and stability.

Many Americans own their own homes. Some say they own their homes so they can have more freedom and privacy. Others need space for growing families. Others decide to use home ownership as a financial investment.

On a long-term basis, buying a home is likely to cost less than renting. When you rent, none of the money you pay will be returned. When you buy, you are investing your money and will probably realize a return on your investment when you sell the home. If you buy a well-built home in a good neighborhood and take good care of it, your investment is likely to be a good one.

Another financial benefit of home ownership is that you can take advantage of certain tax deductions. However, you cannot weigh the decision to rent or buy strictly on a dollar and cents basis. Your personal happiness, for now and the future, has to be a factor.

Cholla Runnels

24-19
Home ownership is still the dream of many Americans.

Condominium Ownership

The word *condominium* means common ownership. It does not refer to a type of building. Condominium units are found in a variety of structures, from duplexes to high-rise buildings.

When you buy a condominium unit, you own the unit and also a share of the common areas such as stairways and hallways. A condominium complex may provide many facilities and services such as swimming pools, tennis courts, and lawn care. The owner is not directly responsible for the cost of these "extras." Instead, he or she pays a monthly maintenance fee that pays for them indirectly.

Condominium owners have many of the benefits that owners of single-family houses have. They are investing their money with the hope of getting a good return. They can also take advantage of the same tax deductions.

Buying a condominium unit is much like buying a house. However, you need to take some special precautions. When you compare prices, be sure to look at both the purchase price and the monthly maintenance fee. You will also want to read the *declaration of ownership* carefully. It states the special rules and regulations of the particular condominium complex. Be sure you understand all the legal issues involved before you buy.

The Process of Buying

Buying a home or condominium is a long and sometimes complex matter. Most people seek the help of a real estate agent and a lawyer to handle many of the details. See 24-20.

Once you have found a house or condominium unit and have settled on a price, you need to secure a mortgage. A *mortgage* is a claim against property that a buyer gives to a lender as security for borrowed money. The mortgage is paid in monthly installments.

24-20
A real estate agent may be able to help you find a house that will fit your needs and your budget. The agent can also help you settle many of the detailed matters involved in your purchase.

David Hopper

You can get a mortgage loan from a bank, a savings and loan association, a mortgage company, or a private individual. Comparison shopping is extremely important and can save you significant sums of money. Mortgages differ in three areas: size of down payment, interest rate, and length of time to repay.

Down payment. The *down payment* is the initial payment you make to buy the home. The amount is usually a percentage of the total purchase price. It is made in one large cash payment.

The institution from which you get your mortgage will probably state the minimum amount of your down payment. Some people want to make as large a down payment as they can afford and thus reduce the size of their mortgage. However, you should be careful not to deplete all your cash resources. You will need money to furnish the home, to pay property taxes, to buy homeowner's insurance, and to cover other expenses involved with buying the home.

Interest rate. In the past, almost every mortgage was a fixed-rate loan. That meant that the interest rate and monthly payments remained constant until the loan was completely repaid.

As a result of rising housing costs and changing interest rates, more types of mortgages are available. Fixed-rate mortgages are still popular, but other types are also offered. Interest rates and monthly payments vary according to the terms of the mortgages.

Comparison shopping for mortgages is necessary. You need to find the best kind of mortgage for your financial situation as well as the lowest interest rate.

Length of time to repay. The length of time you have to repay the mortgage is determined by the type of mortgage you get and your earning ability. The longer you take to repay, the smaller your monthly payments will be. However, you will be paying more interest than you would if you made larger payments over a shorter time.

Transportation Decisions ■ ■ ■ ■ ■ ■

In our highly mobile society, transportation needs seem more important than ever for most people. The types of transportation you choose involve a variety of financial, environmental, and societal considerations. Where you live and how much you travel are the main factors in determining your transportation costs.

Types of Transportation

A number of methods can be employed to move people from one place to another. Walking, bicycles, motorcycles, automobiles, buses, airplanes, trains, subways, and other types of transportation all accomplish this objective. However, various modes of transportation involve differing financial, environmental, and other costs. The most common method—the personal automobile—involves the highest costs of all.

Costs of Buying and Owning a Car

To many people, one's first car is an important milestone of growing up. Some individuals invest a great deal of their personal identity in the choice and upkeep of their cars. Others view their cars as "just wheels." Regardless of your emotional investment, car ownership involves a number of costs and responsibilities, 24-21.

The first cost that you will encounter is the purchase price of the car. Whether you buy the car new or used can make a big difference in your financial outlay. Some people value a brand-new car very highly. It matters little to them that the minute they drive the car out of the lot, it depreciates greatly in value.

Other people willingly settle for a used car. Used cars that are chosen carefully can yield excellent value.

The costs associated with automobile ownership are significant. There is the cost of insurance, for which young people pay higher premiums. There are the costs of an operator's license, annual registration and tag renewal, and—for many urban dwellers—residential parking stickers. There are the costs of gasoline and maintenance, including new tires, muffler replacements, repairs,

Ford Motor Co.

24-21
Automobile ownership involves a number of costs and responsibilities.

tune-ups, and oil changes. There may be other expenses as well, such as paying parking fees and the cost of maintaining a car that will meet state safety inspection requirements.

The environmental costs of car ownership are also high. Gasoline is a nonrenewable (cannot be renewed or recreated) natural resource, which is a fact of concern in and of itself. In addition, fumes from automobile exhaust are a major source of air pollution.

In recognition of this pollution, environmentally aware consumers try to use their cars only when necessary. They carpool or take public transportation (bus, train, or subway) the rest of the time, 24-22.

The following tips may be of value in diminishing environmental and personal costs:

- When shopping for a car, compare EPA (Environmental Protection Agency) ratings for fuel economy. Buy a car with a good rating.

- To save gasoline, drive with a light foot. Accelerate slowly, brake gently, and obey speed limits. Avoid excessive idling of the engine.

- Maintain your car well. Have engine tune-ups regularly. Change the oil as needed, and check the air pressure in the tires often.

Other modes of transportation have advantages and disadvantages as well. See 24-23. Each consumer must choose the mode of transportation that best balances his or her personal, financial, health, and environmental concerns.

With the Courtesy of Asea Brown Boveri

24-22
Using public transportation rather than one's individual automobile reduces environmental pollution.

Leisure-Time Decisions ■ ■ ■ ■ ■

Much can be learned about an individual or a family by observing the decisions they make about the use of leisure time. Some people find themselves in careers that demand a great deal of overtime work. For good mental health, however, it is important to find some time for relaxation. Families who share leisure-time activities are likely to be stronger.

Many people spend their leisure hours on hobbies, projects, social outings, volunteer work, reading, television viewing, listening to music, or other activities. These choices reflect personal tastes and values.

Time for Family

It is important that family members find time to be together as a family during the children's school years. Leisure time should not be filled with activities that take each

Transportation Choices		
Forms of Transportation	*Advantages*	*Disadvantages*
Moped	■ Less expensive than a car or motorcycle. ■ Appropriate for traveling short distances. ■ Better mileage than a car.	■ Not desirable in climates with frequent rain or snow. ■ Safety is a factor.
Bicycle	■ Least expensive of two-wheel vehicles. ■ Inexpensive to operate—no fuel costs. ■ Inexpensive to maintain and repair.	■ Requires human energy. ■ Not desirable in climates with frequent rain and snow. ■ Safety is a factor.
Carpooling	■ Economical. ■ Reduces traffic congestion. ■ Minimizes parking problems. ■ Offers companionship.	■ Inconvenience—allows little flexibility since needs of all must be considered. ■ Doesn't answer transportation needs outside of carpooling.
Bus	■ Convenient. ■ Less worry than owning other vehicles. ■ The overall cost is less.	■ Adjusting your schedule to bus schedule. ■ Getting to and from bus to home during bad weather.

Goals for Living, Nancy Wehlage

24-23
Each transportation choice involves advantages and disadvantages.

member of the family off in a different direction doing his or her own thing. At the same time, your free time should not be spent just taking children to various lessons and activities. Instead, the family should spend some part of their leisure time in activities together. In busy families, this time may have to be scheduled.

Shared leisure time is important for the health and well-being of the family. Participating together in recreational activities helps to pull families together. Communication is sometimes easier when family members are enjoying relaxing activities. Parents and children who find recreational activities that they all enjoy are drawn together be-

Wisconsin Tourism

24-24
Your decisions about the use of leisure time involve environmental implications as well as personal considerations.

cause of their mutual interest and enjoyment. As children enter their teen years, this mutual interest can help to sustain a bond that will keep teens from unnecessarily drawing away from their parents.

Environmental Awareness in Leisure-Time Use

Often, consumer choices related to leisure-time use reflect environmental aspects of personal values. Gas-guzzling vans, snowmobiles, power boats, and other energy-intensive leisure equipment contribute to Americans' status as the number-one users of nonrenewable resources worldwide.

Americans are increasingly seeing themselves as members of the global family in a world of limited natural resources. As their values change to reflect greater concern for their environment, their leisure-time decisions may reflect these concerns as well. See 24-24.

In choosing leisure-time activities, people must find the right balance between personal fulfillment and the responsibilities they have as members of a larger community. The choices you make are uniquely personal, but they affect the society in which you live.

Summary ■ ■ ■ ■ ■ ■ ■ ■ ■ ■ ■ ■ ■ ■

- Families set goals based on their personal values and standards. They must then choose the mix of resources they will use to reach their goals.

- Advertising can serve as a source of information, but it can also stimulate unnecessary expenditures. Thus, advertising can work both for and against consumers.

- Environmentally responsible consumption includes at least two practices: buying items that are safe for the environment, and recycling nonbiodegradable materials.

- Food, clothing, energy, and transportation costs account for a large portion of your budget. Wise consumer practices can help you keep these costs under control.

- Family meals can be planned with an eye for nutrition and appeal and within preparation-time constraints. Cooking and clean-up chores can be shared by family members.

- The food label on food products can convey much significant information, including ingredients, nutrition facts, percentages of Daily Values per serving, and other data.

- Sources of clothing include previously worn clothing from family or friends, home sewing, department stores, specialty stores, factory outlets, discount stores, thrift shops, and mail-order businesses.

- Clothing labels provide information about the fiber content of the product as well as instructions for the proper care of the item and other facts.

- Persons who plan to move often, who do not have a large sum of ready cash, who are not skilled in home maintenance, and who place a low priority on home ownership will probably choose to rent their homes.

- Persons who plan to stay in one area for several years, who enjoy home maintenance, who have growing families, and who want to have the benefits of home ownership will probably choose to own their homes.

- Consumers should be certain they understand the legal aspects of signing a lease or buying a home before proceeding with these transactions.

- Transportation decisions involve environmental as well as personal considerations. Consumers can reduce environmental pollution by using public transportation rather than individual automobiles whenever possible.

- Leisure-time decisions involve environmental as well as personal considerations.

To Review ■ ■ ■ ■ ■ ■ ■ ■ ■ ■ ■ ■ ■

1. _____ gives the consumer responsibility to choose good products. _____ gives merchants the responsibility to sell good products.

2. Match each of the following agencies with its description.
   _____ Food and Drug Administration
   _____ Better Business Bureau
   _____ Consumer Product Safety Commission
   _____ Federal Trade Commission
   a. Watches out for hazardous products such as malfunctioning appliances and has information on product recalls, repairs, refunds, and replacements.
   b. Investigates complaints about the safety of food, drugs, and cosmetics.
   c. Protects consumers from unfair trade practices and false advertising and enforces mail-order regulations, warranty legislation, and fair credit and billing laws.
   d. Promotes and maintains advertising and selling practices that are fair to both businesses and consumers.

3. Which of the following measures will help you control energy costs?
   a. Keep your heating and cooling system running efficiently.
   b. Close blinds and draperies to block out extreme cold.
   c. Insulate the attic.
   d. Use weather stripping on doors and windows.
   e. All of the above.
   f. None of the above.

4. What does environmental responsibility mean?

5. Which of the following statements about food labels is true?
   a. Only low-cholesterol, low-fat foods have labels.
   b. Ingredients are listed in no particular order.
   c. Labels must designate the number of servings that are included within the container.
   d. The Daily Values are based on a 3,000 calorie diet.

6. Which of the following clothing sources is likely to offer the greatest number of customer services?
   a. Factory outlets.
   b. Department stores.
   c. Thrift shops.
   d. Discount stores.

7. List five tips for building a wardrobe.

8. What is a security deposit, and what purpose does it serve?

9. A claim against property that a buyer gives to a lender as security for borrowed money is a _____.

10. Name five costs associated with automobile ownership.

11. True or False. Americans' leisure-time activities are related to environmental quality.

To Do ■ ■ ■ ■ ■ ■ ■ ■ ■ ■ ■ ■ ■ ■ ■ ■ ■

1. Discuss various goals families might have. What needs do families have? What resources are available to meet each of these goals and needs?

2. Bring advertisements aimed at various hidden needs to class. Display these on a bulletin board, and ask class members to name the hidden needs they believe are depicted in the ads.

3. Research the various consumer protection agencies and associations in your area. Ask a representative to visit your class to discuss consumer rights and responsibilities.

4. Work in small groups to do comparison shopping in food stores. First, prepare a list of 15 common products sold in food stores. Give a copy of this list to each group. Ask each group to visit a different store in your area and note the prices of the 15 products. Compare the total costs.

5. Divide the class into small groups and ask each group to visit a different apartment complex in your area. Interview the resident manager to obtain information on the rental cost, utility costs, number of rooms, recreational facilities, laundry facilities, storage space, furnishings, appliances, and security-deposit rules. Compare the findings of the group with those of other groups.

6. Ask a representative of a community environmental advocacy organization to visit your class. Request that he or she make a presentation on "Environmental Awareness," "Tips for Environmentally Aware Household Management," or a related topic.

7. Compare costs of renting and buying a home in your area. Check local rental fees, purchase prices of houses, and interest rates. Compare 30 years of rental costs with a 30-year mortgage. Discuss the results of your findings, including strengths and weaknesses of both options.

Pam Ryder

Washing the car together can be fun for the entire family

Protecting the Family's Resources

Terms to Know

life insurance

policy

premium

beneficiary

face amount

cash value

term life insurance

whole life insurance

adjustable life insurance

universal life insurance

variable life insurance

major medical insurance

deductible

coinsurance

health maintenance organization (HMO)

preferred provider organization (PPO)

disability income insurance

no-fault auto insurance

homeowner's insurance

After studying this chapter, you will be able to

■ identify different types of life and health insurance.

■ describe various types of auto and homeowner's insurance.

■ list the advantages and disadvantages of various types of life, health, auto, and homeowner's insurance.

■ appraise your family's needs for life, health, auto, and homeowner's insurance.

Common sense and numerous statistics tell us that people experience both fortunate and unfortunate events during their lifetimes. Some events can be anticipated and sometimes avoided, but other events are beyond our control.

No one likes to think of all the catastrophes that can happen in life. The fact is that you could get very sick, you could have a car accident, or your home could burn. If something like this happened to you, insurance would help you and your family through the financial crisis. It could protect you from financial ruin. In the meantime, even if nothing bad happens, insurance gives you security and peace of mind.

Spending money on insurance is not as much fun as buying a new car, new clothes, or new furniture. You have nothing but a piece of paper to show where all your money went. However, buying insurance can be one of the smartest ways to use your money.

Life Insurance ■ ■ ■ ■

Life insurance protects against loss of income due to the death of the insured. Life insurance is one of the most misunderstood aspects of financial planning. However, it is an important part of a sound financial program. You may want to consider a life insurance program as a young adult. One reason is that life insurance will take care of immediate expenses at the time of death. No one likes to think of death, but it is a reality everyone has to face. Final expenses are high, and when a death occurs, the family is faced with an immediate need for cash to cover the costs. Life insurance will provide this money.

Another reason for having life insurance, especially if you are married, is that it can help a family maintain an adequate level of living if a wage earner dies. See 25-1. It takes time for a family to work out a new plan for meeting daily living expenses. Until they can do this, they may need money from a life insurance policy to keep them going. Even if the family receives social security payments and benefits from the deceased's former employer, they may need additional funds to meet their living expenses.

The study of life insurance requires knowledge of several terms. The *policy* is the legal contract issued by the insurance company in your name. The *premium* is the amount of money you pay for your insurance. The *beneficiary* is the person you designate to

Cholla Runnels

25-1
If a wage earner dies, life insurance benefits can help the family of the deceased meet living expenses.

receive the benefits of the policy upon your death. The *face amount* is the amount of money that will be paid to the beneficiary upon your death. The *cash value* is the amount of money you, the policyholder, would receive if the policy is surrendered before your death or when it matures.

Types of Life Insurance

You will need to determine the best insurance plan for your needs. Be sure to check with several companies before you buy life insurance. Prices and benefits vary widely. You should do some comparison shopping. Find a reputable agent with a good company that can provide a policy that meets your needs, 25-2. You will want to look at the following types of life insurance.

Term Insurance

Term life insurance covers the life of the insured for a specified term or period of time. Once the term expires, the person is no

Contemporary Concerns *of today's teens:*
Do Young Adults Need Life Insurance?

Some unmarried young adults with no dependents wonder whether they need life insurance. Insurance agents may point out that healthy young adults qualify for policies with very low premiums. Agents also may urge young people to get a policy while they are still healthy enough to qualify.

Many financial experts, however, question the need for life insurance for young people at this stage of life. Death rates among young adults are low. If the young person is working, the wages lost by his or her death are unlikely to be missed by other family members.

It is true that healthy young adults may have an easy time qualifying for insurance. On the other hand, few adults applying for life insurance later in life are turned down for health reasons.

Some financial counselors advise young people to consider a small policy to cover the costs of a final illness and burial. Others believe that funds for insurance premiums are put to better use elsewhere, for example, for savings or continued education.

longer insured. Term insurance has the lowest premiums, but it does not build a cash value. Term insurance is designed to offer protection during a time when financial responsibilities are great, but money to pay premiums is limited. For instance, when people buy a house, they often buy enough term insurance to cover their mortgage. Then if they die before the mortgage is paid, their life insurance will take care of it.

One variation of term insurance is *renewable term insurance.* When this type of policy expires, the insured can renew it without taking another physical examination. However, the premium increases each time the policy is renewed.

Another variation of term insurance is *decreasing term insurance.* At the start of the term, the face amount is large. The face amount gradually decreases to nothing by the end of the term. The premium remains con-

25-2

David Hopper

A reputable agent can help you set up an insurance program designed to meet your needs.

stant throughout the term of the policy. This is designed to provide coverage for debts such as a mortgage. As the debt is repaid and the need decreases, the policy's face amount is reduced.

Whole Life Insurance

Whole life insurance is designed to cover a person's entire life and to build a cash value. The earlier you buy a whole life policy, the lower the premiums are. The premium amount is based on your age when you buy a policy. It remains the same throughout your life.

The advantages of whole life insurance are that it offers protection for your entire lifetime and that it builds cash value. The cash value provides an important asset for a family. It can be used as collateral for a loan. (However, until the loan is repaid, benefits are reduced by the amount of the loan.) It can be left to grow, earning interest, to form the basis for a retirement plan. It can also be cashed in if the insured wants to change or eliminate life coverage.

Today, many whole life policies are interest-sensitive. They offer a current-yield interest rate of return that varies with the economy.

Other Types of Life Insurance

As today's financial options have become more varied, new kinds of life insurance have emerged. The emphasis is on flexibility. A flexible policy can combine term and whole life insurance to give you coverage that changes along with your insurance needs. Benefits can be increased or decreased. Premiums can go up and down. Your insurance can vary to match events in your life such as the birth of a child or the purchase of a home, 25-3. With a flexible policy, you can cut premiums by reducing the benefits or by switching from whole life to term.

Bristol-Meyers Squibb Co.

25-3
Your insurance can vary to match life events such as the birth of a child.

When your financial situation changes again, you can increase benefits and switch back to whole life.

Adjustable life insurance is flexible insurance that allows the insured to alter the coverage as the need for protection and the ability to pay for it change. Within limits, the policyholder can raise or lower the premiums, the face value, and the premium payment period.

Universal life insurance also offers varying degrees of protection and savings. Its main feature is that the two parts—protection and savings—are clearly separated and that the amounts of both parts can be changed. You can increase or decrease the amount of protection (the death benefits of the policy). You can add or withdraw money from the savings part. Savings are generally invested to earn interest at current market rates.

Variable life insurance also offers both protection and savings. You pay a fixed premium. Part of the money goes toward protection. The rest goes into savings invested in equity products such as stocks listed on the stock market. The policyholder can select and periodically change the type of equity products used for the savings part of the plan. Unlike a fixed return with a stated amount of interest, the equity product investments earn a variable return. If the investments perform well, your cash value goes up. If the investments perform poorly, your cash value goes down. However, the face amount of the insurance policy never falls below the original amount stated.

Who Should Be Covered?

Whoever is financially responsible for someone else needs life insurance. The primary wage earner in a family certainly needs life insurance. Any other wage earner in the family needs life insurance if the family depends on his or her income. A full-time homemaker needs life insurance if the family depends on him or her for child care and household tasks that would otherwise have to be purchased. All adults, whether single or married, may want to build equity through life insurance.

Health Insurance ▪ ▪ ▪

A major illness can plunge an uninsured family into financial crisis. You are not immune to an accident or to a sickness that would cause you to need money for your care, and medical costs have soared in recent decades, 25-4. Thus, it is clear that health insurance should be a part of your budget. The question is how to find the policy that is best for you.

There are hundreds of health insurance companies. Each offers several different combinations of coverage. When you shop for health insurance, compare the policies of several reputable companies. Take time to study the details of various types of policies. Talk to an agent you feel you can trust, and choose the coverage that best fits your needs.

Group insurance policies are usually less expensive than individual policies. Most employers now offer group health insurance to their employees, with the employers often paying a share of the cost and sometimes all of it.

Health insurance typically works on a fee-for-service basis. You pay set premiums. When you are ill or injured, you go to the doctor or a hospital. The insurance will help you pay for the health care you receive according to the terms of your policy.

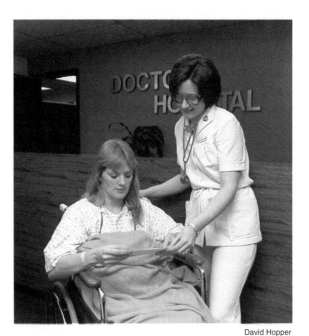

David Hopper

25-4
High medical costs make health insurance a necessity. Without it, a major illness could cause financial disaster for a family.

Costs of health insurance vary a great deal according to the kind of protection, the number of people covered, and the ages of those covered. Basic medical insurance generally pays for hospitalization, which includes room, board, and nursing services. Some basic coverage includes services such as X rays and lab tests. Medications are usually covered.

Major medical insurance is designed to begin paying when the basic coverage stops. It may extend your basic policy and pay for additional days of hospital care due to major illness or serious injury. It also covers many out-of-hospital costs. *Catastrophic insurance* is often included in major medical insurance polices. It covers the costs of intensive care, heart surgery, or long illness. The purpose of this type of insurance is to protect individuals and families against huge medical bills that could ruin them financially.

Health insurance policies may include a deductible clause and a coinsurance clause. A *deductible* clause states that the insured will pay an agreed-upon portion of the total expense, which may be the first $250, $500, or even $1,000 of the bill. The insurance company will pay the balance. The smaller the deductible amount is, the higher the premiums the insured will have to pay.

A *coinsurance* clause states that the policyholder will pay a certain percentage of the costs, perhaps 20 to 25 percent, while the insurance company pays the remaining portion of the costs.

Health insurance policies may include a number of additional features. *Stop-loss protection* is being offered by a growing number of companies. It becomes more important as the costs of deductibles and coinsurance payments rise. Stop-loss protection limits your out-of-pocket coinsurance medical expenses. Typically, it limits expenses, after the deduction, to $5,000 in any one calendar year.

You should try to select a policy that is *guaranteed renewable* so that the company cannot cancel your policy just because you submit many claims. A *right-to-transfer* clause gives you the right to continue your group policy even if you leave the group. This clause could also mean that if the policy was in the name of your spouse, and you divorced, you could continue to be covered by the policy.

A *maximum benefits clause* sets a limit on the benefits that you can collect over your lifetime. It may be as small as $100,000 or as high as $1,000,000. A maximum limit of at least $350,000 is recommended.

Health Maintenance Organizations (HMOs)

One way of receiving and paying for health care is through a *health maintenance organization (HMO)*. When you belong to an HMO, you pay a set fee on a regular basis. Since HMO membership is most often offered to groups of employees, your employer may pay part of the fee. When you need health care, you go to a physician associated with the HMO. You receive whatever care you need, usually with no deductible and no coinsurance payment.

Before joining an HMO, ask about the fees and what they cover. Find out what services and facilities are available to members, 25-5. Check the qualifications of the health care professionals. Then compare the HMO to other forms of health care and health insurance.

Preferred Provider Organizations (PPOs)

A *preferred provider organization (PPO)* has characteristics in common with both HMOs and fee-for-service health insurance.

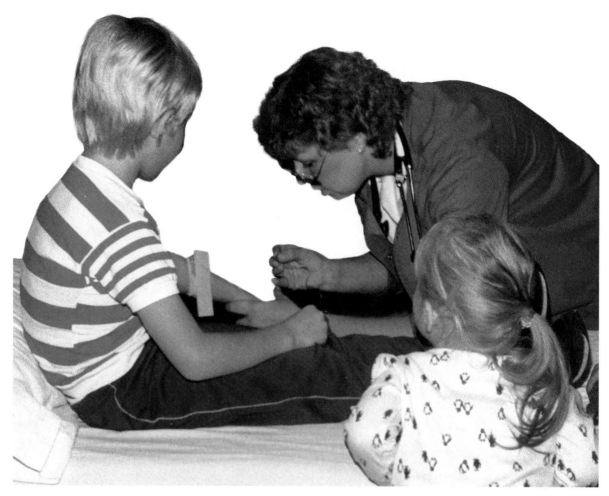

25-5
One way of receiving and paying for health care is through a health maintenance
organization or HMO.

Like an HMO, it offers lower-cost care. It also
allows the freedom of choice that fee-for-service plans offer.

In a PPO, an employer has a contract
with a group of doctors. These doctors agree
to provide medical care for employees at
what is essentially a group discount rate. Although employees are not required to use
participating doctors, they are given incentives to do so. In most cases, this means the insurance company will waive your deductible

and pay all or most of the bill if you go to a
participating doctor. It will usually pay some,
but substantially less, if you go to a nonparticipating doctor.

Disability Income Insurance

Disability income insurance is another
kind of health insurance. It protects a person
or family from loss of income due to a disabling illness or injury. Although some finan-

Cholla Runnels

25-6
As a driver, you are responsible for any damage or injury you cause.

cial help is available through social security to disabled individuals who qualify, many people want additional coverage.

Disability income insurance guarantees the continuation of a portion of the wage earner's salary during the time he or she is unable to work. Short-term disability income insurance generally provides six months of income. Long-term coverage generally provides income for at least two years or until age 65.

Auto Insurance ■ ■ ■ ■

Each year, thousands of persons die and millions are injured in auto accidents in the United States. More than one-third of the drivers involved are under age 25.

Auto insurance is a necessity for several reasons. Without insurance, financial losses due to an accident could wipe out a family's resources. The law requires all drivers to be fi-

nancially responsible for any damage or injuries they cause, 25-6. In many states, you cannot register an automobile without showing proof that the vehicle is insured.

Auto insurance rates vary according to many factors. The amount of coverage you want; the year, make, and model of your car; and your driving record all affect the amount you pay. Rates are also affected by overall accident statistics. Therefore, persons in urban areas generally pay more than those in rural areas. Young persons pay more than older persons. Men pay more than women. Single persons pay more than married persons.

Some companies allow discounts if you or the vehicle meet certain requirements. For instance, if you passed a class in driver's education or if you are a good student, you may qualify for a premium discount. If your car is equipped with certain safety and anti-theft features, you may also be eligible for a discount.

Basic Types of Coverage

Most auto insurance policies provide six basic types of coverage to protect you from the financial risks related to owning and driving a car.

Bodily injury liability insurance pays for damages and legal defense if you or a member of your family injures others while driving. Most policies have two limits on this coverage. One limit is the maximum amount the insurance company will pay for any one injury. The second limit is the maximum amount that will be paid for any one accident.

Medical payments insurance pays for the medical expenses resulting from accidental injury. It covers you and your family for any type of auto accident. It also covers others who are injured while riding in your car.

Protection against uninsured motorists applies to bodily injuries caused by an unin-sured motorist or a hit-and-run driver. It covers you, your family, and other people in your car.

Property damage liability insurance pays for legal defense and the damages your car causes to the property of others. It does not cover damage to your car.

Comprehensive physical damage insurance protects you against financial loss caused by something other than another vehicle. Policies vary in the perils they cover. Some of the most common perils that are covered are fire, theft, hail, water, vandalism, glass breakage, falling objects, or collision with a bird or animal.

Collision insurance protects you against financial loss when your car is damaged by collision with another vehicle or object or as a result of turning over. See 25-7.

David Hopper, *Conroe Courier*

25-7
Collision insurance protects you against financial loss when another vehicle collides with your car.

At the Scene of an Accident

Stop your car and get help for the injured. Have someone call the police or highway patrol. They can then notify the nearest medical unit.

Provide the police with whatever information they require. Ask the investigating officer where you can obtain a copy of the police report. You may need it to support any claim you submit to your insurance company.

Try to protect the accident scene. Take reasonable steps to protect your car from further damage. For instance, set up flares and move the car off the road. If necessary, have the car towed to a repair shop. Remember, your insurance company probably will want to have an adjuster inspect it and appraise the damage before you order repair work done.

Write down the names and addresses of all drivers and passengers involved in the accident. Also note the license number, make, and model of each car involved as well as the drivers license number and insurance identification of each driver. Record the names and addresses of as many witnesses as possible. Also record the names and badge numbers of police officers or other emergency personnel. If you run into an unattended vehicle or object, try to find the owner. If you can't, leave a note containing your name, address, and phone number.

Insurance Information Institute

25-8

If you are involved in a car accident, don't panic. Just follow these procedures.

No-fault Insurance

Accident settlements can be lengthy, costly, and frustrating. In determining who is at fault, and therefore legally liable, both sides may hire lawyers. Because of the huge number of cases, trials are often delayed for long periods of time. Another problem is that court decisions and jury awards are inconsistent and sometimes unfair.

Many states have adopted no-fault auto insurance to solve these problems. In theory, *no-fault auto insurance* eliminates the legal process of proving who is at fault in an accident. This allows the injured persons to receive payment from the insurance company much sooner. Each person's financial losses are paid by his or her own insurance company without concern for who is at fault.

Auto Insurance Claims

The purpose of auto insurance is to help you when you have an accident. You should know how much and what kinds of coverage you have. If you have collision and/or comprehensive coverage, you should know what the deductible is. (The deductible is the amount you will have to pay out of your own pocket if you suffer a loss.) You should also know if your state has no-fault insurance. Do not wait to review your insurance coverage until you need to file a claim. By then, it is too late to change your coverage.

If you are involved in an accident, try not to panic. Chart 25-8 explains what you should do at the scene of an accident.

Filing an Auto Insurance Claim

Phone your insurance agent or a local company representative. Do it as soon as possible, even if you're far from home and even if someone else caused the accident. Ask your agent how to proceed and what forms or documents will be needed to support your claim.

Supply the information your insurer needs. Cooperate with your insurance company in its investigation, settlement, or defense of any claim. Turn over to the company immediately copies of any legal papers you receive in connection with your loss.

Keep records of your expenses. Expenses you incur as a result of an automobile accident may be reimbursed under your policy.

Keep copies of your paperwork. You may need to refer to them later.

Insurance Information Institute

25-9

Follow these steps to file an auto insurance claim.

Report any burglary or theft to the police.

Phone your insurance agent or company immediately. Insurance policies place a time limit on filing claims. Ask these questions: Am I covered? Does my claim exceed my deductible? How long will it take to process my claim? Will I need to obtain estimates for repairs to structural damage?

Follow up your call with an explanation of what happened in writing, at the request of your agent or company.

Make temporary repairs and take other steps to protect your property from further damage. Save receipts for what you spend and submit them to your insurance company for reimbursement.

Prepare a list of lost or damaged articles. Save receipts from any additional living expenses you incur if your home is so severely damaged that you have to find other accommodations while repairs are being made.

Provide needed information to the insurance representative assigned to handle your claim.

Talk things over with your agent and adjuster if you are dissatisfied with the settlement offer. Check your policy to see what settlement steps it outlines.

25-10 Insurance Information Institute

Follow these steps if you need to file a homeowner's insurance claim.

When you have been in an accident or when your car has been damaged or stolen, you need to file a claim. Chart 25-9 lists the steps you should follow in filing a claim.

Homeowner's Insurance

If you own your home, you will also need homeowner's insurance. **Homeowner's insurance** covers damages to (or loss of) your home as well as the personal property inside your home. Most policies also include liability insurance to cover the medical costs of someone injured on your property.

Homeowner's insurance also provides coverage for personal property such as jewelry, clothing, furniture, china, and silver. It protects this property from such perils as fire, smoke, wind, hail, vandalism, and theft. Some policies cover more perils than others. Read a policy carefully before you buy it. Information on filing a homeowner's insurance claim is presented in 25-10.

If you rent your home, you still need to carry personal property insurance. This is often called *renter's insurance*. The building is insured by the owner, but your individual property is your responsibility. See 25-11.

Some property insurance policies offer *replacement cost* for property that is destroyed or stolen. With this coverage, you will be able to replace what you have lost with items of

25-11 Cholla Runnels

Whether or not you own your home, you need property insurance to protect your personal property.

similar value at today's prices. Other policies use the *actual cash value.* The value of items is depreciated according to their age. For example, a $500 TV set that is five years old might have a depreciated value of only $200. If the set were destroyed, you would receive only $200 from the insurance company. Be sure you know which your policy provides.

Re-evaluating Your Insurance Needs

The insurance needs of individuals and families may vary according to many factors. For instance, an owner of an older used car does not need the same amount of collision insurance coverage as the owner of a new car. If the value of a home increases, so must the level of insurance coverage for that property. Young adults who complete their educations and no longer qualify under their parents' health insurance policies need to get their own coverage.

Keeping track of insurance coverage is essential to protecting the family's resources. Families' insurance needs will vary throughout the life cycle as their financial and health situations change. You can increase your knowledge about insurance through such activities as reading financial periodicals, taking courses in family finance, and talking to insurance professionals.

Summary

- Insurance coverage is essential to the protection of family resources.

- Life insurance offers financial protection for families in case a wage-earner dies. Some policies also provide a means of saving.

- Every family faces the risk of illness or injury. Health insurance can prevent financial difficulties resulting from such misfortunes.

- Disability insurance protects a person or family from loss of income due to a disabling illness or injury.

- All drivers must be financially responsible for any damage or injuries they cause. Thus, auto insurance is a necessity. In some states, it is required by law.

- Many states have adopted no-fault auto insurance plans, which eliminate the need to prove who is at fault in an auto accident.

- Homeowner's insurance protects against financial loss resulting from damage or liability in connection with your home and its contents.

- Renters need personal property insurance to replace lost or damaged possessions.

- Families' insurance needs tend to vary over time, as their financial and health situations change.

To Review ■ ■ ■ ■ ■ ■ ■ ■ ■ ■ ■ ■ ■ ■

1. Fill in the blanks with terms related to life insurance.

    Sue and Dan bought a _____ policy, which will protect them for a five-year period but will not build up any savings for them. They pay a monthly amount, called a _____. Sue is named as the _____. If Dan dies, she will receive $20,000, the _____ _____ of the policy.

2. Which of the following statements is (are) true?
    a. Term life insurance provides both protection and a means of saving.
    b. Universal life insurance offers no flexibility.
    c. Group health insurance policies are usually more expensive than individual policies.
    d. Property damage liability insurance pays for legal defense and the damages your car causes to the property of others, but it does not cover damage to your car.
    e. No-fault insurance eliminates the legal process of proving who is at fault in an auto accident.
    f. Homeowner's insurance protects personal property from such perils as fire, smoke, wind, hail, vandalism, and theft.

3. _____ insurance is designed to cover the cost of intensive care, heart surgery, or long-term illness.

4. Explain the difference between a deductible clause and a coinsurance clause.

5. Explain one way in which HMOs and PPOs are similar and one way in which they differ.

6. List five factors that affect premium rates for auto insurance.

7. Name six basic types of coverage provided by auto insurance policies and briefly explain the function of each.

8. If you were buying renter's insurance, which would you prefer—a policy that provided replacement value or actual cash value? Explain your answer.

To Do ■ ■ ■ ■ ■ ■ ■ ■ ■ ■ ■ ■ ■ ■ ■ ■

1. Talk with various life insurance agents in your area. Set up realistic insurance programs for a young single person and for a young married couple.

2. Research the basic features of a proposal for national health insurance reform. How would it work? Summarize your findings in a written or oral report.

3. Ask an automobile insurance agent to visit your class. Ask him or her to explain the levels of coverage appropriate for a "beater," a late model mid-size sedan, and a brand new sportscar.

4. Invite an insurance agent and/or the resident manager of a nearby apartment building to your class. Request their opinions as to whether renters need property insurance. What specific types of coverage do they recommend?

David Hopper

Life, health, and auto insurance can give family members a sense of security and peace of mind.

26

Using Banking Services

After studying this chapter, you will be able to

- differentiate between gross income and net income.

- identify the types of payments that typically are collected through payroll deductions.

- compare various types of financial institutions and the services they provide.

- describe the use of a checking account.

- summarize ways to save and invest money.

You will work hard for your money all your life. If you manage your money well, it will work hard for you and help you enjoy life.

The typical family has periods when money is plentiful and when money is scarce. One period of plenty occurs when a husband and wife are both employed and have no children. Another occurs when the couple's children have grown and left home and at least one spouse is still working. The scarce

Terms to Know

deductions

gross income

net income

exemptions

social security

commercial bank

savings and loan association

mutual savings bank

credit union

cashier's check

certified check

money order

traveler's checks

Automated Teller Machines (ATMs)

endorse

overdraft

savings account

United States savings bonds

certificate of deposit

money market account

retirement accounts

individual retirement account (IRA)

Keogh plans

stages are usually the childrearing years, the college education years, and the retirement years. The retirement years can be especially difficult if the couple has not planned carefully for this period of life. Families who manage their money wisely will be able to take advantage of their times of plenty to help them through the scarcer times.

Your Income ■ ■ ■ ■ ■

Your wages for work done on a job are likely to be your greatest source of income, 26-1. Every job has a certain wage. Some persons are paid by the hour. Some are paid a constant salary, regardless of the amount of time they spend at work. Some, such as salespersons, are paid on a commission basis. They receive a percentage of the amount of sales they make.

David Hopper

26-1
For this secretary, and for the majority of people, the greatest source of income is the wages received for work.

Jobs have fringe benefits that are often overlooked as an income source. These may include sick leave, vacations with pay, savings plans, retirement funds, and health and life insurance. In today's competitive world, businesses often attract potential employees with their fringe benefits. You should assess what these benefits will mean over the years when you compare job offers.

Your Paycheck

Most people who are employed receive a paycheck every week, every two weeks, or every month. Your paycheck may not be as large as you expect it to be. Some amounts of money are subtracted from your wages before you receive them. These amounts are called *deductions.* They are recorded on the stub of your paycheck as shown in 26-2.

The two most common deductions are federal income tax and social security. If you live in a state that has a state income tax, this will be another deduction from your paycheck. If you participate in a group insurance plan—either life or health—you may have yet another deduction.

The reason deductions are made from your paycheck is that they help you pay necessary expenses. If all your income tax, all your social security contributions, and all your insurance premiums were due at one time, you would probably have trouble paying them. These expenses are easier to meet when a little is taken from each paycheck.

The income you accumulate before deductions are made is called *gross income.* The amount of money you receive after deductions have been made is called *net income* or take-home pay. Your personal financial plan should be based on your net income because this is the money that is available to you for spending.

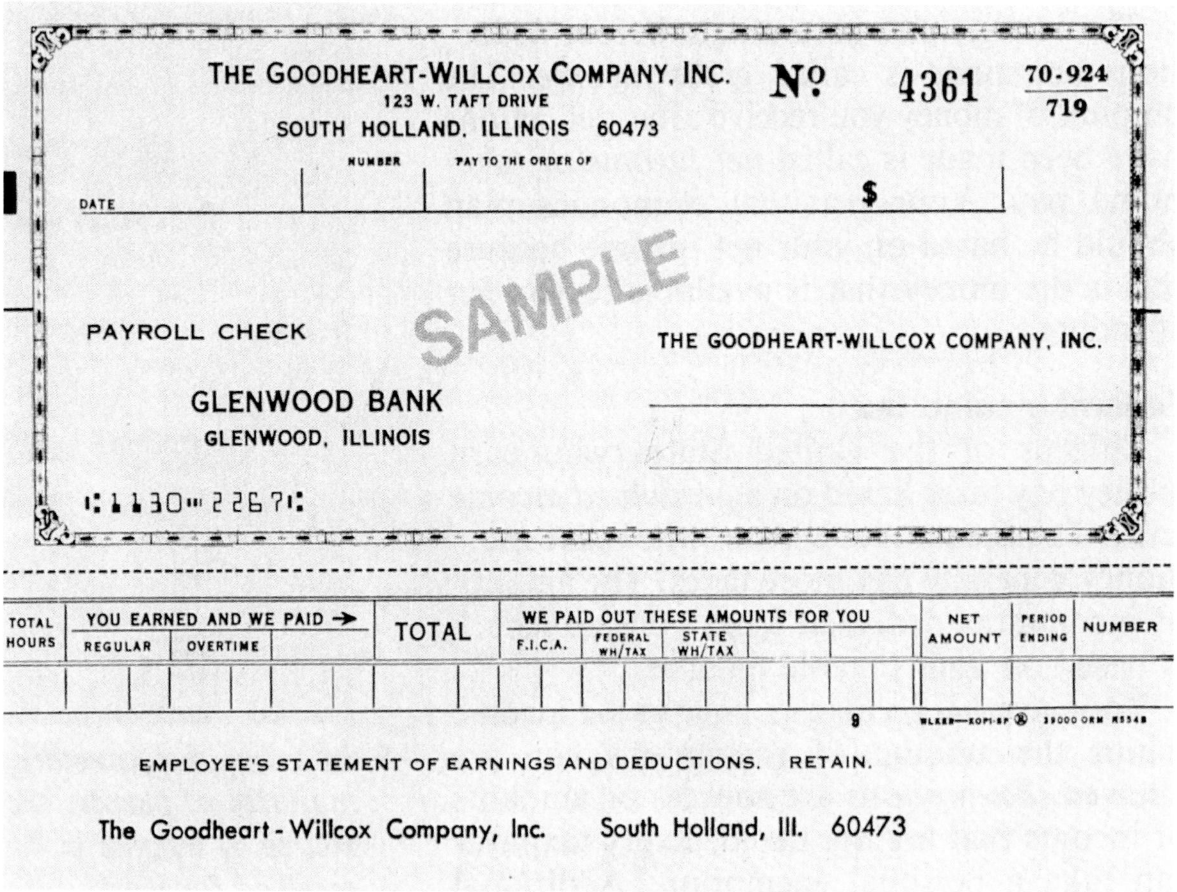

THE GOODHEART-WILLCOX COMPANY, INC. **N⁰** 4361 $\frac{70\text{-}924}{719}$

123 W. TAFT DRIVE

SOUTH HOLLAND, ILLINOIS 60473

NUMBER PAY TO THE ORDER OF

DATE $

PAYROLL CHECK THE GOODHEART-WILLCOX COMPANY, INC.

GLENWOOD BANK

GLENWOOD, ILLINOIS

⑈1130⑈2267⑈

TOTAL HOURS	YOU EARNED AND WE PAID →			TOTAL	WE PAID OUT THESE AMOUNTS FOR YOU					NET AMOUNT	PERIOD ENDING	NUMBER
	REGULAR	OVERTIME			F.I.C.A.	FEDERAL WH/TAX	STATE WH/TAX					

WLKER—KOPI-8F ⊛ 39000 ORM R5548

EMPLOYEE'S STATEMENT OF EARNINGS AND DEDUCTIONS. RETAIN.

The Goodheart-Willcox Company, Inc. South Holland, Ill. 60473

26-2

A typical paycheck shows the gross amount earned, the deductions made, and the net amount received.

Federal Income Tax

Citizens of the United States who earn money pay taxes based on a *graduated income scale*. This means that persons who make more money generally pay a higher proportion of their income in taxes. The amount of income tax deducted from your paycheck is based on your taxable income.

Your *taxable income* is your net income minus the amount of exemptions you are allowed. *Exemptions* are sources or amounts of income that are not taxed. Every taxpayer can take a personal exemption. Additional exemptions are allowed for persons who are blind, for people over 65, for a spouse, and for dependents. See 26-3.

When you begin a job, your employer will ask you to fill out a *W-4 Form* like the one in 26-4. This form tells your employer how many exemptions you are allowed. It also tells of any special situations that might alter your tax obligations. From this, your employer determines how much of your gross income should be deducted from your paycheck and withheld for taxes.

Cholla Runnels

26-3
Taxpayers are allowed a tax exemption for each of their dependents. Dependents are persons, such as children, who rely on others for financial support.

The withheld pay will be sent by your employer to the Internal Revenue Service (IRS). During the year, this will accumulate in your name and will help pay your income tax.

In January, your employer will give you a *W-2 Form* like the one in 26-5. It shows how much money the federal government withheld from your paychecks the previous year. It is your proof of payment. You use it when you fill out your federal income tax return. If your income tax return shows that too much was withheld from your paychecks, you will be due a refund. If you have not had enough money withheld to pay your full tax bill, you will have to make up the difference.

Social Security

Your job will probably place you, along with nine out of every 10 United States citizens, in the *social security* program. The the-

---

Form W-4
Department of the Treasury
Internal Revenue Service

Employee's Withholding Allowance Certificate

▶ **For Privacy Act and Paperwork Reduction Act Notice, see reverse.**

OMB No. 1545-0010

1995

| 1 | Type or print your first name and middle initial | Last name | 2 | Your social security number |

Home address (number and street or rural route)

3 ☐ Single ☐ Married ☐ Married, but withhold at higher Single rate.
Note: *If married, but legally separated, or spouse is a nonresident alien, check the Single box.*

City or town, state, and ZIP code

4 If your last name differs from that on your social security card, check here and call 1-800-772-1213 for a new card . . . . . ▶ ☐

5 Total number of allowances you are claiming (from line G above or from the worksheets on page 2 if they apply) . | **5** |

6 Additional amount, if any, you want withheld from each paycheck . . . . | **6** $ |

7 I claim exemption from withholding for 1995 and I certify that I meet **BOTH** of the following conditions for exemption:
● Last year I had a right to a refund of **ALL** Federal income tax withheld because I had **NO** tax liability; **AND**
● This year I expect a refund of **ALL** Federal income tax withheld because I expect to have **NO** tax liability.
If you meet both conditions, enter "EXEMPT" here . . . . ▶ | **7** |

Under penalties of perjury, I certify that I am entitled to the number of withholding allowances claimed on this certificate or entitled to claim exempt status.

Employee's signature ▶   **Date** ▶   , 19

8 Employer's name and address (Employer: Complete 8 and 10 only if sending to the IRS) | 9 Office code (optional) | 10 Employer identification number |

Cat. No. 10220Q

26-4
Form W-4 gives your employer the information to determine the amount that should be withheld from your paychecks.

a Control number	22222	Void ☐	For Official Use Only ▶ OMB No. 1545-0008	

b Employer's identification number		**1** Wages, tips, other compensation	**2** Federal income tax withheld
c Employer's name, address, and ZIP code		**3** Social security wages	**4** Social security tax withheld
		5 Medicare wages and tips	**6** Medicare tax withheld
		7 Social security tips	**8** Allocated tips
d Employee's social security number		**9** Advance EIC payment	**10** Dependent care benefits
e Employee's name (first, middle initial, last)		**11** Nonqualified plans	**12** Benefits included in box 1
		13 See Instrs. for box 13	**14** Other

	15 Statutory employee ☐	Deceased ☐	Pension plan ☐	Legal rep. ☐	942 emp. ☐	Subtotal ☐	Deferred compensation ☐
f Employee's address and ZIP code							

16 State Employer's state I.D. No.	**17** State wages, tips, etc.	**18** State income tax	**19** Locality name	**20** Local wages, tips, etc.	**21** Local income tax

Cat. No. 10134D   Department of the Treasury—Internal Revenue Service

Form **W-2** **Wage and Tax Statement** **1994**

For Paperwork Reduction Act Notice, see separate instructions.

Copy A For Social Security Administration

26-5
Form W-2 states the amount of money the federal government withheld from your paychecks the previous year.

ory behind social security is simple. Employees, their employers, and self-employed persons pay social security taxes. These taxes are used to pay benefits to millions of eligible people. When a worker's earnings stop or are reduced because of disability, retirement, or death, monthly cash benefits are paid to replace part of the earnings the family has lost. In practice, however, the social security pro-

gram is complex, with many requirements and limitations.

When you are employed and you qualify for the program, you must pay social security taxes according to the Federal Insurance Contributions Act (FICA). The amount you pay is a percentage of your gross earnings. The percentage varies as determined by Congress. Congress also sets a maximum limit on the amount of a person's earnings that are subject to the tax. You will not have to pay the tax on any income you receive over this limit.

For every dollar you put into the social security system, your employer also puts in a dollar. Thus, your employer matches the social security taxes you pay.

Financial Institutions ▪ ▪ ▪ ▪ ▪

As you earn income, you will need the services of financial institutions. Commercial banks, savings and loan associations, mutual savings banks, and credit unions are all financial institutions that can help you manage your money. Other companies, such as insurance companies and brokerage firms, also offer a wide range of financial services. The main differences between the many types of financial institutions involve ownership and insurance.

A *commercial bank* is owned by stockholders and operated for profit. In most commercial banks, deposits are insured up to a specified limit by the Federal Deposit Insurance Corporation (FDIC). This means that depositors will not lose their money if a bank goes bankrupt or suffers serious financial losses.

A *savings and loan association* may be a mutual company (owned and operated for the benefit of its depositors) or a stock company (operated for profit much the same as a commercial bank). In most savings and loan associations, deposits are insured up to a specified limit by the FDIC.

A *mutual savings bank* is owned by its depositors. After deducting operating costs and cash for reserves, earnings are divided among depositors in the form of dividends. Accounts in these banks may be insured up to a specified limit by the FDIC or by state-sponsored insurance.

A *credit union* is a nonprofit financial institution owned by and operated for the benefit of its members. Since a credit union is not for profit and is run by its members, it may lend money at lower rates and pay higher rates on savings than other financial institutions. The National Credit Union Association (NCUA) insures most credit union accounts up to a specified limit.

Financial Services

The services a financial institution offers depend mainly on its size and the needs of its customers. The following is a list of some of the services provided by many financial institutions:

- Checking accounts and savings accounts.

- Money market accounts.

- Certificates of deposit.

- Retirement accounts.

- Credit card accounts.

- Personal loans for autos, education, vacations, and other needs.

- Home mortgages.

- Farm and business loans.

- Cashier's checks, certified checks, money orders, and traveler's checks.

- The sale and redemption of United States savings bonds and other securities.

- Trust, investment, and estate management.

- Automatic bill-paying plans.

Contemporary Topics *of interest to teens:*
Banking at Home

Families with personal computers may soon be able to do much of their banking from home. Bank-at-home programs promise to make many transactions quicker, more efficient, and more convenient for busy consumers.

Using simple software or other equipment, consumers will be able to check their account balances and pay bills. They will also be able to review credit card purchases and automated teller machine withdrawals; stop payment on checks; order checks and traveler's checks; and complete many other banking tasks.

Consumers will benefit primarily from the convenience and flexibility provided by remote banking. They will avoid long lines in banks and will be able to do their banking outside of normal business hours if they wish.

Banks will gain cost savings associated with greater efficiency. Fewer employees will be needed to handle face-to-face consumer transactions in the bank. Fewer branch banks will have to be built. Instead, banks will be able to redirect their resources toward providing a wider range of services (for example, financial counseling and investments) more competitively.

When will home banking become a reality? According to some estimates, one household in three will be using some form of home-based financial services by the turn of the century.

- Direct electronic paycheck deposit and funds transfer.

- Overdraft protection.

- Automated teller machines.

- Automated telephone banking.

- Safe-deposit boxes, 26-6.

- Financial counseling.

Financial institutions can provide checks (other than personal checks) that can be used to transfer money. These include cashier's checks, certified checks, money orders, and traveler's checks. These checks are available at most financial institutions, usually for a small fee.

If you are paying a large sum of money, a cashier's check may be a more acceptable form of payment than a personal check. A *cashier's check* is drawn by a bank on its own funds and signed by a bank officer. Therefore, the receiver of the check doesn't have to worry if there are sufficient funds in the payer's account to cover the check.

Another alternative to a personal check is a certified check. A *certified check* is actually a personal check but with a bank's guarantee that the check will be paid. When a financial institution certifies a check, the amount of the check is immediately subtracted from the payer's account.

People who do not have checking accounts can use money orders to make pay-

David Hopper

26-6
Safe-deposit boxes are one of the many services offered by some financial institutions. They are used to store important papers and valuables.

ments safely by mail. A ***money order*** is an order for a specific amount of money payable to a specific payee. Money orders are sold in a number of places. However, it is wise to buy them from reputable sellers such as insured financial institutions and post offices.

When you are traveling, traveler's checks allow you to avoid carrying large amounts of cash. ***Traveler's checks*** can be cashed at most places around the world. They can be replaced if they are lost or stolen.

Checking Accounts ▪ ▪

When you begin to earn and spend money, you will want to set up a checking account with a financial institution. See 26-7. Being able to write checks will give you a sense of security and will help you handle

monthly bills. It will also provide you with detailed spending records, which are necessary to document your tax and investment expenditures.

Financial institutions usually offer more than one type of checking account. Some accounts, such as NOW accounts, earn interest if you maintain your balance at a specified level. Some accounts require you to keep a minimum balance, and some accounts charge for each check written. You will need to compare the requirements, limitations, service charges, and advantages of each. Then you can choose the type of account that best fits your needs.

When you open a checking account, your bank or financial institution will require that you sign a signature card for their records. This shows the name that you will use in signing all financial transactions. Names are often duplicated, so you will want to choose the combination of your names and initials that will make your signature unique. A man named Samuel David Smith may choose Samuel David Smith, Samuel D. Smith, Sam D. Smith, S. David Smith, or S.D. Smith. A woman named Mary Louise Brown might choose Mary Louise Brown, Mary L. Brown, M. Louise Brown, or M.L. Brown as her legal signature.

When a woman marries, she traditionally—though not always—takes the last name of her husband. Thus, if Mary Louise Brown married Samuel David Smith, she would be able to use any of several names, such as Mary Louise B. Smith, Mary Louise Brown Smith, Mary B. Smith, or even M.L. Smith. If Ms. Smith lives in a small community, she might want to chose a name that would not be duplicated by her mother-in-law or other relative.

Automated Teller Machines (ATMs)

Automated Teller Machines (ATMs) offer convenience by facilitating banking transactions at a number of locations 24 hours a day. To start a transaction, you insert a plastic card (provided by your bank) into a designated slot. Then you enter your personal identification number (PIN) and interact with a computerized menu of choices. For example, you may wish to deposit funds, inquire about your account balance, or withdraw cash.

To avoid being a victim of theft, banks advise persons who use ATM machines to observe several precautions. Do not share your PIN with anyone, and do not write it down in a place where others can find it. Avoid using ATMs late at night or in poorly lighted or isolated locations. If you feel that you are being observed as you enter your PIN, discontinue the transaction and leave.

Remember to keep records of your ATM transactions by entering them in your checkbook. If your card is lost or stolen, notify the bank immediately to limit your liability.

Writing Checks

When you write a check, you are telling your financial institution to take a certain amount of money out of your account and

David Hopper

26-7
Opening a checking account is one of the first steps in setting up a money management system.

pay it to whomever you name. You should be careful to write checks correctly to avoid costly and embarrassing mistakes.

A blank check has space for quite a bit of information, as shown in 26-8. When you write a check, you will want to fill each of the spaces correctly. See 26-9. The following tips may help you.

- Always use ink.

- Date the check the day it is written, even if it is a Sunday or holiday. Some people *postdate* a check (write in a future date), thinking that they will deposit money to cover the check before it is posted at the bank. As a rule, financial institutions will not cash a check before the date that is written on the check. Most businesses will not accept a postdated check as payment. Another problem related to postdating a check is that you might not be

able to get the money to the bank in time to cover the check.

- In the blank after the words "Pay to the order of," write the name of the *payee* (the person or organization whom you are paying). Spell it correctly, and do not use any abbreviations that may cause confusion. If you want to withdraw money from your account, write your own legal name in this blank.

- Record the amount of money to be paid clearly in the space after the dollar sign. Never leave a space between the dollar sign and the numerals. This might allow someone to alter the amount. (For instance, $ 15 could be changed to $115.) Write the cents as a fraction of 100.

- On the next line, write out the amount of dollars in words. Then write the word "and," followed by the number of cents

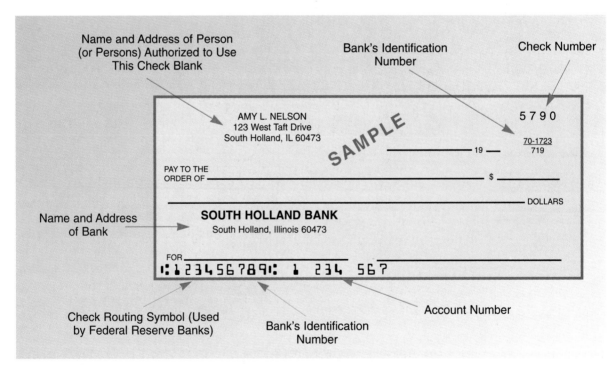

26-8
Space for a variety of information is provided on a blank check.

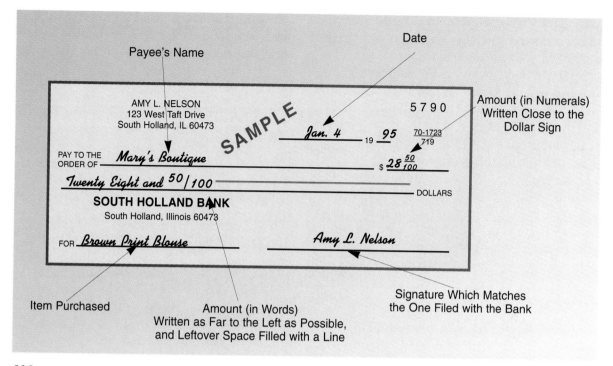

26-9
Checks should be written carefully and neatly to avoid errors.

written as a fraction of 100. Start writing at the extreme left of the blank. Fill any leftover space with a line. This prevents anyone from changing the amount.

- Most checks have the word "for" or "memo" and a blank in the lower left-hand corner. You do not have to fill in this blank, but doing so will help you keep clearer records. When you write a check for a purchase, make a note of what you have bought. When paying a bill, write the number of your account with the company on this line to be sure your payment is credited to your account.

- Finally, there is a blank for your signature. Always use the same signature you filed with your financial institution. Be

sure you have written the name of the payee and the amount to be paid before you sign the check. Once you have signed it, it is negotiable. Any blank spaces could be filled in by anyone in any way.

Immediately after writing a check, make a note of it on your check stub or in your check register. Write the check number, the date, the payee, and the amount. This is necessary for complete and accurate records. Keeping a running balance of your expenditures in your check register will help you avoid overdrawing your account. You will always know exactly how much money you have.

Do not change or cross out any part of a check. If you make a mistake, write the word "VOID" across the check and tear it up. Then start again with another check. Be sure to make a note of the void check on the check stub or in your check register.

If you make out a check to someone and it is lost or stolen, you should report this immediately to your bank. Tell them the check number, the date, and the payee, as well as your name, address, and account number. The bank will then stop payment of the check. You will usually be charged a small fee for this service.

It is wise to keep your blank checks in a locked drawer or other safe place. If your checks are lost or stolen, contact your bank immediately.

Endorsing Checks

To cash a check, you must endorse it. To *endorse* a check, write your legal signature on the back of the check, on the end opposite the dollar amount. This tells the bank that the correct payee is receiving the money.

A problem may occur when the payee's legal name is not used on the face of the check. In this case, the payee should write two signatures on the back of the check. The name that appears on the face of the check should be written first. Directly below this, the payee's legal name should be signed. For instance, a check could be written to Mary Brown. To endorse the check, she would write *Mary Brown* on the back of the check. Directly below this, she would write her legal signature, *Mary L. Brown.*

Once Mary had endorsed the check, anyone could cash it. One way to prevent this from happening is to endorse a check just before it is cashed. Another way is to write *for deposit only* below the legal signature. If you do this, the total amount of the check will be deposited in your account, regardless of who takes the check to the bank.

Suppose Mary's check was for $10, and she wanted to pay Sam $10. Perhaps Mary was busy and wanted Sam to cash her check for her. In either case, she would endorse the check like this:

Pay to the order of
Samuel D. Smith
Mary L. Brown

Then Sam could endorse the check by writing his legal signature under Mary's and could cash the check.

Depositing Money in Your Account

Your checkbook will include printed deposit tickets, as shown in 26-10. When you add money to your account, you will need to fill out one of them.

The date of the deposit and your legal signature should be written in the blanks at the left. On the right is a small chart. If you are depositing cash, write the number of dollars you have in paper bills beside the word "currency." Write the amount of money you have in coins beside the word "coin." If you are depositing a check, write the check number in one of the blanks next to the word "checks." Then write the amount of the check in the space to the right. If you have more checks than the chart will hold, write the additional information on the back of the deposit ticket. Add all the amounts to find the total amount of money you will present to the bank teller. If you want to receive some of the money in cash, subtract this amount from the total. This will give you the "total deposit," or the amount that will be added to your account.

The teller will give you a receipt for your deposit. Keep this for your records. In addition, make a note of the deposit on your check stub or in your check register. Write the date of the deposit and the source and

THOMAS B. ANDERSON   08-92
MARY A. ANDERSON
123 MAIN STREET
ANYWHERE, USA 12345

©HARLAND 1988

DATE_____ 19 _____
CHECKS AND OTHER ITEMS ARE RECEIVED FOR DEPOSIT SUBJECT TO THE TERMS AND CONDI-
TIONS OF THIS FINANCIAL INSTITUTION'S ACCOUNT AGREEMENT.
DEPOSTIS MAY NOT BE AVAILABLE FOR IMMEDIATE WITHDRAWAL.

SIGN HERE ONLY IF CASH RECEIVED FROM DEPOSIT

CURRENCY
COIN
CHECKS LIST CHECKS SINGLY
TOTAL FROM OTHER SIDE
SUB-TOTAL
TOTAL ITEMS   LESS CASH RECEIVED
TOTAL DEPOSIT

DEPOSIT TICKET
PLEASE ITEMIZE
ADDITIONAL
CHECKS ON
REVERSE
SIDE

SOUTH HOLLAND BANK
SOUTH HOLLAND, ILLINOIS 60473

⑆123456789⑆ ⑈ 234 567⑈

26-10
You need to fill out a deposit slip when you add money to your
checking account.

amount of each check. If you need to verify the deposit of a certain check later, you will have the necessary information.

Your Bank Statement

As your checks come into the bank, they will be posted against your account. At the end of every month, the bank usually will send your canceled checks to you, together with your *bank statement.* This will show a record of every deposit and every check that passed through your account during the month.

When you receive your bank statement, check it against your check stubs or register, 26-11. To do this, write the balance given on the bank statement on a sheet of paper. Add any deposits you have made since the closing date of the statement. Then subtract the amounts of the checks that have not cleared or that you have written since the closing

date. Circle the final figure. The next step is to subtract any bank service charges or add any interest earned to the balance in your check register. At this point, the figure you circled should be equal to the balance in your check register. If it is not, double-check your arithmetic. If you cannot find an error, ask someone from your bank to go over your records with you.

Overdrafts

An *overdraft* occurs when you write a check on an account with insufficient funds. Overdrawing your account results in re-turned (or "bounced") checks. The bank usu-ally charges a penalty fee for each "bad" check. Creditors may call you wanting to know when they will receive payment.

Overdrawing usually results from failure to keep track of the amount of money in your

26-11
Check to see that the balance listed in your bank statement agrees with the balance listed in your check stubs or register.

account. If overdrafts occur frequently, your credit rating will probably be affected.

To avoid overdrawing, be careful to keep an accurate and ongoing record of the amount of money in your account. You may also wish to look into automatic overdraft protection through your bank.

Overdraft protection may involve several options. Under one option, for example, the bank transfers funds into your account to cover overdrafts—and then charges you interest on this "loan." Under another option, the bank transfers funds from your savings or money market account into your checking account.

Saving and Investing Money ▪ ▪ ▪ ▪ ▪ ▪

Saving and investing money is important whether you are single or married. Setting aside money helps you finance future goals such as a college education, a down payment on a car or home, or a financially secure retirement. Savings and investments also provide you with a cash reserve that you may need during a period of unexpected illness or loss of income.

Most financial institutions offer at least five forms of savings and/or investment plans. These include

- savings accounts.
- United States savings bonds.
- certificates of deposit (CDs).
- money market accounts.
- retirement accounts.

Savings Accounts

A *savings account* (sometimes called a passbook savings account) permits you to make deposits and withdrawals in varying amounts at any time. The money in the account earns interest. A savings account can be opened with only a few dollars. Although a savings account is a convenient form of saving, it pays a low rate of interest.

U.S. Savings Bonds

Another way to save money is by buying *United States savings bonds.* Savings bonds are issued in denominations of $50, $75, $100, $200, $500, $1,000, $5,000, and $10,000. Purchasers pay half the face amount. For instance, you would pay $25 for a $50 bond. Interest is earned over time. If the bond is held to the maturity date, it will be worth the full face amount.

Series EE bonds that are held at least five years earn a flexible interest rate. They earn a market-based variable rate or a minimum guaranteed rate, whichever is higher. If bonds are redeemed before five years elapse, the interest earned is based on fixed interest rates rather than on market-based rates.

U.S. savings bonds are guaranteed by the U.S. government. They can be replaced without charge if they are lost or stolen. They are a safe way to save money, and they are an investment in our country. The government uses the money to finance the national debt.

Certificates of Deposit

If you have money you can deposit for a set period of time, you can buy a certificate of deposit (CD). With a *certificate of deposit,* you agree to leave your money on deposit in a savings institution for a specific period of time. A CD may pay a higher rate of interest than a savings account or U.S. savings bond. However, it requires you to commit your money for a set period of time such as six months or five years. A minimum deposit is usually required. If you cash in the certificate before the time period is over, you lose a significant amount of interest.

Money Market Accounts

A *money market account* is a type of account that pays interest rates that change with prevailing rates on short-term investments. The rate of interest earned on money market accounts is not a set rate—it changes daily.

A money market account has some advantages. It can provide savers with high returns. If interest rates are going up, a money market account will pay higher interest than accounts with set rates of return. Part or all of the account can be withdrawn at any time. A money market account opened through a bank or savings and loan association is federally insured by FDIC.

Money market accounts have some disadvantages, too. A large minimum deposit is usually required to open an account. If interest rates go down, so does the rate of return on the account.

Money market funds are slightly different from money market accounts. They are offered by private investment firms. They usually offer a higher rate of return than money market accounts. However, they are not federally insured.

Retirement Accounts

Retirement accounts are long-range savings accounts designed to provide income after retirement. Such resources can be an important part of planning for the retirement years, 26-12.

Many employers offer retirement pension plans to their employees as part of employees' fringe benefits. People who either do not have this benefit or wish to increase their retirement income above the amounts their employers offer may open retirement accounts. Financial institutions offer these accounts as part of their services.

David Hopper

26-12
Money is often scarce in the retirement years. Wise money management is needed to meet living expenses.

Retirement accounts have tax advantages that other savings accounts do not have. In most cases, money deposited into these accounts is not taxed until it is withdrawn. The interest earned on these accounts is not taxed until the money is withdrawn.

There are also disadvantages to retirement accounts. In order to get tax-favorable treatment by the IRS, certain federal regulations apply. One of these restrictions prohibits the withdrawal of money from these accounts prior to retirement age. If money is withdrawn early, penalty taxes must be paid.

Several types of retirement accounts are offered by financial institutions. Examples are Individual Retirement Accounts (IRAs) and Keogh plans.

Individual Retirement Accounts

An *Individual Retirement Account (IRA)* is an account to which taxpayers may make annual contributions up to a set amount. Taxes may or may not be paid on the contributions, but interest earnings are not taxed until the money is withdrawn. IRAs are open to every American receiving earned income or alimony. A person may contribute up to $2,000 per year to this account. Contributions are tax-deductible for persons (1) with annual incomes of less than a specified amount or (2) who are not covered by a company-sponsored pension plan. Interest accumulates on a tax-deferred basis until the funds are withdrawn at retirement. During the retirement years, most people have lower incomes and are therefore likely to be in a lower tax bracket than they were in their wage-earning years.

Keogh Plans

Keogh plans are named for the member of Congress who sponsored legislation enabling such plans in the 1960s. *Keogh plans* are designed to help self-employed people establish tax-deferred retirement plans for themselves and their employees. Contribu-

tions are tax-deductible, and interest accumulates on a tax-deferred basis until retirement. Different types of plans are available for persons of various income levels. The maximum contribution is $30,000 per year or 20 percent of earned income, whichever is less.

Employees of financial institutions will provide counseling to help you determine which type of account to open. They can also provide details on current tax regulations and restrictions.

Be sure to compare accounts and plans at different financial institutions. Such institutions offer a wide range of services, types of accounts, and interest rates. See 26-13.

The more money you have to save and invest, the more you can lose as a result of poor financial decisions. That is why it is so important to research your options carefully.

A Comparison of Interest Rates			
If you save $10 a month at compound interest* of			
10 Years	15 Years	20 Years	25 Years
5% $ 1569	$ 2717	$ 4906	$ 6135
6% 1663	2976	4772	7226
7% 1765	3269	5439	8570
If you save $50 a month at compound interest of			
5% $ 7847	$ 13,589	$ 21,032	$ 30,679
6% 8315	14,882	23,860	36,134
7% 8825	16,345	27,196	42,852

*Compound interest is interest which is computed on the sum of the deposits and the accumulated interest. The information in this chart is based upon interest which is compounded daily.

26-13
Do some comparison shopping before you start a savings program. A small difference in interest rates can make a big difference in interest earnings.

Summary ■ ■ ■ ■ ■ ■ ■ ■ ■ ■ ■ ■ ■

- You will work for money all your life. You can learn how to manage money so that money will work for you.

- Gross income is the total amount of money you earn. Net income is the money left after taxes, social security, and any other deductions have been taken from your paycheck.

- The U.S. tax structure is based on a graduated income scale. Generally, the more money you earn, the more taxes you pay.

- During the years you are employed, you have to pay into the social security program. When your earnings stop or are reduced, monthly cash benefits will be paid back to you out of this fund.

- Financial institutions offer a variety of services, such as checking accounts, savings accounts, personal loans, home mortgages, and safe-deposit boxes. The services a financial institution offers depend mainly on its size and the needs of its customers.

- A check should be written carefully and completely, in ink, on an account with sufficient funds to cover the check. If you make a mistake while writing the check, tear it up and start over.

- To endorse a check, write your name on the back of it. Once a check is endorsed, anyone can cash it.

- A deposit to your checking or savings account must be accompanied by a filled-out deposit slip. Be sure to record your deposit on your check stub or check register.

- When you receive your bank statement, check it against your check stubs or register to account for all funds.

- Common savings and investment plans include savings accounts, U.S. savings bonds, certificates of deposit, money market accounts, and retirement accounts.

- Retirement accounts are long-range savings accounts designed to provide income after retirement. Individual retirement accounts (IRAs) and Keogh plans allow people to earn interest on a tax-deferred basis until the funds in the account are withdrawn at retirement.

To Review ▪ ▪ ▪ ▪ ▪ ▪ ▪ ▪ ▪ ▪ ▪ ▪ ▪ ▪ ▪

1. List four possible fringe benefits of a job.

2. True or False. The income you accumulate before deductions are made from your check is your net income.

3. True or False. A commercial bank is a nonprofit financial institution.

4. List five services provided by most financial institutions.

5. Match the agencies listed below with the functions they perform.
   _____ IRS
   _____ FDIC
   _____ NCUA
   _____ FICA
   a. Insures most credit union accounts up to a specified limit.
   b. The legislation that requires the payment of social security taxes on employment income.
   c. Insures accounts up to a specified limit in most banks and in most savings and loan institutions.
   d. The federal agency that handles matters related to income taxes.

6. Explain the theory behind social security.

7. What should you do if your checks are lost or stolen?

8. True or False. Once a check is endorsed, anyone can cash it.

9. Match the type of investment listed below with the item that best describes each type.
   _____ savings accounts
   _____ U.S. savings bonds
   _____ certificates of deposit
   _____ money market accounts
   _____ retirement accounts
   a. Purchasers pay half the face amount; if held until maturity, can be cashed for the full amount.
   b. Examples are IRAs and Keoghs.
   c. Can be opened with only a few dollars, and deposits and withdrawals (without penalty) are possible at any time.
   d. Requires investor to commit money for a set period of time, such as six months or five years.
   e. Usually requires a large minimum investment; deals in short-term investments, with interest rate varying daily.

10. True or False. Once you put your money into a retirement account, you can withdraw it any time you wish without penalty.

To Do ■ ■ ■ ■ ■ ■ ■ ■ ■ ■ ■ ■ ■ ■ ■ ■ ■

1. Refer to the classified section of a Sunday newspaper in your area. Select job listings comparable to your career goals and survey the jobs available. Evaluate salaries, fringe benefits, and other characteristics that are described.

2. Choose one job listing from the previous activity. Use current income tax and FICA figures to estimate the net income provided by the job. Assume you are married but have no children.

3. Research various sources of savings in your area. Set up a savings plan for yourself assuming you would save $5.00 a week for the next 20 years. How much savings would accumulate?

4. Arrange a field trip to a local commercial bank. Investigate all the banking services that are available. Compare these services with those offered by savings and loan associations, mutual savings banks, and credit unions.

5. Invite a personal financial planner to visit your class. Ask him or her to explain the differences in the total savings you would accumulate by age 65 if you were to start saving for retirement at the ages of 20, 30, 40, and 50.

6. Ask a representative from an area agency on aging to visit your class. Request that he or she discuss typical financial expenses of retired people as well as the adequacy of the usual sources of income (such as social security) to meet these expenses.

7. Invite a local social worker to discuss various options available to people who need some type of assisted living or nursing home care, as well as the typical cost of each option.

Managing
Your Finances

After studying this chapter, you will be able to

- describe types of arrangements that couples may use to handle family finances.

- design a budget for managing your income and expenses.

- identify various types of credit.

- evaluate various sources of credit.

- recognize benefits and pitfalls of credit use.

You have studied the many choices you have for managing your personal finances. Now you are ready to determine how this information can help you. Your challenge is to use the money you earn to meet your financial obligations and to reach your goals.

Terms to Know

budget	revolving credit
fixed expenses	collateral
flexible expenses	default
credit	pawnbroker
installment credit	credit bureau
finance charges	credit rating
noninstallment credit	

Handling Your Money ■ ■ ■ ■ ■ ■

Once you have landed a job and have an income, you will have to decide how to handle your money. If you are single, you will set up your bank accounts in your own name, manage your own money, and pay your own bills.

If you marry, you will want to determine the most workable method for handling your money, 27-1. Family income may come from one or both spouses. How to control the spending and how you should set up your banking records are two decisions you will have to make as a couple. Many couples choose one of the four alternatives described below in making these decisions.

- A *joint bank account* allows the maximum feeling of sharing. Both spouses are free to make deposits and withdrawals at will. From a business standpoint, it is a good method because money is available to either husband or wife. In the event of severe illness or injury, money is not tied up, and bills can be paid. If one spouse dies, the other will still have access to the account, though in some states the account is frozen for a period of time. The main problem with this method is that one accurate running balance has to be kept by two people. If one spouse writes a check and fails to record it in the running balance, the couple may find themselves overdrawn at the bank.

- The husband and wife may choose to have *separate accounts*. The couple will have to divide the expenses. One may pay for household items, such as food, clothing, and incidental (minor) expenses. The other may take care of the mortgage or rent, insurance, operating costs, and investments. This method works well if good communication is maintained. Friction may arise if one of the partners feels the division is unfair.

- Some couples have *two accounts*, both funded by one spouse, but each managed separately. For example, one spouse may set up a household account for the other spouse to use in meeting household expenses, needs of the children, and personal needs. Together, both spouses estimate the amount that will be needed each month in this account. One spouse will deposit this amount into the account, and the other will manage the money. As prices rise, or as needs increase, this amount may have to be adjusted.

The second account is managed by the first spouse. It is used for personal needs, for savings and investments, and for any other expenses not met by the other account.

- *One spouse may control all spending.* This method is often used when only one income is earned. In some marriages, the employed spouse controls all the spending. This spouse gives the other money as it is needed. In other marriages, the homemaker controls all the spending. This may be the result of interest, ability, or necessity, such as when the other's job requires a great deal of travel.

This method sometimes leads to marital conflict since most adults feel uncomfortable

David Hopper

27-1

When you marry, you and your spouse should be in agreement about the methods you use to manage your money.

Mississippi Dept. of Econ. & Comm. Dev.

27-2
Some couples look forward to buying a camper for enjoying family vacations together.

having to ask for or hand out money all the time. It can also cause problems if control of the money is equated with power in the relationship.

Budgeting

Planning ahead is the key to successful personal money management. For many, the best way to do this is to follow a budget. A *budget* is a plan for managing income and expenses.

Why Budget?

A budget will help you use your income to meet your needs and reach your goals. If you establish a good budget and live within it, you will have the peace of mind that comes with knowing that your expenses will be met. As you set goals together and manage re-sponsibly, you and your spouse will gain more confidence in each other as financial partners.

The savings for which you will budget will give you a sense of security in facing the future. You will sleep better at night knowing that funds are available for emergencies. You will also be able to look forward to the day when financial dreams become realities, 27-2. You will have a sense of competence and control when it comes to financial matters.

A budget should be viewed as a management device, not as a terrible burden. A good budget does not require complicated math, nor should it force you to become a penny pincher. A spending plan simply helps you recognize where your money is going. It helps you reach both your short- and long-term goals.

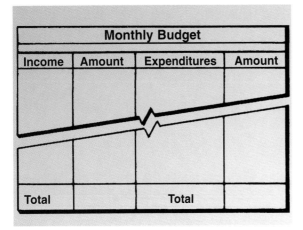

Monthly Budget			
Income	**Amount**	**Expenditures**	**Amount**
Total		**Total**	

27-3
Keep a simple list of all income and expenditures for a month or two when you first marry. This will give you a good basis for preparing a budget.

Setting Up a Budget

There are several steps to follow in setting up a budget. Whether you are single or married, you will want to follow the same procedure. If you are married, you and your spouse will want to work through these steps together.

Define Your Goals

The first step in budgeting is to define your present and future goals. Ask yourself what you need and want now. Then think about what you will need and want during the next year, the next 10 years, and on into retirement. How much will you need to save to achieve your long-term goals? If you are married, you may find that your priorities differ from those of your mate. You may need to make some adjustments and compromises. Clearly defined goals may provide you with the incentive to make your financial future secure.

Yearly Budget			
Item	**Jan.**	**Dec.**	**Total**
Total money income			
Major fixed expenses:			
Taxes:			
Federal			
State			
Property			
Auto			
Rent or mortgage payment			
Insurance: Health			
Life			
Property			
Auto			
Debt payments: Auto			
Other			
Savings			
Flexible expenses:			
Food			
Operating: Household			
Auto			
Clothing			
Personal care			
Fares, tolls, other fees			
Medical care			
Recreation and education			
Gifts and contributions			
Total expenditures			

27-4
You can use this typical budget form as a guide. You may need to add or delete certain categories to make it fit your personal financial plan.

Determine Your Income

The next step in making your budget is to determine your monthly net income or take-home pay. Working with monthly figures is recommended because most household bills are paid once a month. (A few bills are paid only quarterly, semiannually, or annually. These can be averaged on a monthly cost basis.)

Your income may not be based on a regular monthly amount. Perhaps you are paid on a commission basis. In this case, your salary depends on the amount of sales you make. You therefore will have to estimate an average monthly income.

Identify Your Spending Needs

When you live on your own for the first time, or when you first marry, you may have no idea of what your expenditures will be. To be realistic, you would be wise to keep records of your income and expenditures for a month or two before actually setting up a budget. You could use a simple form like the one in 27-3.

It is helpful to divide your expenses into two categories: fixed and flexible. *Fixed expenses* are costs that are predictable and that recur regularly. Examples include monthly rental payments or semiannual insurance payments. *Flexible expenses* fluctuate in amount and may occur less regularly. Examples of flexible expenses include clothing, food, transportation, medical care, and personal and recreational expenditures.

Once you have a good idea of your spending needs, you can list all your income and expenses on a more detailed budget form. See 27-4. Budget books with similar forms are available at most stationery stores. Some financial institutions give them to their customers.

The following paragraphs will give you some suggested limits for major categories of spending. You should remember, however, that no two families' incomes or needs are identical.

Food. The average American family spends between 15 and 20 percent of its net income for food. The amount depends on income, size of family, and individual needs. See 27-5. The percentage spent for food decreases as income increases.

Housing. Your housing will cost about 25 to 35 percent of your net income. This includes mortgage or rent, utilities, and home maintenance costs. You should try not to go beyond this figure. If you do, you may have trouble meeting your other expenses.

Transportation. This runs about 10 percent. If you have two cars and both are used for work, transportation costs may be more than 10 percent of your budget. Carpooling or use of mass transit services may help cut these expenses.

David Hopper

27-5
An average family eats a lot of food each week. Obviously, food is a major category in a budget.

Clothing. About 7 percent of your net income will probably be spent for clothing. This includes new purchases and care of your existing wardrobe. The exact amount will depend on whether one or both spouses work and the type of clothes needed for work. See 27-6.

Health care. Medical insurance and bills vary widely according to your age and state of health. Even if you are not sick or injured, you should set some money aside to deal with the possibility of a major illness or accident. Health insurance is necessary and should be a part of your spending plan from the beginning, unless it is provided by your employer. Regular dental checkups should be anticipated. If you have expenditures associated with special health problems, such as an allergy, these costs should be included.

Savings. You should try to save at least 10 percent of your net income. This includes cash savings as well as your life insurance savings. Be sure to increase your savings as your salary increases, especially if you are part of a dual-career family. Typical long-term goals for which couples save include a house, the children's education, and retirement.

Miscellaneous. Miscellaneous costs comprise the most flexible budget category. Education costs, such as newspapers and magazines, need to be included. A personal allowance for each spouse should cover needs for hair care and grooming supplies. Recreational expenses need to be included, 27-7, as well as charitable contributions. The personal allowance should also include a small sum for each spouse to spend for whatever he or she pleases. Not having to account for every penny to one's spouse can make it easier to live within the boundaries of the overall budget.

Evaluate Your Budget

Once a month, compare the budgeted figures in each budget category with the amounts that actually were spent. It can be interesting to see where your money has gone. How do you feel about the expenditures? Was the value you received from spending in a given category (for example, restaurant meals) worth the expense, or would it have been just as easy to have spent less (by planning a few more meals at home)?

David Hopper

27-6
People who wear uniforms to work may be able to keep their clothing budgets small.

27-7

L. Leslie-Spinks, with the Courtesy of Cullberg Ballet Company

Recreational expenses, such as tickets to the ballet, should be included in a budget.

Revise Your Budget As Needed

If you find that your expenditures exceed budgeted levels, look for places to cut back in the following month. Often, the easiest way to accomplish this is to decrease spending a little in each of several categories.

Deliberately underspending in a category for several months may allow you to spend more at a later time. For example, some people like to postpone expenditures on higher-cost clothing items (such as coats and suits) until these items go on sale and then to make major purchases.

A good budget can help you make financial decisions. If you find that you are spending too much, you will be able to review your records and find the items that are out of line. If you have extra money, you may want to look into investments in addition to a savings account.

Your spending plan has to be uniquely geared to your needs. Do not be discouraged if it does not always fit perfectly with reality. The important thing is that you learn to control your finances and to plan ahead. As time goes by, you will become more experienced in monitoring and modifying your budget.

Using Credit

Another way of achieving goals may involve the use of credit. When you use *credit,* you are spending future income for goods and services you are receiving now. "Buy now, pay later" has become a way of life in our country. We live in a state of controlled debt, buying things on time with wallets full of credit cards, 27-8. Buying on credit is not necessarily bad. Wisely used credit can lead to a higher level of living. However, credit used unwisely can lead to misery.

Types of Credit

Credit can be used to pay for almost anything you wish to buy, including houses, cars, clothes, and vacations. You can choose from a variety of types of credit, depending on your needs and preferences.

When you use *installment credit,* you agree to pay for a purchase in several regular payments. This type of credit is generally used for personal loans or for large purchases such as cars, appliances, or furniture. A plan of installment payments is set up to cover the cost of the item plus *finance charges* (the dollar amount the credit will cost you). Finance charges consist primarily of interest payments.

With *noninstallment credit,* you do not pay for the item or service as you receive it, but you pay the full charge in one payment. Examples of noninstallment credit include 30-day charge accounts, single payment loans, and credit extended for services from doc-

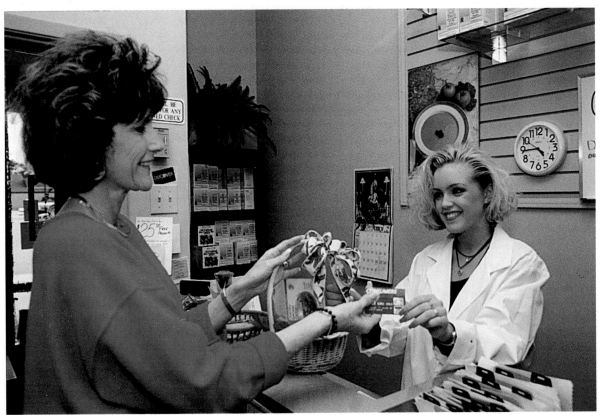

David Hopper

27-8
People use credit cards for many daily purchases. They are using cash less often.

tors, dentists, and utility companies. The amount may or may not include interest, depending on the goods and services you have received.

On a *revolving credit* plan, you are allowed to make purchases up to a specified amount. You pay a percentage of the balance each month, plus carrying charges, to keep the account "revolving." You can continue to charge on this account as long as you pay the carrying charges and the total bill remains within the specified limit.

Credit Cards

Credit cards are the most common type of credit used in the United States. See 27-9. They operate on the basis of either noninstallment credit or revolving credit.

The main advantage of credit cards is their convenience. They eliminate the need to carry a lot of cash. They allow you to pay bills once a month by check. Together, credit card receipts and canceled checks provide you with a record of most of your expenses and payments.

When you use credit cards, you are receiving a service as well as the item you are purchasing. Because stores make less profit on credit purchases, a few stores offer discounts on items purchased with cash. They may accept credit cards only if the amount purchased falls above a specified minimum level.

Credit cards have some disadvantages. Your credit cards can be stolen or lost. If someone else uses them, you may be held responsible for part of the cost. An even more serious disadvantage of credit cards, however, is that spending becomes so easy that you may overspend. You may find yourself with a debt so large that you remit only the minimum payment each month—at the high interest rates typical of credit card arrangements. It may take you months or even years to recover from a "spending spree."

David Hopper

27-9
Credit cards represent the most common type of credit. They can be used to buy everything from gasoline to plane tickets.

If you decide to use one or more credit cards, try to avoid sinking into debt. To resist the temptation to overspend, some consumers strictly limit the number of credit cards they own. Others resolve to use their credit cards only for emergencies or for rare, large one-time purchases. People who abuse their credit card privileges often find that these privileges—as well as their cards—have been revoked.

Sources of Credit

Sometimes it is wise or necessary to use credit. You may want, for example, to borrow money to buy a home or to invest in further education. Besides knowing the types of credit that can be used, you need to know what sources of credit are available. This will help you comparison shop for your best credit deal.

Yourself

You may be able to borrow from yourself with a passbook loan. In this transaction, you can borrow money from your bank and use your passbook savings account as *collateral* (security) for the loan. The bank knows that if you *default* on (don't pay) your loan, the bank can take your savings to pay for the loan. When you borrow from yourself, you pay interest but your savings continue to earn interest. When you pay back the loan, you still have your full savings account along with its accumulated interest.

You can also be your own source of credit if you borrow from your life insurance. Several types of policies build cash values that can be used as collateral. This kind of loan is much like a passbook loan. If you repay the loan (with interest) and continue to pay premiums on your policy, your death benefit will remain the same. If you do not repay the loan, this amount will be deducted from the amount paid to the beneficiary at the time of your death. The passbook loan and the policy loan are usually the lowest-interest loans available.

Credit Unions

A credit union is a non-profit financial organization owned by and operated for the benefit of its members. Credit unions often exist for employees of a company or members of a union or professional organization. Loans from credit unions are available to members only. They usually offer a low interest rate.

Financial Institutions

Banks and savings and loan associations are some of the most common sources for borrowing. They may offer lower interest rates than many of the other sources. They also give you the convenience of completing most of your financial transactions under one roof, 27-10.

27-10
Local banks can be a convenient source of credit.

Store Dealer Financing

If you buy an item such as a car from a dealer, you may be able to finance it through the same company. However, the cost of the credit may be high. The dealer earns a profit from the loan as well as from the merchandise sold to you.

Finance Companies

Money is often available (with less checking of your credit history) from a finance company. Usually you are able to borrow money quickly, but the interest rate is extremely high—sometimes over 45 percent.

Pawnbrokers

If you have an item to use as collateral and you need money quickly, you can seek credit from a *pawnbroker.* If you do not repay the loan within the stated time, with the accompanying high interest, the pawnbroker can sell the item you gave as collateral.

Family and Friends

If a family member or friend offers you a loan and you accept, arrange it as a legitimate business deal. Both of you should sign an agreement that states the interest rate and all the terms. Using family and friends for sources of money is not always the wisest choice, even if they make the original offer. In such cases, resentments or perceptions of personal obligation may complicate a relationship.

How to Obtain Credit

Before a company decides to extend you credit, it must be certain that you are a good risk. You will have to complete an application and provide information about your financial history. Then the company will investigate your background and check on your ability to pay by contacting a credit bureau. *Credit bureaus* collect information on the credit practices of individuals and make this information available to businesses. This protects stores and businesses from phony or misleading applications.

If you have previously had credit, your *credit rating* is determined by how promptly you have paid your debts. If you do not have a credit record, the issuing company will weigh several factors. They will consider your employment, your student or job status, and your assets (such as a savings account or car). More information about getting first-time credit is presented in 27-11.

If you are rejected for credit, you have the right to check your credit report for damaging information. The credit bureau must show you your file. If you claim that the information in your file is false, the credit bureau must reinvestigate. If you are right, everyone who received the bad report in the past six months will get a correction at your request.

Making Credit Work for You

Credit is convenient to use. It also allows you to enjoy your purchases while you pay for them. However, it can be expensive. Before you use credit, you should be sure you will be

---

Getting First-Time Credit

■ Open checking and savings accounts. Responsible management of bank accounts is a sign of good financial character. Besides, savings can sometimes be used as collateral for a loan.

■ Use a layaway plan in a local store. This is a kind of credit, except that the item you are buying stays in the store until you pay for it. After you successfully pay off a layaway item, a store might allow you to open a charge account.

■ Apply for credit with a merchant who knows you. He or she may be willing to give you a chance. If so, start small and repay promptly. That way, the first entry in your credit history will be a positive one.

■ Open a charge account at a store where your parents already have an account. Many stores offer special teenage accounts with low credit limits.

■ If your parents belong to a credit union, check their rules. Many credit unions automatically grant membership to the children of members.

■ Offer to make a big down payment. A lender might be more willing to let you make installment payments if you can pay a large sum of money "up front."

■ Get a cosigner for a loan. A parent, relative, or other adult might agree to "guarantee" that your credit is good. If you repay the money on time, the store may be willing to give you credit by yourself next time.

27-11
Getting credit for the first time can be difficult for young people. These tips may help you.

Contemporary Concerns *of today's teens:*
Your Credit Card: Staying in Control

Due to strong competition among credit card companies, young people are finding it easier to get credit cards—often before they have sufficient financial experience to use them wisely. Consumers with credit cards have opportunities to spend beyond their means. If they overspend, however, they must pay a price—not only in interest but in financial worry.

Financial counselors suggest the following tips for staying in control:

- Keep careful track of each purchase you charge to your credit card each month, so that you are less tempted to overspend.

- If at all possible, pay off the entire balance each month. This allows you to avoid interest charges and indebtedness. It also gives you peace of mind because you know that the maximum amount of credit will be available in case of an emergency.

- Beware if you find yourself making only the minimum monthly payments on your balance. This often shows that you are headed for trouble.

- If necessary, put away your credit card for several months to get out of the habit of overusing it.

- Avoid getting too many credit cards. Each credit card means another opportunity to overspend. Moreover, the number of credit cards you own becomes part of your credit history. Consumers with too many cards are viewed as greater credit risks.

Consumers who abuse credit cards can plunge themselves into debt and financial worry. Used wisely, however, credit cards can play a constructive role in their personal and family finances.

able to manage the payments without sacrificing other important needs.

Think before you buy something with credit. Don't buy an item just because it is easy to use your credit card. Instead, be sure that it is something you really want or need. For a major purchase, consider convenience versus cost. Do you need to have it now? Is it worth the cost of credit, or can you wait until you have saved enough money to buy it with cash?

The main cost of credit is for interest. Because interest can be figured in different ways, comparing credit costs is difficult. To help consumers, the Truth in Lending Law was passed. Now every loan agent must give you the same kind of information, which makes comparison shopping easier. You must be told the annual percentage rate of interest as well as the number and amount of payments you will have to make. You must also be told the finance charge and the total amount

Six Ways to Buy a $750 TV Set				
Buying Method	**Annual Percentage Rate**	**Monthly Payments Over Two Years**	**Total Finance Charges**	**Total Cost**
Cash				$750.00
Credit Union	10.5%	$34.78	$ 84.77	834.77
Commercial Bank	12%	35.31	97.32	847.32
Store Loan or Contract Plan	19%	37.81	157.35	907.35
Credit Card	21%	38.54	174.93	924.93
Finance Company	27%	40.79	228.85	978.85

27-12
Buying an item with credit can be costly. Compare loan information from various
sources to get the best deal.

you will have paid after making all the payments as scheduled. It is to your advantage to shop around. Consider several different credit sources. Compare the information you receive, and choose the best deal. This kind of shopping can save you a lot of money, 27-12.

Before you sign a credit contract, read it thoroughly. If you have questions, do not be afraid to ask them. Be sure you understand everything in the contract. Also check to see that the contract contains all of the same information that you were given earlier as you were comparison shopping. After you have signed the contract, be sure to get a copy of it. Keep it in your files so you can refer to it if necessary.

Once you have established a credit history (good or bad), it is likely to follow you. Protect your credit rating by keeping the promises you made when you signed the credit contract. Make your payments on time and in the correct amount. If for some reason you must miss a payment, contact the creditor at once to make special arrangements.

Credit, managed well, can be a big help to consumers. Managed poorly, however, credit can cause major financial problems.

Summary ■ ■ ■ ■ ■ ■ ■ ■ ■ ■ ■ ■ ■ ■

- Couples have a variety of options for managing family financial matters. The best arrangement is the one that works best for the individual couple.

- A budget is a plan for managing income and expenses. It helps you recognize where your money is going.

- Before constructing a budget, you may need to record your expenses for a few months so you know what your spending needs are.

- By evaluating your income and expenses through budgeting, you will be able to manage your money more successfully to meet your wants and needs.

- Using credit can allow you to enjoy a higher level of living, but it can also lead to major financial problems.

- Common types of credit include installment, noninstallment, and revolving credit.

- Typical sources of credit are oneself, credit unions, banks, store dealers, finance companies, pawnbrokers, and family and friends. Using family and friends is not always the wisest choice because of the relationship complications that can result.

- Before a company decides to grant you a loan, it will investigate your credit history. Your credit rating is influenced by your record of debt payment in the past.

- The main cost of credit is interest. The Truth in Lending Law requires every loan agent to give you the same kind of information so that you can compare various arrangements more easily.

- Before you sign a credit contract, read it thoroughly. If you have questions, do not be afraid to ask them.

To Review ■ ■ ■ ■ ■ ■ ■ ■ ■ ■ ■ ■ ■ ■

1. Describe four arrangements often used by couples to handle family finances.

2. Name three reasons for following a budget.

3. Name five categories of expenditures that should be included in a budget.

4. Describe a revolving credit plan.

5. True or False. When you use installment credit, you agree to pay for a purchase in several regular payments.

6. List five sources of credit.

7. True or False. Finance companies usually offer loans at low interest rates.

8. What is the function of credit bureaus?

9. True or False. If you are rejected for credit, you have the right to check your credit report for damaging information.

10. Once you have been given credit, how can you protect your credit rating?

To Do ■ ■ ■ ■ ■ ■ ■ ■ ■ ■ ■ ■ ■ ■ ■ ■ ■ ■

1. Discuss different methods couples may use to handle their money. Point out advantages and disadvantages of each method.

2. Set up a budget for families in three different stages of the life cycle. Consider the various wants and needs of each family as you prepare a suitable budget for each.

3. Select a car you would like to buy. Compare the costs of purchasing it with cash, a loan from a financial institution, or the financial services of the dealership.

4. Invite a speaker to class to discuss credit bureaus. Prepare a list of questions to ask the speaker, such as the following:
   a. What background information is kept on file?
   b. How is information made available to businesses?
   c. If a person has never bought anything with credit, how can credit be established?
   d. What information can be damaging in a file?
   e. If a mistake has been made concerning a person's financial transactions, what can be done?

5. Ask a family financial counselor to visit your class to discuss
   a. how families get into financial trouble (for example, high levels of indebtedness).
   b. what strategies can be used to help families recover from financial trouble.
   c. how a family can avoid developing financial problems.

Glossary ▪

A

abstinence: choosing to refrain from some activity, such as using drugs or having sexual intercourse. (9)

accommodation: form of marital adjustment in which two partners recognize and accept differences in each other. (14)

acquaintance rape: when a person the victim knows and trusts forces or pressures the victim into non-consenting sexual intercourse. (11)

active listening: type of listening in which a person indicates to the sender that a message has been heard and understood, encouraging further communication. (10)

addiction: the abuse of any drug that results in a physical or psychological need for the drug. (8)

adjustable life insurance: flexible insurance that allows the insured to alter the coverage as the need for protection and the ability to pay for it change. (25)

advertising: information about goods and services given to consumers in order to stimulate sales. (24)

agency adoption: procedure in which the birthparents relinquish their child to an adoption agency rather than directly to adoptive parents. The agency then places the child with a carefully selected adoptive family. (9)

AIDS (Acquired Immune Deficiency Syndrome): condition that develops when the HIV virus attacks the immune system of the body, creating a weakness to infections. (9)

alcoholic: a person who suffers from a condition manifested by compulsive, obsessive drinking that is beyond the person's control. (8)

alimony: money paid by the primary wage earner to the other marriage partner during and after a divorce. (20)

allowance: money given by parents to children for their personal needs. (19)

ambivalence: being attracted to and repelled by someone at the same time. (11)

ambiverts: people who behave as either introverts or extroverts depending on the circumstances. (4)

amniocentesis: process in which a long, thin needle is inserted into the uterus and part of the fluid surrounding the fetus is drawn out and analyzed for abnormalities. (16)

amnio-chorionic membrane (bag of waters): a membrane formed by the joining of two membranes, the amnion and chorion, which forms around the developing fetus. (17)

amniotic fluid: fluid that completely surrounds the fetus. (17)

amotivational syndrome: behavior pattern typical of long-term marijuana users in which they have trouble remembering things and concentrating. They become apathetic and lethargic, adopting a "dropout" personality. (8)

anabolic steroids: synthetic testosterone-like drugs that have tissue-building properties. (8)

anemic: condition in which people have a low level of hemoglobin in their blood caused by a deficiency of iron in the diet. (9)

annulment: a court order stating a legal marriage never took place. (22)

anorexia nervosa: an eating disorder in which people have an intense fear of being obese and a distorted image of their bodies. They therefore starve themselves. (7)

apprenticeship: a formal, registered program for training an individual in a skilled craft or trade. (6)

aptitudes: potential for special talents. (6)

areola: pigmented area around the nipple. (17)

artificial insemination: method of treating infertility in which a physician places sperm directly in the upper part of the woman's uterus or in the fallopian tubes. (16)

assertive: sure and confident, expressing feelings directly, asking for what one wants, and refusing what one doesn't want. (10)

assign the lease: to transfer the entire unexpired portion of a lease to someone else, thus giving up any responsibility for it. (24)

atheist: one who denies the existence of a god. (12)

attitude: a feeling or mental position that causes a person to react to a situation, concept, or object in a characteristic way. (4)

authority figures: people who make final decisions, such as parents, teachers, and the police. (3)

Automated Teller Machines (ATMs): convenient computerized machines that facilitate banking transactions at numerous locations 24 hours a day. (26)

autonomy: the freedom of self-direction achieved by learning to make decisions for oneself and taking pride in one's accomplishments. (4)

autopsy: detailed physical examination of a dead body usually performed to determine the cause of death. (23)

autosomes: any chromosome that is not a sex chromosome. (2)

B

Babinski reflex: reflex exhibited by newborns that causes them to extend their toes when the soles of their feet are touched. (18)

bailout: money loaned by family or friends to finance gambling debts. (21)

bait-and-switch advertising: type of advertising in which a store offers an item (the "bait") at a very low price to get you to come into the store. Once there, the store owner may try to redirect ("switch") your attention to other more expensive items. (24)

bank statement: a record of every deposit and every check that passed through an account during a month. (26)

beneficiaries: persons designated by a life insurance policyholder to receive the benefits of the policy upon the policyholder's death; also a person who is named in a will to receive a deceased person's property. (23)

bigamy: crime in which a person enters a second marriage before the first one is dissolved. (13)

bigots: people who have strong prejudices. (4)

biodegradable: decomposes by natural biological processes. (24)

biofeedback: procedure in which electronic equipment is used to provide measurements of blood pressure, respiration rate, skin temperature, and tension in individual muscles so that a person can monitor stress. (7)

blended family system: family system in which either or both spouses have been married before and may have one or more children from the previous marriage. (15)

block scheduling: option allowing employees to work 40 hours (a typical work week) in three or four days. (20)

blood pooling: the accumulation of blood in the large muscles of the legs, which causes the heart and brain to be deprived of an adequate blood supply. (7)

blood types: one of four main groups into which human blood can be classified: O, A, B, and AB. (2)

body language: a form of nonverbal communication in which a person reveals inner feelings through gestures. (10)

bonding: formation of close emotional ties between a mother and her baby that begins at the moment of birth. (17)

budget: a plan for managing income and expenses. (27)

bulimia: an eating disorder in which people eat large amounts of food and then feel guilty and purge themselves of the food by vomiting or taking laxatives. (7)

bullying: the infliction of physical, verbal, or emotional abuse on another person. (10)

C

cash value: the amount of money the policyholder would receive if the policy is surrendered before his or her death or when it matures. (25)

cashier's check: check drawn by a bank on its own funds and signed by a bank officer. (26)

caveat emptor: "Let the buyer beware." The consumer bears the responsibility of choosing good products. (24)

caveat venditor: "Let the seller beware." The merchants bear the responsibility of selling good products. (24)

ceremonial wedding: wedding performed by a religious officiate. (13)

certificate of deposit (CD): money left on deposit for a specific period of time to earn a higher rate of interest. (26)

certified check: a personal check with a bank's guarantee that the check will be paid. (26)

cesarean section: method of childbirth in which the walls of the abdomen and uterus are cut and the baby is lifted out of the uterus. (17)

character: a sense of right and wrong that guides a person's behavior. (1)

chasing: attempting to win back what one has lost while gambling. (21)

child abuse and neglect: physical and mental injury, sexual abuse, negligent treatment, or maltreatment of a child under the age of 18 by a person who is responsible for the child's welfare. (21)

child support: payments made by the non-custodial parent for the financial support of the children. (22)

chlamydia: widespread sexually transmitted disease that can be cured when detected, but detection may be difficult since most victims have no symptoms. (9)

cholesterol: a fat-like substance in blood strongly associated with heart disease. (7)

chosen role: role a person voluntarily assumes, such as husband, wife, father, or mother. (15)

chromosome: thread-like structure that carries hereditary information in the form of genes. Humans have 23 pairs of chromosomes in every cell of their bodies. (2)

civil wedding: wedding performed by a judicial official. (13)

climacteric: changes that occur in men during middle age when hormone production diminishes, resulting in shifts in moods and emotions. (23)

clique: a narrow, exclusive group of people held together by common interests, views, and purposes. (10)

closed adoption: adoption procedure in which the birthparents do not meet or know the adoptive parents. (9)

codependency: set of maladaptive, compulsive behaviors learned by family members when the family is experiencing great emotional pain and stress. (21)

coinsurance: clause in an insurance policy that states that the policyholder will pay a certain percentage of the costs, perhaps 20 to 25 percent, while the insurance company pays the remaining portion of the costs. (25)

collateral: security for a loan. (27)

collusion: fraud against the court which occurs when a couple want a divorce but have no legal grounds, so they set up necessary grounds for divorce. (22)

colostrum: the sticky precursor of milk that is produced in the female breast during pregnancy. (17)

commercial bank: financial institution owned by stockholders and operated for profit. (26)

common-law marriage: a lifestyle in which a man and a woman live together with the intention of being husband and wife and present themselves in public as such. Common-law marriages are legally binding in some states. (13)

communication: any means by which one person shares a message with another person. (10)

community property: property acquired through the labors of either spouse during their marriage and owned equally by both spouses. (22)

compensation: using a substitute method to achieve a desired goal. (4)

complementary needs: tendency to seek a partner who is strong in areas where you are weak. (12)

compromise: form of adjustment in which both partners give in and find a satisfactory agreement for both. (14)

compulsive gambler: someone who loses control over gambling and continues to gamble despite the harmful consequences. (21)

conception: fertilization that occurs when a sperm and egg unite and pregnancy begins. (17)

concession: form of adjustment in which one person must win and one must lose. (14)

condominium: common ownership of a residential property. (24)

condonation: in a divorce, once the "guilty" party has been condoned or forgiven for a certain action, that action cannot be the grounds for divorce. (22)

conflict resolution: a form of mediation that is used to resolve disagreements in a positive way. (10)

connivance: a defense to prevent a divorce in which the person suing for divorce is found guilty of causing the condition used as grounds for the divorce. (22)

consanguineous marriage: marriage of people related by blood. (13)

consumer: any person who buys goods and services. (24)

contested divorce: a divorce procedure in which a person who wants to fight the divorce files an answer and tries to prove that no grounds exist. (22)

convenience foods: foods that have been partially or fully prepared in order to save time. (24)

conversion: act of transferring the energy of a desire one cannot express into a physical symptom or complaint; a defense mechanism. (4)

cooperative play: form of play in which a child chooses to interact with one or more other children. (19)

cost-effective: economical in terms of benefits yielded by money spent. (20)

cover letter: letter sent with a resume meant to introduce the accompanying material. (6)

credit: use of future income for goods and services currently received. (27)

credit bureau: agency that collects information on the credit practices of individuals and makes this information available to businesses. (27)

credit rating: a rating based on how promptly a person pays his or her debts. (27)

credit union: a nonprofit financial institution owned by and operated for the benefit of its members. (26)

crisis: a crucial time or event that causes changes in a person's life and has no ready solution. (21)

culture: the total social environment of a people or group. (3)

custody: parental right to raise the child in the home and to make decisions about the child's care, upbringing, and overall welfare. (22)

D

date rape: when a person the victim knows and trusts forces or pressures the victim into non-consenting sexual intercourse. (11)

decision-making process: a method of making decisions and solving problems that is a step-by-step process. (5)

deductible: clause in an insurance policy that states that the insured will pay an agreed-upon portion of the total expense, which may be the first $250, $500, or even $1,000 of the bill. (25)

deductions: money subtracted from a person's wages for such items as income tax and social security. (26)

default: failure to pay back a loan. (27)

defense mechanisms: automatic and involuntary ways people react to anxiety-producing events or threats. (4)

depressants: drugs, also called sedatives, that slow down the central nervous system. (8)

depression: an overwhelming attitude of sadness, discouragement, and hopelessness. (21)

desertion: abandoning the marital partner. (22)

designer drugs: manufactured drugs that have slightly altered formulas, but closely resemble other illegal drugs such as cocaine. (8)

destructive quarreling: arguments in which partners attack each other's self-esteem, weakening the relationship and not solving the problem. (14)

Dietary Guidelines for Americans: a list of recommendations developed by the federal government for making healthful food choices. (7)

direct attack: in response to a threat to a person's self-esteem, the person attacks the source of the threat. (4)

disability income insurance: health insurance that protects a person or family from loss of income due to sickness or disabling injury. (25)

discipline: the use of different methods and techniques to teach children self-control and limits. (19)

displaced homemakers: longtime homemakers whose husbands have left or remarried and whose children have grown and who find themselves unexpectedly dependent on their own resources for financial security. (20)

displacement: transferring an emotion connected with one person or thing to an unrelated person or thing; a defense mechanism. (4)

divorce: a legal dissolution of the marriage contract. (22)

domestic violence: violence between intimate friends or family members, including spouses, children, or elders. (21)

dominant: more influential or prevalent. (2)

down payment: the initial payment made to buy a home or item, which is usually a percentage of the total purchase price. (24)

drug: a substance, other than food, that has an effect on one or more systems of the body, especially the central nervous system. (8)

drug abuse: deliberately taking a substance for other than its intended purpose and in a manner that can result in damage to the person's health or his or her ability to function. (8)

drug misuse: taking a substance for its intended purpose, but not in the appropriate amount, frequency, strength, or manner. (8)

drug use: the taking of a drug for its intended purposes, in the appropriate amount, frequency, strength, and manner. (8)

dual-worker families: families in which both the husband and the wife are employed. (20)

dysfunctional family: family system in which one or more family members do not fulfill their responsibilities, throwing the system out of balance. (15)

E

embryo: term describing the developing baby from implantation until the fourteenth week of development. (17)

emotional abuse: parents continually making demands that their children are not capable of meeting, then criticizing and humiliating the children for not living up to their demands. (21)

emotional growth: the continuing refinement of emotions or mental states that causes an individual to act in a certain way. (1)

emotional neglect: the failure to provide children with love and affection. (21)

empathy: the process of seeing things from another person's view. (10)

employee-assistance programs (EAPs): groups that counsel employees faced with problems such as alcoholism or other substance abuse, family illness, financial debt, or finding child or elder care. (20)

empty nest syndrome: feelings of uselessness and depression some parents feel after their children have left home. (23)

enabler: someone who unknowingly acts in ways that contribute to an addict's drug use. (21)

endometrium: inner lining of the uterus where the fertilized egg implants. (17)

endorse: to sign the back of a check in order to transfer it to another person or institution. (26)

Enoch Arden divorce: divorce that may be granted if a married person disappears for a stated period of time, usually five to seven years, and cannot be located. (22)

environmental responsibility: feeling of personal accountability for protecting the environment. (24)

environment: all of the conditions, objects, and circumstances that surround an individual. (1)

exemptions: sources or amounts of income that are not taxed. (26)

extended kinship family system: family system in which several generations of a family, such as grandparents, parents, and children, and sometimes aunts, uncles, and cousins, live together. (15)

extroverts: persons who prefer to be with people and to tell others about their feelings and thoughts. (4)

F

face amount: the amount of money that will be paid to the beneficiary of a life insurance policy upon the policyholder's death. (25)

family: a group of two or more persons, related by blood, marriage, or adoption, who reside together in a household. (15)

Family and Medical Leave Act: a law that entitles workers to 12 weeks of unpaid leave per year following the birth or adoption of a child. This time can also be used to care for a seriously ill relative or to take care of a serious personal health condition. (20)

family life cycle: the five stages of change through which families pass as they expand and contract in size. (15)

family-centered childbirth: childbirth method based on the belief that birth affects the family as a unit as well as each individual family member. (17)

feedback: communicating to another person how you feel about what was said. (10)

fetal alcohol syndrome: a pattern of physical and mental birth defects often present in children born of alcoholic mothers. (17)

fetus: term describing the developing baby from the fourteenth week of development until birth. (17)

finance charge: the dollar amount the use of credit will cost, consisting primarily of interest payments. (27)

fixed expenses: costs that are predictable and that recur regularly. (27)

flexible expenses: costs that fluctuate in amount and may occur less regularly. (27)

flextime: option allowing the worker to choose his or her own working hours, subject to certain rules. (20)

fontanel: open space between the bones of a newborn's head that allow the bones of the baby's skull to move together and make birth easier. (18)

Food Guide Pyramid: a simple guide to good nutrition that gives recommended numbers of servings from six food groups. (7)

foster parenting: system that provides children with substitute families while their parents are unable to care for them. (15)

fraternal twins: twins resulting from two eggs fertilized by two sperm. They are no more alike than brother and sister except that they are born at the same time. (2)

functional family: family system in which all family members fulfill their roles and responsibilities. (15)

G

gene: the basic unit of heredity, which carries all the characteristics that will be transferred. (2)

generativity: concern for others beyond a person's immediate family and especially for future generations. (4)

genetic counseling: advice given by a physician to prospective parents on matters of heredity. (16)

genital warts: sexually transmitted disease caused by a virus. (9)

given role: role acquired when a person is born into a family, such as son, daughter, sister, or brother. (15)

goal: something a person wants to achieve or to have. (1)

gonorrhea: a highly contagious sexually transmitted disease caused by a bacterium. (9)

grasp reflex: reflex exhibited by newborns that causes them to close their hands tightly when their palms are touched. (18)

gross income: the total income earned before deductions are made. (26)

group dating: form of dating in which there is more emphasis on groups of people than on couples. (11)

growth pattern: unique way a person grows; includes chronological, physical, intellectual, emotional, social, and philosophical areas of growth. (1)

H

habituation: a term used to describe psychological dependence. (8)

halfway houses: centers where runaways can receive care as well as counseling. (21)

hallucinogens: mind-altering drugs that cause hallucinations with frightening mental experiences. (8)

health maintenance organization (HMO): a method of receiving and paying for health care where you pay a set fee on a regular basis. When you need health care, you go to a physician associated with the HMO. You receive whatever care you need, usually with no deductible and no coinsurance payment. (25)

hemoglobin: a component of blood that carries oxygen to all the cells of the body. (7)

heredity: the sum of the traits that are passed from ancestors to descendants. (1)

herpes: viral infections that occur in different forms, one of which is a sexually transmitted disease and may be called herpes simplex virus type 2, herpes II, or genital herpes. (9)

HIV (human immunodeficiency virus): virus that attacks the immune system of the body, causing AIDS. (9)

homeowner's insurance: insurance that covers damage to, or loss of, your home as well as the personal property inside your home. (25)

hospice: a medical facility designed for people who have only a few weeks or months to live, which provides a more homelike atmosphere than that of a hospital. Hospice-type care can also be provided in the home. (23)

human resources: resources that come from within a person and from other people who give support in some way. They include health, energy, time, personality characteristics, and character traits. (5)

I

idealization: valuing something far more than it is worth; a defense mechanism. (4)

identical twins: twins resulting from a single fertilized egg that divides. They have the same hereditary factors, so they are always of the same sex. (2)

identity: sense of who you are and what your roles are in society. (3)

incest: sexual activity between persons who are closely related. (21)

independent adoption: birthparents go through the legal process of placing their baby directly with adoptive parents without the assistance of an adoption agency. (9)

Individual Retirement Account (IRA): an account to which taxpayers may make annual contributions up to a set amount. Taxes may or may not be paid on the contributions, but interest earnings are not taxed until the money is withdrawn. (26)

infatuation: foolish, extreme attraction that does not last. (11)

inferiority: feelings of inadequacy and unimportance. (4)

inhalants: substances that give off fumes that may produce a sensation comparable to alcohol intoxication when inhaled. (8)

initiative: desire to begin action. (4)

installment credit: credit plan in which a person agrees to pay for a purchase in several regular payments. (27)

integrity: a state of being complete and satisfied with life. (4)

intellectual development: development in the areas of perception, attention, association, and other aspects of the mind. (18)

intergenerational care giving: care provided for both older and younger generations by the middle generation. (23)

intermittency: process of coming and going; occurring in interrupted sequences; not continuous. (14)

intervention: a means of forcing a person such as an alcoholic or addict to look at his or her behavior without the mask of denial. (21)

intestate: having died without leaving a will. (23)

intimacy: a sense of familiarity that develops over a long and close association. (11)

introverts: persons who prefer to be alone and to keep their feelings and thoughts to themselves. (4)

in vitro fertilization: process to achieve pregnancy in which an egg is removed from a woman's ovary, fertilized in a glass dish, and implanted back into the uterus. (16)

J

job sharing: option in which companies allow two employees to share one full-time job. (20)

K

Keogh plans: plans designed to help self-employed people establish tax-deferred retirement funds for themselves and their employees. (26)

L

lactation: the secretion of milk from the breasts. (17)

Lamaze method: method of childbirth based on the theory that the pain of childbirth can be controlled by the woman. (17)

large muscle development: improving ability to use the large muscles of the body, such as those of the trunk, neck, legs, and arms. (18)

latchkey children or children in self-care: children who are regularly left without direct adult supervision before or after school. (19)

leadership: the ability to lead and influence others. (6)

lease: a written, legally binding rental agreement. (24)

Leboyer method: method of childbirth focusing on making the birth experience of the baby less shocking and more comforting. (17)

legal separation: court order that allows a couple to live in separate households but does not end their marriage. (22)

leisure time: time free from work and other duties. (19)

life insurance: insurance protection against loss of income due to the death of the insured. (25)

lifestyle: a set of behaviors adopted by personal choice. (9)

lightening: term applied to the sinking of the uterus downward and forward toward the end of pregnancy; allows the woman to breath more easily because it relieves abdominal pressure. (17)

living will: legal document allowing people to choose whether or not they want to be kept alive when there is apparently no hope for them to recover. (23)

long-term goals: goals a person hopes to achieve next year or several years from now. (5)

love: a strong feeling of personal attachment between friends or family members; tender and compassionate affection shared between two people. (11)

lunar month: month consisting of exactly 28 days or four weeks, often used in describing fetal development. (17)

M

major medical insurance: policy that begins paying when the basic insurance coverage stops. It extends the basic policy and pays for additional hospital care due to major illness or serious injury, protecting people from huge medical bills that could ruin them financially. (25)

marijuana: a product of the hemp plant that acts as a stimulant, depressant, and hallucinogen, depending on the amount used and the stability of the user. (8)

marriage of affinity: marriage between persons related by marriage, such as stepparents and stepchildren. (13)

martyrdom: form of adjustment in which one partner avoids trouble at all costs by always giving in to the other partner. (14)

mediator: a third party who helps in resolving a conflict. (10)

menopause: period of time during a woman's middle years when certain biological changes occur in her body and the ovaries cease to mature a ripened egg each month. (23)

mirror imaging: condition which sometimes occurs in identical twins. Some body details that appear on the right side of one twin appear on the left side of the other. (2)

miscarriage: the birth of a baby before it has developed enough to live in the outside world, usually before the sixth month. (17)

mitten grasp: grasp using the palm and fingers opposing the thumb. (18)

mixed marriage: marriage involving persons from different countries, races, or religious faiths. (12)

money market account: a type of account that pays interest rates that change with prevailing rates on short-term investments. (26)

money order: an order for a specific amount of money payable to a specific payee. (26)

monogamous: married to only one person at a time. (13)

morals: beliefs about right and wrong behavior. (4)

mortgage: a claim against property that a buyer gives to a lender as security for borrowed money. (24)

motor development: the achievement of control over movement of different parts of the body. (19)

mutations: chemical changes in genes caused either by spontaneous error in genetic mechanisms or through some outside influence. (2)

mutual savings bank: financial institution owned by its depositors. (26)

N

narcotics: addicting drugs, such as opium, heroin, morphine, and codeine, that induce sleep or stupor and relieve pain. (8)

natural fibers: fibers made from sources found in nature such as the cotton plant or sheep. (24)

natural resources: resources available to everyone, such as air, water, and soil. (24)

needs: those items or conditions that people must have in order to survive. (24)

negotiation: process of conferring with one another and arriving at a settlement of a matter. (14)

net income: the money received after social security, income tax, and other deductions have been taken from the paycheck. (24)

networking: making professional contacts. (6)

nicotine: a toxic substance found in tobacco. (8)

no-fault auto insurance: a type of insurance that eliminates the legal process of proving who is at fault in an auto accident. (25)

no-fault divorce: a divorce procedure that eliminates the need for proving one partner guilty. (22)

non-contested divorce: a divorce procedure in which the spouses agree to the divorce. (22)

nonhuman resources: resources that are not physically a part of any individual, including money, material possessions, and community resources and facilities. (5)

noninstallment credit: type of credit in which the buyer agrees to pay for purchases or services in one single payment. (27)

nonverbal communication: type of communication that uses factors other than words, such as gestures, facial expressions, eye contact, and body movements. (10)

nurturance: affectionate care and attention. (19)

O

officiate: a person who can legally marry a couple. (13)

ongoing hostility: situation in which the couple never really settle their conflicts. (14)

on-site child-care facility: child-care facility that is provided by the employer at or near the job site. (20)

open adoption: adoption procedure in which the birthparents and adoptive parents meet or know each other. (9)

organ bank: place where parts of bodies are kept until they can be donated to other people. (23)

osteoporosis: condition affecting mostly women in later life in which bone mass is lost, causing bones to weaken. Vertebrae may collapse, causing stooped posture, and bones may break easily. (7)

overdraft: occurrence in which a check is written on an account with insufficient funds. (26)

over-the-counter (OTC) drugs: drugs that are used to treat or prevent illness and are available without a doctor's prescription. (8)

P

parallel play: form of play in which children like to play next to their peers but do not play with their peers. (19)

parent image: theory that a man looks for a wife similar to his mother and a woman looks for a husband similar to her father. (12)

part-time workers: people who work less than a full work week. (20)

passive listening: taking in another's words, but offering no sign of hearing or understanding the message. (10)

passive smoking: inhaling second-hand smoke. (8)

pawnbroker: a person who will give collateral for an item if money is needed quickly. If the loan is not repaid within the stated time, with the accompanying high interest, the pawnbroker can sell the item given as collateral. (27)

peer group: group consisting of persons who are similar in age or status. (3)

peer pressure: the influence of members of the peer group. (3)

personality: the group of behavioral and emotional traits that distinguishes an individual; the sum of all inherited and acquired characteristics. (1)

phobias: exaggerated fears of everyday objects or events. (4)

physical abuse: the infliction of physical injury upon a person. (21)

physical dependence: condition that occurs when the body chemistry of a drug user is altered by repeated use of a drug, causing the user's body to develop an actual physical need for the drug. (8)

physical neglect: the failure to provide sufficient food, clothing, shelter, medical care, education, guidance, and supervision for a child. (21)

physically disabled: having an abnormality of body structure, function, or metabolism that interferes with the ability to walk, lift, hear, or learn. (18)

pincer grip: grasp using just the thumb and index finger. (18)

pituitary gland: small organ attached to the brain that produces secretions that affect basic body functions. The gland triggers the growth and changes that occur at puberty. (1)

placenta: a special organ that functions as an interchange between the developing fetus and the mother. (17)

policy: a legal contract issued by an insurance company. (25)

polygamous: married to more than one person at a time. (13)

postpartum period: period of time following the delivery of a baby. (17)

preferred provider organization (PPO): organization that offers lower-cost health care by providing a group discount if participating doctors are used. It pays some of the costs if a nonparticipating doctor is used. (25)

prejudices: attitudes based on false or insufficient information. (4)

premium: the amount of money a policyholder pays for an insurance policy. (25)

prescription drugs: drugs available only with a doctor's recommendation. (8)

productive quarrel: an argument that can strengthen a marriage as partners clarify issues and realize their viewpoints are not so different. (14)

projection: blaming other people or things for one's own failures; a defense mechanism. (4)

proximity: nearness. (12)

pseudo-truths: false statements made to sound as if they were true. (24)

psychological dependence: condition which occurs when a drug user has learned to use a drug as a mental and emotional crutch. The user's need is real, but it is psychological rather than physical. (8)

puberty: the time when the body changes from that of a boy or girl to that of a man or woman. (1)

puffery advertising: advertising that makes an exaggerated claim that attracts the reader or listener. (24)

Q

quality time: time spent giving full attention to another person or persons. (20)

quickening: active movements of the fetus felt by the mother. (17)

R

rape: any sexual intimacy forced on one person by another. (11)

rationalization: explaining one's weaknesses or failures by giving socially acceptable excuses; a defense mechanism. (4)

recessive: less influential or prevalent. (2)

recycled: used again to produce new products. (24)

regression: a defense mechanism in which a person reverts back to a less mature stage of development. (4)

rehabilitative alimony: financial support for job retraining rather than lifelong support. (20)

resources: the various ways and means that a person has for reaching goals. (5)

resume: an information sheet about a person's educational and job background. (6)

retirement accounts: long-range savings accounts designed to provide income after retirement. (26)

revolving credit: a type of credit in which the buyer is allowed to make purchases up to a specified amount, paying a percentage of the balance each month plus carrying charges to keep the account "revolving." (27)

Rh factor: a specific blood element. Persons who have inherited the element are called Rh-positive. Persons who have not inherited it are called Rh-negative. (2)

role: a socially expected behavior pattern. (3)

rooting reflex: reflex exhibited by newborns. When they are touched on one of their cheeks, they turn their heads in that direction and open their mouths. (18)

S

sandwich generation: middle-aged couples often "sandwiched" between caring for their children and caring for their parents at a time when they would really like more time for themselves. (23)

saturated fat: a type of fat that tends to be solid at room temperature, comes from animal sources, and is a factor in high blood-cholesterol levels. (7)

savings account: an account that permits the saver to make deposits and withdrawals in varying amounts at any time. (26)

savings and loan association: a financial institution that may be a mutual company (owned and operated for the benefit of its depositors) or a stock company (operated for profit). (26)

scapegoat: in the defense mechanism of projection, the common term for the person who bears the blame for others. (4)

security deposit: a sum of money, usually one month's rent, that a person pays a landlord before moving into a rental unit. (24)

self-actualization: the realization of a person's full potential. (4)

self-concept: the way a person sees him or herself. (1)

self-esteem: how one feels about his or her self-concept. (1)

self-worth: a feeling of worthwhileness, adequacy, and belonging that is influenced by a person's self-esteem. (1)

separate property: property owned by one spouse prior to marriage or acquired during marriage by gift or inheritance and retained as separate property. (22)

separation anxiety: emotion shown by babies when adults they love leave them for a short time. (18)

sexual abuse: forcing a child to engage in sexual activities. (21)

sexual harassment: unwelcome sexual advances, requests for sexual favors, or other verbal or physical conduct of a sexual nature. (10)

sexually transmitted diseases (STDs): illnesses spread by sexual contact. (9)

shelters: establishments that offer food and housing for people who have nowhere else to go. (21)

short-term goals: goals reachable in the near future—the next hour, day, or week. (5)

Siamese twins: identical twins who are born physically linked because the fertilized egg failed to split completely apart. (2)

sibling rivalry: sense of competition between brothers and sisters. (3)

siblings: a person's brothers and/or sisters. (3)

single-parent family: family system that occurs as the result of divorce, separation, death, or having children outside of marriage. (15)

small muscle development: improving ability to use the small muscles, such as those of the hands, fingers, feet, and toes. (18)

smokeless tobacco: snuff and chewing tobacco. (8)

social development: the process of learning to relate to other people; shaped by how other people affect the child and how the child affects other people. (18)

social security: plan whereby employees, their employers, and self-employed persons pay social security taxes that are used to pay benefits to eligible people. When a worker retires, becomes disabled, or dies, monthly cash benefits are paid to replace part of the earnings the family has lost. (26)

stages of dying: clearly defined stages in the acceptance of death. (23)

stages of grieving: the grieving process of survivors, which generally follows stages similar to the stages of dying. (23)

standards: levels of achievement that help a person determine if goals have been achieved. (5)

startle reflex: reflex exhibited by newborns. When they are tapped on their abdomens or when their support is suddenly removed, they respond by spreading their arms and legs apart and then bringing them together again in a bow. (18)

steady dating: dating only one person for a period of time. (11)

stereotypes: widely held beliefs that all members of a group share the same characteristics. (4)

stimulants: drugs that speed up the central nervous system and accelerate body processes, often to a dangerous degree. (8)

stress: a state of bodily or mental tension resulting from change. (7)

sublet: to let someone else rent your property for a period of time while still retaining responsibility for all terms of the lease. (24)

subliminal advertising: flashes of suggestive advertising repeatedly shown on a television or movie screen designed to stimulate your subconscious mind. (24)

support group: group usually made up of people with a common concern who offer emotional help, information, and the benefits of shared experience. (7)

synthetic or manufactured fibers: fibers made from non-natural sources. (24)

syphilis: sexually transmitted disease in which sores develop at the site of infection. (9)

T

telecommuting: the practice of working at home—rather than commuting, or traveling, to work—by using a computer and a modem. (3)

telephone hotlines: telephone numbers that people can call for immediate information in a crisis. (21)

temper tantrum: a violent outburst of anger. (19)

term life insurance: type of life insurance that covers the life of the policyholder for a specified term or period of time. Once the term expires, the person is no longer insured. (25)

theist: a person who believes a god exists. (12)

tonic neck reflex: reflex exhibited by infants. When babies lie on their backs, they turn their heads to one side. If they turn to the right, their right hands extend outward, and their left arms extend upward. If they turn to the left, the movements are reversed. (18)

toxemia: condition during pregnancy that results in fluid retention, causing swelling of fingers and feet, and weight gain. (9)

traveler's checks: checks that can be cashed at most places around the world and replaced if they are lost or stolen. (26)

two-parent family system: family system consisting of a married couple and their biological children. (15)

U

ultrasound examination: process using sound waves to provide an outline or picture of the fetus inside the mother. (16)

umbilical cord: cord that links the fetus to the placenta. (17)

United States savings bond: a type of bond in which purchasers pay half the face amount and receive the full face amount if held to the maturity date. (26)

universal life insurance: a type of life insurance in which protection and savings are clearly separated and the amounts of both parts can be changed. (25)

unsaturated fat: a type of fat that tends to be liquid at room temperature and comes from plant sources. (7)

V

values: the concepts, beliefs, attitudes, activities, and feelings that are most important to a person. (5)

variable life insurance: a type of life insurance in which part of the premium goes toward protection and the rest goes into savings that are invested in equity products such as stocks. (25)

verbal communication: form of communication that uses words to send and receive messages. (10)

violence: any harmful physical contact that results in serious injury or death. (21)

visitation rights: following a divorce, the legal rights of the non-custodial parent to see a child during specified times. (22)

volunteering: choosing freely to provide a service for others without pay. (1)

W

whole life insurance: a type of life insurance in which the premium is based on the person's age when the policy is purchased and remains the same throughout his or her life. This type of policy builds a cash value. (25)

will: a legal declaration of a person's wishes concerning the way his or her property will be distributed after death. (23)

Index